In This There Tigers

By: Charles A. McDonald

Charles A. McDonald

Copyright © 2015 by Charles A. McDonald

All rights reserved. This book or any portion thereof
may not be reproduced or used in any manner whatsoever
without the express written permission of the author
except for the use of brief quotations in a book review.

Printed in the United States of America

First Printing, 2015

ISBN 9781508819004

This book is for my wife Louise, with all my love.

SSG McDonald

Acknowledgements.
 To Navy Chaplin Ray William Stubbe for his help with this book and his military service during the siege at Khe Sanh. Chaplin Stubbe served at Khe Sanh for nine months from July 1967 to March 1968. To Else Krakow who read my manuscript and corrected my grammatical mistakes. And finally, to my daughter Cheryl and her husband Arthur Moore for their technical expertise.

In Memory Of
 To all the men who proudly served at Khe Sanh, especially, Corporal Lionel Guerra, and the other Marines with Bravo Company, 3rd Reconnaissance Battalion.

Jacket Design by: Arthur J. Moore Jr.
Jacket Photo by: Lionel Guerra

CONTENTS

Prologue   7

Chapter 1.	*Red Hat*	29
Chapter 2.	*Ben Suc*	71
Chapter 3.	*Khe Sanh*	99
Chapter 4.	*Ryukyu Islands*	143
Chapter 5.	*Vietnam*	161
Chapter 6.	*Camp In The Clouds*	201
Chapter 7.	*Border Surveillance*	229
Chapter 8.	*Return to Okinawa*	269
Chapter 9.	*Project DELTA/Operation Mallet*	283
Chapter 10.	*Project DELTA/Operation Masher*	335
Chapter 11.	*Tou Morong*	423
Chapter 12.	*Hospital*	477
Chapter 13.	*The Phu Yen Prison Raid*	509
Chapter 14.	*Eagle Flight*	535

Glossary of Terms and Abbreviations   555

Appendix: Cast of Characters   564

Pacifists seek to lower the soldier to the caricature of gladiator, for they have no conception of true manhood. They have no understanding of the greatness of the sacrifice and suffering which war demands. Nor can they understand that there are men who can look upon a glorious death as the great achievement of their lives.

Major General Baron von Freytag-Loringhoven

Journalists say a thing that they know isn't true, in hopes that if they keep on saying it long enough it will be true.

Arnold Bennett (1867-1931)

Prologue

It was 1964, the Year of the Dragon, a time that would dramatically change my life. Eventually, I would learn that one has to live with the choices that are made when you are young and naive. Special Forces soldiers were being sent to help and fight in emerging agrarian nations around the globe, from Africa to South America to Indochina.

All of us in Special Forces had spent one year in Special Forces Training Group to qualify and prepare for a guerrilla or counter-guerrilla warfare mission. One thing we had learned was that this war would be psychological as well as physical. Everyone who had earned the Green Beret in Special Forces loved the United States Army. We were triple volunteers and were considered the cream of the crop. As quiet professional soldiers, we had a different manner and were usually, older and self-confident, but our futures were very uncertain.

For those of us sent to Indochina, never in our wildest dreams would we have believed how long the Vietnam War would go on or the extraordinary price which would be paid for our service, sacrifice, and commitment. We were to personally learn from hard experience, and at close quarters, the mettle of the People's Army of North Vietnam (PAVN).

Politics, Religion and Opium

Many Vietnamese Airborne officers and NCOs told me stories of intrigue, and I listened well. I quickly learned the historical background of the 7th Battalion's first combat jump. In the early days, Vietnam was a French colony. The Frenchmen who occupied Vietnam were the right-wing Vichy French, who were allied with the Germans in World War II. They jointly administered Indochina with the Japanese until 9 March 1945. The Gaullists, or Free French, who were allied with the Western powers, were never successful in establishing themselves in Vietnam. To the Vichy French, Charles de Gaulle, the leader of the Free French, was an outlaw. The colonial French were primarily Catholic and anti-communist, although a few were socialist or communist.

In 1945, President Harry S. Truman abandoned President Franklin D. Roosevelt's proposal for transformation of Indochina into a United Nations trusteeship and yielded to Charles de Gaulle's demands for assistance in restoring French control in return for cooperation in Europe. This was done to appease its defeated, temperamental and proud French ally. Truman never replied to eight appeals by Ho Chi Minh for American support of independence.

The Vietnamese were anti-colonial and therefore anti-French. They were a deeply divided people, split along religious and ideological lines: Catholic, Buddhist, and communist. They were further divided by urban and rural attitudes, and by the cultural and racial attitudes of the Vietnamese, Chinese, and Montagnards. Tying them all together was the Confucian philosophy they practiced, as it valued loyalty and devotion to family and friends, ancestor worship, and the maintenance of justice and peace. One nationalistic man who followed these ethical teachings was Ngo Dinh Diem. Diem and the Vietnamese people saw the US as "replacements" for the French and they became increasingly anti-American as more and more American troops came into the country.

In 1949, after the Chinese communists took control of all Mainland China, the 1st Indochina War started in earnest. The reentry of the French Foreign Legion into North Vietnam led to heavy fighting in the western mountains, with the Americans aiding the French, and the Chinese and Russians aiding the Viet Minh. By 1950, the U.S. Defense Department was providing seventy-five percent of the material aid. On 12 April 1953, North Vietnamese Army (NVA) regiments began reinforcing units already fighting French-led Laotian commando forces in Laos for the network of roads on the Plaine des Jarres. On 28 April 1953, the American role further expanded. The U.S. Air Force 50th Troop Carrier Squadron (C-119s) departed the Philippines after painting their aircraft with French markings to support French Forces.

On 20 November, in response to North Vietnam's General Vo Nguyen Giap's plan to invade Laos, the French launched Operation Castor. Within a matter of days, they conducted the largest drop of paratroopers in the war. French paratroopers parachuted into the valley location of Dien Bien Phu (North Vietnam) in northwestern Tonkin. This made the French dependent upon aerial re-supply. The village garrison at Dien Bien Phu was surrounded by high mountain terrain on all sides, which proved difficult to defend and hold.

Communist Chinese advisors under General Vy Quoc Thanh were helping Gen. Vo Nguyen Giap's army of five divisions. Well-camouflaged Chinese communist artillery, was deployed by hand into the high surrounding mountaintops, and inflicted punishing numerical losses on the French. The French Expeditionary Corps was surrounded and vastly outnumbered, as communist soldiers slowly closed in on the valley and cut off reinforcements. The French soldiers soon found themselves abandoned and unsupported by their own politicians, much as the American Army would be in later years. Under the command of General Thanh the Chinese Army, equipped with superb artillery and antiaircraft batteries, was largely instrumental in defeating the French at Dien Bien Phu. On 7 May 1954, after fifty-nine days of heavy fighting, the valley fortress fell. This resulted in the loss of the French colonial empire. The French role in Indochina ended, and the American role in Southeast Asia expanded overnight.

Immediately after this communist victory, France agreed to discuss a peace settlement at Geneva. There were by this time hundreds of Americans already serving in Vietnam, advising and assisting in the transition from French to American rule. President Eisenhower declared Vietnam vital to

U.S. security and planned to safely reintegrate Japan into the world economy without allowing Japan to normalize relations with the Ho Chi Minh government.

It was President Eisenhower who sent U.S. Air Force Lt. Col. Edward Geary Lansdale to Vietnam. Lansdale was skilled in the use of psychological warfare. As chief of the CIA-sponsored Saigon Military Mission (SMM) since June 1954, he was assigned to covertly help Diem become democratically elected, and then to democratically rule the South Vietnamese people, thereby strengthening the South Vietnamese government while instituting social reforms. Diem's election was aimed to turn Vietnam away from the French and toward the Americans. Lansdale, nicknamed "Colonel Ed," was well liked by the Vietnamese. He had helped President Magsaysay defeat the communists in the Philippines, and his reputation was well known. In Vietnam, however, the people were already ruled by a criminal brotherhood known as the Binh Xuyen.

Col. Lansdale was also ordered to establish a covert operation in North Vietnam utilizing defectors, employing an underground force made up of operational cells: intelligence, to plan and organize activities; sabotage, to attempt to withhold resources from their war effort; and assassination, to reinforce government policy. To this end, in South Vietnam, he recruited Col. Duong Van Minh to help break up the French-sponsored United Front, a coalition of the Binh Xuyen criminals and the Cao Dai and Hoa Hao religious sects. Once the U. S. Central Intelligence Agency saw that Diem had defeated the United Front, they understood that he was a survivor worth backing. He was a hard-working, deeply religious man of integrity.

Diem had four brothers who also played significant roles. Ngo Dinh Nhu, his younger brother, ran the secret police, and his wife, Madame Nhu (Tran Le Xuan), was a relative of the emperor. In addition, because Diem never married, Madame Nhu acted as Diem's surrogate first lady. Ngo Dinh Canh lived with his mother in Hue and controlled the northern and central provinces with his intelligence and private police force. Diem's youngest brother, Ngo Dinh Luyen, was ambassador to Great Britain. The Catholic Archbishop of Hue,

Ngo Dinh Thuc, was Diem's eldest living brother. The communists had, previously killed a fifth older brother.

On 11 February 1955, the French Army and its 2eme lost financial and training control of the Hoa Hao, Cao Dai, and South Vietnamese Army to the United States. This happened after Col. Edward G. Lansdale foiled a coup by pro-French General Nguyen Van Hinh, a French citizen and also a French army officer.

On 27 April 1955, President Diem, backed by the CIA, directed the Vietnamese Army against the Binh Xuyen. The month before, the sects had openly opposed Diem, resulting in heavy casualties on both sides. Diem was then fighting French colonialism, the Cao Dai, Hoa Hao and the communists. He was advised by the French and the Americans, and had to tolerate their clandestine war in Saigon. In early May, after six days of house-to-house fighting for the control of Saigon, the Binh Xuyen, Avant-Garde Youth, Hoa Hao and Cao Dai were driven out of the city and into the mangrove swamps of the Rung Sat (Forest of Assassins), southeast of Saigon. Long An Province, immediately southwest of Saigon, now became a communist stronghold. There, the Communists redistributed land and collected taxes without interference from the government. By 1956, when Ba Cut, the leader of the Hoa Hao, was guillotined in Can Tho, the war between the sects was largely over.

On 23-24 September 1955, the 7th Airborne Battalion made their first combat jump, parachuting into the Rung Sat special zone and began to eliminate the green-beret wearing Binh Xuyen soldiers. In April 1956, at Diem's request, the last French troops were withdrawn from Vietnam. Colonel Lansdale went as well. Col. Lansdale was later fictionalized in two best-selling novels, William J. Lederer and Eugene Burdick's books, *The Quiet American* (1955), and *The Ugly American* (1958) by Graham Greene. Later, President Kennedy considered Col. Lansdale as ambassador to South Vietnam because he was one of the few men who had a vision of how to fight the counterinsurgency with the use of Special Forces and indigenous troops. But the State Department and the conventional-minded soldiers in the Pentagon stopped Col.

Lansdale's appointment as ambassador. Diem's problems with the communist-supported, militant Buddhists had by then led to organized civil protests by Catholic and Buddhist groups.

The Buddhist leaders in Vietnam were the most politically astute group in the country and truly sincere in their desire to free Vietnam from any colonial presence. They thought that America wanted to replace France, and the Buddhist leader, Thich Tri Quang, believed the United States should leave Vietnam.

Diem suppressed religious freedom and all political opposition. He also appointed primarily pro-Diem Catholics to important government positions. Diem's troubled relations with his political opposition were greatly magnified by the Western press and by his outspoken sister-in-law, the outrageous Madame Ngo Dinh Nhu (Tran Le Xuan), known as the "Dragon Lady." It was she and her husband, Diem's younger brother, Ngo Dinh Nhu, who contributed to Diem's unpopularity, largely alienating the country.

Ngo Dinh Nhu headed the intelligence units, the Vietnamese Special Forces, the secret police, and the covert Can Lao Party. Also known as *Can Lao Nhan Vi Cach Mang Dang* or Revolutionary Personalist Labor Party, the Can Lao Party was the political and intelligence apparatus headed by Special Forces commander Le Quang Tung. Made up of some 20,000 Catholic followers, this clandestine intelligence network kept Diem and Nhu in power. They were rewarded monetarily with grants of land and political favors. During the early 1960s, this reward system caused few problems. Since the time of the French, opium had been the Vietnamese government's financial prop. The government-run Opium Monopoly was banned when the Vietnamese started working with the Americans. However, the Opium Monopoly was secretly restored to pay Ngo Dinh Nhu's secret police and informers and finance the costs of coping with a mounting insurgency and other political problems with funds from the opium trade. The opium fruit matures between January and February, and the Montagnard women cut the gray-green globes and wait for the gum to ooze out. The crude opium was collected and refined to a morphine base for shipment. Nhu used the thirty-two C-47s of the First Transport Group of the Vietnamese Air Force to fly back and forth between the northern poppy fields in Laos to Pleiku and Saigon.

The First Transport Group aircraft flew intelligence missions into Laos for the U.S. Central Intelligence Agency directed by the commander of the Vietnamese Air Force, Nguyen Cao Ky (future president of Vietnam), who controlled Tan Son Nhut Air Base. The opium in Laos was flown from Ban Houei Sai and Long Tieng to Pakse. Long Tieng was a top-secret CIA base, located southwest of the Plain of Jars. It was the base of Gen. Vang Pao's Meo guerrilla force in Military Region II. The hills surrounding the base were covered year-round in white and yellow poppies. From Laos, opium was shipped to Pleiku and Ban Me Thuot in Vietnam, or from Pakse to Phnom Penh and then to Saigon. It was then flown to the United States.

Between 1953 and 1956, during their land reformation program in North Vietnam, the communist regime executed 100,000 wealthy landowners. This brutal "reform" forced 900,000 Catholics to flee to South Vietnam. On 7 August 1954, after Diem requested help, President Dwight D. Eisenhower gave the order for Operation Passage to Freedom to commence. The United States Navy conducted the largest sea evacuation operation in military history. The evacuees were subsequently given land and jobs in South Vietnam, causing friction as the American press took up the Buddhist cause. The Buddhist and communist factions both resented the earlier 1954 evacuees.

By 1959, North Vietnam had decided to take armed action against the South. Main force units, organized and equipped along conventional military lines and backed up by regional troops and guerrillas, began to attack isolated South Vietnamese army posts more frequently. Assassinations increased countrywide.

Early in the morning of 12 November 1960, three airborne battalions attempted a *coup d'état* against Diem, encouraged by Lt. Col. Lansdale. The airborne troops secured the Saigon radio station and announced Diem's removal. These troops were led by a cabal of paratroop officers commanded by Colonel Nguyen Chanh Thi, a Buddhist who discontented with

Diem's favoritism toward Catholics and who was aligned with the militant Buddhist monk leader Thich Tri Quang. After seizing the General Staff Headquarters, police headquarters and Tan Son Nhut airport, the troops surrounded the presidential palace, entered, and cut the phone lines. An overlooked emergency system in the underground tunnels was used to summon help from the Seventh Division, commanded by Nguyen Van Thieu. The airborne troops tried to extract the promise from Diem that he would broaden the government by minimizing the dominance of the Can Lao party and members of his family. The CIA station chief stalled negotiations. At 9:00 a.m., after Diem stated he would carry out the reforms wanted by the United States, troops under the command of Col. Tran Thien Khiem liberated Diem and the coup was over.

During these early years of the war, President Diem maintained control over the communists in South Vietnam. The initial spread of communism had caused him to arrest and detain his political opponents and to abolish all elected village councils in favor of the village chiefs he himself had appointed. The Vietnamese press, manipulated by the CIA, took advantage of Diem's many problems with the communists and Buddhists who sympathized with the communists. The most problematic of these were the sympathetic militant Buddhists from the Chinese Cholon "Big Market" district of Saigon. Their headquarters were in the An Quang Pagoda (Pagoda of the Shining Seal) on Vinh Vien Street in the city's District 10, and the Xa Loi Pagoda at the eastern corners of Cach Mang Thang Tam and Nguyen Dinh Chieu streets.

As of May 1961, there were an estimated four hundred U.S. Special Forces personnel serving with the Vietnamese Special Forces in Vietnam. The elite, American-trained-and-funded, Vietnamese Special Forces troops were independent of the Vietnamese Army. These Special Forces units commanded by Col. Le Quang Tung were under the direct control of Ngo Dinh Nhu. These troops raided pagodas throughout Vietnam, brutally arresting and often killing monks. In November 1961, the forerunners of the air commandos, the U.S. Air Force 4400th "Jungle Jim" units, arrived in the country with World War II vintage aircrafts to conduct tactical operations. From the beginning of 1961 until 4 January 1965, the United States armed forces casualties in South Vietnam totaled 356 dead, 1,546 wounded, and nineteen missing.

Ap Bac

On 2 January 1963, left-wing journalist David Halberstam of the New York Times began trying to convince the American and Vietnamese military, as well as the American public, that during an engagement in the rice fields of Ap Bac, the Vietnamese had tried to avoid combat. In actuality, the communists were being reinforced from North Vietnam and had changed their methods of fighting, having been resupplied with better weapons. The Americans had tried to use conventional military tactics against guerrillas, and it hadn't worked. At the point of being surrounded, the guerrillas had slipped away underground and into the vast Plain of Reeds. The early American advisors were not prepared for this type of warfare. This battle against elements of two Viet Cong battalions ended in a shattering defeat for the ARVN forces of the 7th Division. The entrenched communist 261st Main Force Battalion and the 514th Regional Battalion withstood napalm, artillery and the heavy machine gun fire of the armored personnel carriers (M-113). The communists shot down five helicopters and damaged 11 others, and during the course of the battle killed 80 Vietnamese, six Americans, as well as wounding over 100 Vietnamese. The Communist forces had an advantage: the American-Vietnamese radio net was being monitored by a communist radio transmitter in the nearby village of Tan Thoi, which allowed their field commanders to be informed of every move the Americans made.

The ARVN forces during the battle of Ap Bac were commanded by Brigadier General Huynh Van Cao. John Paul Vann, an emotional officer who clashed with his Vietnamese counterpart, Colonel Bui Dinh Dam, who charged the ARVN commander with cowardice and incompetency for failing to block the enemy's retreat. Colonel Vann had been in an aircraft rather than on the ground during battle. General Huynh Van Cao was guilty only of following President Diem's orders to avoid too many casualties. The 350 encircled Viet Cong used a gap left open by General Cao for the communists to escape in the night. Because General Huynh Van Cao was a Diem loyalist with three divisions under his command, he had to be neutralized in any way possible.

The reporter Halberstam, however, had been briefed by Col. J.P. Vann whose reporting misled the American and Vietnamese public into thinking that the communist guerrilla forces were superior and could stand up against a multi-battalion ARVN operation supported by U.S. The early exaggerated reporting by American correspondents had profound consequences on American personnel for the rest of the war. The American advisors used this operation as an argument to widen the U.S. involvement in the war. Ironically, in May 1967, the American 9th Infantry Division made the same mistakes with the entrenched communists, and despite their superior firepower, would suffer the same casualties at the village of Ap Bac.

The New York Times published a front-page article in August of 1967, headlined "Vietnam: The Signs of Stalemate," that gradually altered perceptions of American success for the remainder of the Vietnam War. The secret military source was General Frederick Weyand, the commander of III Corps in the Mekong Delta, who told the reporters that the war was unwinnable.

*   *   *

There are two primary schools of Buddhism: Hinayana Buddhism in India and Mahayana Buddhism of China, Japan and Southeast Asia. With the Chinese communists' victory in China in 1949 came a renaissance for Mahayana Buddhism. Communists won many converts among the Buddhist monks by drawing upon the similarities between Marxism and Buddhism, and by endorsing the shared goal of a classless society. The Buddhists in Hue were not the older, traditional Buddhists, but the younger, reformist activists. The Buddhist leaders drew intense emotional reactions from the people in their committed opposition to Diem. Thich Tri Quang, a former Viet Minh, was a powerful dissident Buddhist monk who sided with the communists against the French. On 8 May 1963, he became the headstrong leader of the Buddhists in Hue, who wanted the United States out of Vietnam in order to pave the way for reunification between South and North Vietnam. Their headquarters were the Tu Dam Pagoda, located on the south bank of the river in the western outskirts of Hue. Its monks were pro-communist and the source of many violent protests against the United States and South Vietnamese governments. Due to strained relations between Diem and the representatives of the U.S. government, Diem's brother Nhu began clandestinely negotiating with the communists in Hue.

Diem's eldest brother, Ngo Dinh Thuc, the Catholic Archbishop of Hue, an anti-communist and a nationalist, further exacerbated tensions in Vietnam. On 8 May 1963, Diem prohibited Buddhist flags from being flown in celebration of the birthday of Buddha. The law in South Vietnam already prohibited the display of any flags other than the national flag of South Vietnam, but Diem allowed the yellow and white Vatican flags to be flown to honor his brother. The Buddhists claimed this action limited their religious freedom and that they had Ngo Dinh Canh's permission to fly their flags. (Ngo Dinh Canh, Diem's younger brother, ruled Northern and Central Vietnam.) The resulting march and celebration of ten thousand followers was the key incident and immediate catalyst in this political turmoil.

The Buddhists, bearing anti-government signs, marched from the Tu Dam Pagoda eastward to the Hotel Morin, and on to the radio station. The plan was to use the radio station to broadcast the speech of Tri Quang, but the station refused. The radio station called the deputy province chief, as the crowd became unruly. Some fifteen grenades were thrown, killing eight children and one woman. This incident was rumored to have been initiated by the American CIA, because of the types of wounds observed on the dead by Dr. Le Khac Quyen, the examining physician. This led to a violent confrontation between the communist-agitated Buddhists of the Tu Dam Pagoda and the Catholics, causing many casualties. Armed troops were called in.

On 6 June 1963, supported by tanks under the command of Major Dan Sy, the ground troops surrounded the pagodas in an attempt to stop the hunger strike of forty Buddhist monks. An estimated forty monks were killed, and hundreds more were wounded. Armored vehicles crushed some of the demonstrators. Finding their niche, the left-leaning American press began to focus on the Buddhist problems. This approach was much safer than going into the field and trying to report on the war. The Buddhists insured that the Western press covered all their events through meetings and phone calls with Duc Nghiep, their spokesman. On 16 August 1963, a monk's suicide instigated another riot. The militant Buddhist monks and nuns continued to cooperate with the communists. Their political activity never stopped.

On 11 June 1963, my twenty-eighth birthday, a political protest by Reverend Thich Quang Duc, a frail, 66-year-old, militant monk from Hue, made headlines in the Western press. Early in the morning, Duc departed the tall tower of the Xa Loi Pagoda with a column of other militant monks. Upon reaching the intersection of Phan Dinh Phung and Le Van Duyet streets on the western side of Saigon, he sat down in the street and assumed the lotus position. He meditated while other monks poured a mixture of diesel fuel and gasoline over him and then set him on fire. This mixture produces an intense and long-lasting heat and flame. He remained in the lotus position as he burned to death. Duc was the first bonze to self-immolate in public. His suicide caught world attention through the photographs in The New York Times, taken by the overly aggressive AP bureau chief Malcolm Browne.

Rumor in Saigon had it that reporter Malcolm Browne had paid for the privilege to set himself up for the pictures of the burning monk, and was informed in advance, by Nghiep, who accompanied him to the demonstration. This one picture of the burning Reverend Quang Duc led to later pictures of the sacrificial burning of other monks and nuns. Together, they helped sway the American public against the Vietnam War. The practice of self-immolation was common in Vietnam; however, the American Press did not bother to inform the Western public of this fact. Instead of putting it into perspective, Halberstam chose to deceive the world. Again, on 6 October, New York Times correspondent David Halberstam was involved with headline news of a self-immolation.

The insensitive Madame Nhu referred to these self-immolations as "barbecues." The Western press was all too eager and delighted to quote her remarks in the newspapers. The Communists leaning Buddhists had found a useful tool in the American press.

In 1972, Ambassador Lodge finally expelled Malcolm Browne from Vietnam. President Kennedy had hated the reporter David Halberstam. Reporters like Browne and the Halberstam won Pulitzer awards for exploiting the Buddhist unrest in Vietnam. They used their positions as reporters to attack and question U.S. policy, helping to polarize the American public and the Vietnamese by reporting the actions of the communist converts among the Mahayana Buddhist monks. They had firmly decided to help bring down his government with their biased and inaccurate reporting. They created division between the American and Vietnamese military, helping to erode American military credibility and political support with the American public. These two left-leaning reporters and others like them did not represent the best interests of the United States.

During Operation Bravo I, on 21 August 1963, all senior military commanders and key cabinet members of the South Vietnamese Government met to discuss the ongoing problems with the Buddhists. Martial law was declared in compliance with the instructions of Ngo Dinh Nhu, Diem's political adviser and head of the secret police. This martial law justified the raids on the pagodas, which were in defiance of the United States. Much of what happened in the days and years ahead would be guided by these conflicts within the Vietnamese military and society, as one faction struggled with another for supremacy.

The Vietnamese Special Forces and the elite police forces of Ngo Dinh Nu were disguised as regular army troops. The units paid directly by the CIA, conducted a brutal raid on the city's most sacred Buddhist shrine, the Xa Loi Pagoda. Approximately 1,500 monks and nuns were severely beaten and arrested. Government troops took about forty of the most militant monks to the top of the seven-story tower and threw the monks to their deaths. At the same time, other raids took place in Hue and other cities, resulting in the mass slaughter of Buddhists. Months of trouble between the government and Buddhists monks followed.

On 23 August 1963, Lieutenant General Duong Van Minh, known as "Big Minh" due to his size, began to plot a military coup to overthrow Ngo Dinh Diem, who had refused to be an American puppet. In response to Minh's plot, Saigon University students and Buddhist monks rioted into September, demanding the release of the imprisoned monks. Diem, dissatisfied with the rising numbers of American advisers, requested the removal of a substantial number of them. On 7 September, Rome requested that Diem's brother, Monseigneur Thuc, come for an extended visit. Two days later, Madame Nhu departed for Europe. The handwriting was on the wall.

The Young Turks

LTG Duong Van Minh (Big Minh) was a competent general, who was feared by Diem. He was the army's senior general, but had no authority to issue orders directly to troops. He had formed and commanded the Revolutionary Command Council of senior army commanders, who were supported by the Cao Dai and Hoa Hao sects and the Communist National Liberation Front (NLF). This was one of the major reasons for the South Vietnamese Army's reluctance to engage the communist forces. The Revolutionary Command Council wanted all foreign troops out of Vietnam in order to establish a working relationship with North Vietnam.

In the planned coup d'état against Diem, all the members had initially pledged to guarantee the safety of the president, his brother, and their respective families. The senior army commanders in charge of Vietnam's four Corps Tactical Zones were LTG Do Cao Tri, a Buddhist who commanded I Corps; LTG Nguyen Khanh, leader and former communist Viet Minh soldier who commanded the II Corps; LTG Ton That Dinh, whose support was vital due to his command of the III Corps and the Capital Military District (CMD); LTG Tran Van

Don, who commanded the IV Corps area and acted as the liaison with the U.S. Central Intelligence Agency for the coup; and Col. Albert Pham Ngoc Thao, a former Viet Minh whose brother was a high official in the Hanoi government. Colonel Thao served as a clandestine communist agent in charge of the strategic hamlet program, running the espionage network in South Vietnam. Thao's program, administered by CIA-advised province security officers, moved peasants into fortified villages in order to secure them from guerrilla attacks and to prevent them from aiding the insurgents. His policies insured that those officials who were working at the village level for the government would remain haughty, arrogant, and aloof in their behavior. To this end, Thao's mission for North Vietnam was to create division within the Army and cripple its effectiveness. Until his execution in February 1965, he played a major role in destroying the credibility of the South Vietnamese government.

CIA officer Lucien E. Conein served as liaison between Ambassador Henry Cabot Lodge, General Duong Van Minh, and vice president Nguyen Ngoc Tho. He was assigned to the Interior Ministry from the CIA-sponsored Saigon Military Mission (SMM). Vice President Nguyen Ngoc Tho was a Buddhist and wealthy landlord who oversaw Vietnam's land policies. The North Vietnamese and the National Liberation Front favored the landless peasants in land reform. However, President Diem's land policies favored the powerful landlords. Nguyen Ngoc Tho and the Revolutionary Command Council learned that Nhu was negotiating an accommodation with the communists, a discovery that marked the beginning of the end for Diem and his brother Nhu. On 23 September, economic aid was cut to the units responsible for the raids on the pagodas. In October, demonstrations by students and Buddhist militants escalated. Thousands of students were arrested and tortured.

By 27 October 1963, President Kennedy had already sanctioned the overthrow and assassination of President Diem. Lansdale had been the only man who disagreed, arguing with both Kennedy and McNamara. Kennedy acted on the advice of Henry Cabot Lodge, Robert McNamara, Averell W. Harriman, Lyndon Baines Johnson, George Ball, and Dean Rusk. Over the years, Robert McNamara's plotting of political and military strategy in Southeast Asia made him the worst of the suits in Washington. McNamara completely misjudged the capacity of North Vietnam. This mistake became evident on 19 October 1965, when the North Vietnamese Army attacked the Plei Me Special Forces Camp, and on 14 November 1965 when the 1st Cavalry Division lost many men in the Ir Drang Valley. Secretary of State Dean Rusk's misjudgment in refraining from creating a war psychology in the United States, bordered on the criminal.

Averell W. Harriman, who had always opposed U.S. intervention in Vietnam, preached the neutrality of Laos. The Laotian Neutrality Treaty of July 1962, in turn, allowed the North Vietnamese to remain in Laos and keep the Vietnamese and Americans out. This vicious diplomat and Undersecretary of State for Political Affairs sold the US "a bill of goods" by creating the Laotian neutrality at Geneva in 1962. That swept the military out of Laos, except for the North Vietnamese, Chinese, and Russians. This resulted in the PAVN forces building their supply line in Laos to supply their troops in South Vietnam. Harriman tied the hands of the US for years to come. Harriman's close ties to the Quakers, who were sympathetic to the North Vietnamese, put his motives into question. Their supply of North Vietnam was well reported upon in the press during the war. Later, many Vietnamese and Americans referred to the Ho Chi Minh Trail as the Harriman Memorial Highway. Harriman openly hated Diem, and American policy in Vietnam reflected his hatred. This is the reason that Diem, an anti-communist, gradually decided to try to reach an accommodation with North Vietnam. Harriman sent a cable to Ambassador Lodge, authorizing U.S. support for the coup. Lodge had been systematically deceiving Kennedy and undermining Diem by withholding State Department information from the pro-Diem General Paul D. Harkins. The commander of U.S. Military Assistance Command, Vietnam (MACV) Gen. Harkins was in complete disagreement with Lodge. On 29 October 1963, Special Forces troops under Col. Le Quang Tung, and loyal to President Diem's brother Ngo Dinh Nhu, were ordered out of Saigon by LTG Ton That Dinh.

The Vietnamese generals were afraid to attempt a coup as long as the ten independent Special Forces companies were nearby.

Operation Bravo II

On 1 November 1963, an hour after midnight, the Revolutionary Command Council began carrying out the Diem coup plan known as Operation Bravo II. For the duration of the coup d'état, Col. Conein set up his office at the Vietnamese Joint General Staff Headquarters with communications links throughout the city to his CIA operatives and to Washington. In Danang, General Do Cao Tri, the commander of I Corps, kept government officials busy to preclude their contact with the Republican Youth and defend Diem. The Republic of Vietnam forces, led by Colonel Pham Ngoc Thao, a clandestine communist agent, seized control of strategic installations. Diem had initially believed that he could trust LTG Tran Van Don, his advisor, but Don convinced him to station troops throughout Saigon and declare martial law. Troops under the command of LTG Ton That Dinh seized the radio station and police headquarters. Dinh had already betrayed Diem's plans for a counter coup against the plotters.

The Special Forces commander, Col. Le Quang Tung, was the one officer loyal to the President's brother, Ngo Dinh Nhu, and the most dangerous to the coup plotters. Diem and Nhu had ordered Col. Tung to round up and shoot the coup plotters. Instead, Tung and his brother, Maj. Le Quang Trieu, were summoned to the officers' club inside the JGS headquarters near Tan Son Nhut airfield. There, Minh's personal bodyguard and executioner, Captain Nguyen Van Nhung, murdered them. Navy commander, Captain Ho Tan Quyen, loyal to Diem had already been killed earlier by his aide. Meanwhile, the III Corps Commander Dinh withdrew all Special Forces personnel from Saigon.

Col. Nguyen Duc Thang furnished troops for this coup d'état. He commanded the 5th ARVN Infantry Division stationed at Bien Hoa. In addition, a future President of Vietnam, Col. Nguyen Van Thieu, who had fought for the French, led elements of the division to take up positions around the presidential Gia Long palace. Meanwhile, the Airborne

Brigade seized the airport. The independent Vietnamese Marine Battalions, led by LTG Du Quoc Dong and the 6th Armored Squadron seized two Saigon Radio Stations, the communications site at the central post office, naval headquarters, and presidential guard barracks. They also set up roadblocks around the city.

Day of the Dead

Saturday, 2 November 1963, a holiday celebrated as All Souls' Day, was ironically, also known to the French-speaking brothers, as *La Fete des Morts*, the Day of the Dead. Early that morning the units of the 5th Infantry started their assault on the palace under the cover of darkness. After about three hours, the soldiers entered and searched the palace and the underground tunnels, only to find that both President Diem and Nhu had already escaped and entered the city the previous day.

Diem and Nhu fled to the Cholon district home of Chinese businessman Ma Tuyen, a leader of the Chinese community, where they had previously engaged in secret negotiations with the communists of the National Liberation Front. The house was maintained just for such an emergency situation. Unknown to the two brothers, this residence was under American surveillance by the 704 Military Intelligence Detachment. It was suspected of being a secret communist communications site belonging to the Central Office for South Vietnam (COSVN), and was kept under constant clandestine surveillance.

The two brothers soon left the Ma Tuyen residence and headed for their church, the Cha Tam Catholic Church in Cholon. They tried to contact supposed loyal military officers by phone, but they failed. Their fatal early morning phone call to Gen. Ton That Dinh at 0620 hours led to the discovery of their hideout and their subsequent agreement to surrender.

At 0630 hours, LTG. Tran Van Don ordered Captain Phan Hoa Hiep to take two M-113 armored personnel carriers (APC) and four jeep-loads of soldiers to pick up the brothers. The ranking officer for the escort was General Mai Huu Xuan, a general who had served with *doc phu* Tam, "the tiger of Cai Lay," and who was known for brutal methods. In the two APCs were General Duong Van, Big Minh's brutal bodyguard, Captain Nguyen Xuan Nhung, and Major Duong Hieu Nghia with instructions to kill the brothers. Diem and Nhu were driven to Hong Thap Tu Alley and repeatedly stabbed, then shot at point blank range. Vice President Nguyen Ngoc Tho, became head of the newly established military government.

This assassination destroyed the base of the South Vietnamese police apparatus, resulting in the communists' resurgence around the country. At the same time, inexperienced administrators replaced many provincial and district chiefs loyal to Diem. This incident took place while I was completing training in Special Forces Training Group (SFTG). Three weeks later, on 22 November, the day I graduated from SFTG, another assassination occurred: that of President Kennedy, who had wanted to withdraw a substantial number of American advisors.

On 25 November, the new President, Lyndon Baines Johnson, signed National Security Action Memorandum 273, authorizing planning for covert military operations against North Vietnam. He utilized the Military Assistance Command Special Operations Group (MACSOG) and its Maritime Operation (MAROP) unit 34-A to conduct and electronically assess North Vietnam's radar, air defense, and coastal patrol capabilities. On the night of 31 July 1964, a raiding force of U.S.-led commandos attacked two island installations off the coast of southern China and North Vietnam. One of these was a radar installation. The diesel submarines USS Perch, USS Tunny, and USS Grayback were used to land commandos on covert missions in North Vietnam. To create a planned response from the North Vietnamese, the unit deployed four armed Fast Patrol Type boats (nicknamed "Nastys") for the raid on their installations. In the event of pursuit by North Vietnamese PT boats (SWATOWS), this unit would be backed up by the destroyer USS Maddox (DD-731), and the aircraft carrier, USS Ticonderoga, which would be ready to launch aircraft. On 2-4 August 1964, the four PTFs (PTF-2,3,5, and 6), while under the pursuit of three North Vietnamese Navy PT boats, escaped by running past the destroyer Maddox. The

North Vietnamese torpedo boats were taken under fire by the Maddox, but none were sunk. The United States claimed that the North Vietnamese attacked the U.S. destroyer Maddox, resulting in the Tonkin Gulf Resolution. On 7 August, President Johnson used these North Vietnamese PT boat attacks as the legal basis for gaining congressional approval for legal intervention in the Vietnam War. He won this approval through guile, encouraging Congress to pass the Tonkin Gulf Resolution, which transformed and escalated the war in Vietnam. As a result, hundreds of thousands of American and Free World troops were sent to Vietnam. By utilizing these raids, President Johnson achieved his goal of provoking a response in the Gulf of Tonkin, which led to the escalation of the Vietnam War. This overt, act-of-war provocation policy had been earlier adopted by President Polk in the Mexican War, President Lincoln in the Civil War, and President William McKinley in the Spanish-American War.

By 1964, the city of Saigon was encircled by communist troops. The U. S. politicians had trouble finding anyone that they could mold into their own image to lead South Vietnam and pursue the war against the communists, until they found LTG Nguyen Khanh. In the meantime, the self-immolation of Buddhists continued, but they managed to stay out of the Western press.

In December 1964, LTG Nguyen Khanh secretly started his own serious exchanges with Hanoi in order to end the war. On 30 January 1964, he conducted a coup overthrowing Gen. Minh, in which he had Minh's bodyguard, Captain Nguyen Van Nhung, executed. In February 1965, the CIA informed the President of Khanh's message intercepts, and the Americans initiated yet another coup. The communist double agent, Col. Pham Ngoc Thao, who had been involved in the unsuccessful 1965-coup attempt against Khanh, was the chief of Ben Tre, the capital city of the island province of Kien Hoa until 1965. He was then killed by the future President, Nguyen Van Thieu. On 3 September 1967, Nguyen Cao Ky came to power, and he was elected vice-president, while General Nguyen Van Thieu was elected President. They held office for the duration of the

Vietnam War. Throughout the rest of the war, the Diem coup and the later, resulting coups were responsible for the distrust and poor working relationships between many uninformed, bewildered American advisors and their indigenous counterparts. Many American advisors feared for their lives.

The Diem assassination was America's very first betrayal of the South Vietnamese people, but it wasn't the last. President Diem's fourth brother, Ngo Dinh Canh, an administrator in Hue, controlled the city and the central provinces with his own political and intelligence network. Canh was transported to Saigon by American military personnel, and in May 1963, turned over to the Vietnamese on the orders of Ambassador Henry Cabot Lodge, and shot on 9 May 1964 in a public execution.

Prior to the 1968 Tet Offensive, the An Quang Pagoda in Saigon took over as the new center of anti-government agitation from the Tu Dam Pagoda in Hue. Later, the An Quang Pagoda served as the Viet Cong command post for the attack on Saigon. In 1968, Vu Ngoc Nha, a close friend and special adviser to President Nguyen Van Thieu, and a covert North Vietnamese agent, convinced Mr. Thieu to let soldiers go on leave for Tet, before the communist attack during the Lunar New Year. The Tet offensive helped drive the United States out of the war.

In 1969, President Thieu's special assistant for political affairs, Huynh Van Trong, a close friend of Vu Ngoc Nha, kept him informed on President Thieu's meeting with President Nixon on Midway Island, and their planned negotiating strategy with the North Vietnamese at the Paris Peace Talks. In August 1969, while the United States was encouraging the South Vietnamese to refuse negotiations with North Vietnam, Henry Kissinger began secret talks with the North Vietnamese in Paris, in which the DRV demanded withdrawal of American forces and the existing government of South Vietnam. The Paris Peace Talks became deadlocked. In May 1970, American and South Vietnamese troops invaded Cambodia, resulting in antiwar demonstrations. The rest is history.

Captain Jim Kern
Senior Advisor to Vietnamese 7th Airborne Battalion

CHAPTER 1

RED HAT

Six parachute jumps were required to qualify for my Vietnamese Airborne wings. By January 1967, I had made all six from the venerable Douglas C-47 Gooney Bird, on Ap Don Drop zone, some 10 miles from Tan Son Nhut airfield. The first jump was memorable. It had been with the women paratroopers assigned to the division. They served as field nurses, parachute riggers and in various administrative positions. I was amazed at how beautiful they all were.

I had been assigned to the Vietnamese Airborne Advisory Detachment-162. They were headquartered at Tan Son Nhut Air Base, located on the outskirts of Saigon, under the command of Col. Le Roy S. Stanley. There was only one Airborne Division in the Vietnamese Army. The division was made up of the 1st, 2nd, 3rd, 5th, 6th, 7th, 9th and 11th Airborne Infantry Battalions, and was the National Strategic Reserve force, the shock troops. If any Allied unit fell into trouble during combat operations, the Vietnamese Airborne was thrown into the battle.

Assigned to the 7th Airborne Infantry Battalion I traveled twelve miles northeast of Saigon, across the large Newport Bridge, up Highway 1, to Bien Hoa Airfield, on the north bank of the Dong Nai River. The 7th Battalion was very small made up of its headquarters company and four infantry companies. The 7th Battalion had only 590 paratroopers assigned. There were three American advisors assigned to this battalion, the Senior Advisor was Captain James C. Kern, Captain Thomas C. Kerns and myself. The members of the 7th were older, veteran fighters, many of whom had served under the French.

I had barely settled in when the battalion was alerted for movement to the 1st Marine Division-built airfield at the coastal city of Chu Lai, in southeastern Quang Nam Province. Chu Lai was a huge, tin shantytown, located in north-central Vietnam about 30km north of Quang Ngai. I was about to witness, first hand, the reputation, courage and sense of honor of this paratroop battalion.

* * *

On 14 February 1967, our preparation plans for movement were completed at the airfield and everyone was broken down into his loading sequence. Our mode of transportation was the U.S. Marine Chinook air cargo helicopter. This medium-sized twin-rotor helicopter was extremely noisy, and had a range of 115-miles. It could carry 44 well-equipped American troops, which meant we were able to put a lot more of our Vietnamese paratroopers into it. We would fly south into Quang Ngai Province, and then go up the Tra Khuc River valley. We received a briefing on our landing and tactical plan for locating the North Vietnamese Army's 21st Regiment, 2nd NVA Division. Then came the hard part-- the waiting.

I double checked my radio by turning it on, turned the night Lite on to see that it would work. It lit. Then I checked to ensure my primary and alternate frequencies were correctly set. I studied my map-So'n Ha map sheet 6739 III. We were being used as a target of opportunity, bait, to draw the NVA out long enough to make a battle of it. The 7th Battalion was to be the sacrificial lamb. Airborne troops were trained to respond effectively in the event of being surrounded by an enemy force. I checked the troops and closely looked over the individuals who made up these ranks of camouflaged soldiers. They looked prepared and conducted themselves professionally. I was both impressed and satisfied with what I saw. The personal maturity of these Vietnamese paratroopers made me proud to wear their uniform.

Finally, the transportation arrived, blasting everyone with wind, fine dust, and sand. Engines idling, the transports lowered their ramps. The CH-47 Chinooks had straight-in rear loading, and the troops entered through the dark opening to settle onto the tubular web seats in the dim interior. No one was able to talk, their voices drowned out by the roaring of the engines. Only the lips of the door gunners moved silently, headphones on, responding to commands by giving answers. The formation of Chinooks rose slowly from the airfield. As we flew south over the Tra Bong River and the Batangan Peninsula, I looked down upon the dark-brown roofs of the densely populated villages, surrounded by dark-green islands of trees that dotted the flat, sandy areas between the sea and the

---

NOVEMBER 1, 1967   67-0499-F

DANANG --- The 7th Airborne Battalion of the Vietnamese Airborne Division won America's military group award -- The Presidential Unit Citation -- for heroism in an eight day battle near Quang Ngai in February, 1967.

The Presidential Citation commended the battalion for exemplary conduct in the highest military traditon and reflecting "great credit upon the battalion and the Army of the Republic of Vietnam."

The 7th Battalion was one of three Vietnamese battalions airlifted to complete the encirclement by U.S., Korean and Vietnamese forces of a North Vietnamese Regular Army regiment. After closing the trap, the communist regiment concentrated its forces against the 7th Battalion in a breakout attempt. Withstanding three human-wave attacks and hand-to-hand battle, the Vietnamese "Airborne Troopers" left 813 dead enemy on the battle field. They captured 41 heavy machine-guns, mortars and other crew served weapons along with 138 individual weapons. 22 Of the enmy were captured. Allied forces casualties were 54 killed and 187 wounded.

Vice President Hubert H. Humphrey tied the citation streamer to the unit colors during ceremonies at DANANG, November 1, 1967.

---

mountains. I could not imagine the unimaginable agony that was soon to take place. In Quang Ngai Province the mountains closely crowded the coast. The Chinook formation turned west and flew inland, passing over Highway 1, and then the National railroad line. I began to notice the absence of villages and people. The area was pockmarked with bomb and artillery craters, and the villages marked on the map were long gone. We were now in our operational area, the Son Tinh district.

We were inserted on the northern side of a large valley, split down the middle by the winding Tra Khuc River. The river acted as the dividing line between Son Tinh district and the more southern Tu Nghia district. Further east, the small town of Quang Ngai sat on the southern bank of the Tra Khuc River. There were mountains further up the valley, to the east, and to the north and south. Using my compass, I oriented the map to the terrain, checked the land features and cross-reference them to the topography shown on my map, and within minutes accurately had my exact position. It was a bright, clear day, but this was the winter monsoon season, the period from November to February when the onshore winds out of the northeast shed moisture over the northern provinces of South Vietnam.

After the rackety clamor of our insertion, we formed our units and moved cross-country in a formation of columns, across the open terrain toward the river, where timber grew in isolated tracts. When we received sniper fire, I thought we were really in for it. All my previous experience told me, this one shot was a signal. We were in for some kind of a surprise. The sky quickly turned from blue to lavender to pale blue with the setting of the sun. This area showed a lot of recent signs of agricultural activity; there had to be a lot of people somewhere nearby.

We settled into our chosen, slight defilade position night defensive position at grid coordinates BS 486768, just south of a village named Minh Long 1. The village consisted only of a few empty huts. The battalion dug in as soon as individual fighting positions and fields of fire had been assigned. Capt. Kern was in the center of the perimeter with Major Le Minh Ngoc, the Vietnamese Commander. The Assistant Battalion Advisor, Capt. Kerns was assigned to the northern portion of the battalion perimeter, and I was assigned to the eastern side of the perimeter. I walked around my company's assigned portion of the perimeter, memorizing the terrain, marking the low areas, where men could hide in the open, below the line of fire in the coming darkness.

The best enemy approach cover was a nearby sugarcane field and forest to our southeast, suitable for a daylight attack.

The best approach routes for quiet night movement lay in the open areas. The Regular North Vietnamese Army infantrymen (Bo Doi Chu Luc) would have to attack from open areas to put enfilading (direct) fire onto us, as we had sufficient cover of our own, with hedgerows sheltering our foxholes. In addition, the river covered the southern portion of our perimeter. That meant we had just three directions to worry about. It gave our under strength battalion an unusually strong defensive position. To our east and west, the terrain was open. Immediately to the north, across some 200 yards of open space, was the only danger, a large wooded area.

By this time in the war I was habitually paranoid, and even turned around to study the hedgerow behind me. Nevertheless, I felt somewhat secure; in the broken shadows, with the dark background behind me, I would be difficult to spot. I had already plotted the areas from which the NVA (*bo dois*) could aim their supporting fires, just in case. I checked the two butterfly-wing locks on my radio. They controlled the tuning knobs for setting my frequencies in megahertz and kilohertz. My radio was already preset for switching from my primary frequency to my alternate frequency so that I wouldn't have to fumble around in the dark. I turned them both simultaneously, first to the left, then to the right, to make sure their settings were correct. I turned my switch to "Lite," to check that it was still working. I had already called in my pre-plotted defensive concentrations to Captain Kern, and had also dug my foxhole, nice and deep.

Like so many times before, I watched the last rays of the setting sun spread crimson fingers across the western sky, and prayed to see the next new day's dawn. The pale blue sky continued to shift, turning to gray, then to black. It was February, and a clear night, so I knew that as it cooled off, the fog would come. River valleys tend to fog. I felt like praying for fair weather in the morning. As it was, there was hardly any wind and unless the wind picked up, the morning fog might remain. My mood dampened. Adverse weather of any kind meant the NVA would move, if they'd planned to. In the absence of wind, everything was unnaturally still, like a bad omen. Even worse, there would be no moon or starlight. I sat wakeful and tense, spending much of the long night peering into the dark, listening to nature's sounds with an air of anticipation, hearing only the shrill moaning of the insects and croak of frogs next to the river. In my uneasiness, I kept a keen watch, until middle-of-the-night weariness finally overwhelmed me. I had not heard, seen or smelled any clear sign of danger. Little did I know that as a heavy mist settled, death was stealing upon us. My senses dulled by encroaching drowsiness, I sank into sleep. The moon had long since disappeared behind a fast emerging bank of clouds.

Early in the morning, the base of the clouds was sitting right on the ground. Their moisture hung in the air reducing visibility. The *bo dois* moved quietly in file formations, to position themselves to attack just prior to their supporting preparatory fires, through the ground fog. They had waited and timed their attack for the most dangerous period, between 2:00 A.M. to 4:00 A.M., when the biological rhythms and temperature affect tired soldiers the most, and leave them at their least vigilant.

The 7th Battalion's listening post (LP) was still alert. They had heard the faint sounds of overwhelming, mass numbers of *bo dois* assault force personnel, emerging in formation from the thick, wet gray ground fog and moving toward our lines.

The NVA always made their assaults from an attack position, as close to any unit's forward edge of the battle area as possible, so indirect fire weapons could not be used effectively. Several long files of the NVA were already moving past the LP position, when the LP personnel decided to form up and tag along with them. The NVA stopped just short of our perimeter. They then quietly formed into their attack formation and lay down in the prone position to wait. Soon the NVA quickly lifted to one knee and extended their bayonets to the raised position, locking them, poised for the assault, the soldiers who had been manning our listening post took an enormous gamble. They slipped quietly by and breathlessly reentered our lines.

At 3 a.m., the NVA advanced in force, and mortars began to fire. Thanks to the courage of our listening post, the

7th Airborne Battalion had received warning of this attack just minutes before it started. Runners had to make sure everyone was alerted silently. Most of the battalion was ready and waiting, peering into the dark, their senses fully alert. There's always that 10 percent of the men, however, that don't get the word.

My heart-stopping awakening came when the first loud shrieking incoming rounds hit. Krumppp. . . krumppp. . .krumppp. The compression waves from the blasts knocked me out of my hammock and down into the hole I had dug. I woke immediately with a start, my heart beating wildly in my chest with sudden terror. I had been in a deep sleep, where the heart slows, and the mind is inert and dreamless. Now awake, my brain's "sleep clock" kept me drugged with sleep. I lay there stunned in mild shock for however long it took me to register that my poncho, strung above my hammock, had not been full of holes when I went to sleep. My first conscious thought was for my radio, and I pulled it into the hole with me. The poncho was shredded, but my hands told me the radio had not been hit. As long as the radio worked, help was always near.

The devastating sound of incoming rounds came again. Krumppp. . . krumppp. . . krumppp. The ground trembled and shook from each series of colossal flashes and head-slamming explosions. The air whistled with fragments of metal and chunks of earth leaping skyward. Debris showered downward upon me. The smoke enveloped us. The air reeked of high-explosive powder. It seemed to go on forever and intensify as the large shells drowned out all other noise. There was now sporadic gunfire, then a long thunderous volley. The NVA were attacking through their own mortar fire, counting on us to take cover and hide in our foxholes. Those who did this would die there, unless they were just plain lucky. The dry tap of small-arms fire started gradually and then built to a massive roaring eruption. I tried to make myself as small as possible. I was still stair stepping up from the depths of deep slumber. A third and fourth concentration exploded, all within twenty feet of one another, as men screamed in agony. Again there came a high, swift whine. A brief shrieking roar, Krumppp. . .

krumppp. . . krumppp, again followed by concussions and shock waves.

I watched in awe, as impact after impact of exploding enemy mortar shells blanket the entire area around me. Jagged bits of steel death flew in every direction. The trees around me splintered. The NVA was using high-explosive fuze quick. The explosions temporarily deafened me. I instinctively knew the direction from which the NVA were firing. Whoever that NVA forward observer was, his range determination had been very accurate, meaning that he had excellent knowledge of the area. With wide eyes, I watched this dance of death continue to light the darkness. Miraculously, I hadn't been hit right away. I couldn't believe it. Beset by dread, I fell prey to my darkest, ugliest, and most unimaginable fears, which weakened me. As long as I was afraid, I was more vulnerable. I knew I had to do what I didn't want to. I had to be brave and strong, and not let panic grip me. Keeping my head down made me an ineffective fighter.

We were in the merciless embrace of the heavy ground fog that had settled in and choked the valley. The whooshing sound of an illumination round went up and popped. The flare lit, and the night bloomed with white flickering Illumination. The thick night fog diffused the light. The flare floated down under a tiny parachute. We would have two minutes of light before the flare burned itself out. An irregular line of smoke marked its spiraling, hissing descent, and sparks showered down from the flare as it floated toward earth. I dared not move as I stared into the contrast of light and dark images, of growing long shadows cast by the flare that grew brighter as it fell. Then the light started fading, burning itself out, still in the air. My ears still rang.

As the fire at last began to slacken, I moved at a fast low-crawl into the line through the distorting ground fog. It was something like jumping out of the frying pan and into the fire. Immediately after I crawled out of my hole and started toward our main line of resistance, salvo after salvo of projectiles were bursting around the immediate area. The thick mist obscured everything beyond 20 paces. I peered over the crumpled human bodies that lay before me in clumps, trying to catch a glimpse of the ghostly human forms that would surely appear again out of the ground fog. I laid out some magazines in readiness, waited, and listened. Nothing moved save my eyes, hunting. There was an ominous quiet. I strained to listen, for sound carries far at night. The darkness was charged with electricity. Then I felt it, the ground vibration. The subtle pressure of running feet that betrayed their approach, that quickly grew like a fast swelling thunder. They were coming. I heard the familiar slight metallic rustle of weapons.

Faint shadows moved in the drifting mist, surreal shadows that loomed larger, no longer blending with the grayness. The specter-like figures of the *bo doi* slipped out of the night. Then mortar rounds were again exploding around the area. My mouth was dry and my heart was hammering in my chest and ears. I felt like a man condemned to death. Hands sweating, I set my selector switch on semi-automatic fire, to conserve my ammunition.

Their massed ranks emerged from the darkness hunched in a beastial crouch as if from the bowels of the earth, advancing with a blind heroism, like death's foul hand. I could already make out the flickering, lethal gleam of long-steel bayonets that silhouetted our targets, and it had a terrifying effect upon me. The NVA, with no sign of fear or hesitation, with complete and total disregard for their own lives, were suicidally attacking through their own mortar fire. I could feel in my bones the menace of their approach.

They came quickly. Machine guns crackled in hysterical unison and the khaki figures exploded into violent movement as the rounds struck them. A whispering rush arose as bullets cut holes in the air nearby. Much closer I heard the sonic crack of bullets just over my head. The sounds of the attacking NVA were answered by the detonation of claymore mines, and by the many screams and cries of the terribly wounded--these were enough to unnerve the best of men. A stuttering of gunfire started, almost taking my breath away. As I lay there in the dark, shoulder to shoulder with my men, I still felt mortally alone. *Swoosh!* A flare burst overhead. There was an explosion of light. *Pop!* The flare went down and out, plunging us back into darkness again. Around me, I heard the sound of hand-fired flares. Then other flares were popped. *Swoosh! Swoosh!* The thump of illumination rounds fired by the mortar crew sounded clearly through the din. The intermittent, swinging, brilliant artificial half-light of descending parachute flares and ground flares lit the fog, making it shimmer, making the shadows move. I diverted my eyes from the illumination and closed one eye, so I would not lose my night vision once the dark returned. Before me, the blackened landscape had been lit up and turned it white.

My heart rate was greatly accelerated--I could feel the tingling in my fingertips. Rifles fired around the southern perimeter. The sight emerging before me somehow seemed unreal. Now, all too fast they appeared. The crack of rifle fire began to build like a faraway storm. The sustained sound swept in from all around our perimeter, giving witness to the size of the attacking unit. The individual noises of small arms fire were now no longer distinct from one another, and my eardrums swelled and quivered. The NVA charged boldly on line, a wall of steel, without fear. Ejected brass cartridges flew from my weapon. The human wave shuddered as our return fire reverberated throughout the area.

In the gloom, I could hear the electric sound of shrapnel passing above, the unmistakable sonic pop of bullets high overhead, the terrible, loud meaty thumping of bullets hitting bodies, the shrill singing of bullets hitting leaves *frip! frip! frip!* The many sounds of bullets was everywhere, ricocheting off branches, snapping reports that hurt the eardrums, and flitting sound of bullets passing close beside my head.

A body rolled down beside me, and convulsively flopped, jerking in spasms. Someone set off another ground flare. There wasn't a lot of light, but it was enough. I saw the rapid winking of too many assault rifles, meant to suppress our fire as they moved over us. Many NVA were falling and being flung to the dirt, tumbling and colliding with each other. The ground nearby was covered with crawling and semi-still men, writhing in agony, retching blood. Volleys from automatic weapons began across the intervening darkness. I could hear the sound of countless shots building and merging to a crescendo, like one continuous, furious rattling roar of thunder.

Lines of red tracers swept the onrushing ranks of the collapsing NVA.

Every fifth round was a tracer, and the flicker of tracer rounds was everywhere. Their shifting colors of red and green, made pale by the mist, crisscrossed the perimeter. I fired slowly, making each round count. My eyes darted everywhere. My face felt the sting of bark chips, dirt and stone grit, kicked up by the many rounds striking and splintering the tree trunks and limbs and ground around me. Grenades detonated everywhere. Dirt kicked up, stinging my face, neck and hands. The incessant firing made my ears throb with pain. The light from flares hanging in the sky around our perimeter transformed the groups of running men into shadows. I felt as if I couldn't get enough air into my lungs.

Throughout the war, the PAVN never wanted us to know how badly we had hurt them. After each attack the NVA, covering each other, began picking up or dragging their dead and wounded away. They were very disciplined. There was a brief, mercifully quiet lull. Suddenly I could breathe again. *The attackers had come near breaching the defense line, then wavered.* The enemy began pulling back, shocked and badly beaten up by the determined defense.

Adrenaline pumped into my overtaxed system. My ears were ringing from the muzzle blast. I reached in my pack and grabbed a cloth bandoleer and draped it over my head. I ejected my magazine, and with great difficulty and shaking hands, refilled them from another cloth bandoleer. In the immediacy of what I had been doing, I couldn't remember changing magazines during the fighting. I sincerely repeated the Lord's Prayer and the Twenty-third Psalm, over and over, while waiting for whatever was to come next.

Yea, though I walk through the valley of the shadow of death, I will fear no evil: for thou art with me; thy rod and thy staff comfort me.

There were now minutes of breathless silence as I waited for the inevitable to come again, knowing that whether I lived or died would be determined here. The muscle beneath my left eye was out of control and one leg twitched uncontrollably. My throat felt tight. Fear pounded through my chest. Once more, I could not breathe. My flesh crawled as I felt the shock of being trapped; my body and mind felt numb. Waiting in the darkness, the parachute flares gone, there was no relief from the tension. Gradually my throat loosened and let me breathe again. I knew the advantage usually lay with the defender. My nerves were being stretched. We watched, with every sense alert. Everyone was uncannily calm--silent, anesthetized by fear. How many times during those last years, facing imminent death, had I experienced that feeling? The tension between my eyes became so great that I felt I could no longer bear the strain. Reluctantly, I closed my eyes and listened. A weird and unnatural quiet fell over the battleground, broken only by the groans of the wounded. It lasted but a few minutes. A succession of flares burst high above the area, illuminating it with a garish light.

I felt the earth's vibration, the vibration of the attacking force, palpable in the ground. I felt crushed by its intensity. It was barely audible in the close silence of early morning. It was only a slight breath of sound. No louder than that of trodden grass. I could hear them now, the gentle rustling of grasses, and the sound of dry dirt crunching beneath many feet. A familiar prickle crept down my spine. Quickly reassuring myself that I wasn't alone, I glanced to both sides of me, seeing the flare-lit faces of those closest to me, 5 meters away. They too could hear the approaching soldiers. They too were ready. Again I caught the flickering points of light, the lethal gleam of bayonets, winking as they caught the distant, burning flares. Then the first ghostly shadows loomed in front of us, and quickly charged in. Their ranks were closely packed.

I saw the blur of their light-brown uniforms and the shimmer of bayonet points. I could feel and hear the rhythm of their feet as they emerged from the mist. They voiced a brutal, primal yell. There were so many, that I felt they must break under the punishment of our weapons. Yet, they came on, never wavering, scornful of death. I felt lost. I brought my carbine to bear on a moving shadow. Our aimed, sustained rifle-fire was soon drowned out by a roaring. Many PAVN flipped forward, hit low. Others were thrown backward. Some crumpled and flopped crazily. The staccato chattering of many machineguns firing their killing line, belly high, was maddening. Our streams of red tracers washed into them, and their dead and wounded were knocked into crazy heaps. Flares were fired. They went high overhead and before us, lighting the area behind the attacking NVA, increasing our vision, preserving our night vision. The NVA could see as well, but they were looking right into the light. When the flares went out, they would be blind for minutes. Darkness is an enemy only to the untrained. Low to the ground, with my hat brim pulled down, the light would not strike my eyes directly.

Suddenly a fusillade of fire erupted, as if all of us had waited for the same moment to shoot. The vicious whine of ricocheting rounds sounded everywhere. The line of khaki uniforms faltered as they encountered our return fire. My eyes darted, examining the dark shadows, and I saw the faint wisps of men and their moving faces, and then NVA soldiers raced toward my position. I distinctly heard the slow, loud rattle and sharp cracks of the staccato beat of the AK-47's.

As they assaulted our line, they built up a massive roar of intense small arms fire, interspersed with the crackling and then the rush of close-passing 82mm rocket-propelled grenades, fired from their RPG-7 launcher. The hair on the back of my neck and arms was standing up.

Fsssssssttttt. A familiar sound.

I watched the RPG wobble coming in, passing above me and just behind me.

Booom!

The NVA's constant and accurate mortar fire was a terrible wonder to behold. It wore on the nerves.

Krumppp! Krumppp! Krumppp!

We froze, but our psychological shock was only momentary. Our line erupted with the frightful return of small arms fire, tearing into these suicidal troops. Aiming instinctively, I dropped one in mid-stride. Luckily, the Browning automatic rifleman (BAR) got the others. They fell face down and rolled several feet, legs twitching in the throes of death. One soldier almost got up on me, when a feeling of calm came over me. Surely blinded by the illumination and the muzzle flash of his weapon, he couldn't see me. He was firing too high and off to my flank. I knew that I couldn't miss and fired several rounds

Troopers in fighting positions on both sides of me were moaning. I had been splattered with blood. The salty taste of it was in my mouth. The fighting in the dark fog was bitter. At many points, our line developed into brief struggles of hand to hand combat between men of both sides, as the airborne troops stubbornly resisted the NVA advance. Then, the attack was quickly broken off.

My hands flew over my body, checking for a wound. The blood I wiped from my face did not seem to be mine. Depressing the magazine catch and removing the empty magazine with fumbling hands, I managed to recharge it and re-insert it into my carbine. I recharged my other empty magazines and waited. Everyone nearby checked the persons lying nearest to them to ensure they were not partnered with an NVA soldier.

Of all the major things that could have gone wrong that morning, communication failure was thankfully not one of them. I managed to call over the radio and request that all my pre-plotted defensive concentrations be fired upon. I knew that we had to eliminate all the unnecessary radio traffic now tying up our communications net. Until then, things were not going to get better. I waited for Capt. James C. Kern to get everyone off our frequency. A marine artillery unit was on standby to support us with indirect fire. The PAVN had been busy adjusting their own supporting fire, and keeping its fierce continuous pressure crashing in on us at point blank range where our two lines met.

The NVA's neutralization fire had killed and wounded a lot of men at the outset of the attack, but they hadn't destroyed our combat effectiveness, or our will to fight. All of our able-bodied, and many of our wounded, still bleeding, with field dressings on their arms and legs, stuck to their fighting positions. I felt the hair on the back of my neck rise to attention. Trying to remain calm, I checked my rifle and magazines. *This is it*, I thought again. "Stay calm," I kept repeating to myself as I waited in a daze. "Don't panic." I caught sight of our men moving around to redistribute themselves, taking the places of the many who had already paid the full price. My head, eyes and neck ached from staring into the dark. With growing despair, I felt as if the weight of the world was physically pressing down on my upper back. I felt as if a rock were lodged in my stomach. When things were hot and heavy, I didn't experience much of anything, except the kind of detachment assumed by a spectator, watching all this happen. Then there were periods when I was completely terrified. Since early in the morning, I had already run my hands over myself several times expecting to discover a wound.

Suddenly, we saw the running shadows emerge once more. They were almost on top of us, firing on the run. It made my breath come quickly. I aimed into the dark, looking down the top length of my rifle, at their waist level, and fired. We had no trouble finding another target, as more khaki uniforms appeared. Watching them race closer, my eyes were clenched against the glare, waiting until I couldn't miss. The attack seemed to break off as quickly as it started. I could hear and see the NVA noisily dragging their dead and wounded. I prayed.

Thou preparest a table before me in the presence of mine enemies: thou anointest my head with oil; my cup runneth over.

Waiting frays the nerves. As I waited and listened, there came the sound of movement through the grass. It swelled in my ears and mingled with the pounding of my heart. I took a big breath. Blinding white flashes, followed by the explosive cracks of hand grenades. It had started again. I heard the sickening crunch of bone as a bullet passed through a head somewhere on my left. Crouched in my depression, I felt exposed and vulnerable, without any hope. The crackling din of rifles was followed by the chatter of machine-guns.

The noise became incredible--a fluctuating chorus of screams, harsh cries, gunfire and hand grenades. Suppressed fear now overwhelmed my senses. I had glanced toward the BAR gunner, next to me just in time to see a bullet glance off the receiver of his weapon and slice open the side of his face. He paused just long enough to touch his wound, looked at the blood on his hand, then returned to his weapon with no sign of distress. He initiated immediate action. He attempted to make it fire, but found the Browning unworkable. Throwing it aside, he grabbed a nearby rifle and continued fighting. Others nearby lay twitching and writhing, until the medics carried or dragged them off to the aid station.

My carbine was quickly ejecting its spent rounds, as men in front of me grunted in pain, fell and screwed themselves into the ground. They were getting too close for comfort. The coughing roar of hand-grenades sounded everywhere. Beneath it, I could hear the more deliberate semi-automatic firing of our rifles. I could tell that the men on my portion of the perimeter were aiming at their targets. Then it was over again. These NVA soldiers were truly strong-hearted men, men with spirit.

My PRC-25 radio lay at my elbow, in its own depression. I knew that nothing must happen to it. I was more terrified for my radio than for myself. I knew Captain Kern was still alive, because I had heard him over the radio, trying to make our situation clear to everyone listening and talking on our frequency, so they would stay off the radio so we could get down to the business of trying to stay alive. When the fog lifted my turn would be at hand, if I were still here. With the radio, I fully intended to bring the world to me. To this day, I still think about all the times I spent worrying about radios.

I heard the soapy smack of a bullet hitting flesh in someone on my right, and felt bits of his flesh and blood splatter onto me. There was the sound of legs thrashing. The body noisily voided its bowels in a gaseous explosion. I didn't have to look. I knew he was now dead. Somehow, the *bo doi* were all stopped and lay in a lifeless sprawl to our immediate front. The seconds and minutes were passing slowly, and in the heavy silence, my eyes, wide with terror, burning with accumulated distress were fixed on the terrain to my front.

Surely goodness and mercy shall follow me all the days of my life; and I will dwell in the house of the Lord forever.

The bloody night had begun to gray into false dawn. The moment I saw that, I knew I wanted more of this life before I died. Finally, daybreak! Dawn never really broke--with fog, the quality of light was poor--but there was light at long last, and where there was light, there was hope and I felt as if the hand of God had touched me. The mist was lifting. Looking around, I could see that those nearest me were alert and visibly calm. I saw several low-flying, slow-moving rocket propelled grenades coming in and passing over us, as I heard the hysterical outbreak of small-arms fire on the distant side of the perimeter. One rocket passed directly over my head. From the slant they came in on, I could tell that the gunners were about 75 yards away. The Soviet RPG-2 gunners were evidently lined up out there--somewhere, close--firing their shoulder-fired 40mm HEAT rockets.

Faces of the Enemy

The mist at ground level had almost cleared. Again, I heard the light but audible slap of running feet. I looked at those nearest me and saw their eyes reflecting what mine must have looked like. A good number of *Bo doi* rose up, delivered fire, and charged. We held our fire. Their eyes were filled with a terrible desperation, their bayonets pointing the way. They just kept coming. I felt as if my self-control was almost gone. Both sides were firing at point blank range. I aimed low. Many collapsed without a sound, others lay writhing and screaming, clutching their bodies, blood misting out from terrible wounds, weapons discharging into the air. Ricochets were everywhere, and direct fire stitched the ground all around us, throwing dirt and leaf litter over us. I watched bodies rolling, arms flying wide as they were struck and lost coordination. Tears ran down my cheeks. Shots were still fired as the NVA retreated from sight, dragging their dead and wounded. Not trusting my eyes, I watched, reloaded a fresh magazine, and began filling the others from my cloth bandoleer. The area was covered with spent rounds, and the perimeter was strewn with twisted corpses and wounded from both sides. I could see bodies twitching and jerking in the epilepsy of death. The khaki uniforms of the NVA mingled with our own. Then as fast as it had started, it was over. Somehow, we had held. Our numbers were now meager, our ammunition dwindling. It was still foggy and dark. The gray ceiling was lifting, but very slowly. Cordite fumes hung heavily over the area.

In the next several minutes, I saw as many as three dark-colored rifle grenades at one time. They were wobbling my way, a couple feet too high, and exploding somewhere behind me. Eventually I knew one of them would manage to find me. Sure enough, I felt a blast of wind at my back and head, followed by the stinging and burning sensation of the grenade fragments. I felt something running down my neck and wiped at it. My hand came away bloody. I radioed Captain Kern. "I've been hit in the head," I said. "Well if they hit you in the head, they couldn't have hurt you much" was all he had to say. I felt better instantly, and, with blood still oozing from the wounds, I went back to work. Nearby, I saw one wounded trooper, fighting to stay conscious as foamy pink blood leaked from his nose and mouth. He was hit in the lung, wheezing and coughing, each jarring cough bringing an explosive new agony, consuming him in pain.

The cloud ceiling was still very low. Dark, ragged clouds covered the sky. At this rate it would be well past midday before the fog lifted, if it ever did. Visual aerial observation by Red Marker, our Forward Air Controller (FAC) was out because of the fog. However, he was already flying in the area above us, searching for a hole in the clouds. We knew that the PAVN could also hear the ominous droning overhead. The FAC had told me to be prepared to mark my forward edge of the battle area. He had already had some jet fighters stacking up and orbiting the area, waiting at a much higher altitude, saving fuel in the thinner air. But they were now low on fuel and had decided to leave. Deeper than our fear was our awareness that we were alone. The FAC informed us that he would fly further inland and probe for a hole in the clouds. Then he was gone.

Around 0800 hours, Captain Thomas C. Kerns was placing panels out on the northern perimeter for aircraft identification when another frontal assault started. He quickly took cover in a shallow foxhole, much too small for his bulk. Kerns left it and took cover behind a tree. By then he had seen four NVA coming quickly toward his position, 30 feet away.

In the quick exchange of fire, Kerns was shot twice, in two places with an AK-47 round, known as the "piggy-back"-- two bullets fired as one. The first penetrated and the other tumbled and destroyed. The initial round struck his hand and entered the palm above his index finger, shattering bones. The piggyback round struck and fractured the bone in his upper thigh, as it glanced off, leaving a terrible exit wound. He was bleeding profusely. His serious leg wound left him unable to walk or move, and he fell backward into the foxhole he had just left. He lay exposed, incapacitated. I heard his dazed plea for help on the radio. Sometime much later, our medics found Kerns unconscious. They managed to stop his bleeding and administered morphine. Amid the maelstrom of small arms fire, exploding grenades and mortars, it took six Vietnamese soldiers to carry the 6-foot, 185-pound Kerns to the aid station.

How dangerous our overall tactical situation was, I didn't know. It was a good thing too, because I was already almost scared to death. The next time I contacted Capt. Kern his voice sounded different. He told me on the radio to hold the perimeter at all cost. His voice was pleading, in a desperate tone, thick with shock. We were now in serious trouble. *Winning a battle is about holding the line and sticking with your comrades. Discipline!* We had expended a lot of ammunition in fending off the previous attacks. I could hear the firing getting louder. It had changed in pitch, a great volume of automatic fire and the flat-hollow crack of grenades coming from Kerns' northern portion of the perimeter. I exchanged worried looks with Vietnamese troopers on my left. We all knew the NVA might have broken through. In fact, part of the perimeter on the north side had indeed already been overrun by the human-wave assault. I was unaware that my fears had been realized, that a macabre drama was taking place on the northwestern side of the perimeter.

Captain Kerns' men were engaged in close-in fighting, and for many, it was hand-to-hand fighting, where no quarter was given. The NVA penetration of our perimeter managed to isolate many of our men in the northern sector. This accounted for our many missing after the battle. The NVA were determined to push us back toward the river, where our movement would be hampered and they could cause greater casualties. We were determined not to be pushed back. The battle in this small area was savage.

The breach had been closed by pulling a few Airborne troopers out of their assigned positions on the south and east sides of the perimeter. Headquarters personnel were also used to fill in to the front of the NVA penetration and close the gap. From my own position, I saw some of these able bodied men moving double-time back toward the headquarters element. At the time, I thought they were going for more ammunition and hand grenades. Reinforcing the perimeter in the overrun areas left me with only a few men. It was this thought, of men running out of ammunition, which really put a chill in me. Overhead, I heard the sound of the Forward Air Controller's aircraft, as the fog slowly continued lifting.

He was flying in from the east, under the ceiling. I couldn't believe it. Flying that low, he was really sticking his neck out for us. There was barely one hundred feet vertical clearance between the treetops and the clouds. He also brought good news: a flight of A-1 Skyraiders, were now orbiting above the clouds. Just knowing they were there helped to restore my faltering courage. We had, at this point, been fighting for seven and a half desperate hours. The FAC told me to talk directly to the A-1 Skyraider flight leader when he arrived.

The A-1 pilot would have his hands full, as his radio traffic was about to intensify in order to reduce confusion over the battalion's perimeter. While concentrating on flying his aircraft, observing the ground situation, taking and giving instructions, operating his three different radios--VHF, UHF and FM--he would also be busily writing locations, altitudes, and axis of attack on the Plexiglas window with a grease pencil. At present he was talking to me on his FM radio. His midair briefing and instructions to the fighter pilots would be on his UHF radio. The VHF radio was used for communicating to his command post. All the while, he had to try and ignore the fact that he was under fire. I could clearly hear and see the multiple streams of green tracers lacing upward, and told the FAC he was receiving fire.

Help was on the way. Each Skyraider, fully loaded, would have 8,000 pounds of mixed weapons: four 20mm machine guns, napalm, bombs and CBUs (Cluster Bomb Units). On the ground, the hand grenade duels were still going on. Hope and dread stirred simultaneously within me. As I waited, I removed the blue-gray cylindrical body of an M18 colored smoke grenade from my harness. I still had the presence of mind to scrape off the tape covering the holes and to straighten the pin. The chemical grenade had a 2-second delay. The FAC requested that the perimeter be marked, so I threw the smoke out to my front, as did the rest of the men waiting on the perimeter. The cylinder popped, and the angry swirls hissed out of the spinning grenade, spreading smoke quickly along the ground and slowly up into the air.

Just then, the intensity of fire picked up a little. The NVA must have been listening in. Then, surprising us momentarily, the small-arms fire began to subside. Even as I wondered what would come next, I caught that wonderful raw throbbing of a powerful, propeller-driven engine, droning up the valley. I told the FAC to start with the cane field. It was full of NVA. I was told that the Skyraider flight leader had flown west, looking for a hole to fly down through. He was going to try coming down on the deck with us! The FAC, just under the ceiling, slowly circled above our perimeter, watching. I knew what was happening, and had the line again marked with smoke. This time, the NVA must have definitely seen or heard what was coming. Their automatic-weapons fire abruptly ceased. It was now deathly silent and still, except for the distant sound of the approaching aircraft. I knew for certain that the NVA were well aware of what was happening. Now it was their turn to be terrified. Anyone who had ever been in serious trouble in country with the NVA knew that the A-1s were some of the best help you could get.

The unmistakable roar slowly approached from the east, swelling in volume, the deep thundering increasing rapidly in strength, as it got closer. That first brave, ballsy American fighter pilot came droning in from the east in his beautiful, loud, fully armed Douglas A-1 Skyraider. He flew low and slow, just above the treetops, looking at the target, then passed overhead 50 yards away, above and slightly south of the sugarcane field, talking to me on his FM radio. "*Burn it*," I said. I could see the pilot take a good look at the situation on the ground. I could see him looking down at the cane field, as he replied. "I will make the attack flying from west to east," he told me," flying directly over your position and release my ordnance." Then the flight leader made a long, slow turn, started his first run, and dropped a 150-gallon canister of jellied napalm.

That first six-foot-long canister wobbled downward and blossomed into a giant tumbling fireball. One by one, the other pilots commenced their attacks. A single burst of a canister of napalm covered a 100-foot radius and would stick to anything it hit. If there were any underground entrances out there, it would asphyxiate those inside and outside for a hundred yards around, drawing out the air and depleting it of oxygen without burning them. I watched the canisters tumble end over end, glittering in the light. I watched, gape-jawed with awe. The NVA soldiers panicked when they saw what was happening, and started a mind-bending screaming and howling before the enormous explosion occurred. They ran, trying in vain to get away.

 The canister lit off and exploded in a "whoosh." A yellow-white fireball erupted and splattered as air rushed in to feed the jelled gasoline. Then a thick, black cloud of noxious smoke billowed straight up and drifted. The field was turned into an impenetrable wall of flame. The sound could not drown out the screams of the wounded and of those burning to death. The heat wave blasted over my face with terrible strength. The pilots now had an accurate reference to carry out the rest of their attacks.

 While I was coordinating the air strike on my right flank, I had looked around and saw the fierce face of the 7th Battalion Executive Commander, Major Le Minh Ngoc. His expression radiated intense will power. We watched the flames trailing from the screaming, flailing and running figures, as the jelled gasoline burned their hair, clothing and bodies until they crumpled. We could hear the sound of heads popping from the burning heat. We saw and heard the hysterical and terrified screams of upright, running figures trying very briefly to wipe the flaming fuel from their burning uniforms, then fall and thrash upon the ground with blackened arms and legs. It cooked them, turned them black. The lucky ones had not been in the splashdown and had not breathed the flames; it killed them more quickly. The screaming continued for a bit, and ammunition started cooking off. The smell of napalm was heavy. The cane field and its cover were now mostly burned off.

 Now, the Skyraider was vulnerable to enemy anti-aircraft fire, and green tracers from Chinese-made .51-caliber heavy machine guns could be seen going over the aircraft. Luckily, the Skyraider was made with heavy armament, helping to protect the pilot from small-arms fire. I took mental note of the locations where the streams of tracers had originated. The next fighter swooped in and dropped his canister raining napalm. All the Skyraiders were taking heavy ground fire. Below, the NVA caught in that large cane field were incinerated.

    I next requested that the rest of the canisters be dropped immediately east of my position. It was from this area that we had been receiving intense fire, and most of the ground attacks. We would learn later that day that our carefully selected defensive position, in which we had remained overnight, had an NVA trench system just outside of the perimeter. The Skyraider flight leader conducted the attack, flying from south to north. It was a close strike; it had to be. Watching the approaching Skyraider flying through the heavy ground fire, I was very frightened for him, and for myself. I remembered other American infantrymen who had been hit in splashdowns. Napalm was risky to deliver in close proximity to friendly troops because there was an extreme range error potential, but it was now necessary. The canisters dropped, end over end, exploding in flames, and splashing upward, forward and then down. The outer burning edge was just a few yards away. Its smell was unique. I could feel the superheated air burning at 2,000 degrees Fahrenheit, starving the life-giving oxygen. It burned my face.

    The air strikes continued. Each aircraft dropped a pair of bombs. A bright white thundering of flashes would be followed by great concussions. Each aircraft would then peel away to the east and prepare for another run. Black smoke was everywhere. I watched in fascination as the antipersonnel cluster bomb units (CBU) separated from the low-flying aircraft and fell. The free-falling container detonated and the outer shell of the CBU peeled away, scattering hundreds of smaller shot-put sized bomblets. I felt the tooth-rattling vibrations of pressure waves shudder through me as I lay there. The hundreds of mighty concussion waves rocketed across the ground. Well within their range, I heard them passing over my head. Dirt and debris was thrown everywhere, and smoke engulfed everything, remaining for a good while. Then the A-1's conducted their strafing runs, each with their four 20 mm cannons. Ground litter flew everywhere as the A-1's expended their ammunition in high-level attacks.

Then another chilling reality settled in. The flight had exhausted its ordnance and was on minimum fuel. I watched them wave off and speed away to refuel and rearm. The A-1's were gone. Enemy small arms fire picked up again, and deadly streams of slugs ripped through the leaves. The FAC told me he had some Canberra B-57 bombers standing by. The solid cloud cover and low ceiling was still in place, so the aircraft made their only approaches, one by one.

Flying from the south to the north, they were coming in on us so closely that I found myself screaming into the radio that they were too close. This versatile and highly maneuverable aircraft, normally used in ground attacks, had a two-man crew seated one behind the other, and I could see them in the bubble canopy on their approach. From their insignia, I could see that they were Australian aircraft. The FAC told me that they were not armed but merely flying dummy runs without ordnance.

The Royal Australian Air Force (RAAF) Canberra's of No. 2 Squadron were returning from another mission and decided to help us stall for time. With their ordnance already expended on another target, these Australians braved the heavy machine-gun fire to make these extremely low and slow runs over our position to our immediate front. The straight-winged bombers, known for their accuracy, did this by opening their bomb bay doors to fake out the NVA. It must have scared the NVA, because it scared the hell out of me.

The weather and suppressive fire hampered our medical support. The first of our wounded personnel had been waiting until after mid-day to be evacuated. Forced by circumstances to remain above ground level, trying to repeatedly retrieve the many wounded from our perimeter, our medical personnel suffered eighty-percent casualties.

After the Marine medevac missions started, I couldn't help but marvel, again and again, the raw courage displayed by every single pilot. They were flying the old H-34 Choctaw, and the arrival of the first, lone helicopter signaled to the wounded that they had hope. The sound of the choppers engine was faint and distant coming in from the east flying well around and outside our area to make their final approach from the west. This was the only approach that could be used to avoid enemy ground fire. Coming down river, the medevac chopper flew low until they neared our position, where they had to gain altitude. The whistling whine of the rotor grew swiftly shriller coming in quickly on the approach to our landing zone. The roaring whine of the helicopter erupted as it popped up over our position like a gigantic bird. They maneuvered over our landing zone, into the intense heavy machine-gun and small-arms fire unleashed against them. They had to slow abruptly to a hover, set down in a roaring hurry, load our wounded as quickly as they could, and then lift, bank left, and fly out the way they came in. It seemed to me that it took too long to load, but in reality it probably took only a couple minutes. These medevac missions went on for three hours that day, receiving intense ground fire the whole time.

Around 1500 hours, Kerns witnessed the Marine medevac helicopter coming in under intense anti-aircraft fire. He was finally placed aboard. There were so many wounded that three wounded Vietnamese were lying on the floor under him. Kerns managed to look at the man he was laying directly on top of; he had a sucking chest wound. The aircraft lifted. The anti-aircraft fire intensified and stitched holes through the chopper. The skillful Marine pilot soon had his helicopter up and down to the river to escape the direct fire. The chopper made it out, heavily peppered with holes.

At one point, I looked around behind me, my attention drawn by the terrible intensity of concentrated machine-gun fire directed against the medevac crews, and the sound of the rounds going overhead and slapping the chopper. Green tracers from several NVA gun positions were hitting the Choctaw. The green tracers were still coming from the same general area that I had noted earlier, while they had fired on the Air Force.

At the helicopter's most vulnerable moment of exposure, when the pilot brought it to a hover, I watched 12.7mm green tracers envelop him and the aircraft shudder from the numerous hits. I saw the helicopter lurch. I could imagine the controlled panic and terror of the crew. The pilot pulled up as the impact of the rounds ripped through the length of its side. I saw one of the rounds hit the crew chief. Then the tail fin assembly was blown halfway off and went flying through the air. The helicopter vibrated, spun and oscillated into circles, then lurched from side to side as it began to stabilize. It tried to gain altitude while leaving the area. There was no doubt in my mind that these pilots had given their best for us and our wounded under intense fire, and were now doing their best to get out of there with their lives, with the helicopter and with our wounded. The wounded who were conscious and still on the ground had to endure not only the pain of their wounds, but the special hell of watching the helicopters come and go under direct intense machine-gun fire. The thought was terrifying, knowing their turn would come.

Finally, the friendly U.S. Marine artillery battery was turned over to me. The artillery battery of six 105mm guns was finally mine. I remembered. *Each of the six guns could fire at a sustained rate of 3 rounds per minute, for a total of 18 rounds. The battery could fire faster, but this rate of fire was best for the life of the guns.* Then in moments, I was finally talking to the Fire Direction Control (FDC). After identifying myself, I repeated those beautiful words: "fire mission." Proceeding with the elements for calling fire, I gave him my grid and direction to target, followed by "Little Brown Mother Fuckers in the open." I requested High Explosive (HE) fuze quick. The last element was: "will adjust."

The flash blossoming of the first rounds were beautifully close, as the clouds of black smoke and dust towered and drifted in the air. Shrapnel whizzed overhead, smacking branches and trees dully. They were less than 50 meters in front of me. After the area was saturated, I made small range changes, 50 meters at a time, and walked the fire back where the NVA had originated their attack. The NVA knew where I was and what I was doing. Each time I barely lifted my head, the automatic weapons fire, small-arms fire and rifle grenades directed my way became more intense. Rounds were cracking and popping all around and over my head. I noticed a trooper to my right, head down and hands fluttering. The PAVN's tracer ammunition had been a great help to me. The machine gunners, directing their fire so effectively at long range, had also revealed from where that fire was coming.

I had to switch to white phosphorous (WP) periodically because I could not get my head up far enough to see, so I just watched and waited for the burning, dense, gray smoke of the thick white phosphorous cloud to raise and waft over the area, and then went on with my adjustments. The incendiary effect of the flying, bright spikes of white phosphorus flowers, burning without oxygen, would also set fire to the surrounding vegetation, destroying the PAVNs available cover.

The waxy particles adhered to flesh, and when it was exposed to air, it burst into flames. It was a great casualty producer; it would burn its way into a body and keep burning until it burned itself out. The acrid fumes from these bursts hung over the area. After adjusting the correct deviation and range on the target, the command "fire for effect" was given. I now felt much better, knowing that the bursting radius of one

105mm round of high explosive (HE) was killing everything in a 30 meter radius plus. The six guns of the artillery battery covered a 200-meter area of my front, shifting on my command.

Looking at the map, I made an educated guess as to the location from which the NVA had directed the heavy machine gun fire, and where their rally point would be. It was payback time. I decided that the wood line in the far distance, directly east of my position, was the right place. I plotted it, called it in and asked the artillery battery to hit that area hard. They saturated that area well. I heard later that it had been a good guess.

Some American staff puke, far removed from our location, had tied our communications net up for quite a while earlier that day, talking nonsense to us, in his attempt to second guess the decisions of Captain Kern and myself about the close proximity of the artillery fire we were directing. This was a perfect example of the flightiness of the human mind in combat, and of a staff officer whose only experience in this type of situation is academic. In this case our brigade liaison officer was trying to get into the operations business, instead of staying in the liaison business. What he didn't understand was that the most important thing was to attack your target in the shortest possible time. In close-quarter combat there are no rules except survival. Artillery fire has to be very close, or the advantage is given to the enemy. It was something I had come up against while serving in the infantry with the 101st Airborne, the cautious reluctance of the commanders and forward observers to bring in artillery fire closely. That liaison officer had cost us many lives and didn't have to accept any responsibility for his actions.

* * *

I briefly remembered one of my relatives, Commander J.D.P. Hodapp, Jr. USN (Ret), who had once commanded the U.S.S. Hall in World War II in the Pacific during the battle for Okinawa, relating to me about the firing of the big guns. Commander Hodapp, a well-decorated Pearl Harbor Survivor, had served aboard the USS Iowa for three months during the summer of 1947 as the Seamanship Department head for the embarked Naval ROTC midshipman on their first postwar training cruise (He had just been assigned to the University of California, Berkeley, as Associate Professor of Naval Science in April of 1947 after nearly eight straight years of sea duty, and he went back to sea for the summer). The Iowa had been permitted to fire all the weaponry aboard. He witnessed the 16" guns as a spectator—his place for viewing was high up on the foremast—the first firings were individual turrets (three guns) and then a full nine-gun broadside. He had been told what would happen, but had been hard to believe until he saw it for himself—the blasts of nine guns each throwing out a one ton projectile at the same time over the starboard actually shoved the 60,000 ton ship a few inches to port—the movement was noted in the water cascading down the side of the ship. He had said the blast was something out of hell, even though he had big cotton wads stuffed in his ears. I shrugged off the flight of memory, and returned to the present.

* * *

There were still NVA troops in the deep, narrow trench to our front. I realized this when I saw the intense fire they unleashed during and after each overhead run by the Air Force, and after each artillery strike. Those troops were not going to get burned up or exposed to any other type of fire as long as they remained in those trenches and didn't get a direct hit.

I was beginning to feel distressed, when I again saw Major Ngoc nearby, observing to the front of my portion of the perimeter. I got myself over to him and asked what we were going to do. He looked at me for what seemed a long period of time and then said, "There's nothing we can do, except counterattack." I thought about this and knew he was right. Our only recourse out of this present situation was the old maxim of war, to do the unexpected: take the offensive and counterattack. There was no alternative. I will never forget this as long as I live. I'm certain I had anything but a stoic look on my face. I knew that there couldn't be that many of us left who were still holding on. All we really had left was our defiance.

There we were, with these immense numbers of dead and dying, with no room in the evacuation area because there were so many wounded, and we were about to take a greater risk and counterattack a vastly superior force 25 yards away. Our little battalion was almost used up, as was our ammunition. Hand grenade duels still continued intermittently. So far we had been on the defensive, surrounded, fighting for our very lives. One more determined assault by the NVA would finish us. But frightened as we were, we had to ignore the reality of the situation. We had to find the courage to get up out of the security of our fighting positions and move through the open to counterattack. I thought. *Well, at least it's a short distance to the trench. The unexpected will often cause panic. Surprise and momentum is everything!* The desperate paratroopers of the 7th Battalion were given only a short time to prepare themselves for the counterattack. We waited, tense to charge, each man staring ahead fixedly. *Do not think, just act.*

The NVA trench was only 25 yards away. *Father, protect me.* Then the command was given: "Follow me."

"Now!" With a roar, the paratroopers got up on command, as one, with teeth bared in a grimace, we surged forward, quickly crossing the open ground and swept over their trench in one quick movement, roaring and shooting, into the shocked and dazed enemy. Crumpled and formless bodies littered the area; the only ones moving were those of our wounded comrades, lying outside the trench to our rear, hit in the counterattack. We shot down into the trench, until all movement stopped. Their bodies became mangled and grotesque.

The counterattack had caught the NVA by surprise, and we killed them all. We quickly reloaded. In my sector it was over swiftly, we had killed a large number of men in just minutes by a quick move of surprise. They had not even had a chance to get up to give a good fight.

They'd had the means of escaping, if they'd known we would counterattack. But they didn't know, and didn't have time to get away. The bottom of the trench had small holes intermittently spaced so that their soldiers could crawl into or out from an underground tunnel connected to the trench system. I don't think very many people noticed this, because they were mostly covered with the dead bodies of those who had not had time to get into the exit tunnel. The field was now littered with enemy casualties, abandoned equipment and weapons. As I looked around at those airborne troops still standing, I realized that something extraordinary had happened that day. We had defeated an NVA unit four times our size. All I felt was weary.

After this, as the North Vietnamese begin to break away, snipers focused on my sector of the line and slowly went to work on us. One Vietnamese paratrooper was shot down in front of me, in the open, while retrieving an enemy weapon from one of the dead NVA soldiers. Before the bullet hit him, I had seen it cutting through the air, and I watched as he threw his shoulders back and shivered. His breath exploded as the round struck him in the left breast, through one lung. When it struck, the explosive spray of blood, bits of bone, fabric and dust shot out towards me. The trooper was running, and the force of the bullet lifted him into the air in mid-stride. Then he buckled, collapsed and limply rolled to a stop. He was alive, but shot solidly through the chest. I witnessed the shock in his eyes as the bullet hit him. I watched him try to get back on his feet. His back rose and fell impotently. In his pain, blood coming from his lips, he waved "no" to everyone wanting to help him, concerned that we too would be hit, and went limp.

    I had always been a fast runner, and I gambled that I could dash out there, grab his web gear, and run him back before the sniper could see me, aim and fire. I prayed that the sniper was still congratulating himself on his last shot and was not yet ready for another target so quickly. The wounded trooper looked up again and saw me coming. "No!" the trooper grimaced. Again saying, "No, no," and motioning the same with his hand, he ended with a groan of pain. He sighed a terrible moan of pain as I lifted him by his web gear with one hand. I felt my adrenaline surging. It must have been pumping, because the trooper felt as light as a briefcase on the way back. I had beaten the snipers. I laid him face up on the ground under cover. He attempted to talk as pink foam bubbled from his mouth. Then the blood spewed out. Breathing in shallow gasps and still trying to talk, he gurgled. He tried to rise but could not. More blood gushed from his mouth and nostrils. I quickly rolled him over, so he would not drown in his own blood. Then the medics were there. They carried him face down, and the blood dribbled from his mouth as they hurried him away.

    I reported to our medic and asked him to check the grenade fragments from a rifle grenade in the back of my head. Our medic examined the small fragment wounds and told me that my skull had stopped the fragments. He proceeded to take the small fragments out with tweezers admonishing me the whole time because of the moans and groans I made as he pulled each piece from my head. It seems that I had made more noise than all of the seriously wounded still present. The area was a nightmarish scene. There were so many dead that the raw smell of death filled the air with the peculiar stench of rendered flesh and blood. The area smelled of pus, blood, sweat, urine and excrement.

    What struck me most was how the wounded suffered their terrible wounds in silence--accepting their fate. There were no wails of agony. Men rolled their heads and held them back, tilting their face to the heavens, with their lips drawn back and eyes rolling, silently crazy with pain. I saw and felt the real agony of intense pain being suffered by so many. It was as if each man knew the other was worse off than he. Looking at the exhausted, disheveled and sweat-dampened faces of these mangled men, laying on the ground, still waiting for evacuation, suffering terrible pain in quiet dignity, I felt many emotions. Many looked almost gone. I saw the haggard and stunned eyes of a bandaged half face, of one man whose jaw had been blown away. I watched the frantic work of the sweaty medics moving among them, squatting beside them. I could smell upon them the fetid stench of old blood and the coppery smell of fresh blood. Many of those wounded had shockingly mutilated bodies and were barely conscious. Others were already in the merciful oblivion of unconsciousness. Most of the wounds were upper body wounds. Medics were changing reams of bloody bandages and administering intravenous fluids, trying valiantly to stanch the flow of blood and prevent shock. The IV's would enable many of the wounded to make it to the hospital.

I heard the respiration of many of these critically wounded men, as they fought for breath. They were raggedly breathing their last breaths, the unnatural, hurried-air catching in the throat, creating the raspy and hissing sound of a chest wound. I knelt by one friend. I held his hand and watched, as the flicking of his eyes grew weaker, the lids pulling back. I saw his eyes widen, go fixed, and suddenly dilate as his last ragged breath went out of him with a sigh. *Gone!* His fingers slowly curled. Gone with so many others. Still kneeling, as I lifted my head, I saw other drained faces. I wanted to speak with some but could not, for fear they would cough, spit blood, and strangle. One man's face, eyes opened inordinately wide, was purple. He wasn't breathing. A medic tried to force air into his lungs. No response. With another attempt, his chest heaved, and then he coughed. His body stiffened, he coughed again weakly. His eyes fluttered open. He had made it back.

I saw one soldier with a terrible, sticky stomach wound, with a purple bubble of intestine partly protruding. The stench of torn intestines was overpowering. The odor mingled with the smell of blood. Only a bubbling whisper of sound escaped the man, his eyes fluttered open. The entrails were trying to burst through. His eyes, filmy and misted, were filled with pain and fixed with the ashen color of death. He coughed and wheezed. Agony was on his face--with each flush of pain, his jaw muscles tightened and he gritted his teeth. Blood was gushing out, as if from a small hose. Rivulets of blood turned into dark puddles beneath the wounds. The wound was quickly wrapped. Then another gaping abdominal wound presented itself to my eyes. Momentarily, I watched the guts trying to puff out as the medic worked frantically. I wondered how long the men would have to suffer, strangling in their own blood, before death mercifully took them.

I saw ruined legs, where the white of jagged bones showed in torn and purple swollen flesh. There was one soldier with a terrible leg wound, who was silently moaning in tremendous pain; his left femur, the heaviest bone in the body, had been shattered. They twisted and struggled feebly, their bodies arched in spasms of pain. Some would let out a long breath and mercifully go unconscious. As I turned to a nearby sound, I saw heels drumming the ground as death touched yet another. Another white-faced trooper with glazed eyes was leaning against a tree in muted agony, one hand over his belly, blood running through his fingers, soaking his crotch. He tried to talk to the medic, but without success. His indrawn breath hissed sharply through his teeth. Then, came the sound of more labored breathing. As I passed another with a bloody but intact nose, I saw a bubble of blood form in a nostril and then burst.

Turning my head, I saw a bandaged chest. Blood was seeping through the layers covering the wound on the right side, about where his kidney was located. As I looked into the face, my friend looked up at me and tried to smile. Concerned, I tapped a nearby busy medic who spoke English and pointed to my friend. He said that my friend had said he felt all right. When I went back over to him, he was dead. Later, it was explained that the shock of his wound to his other organs had killed him. I was strongly affected by the sickening carnage of all the broken bodies of those fine infantrymen. I shut my eyes to the horrific sight.

RED HAT RENDEZVOUS
EXPLOITS OF THE VIETNAMESE AIRBORNE DIVISION

DATELINE: FEBRUARY 22, 1967

The South Vietnamese Parartroopers and Marines were the National Reserve Force. As such, their areas of operation were anywhere in the Republic of Vietnam that the military situation required them. Their courage and determination are exemplified in this PRESIDENTIAL UNIT CITATION awarded to the 7th Airborne Battalion.

The President of the United States takes pleasure in
presenting the PRESIDENTIAL UNIT CITATION to the:

**7th AIRBORNE BATTALION
AIRBORNE DIVISION
ARMY OF THE REPUBLIC OF VIETNAM**

For heroism in connection with military operations against North Vietnamese Army forces in Quang Ngai Province, during the period 14 February to 22 February 1967. An enemy regiment, encircled by a tri-nation operation, launched a full-scale, predawn attack against the 7th Airbrone Battalion on 19 February 1967, under weather conditions which prevented U.S. tactical air support. The 7th Airborne Battalion, in a matter of a few hours, was heavily engaged in repelling human-wave attacks from three sides in hand-to-hand combat. Inspite of heavy casualties after a five-hour battle, the gallant paratroopers continued to counterattack deeper and deeper into the attacking force, alternately returning to their lines, as weather conditions permitted elements of fighter aircraft to make passes, and using captured weapons in their defense.

With over 200 enemy dead lying on the 7th Airborne Battalion perimeter, the attackers continued to assault in an attempt to break through the hard-pressed Airborne lines. Following an emergency resupply by U.S. Marine Corps pilots, the South Vietnamese paratroopers successfully held their positions for another seven hours during determined enemy attacks. At the opportune time, the Airborne soldiers valiantly counterattacked in three directions from their positions, routed the enemy, killed many of the fleeing members of the North Vietnamese Army regiment and captured huge quantities of weapons and equipment.

Their determination was clearly evident, as individual soldiers refused to give ground to the enemy and noncommissioned officers quickly took command where necessary. The gallantry and fighting ability of the 7th Airborne Battalion in the face of exceptionally strong opposition, reflect great credit upon the Battalion and the Army of the Republic of Vietnam.

LYNDON B. JOHNSON

The American Advisors to the 7th BN were CPT Thomas C. Kerns, CPT James R. Kern, SFC Isaac Patino, MSG James C. Ferguson and SG Charles A. McDonald.

To prevent whatever expression may have been on my face from being misinterpreted by the wounded, I hurried away from that place. The familiar smell of death never left me, it followed me everywhere throughout the war. During the years, from 1964 to the present, a kind of slow, emotional paralysis set in on me. I felt completely empty inside--drained and like a different person.

I went to the hut where our headquarters element was located and they made me a cup of coffee. I was deathly tired. Hardly anyone spoke, and those that did, did so in very low tones. The earlier ringing in my ears had now become a steady hum. The years spent on the rifle ranges and the firefights and battles in Vietnam were taking their toll on the auditory nerves. This was a source of irritation, but it had always gone away. After I was handed my coffee, I spilled some on my hand and burned myself. Looking down at the cup in my hand, the coffee was rockin' and rollin.' I realized that my hands were shaking. I knew that, besides the noise-induced stress, I was experiencing another adrenaline rush, one of just many I had experienced after surviving so many close encounters over the years. The muscle in my left cheek quivered, and a nerve in my eyelid began to twitch insistently, I could not get it to stop. I put the coffee down, leaned back against the post, closed my eyes for a few minutes and noticed that my eyelids had a nervous twitch. I spent the time blowing the steam off the surface of the strong, sweet coffee to cool it, and watched my hands shake uncontrollably. Burning my lips periodically to sip the liquid helped me, momentarily taking my mind off my immediate surroundings. Besides being more fatigued than I had ever been, I was emotionally spent.

Before I left, I pointed to a locked trap door in the floor of the hut. They said they were getting to that. I finished my coffee, got up, put my hands in my pants and started walking around to relax. After the lock was blown off, an amalgam of stenches arose: the noxious, stagnant and fetid emanation of odors from many people living in a confined space. It was an odor associated with the relinquishment of muscular control resulting in excrement, urine, and vomit, bodily effluvia and organic remains. It made us wonder. What or who was down there. The vigilant nose had anticipated and warned of danger. Acting out of self-preservation, we decided to investigate the underground structure.

Interrogating Prisoners of War

Paratroopers descended the eight-foot shaft and searched the immediate underground complex. The little hut that was our battalion command post area with the locked trap door proved to be an underground NVA field hospital. The NVA prisoners that were discovered were brought from underground. The prisoners included four female army nurses who had remained behind to look after the wounded soldiers. The only others were the dead, not yet disposed of. It was in this vast, labyrinthine system of tunnel complexes, found throughout Vietnam, that the PAVN hid their large units, and to which they carried their dead after a battle. There were some two hundred North Vietnamese regulars counted dead within, on, and in front of our perimeter.

I went to have a look at our prisoners. The guards had slightly evil grins and a rapacious, ghoul gleam in their eyes. The prisoners' ashen-hued faces were sweaty, some twitched, feeling psychologically threatened. For a long moment, my gaze rested on the women. Oddly, as I searched their eyes, I decided the women soldiers looked to be in the best shape psychologically. Those exhausted NVA had been well equipped, looked very well fed, and had stocky builds.

I had decided to conduct my own personal terrain walk of the 7th Battalion's battle area because I had to know for myself what had happened. What I found during my walk was that the 7th Battalion had moved into the middle of an area which was heavily fortified by the NVA, and which had even included underground fortifications. I was able to observe how the NVA had made their close approach without being seen from any distance, and where they had buried their men killed in action in many places. All the areas that showed signs of fresh excavation, I dug into, to verify that there were fresh bodies there, before going on looking. In many instances, the bodies had not been taken away, as could be seen by the pictures of those killed in my area. The ever-present bluebottle flies were already laying their eggs in the flesh and feeding on the dead.

One of the first areas I checked over the hill from our lines was a freshly planted field. My first thought, upon seeing fresh dirt, was that a tunnel entrance could be concealed here. I could smell a slight, unmistakable, sugary porcine smell. I walked down the top of the first furrow, and it gave away under me the whole way. I squatted down and the smell was stronger. I bent down and over, bringing my nose to the soil. A familiar disagreeable odor rose from the ground. There was the smell of fresh soil mixed with something obscure, fetid, and penetrating. This was a smell with which I was well acquainted. It was not a typical terrestrial odor. It was the vile-smelling, organic odor that bears witness to the presence of death. This was the smell of man and the stench of death.

    I raised my head and examined the furrowed field from one end to the other. Then, I noticed it had very neat furrows and no sign of footprints. That seemed extremely odd to me, after all the human activity that day. I straightened back up and used my foot to find a hard place. Finding what I wanted, I then began to carefully brush away the soil from this area, eventually revealing a fresh dead face. As I stared, the lips immediately under the nose parted slightly and began spewing forth a white cranial liquid. There was an immediate putrid emanation that rose from the corpse. I jerked my head back. I grabbed a handful of soil and covered the soldier's face and stood looking at the field. I estimated it to be about 40 paces long and 30 paces wide, so I guessed that maybe as many as 16 NVA soldiers could be in just one row. The hot, sun-warmed earth was already saturated with the fatty acids of soft tissue from their decomposition. I wasn't going to unearth them for something as sadistic as a body count. I leave the math to the reader, because if my estimate is correct, the body count that day was grossly underestimated and it still makes me sad to think of it.

    The cost and waste to our own brave Airborne Battalion was 392 casualties. Of the 590 men we had started with, 150 men were killed in action. Some 200 more had been wounded, many of them badly, with multiple wounds. Many would die later. A total of 42 men were missing in action. The latter were most likely captured and eventually shot. It made me shudder to think of what their fate would be. When it came time to silently depart from this valley, only 198 men of the original 590 men were able to walk away from the position so valiantly defended against insuperable odds. Many of us were lightly wounded. During the Vietnam War, over 20,000 Vietnamese Paratroopers from this lone Airborne Division were killed in action, more than a third of the total casualty list for the entire American military.

Captain Thomas C. Kerns of Chesapeake, Virginia, was evacuated to the Army hospital at Chu Lai, where he remained three days until he stabilized. He was then transported to the naval facility at Danang, until again stabilized. Subsequently, he was flown to the Air Force hospital at Kadena Air Base on Okinawa. After six weeks, he made the rest of the journey to Valley Forge, Pennsylvania, where he remained for another six months, having both hips replaced.

Our isolated 7th Airborne Battalion, completely surrounded, had held against repeated determined close-range bayonet assaults from a unit four times our size. It had made one of the most heroic and gallant stands of any battalion in the entire war. I likened the battle to an abattoir. Adversity had brought out the best in these troopers. They never faltered in their attitude during that long, intensely bitter battle. The 7th Airborne Battalion's iron bravery and passion in this battle was to be remembered with the award of the United States Presidential Unit Citation. Since we had inserted on February 14th on this operation, I heard that this operation was referred to as the "St. Valentine's Day Massacre." Our lone battalion was in reality decimated, losing up to 66 percent of its strength. I came to realize that I had had the honor of serving in the company of heroes.

**This is courage...
to bear unflinchingly whatever
heaven sends.**
Euripides

CHAPTER 2

BEN SUC

After the battle in the Quang Ngai Province, our 7th Airborne Battalion's first mission was to provide convoy security from Bien Hoa, past Long Thanh, Phu My, and Ba Ria to the peninsula of Cape Saint Jacques. Along Highway 15, each small town we passed through had been a past site of heavy fighting. Our destination was the city of Vung Tau, "The Bay of Boats," a port city in Phuoc Tuy Province, which lay 78 miles southeast of Saigon. This type of mission kept the Viet Cong from controlling the transportation routes and collecting tolls to finance their operations, from cars, buses, and trucks. As we drove, I saw the high, lonely, and heavily forested mountains of Nui Toc Tien and Bao Quan to the east. I had once patrolled there with Ronald Terry and Frank Badaloti while with Project Delta in 1964. My mind drifted momentarily as I thought of my dead friends. Our Escape and Evasion (E&E) plan, if we were compromised during our patrol, had been to get to this very highway and follow it to Vung Tau. I had been in the war for three years since then.

Our convoy arrived in Vung Tau without getting ambushed and I had time to explore the city. The town, with its hotels, villas, cafes, restaurants and palm trees, had been a seaside resort in colonial times, and in 1967, it was used as a rest and recreation center for Allied soldiers. The most memorable things about the city were its jewel-blue water, its white sandy beaches, and sweet fragrant frangipani and bougainvillea. Vung Tau was nestled between Phu My and Ba Ria, opposite the extensive mangrove swamps of the Rung Sat (Forest of Assassins) to the west, which was a haven for guerrilla and NVA units. Two days later we returned to the outer perimeter of the Capital Military District of Saigon, and began to constantly patrol the countryside.

*   *   *

The companies of the 7th Airborne Battalion covered a large area. The headquarters element and the company that I was assigned to were fortunate enough to spend most of their time in a small village, allowing us to rest. I recognized that the village was old and established by its people and their traditional behavior. Every morning, there was the same enduring bituminous stench. The village had all of the diffused odors of the peasants' hovels, mold, excrement from their open latrines, rot and rubbish, and the stored human fertilizer for the local crops, complete with the fetid sweat of the crowd of workers. Flies swarmed and droned everywhere. Small children were all around, walking about with bare bottoms. Men and children urinated along the streets anywhere and everywhere. Over the top of vegetable and animal life in the market, floated the smell of mud and earth streets, impregnated with putrid materials of passing people and livestock. All these odors filled the air and my lungs, making me long for the industrial odors of my own country. Taking a bath meant standing at the well, drawing several buckets of water and dumping it over my head, soaping up and rinsing off with the others. Bathing was always in public view unless it was dark. It was common to hear hidden females giggling.

Luckily for me, the village had a noodle shop right outside the house where I slept. Street stalls opened early and closed late everywhere in Vietnam. The traditional Vietnamese breakfast is a soup known as *pho*, a rich broth with noodles, meat and vegetables. If the soup was chicken, you would be eating *pho ga*; if you chose beef, you would be eating *pho bo*. Well made *pho* broth came from the marrow, not the fat. The cook would skim off the fat. I always stopped in the small shop to eat my breakfast--a bowl of soup filled with beef, rice noodles, chilies, scallions, a dash of lime, herbs and bean sprouts, and a cup of coffee (*ca phe sua*). Every morning, I longed for the traditional cup of coffee. *Ca phe sua* was a very strong coffee. Sweet and dark, swirling with a large helping of sweetened condensed milk, the coffee was worth the wait.

The many green and red jars on display in the shop had always intrigued me. Upon a casual inquiry, they turned out to be herbs and spice pastes, much to my delight. They represented the concentrated tastes of Southeast Asia: chilies, mint, cilantro and lime.

While eating, I would watch the cook at his work, slicing the reedy, fragrant, ramrod-straight stalks of lemongrass, into tissue-thin strips, a staple ingredient of Vietnamese cooking. The cook was a man. I mostly remember that his back was always to me, except when being served and then my eyes were on the coffee and food. Lemongrass flavored their chili and curry paste and sauces, and fried rice. The young, tender outer leaves were used for their aromatic tea. The minced lemongrass went into the cooking of whole chickens. The cooks' hands smelled of lemon.

I also always had a half loaf of French bread that was made with rice flour. For a very long time I thought that the black specs were seeds, but eventually found out that they were weevils cooked with the dough. I might add that I never ate one bad meal on the economy in Vietnam. Every meal was different, delicious, and I was always hungry. While eating in this little shop, I daydreamed about my last Vietnamese meal in Saigon.

* * *

Saigon was the "Paris of the Orient." As the years of the war went by, however, the squalid shanties of the poor grew, and the beggars and hawkers took over. But in 1967, it was a beautiful city located on the Sai Gon River. French-colonial style buildings and high-walled private villas were surrounded with flowering vines of purple bougainvillea climbing the sunny areas of the walls. Many of these structures were cream or yellow, the Vietnamese royal color. Often, they were shadowed by tall, handsome, thick-trunked tamarind or flame trees with hard, scabrous bark, which grew throughout much of the city. Their splashes of vermilion were everywhere. The Vietnamese called these trees "cay Hoa Phuong." The trees were recognizable by their ash-gray bark and their clustered yellow-orange-red veined flowers with purple filaments. They bore sweet, dark, date-like fruit. If you walked under one in the night, you generally knew it, because its moisture would drip onto you. Walking to a restaurant, I often stopped to stare up into these trees thinking it was beginning to rain, bewildered because I could still see stars. The Vietnamese NCOs always laughed at me. Large, sweet-toothed fruit bats ate from the flowers that opened primarily at night, pollinating them in the process. They could seldom be seen, but could often be heard fluttering from tree to tree. The bat activity around these trees was of great interest to me. There are several species, which are considered delicacies by many people of Southeast Asia.

We had found our Vietnamese restaurant. While I listened to the music, I sipped my beer and watched the Vietnamese troopers drink and argue about their selection of dishes. The table always ended up filled with plates of food. Everything on the round table was on communal plates. We all helped ourselves, filling our own rice bowls, picking at what we wanted with our chopsticks. Troopers sitting near me continually put something new on my plate, most of it was strange and unknown, but unique and delicious. Herbs and spices were ground into everything. In Vietnam as in Japan, proper etiquette demands transferring food on other plates to your rice bowl before eating it with your rice. Since my wife is Japanese, I didn't offend anyone.

We had chicken with lemongrass and chili, sugar cane prawns and steamed fish with ginger. Large, fat shrimp were staples of the restaurants of Saigon, since they were caught in the nearby Mekong Delta and its many small canals. The chickens in Vietnam were much smaller than those in the United States, but they were delicious. We also had shredded chicken salad with herbs, steamed rice cakes with shrimp, and the crisp little pork rolls called *Nem ran*. I really loved these. There were also frog legs sautéed in lemongrass and chili, with wedges of tomato and pineapple. We also had a pancake filled with shrimp and bean sprouts called *Banh Khoai*. All the Vietnamese troopers piled my plate with rice and cooked pork fat. Luckily, I love fat. Later, I was told that it was an honor to receive these portions of fat. The smell of garlic was strong. I had been made to feel like I was at home. I really loved these troops.

Traditional Vietnamese music accompanied the meal, played on instruments, mainly stringed and percussion. Over the top of them, a beautiful woman sang emotive songs. The night passed too quickly, and we returned to our post.

Meal Time

The next morning, I was going about the business of feeding myself and enjoying my cafe *sua*, when a runner told me that I was needed for a meeting with my commander. Upon reporting to him, I was informed of our immediate movement to another operational area. Shortly thereafter, we loaded on to trucks for transportation to a point where a riverine unit would transport us upriver. We would conduct search-and-destroy missions and provide security for an American artillery battery.

* * *

By 1967, American forces in South Vietnam were sufficient enough to conduct large-scale offensive operations for the first time. In September, the decision had been made by General Westmoreland to invade the notorious, strongly defended area, known as the Iron Triangle, in War Zone C. The Iron Triangle was a 115-square-mile area, heavily defended, and fortified with huge bunker and tunnel complex. Over a period of several months, an operational plan called "Cedar Falls" was drawn up, based upon intelligence produced from documents exploited by the Military Intelligence personnel of the Combined Document Exploitation Center in Saigon.[1] They had been captured by Vietnamese Rangers and U.S. Special Forces operators in the area. "Operation Cedar Falls" was initiated during the period of 8-26 January 1967. This III Corps multidivisional search-and-destroy operation was the largest classic "hammer-and-anvil" coordinated offensive operation of its kind in the Vietnam War to this date. A natural obstacle, the Saigon River, served as the anvil. General Westmoreland was attempting to engage the larger enemy units in a set-piece battle.

The Iron Triangle area in Binh Duong Province is located twenty-five miles north-northwest of the capital, Saigon. Defined by the Saigon River to the southwest, the Thi Tinh River to the east and the Than Dien forest to the north, it had been a fertile, 60-square-mile area of dense forest, paddy fields, orchards and rubber plantations. As many as 10,000 people were reportedly living in the operational area that contained four principal villages: Ben Suc, Rachhap, Bungcong and Rachkien, all of which were to be destroyed.

The largest village was Ben Suc, located at the northwest corner of the Triangle. A staging base for attacks on the Capital Military District of Saigon and Bien Hoa Air Base; it was centered over the heart of the labyrinth of underground tunnels. These tunnels, known as the Cu Chi tunnels covered a 50-square-mile area, extending to Bien Hoa and Saigon. They were constructed between the Thi Tinh River to the east and the Saigon River to the west, in an area not easily waterlogged. They were dug in a laterite clay set as hard as concrete and concealed hospitals, living quarters, classrooms, storage facilities, arms depots, kitchens, mess halls and factories. Ben Suc also served as the PAVN Military Region IV logistical and political center, a meeting place for political cadres. Ben Suc was also an enemy communications network and supply point responsible for moving supplies down river by sampan. The 6,000 civilians in and around the village had been organized into four service transport units, charged with supplying communist troops to the southeast. The nearby Thanh Dien Forest reserve covered most of the area to the north of Ben Suc. The Boi Loi Woods were to the west and the Ho Bo Woods, to the southwest of Ben Suc. The villagers were to be rounded up and forced to evacuate with only the personal possessions they could carry. Then they were to be relocated further down river to the southeast, some twenty miles to Phu Cuong and Phu Loi. Their communities and homes would consequently be burned and flattened by bulldozers. At Phu Loi, no advance preparations had been made for the refugees.

It was here, north of Ben Suc, that the enemy's mobile political and administrative Central Office of South Vietnam (COSVN) for the War in South Vietnam was believed to be located. COSVN directed the activities of the North Vietnamese Army, the National Liberation Front and the Viet Cong's Liberation Army. The executive committee of COSVN took their orders from the Lao Dong Central Committee Reunification Department in Hanoi. COSVN's Viet Cong Infrastructure (VCI) was active in every province, district and village. And inside the South Vietnamese Government were two of COSVN's agents: Vu Nhoc Nha, President Thieu's friend and chief advisor on Catholic affairs, and Huynh Van Trong, Thieu's director of the Central Intelligence School and also his special assistant for political affairs. Nha was the leader of the COSVN spy ring. The major enemy unit located there was the 10,000-man Viet Cong 9th Division, commanded by Lt. Col. Hoang Cam. The Division, consisting of three regiments, was supported from the large NVA supply complex with sanctuary inside the Fishhook region in Cambodia. The division political officer was Col. Le Van Tuong. The NVA's Rear Transportation Unit 70 supplied the Fishhook region.

My Radio Operator

The 9th Division, reinforced with NVA replacements, was composed of the 272nd Viet Cong Regiment, the only known regiment in the immediate area, along with the 1st and 7th Main Force Battalions, the independent Main Force Phu Loi Battalion, and local force companies. The 165th Regiment's base camp was thought to be in the Ho Bo Woods. One of the communist guerrilla units remaining beneath Ben Suc throughout the entire operation was Ben Suc's own 300-man guerrilla force, commanded by Pham Van Chinh.

The NVA troops were masters of camouflage. The very few facilities located above ground in the jungle were impossible to spot until you were right on top of them, or looking down from the air. Most were hidden below ground. The majority, such as quarters for troops, food storage, ammunition storage and hospitals, were deeply dug, and well-constructed underground. A tunnel that ran clear to Saigon was a prime example. In every area of Vietnam where American units initiated an operation, they had difficulty finding the enemy, because entire battalions were hidden well below ground. Enemy fighting positions were usually located in thick clumps of old-growth bamboo that could withstand heavy incoming fire. In building these positions, the NVA would burrow into the center of a bamboo grove from another location, coming up in its center. The entrance and exit points were concealed with natural objects. There was no way into these thickets for attacking troops. Except for small cut fields of fire in these bamboo thickets, there was really nothing to see. Friendly troops could receive fire in one area or another, and by the time we discovered its location and converged on it, the enemy was gone--unseen.

Some members of my unit spent many days with long, solid poles in their hands, just moving around the area south of Ben Suc, and tapping the ground. This enabled us to locate the underground rice storage areas, tunnels and bunkers.[2] The bulk of this food was meant to feed the Communist forces. It came from the agricultural taxes, the most important being the rice tax. These large tunnel systems were spread over the entire operational area. Small numbers of Communist troops were constantly emerging to ambush and kill American troops. One can only imagine what it was like for them enclosed down there, waiting.

At any NVA base camp discovered above ground, the jungle was so tangled that it had to be destroyed by Rome plows. The thick undergrowth had to be cleared with M-113 Armored Personnel Carriers and their assigned infantry, and their attached engineers equipped with bulldozers. The Rome

Plow had a heavy-duty protective cab and a special tree-cutting blade that was used primarily for land clearing. Many base camps were found, and at each one, the APCs were dug in and a perimeter defense was established while an effective underground search was made of the facility. These operations provided the largest amount of documented intelligence in the war.

Hundreds of enemy soldiers trying to pass themselves off as civilians were taken prisoner, including the enemy's Military Region IV operations officer, with documents found on his person. The captured military documents and personnel histories in this operation conclusively proved the intervention of the NVA in the war.

* * *

National Liberation Front Headquarters in Tay Ninh Province

On the 16th of January, I listened to the report on the radio that a platoon-sized element of NVA had broken contact successfully by using tear-gas. During this operation, a cache of 1,300 China-made tear-gas grenades and gas masks were located. This was the second reported use of gas in this area, the first having occurred the year before. Earlier in the war I had heard of nerve gas in Chinese hand-grenades being used against the marines in the North, but had forgotten the exact date by this time.

The Special Forces team A-322 was located at Camp Prek Klok, in War Zone C, along the Cambodian border, 9 kilometers north of Nui Ba Den (Black Virgin Mountain) in Tay Ninh Province. Capt. Joseph M. "Joe" Lukitsch, a friend of mine, commanded the camp. We had served at Khe Sanh together in 1964.

The camp was built as the first III Corps fighting camp. It was constructed from used Conex containers, in which the troops lived and from which they fought. Its "berm" was bulldozed over the Conex containers. In this manner, they employed interlocking machine-gun fire down the walls of the camp. They also had 175mm artillery support from the 25th Infantry Division. Camp Prek Klok, was rumored to have been built on the site where Lt. Col. Alexander Haig, commanding the 1-26th (Blue Spaders), 1st Infantry Division, killed some 450 NVA in one good battle with the 271st Regiment and a battalion of the 70th VC Guards Regiment in the last major engagement of Operation Junction City. During operation Junction City, A-322 conducted an operation, leading to the discovery of a dozen 50 to 75-pound bags of powdered mustard gas stacked underground. They were made of a type of plastic and neoprene. The PAVN regional chemical officer was Nguyen Van Binh. The Chinese and North Vietnamese had added another dimension to the conventional warfare battlefield.

At that time, our first American incursions were taking place while the enemy was already dispersing. The 9th Division's 271st and 273rd Regiments were closer to the sanctuary of the Cambodian border, where they had the advantage of withdrawing across it in a hurry, if needed. The

9th Division's supporting 84A North Vietnamese Army Artillery Regiment was equipped with 120mm mortars and 122mm rockets. In addition, they had surface-to-air missile capability. The 271st Regiment was made up mainly of Chinese, many serving in the units as advisors to the 9th Viet Cong Division as well. It would not be until May 1989 that the People's Republic of China would finally disclose that out of 320,000 Chinese soldiers sent to serve in the Vietnam War, only 4,000 were killed in action. The actual figure, however, is reportedly much higher.

* * *

Our unit was transported up the fast-flowing Saigon River to the hostile village of Ben Suc, the Triangle's main village of 3,500 people, and political center. The river flows southward on the northeast side of Saigon, where it joins the Dong Nai River in its flow to the sea. We had been trucked north on Highway 1 toward the direction of Tu Duc, where we crossed the Saigon River. Then we turned north onto Route 13 and tailgated our trucks at Phu Cuong.[2] Our transportation was a U.S. Army steel-constructed vessel known as a LCM (Landing Craft Mechanized). Used for limited inter-coastal and inland waterway operations, it had a powerful diesel engine. When the bow ramps of the LCM were lowered, we entered the craft. I went up to its narrow top deck at the stern. The U.S. Army and Marines had used them in amphibious operations since World War II. We then embarked, following the Saigon River's serpentine meandering upstream. During the trip we mostly passed abandoned fields covered with tall, dry grass and low scrub brush lining the river. Although rice is the staple food crop of the country, from what I had seen on the ride up the river, we had already destroyed all of that. Ben Suc, our destination, was a recently established site for a U.S. Military Intelligence POW unit. The Headquarters of the 1st Infantry Division was at Lai Khe, north of Ben Cat.

* * *

    We left the Saigon River, passing the forks of the Thi Tinh and the Prek Klok. I was relaxed and resting, keeping an eye on the forest and mangrove shadows. We took the left fork, moving up the Prek Klok River. The Iron Triangle was formed by the junction of the Saigon and Thi Tinh Rivers, between the villages of Ben Suc and Ben Cat, the former located at the southwestern boundary of the Triangle. Some of my troops were trying to sleep, rocked by the soothing rhythm of the boat, while others, enjoying the ride, ever watched the shadowed foliage on the banks. The sky was cloudless, an endless sapphire blue. The wind was still and the hot air shimmering, dancing in quivering and spiraling columns to our front, as the sun bore down on us.

    We passed the enemy-based area of the huge Filhol Rubber Plantation on the south bank. Cu Chi was far to the south from this point. I thought of a letter I had received in February 1966 from an old friend of mine, Psgt. Herman L. Trent, who was in the hospital. While serving in the 173d Airborne Brigade (Separate), he had been wounded twice in the Ho Bo Woods.[3]

    The letter was dated 11 January 1966, after "Operation Crimp." His unit was here, in these very woods, on the left bank that we were now passing. Unbeknownst to his company, they were passing through a well-fortified ambush position. Herman's platoon was bringing up the rear in his company file, and as soon as they came into the kill zone, the enemy hit them from the front and both flanks. The enemy had seeded the area with anti-personnel mines, hand grenade booby traps, and command-detonated 60mm mortar rounds. Three machine guns were set so as to fire effectively on the paratroopers. Overcoming their initial shock, with great self-control, they quickly met the enemy head-on. For two and a half hours, they were hotly engaged, trying to fight their way through their dug-in positions to dislodge them. Their pride and dedication finally won the day. Six troopers were killed in action, and eighteen wounded. In this action, Herman received his second wound of the war, a bullet through his right hip. I thought, in tribute to him and to the others: "Airborne, all the way."

*   *   *

My mind had been drifting. I quickly awoke from my daydreaming to the reality of heavy firing of mortars, cannons, and the ceaseless stuttering of machine-gun fire, barely audible in the distance. Suddenly I heard a clamoring volume of tracked vehicles. It became a deep, loud and humming growl. I watched the menacing silhouettes of tracked M113s Armored Personnel Carriers (APC) and M48A1 tank vehicles of the 11th Armored Calvary as they conducted a mechanized attack. They were crossing the open, shimmering plain that extended unbroken to the distant horizon. The APCs had a 50-caliber machine gun and a 7.62 mm machine gun mounted over the crew compartment. They were attacking westward. Our heads craned, we watched the red clouds of dirt pouring from their tracks as they tore through the dry scrub. I saw one aggressive tank, an M132 flame-thrower vehicle, firing its liquid fire into a hidden enemy position. I watched from the LCM on the river until they were lost from my view, obscured by the high riverbank. I was most impressed with their rapid fire, as well as their movement while under fire; they were a bold and fearful sight to behold. The terrain was well suited for mechanized warfare.

As we passed the Ho Bo Woods, a disagreeable organic odor rose from the glassily calm river, an odor that saddened my soul. I was again bearing witness to the smell of death. I noticed three separate bodies floating in the water at different points along the river. I wondered how many more bodies there were still on the bottom, waiting for the gases to float them to the surface. Evidently, the NVA had gotten caught earlier in a fighting retreat, trying to cross upriver. This had been the night work of the 34th Armored, with their tank-mounted searchlights. During the daylight hours, armed helicopters patrolled the river.

Taking A Break

We caught up, moored alongside a wooden quay and landed shoreside. The first thing I noticed was the fatigue of the women and hungry, crying children. The familiar putrid odor of vaporous gases came from fresh excrement in the nearby village latrines. The odor was the product of the crowded living and collective putrification. The unhealthy stench diffused and infected the air, penetrating our lungs. I saw a tall, uniformed man watching the loading at the dock. I recognized him as Gen. William E. De Puy, the Commander of the First Infantry Division. With their few possessions, the traumatized people were waiting to be loaded on Chinooks or patrol boats for the trip downriver. They stared silently, numbed by physical exhaustion and the psychological emptiness of having been forcibly removed from their traditional homes. The people gave us only fragmentary gazes.

Women sobbed in their confusion of having been separated from other family members. They were leaving one nightmare to face another nightmare of a hand-to-mouth existence at the refugee camps at Phu Cuong and Phu Loi. By now, I was well aware of what this meant for the new refugees. These people were farmers, and in the area where they were going, the land belonged to someone else. There would be no jobs. Some 6,000 civilians were relocated to these camps. There were also over 100 detainees in a POW compound, awaiting interrogation. This operation had started with the taking of Ben Suc after an airmobile operation had landed right outside of the town. The entire area of operations then became a free-fire zone. The largely innocent villagers were now the human debris common to every war--refugees, for whom nobody wanted to be responsible. These simple people would now struggle and suffer for the sins committed by the Communists.

During the days along the river, I enjoyed taking breaks and entertaining myself in the long, dark shadows of the great trees. It always amazed me how quiet it became at dusk, when the last light turned to dark gray. I would hear the shrill pitch of the multitude of mosquitoes as they drifted in on us. The only way to hide from them would be to stop breathing, to avoid leaving an attractive trail of carbon dioxide for them to follow.

I listened to the faint hydraulic whine of an individual mosquito. I watched as she landed on my bare arm and stalked slowly and deliberately into position. As her legs stiffened to penetrate my flesh and feed, I struck. I wished that the nights were so easy. At night I spent my time watching, listening and investigating the area. At the beginning of this war, I had learned from the tribesmen that in order to develop and improve a fine critical ear to perceive more night sounds, I must regularly close my eyes to listen during the night. By long careful habit, I took several small sniffs with my mouth open. I could detect the fragrant and fresh smell of the earth mixed with the rising gases of the wetlands carried on the breeze. I listened to the chatter and clicking of insects in the tall trees. The smell of the land and river was strong. Terrestrial vapors escaped and spread along the river, the products of fermentation coming from the waterlogged soil and putrefied ooze of the swamps. In the distance, I could hear air and artillery strikes taking place.

    The sky was alive with big bright stars, and the visibility was disconcertingly good. I watched the lighting of the distant horizon and felt the earth shaking from a B-52 strike. I later learned that during the first seven days of this operation, there had been over 600 tactical air strikes.

    The nights were never empty of sound unless men were moving around. Usually, with the approach of dusk, the surrounding forest would come alive. The familiar sounds would have been comforting. Along the river, the lack of these night sounds worried me; it was a suspicion imprinted over the years on my subconscious. My inner voice of intuition always warned me. I decided that I would continue to listen for a while and then tell my fears to the battalion commander.

    About two and a half hours later I was still up, observing the moon-gilded plain. I felt like the mystery of the moon was working its magic on me. As the night's chill had set in, my brain became fuzzy with fatigue. Earlier, there had been only a few distant natural sounds and then nothing more. I worried about the quiet. Suddenly, a distant half-heard noise mesmerized me and had me listening. The echoed sound of trunks of bamboo knocking together in the wind reached my ears. I quickly realized that there was not enough wind to have created that sound. Somewhere to our front, in the marshes and swamps, NVA scouts were communicating their location to each other by tapping two pieces of bamboo together. The moonlight no longer seemed beautiful to me. It was now menacing. Now restless and worried, I took a careful walk, checking and alerting the guards. Then I went and found Major Le Minh Ngoc. I reported the lack of normal night sounds to him, the sounds of clicking bamboo, with no wind to cause them. He sent men to check and question the guards on the perimeter. The night passed without incident, but we knew that the artillery battery was targeted.

* * *

After that night, I constantly checked the guards. The listening posts reported the slight sounds of movement, and there were indications that could not escape us. We didn't see them, but we knew they were there, somewhere. Our commander had been plotting each of the reported sounds, and they were always in and around the swampy, depressed areas on our map. The men must have crossed the river in small units under the cloak of darkness from the dense bordering forest of the Boi Loi Woods and the Ho Bo Woods. An enemy reconnaissance unit had covertly taken advantage of the numerous small marshes and dense vegetation scattered along the river on our side of the stream. They prepared for an attack on the artillery battery.

* * *

On 15 January 1967, our tall Vietnamese commander, Major Le Minh Ngoc, made the wise decision to conduct a sweeping search. We were about to administer due process-- bullets to these brave and daring enemy soldiers located in the swamp. Just as the red dawn colored the horizon, we moved out. The sparkling day dawned as we began to sweep the flats in a 180-degree arc, from the east of the artillery position. These wide, slightly depressed areas of dead space were timber-covered, and made up of mounds, depressions and buttresses formed by fallen trees. The dead ground was barely noticeable to the eye. The gullies were only a few feet in depth, but anyone in them was invisible from any angle, unless you were inside them and looking.

Each punishing moment of moving in the open through the wavering and shimmering heat toward our first suspected tree line seemed like an eternity. I knew that the silent and unseen enemy would be watching. The air was filled with the loud, rhythmical buzzing of cicadas.

Suddenly, there was a whine and crack of shots overhead. It was the distinctive, automatic sound of Kalashnikov AK-47 assault rifles. The 7.62mm rounds, fired by the NVA, kicked up the dry debris amongst us. Our M-79 gunners pumped round after round into the tree line. Deciphered by intuition of the sound, the soldiers charged across the open toward the sinister, sheltered gloom of the tree line. The sound of firing gave me the power to lengthen my stride into long, ground-eating steps. I made the run across the open in one piece. I crouched, gaping, incredulous that I had made it. Already in cover, I heard the quick, soft slap of running feet behind me. Turning my head, I saw the less-experienced troopers, now over their startled response, running lightly over the undulating ground and falling quickly into the dense cover of the trees immediately behind us. I was dry-mouthed and fearful. My starving lungs gasped for air. I could taste bile at the back of my throat. The NVA's firing intensified again at close quarters. Unable see anything, all I could do was listen. Time passed slowly as stinging sweat ran into my eyes. I shifted my scarf from my neck to my head to keep it out of them. I inched slowly forward, a foot at a time, holding my head in such a way as to make no motion, but giving my eyes a chance to look around ahead. I was still unable to see anything. Nothing stirred ahead of me.

The hammering of solid hits striking the trunks of the trees, and the evil whine of misshapen ricocheting rounds continued on. Tree bark exploded in all directions as the rounds chewed up the trees. Fear hit me. REAL FEAR! The brutal conditions that gave you the sensation of doom, making breathing difficult, causing light headedness and your stomach to churn and feel like there was a small stone there. I felt the pain between my eyes and shoulder blades, from the pressure of their unseen eyes. My greatest fear was always the same, that of "letting the others down."

Then the air was tense with silence for scant moments as the NVA took cover in their holes. Answering the hostile fire, an M-79 gunner sent deafening shock waves through the area from his exploding 40mm rounds. Close by, a Vietnamese friend was firing alongside me. I could feel my hammering heart jump against my rib cage. A Chinese stick grenade came flipping end-over-end through the air, and burst so close that it whipped the small trees around me. Immediately, I changed my position, during the bright-white flash. I rolled over behind the next larger tree to my right, using the cover of the exploding debris. Remaining utterly motionless, I watched ahead with one eye from the side of the tree. I felt the now-familiar hollow feeling of nausea in the center of my stomach, and my mouth went dry. The large canopies and liana-vine festooned trees effectively blocked out the sun. I saw that the faded colors of our French-designed camouflaged uniforms blended cunningly within the mottled tree trunks and foliage. The dim light under the huge trees was strangely unreal. Sweat-soaked, I eased myself slowly forward, using my elbows and toes, and intuitively taking in my surroundings. My gaze was steady. Moving my eyes in and out in grids, I tried to sense a presence ahead before it would come into view. I knew they weren't in the trees, because the ground was not erupting and giving me a dirt shower. They were hugging the ground just as we were. We had to crawl forward. Anyone who got up to rush forward was dead.

Death was now measured in a split second. Each move had to be calculated carefully. There would be no second chances. Every little while, my paranoia would manifest itself and I would glance to the background, making sure that I wasn't silhouetted or skylined. I heard a slight noise ahead. *The wind? Whispering? Silence!!* I was just beginning to turn my head, but stopped. I saw a shadowed movement up ahead. But it was gone before I could bring the carbine to bear. The shadow had been backed by trees, which made it extremely difficult to see. I felt a chill at the back of my neck. I watched apprehensively as one of my friends, up ahead and to my right, got up from his shadowy place of concealment and crouched, peering forward into the gloom. Then, he moved quickly ahead through the dense overhanging branches. I yelled "NOoo," but not quickly enough. I felt an electrifying terror as he moved forward. My eyes widened and my body went rigid, my hand half-reaching out to him. Then the inevitable automatic burst came, and the foliage shredded around him. Bullets were ricocheting wildly. I saw a bright spray mist from his back, caught by the small shaft of sunlight amongst the trees just beyond him. I heard the explosive exhalation of pain.

Another trooper used this time to crawl forward. I heard a hoarse gasping. Despite the wounds, my friend slowly and weakly crawled back toward us. He drew each agonized breath with a bubbling sigh, the garbled choking of a man drowning in his own blood. If he could crawl a little further, there would be enough cover to extract him from the heavy line of fire.

Moments passed. He laid one side of his head down upon the back of one hand and quit moving. Then his body arched, straining. He sagged and relaxed. A small noise came from the movement of his feet, kicking his life away. My heart was pounding as I listened. I was almost afraid to breathe. A long rattling sigh emanated from his throat and I knew he was dead. He would come no further. I reached him, crawling. I rolled him on his back, looked into his agonized eyes, and saw that the once-fierce dark eyes were dull and clouding. The fat tears of pain were still wet on his filth-caked cheeks. Another friend was gone.

I lay flat to the ground, in a slight depression, with only my head up and one eye looking out from behind a tree, as I scanned the way ahead. The musky aroma of the forest floor filled my nostrils. Watching for the faintest movement, I searched as far as I could into dim shafts of pooled light between trees and dense shadows. My eye searched up and then down slowly, focusing on every thing. The only horizontal lines I could see were downed trees. I was about to lift up to see better, when I noticed that there had been a long pause in the firing. Instinct or my subconscious hearing of an almost indiscernible sound warned me. Again, I picked up the stirring of whispered sound ahead. There was a faint rustling--a compressing sound. Someone up ahead, silent and unseen was moving. I tried hard to separate movement from shadow and the dark background of the trees ahead. I saw the muzzle flash from a dark shadow as bullets chewed the foliage and tree trunks. Then there was a movement so slight that my eye scarcely detected it: a blurred and fleeting dark form in the shadows, keeping low to the ground. He changed his position after firing. I fired a quick well-aimed burst, but I could see nothing. From my left flank, someone else had seen the NVA fire and sent a burst his way.

Someone threw a hand grenade. After the debris from the explosion settled, from my right flank, I heard the slight rustling and a trooper moving forward fast, and then going to ground. Then silence. We moved very slowly, but we were almost upon them. An eerie calmness washed over me. The cracking of small twigs came from my left, as another trooper moved forward in the attack. He was up and moving fast. His arms flew wide, and he went down, crashing heavily, as if dead, to the crack of a weapon. He twisted sharply with the impact of the bullet. His fingers digging into the ground, and he dragged himself to the cover of a large tree. He heaved himself, trying to rise, and then raised himself on his left elbow, coughing. As I watched, he gave another bubbling cough, and bright blood trickled down his chin. His eyes were glazing and his supporting arm seemed to go slack. Then the trooper fell backward, his head striking the ground with a thump. I knew he was dead or had passed out. The smell of blood pervaded the air. Ahead of me and off to the right side, two upright forms ran forward, exchanging fire with the enemy. There was a brief firefight, and voices yelled something out in Vietnamese. The others around me slowly rose and cautiously moved forward. It was over.

I waited and watched them move, cautiously looking around. Then I rose up and moved slowly forward. My throat was parched, and I could barely swallow. As I moved by one spider hole, I saw one NVA with a hole in his forehead, the back of his damaged head resting against the dirt wall. It seemed as if he were looking at the sky one last time. I saw two of our troopers outside of the trees, next to the river, walking upright. I walked out of the forest and into the light.

The uniforms of our dead and wounded were saturated with blood. The wounded labored to breathe. One pale trooper had faded into the merciful oblivion of unconsciousness; his jaw hung loose and his eyes were open, empty and devoid of color. A small bullet had hit him in the forehead over the eye, sending it skidding around the skull under the skin. Another soldier sat upright. The bloody bandage on his head testified to the open part of the wound. He would have a concussion. Near him two more were lying on their wounded sides, allowing the good lung to breathe without filling with blood. One was gently moaning with pain, twisting and breathing with a snoring sound through his open mouth. Another, ashen-faced, was breathing shallowly, in shock. I noticed the inside of the plastic wrappers face down over the entry wounds and already soaked bandages on his exit wounds. These had been the brave but foolish ones who had gotten up to move forward. The medic was attending one wounded man who had sat up. He was finding it hard to take a breath, and was sweating with pain. Consciousness had returned to one man and he was trying to talk through barely parted lips. The others, weakened from loss of blood, lay still. Only their pain-filled eyes showed they were alive. Looking small, the dead were completely limp with empty, lusterless eyes.

I cocked an ear toward the sky. I could just make out a gradually rising thumping. *Helicopter rotors*!! The sound gradually grew into the faint rackety clamor of an approaching Huey. They were coming for our dead and wounded. The helicopter came fast from over the direction of the river, lost altitude rapidly and made its final approach directly above from between Ben Suc and the river. The helicopter flared out, its nose going up and the tail dropping to lose speed, and settled down gently to the ground. The rotor wash buffeted our headbands, pants and shirts, as they slowed into their drooping turn. The wounded were quickly loaded, then the air thundered as the engine reverberated. The pilot pulled pitch and lifted off, banked to the right, made its run, and then climbed high. The flying time to the nearest medical facilities at Bien Hoa was only 10 minutes. The furnace of their suffering and pain would soon be over. Eyeing the ever-widening arc of the sun, I knew another day would soon be gone.

We continued the sweep across the rolling open terrain. We approached another forested area, surrounded by tall, thick grass. Further in the trees was a russet, wind-combed reed swamp that could easily conceal many men. Soon, and without incident, we were at the swamp's edge. Another element had been sent around the swamp to watch for any movement as we slowly pushed into it. There were a few trails beyond the screen of reeds through the wet marsh. As we entered, we let our eyes do most of the walking.

The only sound was the rustling of birds winging out of the reeds a good distance ahead of us. I followed in the wake of two troopers. We stopped, watched and listened. *Nothing*. If any NVA were inside the screen of trees at the edge of the forested area, they would know we were here. The reeds rose up all around us. Our exposed arms and faces itched from the grass and reeds. Our feet were wet. The lead trooper stopped and squatted, waving us forward. We paused and squatted, examining the tracks in the muddy ooze. They were rounded animal tracks, not the elongated, narrow track of a human. I felt a little more at ease.

We moved slowly. The stalks were noisy to push through and fast movement would be easily heard. There was only the whispered, sucking sound of someone's boots getting stuck in the mud. We moved slowly inside the dark cover of the trees, searching through the shadows. We found only prepared positions, spider holes and recent sign of movement. We approached the open on the other side, and reentered the reeds. The only sign of humans was that of a fresh attempt to erase the tracks leading out to the river. They had heard the fight and withdrew. We communicated to those waiting that we were entering the open again. Our sweep was over.

Once again I was awed that I was walking away intact. I knew that I should be tired, and I really was. But the psychological change from the battle had given me energy. I was impressed with the defense of this small number of NVA soldiers who had fought and died. There were no prisoners. I was convinced now that the NVA firmly believed in their cause. They always fought well. After our unit was relieved, we departed back down river. I felt refreshed by the clean, cool breeze as it came off the river. Everyone was intent on their surroundings, watching the nearby woods. "Operation Cedar Falls" ended.

* * *

On 22 February 1967, another operation, known as "Operation Junction City," started, just to the northwest of us. Elements of the NVA 9th Division who had remained in our operational area took casualties, but emerged intact from their deep underground, complex tunnel systems. They regrouped in the Tay Ninh province, closer to the Cambodian border, only to return again in the days ahead to become the springboard for the 1968 Tet offensive.

Preparing for Operation "Junction City"

It was during this time that by scuttlebutt I learned of the death of the great author Bernard B. Fall, near the city of Hue. On 21 February 1967, I learned Mr. Fall, had been killed by a mine in Thau Thien Province. He was on patrol with the 1st Battalion, 9th Marine Regiment. With great interest, I had read his classic book, <u>Street Without Joy</u>, four years earlier while in Special Forces Training Group at Fort Bragg. Over a period of several months

* * *

My time in Vietnam was coming to an end again. I soon found myself on the Freedom Bird. The journey homeward held many incalculable differences from the uncertain doubts, fears and unsettling unknown that had tormented me on the outward trips. Seated next to the window, I watched Vietnam disappear. Solemnly I recalled all that had happened. The emotional wounds, scars and images were burned into my mind, always to remain. The grinding years of paranoia had made a nervous wreck of me and the psychological toll had been physically draining. I knew that I needed a long rest, in order to escape all knowledge and all thought. I needed to feel again that sense of well being that only being home in the United States would bring. Little did I know that in the months ahead, I would face the beginning of another year's tour of duty.

Our army was winning all the battles, but our politicians were losing the war. The casualties were enormous despite the quick evacuations by helicopters to hospitals. The cream of the army forged in battle had disappeared. It had been killed, missing-in-action, captured, and wounded in body and mind. We were fighting the largest manpower source in Asia.

Even as I wrote this story, I suffered occasional nightmares. There will always be plenty of ugliness floating around, printed in my subconscious, but that will pass. The greatest hurt, however, came from the organized psychological attack faced by myself and other soldiers, from the great many misguided citizens of the United States, for whom we willingly went into battle. I now know how precious life is and how quickly it can be taken. Civilization is only skin-deep. The weight of my sorrow has made me wiser, helping me understand that the most important thing in my life is to try and live well and love my family and friends. But then, very few people learn these lessons.

On the flight home, I felt that I could not sleep. I could not feel safe until my arrival at Travis Air Force Base in California. I closed my eyes to try to relax. I don't know if I slept or not, but I found myself once again back on the border of Laos and North Vietnam at Khe Sanh. In a mixture of fear and anticipation, the events were once again re-lived vividly clear in my mind. These sensations, images and thoughts were all too real. These nightmares occurred for so many years that I became afraid to fall asleep.

U.S. NEWS & WORLD REPORT, Aug. 4, 1975

★ ★ ★

Washington is hearing that anti-Communist guerrilla operations are being stepped up in Vietnam. Latest reports tell of hit-and-run attacks on Red forces in two coastal areas—one in Phuoc Tuy Province, the other near Vung Tau, a resort city. Former South Vietnamese paratroopers are credited with the raids.

Footnotes:

1. Operation Cedar Falls was named for the hometown of 1st Division Medal of Honor recipient Robert J. Hibbs, killed in March 1966.

2. The Vietnamese paratroopers found tons of buried rice and a major logistical site, a three-story-deep complex of tunnels and chambers covering several acres underneath the town of Ben Suc.

3. Phu Cuong was the provincial capital. It became the temporary resettlement camp for the people relocated from Ben Suc.

4. Psgt. Herman L. Trent, with one lung, survived the war. He was wounded three different times--shoulder, hip and leg. He is one hundred percent disabled, and now lives in Hazard, Kentucky, cared for by a nurse, his wife Sharon. I called him on the phone, but sadly he no longer remembered me.

A man who has nothing
for which he is willing to fight,
nothing he cares more about
than his own personal safety,
is a miserable creature
who has no chance of being free,
unless made so and kept so
by the exertions of better men
than himself.

John Stuart Mill (1806-1873)
English Philosopher

CHAPTER 3

KHE SANH

The old camp Khe Sanh was the most remote and isolated Special Forces outpost in the northern part of South Vietnam. It connected a series of mountain valleys. Our "A" Team-323 out of Okinawa had replaced A-728, originally under Captain Floyd James Thompson from Ft. Bragg, North Carolina. A short distance away, North Vietnamese army units were hard at work building a complex of trails used by infiltrating units and securing them. Our team's mission was to build a new camp Khe Sanh on the plateau at the airfield, conduct reconnaissance and block enemy infiltration.

Luckily, I had the right patrol partner to learn from, Staff Sergeant Ratchford P. Haynes. This veteran of Mobile Training Team "White Star" in Laos, responsible for training the Royal Lao Army to fight the Pathet Lao and PAVN, was now our senior team communicator.[1] His eyes reflected depth and experience. I always felt secure with Haynes because he commanded with cool objectivity, sharp reflexes, and good judgment. My first patrols with Ratchford, had been conducted around the outer areas of the different Bru villages to provide security, to assess our surroundings while adjusting to our vast operational area. He was always seemingly in complete self-control and exhibited an inherent awareness of everything about him. He seemed to have the ability to anticipate events in advance of their occurrence. His character and personality helped me gain the experience and self-assurance needed to effectively survive the long war.

Haynes and I were to conduct the first long-range border surveillance patrol south, twenty klicks along the Laotian border from the Bru village at Lang Vei in the area of Highway 9. We would be on the mission for over two weeks and would take our patrol twelve miles down to La Man (1), to where the border came to a point and briefly turned back in a northerly direction. We made a careful map study, to imprint upon our minds the lay of the land far to the south. We familiarized ourselves with the names and noted the highest features of the land marked "Dong Co Ac" and "Dong Cai Ong." "Dong" in French means "massif," in English, "massive." The word "Co" on our map translated to "narrow passage." The name "Khe Sanh" meant "gorge," anyone who has been there has seen the gorge. The names were taken from the French maps and were ethnic minority names of the primitive Montagnard Ta-oi tribe, the only people known to inhabit the area south of the Bru tribe. The Ta-oi were rarely seen. Further down in South Vietnam, "Nui" was the word used for "massif," or "massive." An aerial recon was also scheduled and I was to make the flight, checking our route along the border through the mountains.

Early the next day the Cessna O-1 Bird Dog (L-19) pilot arrived. The high-winged, single-engined Cessna was sitting on the parking ramp. Except for the clouds to the east and a few scattered clouds above the airfield, the sky was an untrammeled blue. The pilot gave me the routine emergency instructions and showed me how to communicate with him during flight. In the event we received ground fire, he would attempt to mark the target for a possible airstrike with his 3.5 white phosphorus (WP) wing rockets. The WP rockets were highly flammable and were used to create fire and smoke in marking targets for a tactical airstrike. In addition, the WP rockets were casualty producing, and if any of the chemical hit human flesh it could only be extinguished by removing its source of oxygen. I sat behind the pilot in the two-seater aircraft. We could cruise easily between 60 and 100 mph, and with its tanks full the aircraft could fly over 500 miles. While in flight, I thought about the original Special Forces A-728 team leader Captain Floyd James Thompson, who had been replaced by Capt. Imes. Their team had been assigned to Khe Sanh in March of 1964. On 26 March 1964, Captain Thompson had taken off from this same airfield. He had been shot down by small-arms fire and captured by the NVA while conducting an aerial reconnaissance in an L-19 at the reported grid coordinate of XD 890419.[2]

With Capt. Thompson in mind, I paid close attention as the pilot explained to me where the emergency flight stick was located, and where to insert it on the floor in front of my seat. If anything happened to him, the aircraft could still be flown from the back seat. Soon we were climbing through the clouds that were illuminated and gilded with the hues of the blazing morning sunlight and were airborne. We soon passed over the French plantation, Route 9, the small town of Khe Sanh with its surrounding patchwork of fields and paddies, and its network of trails and villages. I closely watched the worn and beaten trails in the reddish soil leading off into the desolate and forbidding real estate surrounding us as we snaked along the river valley, then all too quickly the forest covered everything. The spectacularly beautiful view was an awe-inspiring sight. The unbroken rich hues of blue and dark-green of the high mountain forest immediately rose and stretched from horizon to horizon, as far as the eye could see. Only the silver reflection of the Se Pone (Tchepone) River punctuated the landscape. I watched for visible trails approaching the border on the far side, and for evidence of trails below us and saw nothing. We flew south for quite a distance, and then after turning east for a short while, we flew back north in the direction of Khe Sanh.

On the day of our first really long patrol, the weather was so beautiful, with blue skies, gentle winds, balmy temperatures and no scent of rain in the air. Prior to departure, we checked our tough, musky-smelling tribesmen and their equipment. All the Bru, Nungs and Vietnamese carried older weapons, mostly World War II and Korean War vintage M-1 Garand Rifles and M1 Carbines. A quick weapons check revealed that all weapons were well cared for. I carried the old and compact 30 cal. M2 Carbine that weighed a light five pounds. My M-2 held a 30-round magazine that suited my needs for close range fighting. The M-2 was very accurate and capable of both semi-automatic and automatic fire. I had zeroed my weapon at 100 yards and test fired it prior to the patrol. My patrol partner, Ratch, was carrying a new experimental rifle, the AR-15. His rifle fired the 5.56-mm (.223-caliber) cartridge. While inspecting the older weapons, I realized that the PAVN carried the reliable 7.62mm, AK-47 Russian "assault rifle" invented by Mikhail Timofeyevich Kalashnikov. The AK-47 was the superior weapon of the times because it was simple and reliable, and still fired even when extremely dirty.

I surveyed each man's weathered, dark, and often wrinkled face. All too many of these soldiers were just young boys. They were a proud and assured people with high cheekbones and powerful, lean builds. They had strong arms and broad shoulders for their size. Their hands were made sinewy from working in the fields and forest. I could smell the musty tang of sweat, and noticed that they all had smiling faces. Some had tattooed faces with wide noses. They had pierced ears and filed-down upper front teeth. Their dark almond-colored eyes flashed brightly, showing a fathomless wildness, which was deep and seemingly impenetrable. Most were smaller than us, on an average of five feet and four inches tall. The only people who didn't like the Bru were the Vietnamese, but even the Vietnamese respected them.

Laotian Border on Patrol 1964

On patrol, our older Bru tribesmen, whose knowledge of the forest was unmatched by anyone, were careful guides. These Stone Age warriors were suspicious and fearful by nature, and always alert. We maintained the strictest scrutiny and no one ever lagged behind. The ever-smiling Bru guaranteed the greatest amount of security to every chore. They were on guard with their weapons while any small number of men went about the camp business of obtaining water, eating, cleaning weapons, resting and planning. They convinced us that the eyes of the PAVN were always upon us. Just because we didn't see them, didn't mean that they weren't there. The tribesmen noticed details and subtle things that were close by and were careful to always point out the prepared ambush areas before we got to them. I was learning.

    The kunai grass covered the surrounding hills leading toward a mist-covered mountain ridge that was over 2,165 feet high. I listened to the shrill call of insects emanating from the high, rank grass. I could see the route ahead: a vast expanse of grassland. The wind carried its sweet scent. As we moved through the open sea of sun-lit grass, I watched the patterns of the warm wind rippling through the swaying, open fields of grass. I soon learned not to wear my sleeves rolled up, because the broad, tall elephant grass was razor sharp.

    After we reached the crest of the mountain, we entered the shadowy forest, where the sun came meagerly through dense treetops. The mountain forest was dense, closed and protective, designed to conceal. Subconsciously, we kept track of the sun and its direction, using it as a reference point while moving. The vegetation thinned at ground level in the mottled light. Now the forest began to thicken as the green veil closed around us. As we moved further into the forest the trees became taller. Dark tree trunks were like huge cathedral columns forever hidden from light. Large insects whizzed past and it felt as though a thousand invisible eyes gazed from the depths of the shadows. The forest echoed a frequent, multitude of sounds that reverberated throughout the surrounding forest. There was a cacophony of melodious calls, random drills and trills of notes, whose pitch, rhythmic variations and harmonic patterns of high, mellow and low staccato calls came from a myriad of bird's overhead. They were matched by their nearby neighbor in a call-response pattern, filtering through the trees in every direction. My hunter eyes were irresistibly drawn upward and I saw many birds twittering about, dancing through the treetops back and forth, chasing, and hunting for food in the high branches. Some had scarlet-striped backs and others were more noticeable with their yellow-colored bellies.

There were spiritual omens to be read in the tracks of the animals and birds. Our Bru scouts were very sensitive to their environment, very superstitious, often grave and heavy-spirited. Always seeking omens and portents, they searched the foliage above and took notice of the direction in which the perched birds flew. If they flew to the right it was considered a good sign. When flying to their left, it symbolized impending danger. If the Bru, with heavy fear and reluctance began dragging their feet, it might have meant that they would go back to Khe Sanh. They believed that the spirits sent omens of misfortune--of accidents, illness, and death--to them in the form of signs or dreams to warn of future good or evil. It was here in the forest that the spirits had always dwelled and exerted their power, and where the Bru strained their eyes and ears.

An animal track--a single imprint of a deer's split hoof, found on the trail at the wrong time or facing the wrong way-- would be seen as an evil omen that could send our tribesmen home. They believed that to ignore the warning would result in meeting the devil or being killed by a snake or eaten by a tiger. As for Ratch and myself, having grown up hunting and fishing, we could sense when flocks of birds were formed to search for food and water, or possibly gathering to wait out an approaching storm.

It was an exhilarating experience being around the tribesmen. I loved the wilderness and its tranquility. It was deep and dark and dangerous. I came to realize how little religious faith the Western man has compared to the Bru tribesmen who live their religion day by day. To them the forest was crowded with spirits, and no matter what activity they were engaged in, they always seemed to be watching, waiting and listening to the voices of passing spirits in the wind to guide them. Every major or minor catastrophe was due to the spirits. The spirits from beyond this world would punish the Bru for any violation of their belief. They believed an offended spirit might transform itself into a phantom--clawed or fanged, malevolent carnivore or snake---to kill them. These tribesmen were very religious and had complete faith in the spirits that crowded their surrounding forest, influencing their well-being. They lived in constant fear of punishment from malevolent spirit incarnations. They, therefore, lived a pure-of-heart existence. These were the noble savages-John Locke would've been proud of. The spirits would guide the good hunters to game and warn of danger by way of omens and magical signs. Their eyes were never focused long on a single object, as they stood silently listening to the wind in the forest or gracefully moving about on patrol. The eyes and ears of the hunter were always alert for every change of the sky that promised a change in the weather. They probed the shadows carefully, searching the forest sounds for every scuffle of leaves, for every animal call or cry. These were wise men, who lived with their fear. It had taught them caution since childhood. Only a cautious man could hope to survive in that wilderness.

They were animists who believed that a living spirit Yang, or the supreme god, was imminent in nature and manifested in trees, plants, animals, stones, rivers, mountains, particular pieces of ground and the sky. The spirits of the sky received the most attention, because they were regarded as being filled with omen and portent. Fear, anxiety and dread of the evil spirits and omens from dreams and signs were dynamic forces controlling their daily lives and existence. Every minor and major catastrophe was due to the spirits. Because of the Bru religious spirit worship, they were constantly attempting to communicate with the spiritual world. They even paid great attention to their dreams. I learned while on boarder patrol that these indigenous people took their dreams very seriously, and based many of their decisions on such phenomena. For many Americans there is little spiritual dimension. Our rapport with the Bru depended upon our complete respect for them and their beliefs. Our welfare and the accomplishment of our mission required us to abandon logical thinking regarding these people and to accept them the way they were.

*   *   *

We emerged into an ancient "cathedral grove" of trees that appeared to be a thousand years old. The trees, 200 feet tall with perfect vertical trunks, formed a continuous canopy entwined overhead, and a smaller second layer formed a level of foliage some 80-feet tall. Thick entwining liana vines dangled to the ground from the intricate interwoven support of the trees and dense canopy. Only splotches of suffused light from the sun filtered through, creating interplay of light and shadow. The wind moved laterally through the giant trees, not upward. We moved carefully, up and down the steeply sloped, well-beaten trail, shifting our packs, following the turns. Our eyes darted from one shadow to the next, trying not to leave any trace of our passing.

At night, those of us who were allowed to sleep slept lightly and fitfully, waking at every sound. It was at these times that I remember the tribesmen telling us we were going to be wet. Night fog would roll in. The suspended water in the fog would accumulate on the branches above during the night and drip down from the leaves and run down the trunks of the trees. The fog drip from the gigantic trees kept us wet and cold constantly.

Our biological clocks--the built-in timers that synchronized our bodies with our environment, awakened us before dawn each day--were by now working well. Before dawn our equipment was ready to go and we were waiting uneasily for the light and the fog to dissipate. If we were attacked, it would be during the hour before dawn. The overpowering silence was filled with the whoops, caws and cries of the surrounding jungle, as monkeys, birds and frogs wildly greeted the sunrise. When the sounds of our surroundings again became normal, we were slowly once again on the move.

From the state of the trail we knew two things: men used the trail regularly, and they would do so again. I wondered if the young trees had been stripped of their leaves by the PAVN for camouflage or by the roaming resident jungle experts--the slender-limbed langur, and gibbons. We crossed deep ravines with cool, shady brooks that rushed forth foaming up through all the defiles. I could smell the gurgling water. As we neared a small watercourse we would hear a series of flute-like whistling notes from small birds perched in the trees over the tumbling of the water. Near wet areas, the snuffling of piglets could be heard. The sight of adult pigs without any accompanying piglets was usually an indicator of an actively hunting tiger in the area. Now and then, we caught a glimpse of the shining, silvery Se Pone River below.

Our planned destination was a point twenty kilometers south of Khe Sanh. We passed the line-of-sight from the top of the mountain, that invisible barrier where we no longer had line-of-sight radio communications with anyone. The radios we carried were the old AN/PRC-10 radio sets and the HT-1s. The low-powered PRC-10s were backpacked and weighed 22 pounds each. It was common for my patrolling partner Ratchford P. Haynes, making an operational inspection and check of the radio each day. He religiously examined the long and short antennas and battery box for corrosion to ensure their operational reliability. The small, lightweight, HT-1s were hand carried. We used a jungle-antenna with both types of radios for the best ground-to-air communications. We either climbed a tree or tossed a rock with a line attached to the jungle antenna over a high limb and pulled it up. It had to be erected 30 feet high. The higher the aerial was placed, the greater the distance the signal could carry.

The jungle antenna was cut to the frequency range we were using for our particular patrol. We could make sporadic contact with Khe Sanh using the AN/PRC-10 with the jungle antenna if we were high enough up on a mountain promontory and weather conditions were not too bad. The antenna was omni-directional.[3] Our transmissions were quick and short. Sure that our brief signal was the only source of an electrical disturbance in the mountains; we knew we would be easily located and tracked by any enemy radio direction-finding operator. After any transmission in the mountains, we had to be prepared to move quickly in order to prevent the PAVN from triangulating our position. It wasn't safe to remain for too long in one place. When we stopped each night, we got out our maps and studied them in the rapidly fading evening light.

* * *

The period just before daybreak always brought a certain quiet intensity. Our gear was packed and ready. A sense of ethereal quiet pervaded the air as a profound silence settled over our encampment. Sitting poised like wild creatures, we listened in stoic silence for the sounds of well-being. As the dim light sharpened, a soft breeze stirred the rising, waking sound of raucous birds to a crescendo nearby. Suddenly there were all sorts of noises, and I had to learn to sort them out, to develop a sense of awareness of what was normal and what was not, of what was dangerous in this environment. In the distance, the hooting of gibbons greeted the day by calling to one another for comfort, to be on the alert. There was a deafening cacophony of hoot-like shrieks and screams of alarm in the distance, telling all within hearing range that danger was nearby or within full view, usually a large panther or the much larger tiger. I had already seen a few gibbons close up. They traveled in groups and at times could be seen trudging upright on the ground to forage. They usually sought cover among the branches, where they walked upright on large limbs or hanging from one arm, while picking fruit with the other. They quickly disappeared with little sound when they were encountered while walking on the ground trails.

* * *

The stillness, broken only with the low hum of insects, barking deer, and the sound of waking birds, rose to a melodious peak as we continued our patrol. I could smell the sweet, rotting flower fragrance of swamp gas. It was not completely hidden from our awareness that the forest fed upon itself. *Mildew and mold was quickly ruining our clothing, equipment and food.* As we were walking, the breeze stirred. The movement of our file stopped. Being close to the point, I went forward to see why. There was a heavy, rank smell hanging in the air. Transfixed, I saw the tribesmen on point, listening closely to the deer. The barking was considered an omen. The alarm-call and panicked flight of the nearby, hysterical deer were followed by the explosion of hoof beats. These sounds meant there was a tiger. "He is close and watching us," the tribesman said. "He has just crossed the trail ahead of us and is there in the dense scrub." Ratch had come up quietly and was standing close behind me and said over my shoulder, "Tigers posses a supernatural ability to stay out of sight." I stared into the thick brush seeing nothing, thinking of the tiger.

The jungle ghost is camouflaged by its striped coat in the dim, green light of the dense groundcover. It kills water buffalo, an animal four times its own size, snapping its spine with its long canine teeth.

Imitating the Bru, tasting the air with my nostrils and open mouth, I noticed that the meat-eating, acrid stench of the tiger was overwhelmingly foul. The tiger's chief prey were wild boar, deer and man. They hunted upwind because of their own smell. We saw the tracks. The four large toes of the tiger's enormous pugmark impressions clearly discernible. The tracks were huge--a handbreadth across--firmly set in the ground. One of the older Bru tribesmen, with the tattooed face and a raptorial look, filed teeth, and wood pegs inserted in his ears, pantomimed with his hands while explaining through an interpreter about the great round tracks. He pointed out that the back feet were marked by a convex indentation, stopping short of the front feet. A stalking tiger would have placed his back feet exactly over his front feet to eliminate making a noise. The Bru stared at the tracks, eyes big and round, whispering among themselves. "This is a large, healthy male tiger, because the hind foot was more square and his four toes were shorter and more blunt. An old tiger would have elongated toes and splayed feet, with heavily rutted pads," The older tribesman explained. Then with a dead serious face, the interpreter explained, "The presence of a human-like fifth toe would indicate to the superstitious Bru the presence of a man who had transformed into a tiger." As usual, the Bru were searching for an omen in reading the tracks. I touched the edge of the track with my finger; it was soft. The wind had yet to mar the edges. As I looked at the faces around me, I saw the seriousness of what had been said. I was learning about superstitions. The distant chatter and screams of monkeys was heard in the distance and we knew the tiger was gone. The birds and animals on the ground paid attention to what the others were doing and reacted to the situation.

As if arriving from hell, the incessant, electrical hum of the large, Asian Tiger mosquitoes constantly increased in numbers to launch aerial attacks through our clothing.[4] A fact of life that we had to learn to live with. During the cool season in the mountains, we were rarely bothered. When the weather warmed or we went to lower elevations, the air was alive with the hum of them. Thankfully, the smaller bats ate large amounts of mosquitoes. Our worst enemy was the P. Falciparum mosquito that sought our blood in order to foster the development of its larva.[5]

The trail became steeper. As we climbed higher on a path that rambled through ancient forest, a blast of cool wind greeted us, making me instantly grateful. Here on this high periphery of the valley, the wind blew erratically from every direction. The force of the mournful wind felt good on our sweat-dampened faces, tugged at our clothes as the trees groaned, and branches and foliage swayed in the last bit of sunlight. At this time of year, the air freshened and cooled quickly. The air was invigorating, much cooler than the steamy lowlands near the river. We stopped on the shoulder of the mountain where I had time to notice the luminous blue sky. Looking west, the view seemed infinite from my location on the ridge. My first good view of the vast karst formations of Laos and Co Roc Mountain was from a high promontory at grid XD 805304. The landscape was a humbling reminder of the smallness of man. We were on the western most promontory of Vietnam, which afforded an unobstructed view. Across the steep-sided Se Pone River valley we saw a stunning panorama of undulating green landscape of ragged limestone karst jotting the ridges along the Laotian border. The porous limestone karst accounted for the many caves and underground rivers in the area. We watched from the top of the mountain ridgeline for signs of PAVN activity in the fading light at the end of the day. The PAVN forces were reportedly well dug into the karst formations.[6] Our mission was to help keep watch on this activity, and soon it was also my turn to go on patrol. In the supposedly neutral Laos, the Central Intelligence Agency (CIA) had organized and was financing tens of thousands of Laotian and Thai guerrillas led by American Special Forces, fighting the Pathet Lao and PAVN troops who used it as a sanctuary. They had a supply depot at Muong Nong on the Laotian side below Route 9. The PAVN forces were busy preparing themselves logistically for a long war. However, they were capable of living off the land.

I felt the mystery and thrill of the unknown, and a stimulating sense of isolation. It was as if my eyes were seeing the world for the first time. I noticed the Se Pone River winding like a dark snake below. In my mind, there was a mysterious, serpentine beauty to the often shallow, Se Pone River, which slipped smoothly along, coiling quietly in pools. The glassy, calm river meandered gracefully through the endless green, among towering forests and mountain ridges, separating Laos and the northern part of South Vietnam.

With the evening hours approaching dusk, the forest appeared to come alive. The buzzing of the flies had ceased as they sought shelter under leaves and grass stems. I enjoyed watching the night rising over the river far below. In the distance I could hear the waking rattle of the benign, nomadic bats in the large trees. The bat "camp," ghostly and dark, became noisy prior to their hunt for papayas, litchi nuts, mangoes and other ripe rain forest fruits. Their distant black silhouettes, seen hanging on the trees all day, were like giant pods or hanging fruit. They emitted high-pitched faint ticking social sounds as they awakened, squabbling and communicating to each other. Their squirming was not easily noticeable against the movement of the leaves, but their slowed body processes were rapidly coming to life again. They were uncloaking themselves after being wrapped in their great wings for their daytime dormancy on hanging perches in the darkest shaded recesses provided by the ancient trees. Then came the great sound of their emergence--the flapping of their 5-foot-wing span as they soared out, accelerating slowly toward the rose-colored horizon with the sunset behind the western mountains. By listening closely, I could hear the sound of their erratic flying in the twilight. Birds were flying to favorite roosts to settle for the night. Standing motionless, watching and listening, my attention was drawn to the sound of rapid wing beats--a winged hunter. A large, almost ebony colored hawk caught a bat in flight. I had noticed the broad-winged silhouette before, hunting bats. The fast and fluid smaller bats in pursuit of insects flitted in the dark sky in and out between branches in an aerial dance for their nighttime feeding. The small bats could often be seen flying slowly, fluttering about like butterflies.

*   *   *

In the morning, the ridge, with its great trees and cloud-hidden top branches, was covered in a mist. I was always watching the dissolving vapors rising above the river, thinking of the enemy and watching for men crossing the river. As we traveled through this wilderness, we searched the black shadows of the forest along the ridge top. Then again we were gradually working our way down from the mountain ridge in order to move closer in toward the river. The constant up and down movement was necessary in our search for bad guys. A thick green gloom was caused by an overhead curtain of vines, which climbed from branch to branch and tangled together in the tops of the smaller trees. As each night fell in the deep solitude, my ears were attuned to all the sounds and vocalizations of the animals and birds of the mountain forest. I would concentrate on watching and listening, turning my head slightly to catch each sound and arrange it in my mind for future judgments, as the wind softly whispered in the night, mingling with the normal nighttime sounds of camp. *The Bru believed the night was ruled by evil spirits, death and witchcraft.* They were ever alert for omens from the spirits. I often observed them standing still and quiet, studying the area where I saw nothing, and sensing things that I could not. On the clear nights I listened to the night insects and their incessant songs--low, monotonous, plaintive. Tree frogs joined in with their sweet, mellow, melodious trill. Keen aural response to what we heard was absolutely necessary to detect unseen movement. Haynes and I also paid attention to the periods when there was a lack of sound. These intervals were just as important--a warning. We knew it should be monitored constantly. I was learning to identify the smells, recognize the different sounds of animals, as well as the plants utilized by our native troops. I felt the wildness and loneliness of the place.

As we moved into the deeper darkness of the forest solitude, we periodically came across small wooden structures placed by unseen primitive tribesmen. There were temples to placate the evil spirits believed to lurk there. We looked at them, but no one touched them. Seeing we were curious, our tribesmen often warned us not to go near them. The Bru muttered about dire consequences and forces beyond our understanding. *Spirits haunted these deserted places.*

These sacred places were an integral part of the religious lives and superstitions of hunters past and present. These were places where primitive man, feeling vulnerable before the forces of Creation, attempted to commune with the spirits for his well being during a safe journey or a productive hunt. There you came to know the sound of silence. The Bru believed that they could influence the spirits through the power of their beliefs. For the lone, primitive hunter, these means of intuitive communication could tip the survival balance and bring life or death to him and his family, dependent upon him. The Bru understood death must come to us all. In their case, it would come from the ghostly and unseen tiger or large cobra for any transgression committed against their beliefs. There was a certain power associated with these creatures. With a superstitious reverence, they avoided killing the reptile. But they could not avoid the tiger, since the great cat would quietly attack. It would lower its head, flick its tail, and move forward silently in a partial crouch, pacing itself, and when close enough, spring up on its victim. The assailant's frame was massive and designed to kill quickly, unless it wanted to play with its victim first.

We often encountered unoccupied, well-prepared ambush positions, with planted pointed bamboo stakes in the undergrowth, usually on the opposite side of those conducting the ambush. Anyone taking immediate cover had to be careful where he jumped. At times, pits were lined with these stakes embedded in the bottom and sides, enabling them to bend just enough before closing on any unwary victim unfortunate enough to get into one. The great numbers of punji stakes made us more watchful.[7] Punji stakes were meant to impale anyone quickly seeking cover in the undergrowth when fired upon at close range.

    We knew people had recently been moving through the area. Fresh tracks found in the trail, unmarred by the settling of dust or insect tracks. Physical warnings cut into a large tree trunk were visible to the immediate right side of the trail. The warnings indicated that we would die if we went any further. One such sign was a skull and crossbones noticeably cut into the trunk of a large tree. The Bru paid scant attention to the man-made sign, because it was meant for Ratchford and myself. "I wouldn't go any further if I were you," Ratch said smiling, standing behind me. I smiled and moved on. But the warning registered deep in my consciousness.

    Well away from the trail, the wary eyes of the Bru scout found fresh, yellow-colored human feces. Two older Bru approached the pile and squatted, and motioned for us to remain back, their eyes examining the site. I watched and listened as the Bru said a few words to my South Vietnamese Special Forces counterpart. The Bru indicated that it was still early in the day and the ground was slightly damp, while they pointed out with a stick where the still-pliant, fresh leaves were pressed together from the weight of the person who had stood and squatted there. None of the leaves were dry and therefore none were broken. Two other spots were pointed out, just a couple feet away. One small depression was most likely caused by the weight of his pack. There was an indentation apparent where a weapon had been leaned against a tree.

    My counterpart explained further, that the flies on it indicated that it was fresh. I watched as the Bru tribesman pressed it with a stick, picked at its soft state, and pointed to the outside and then the inside. My counterpart, after listening to what the tribesman had to say, remarked that since the surface of the feces was the same as the inside in color, it was fresh. Whoever had squatted there was not far away. When I pointed to the strips of red in the stool, the Bru explained that it was caused by red peppers eaten with a meal. The stool emitted a faint odor of fish sauce.

The native stools characteristically were quite different from the stools of Americans. From the larger size, color and near lack of odor. We could tell that the NVA were on a poor diet. Their rations were made up largely of cellulose roughage, which is not digested well by the human body. This accounted for the large size of the stools. This was characteristic of the anemic PAVN soldiers who lived on a bland diet, consisting largely of rice and leafy plants. By comparison, speaking of Ratch and myself, our protein diet included large amounts of iron; our feces were normally a darker color. Our feces always smelled badly and we always buried it.

The low ground near the river had some mature timber but mostly of single canopy growth with a lot of dense underbrush. Always remaining immersed in the shadows, we had come to a point where our side of the river boundary was higher and overlooked that of the Laotian border. The entire patrol came to a stop. Sniffing the wind, we detected a new scent wafting our way. *Wood smoke. Smoke, where there should be none.* The strong smell of burning wood rode the rising breeze up from the river, greeting our nostrils with a faint odor of cooking meat. *The low-hanging pall of smoke against the pewter-blue sky meant that they felt secure. No native worth his salt would build a fire big enough to give off that much smoke. It would announce their presence. It had to be the red-star city-boys from the north.* The expressive eyes of the Bru said it all. As we listened silently, our eyes roamed the low-lying area for any movement. There was only the gray smudge of cooking fires hanging in the air. In the thickening darkness of twilight, we gazed down across the rolling gray river and up the slope toward our target, checking for movement; there was none. There was only a tiny maze of three large, relatively harmless-looking long houses in the gloomy shadows of a grove of tall trees and some lesser structures. We decided to booby-trap their rest station and the long house where they were gathered. We knew that by deploying the booby traps they would not be able to exit without incurring heavy casualties. After quickly and silently establishing our security, we sent out one scout team to find a position well away from the PAVN camp for us to move to after our attack and remain overnight. We waited until after dark, then, our scouts crossed the river to conduct a reconnaissance mission.

Nothing moved. My eyes took in everything. Our two scouts stealthily slipped into the water, taking care not to create any ripples on the surface. They left no wake in their progress across the river and their heads could no longer be made out in the darkness of the water. The security team watched the sand embankment on the other side of the river. The two scouts made swift progress swimming across the river. The team stopped at the river edge with just their heads above the water. They listened and watched. The scouts had determined that no guards were posted on the riverside of the PAVN camp. Slowly they emerged to the edge of the slow-moving river so that there would be no sound from the water draining from their bodies. They were briefly outlined against the sand as they moved across that only danger area, and then the two dark figures slithered quickly on their bellies and disappeared silently into the dark background, entering the PAVN rest station.

After a long, silent and suspenseful interval, they were seen returning. Upon returning, we learned that the scouts had discovered an occupied rest station. The infiltrating PAVN had earlier been in the process of preparing an evening meal prior to darkness, before the cooking fires would compromise their location. Our scouts had successfully booby-trapped the area without incident. The scouts said that for some reason, the PAVN were all located in one long house. I visualized the images of men sitting inside, warm and relaxed by the fire. We could hear them singing. *I reasoned that they had probably gathered there for entertainment by a mobile cultural team from the PAVN's Ministry of Propaganda and Culture. The entertainment would most likely be followed by a political indoctrination session taught by Communist Party cadre from the General Political Department in Hanoi. It was quite common for Infiltration Groups traveling from the North into the South to undergo political "pep rallies" just prior to infiltrating into the Republic of Vietnam.* As soon as we were reassembled we quickly moved out of the area.

    A day later, the weather was still holding out during the morning hours. Again the point element had stopped. They had spotted movement ahead of us moving rapidly through the sun-dappled forest ahead moving toward us. It turned out to be our scouts returning. They reported NVA troops on the opposite riverbank just south of us, looking to cross the river. Ratch and I quickly pinpointed the location on the map. It showed that our side of the river was higher ahead of us. I watched the glittering eyes of the small unit leaders, as Ratch issued a fragmentary order of what we were going to do and how it was to be done. Choosing our route and using the available higher terrain to our advantage for concealment, we moved. There was only a whisper and rustle of our movement. Our deployment was fast and tense. We were as silent as the great brown fish owl in flight that haunted the streams and forest. Bent forward in a crouch, we stole silently through the dark forest, hurrying under out flung branches to the designated area--a bend in the stream. Our bodies were surging with adrenaline as we quickly organized ourselves and deployed in absolute silence for a hasty ambush. The forest crowded the bank, which was overgrown with large trees right to the water's edge. The opposing bank was open, high and steep but lower than ours. We selected and took our positions in the shaded darkness along the covered high bank of the large trees along our side of the river. The rising sun was placed at our backs. The enemy had the sun in their eyes. They would not be able to see through a leaf curtain from the intense light into the dark. Watching through the leaves we had a good view of the river and the far bank. My eyes scanned along the opposite bank and back to the waiting tribesmen. Only their eyes moved. Like ancient warriors of old, the Bru had an exalted look of triumph burning in their narrowing eyes. Their faces were aglow with vengeful purpose, inspired by what lay ahead.

    Large limbs overhung the stream on our side. There was no sound but the drone of insects, the whisper of the wind and the singing of birds. Some of the tips of the branches overhung and trailed the water. As I leaned forward and cupped a hand behind my ear, I could hear the slight sound of voices; they were coming now. My scalp prickled from the distant sound. My patrol partner told me that I was to fire the first shot to initiate the ambush, when they were all in the kill zone; the river. They would not be given the opportunity to surrender. My blood ran cold. A cold chill had crept between my shoulder blades and up my neck. I almost choked. I closed my eyes for a minute. I sensed the hair standing on the back of my neck. Above the river, the leading figures signaled for a halt. It was apparent that their purpose was to search for any possible danger. Below, the river flowed over the fording place. They watched suspiciously at first, studying the ford, the higher bank and dark foliage for a long time. The only sound was of our own breathing. Tense minutes passed. Then we faintly heard one man say something to another and they started forward. In the cool, quiet dark of the forest, I watched, fascinated, as they considered it safe to cross. They had that casual look of a little too much carelessness as they started down the slope and started to splash across the ford into the ambush. I made the range something less than fifty yards, which meant the bullet would still be rising. With my slower bullet, I would aim a little low to compensate for a killing shot. I checked for semi-automatic fire, examining the position of the selector switch on the left side of the receiver opposite the operating slide handle. They never bothered sending an advance party across to check the area out ahead of them. They started crossing in a relatively closed formation with their weapons on their shoulders. This was my first look at the best light infantry in the world, the Bo Doi Chu Luc.[8]

    Since I was the one to initiate the ambush, I quickly studied the movement of the water, the tips of the tree branches to my front, and also the tips of the high grass on the opposite bank for the wind's effect on the first bullet to be fired. I used my thumb and forefinger to check that the rear sight range scale was seated firmly for 100 yards. *Okay. There is little wind.* My eye quickly checked the windage yoke. *Okay. The sun is high and behind us. They will have to look into the sun and shadows. We have surprise, cover, range and accuracy on our side. It will be difficult for them to spot any movement on our part.* I was close enough that my bullet would not drop. We had all the elements in our favor. In the taut silence, kneeling in the shadows, I saw what appeared to be the last man coming down the steep open bank. They looked a formidable group, heavily armed, all giving an impression of ruthlessness.

I tensed and looked at the waiting Bru warriors to see whether they, too, might be nervous. I sensed that they were not. The alert and watchful Bru waited with grim enthusiasm. I sensed the waiting tension in their bodies. I had eagerly trained for years for this. Now I was at the test, and only wanted to be away from it. I settled into a firm position and picked my target. My mind completed the complex process by releasing the safety on my weapon. The enemy was now completely in the kill zone. I eased my M-2 carbine up against my shoulder and lined up my shot through the sight. The 110-grain bullet with a velocity of 2,200 fps was sufficient for close in work. I leaned into the butt of my carbine.

My sight rose and fell with my breathing. I could feel the faint pulse in my arm and throat. I took a deep breath and then let it halfway out, coming to a natural pause while concentrating on my aiming point. Squeezing slightly, the tip of my index finger took up the slack in the trigger. It was the moment of truth. *I hated this moment.* The continued squeeze was smooth and steady, as the sear released, the weapon's muzzle exploded. The sound seemed to follow the flight of the bullet. I heard the resounding, meaty slap as it struck flesh. A faint plume of dust and cloth resulted from the explosive impact. The single round must have mangled my human target's lungs. Still upright, foamy, pink froth ooze billowed from his lung, as he looked down, shivered and convulsed and fell into the water. As I shifted to another target, more brass kicked out of my carbine to the side and away. I took a brief look at the PAVN over the top of the barrel as our hillside erupted in a storm of gunfire. Without hesitation, the Bru tribesmen shattered the silence of the forest with the thundering sound of their rifle fire. I clearly saw the horror-struck facial expressions as the enemy momentarily turned wild, with absolutely terrified eyes staring in our direction. They stopped, standing motionless and silent as the first volley ripped into them and through them. Anesthetized by terror. Caught completely by surprise, they struggled to see into the shadows where we were hidden. My round caught a man in mid-stride; meat, blood and bone fragments were blown away. He staggered, lost his weapon, toppled slowly forward, the splashing sound reaching my ears as his body and others hit the water, face down, legs twitching, and finally went limp in death. Nothing sounds as mad as rifle-fire, staccato, furious.

The slate-gray river erupted in spraying geysers of water like a powerful fall of rain that glittered in the sunlight all around them. I saw the bullets slamming into the water and tracking around their formation. Hundreds of rifle rounds smacked the surface of the water, creating spouts of spray that danced on the calm surface. Many of the Bo Doi Chu Luc were thrown backwards. Disoriented, some just stood in frozen terror. Others were attempting to run back for cover, or standing and shooting, colliding with each other, limping, dragging, or carrying each other, yelling and bawling for help, and pitifully screaming until they fell floundering, dying in the water. They never had a prayer. There was a rush of sound. There was a slight pause as the Bru quickly changed magazines. Then the firing became so fast and furious that it blended into a continuous roar as the other rifles almost simultaneously started their automatic fire. Bright silver gouts of water completely engulfed them. The effect was shattering. The volume of fire of the attack was fast and violent. The formation was shredded. Blood spouted from their mortal wounds. Features torn, many collapsed silently, while others flopped and flailed helplessly. Their shock, anger and despair, was to be short-lived.

The pitiful momentary screams and cries of other wounded soldiers reverberated as the concerted hammering of sustained rifle-fire continued, causing my head to ache. When the initial wounded survivors turned to stagger toward the bank, they were severely slowed by the water as their legs moved against the current. A second element fired on them, while the first element reloaded, before the echo of the first came back from the forest. Their bodies, stitched by many rounds of automatic fire, were jerking and twitching from the impact of repeated hits, spinning around, staggering and punched over backwards. Others were losing balance, slithering down into kneeling positions, until they finally lacked the strength to move. Some, in awkward postures, struggled in pain to rise, writhing, as more bullets hit them, ripping fabric and flesh into broken heaps. The low sound of mortally wounded men with faces twisted in agony could barely be heard. We had to keep firing until they were all down. There had been many rounds fired, and although the most accurate ones had destroyed a lot of tissue, they had not proven to be instant kills. I thought there had been a loss in accuracy, but it was simply that people were hard to kill.

Men lay dead or seriously wounded in the water, life running out in crimson rivulets, legs churning in their death throes. Wounded men still rose and fell again, staggering forward in the water a few more steps in a lurching death gait before collapsing again or being vaulted over, slithering in a red spray with arms out flung to either side. Some of the bodies closer to shore could be seen kicking their feet in the sand until their bodies relaxed in death. One man still on his hands and knees, without strength, his head dangling downward, struggled to get up. He collapsed, rolling weakly to one side into the water under the continuing fire. One soldier almost made it over the top of the bank and out of view, in the direction from which they had come, when he was punched forward by the impact of several bullets. The many rounds fired at him sprayed blood, dirt and foliage in all directions. The impact spun him into a stumbling fall, causing him to go down with a harsh bounce and hit the ground in a lifeless heap, spewing crimson. Twitching feebly face down, he relaxed and was still. It was all over within minutes. The echo of the firing, now withered away to stone-cold silence, made the scene even more appalling. Confined in the river, they had no chance. The carnage was over. The river fell into silence. What I had just done and what I had just seen hurt my heart and soul. The sound was still ringing in my ears, and the image was locked in my mind. I prayed that this would never happen to me. Still behind cover and now fearful that fate would turn on me, I fed in another magazine quickly. I was slowly overcome with the realization that this incident would now be a part of me always; nothing would ever be the same again.

No one had been spared. The many dead men, stretched out, were littering the stream and its bank. There was a massive, compressing silence. Nothing moved. I stared hypnotically as the river turned red and trailed off downstream. I heard the metallic sound of the Bru reloading. An abrupt and heavy silence prevailed in the mountain forest--and there was the smell of cordite. Now that we had revealed our presence, we would be the hunted. The scene was graphic in our minds and we were now overwhelmed by a definite sense of primal fear. I felt chilled by the magnitude of what I had done. I began to experience an adrenaline rush and started to shake. I felt sorry for what I had done. I fought to bury my emotions. My eyes were opened for the first time, and I saw no glory in this, only horror. In the future, I would go on to serve in Indo-China in 1964, 1965, 1966, 1967, 1969-70, and this incident, more than any other, would continue to hang like an intense darkening gloom over me. A strange foreboding clutched me. Then, I knew this could happen just as easily to me. For the first time I realized that this war was going to be up close and personal. I silently resolved to myself, like these warriors we led, that I would take notice of anything and everything the rest of my time here. I wouldn't let my eyes miss anything around me: I'd be always ready. Like the Bru, I had to learn everything about my new environment. Like the Bru, only through understanding could control of people and situations that would affect my own life and the lives of others be attained. I realized that if you had to fight, you do it on your ground, not theirs. A single mistake in these mountains on patrol was all it took to finish us. I would give my full attention to the landscape, tracks, sign, night sounds, and the behavior of the birds and animals, to stay alive in terrain where at any moment the PAVN could have us in their kill zone. Looking at Ratch and seeing him deep in thought, I went and stood by him. When he turned and looked at me, acknowledging me, I asked what he was thinking about. *"Our options."*

Looking me in the eyes, Haynes began to talk. "*These men we ambushed may have been crossing the river to look for us. We are no longer able to obtain good information because now, we are the hunted and far from any help. We can't afford to be reckless. To safely return to our camp, everything will depend on how we use our time and the terrain, using our own resources, before a much larger force finds us and tries to do the same thing to us.*" We were well aware that those left dead in the river would stir a rage for revenge, regardless of consequences. We knew they would try to think like us and figure out which way we would be going. Logic dictated that the PAVN would expect us to head off in the direction of our destination, using the most efficient and quickest route. This, they would know, would minimize our time and distance, and place us on the shortest, straightest, and known way home. We reckoned that our enemy would quickly set off to ambush the route we came down on, hoping we would return the same way we came. Did they have enough resources to cover all the trails going north? We knew the PAVN would send out trackers to trail us, and send other forces to hopefully cut us off and kill us. It would need to be a large one. The more men they sent, the slower they would travel, and the less likely they would be to catch us.

The trackers, however, could catch us. We gathered the small unit leaders and quickly discussed our plan. Our rear guard was instructed to alert us immediately if there was any indication at all of someone tracking us. That would give us time to arrange another ambush. Haynes stated that the best way home was the longest way. We decided on the bold, perhaps desperate move, to take the long way home by going deeper inland from the border: we would travel east into the deep mountains, find our river that flowed north and follow it to the Bru village of Huong Hoa on the south side of the river from Highway 9, below the last bridge.

Haynes gave the word to move. As we changed direction, I checked the position of the sun. We lengthened our stride. We plunged forward into the deepest forest we had yet encountered. We literally could not see the forest for the trees. Gone were the visible landmarks. In these areas we would depend on "dead reckoning:" keeping track of our direction, distance and speed of travel. Here, sensory navigation was essential, using the external guide, the position of the sun in relation to our direction of movement. We had to make sure that it remained in the same relative position for short periods of time as we moved from point to point, because the position of the sun was constantly changing. Only my nervousness kept me from appreciating the strange green world of large trees, plants, fungi, bugs and birds. The night was black and the air was heavy with moisture that constantly dripped on us. We slept without any covering in dry creek beds. At the higher altitudes the cold kept those of us watching alert, while others rested. There had been no disruption in the sound patterns made by the night creatures, so we knew that the enemy was not in close, watching and listening.

* * *

The tops of the trees swayed gently in the wind, which seemed to be blowing from the east. I estimated the wind blowing at 10 mph. We were always mindful of the direction of the wind, which remained constantly in our faces. We stopped frequently to watch and listen. Instinct told me a bad storm was building. There was the distinctive, penetrating odor of ozone, which told me there was a passing storm nearby. Sharp smells of our surroundings were becoming stronger. The air remained mild, almost balmy. The thick clouds meant that darkness would come early. Rain would only mean one thing: a trail would be left wherever we had been. Where we had once boldly pushed ahead, we were now cautious, fearful. We relentlessly climbed through the brambles and spiked trees and descended trackless ridges into a rugged, wild, beautiful green country trying to disappear into the landscape. Any noise would carry a long way in the forest. For a while, I brought up the rear. I watched our back trail. It was frighteningly quiet back there now. Jungle vegetation was so thick in some places that it was mind-boggling. We knew that we were pursued, and our senses were fully alert.

For a while it was mostly hands-and-knees stuff, then the trail rose steeply. We navigated the wet and slippery, harsh elevations through the climbing lianas vines that twined around the trees, creeper vines with orchids growing on them, and endless "wait-a-minute" vines that would completely stop a man. Each time I didn't look at where and what I was grabbing, it seemed I grabbed a small tree trunk surrounded with sharp thorns. One moment there was no wind; the air was damp and still. Then there was wind flailing the leaves. The trees swayed. I estimated that the wind was now blowing in excess of 15 mph. The sky blackened. Then the wind dropped and the front unraveled over the eastern ridge moving south. High above, through the thick, sinewy forest canopy, we could see bits of the sky. It had again turned blue. Thick serpentine roots laddered the trail, clinging in every crevice and cranny, mortally embracing the giant rocks, twisting and crushing, surrounding us. I kept hoping to find an opening through the timber. Small birds were constantly making unnerving mournful whistling sounds. I thought that if we got onto high ground, we could see what was out there. I glanced at the position of the sun through the trees as it kept to its expected course, and saw the day was late. We knew we wouldn't lose those tracking us, but hopefully we would stay far enough ahead of them that they would not catch us. The slope was soft and springy, and easy to step on without noise. Our only break in the monotony was a false step that would send us rolling and crashing down the slope, until some tree would stop us. We moved slowly and quietly, because the loud shriek of alarm from the gibbons or peafowl would give our position away.[9] My mind harbored only sensations of misery. I worried about growing weak from lack of food and the delirium that would follow if we didn't find something to eat soon. I drank water and even though I didn't smoke, I accepted a Vietnamese cigarette and smoked it to help curb my appetite.

Late the next day while we were still moving down the mountain, I had caught a glimpse of a silver sparkle in a shallow valley below, reflected from the sun, through the trees. Lower down the mountain, I caught a glimpse of the eastern horizon. A gossamer white veil showed cloud-drift creeping to the west beyond the eastern range of mountains. We could see a storm building; the seasonal wind would soon be upon us. The high, thin clouds were the type that ran before the monsoon. We moved through the heavy undergrowth that scratched our hands and faces, and then broke out upon the slow moving, solid and rocky tributary we had been looking for. The sound of an awkward flap of wings caught our attention. I saw a long-legged wading bird, standing like a dignified sentry, tall and stilt-legged in the water. Another marsh high-stepper was already in flight, its silverbright wings gilded by the sun, soaring on the warm-air thermals in a leisurely fashion, low over the landscape. The remaining stiletto-billed bird still standing in the water, amidst tall growing grasses and reeds, told us that all was normal ahead and that the water was shallow. Then the great heron-like bird croaked its raucous cry in alarm and took flight into the sky, loudly berating us as we appeared in the open.

    Well ahead of us, two scouts flanked both sides of the stream as security. We were likely to encounter the enemy following a stream. We entered the stream at a low place where the bank met the water, so as not to leave so much of a disturbed entry point and to help conceal our trail. The stream provided the advantage in this strange country, acting as a guide and definite course, leading to the river. The water was cold and clear. We waded in along the rocky-bottomed bed of the small, sluggish, level stream, following it a long time. For hours we had been looking back in fear, certain that we were being followed. Now we were hoping to hide our tracks, sloshing along in knee-deep water, and hoping to slow, if not confound our pursuit by trackers. The meandering stream was protected by thick bush scrub and bamboo on both banks. We were going to follow it to the larger Da Krong River, that flowed north and eventually into the Quang Tri River that flowed east along the south side of Highway 9. The highway went east, and turned north at Ca Lu. We would eventually come out at the village (Lang) Ruou, located at XD 968426. These directions were important to know, just in case things went terribly wrong. I saw several of the red jungle fowl, the ancestors of our domestic chicken, feeding in the open next to a bamboo thicket. The males were red, gold and green. These beautiful creatures offered a refreshing sight. We made communication with an overhead aircraft to relay a message for an aerial re-supply of food and ammunition.

The pace was not tiring. The temperature and humidity were rising, however, causing the mosquitoes to bite more. I was irritated because I felt the scars on my body contracting and stretching. We all felt the ache of our empty bellies. Our rations gone, we were living by foraging along the way. We knew hunger. It was a dull, inside disturbance, which was easily banished by the eating of roots or drinking of water. I felt light-headed but in control of my body and more aware of my senses than usual. The sounds and different textures of colors were louder and seemingly brighter. We had been eating the fast growing leaves of lemon grass, boiled bamboo shoots, the core of banana trees and colocassia root with what little rice remained. The native troops were a wealth of information, which they parted with readily. Evidently, this stream was used by the PAVN to move inland, because of the food items that could be foraged.

Our scouts caught scent of an encampment and held everyone up. A quick search of the area by the scouts revealed an empty but active PAVN rest station obscured by trees and brush. It consisted of several empty huts maintained by one family: a healthy man, a pregnant woman and a crippled boy. A ragged breechcloth hung from the man's lean hips, and a faded khaki shirt tattered with threads covered his upper body. The tribal man wore his hair loose. The woman wore a tribal dress that had seen better days. The boy wore only an old khaki shirt. They would travel with us to Khe Sanh to be interrogated. The banks of the stream were not high and we merely signaled for everyone to move onto the bank from where they were. This would help cover our trail, instead of everyone coming out at the same point. I studied the stream: there was a lingering discoloration from our movement down its length. A slow methodical search of the area soon revealed a clearing with cultivated food being grown. It consisted of large-leafed taro plants, and the 5-foot high perennial manioc plants, also known as cassavas, a hardy plant that can grow almost anywhere and produces a waxy, rather insipid-tasting root. This ugly, pallid root staple is a virtual carbohydrate factory, producing six times more calories than corn. It is boiled and eaten like a potato. It is eaten when there is nothing else and has extraordinary nutritive power. The taro patch was cultivated and had water channeled into it. The troops dug and cut the underground tubers and leaves of the taro plant, and wrapped them in their packs to carry along. The tubers are edible when cooked, but raw taro will give a burning sensation to your throat and mouth. This particular area must have been under cultivation for over a year, because that was how long it normally took before it was ready to be harvested. Although food was plentiful, it would have been unpalatable for most American troops.

These days of forced fasting were beneficial for Ratch and myself, ridding our bodies of toxins. However, a prolonged period of survival food will eventually lead to a mental and physical collapse unless enough fish and wild game supplements the diet. There was no time to eat here, but if we hurried we would be able to take time somewhere along the trail home. The troops cut the clusters of tuberous roots from the stem base of the manioc shrubs. Banana leaves were cut and packed away by the troops in their packs. The banana trees were cut. There were chilies, wild watercress, colocassia root and bindweed, a deep-rooted, prostrate climbing vine. To the Bru, the watercress was good for mouth sores, headaches, and skin ailments. It was used as a diuretic to eliminate accumulated fluids in body tissue and for clearing mucus congestion from the lungs. There were a lot of slender long-stalked cassavas plants, whose large fleshy, tapering roots were immediately harvested and packed away. I didn't know the difference between cultivated cassava and wild cassava. However, I was informed that the wild cassava produced cyanide. Cooking it would not help. Dense clumps of the long, strongly scented lemon grass were harvested from the open areas near the stream.[10] It could also be used for flavoring tea. We weren't going to starve. As long as we just got the time to eat, we had enough to sustain life. We moved the troops back to the stream. I checked our back trail in the stream: the lingering discoloration was gone, but the few muddy and largely sandy areas of the stream would hold our prints for some time.

We hurriedly moved back into the stream and moved on. Eventually, we came to the wide-open stream channels that signaled the lower reaches of the river system. The sun was low in its western quadrant as we changed direction again: we were now moving north. In total silence and extreme caution, we left the water at a hard area covered by rocks and followed along the bank of the river. We searched the far distant bank for any sign of movement, with weapons always at the ready. The smell of fish and the wet river rocks was strong in our nostrils. We eventually found our fording area. We first had to cross a deep, side channel tributary in a hard rocky area that would leave little sign of our passing. Based on our direction of travel, the tracker could make an intelligent appraisal of our route now and deduce that we were going back to Khe Sanh.

We quickly studied the deep-water current at our crossing point: a surging torrent, which proved to be chest-deep for Ratch and myself. The river was cold. The loud roar of dangerous running water filled our ears, and the wind running wild off the river snatched at our uniforms. Before crossing, I noticed a lowering storm sky that seemed to be miles away to the east. While we waited to receive our aerial re-supply, we were conscious every second of what was behind us, closing in. The PAVN were of a single-mindedness when it came to closing in on their enemy, and we were a small force isolated deep within their territory. The sun was no more than a pale glow in the sky. We could now feel the weather changing. The monsoon would soon be upon us.

I heard a faint sound to the northeast, then after a bit, the throb of engines. The aircraft was still unseen, but from the sound we knew he was coming fast and low. Then suddenly he broke over the tree line. The pilot banked, searching, saw our panels, verbally identified them and flew even lower. Then he was right over us and made the drop. He free-dropped our supplies on the first pass and kept going at treetop level. It had been an Australian CV-2, identified by its circular insignia on the side. The free-drop destroyed most of our food. We gathered what little supplies we could and pushed on. Sergeant Haynes noticed during this break that some of the tribesmen seemed exhausted and were simply staring at the ground. They were malnourished.

    The sky was now heavy with dark-white cumulus clouds. The main part of the river had to be crossed--now. We sent a security team of taller men ahead across the river while our troops got their gear back in order. Many of our native troops crossed with the roaring water swirling over their heads, then submerged under the water, with just their forearms and rifles held above the water level. All of them were soon smiling from the experience.

    The main part of the river turned out to be wide, with solid footing. There were many deep and shallow pools connected by slower-moving water rushing over shoals that were capable of being waded. The pools were crystal clear. The swirling currents of the runs and riffles were broad and shallow, eddying around the boulders as we crossed the gravel-strewn island bars toward the opposite side, then waded out of the shoals and up the river bank and high into the forest. I noticed both, the sudden shift in the wind and the thickening, dark churning clouds were coalescing into black thunderclouds. The leaves on the trees were showing their undersides: a sign of rain. Watching our back trail, the tribesmen still observed no one, but we had the feeling that we were not alone.

    The sound of the cicadas and birds in the mountain forest suddenly stopped, which meant danger to us or that, the storm would soon be upon us. Not a breath of air stirred. Tall cloud formations were gathering, dark and swift, shadowing the land to the east. I was entranced by the low, dirty-gray and black clouds swirling in a writhing and twisting mass, forming in a squall line. The weather was changing. Not a bird was to be seen. There was a sudden cool breeze and it was getting colder. We moved higher up into the embrace of ancient trees. The forest floor was a jumble of great, old smooth boulders covered with twisted roots, damp green vines and mosses. We heard the first distant ominous thunderclap reverberate in the cloud cover. I could hear the soothing sound of rustling leaves high up, indicating a strong wind. The storm would add to our misery, but would help obscure our movements. As I watched, the din of the chattering leaves grew more powerful. Strong sustained winds of a quick-moving front were now rocking and twisting the upper-most tops of the trees.[11]

    The thunder caused a terrific din overhead. Then lightning struck again and again. The noise was unlike anything I had experienced before. White veins of pure light and power crackled and danced through the sky. Raindrops began to fall and the wind came, whistling a low, howling song, hitting the tops of the trees, making them dance. Tree limbs were whipping back and forth. By the onset of darkness, a driving rain was upon us. The rain made a loud banging noise on the large leaves of the canopy overhead. The force of the weather hit us. The clouds were so dark. The giant trees trembled to their very roots. This was no tropical storm, but a typhoon. There was a wild cry of wind. It sounded like the wailing of a million lost souls. A quickening staccato of fat, stinging raindrops hammering at us, as our soaked uniforms clung to us. Our visibility was soon reduced to near zero. When the wind gusted, I was hit with a heavy spray of cold rain. The sky turned dark. A piercingly bright, blue-white, ragged streak of lightning flashed down with a splitting report. The roll of thunder grew louder, closer and more ominous. I felt a buzzing sensation, and was startled by a tremendous crack of lighting. Crooked, white-hot fingers of lightning veined the sky, and struck directly above, striking a nearby tree. Luckily, no one was near it on the ground or it would have come up from the root system and hit some of us. I could smell the peculiar burnt-wood odor caused by the strike. I heard trees breaking apart. The sound of snapping trees really grabbed me. The wind gusts kept getting higher and higher. Lightning ripped across the sky, lighting up the deeper darkness beneath the great trees. Thunder rumbled and boomed relentlessly. I was terrified that our grenades would go off because of the storm. The sky burned white and green. Like the Bru, I felt the hand of God closely. The rain came down harder. The air became sharper. Cold water was quickly running down our backs, as we huddled down. The exploding white incandescence of lightning flashes became fewer and farther between, and now grumbled farther off. The storm was receding. Then the storm grew strong again. With a flash and a clap, lightning broke over us again. The dark trees and clouds were illuminated above us in all their tumultuous glory. I felt as if we had been swallowed up by the storm. Soon the wind had died with the setting sun and was gone. The receding sound of thunder echoed in the distance. Like a black mantle, the night settled over us, and within an hour the storm was gone. Whenever the cold wind stirred the treetops, a shower of rainwater would come down. We would spend the night tired, forlorn and hungry. Whispers spread among the tribesmen because the storm was so powerful and malevolent. They were consumed with fear. I heard them muttering about Bok Claik, the storm spirit--an evil omen of some dreadful thing to come. The thunder was his spirit announcing his presence.

*　*　*

The next morning, after a cold, wet night the forest took on a mysterious quality, with its drooping and dripping tree branches, tree ferns and wisps of ground fog. The troops silently straightened out their uniforms and settled into their harnesses, checked their weapons, then combed their wet, long black hair backward with their fingers, put on their soft caps and were ready to march. The large, striated boulders encased in great roots were scattered about on both sides of the trail. The smell of decay in the soil rose around us. Silver raindrops outlined the strands of spider webs, making them stand out clearly against the dark and green areas around us. There was still a long way before us, through hostile country. Everything about us was wet. The daylight hours were held in a constant twilight. The soggy forest was threaded with filigrees of mist. After the heavy rain, the weather warmed up a little. The nighttime temperatures were above 60 degrees, and the mosquito activity was accelerated. Their ominous buzz was everywhere. A fresh, cool fragrance of a renewed soil filled the air.

Whenever we stopped to rest I watched the leeches, attracted by our body heat, coming in platoon formations in their looping motion on the ground. The trees continuously dripped rainwater. The leeches had suckers at both ends, the larger one located at the posterior end was for attachment purposes. The smaller one was used for feeding.[12] We used salt, mosquito repellent, or a match to get them off, usually long after they had done their damage. We paid attention to our legs and groin area, because it was possible that these wounds could become infected and ulcerated. At night we had to take precautions not to allow them to get into our nose or any of the other apertures of our body; specifically our penis. Once there, they would bloat and become distended with blood, requiring evacuation and a surgical procedure.

Ratchford P. Haynes
My Patrol Partner at Khe Sanh 1964

Finally, late one afternoon, our troops reached "that point"--the limit exceeding our limit of endurance, a deceptive weakness that caused our legs to tremble and robbed our power to endure the heat and cold. We needed to stop long enough to appease our exhaustion and to eat, so we stopped in a protected hollow draw that would help conceal the glow of our small fires. As we walked to the river, others assembled the fire circles and searched the high ground for scattered dry wood. Above and along the river we searched for the deep holes of water. We located a few deep, small quiet sections of pocket water with irregular subsurface rocks, protected by large boulders and containing large woody debris that would offer cover and security for fish. The cool air and water in this area smelled of fish and mud. There was one really nice right-angle pool, where the current hit a shelving rock, and turned on itself to make a foam-flecked eddy. The visible telltale disturbance of water was followed by a flicker of movement revealing fish holding in the water. We fished in these holes using what we referred to as DuPont Lures (hand grenades). The results were better than we expected; the river holes were full of fish.

The Bru gathered the stunned fish as they appeared on the surface. Sites for the cooking fires had been dug and sunk in pits, behind the covering shadow of large boulders, which would help conceal the glow of the small fires. The dry hardwood selected for the fire by the Bru gave off minimal visible smoke, which helped to secure our presence. Soon the blue flames flickered to orange and then glowed radiantly. The fires burned hot and clean and there was a minimal amount of ash produced. The dancing yellow light cast shadows on those of us around the fire. The fire was friendly, and felt intimate and warm. It was quickly reduced to glowing coals. Unlike many of the camp fires I had stood around at Fort Bragg with my eyes watering, unable to breathe because of the oily, noxious and acrid smoke of pine that burned so quickly, these fires lasted a while. The small fish were baked in coals with guts, heads, and skin intact, because the guts congeal and are easily removed after cooking. The larger cleaned fish were cooked either on flat, fire-heated rocks, boiled in helmets or baked in mud. The best were the fish wrapped in the banana leaves and encased in airtight-sticky mud that baked in the coals steaming in their own juice. Rice from the PAVN rest station had been cooked. The mud was baked hard and cracked open with the large end of our knives after cooling. When the mud was broken away and the leaves opened, the fragrant and tender white flesh of the carp was revealed. The cooked rice had been allowed to sit and steam for about twenty minutes while the fish cooked. Rice is best when allowed to sit and steam. Other fish were just cooked in a thick coating of sticky clay mud and cooked on top of the coals. When done, the hardened clay mud-shell came off in chunks along with the skin of the baked fish, leaving succulent white meat behind.

 I helped myself to large pieces of white meat from the fish that had been baked in the mud, blowing to cool it. The sumptuous flakes were mild yet full-tasting as I chewed. I seasoned them with my small C-ration packets of salt before popping them into my mouth. As we picked them apart and stripped the bones, we flipped them into the fire. We ate hurriedly, eyes on the food. The leafy plant we ate was boiled taro leaves and resembled spinach. It was good with the salt. The baked or roasted tuber from the taro plant and sweet potato, a staple of the mountain people because it furnished carbohydrates, also tasted good with salt. It would sustain us, and I was hungry. I slipped into the shadows, away from the smoke. I watched, listened and worried about the fragrance of wood as the gentle wreaths of pale blue smoke began to curl serpentine-like down the slope in the breeze among the trees. I worried most about the glow in the trees overhead being seen at a distance. I was entranced and frightened by the dancing light of ghostly shadows cast from outside the glow of the fires. I was surprised at how quickly I became full and was unable to eat anymore. My stomach had shrunk.

 The fires were well concealed from the river, but a sharp eye would make out the upward glow lighting up the limbs on the close-set trees. I watched as several native soldiers sifted the white ash to rid it of small chunks and mixed the ash with a bit of water to create a dentifrice. The frayed end of a chewed stick was the toothbrush. A few soldiers seemed totally oblivious to everything, staring at the fire, lost in thought. I listened to the soft and sharp little sounds of the fires as a gust of wind swirled hot sparks from the dying embers of the fading flames. The fires dimmed to silent shimmering embers, and again nearly went out. I concentrated on gazing into the darkness out of the corners of my eyes, watching for the faint gleam of strange eyes reflecting the flickering firelight from the shadows of the dark woods. I listened to the crackling, wind-blown fires that scattered a few ashes over the blackened stone rings that contained them, causing the coals to glow again within the ash. In my peripheral vision, I saw the flickering shadowed forms and movements of the fires-- rhythmic, moving back and forth against the dark background of the trees.

I could sometimes see the deliberately unhurried movement of small nocturnal soft-furred lemurs, with their large eyes, against the skylight as they searched the trees for food-leaves and buds. I heard a night bird across the river. The draw we were in would protect us from observation. Our native troops had managed to select mostly smokeless fuel. After the sun had gone down, all we had to worry about was the scent of smoke flowing downward with the cooling air. We listened in the heavy silence for any change in the song of the night creatures, but there was none. Our troops were highlighted against the dimming coals of their fires, their eyes shining bright from shrouded faces. I heard only the soft whisper of their voices and the deep regular rhythmic breathing of those asleep with full stomachs. Anyone who chanced to be along the river for a short distance could possibly scent the smoke, but it would quickly be diffused by the strong breeze blowing northward. The little blazes burned out. There was only the rushing sound of the river and the wind, the voices of the night creatures, and the smell of baked river mud and fish.

My physical condition was deteriorating. I had noticed my urine was turning a darker yellow. I knew that when it got to the orange stage, I was in serious trouble. I had to force myself to drink more fluids and be careful not to leave any telltale signs for those that would track us when I urinated on the ground. I faced another problem as well. Between the rain and all the hard walking, I had to pay more attention to my feet. Whenever the opportunity presented itself, the boots came off to allow the feet to air dry and harden, to be powdered and change into socks only a little dryer than those I took off. I wrung my socks out and hung them on the outside of my backpack. The constant moisture had turned the skin on my feet white. My feet were swelling, and there was a lot of rubbing inside my boot.[13] While applying the standard Army issue foot powder, I literally rubbed off the dead white skin around and inside my toes. The years of calluses built up serving in the infantry were gone--rubbed off. Our leather-canvas jungle boot had two air holes, which were a great help in draining water from our boots and allowed our feet to stay half-dry and breathe better. Luckily, our new, lightweight jungle uniform would dry with our body heat when it wasn't raining or the trees dripping on us.[14]

* * *

At last, the day came when we emerged from the cloud-covered forest, out of the mist around us and into the open. Finally, we were at the last high point of the ridge and the invisibility of the clouds. Peering through the mist, we realized we had a direct line-of-sight of the long houses of the village Lang Ruou. We felt a little more comfortable in this awareness. It was here that Ratch confided in me about the AR-15 he carried. It had jammed on him. We spent some time watching the village and a long empty road on the other side of the river. Finally, we moved down to the village. There remained only one more river to cross and then we would move up Highway 9, climbing the massive escarpment at the bridge located at XD 913402, into the Khe Sanh plateau. Before crossing, our scouts, who had been watching our rear, reported seeing a tracker, a shadowy figure standing in the forest. Haggard and wary, we crossed the river without incident in log canoes that belonged to the village. Our faces were drawn with lack of sleep and pale from weariness. We had been lucky enough to elude their patrols and ambushes. Our fatigue and hunger were forgotten. We did a tactical road march up to the head of the gorge where the Communists had blown the bridge. The steep road in the massive gorge was a one-lane ledge; shelving built into the precipice of the deep gorge with many kinks and twists on the way up. I felt an electric thrill rush through me, as we were met at the top by a small convoy of our camp vehicles, waiting for us to be trucked home. I had made my first really long trek through forbidding and hostile terrain; but more importantly I had completed an inward journey as well. I was becoming more responsible, self reliant and independent. And I had learned that our small tribesmen were loyal and courageous, and that made them the greatest among men.

After returning to camp and ridding ourselves of our uniforms, stinking of stale sweat, we were debriefed by our Intelligence Sergeant, SFC Williams. The elements of infiltrating North Vietnamese Army troops were too large for our small patrols to handle, but we could nip around at their edges. This same scenario was being played out by other A-teams, similar to ours at Special Forces border camps all over the country of Vietnam. Later, while having a beer and listening to the radio, we heard Hanoi Hannah on the radio mention how busy the boys at Khe Sanh had been on patrol along the border. "We will be paying you a visit," she said as she signed off. We now knew that Hanoi was thinking about us. It's always nice to be remembered.

Footnotes:

1. In October 1961, Special Forces soldiers from the 7th Special Forces Group, arrived in the Kingdom of Laos. The clandestine, Mobile Training Team, named "White Star," was led by Lt. Col. Arthur "Bull" Simons.

2. On 16 March 1973 during Operation Homecoming, at Gia Lam Airport in Hanoi, Cpt. Floyd James Thompson who was the longest held prisoner-of-war in history was returned. He spent a total of nine years as a prisoner. The Air Force pilot

of their shot down aircraft, Cpt. Richard L. Whitesides, was never recovered and is still unaccounted for.

3. The manner of radiation in which the radio transmission wave was propagated or skipped depended upon the clouds, sun, and general atmospheric conditions.

4. There are some 3,000 species of mosquitoes in the world, and some 800 are capable of transmitting such diseases as malaria, yellow fever, dengue fever and encephalitis. The striped, disease-carrying Asian Tiger mosquito (Aedes albopictus), was a vector of Dengue fever and encephalitis in Asia. These diseases are sometimes fatal. Their bite creates spiking fever, pain in the body (mainly in the joints and behind the eyes) and an accompanying rash. It caused soldiers to become nervous and irritable.

5. These parasites would invade the liver and quickly begin to multiply. Within a month, the person bitten would be slightly ill, and then with each two or three day cycle the condition would worsen.

6. In the latter part of 1964, some 12,000 PAVN regulars from North Vietnam were working their way south to their various destinations. Depending on the distance individual PAVN units were covering, it could take from several weeks to several months to reach their final destination.

7. The punji stake was made of a four-foot long piece of bamboo. One end was razor sharp, and the other end was trimmed to a point for insertion into the ground at an angle. A notch cut into the shaft about halfway down facilitated pounding the shaft securely into the ground. The tips were hardened over a fire prior to honing, in order to increase the degree of sharpness. This would also make the stakes more brittle, causing them to easily break off inside the wound of the victim, leaving small pieces of wood to cause infection. The stakes were often coated with poisons, and in some cases human feces, to further complicate the wounds.

8. North Vietnamese regulars or People's Army of Vietnam (PAVN).

9. The Peacock was found in the thick undergrowth and thorny creepers of the deciduous forest.

10. The sweet lemon grass is a cattail flowering plant with a hollow stalk, with many uses. Dried lemon grass is eaten. Its oil and its stems are used for making traps and rush baskets. The lemon-grass leaves make a fragrant and tasty medicinal tea.

11. Winds in excess of 30 mph.

12. With their anesthetic saliva, they numbed the skin painlessly, then pierce it with their teeth and release an anti-coagulant blood-thinner, which widens the hole to ensure that the blood will not clot for several hours. This procedure prevented scabbing. Leech wounds would bleed profusely for long periods of time if not treated.

13. Feet under considerable physical stress give off a pint and a half of moisture every day.

14. The old, Army-issue heavy fatigues stayed wet forever in rainy weather, and in good weather they allowed too much body heat to build-up and caused jungle rot.

Khe Sanh Medical Evacuation H-34 Helicopter (1964)

**To save your world you asked this
man to die:
Would this man, could he see you
now, ask why?**

W.H. Auden (1907-73) British Poet

CHAPTER 4

RYUKYU ISLANDS

I entered my new company assignment of Company "C," 1st Special Forces Group (ABN), on Okinawa. I was waiting in the hallway to be interviewed by Sergeant Major McDonald. The first thing I noticed upon entering the company was the little names on bronze plaques in a display case in the hallway for those killed-in-action (KIA) and wounded-in-action (WIA). I thought about the Special Forces motto, "De Oppresso Liber" (to liberate the oppressed). As qualified Green Beret Special Forces soldiers, we were trained as unconventional warfare fighters. We were trained to perform reconnaissance missions, conduct direct action operations, defend the infrastructure of friendly countries and fight terrorism. Our unit had been created in 1952 to combat the spread of communism around the world. Our lineage went back to the Office of Strategic Studies (OSS) Jedburg teams fighting behind enemy lines in World War II assisting guerrilla resistance movements.

Wounded

The first name I saw was Sp5 James P. Gabriel, Jr., a Special Forces soldier killed in Vietnam. I had not realized that Gabriel had been a member of this company. During our time in Special Forces Training Group, we all had spent a great deal of time working in the Gabriel Demonstration Area at Fort Bragg, North Carolina. It was here on Okinawa that I learned the story. On 8 April 1962, in a battle near An Chau hamlet Sp5 James P. Gabriel Jr. and Staff Sgt. Wayne E. Marchand, while serving on temporary duty (TDY) status to Vietnam from Okinawa, had been in a CIDG unit that was overrun by North Vietnamese Army soldiers some ten miles outside Danang early in the morning. They had both been seriously wounded several times when captured. During the hurried PAVN withdrawal, both were shot in the head because they could not keep up. They were found in the trail lying one upon the other. There were many other names on that wall. Those of us sent to the 1st Special Forces Group (Airborne) found that they had already begun to prepare on Okinawa for an increased military deployment to remote regions of Southeast Asia. My company had already lost more men than any other unit in this escalating war. More were to come.

Okinawa, part of Japan's southernmost Ryukyu Islands, was the site of America's bloodiest Pacific battle of World War II. Isolated from the mainland, they are Japan's poorest prefectures. Under United States control, they were dependent upon the military bases. Those bases are crucial to America's strategy in Asia, to maintain a balance of power and to respond to security threats from China, North Korea, North Vietnam and Russia. The Ryukyu Archipelago stretches some seven hundred miles, and is made up of 140 rugged islands and reefs, of which only thirty-six have permanent residents. The southernmost island is Yonaguni near Taiwan, and the northernmost lies just off the tip of Kyushu Island in Japan. Rugged mountain peaks thrust out of the ocean and form the main island of Okinawa. In the course of a year, the residents of Okinawa experience between twelve and forty-five typhoons. Most of the people are farmers and fishermen. Once a separate kingdom, Okinawa, became part of Japan in 1879, and had developed their own distinct cultural forms, dialect and cuisine because of their long trade with China, Taiwan and Thailand. The U.S. Army's Ninth Logistical Command on Okinawa provided support for U.S. forces in Vietnam. On 17 December 1961, it had sent a logistic support team to Vietnam.

Underwater Warfare School

My Special Forces training continued. It was here that I was sent to the Underwater Warfare School, picking up my demolition training in the school operated by the 1st Special Forces Group, which was prior to being selected for a deploying A-team assignment. Here, I became better acquainted with wind and water, two of the strongest forces in nature. I learned to respect them. The school was both physically and academically demanding. The better physical condition of a diver, the longer his standard 2400 pounds of pressurized air in his tank could last. We trained with open circuit and the Emerson closed-circuit scuba rigs. The former is what most sport divers use for recreation. The latter is used for clandestine entry into hostile areas or countries, because it does not emit bubbles that can be detected by sentries. The only really hard part of the school for me was the most important subject taught--physics. To be a competent diver, you had to be in complete control of mind and body, and you had to be knowledgeable of the science behind it. In diving physics, there is no room for error. Diving physics governs the human body under pressure in deep water. It is pressure that causes the buildup of nitrogen, which comprises 79 percent air, to build up in the bloodstream. As a diver descends the lungs contract, and during ascent the lungs expand. Without proper training and control, divers are subject to one of the diving diseases; your main enemy is pressure, and anything over one hundred feet usually results in nitrogen narcosis, rapture of the deep, or the bends' upon ascent. We trained in hostile beach reconnaissance, day and night compass swims, high-speed pickups in open blue water, and extensively in underwater demolition. After each day's training I had to go to a massage parlor and point out on a wall chart of the human body where I hurt the most, and the old mama-san would instruct her girls on what to do. I would meet each new day's training completely refreshed. Our graduation exercise consisted of being dropped in teams of two out in the South China Sea at night with our satchel charges and accompanying equipment. We were to swim in to the coast on a compass heading and hit a river. All the teams had to bypass a large, guarded bridge and reassemble at a designated smaller bridge on the north side of the river over a small tributary. Here we received the order to individually place and rig our charges. Our satchel charges consisted of blocks of C-4, primed with detonating cord. Our instructor would grade the individual teams and their placement of charges, connections and firing system. We then dismantled our equipment and made the swim back out to sea for pick-up. The simulated blowing of this bridge on the northern tip of Okinawa was an exciting adventure, one that would be repeated in daylight on a distant off-shore island whose small fishing village needed the reef entry for its boats widened.

In This Valley There Are Tigers

In This Valley There Are Tigers

The Sharks

The scariest and most intense life-force experience of all our night compass swims was seeing the large phosphorescent outline and wakes that sparkled and withered below us or along side of us. Sharks would move in close, eye us briefly out of curiosity, then move away. My adrenaline flowed. My reaction was always rapt fascination and a certain amount of tension as something that large leisurely cruised in between or below us. Divers could just make out the shape of a large shark below them. Once at night, unknown and unseen by me, a member of another swim team, losing something in the dark, untied himself from his partner and went back and retrieved the item. He was swimming quickly to catch up, when I happened to turn to check behind me and saw this fast moving phosphorescent wake of bubbles coming up behind me. Thinking that I was about to be hit by a large shark, I turned my head and tried to hide my head in my shoulders, awaiting the pain and terror. Then I saw the wake of another swimmer passing me. I almost had a heart attack. I was so relieved, but was still in the dark ocean. The commander of the school, Capt. Grace, one earlier dark night thought that it was his swim buddy along side of him swimming too close and when he nudged him, realized it was a shark. The story was that it was merely curious and swam away, although that fact didn't help calm him much at the time, as he had to worry that he might still be hanging around somewhere. Years later, I had another life-force experience with three sharks while diving in Samoa, but that's another story.

Sea Snakes

In class I was made aware of the sea snakes, but I never actually expected to see any. I was told that they ranged from Southern Japan to Indonesia. Once while performing a beach reconnaissance, however, I swam over several yellow-black banded sea snakes nosing their way along the bottom. Their venom is among the most toxic of any creature. Those around Okinawa were about 4 feet long and had vertically flattened, paddle-like tails. In Vietnam, I saw a specimen that was about

8-feet long. They could remain underwater for as long as I could with my equipment before having to refill their lungs.

The Aircraft Carrier

Our ship bottom search for attached limpet mines was conducted under an aircraft carrier that had just returned from Southeast Asia. I never realized how large an aircraft carrier was until this episode. The cooling intakes on the bottom are huge, as are the screws. We had been briefed that if the intakes were accidentally turned on during this exercise that we were to hold our face mask and mouthpiece with both hands until they could turn off the intakes. My swim partner and I were the middlemen who checked the areas of the hull in the vicinity of the intakes and the screws. My picture was taken at this time, but unfortunately I never got a copy of it before I left for Vietnam.

Community Service

As part of a community service, we were sent to a remote and distant island to widen a reef entrance for a fishing village. We made a long boat trip to a remote fishing village off Okinawa, and upon our arrival checked the work site and then started on our way a quarter of the way around the island. I inquired about what we were doing, and was told that we would throw a few satchel charges overboard and detonate them underwater in order to attract the sharks to the location. The sharks could be counted upon to investigate the source of the noise. They would find the dead and stunned fish and then remain in that area to feed for about an hour. That was long enough. We would go back to our work site, and about the time we should be through the sharks would be back. We anchored and one diver descended to the bottom and waited as we threw our satchel charges overboard. The diver underwater collected them all in one place on the bottom. We then spit in our facemasks and polished the lens of our mask, rinsed them and made our entry and went to the bottom. Each man took off his UDT fins and placed his forearm through the straps, and picked up two satchel charges and placed them over one shoulder, another man placed two more over the other shoulder, and in this manner we walked along the bottom toward the reef entrance. We came to a large drop-off and merely jumped out, allowing ourselves to again settle to the distant bottom before continuing our walk. We rigged our charges and extended a long line of detonation cord back toward a small floating platform on top of the water where our detonator was located. We saw our first sharks coming back into the area just as we were getting out of the water.

After our graduation from the underwater school, we had one additional duty. A young marine had drowned while swimming and free-diving. We were sent to make a search for him and we found him quickly enough. He had evidently been trying to catch a lobster or a striking polished cowry shell in a hole in the rocks on the bottom. A surge of water had jammed his head into the hole and he was unable to extract himself before drowning. I remember he was a very strongly built man.

Okinawa was an outstanding assignment. The only drawback that those of us in Special Forces had was being under USARYIS Command for our promotions. Naturally, they gave their own people the majority of promotions and meted out ours grudgingly. This hurt us extremely, since we were fighting a war while they had it easy. This situation caused me to take much longer to be promoted through the lower echelons.

Our parachute pay jumps were made at the drop zone (DZ) at Yomitan, an old Japanese Army airfield. This was an unforgettable experience for many jumpers because, in addition to making the hard landings on the runways, there were ocean cliffs to the west and the remainder of the DZ was surrounded by Japanese housing areas, an area training military war dogs, and an area of rock piles and power lines. Jump injuries were not common because most of the Special Forces personnel were well-experienced jumpers with many years on jump status.

The Secret War

We read everything about Vietnam and listened to everyone's stories. Vietnam was an exotic place to me then, and it still is. We were made aware that the government of

South Vietnam was like that of the North Vietnam. It had absolute political power, forbade rival movements, censored the press, and its plain-clothed special police had the power to kill on the spot.

In 1963, a 100-man, U.S.-led Taiwanese commando force had entered Vietnamese waters to raid rail and bridges in the coastal North Vietnam's Quang Ninh province. Only 25 commandos survived this raid of sabotage and psychological warfare.

By 1964, the Peoples Army of Vietnam (PAVN) had expanded its operations with great success in Laos and South Vietnam, and the total of American war dead had reached 225. Communist terrorists and sapper squads raided South Vietnamese military installations; routes of communication, such as railroads, highways and bridges, commercial aircraft, and industrial plants; plantations, and villages. The systematic assassination of local administrators helped to destroy the social and economic programs throughout Vietnam. The border areas of Laos, North Vietnam, and Cambodia adjoining South Vietnam, as well as much of the coastline, had fallen to the communists. The rice-bowl of the Mekong Delta was also in the hands of the communists. Special Forces personnel were first-in-line at experiencing this violence, as we tried to halt the communist advances. We had a common goal and a common end, true to the Special Forces motto: "Liberate the Oppressed."

Deployment Orientation

On Okinawa, as many Special Forces companies were alerted, they selected their teams for deployment. We went through a prolonged period of pre-deployment training. One phase that opened my eyes was the instruction received on the Small Atomic Demolition's Munition, or (SADM), in an enclosed compound in the Northern Training Area of Okinawa. This miniaturized, 70-pound, man-portable nuclear weapon (1 kiloton) could be broken down small enough and very easily concealed in a pack to be transported by a small team or carried as a complete unit by one man. An infiltration team could disperse and later come together or travel as one unit. Upon reaching their destination covertly, they would assemble it and set the timer for detonation. Two men were needed to set the device. For a while, I was greatly worried about how we could get far enough away from it when deployed. My mind was laid to rest later when I was told that this was just training orientation.

At the post theater at Machinato, the Special Forces Group commander, Col. Kelly, explained to all of the men selected for deployment to Vietnam that the American government had decided to expand the U.S. Advisory role. He went on to explain that our A-teams would be assigned primarily to very remote areas of Southeast Asia to carry out our missions. The number of American Special Forces advisors in Vietnam received an adrenaline kick from the 1st Special Forces Group on Okinawa with the large deployment of additional teams. The total number of Americans serving in helicopter units and other advisory roles brought our strength up to 35,000 men. All the men assigned to Okinawa were highly trained and motivated, and the selection of 12 team members per A Team went easily. After forming for the briefing, I gazed around the group of men gathered there.

We got along well with each other, or we wouldn't have been there. All were committed to the same goals that would impact our future performance during these missions. I realized that these men were among America's iron men, the roughest and best cut of mankind. A bond of trust with each other, necessary for combat effectiveness, had already been formed. These were men who, in their earlier service years, had been unafraid to take those steps that would make them outstanding. These were men with the quality of character to match the uncompromising wildness and terror found in the mountains of Southeast Asia. Special Forces soldiers were more knowledgeable and appreciative of the world around them; we were unafraid of commitment and welcomed the challenge. Each of us had the training, experience and fiber in our soul to train, work with, and lead primitive tribesmen in combat.

Looking around the theater where the orientation was taking place, I could see that every man was proud to be there. Regardless of the outcome, a great adventure was at hand. We were about to leave our mark on Indo-China's trackless wilderness. Many were already veterans of earlier missions in this war and of earlier wars. Their intellect was whetted by combat and the struggle for self-preservation. All too many were to die in obscure graves. The only thing that could not be explained was that America was going to lose more arms, legs and eyes in Vietnam than in any other war. Little did we know we were literally on the eve of destruction, for fate was about to take control of our lives. The Vietnam War was to be unlike any other war fought. The American conventional units hunted by daylight and the PAVN moved and hunted by night. In the years ahead, nearly 60,000 American men would pay the supreme sacrifice by being killed-in-action. Fifty-eight brave American civilian and military women were also killed there. The Vietnamese were to lose 3,200,000 people. This was to be a war in which the armed forces of the United States would win all the battles, but lose the war. The war was to be lost in elegant meeting rooms by self-serving politicians, and on the streets of America, in the minds of our own people.

Although the fighting in Laos was well-reported, no one in the American public even knew there was a war going on there, much less where it was. Thousands of PAVN troops were tied down in Laos, fighting the U.S. Special Forces and their Hmong tribesmen. In early 1964, the communist North was moving thousands of soldiers and supplies through base areas along the Ho Chi Minh trail in Laos into Cambodia and South Vietnam. Two PAVN communication battalions and labor gangs made up mostly of women, infantry units, and anti-aircraft units supported this dangerous and complex communications trail system. The trail defenders grew and hunted their own food. The trail system supported every front of the war in South Vietnam, A vital piece of intelligence not commonly shared with the press or conventional army units of the United States. The best intelligence in the world is not worth a thing, if it is not shared with those in need of it.

The A Team

We had taken pride in being selected to an A Team. We believed our efforts were in a brave and worthy cause and that our mission was absolutely necessary. Our twelve-man team, A-323, 1st Special Forces Group (Airborne), was stationed at Machinato, Okinawa, and had been alerted for deployment for a six-month tour in June 1964. Temporary Duty Orders (TDY) number LOT-352, dated 21 October 1964, ordered our 12-man A Team from Kadena Air Force Base, Okinawa, to the Republic of Vietnam. The members of A-323 Team were: Capt. Charles A. Allen (Team Captain), Capt. Joseph M. Lukitsch (Executive officer), MSG Thomas Barrett (Team Sergeant), SFC Donald E. Williams (11F Intelligence Sergeant), SFC Thomas D. Dennis (12B Weapons), SFC Edward A. Coffey (11B Weapons), SSG Donald B. Brady (91B Medic), SGT Robert Froetschel (91B Medic), Sgt. Ratchford P. Haynes (05B Commo), SGT John L. Burris (05B Commo), SFC William A. Borgardts (12B Engineer), and myself, Sgt. Charles A. McDonald (Weapons/Demolition).

We went through all the phases of our pre-deployment training: receiving physicals, dental checks, and then when we had time we scrounged all the food and material items we would need from other units. Our physicals and dental checks were thorough. The dental checks of our teeth had to be perfect before deployment. Our physical naturally included urine and stool samples, and periodically someone would be called before the company commander for submitting a sample of dog feces to the medics. Luckily, it was explained away with humor, to see if the system was really working. It was. Our medical care was great. Our shot records were brought up to date. Our arms and rear-ends were soon hurting from the many immunizations.

During the hours of darkness on 21 October 1964, under blackout conditions, our team loaded into two trucks in the company area. With the canvas down and secured, we drove to Kadena Air Force Base. The air base, the largest in Asia, covered over 3,000 acres. Our vehicle, still in blackout conditions on an isolated section of the airbase, backed into a Fairchild C-123 Provider transport where we dismounted the truck. It drove out and the ramp went up. We settled into the metal-framed nylon webbing of the seats. The seats were not designed for comfort. The aircraft echoed and reverberated with the pressure building. Then with the engines roaring to a rumbling crescendo, it began to move. Soon we were accelerating down the runway--faster and faster. With a sudden lift we were off the strip, rising easily in a steep climb into the low clouds off the tarmac and into the night sky. The buffeting of the aircraft was mild as we climbed into the jet stream. I closed my eyes and, leaning comfortably back, resigned myself to wait and to endure. The roar and creak of the aircraft throbbed in my ears. We were due to return to Okinawa in April 1965. True to my Special Forces recruiter's word, we were on our way to an assignment to do something useful and interesting, something that promised great adventure after so many years of training. We were going to build and fight for another country's freedom. The sky would remain dark for most of the trip on the plane. I went to sleep and never woke up until the pilots eased back on the throttles and started their descent, waking me up. It was daylight.

SFC Belcher 1st SFGA

The Angel of Death has been abroad throughout the land: you may almost hear the beating of his wings.

John Bright (1811-89)

CHAPTER 5

VIETNAM

According to the Asian lunar calendar, it was the year of the Dragon. My eyes roamed around the plane, and then, I looked out the port side of the aircraft. Far below us was Vietnam. We were flying north along the Vietnamese coast to Danang. High above the South China Sea, I watched out the port window, I listened to the throbbing roar of the engines, and watched the city and airfield at Danang fifteen-hundred feet below us, under the banking wing as we lost altitude. Although we were arriving during the monsoon season, the weather was beautiful. I saw the fantastic, natural beauty of a half-dozen shades of blue that tinted the clear, unveiling morning waters along the coast. The lap of waves was spilling on the unsullied white coral beaches under a limitless sky. I saw long, velvety-green stretches of rice fields and irrigation canals reflecting the morning sun. This was the alluvial soil and hot humid weather that grew the quick-cooking, short-grained, white rice, which sustained both the Vietnamese people and our enemies. High mountains with thick forest covering them rimmed the distant horizon.

Landing in Quang Tri Province

The C-123 oriented itself off the coastline and started descending. On 27 October 1964, the shrieking of tires announced our arrival in Southeast Asia. We had landed on the single concrete airstrip at Danang Air Base. We could see that aircraft belonging to the United States Marines were already here, the F-4 Phantoms of VMFA-513 (Flying Nightmares) and the Marine UH-34 helicopters, already supporting combat operation. Our aircraft finally stopped taxiing. It shuddered like a great beast as the fuel was cut off, and its two Pratt & Whitney turbo-jet engines ended with a whine and then was still. Then there was the high-pitched whine as the cargo door descended. The humidity rushed in, and we cursed the stifling heat. We were blinded by the blazing sun as we departed the rear of the aircraft. We had arrived in one of the world's most destitute countries, with a fiery arrogance. It was here in this country that I was to learn that "suffering is the one promise that life will keep." We were now a part of the still-secret conflict in Indochina. Earlier that same month, China had just exploded her first atomic bomb.

Danang

The weather was hot and humid in the capital city of Quang Nam Province. As we unloaded onto the tarmac, sweat spots darkened our uniforms. The humid air felt heavy and smelled acidic. Convection waves rose from the asphalt. This was the time of year when the coastal area was stricken by typhoons from the Pacific Ocean. Danang, known under the French as Tourane, was often referred to as the "Saigon of the North." Earlier in history the French conquest of Indochina had begun with the capture of Tourane in 1858. It was Vietnam's second largest city. While our team commander, Captain Allen, was being briefed, receiving our assignment and mission, we were given time to get acquainted with the city or whatever else we wanted to do.

I chose to spend my time getting acquainted with the city and its delights. I briefly visited the Riverside Hotel (Khach San Tien Sa) on Bach Dang Street, overlooking the mighty Han River. I would return here a number of times during my tour because it had a bar, restaurant and other social activities. Across this wide river to the northeast was Monkey Mountain (Nui Son Tra). At the base of this mountain, on the Bay of Danang, was the location of Camp Fay and the U.S. Naval Advisory Detachment (34-Alpha) that was currently running clandestine infiltration commando operations into North Vietnam. In town, as I walked along the river front, looking up at the Hai Van Mountains to the northwest, I inhaled the mixed odors of stagnant urine and vile-smelling piles of garbage rising with the heat that seemed to become thicker as the sun climbed higher. I crossed the river briefly to the north side and was told by the Vietnamese there to return to the other side because it was too dangerous. I made a small tour of the city in a "cyclo," the pedal-powered, three-wheeled bicycle rickshaw, with a carriage on the front. It was the main means of individual, short-range transportation for the Vietnamese.

My eyes registered the graceful architectural character of the city with its narrow streets and low-rise charm, a relic of French colonial-style elegance. Small impromptu businesses were everywhere, and people shopped and haggled in a musical, tonal sound. I detected the constant smell of gasoline in the downtown area. Away from the center of town came the smell of lust mixed with jasmine. I detected the sweet smell of fragrant wood smoke mixed with the presence of fresh blood from animals slaughtered for consumption. Everywhere, the strong smell of stagnant water mixed with the disagreeable stench of vapors rising from public toilets filled with fresh excrement.

Vietnamese Restaurant

Walking past a small dingy, hole in the wall shop, emanating a pleasant smell, I stopped to observe a cook cutting red and white layers of raw pork. The smell of garlic was strong. I decided to eat a meal in their dimly lit, single-room. It was filled with cigarette smoke, with a small kitchen on one side and tables and chairs on the other. It was lit only by oil lamps. I listened to the sound of chopsticks clicking on the sides of the bowls, and ordered a plate of spring rolls, and watched as the cook quickly prepared the meal. The shells of the spring rolls were made of translucent sheets of rice paper. Each roll was filled with shreds of seafood, pork, herbs and vegetables. I dipped my first warm aromatic roll into a spicy sweet-and-sour sauce. After my first bite, I felt like I was home. It was beautifully delicious. The next time I would try a better restaurant and see if the food was any better, but I wouldn't forget this place.

Afterwards, I just walked and took in the sights. Soup stands were everywhere. A staple of the Vietnamese diet is a bowl of noodle soup (pho) with meat. I liked mine with lots of red peppers. People huddled together and begged everywhere on the pavement. Outside the city in the shimmering paddy fields, peasants were bent over planting and harvesting rice. From what I had seen, I knew that I would be back when time permitted.

Away from the center of the city lay a frightening squalor of rows of claustrophobic, ramshackle dwellings made of wood and corrugated aluminum with no electricity, water or toilets. At night, large rats scurried around. These spread-out hovels were often the homes of soldiers, packed with grandparents and infants, many sleeping in the same room. Congested motorbike traffic zigzagged everywhere.

Arriving back at the compound, we learned we would be transported to the most northern site in the country to live and work with tribal mountain people, near the North Vietnamese and Laotian border region. The area was Khe Sanh. The village of Khe Sanh was the seat of government of Huong Hoa district. We were replacing A-728, a 7th Special Forces team from Ft. Bragg, staying in the old French Foreign Legion camp near the town of Khe Sanh. All the previous Special Forces teams assigned to Khe Sanh area as early as August 1962 were responsible for constructing the new camp on the Xom Cham Plateau. In this assigned mission they failed. We made our qualifying jumps for our Vietnamese Special Forces wings, finished our in-country briefing. We were scheduled to build a new camp at the airfield on the plateau. Special Forces A-323, under Captain Charles A. Allen would build the new camp.

Australian Aircraft

Damp with perspiration, we loaded our equipment and ourselves into a Caribou, an Australian CV-2, a high-tailed, twin-engine, all-weather STOL tactical transport and took off for Khe Sanh. We left the white-capped South China Sea behind and flew west, high above green-forested mountains. I found no comfort in the metal-framed webbing of my seat. At that time of year, it was a rare day when the clouds lifted, but that day they had. The patchy sunlight caught the rich foliage of the virgin forest. We followed the valley up into the mountains and were fired upon, taking heavy fire in one area. Visible streaks from green tracers slithered up into the sky close by. The loud impact of several rounds hammering into the tail of the aircraft was sobering. We all realized at the same time that we had taken several hits from a Chinese anti-aircraft 12.7 mm (.51 cal) heavy machine-gun. We had not even reached our final destination and we had already been shot at--a harbinger of things to come in the months and years ahead. In the deep gloom of the aircraft, we exchanged cynical smiles. Then each of us became lost in our own thoughts as we flew northwest. Shortly, the aircraft made a slow turn to the southwest, not far from the mountain marked on the map as "Dong Toan," following the river marked "Song Quang Tri." Through the starboard window, I saw the dark green, cloud-shrouded mountaintops of "Dong Ca Lu" in the distance, and "Dong Che" below. The aircraft turned slightly south and then east again. We flew above a narrow valley, following between the dominant, central mass of two high mountain ridges.

The Beginning

As I stared out the window through the gloom and low clouds at the unbroken dark expanse of dense forest that stretched as far as the eye could see, I began to realize that I was taking my first steps onto the dreaded mountain trails of Southeastern Asia, into an adventure that would last for years. Far below and to our front, I could see a large plateau. It was like a wall ahead of the aircraft. The mountainous terrain was high, extremely rugged, sinister and hostile. An impressive sight. A score of dominating mountain peaks overlooked Khe

Sanh. As we gained altitude, the landing strip dead ahead, a ribbon outlined by red dirt that stretched through the smooth, otherwise unbroken expanse of tall grass on top of the plateau. We went straight in. I heard the wheels chirp. The aircraft slowed down quickly, steadied its speed and turned left into the parking ramp. The Australian pilot had not even used half of the airstrip when we began taxing into the unloading pad. The aircraft turned and cut its engines. No one was at the deserted airfield to meet us. I hoped that nothing exciting would happen. The cool mountain air came as a pleasant shock as we unloaded the aircraft. When we finished, it made a short run and climbed steeply away. We were alone. Although the commander of the A-team we were relieving at Khe Sanh had been notified of our arrival time, they were not there to meet us. They let us wait at the airstrip, unarmed, for an hour. Needless to say, the short time we would spend together was strained. The commander of Special Forces Detachment A-728, Captain Allan B. Imes, had failed to initiate the construction of the new fort at the airstrip. We were determined to demonstrate what a real A-team was capable of when under proper leadership. Captain Allen told us to take a good look at the immediate surrounding area, at its emptiness, because we would remain there until late April 1965. By that time we would have built a new camp from scratch. I had no idea at the time just how much work was ahead of us. To top it off, the winter monsoon was just beginning.

Only one old Vietnamese soldier was on guard at the airfield. He merely looked up from his squatting position and grinned and went on with the preparation of his supper, a chicken whose feet were tied. The chicken was braced between his forearm and knee. I watched as he picked the neck feathers off the live chicken and promptly made a little slice in the chicken's neck, while lightly squeezing with the other hand. He bled the chicken into a bowl of peanuts and set it aside. He then decapitated, gutted and plucked the chicken, all without becoming stained or splattered with blood in the process. There had been no thrashing around. We were in the feral past, where killing one's food was both a necessity and an ordinary event. Vehicles arrived and we loaded our gear.

Our Tactical Area of Operation

Our tactical area of operation was just below the Demilitarized Zone (DMZ), and was often obscured by mist and fog. Astride the Seventeenth Parallel, the DMZ was a fifteen-mile-wide buffer zone between South Vietnam and North Vietnam. This zone had been established by the United Nations in 1954, the year I had entered the army. Our operational area was Huong Hoa, the largest and most western district of Quang Tri Province. It also had the smallest recorded population. All that existed on the plateau in this rugged Annamite chain of mountains was a graded dirt surface and a 3,900-foot Perforated Steel Platform (PSP) runway, surrounded by a sea of grass. The airfield was originally leveled and graded by the French. South of the airfield was the narrow, twisting, and largely unimproved single-lane Quoc Lo 9 (National Route 9 or "Ambush Alley," as the Marines called it). Called QL 9 or Highway 9, it led west from Route 1 near the coast, through Khe Sanh to Tchepone in Savannakhet Province of Laos. One of the missions of Camp Khe Sanh was to block the use of this road by the PAVN. Daytime highs were cool and the nighttime temperature was often cold. Located in the northwestern corner of the province, the plateau lay at the center of an awe-inspiring environment of four valley corridors. I envied its isolation. Very often, cool dense air from the South China Sea would descend into the mountains and replace the warmer rising air, creating a lot of wind and making the surrounding grass lands and forest literally dance. From the start the dark clouds had followed us, and soon the torrential rains were beating down upon us. Nothing could darken my mood, not even the gloomy start.

Weather Forecast

We had arrived at the beginning of the winter monsoon in the Khe Sanh area. The monsoons come from the northeast out of the South China Sea between October and March. With 116 inches of rain recorded falling in the northern province before the end of the year, our team would have a wet, chilly winter. Our entire tour would be during the winter monsoon.

We could count upon receiving more than 65 inches of precipitation during our stay.

The monsoon rains had already started in the region. Luckily, it was not raining when we arrived, but the conditions indicated that they weren't far from starting. The ground was already very wet. The weather during our tour in Khe Sanh would be filled with low-lying fog or high-flying mist and torrential rains. When we were lucky, we had only drizzling rain. Long periods of blue skies would not return until sometime in March.

The Truong Son Trail

The Truong Son Trail was born 19 May 1959, when the Communist leadership decided to conduct an insurgency against the South. The string of high mountains that formed Vietnam's western border were called the Truong Son Mountains (i.e. the Long Mountains) by the Vietnamese or "the Chaine Annamitique" by the French, ran south to within 60 miles of Saigon. The Truong Son Mountain Trail began outside of Hanoi in a gorge known as Heaven's Gate. This system of trails was the world's most dangerous route and also considered one of the great feats of warfare, and became known as the Ho Chi Minh Trail.[1] A camouflaged, spider web network of thickly layered mountain forest paths, rickety bridges, high-speed trails and mud roads used for the infiltration of agents, PAVN units, and columns of porters into South Vietnam.

The PAVN dominated a vast region. Immediate area terrain features dominating the Khe Sanh Plain were Hills 881, 881 South and 758. Further in the distance, the two dominant terrain features were twin mountain peaks, the ominous 1,015 meter (3,330 feet) Dong Tri mountain located at grid coordinates XD 853455, and the smaller 950 meter (3,116 feet) peak located at XD 844455, immediately west of Dong Tri. From these two points immediately north of the airfield and across the Rao Quan River, the PAVN watched our every move and our progress building the camp. In 1957, the

Communist Party Committees of Thua Thien and Quang Tri Provinces established base areas in the mountainous regions of neighboring Laos, centered on the town of Tchepone. Tchepone was selected because of its crossroads and cave system. In January 1959, North Vietnam's Lao Dong Party had decided to use armed force to overthrow the Diem government in South Vietnam. And by June, the real campaign to liberate the South began. The original infiltration trail during this time came right through the French "Poilane" plantation just west of the site of the new camp we were building, but this route drew too much attention. The enlargement of the trail had been initiated in 1959 by the *Binh Tram (i.e. Military Station)* subordinate to the 559th Rear Services Group, a logistical unit of the Peoples Army of Vietnam (PAVN). In 1963, control was ultimately transferred to the logistics group 559, which had supporting engineers, antiaircraft and infantry security units. By 1964, the Ho Chi Minh Trail was a well-established communications network on South Vietnam's 800-mile western border. By 1962, North Vietnam had been supplied with 90,000 rifles and machine guns, and the 919th was airdropping supplies in the Central Highlands. In 1963, they were landing at Tchepone on Highway 9. The infiltration route was moved west to the base areas in Laos, and a corridor of the Truong Son Trail was extended into Quang Nam Province. The Tchepone valley in Laos would eventually become a giant PAVN airtrap for American aircraft. By 1963, there were 24,400 troops and six motorized transport battalions and a regiment of engineers. PAVN women did much of the construction and maintenance work under the leadership of chief engineer Tran Huy Hai. Two communications battalions supported the PAVN radio net along the infiltration routes.

It was often under the cover of bad weather, mist-shrouded valleys, and thick clouds. It had a permanent, impenetrable thickly layered overhead green cover, and was supported by a primitive technology of elaborate tunnel and cave systems from World War II. The entire road system was some 8,000 miles long, much of it nothing more than high-speed trails twisting through the mountain forest and running along the length of the border between Vietnam and Laos.

Early in 1964, the infiltration of 10,000 PAVN regulars was taking place. Men and materials had been substantially increasing each year. It took the PAVN four months to travel its length to their destination in the South. Although Hanoi's strategists attempted to create the illusion that communist military forces in the North were separate from the so-called "Viet Cong" in the South, the "PAVN" was the term accurately denoting the parent organization for communist forces of both regions. A new engineer unit, regiment 559 under the command of PAVN Major Vo Bam, a logistics specialist began the early clandestine construction. In 1962 this unit consisted of 6,000 troops organized into two regiments. One of the first units to utilize this system in August 1964 was the PAVN 808th Battalion, soon to be followed by many other units. Rigorous camouflage and physical training was conducted west of Hanoi at the Son Tay infiltration center prior to deployment for the South. During our team's tour at Khe Sanh, North Vietnam's 95th, 32, and 101 regiments of the 325th PAVN Division moved south to infiltrate South Vietnam's border. In 1965, the PAVN logistical unit was enlarged and General Phan Trong Tue, in an expanded command role, took charge under the direct authority of North Vietnam's Central Party Committee, and heavy equipment was then used for expanding the Trail. Maj. Vo Bam became his deputy. From 1966 to 1975, LTG Dong Si Nguyen would be given the overall responsibility for the construction of the trail. There were more than a dozen of the major bases located along the trail system, and all were well defended. LTG Nguyen would shift his anti-aircraft artillery around to place them near the most frequently targeted site of the American Air Force. The PAVN only had five minutes of warning of impending air attacks provided by observation posts in the mountain heights. Newly installed radar installations provided more warning of impending air attacks. Each convoy would be accompanied by mobile anti-aircraft vehicles forcing the Allied bombers to fly higher, cutting their accuracy. The center and heart of this logistical military station activity in Laos was located in a valley on Highway 9, at the crossroads west of Tchepone. It was at the Tchepone airfield that Soviet aircrews flew in all manner of supplies, staging them for movement into South Vietnam. Since 1959, Vietnamese, Russian and Chinese pilots of the 919th Transport Squadron, flying the Ilyushin-4 and Ilyushin-12, had been airdropping supplies to the logistical units in Laos.[2]

Two PAVN infantry divisions were used to provide security for this network. In the years ahead, the trail would encompass five roughly parallel routes, a network of 21 crossroads that covered 10,000 miles by the end of the war and linking first aid clinics, air raid and rest shelters, and training facilities. Another 2,500 miles of access roads would lead to supply storage areas. A gasoline pipeline supplying underground storage tanks would stretch 870 miles to the south within 60 miles of Saigon. At night, trucks could cover 60 miles driving in blackout conditions.

The Bicycle

Intelligence reports cited the key transport vehicle on the trail was the bicycle. The production of bicycles became a leading light industry in North Vietnam. Bicycles were also imported in large numbers from France and Czechoslovakia.[3] Up to 500 pounds could be mounted on a bicycle and moved 18 miles in a night. The bicycle supplies of ammunition, rice, salt, medicine and weapons, were moved at night to protect against air attack. PAVN forces built hardened underground facilities and prepositioning their battlefield commands, communications systems, heavy equipment and supplies of ammunition. They were deployed to forward positions from which the PAVN forces could mount strong future offensives with only minimal preparation.

During October 1964, when we arrived in Khe Sanh, elements from the North Vietnamese army units were hard at work a short distance away securing this complex of three trails, which were used by infiltrating units. Thousands of man-hours were required to maintain the supply routes. The network depended on its many rest stations and agricultural areas and the people that supported this effort. The PAVN troops crossed the many streams quickly with portable bridges. When needed, they set up dugout canoes lashed together in pairs, and bamboo poles laid across as a light frame. During the rainy season, the roads would be washed away by flash floods only to be later rebuilt.

    By the time I arrived in Vietnam, I had already learned that the most endearing quality of Special Forces and its selected personnel was its ability to teach others. Above all other things, we had to have the capacity to be able to recruit and train large numbers of indigenous personnel. Most of us had a type of interpersonal relationship with the natural world, which came in handy since we were recruiting and training primitive tribesmen, who were hunters and gatherers. I remember my first good look at some Bru tribesmen. They were wearing only loincloths and heading into the forest to kill a marauding tiger. They carried only a net and crossbows. The Bru crossbow, although used for hunting, was more widely used as a booby trap, activated by an inconspicuous vine in the trail.

    In 1964, South Vietnam was, in my opinion, one of the most beautiful countries in the world. I always felt something surreal about the remote area surrounding the plateau, with its endless expanse of beautiful untamed and unchanged forest and grasslands. The mountainous Khe Sanh plains and much of the surrounding hilltops were covered with coarse kunai grass, one of the tallest grasses in the world. Kunai grass reached from waist height to 10 feet and its leaves had razor sharp edges. Breezes nudged the dry, brittle grass into movement that was always mesmerizing. It had knife like edges in its movement that would cut easily and often, unless your limbs were covered with clothing. We were often cut and scratched by the grass while on patrol, and the wounds often became infected.

    There were tilled open fields and pockets of timber and brush in the deeper ravines. Our nights and mornings were cold and the mist would hang low for days at a time. The landscape was in balance with the natural order of things and was marred only by our fear of what waited there for us. Here in the solitude of these mountains were large, dark-colored Sika deer, the small Muntjac barking deer, wild elephants, gaurs, apes, monkeys, bears, tigers and panthers.

The Coffee Plantation

From our airstrip, we shipped loads of coffee for a French planter by the name of Felix Poilane, the son of Eugene Poilane. Driving in the area past the coffee plantation, it was common to see the Bru along the dirt road harvesting the slender 30-foot areca palms for their betel nuts. This was the finest coffee plantation in Southeast Asia. In the United States coffee from Vietnam was sold under the brand name of Arabica and Robusta. Robusta coffee, known for its coarse flavor, is often used for instant blends. For the few days that the neatly ordered 15 foot coffee trees bloomed their brilliantly white flowers, the area was beautiful and amazingly fragrant with the smell of their jasmine-scented flowers. These flowers were replaced by green cherries that gradually turned brown, and finally brilliant red. The fruit that follows is a berry about the size of a cherry tomato. The long branches bent toward the ground when heavy with fruit.

They also produced black pepper and cinnamon on this plantation. Black pepper plants required a long rainy season and were therefore interplanted on the coffee plantation. Vietnam is the largest producer and exporter of black pepper. The leaf reminded me of a dogwood, which was the reason I first noticed it.

Felix Poilane was a slender, dark haired man. The elder Poilane had settled this area long before World War II with his first wife, commonly known as Madame Bordeauducq. They had five children before being divorced. Eugene Poilane's second wife was a Chinese lady from North Vietnam, which added to the intrigue surrounding the family. Eugene Poilane's Chinese wife eventually bore him five children. Madame Bordeauducq after her divorce established a plantation nearby. The Poilane family had established this plantation in 1926. The Poilane plantation trees were destroyed by the Japanese and the Viet Minh in 1945 and 1953 respectively. In April 1964, only six months prior to our arrival, the communists executed Felix Poilane's father, Eugene. At the time of his death, Eugene

Poilane was traveling by car on Route 9, with another Khe Sanh coffee plantation owner, M. Linares. After being stopped on the highway he was pulled from his car and executed for failing to pay taxes.

Our team captain, Capt. Allen, spent many an evening dining with Felix and Madeleine Poilane at their French style mansion on their plantation, and I was always eager to hear of their conversations. One of the guests at one of these dinners was the commander of the communist forces in the Khe Sanh area. The most intriguing stories were those of Madame Bordeauducq. At our airstrip one day, while Felix Poilane was waiting on an aircraft, I asked about tigers. He very briefly told me about Madame Bordeauducq, who had killed a large number of tigers. As a young man and being a hunter, I had grown up reading about the great hunters of the world. Among the stories that fascinated me were *"The Man-Eaters of Kumaon,"* by Jim Corbett. Now, I was assigned to an operational area where one of the world's best tiger hunters lived and hunted, Madame Bordeauducq, a woman of great courage, who has never been acknowledged. To my great disappointment, I was never to meet Madame Bordeauducq.

The plantation was an isolated work area that had many small Muntjac deer and isolated Bru workers. These alert, dainty, deer were characterized by the small, single-tined antlers, the high lift of their hooves when they walked and the barking sound they made when alarmed. Their bark indicated the presence of man or a tiger on the move. The deer and the isolated workers on the plantation drew many tigers into the surrounding area. The tiger's random calling; *Aaaaauuuunnnnn,* at short intervals during the night haunted the villages of the area. The sound at night would carry more than a mile. However, the tigers silently hunted the cultivated land in the daylight. With so many Bru plantation workers out in isolated areas of the plantation, many were killed, by tigers, over the years.

Since no one had really seriously hunted tigers in the area, the undisturbed tigers were killing as readily in the daytime as they were at night. Madame Bordeauducq, in order to protect her workers, had become known as a great hunter of tigers and reportedly had killed many. The tiger used its sense of smell to hunt in two ways. One method was to wait downwind along a frequently used trail for its intended victim, but there were too many villages in the area and therefore too many trails to watch. Knowing that the tigers' alternate method was to approach their prey upwind, she would position herself to watch the work area to one side and down-wind of the workers, and wait. Felix Poilane went on to explain, that the tigers, with their ability to approach without a sound, were considered evil spirits around the plantation. Their color pattern of orange, black and white provided fine camouflage in the dappled light. It was not hard to understand why the Bru considered them to be evil spirits, because the tiger is the largest cat in the world, weighing nearly 400 pounds and reaching 13 feet in length. A tiger standing on all four feet was as tall as many of the Bru tribesmen who were only five-feet tall. During the long course of the war, many Vietnamese would die from malaria, hunger, snakebite, ambushes and airstrikes. But much worse was the fate of many PAVN regulars from the North (*bo doi*), who would discover that they were part of the food chain. Many *bo doi,* would be killed and eaten in tiger and bear attacks. Many would be killed and later eaten by wild pigs and a host of smaller animals.

Old Camp Khe Sanh

Our camp was composed of three CIDG companies of Bru tribesmen, one Nung platoon (Chinese mercenaries), one Vietnamese artillery battery with 105 howitzers and a 12-man, Vietnamese Special Forces team (Luc Luong Dac Biet, or LLDB for short). Initially, we lived in the temporary campsite of old Camp Khe Sanh located on the south side of Highway 9. Located at grid coordinates XD 848383, it was activated 8 July 1962, with its first Special Forces team on the rugged mountain frontier. The area was usually shrouded in rain, fog, mist and its accompanying mud. Our sleeping quarters were an old wooden building built on a concrete slab with partitions for each team member's sleeping space and gear. Our beds were army issue wooden folding cots. The team house, mess hall and commo room were in the site's only concrete structure, which was a small building built by the French Army. During many a night spent on guard duty in this old hilltop French Fort, I would watch the fog spread all around the bottom of the hill, often enveloping the hill itself. Everything stayed damp and musty. The fog, like the breath of a dragon, was a constant reminder of the hidden dangers; keeping me alert for fear that it would consume me.

We had a water truck that periodically filled our tanks as needed. Inside the old French Fort we had a cistern that was filled by runoff. Heavy rains occurred in September and October, and you could count on rain at most anytime to fill the cistern. Military manuals dictate that 6 pounds of water are required a day per soldier. At Khe Sanh, we used water for personal hygiene, food preparation and laundry. We didn't drink the water in camp. On patrol we drank the water we found along our way. Our camp's water was obtained from the small Rao Quan River that ran from the hills north of Khe Sanh.

Booby Trap

Communications and Generators Operations

Our old French Legionnaire fort often blanketed in darkness and fog was only detectable by the faint steady drone of one of our generators in the early morning and evening. Inside the radio shack, the crackle of radio static and hum of electronic equipment filled the room. Each morning and evening our operators would be preparing to send, receive and decipher messages in International Morse Code (IMC). Very early each chilly morning as the rain poured from the dark sky, feet sinking in the water and mud, we had to inspect the generators to make sure that they had sufficient oil and gasoline. We all had to have a working knowledge of the starting and stopping procedures, and of general maintenance. The generator's start-up and continued throbbing for our first communications check with headquarters was our wake up call. No one ever had to be told to get up or be rousted out of the bed.

We had two sizes of generators. One, the 1.5 KW portable that was a 120-volt engine, had to be cranked with a rope early every morning, and was a real pain sometimes when it was really cold. At Khe Sanh it got very cold. The 30 KW was started, merely by pushing a button. We had to make two daily radio reports, the first being early in the morning, which was the weather report, then in the evening around 5 p.m. for the Situation Report (SITREP). Sporadic spot reports were made at any time.

Our communications equipment consisted of our generator-operated radios, with the KWM-2 Collins single sideband, which had voice and CW capability, and our AN-GRC-109, that was strictly Continuous Wave (CW). We also had our UGP-12 set, which was a hand-cranked generator for our CW set. Our battery-operated radios were the HT-1, that were used for ground-to-ground and ground-to-air communications, and the TR-20, which acted as a base station for our use of the HT-1's.

Guard Duty

If I had the first early evening guard shift, I checked the oil, fuel and fuel filter on the generator, and told the radio operator that it was checked and serviced. Then, as the shadows lengthened and crept across our hilltop camp, I could enjoy watching the terrain as the sun went down and the silence spread across the valley. Something interesting always happened. During the good weather, the night flyers always brought the evenings to life magically as they wheeled about. It was during one of these early hour watches that I saw the sudden appearance of a large black hawk. I watched it soar. Spiraling high, it dipped its wings and rode the thermal updrafts overhead nearby, then dropped and circled. Then it suddenly dove and caught a large fruit bat in his slow-moving flight.

I watched the forest edge below the camp from the northeastern wall. The sun, glimmering on the natural scene surrounding the camp never failed to awe, and delight me. At twilight, with the first shift of guard duty, we fired five or six rounds of high-angle surprise fire from our 81mm mortar for our PAVN friends on the other side. The nightly harassment and interdiction (H&I) fire was placed on selected targets picked from patrols and the map, mainly on trail junctions and curves in the trails just to let the PAVN know we were awake.

During October there was very heavy rain. Guard duty was cold, wet and lonely. It was this extreme weather that had necessitated so many shots on Okinawa, to take precautions against disease. The heavy rainfall in Vietnam was associated with the heavy transmission of mosquito-borne diseases, such as malaria and the outbreaks of diarrheal diseases in those whose immune systems were depressed. I thought about the Montagnard tribes and the Vietnamese peasants that did not have closed houses with doors and windows. They suffered greatly. Any standing water was a breeding ground for mosquitoes. During the monsoons, cholera could break out anywhere along the coastal areas of the country.

Often, our camp was shrouded in fog, looking like nothing more than a cloud on the ground. For our first month on site, hammering rain and dark clouds were the norm. The mountains were hidden from view. It was hard to hear because of the big, heavy raindrops drumming on the galvanized iron roofs, droning a steady note. After listening in the dark to the monotonous patter of raindrops for so long, the area would be turned into a quagmire. Every drain and ditch was full. During such times, it was difficult to move around without making a sound.

The buildings trembled as the squalls of wind and rain from the South China Sea swept across the mountains and battered our hill. At times the drizzle lasted all night and the old French Fort was often shrouded in a cold and penetrating mist. Any sound out of the ordinary, when the storm let up, would find me holding my breath and my heart beating faster. When I replaced one of the team members at night, I hated opening the door and being greeted by the wind gusts carrying the force of the rain gale into the room. Stepping into the night, I was immediately swallowed in darkness. The first of my many secret stops, I made my way to a dry spot under a dripping roof along our eastern wall to watch and listen.

During these very late hours, when everyone was sleeping, I always stayed hidden outside in the dark. I located myself in the darkest shadows to observe and listen, where I felt I could best see our team house, generators and communications center at the same time, while listening for the slightest sound in the perimeter wire. On the nights it didn't rain, the only sounds to be heard were those of the rats constantly scurrying from point to point, or a large snake or wildcat hunting the rats, or a night bird. We soon memorized the rustle of the wind throughout the camp, depending upon where we watched and listened from.

A fresh pot of coffee was always brewed, for personnel standing guard at night, in the team house that served as our kitchen and communications site. When darkness fell over the camp, the window shutters and doors were closed. The only light came from a lamp in the team house, a lonely aureole of light from the Coleman lantern in the kitchen. Candles were there for backup. The camp was always on blackout at night. Only by opening a door would a dim glow escape into the night. Sometimes when it became too cold and wet, I took a coffee break. But for me it seemed spooky inside the building. Although the Coleman lantern gave the interior of the messhall a comfortable aspect and shone brightly around the room, chasing the shadows up the inside walls, it was still lonely. Inside listening to the wind whispering in the eaves outside the door, I always worried about the door being opened suddenly by an unwanted guest. Only inside, during a coffee break did I feel vulnerable to the unknown.

    The last guard shift was the worst one to catch. The start of the generator was the signal for everyone to get up. In the dark I had to wrap the rope knot of the starter rope in its slot on the pulley and position the handle for a pull. I would then find and open the fuel shut-off valve, and after turning the rheostat knob fully counterclockwise, I would close the choke. While bracing one foot on the frame I gave a quick steady pull and prayed. As the engine began to run smoothly I gradually opened the choke. Hopefully, it was running on time. Then I would walk into the radio shack and have coffee with Ratchford, and tell him about weather conditions as he prepared to send traffic.

Intruders

    One night I heard a scurrying noise on the other side of the parapet on the outside portion of our defensive wall. I peered from the camp into a cloud blanket of cold, low mist that closed in, masking the camp and leaving only a dozen yards of visibility. I could not see the forward edge of the double-apron wire. I silently moved to the edge of the wall and held my small light out at arm's length with the lens facing inward and down. With my pistol cocked, I leaned silently over and flipped the light on. A big, beautiful lynx with its large translucent eyes stared at me transfixed. I quickly turned out the light. The lynx was hunting for rats. The Vietnamese believe that the sighting of a lynx is an omen that evil will come. Thinking of the Bru, I would say nothing of it to anyone, even though I was scheduled to leave on a long patrol the next day I was concerned about omens.

    On another clear moonlit night, I again heard a noise, and quickly checked the wire below our eastern bunker with my flashlight. In my beam, I saw the two red glowing and piercing eyes of an enormous Indochinese tiger stalking the perimeter. Then, like a cloud passing the moon, the great cat was gone.

New Camp Khe Sanh

After turning off Highway 9, the large tropical deciduous forest crowded up to the roadside on both sides. The elevation of the airfield on the plateau was 505 meters (1657 feet). The camp was approximately 10 square acres in size. Khe Sanh was the only hardened camp in the 1st Corp area, and the most northern border surveillance camp in South Vietnam when officially built in 1964. It was located just under the DMZ only a few miles from Laos. While the confrontation between leaders in Hanoi and the U. S. intensified, our A-Team, designated A-323, continued to build the new Camp Khe Sanh at a frantic rate. We worked hard. The sooner we made it livable, the sooner we could move in. Luckily, we had received plague shots on Okinawa, because our present site was overrun with large rats. The rats attracted too many snakes. More than once, I would wake during the night and find a rat for a companion in my bed. The rats easily chewed through the net and blankets. We kept our mosquito nets tucked in under the mattress to keep out the snakes as well. We had to be careful at night, moving around in the dark on guard duty, or even just going to the latrine, for fear of being struck by an annoyed or disturbed cobra hunting the rats.

Our First Wounded

Not long after our arrival on site, our first casualties to be treated in camp arrived from the Royal Lao 33rd Battalion. This was during a period of very bad weather. I went down to watch our medics at work. The Laotians had been wounded on patrol and were days in getting to us, for further evacuation. As soon as I arrived at the door, there was an unavoidable smell, the rotten, sweet smell of necrotic flesh. *Gangrene!* The nauseating smell that can twist anyone's insides. Once smelled, it can never be forgotten. As I walked in, I saw arterial blood pumping out and the medic, SGT Robert Froetschel, was just clamping it off. I watched him work, quick, competent and efficient. He was cutting away a lot of dead tissue. "When in doubt," he said, "cut it out." After watching Froetschel work, I knew that the wounded soldier was in good hands. Discarded bandages on the floor were stained with a custard-yellow discharge. The stench from the wound was to become familiar in the years ahead.

Village of Khe Sanh

The small village was set among the hills and valleys at 1900 feet elevation. The village of Khe Sanh was marked by the screening growths of palm, banana trees, where there was level ground, and small plots of rice. The isolated town was the Vietnamese government center that straddled the narrow, rutted two-lane Highway 9. Three miles west of the town of Khe Sanh was the village camp of Lang Vei, on the south side of the road. During our tenure at Khe Sanh, only an ARVN artillery company was stationed at Lang Vei. However, it was marked on the map and reported as an ARVN battalion. South of Highway 9 was Lao Bao. Along the Sepone River on the north side of the road was the site of an old airstrip and an old French colonial prison, called Lao Bao Prison, located at grid coordinates XD 697369. The prison-a labor camp-was located in a low, hot area and built long ago for political prisoners. The numerous, old wrought-iron tiger cages that had exposed the prisoners to the elements were still there, but not visible from the road.

Of historical interest was the fact that in 1927, the commander of the PAVN, Gen. Vo Nguyen Giap, at age sixteen was imprisoned here for being an underground member of the Communist Party and for his anti-French political activities. The commander of all PAVN political forces operating in South Vietnam from 1950 to 1961, Gen. Nguyen Chi Thanh, second in importance only to Gen. Vo Nguyen Giap, at age 19, also shared a cell at this prison during the same time period. From 1964 to 1967, Gen. Thanh served COSVN Military Affairs Party Committee as one of the first secretaries. A co-founder of the Indochina Communist Party and secret negotiator at the Paris peace talks, Le Duc Tho had also served time in this remote prison. We had ample reasons to always be in this area: it gave our executive officer, Capt. Lukitsch, opportunity to covertly meet with and pay our two clandestine agents in the area for their reports of the day and night movements along Highway 9. The intelligence collection effort never stopped and dealt with every local social, economic, and political program.

In 1938, a communist named Truong Chinh had developed a political and armed strategy known as "Dau Tranh" (people as an instrument of war). The cornerstone of this protracted strategy, used in South Vietnam, was meticulous organization to include all different ethnic and social groups. This political strategy, one of systematic coercive activity, involved individual and societal mobilization and motivation. This meant gaining the support of the people at the village-level, infiltrating the South Vietnamese military at all levels, and organizing and leading the people under the control of the National Liberation Front. The military strategy included guerrilla and conventional military action, public executions, assassinations, propaganda and kidnapping. During 1953 to 1956, Truong Chinh was responsible for North Vietnam's land reform and its subsequent mass executions of 15,000 village people classified as "landlords."

Order of Battle

In mid-1959, the Communist Party apparatus, with over 20 villages organized under their control, established base areas in the Khe Sanh area of Huong Hoa District. In the beginning, platoon-sized units operated at the district level and company-sized units operated at the provincial level. During this time, two armed military units, the 59A and 59B companies, were operating in the area. By 1960, the armed struggle had begun. Early in 1961, the Quang Tri Liberation Front was established, and a new company-sized unit designated as K105 was deployed in Quang Tri Province. These early company-sized guerrilla units were planned and formed as the nucleus for future expansion by incorporating regular PAVN units moving down from the North into them. These units were well dispersed and hidden. In 1964, the 1,500 men of the PAVN 18th Regiment and 95th Regiment, 325th Division were a direct threat to Khe Sanh. The other regiments of the 325th Division were located further south in the country. In addition, due to the 4 August 1964, Gulf of Tonkin incident, some 20,000 PAVN reportedly moved to the area of the DMZ, just to our North. By 1965, all these units would eventually expand into regimental-sized units. In 1965, the 6th PAVN Regiment, with its 800, 802, 804, 806, and 808 battalions, began operating in Quang Tri Province. During these early days, the North Vietnamese were fighting a protracted war in which the population was encouraged to participate by providing food supplies, labor and replacement personnel to their troops. The PAVN conducted frequent political and military proselytizing activities. When darkness masked the movement of armed men, combatants set out to destroy small U.S. and South Vietnamese units by raids and ambushes and by deception. However, this type of warfare was to quickly change.

Intelligence Collection

On patrol we had to think for ourselves. We knew what we were there for and what information was of value. After every patrol, we were debriefed by our Intelligence Sergeant, SFC Williams for information on enemy activity such as PAVN infiltration routes, rest camps, travel routes, and crop producing areas. SFC Williams was our third eye, the inner eye so to speak, of human logic and deduction. It was always open, watching and listening. With the help of Capt. Lukitsch, he collected information and names of the local infrastructure, underground, local guerrilla force's, regional and main force units of the National Liberation Front (NLF) or *Mat-Tran Dan-Toc Giai-Phong Mien-Nam,* for his black list. The NLF was more commonly referred to as the Viet Cong. We all kept our eyes open for those who appeared to have an abnormal interest in something about which they would not normally be concerned, or someone who would seemingly be in or around an area where they had no business being. I was determined when I was at Khe Sanh, that in the years ahead I would go to the Special Forces Operational and Intelligence school and the Army's Intelligence School to become a team intelligence sergeant.

The basic unit of the underground organization was the cell, composed of a leader and its members. The cell was usually compartmentalized to protect the overall organization from capture or compromise of any member. There were mainly two types of cells: the operational cell and the intelligence cell. These types of cells could be found in every village, district and province of South Vietnam. The local Communist operational cell functioned to collect money, distribute propaganda and carry out political functions. The intelligence cell was different since its leader rarely came into contact with its members. Cell members rarely knew each other's real names or addresses and they avoided coming into contact with other members. A Communist cell member infiltrated into the South Vietnamese Army, government or police would contact his leader only through an intermediary such as a mail drop (shop or restaurant), cut out (note left in a hole in a tree, wall or under a rock) or courier (child or woman) with a prearranged signal that there was a pending communication. There were also terror cells and sabotage cells.

The Communists relied heavily on food and money that they obtained from the local economy by levying taxes on the people. The rice tax was levied on small-scale agricultural production, as well as on large plantations. Other sources of finance included the transportation tax on transients and the market tax. Our agents closely watched the large, local market. The guerrillas lived and operated outside of the control and surveillance of our government forces around the Khe Sanh area, and conducted insurgent military operations. Communist underground cell members in the local villages and town would agitate any grievance and turn people's attitudes against the government. Later, armed guerrillas would turn up and execute those displaying incorrect attitudes. The local people just wanted to live their lives, but the war was making them choose sides. There was no right side. The underground operated within the control and surveillance of our government forces in the Khe Sanh area and was made up of the local villagers and citizens of the town of Khe Sanh. They collected intelligence, a prerequisite for all acts of terrorism. SFC Williams was always looking for the names of the disloyal Bru or Vietnamese. In order for the communists to create mass support, credible agitation was essential. SFC Williams ran a covert agent net to collect information on the activities of these covert and clandestine Communist organizations and their members. His operational funds paid for existing sources of information and for developing new sources. No one ever saw his lists of names. The black list contained the names of confirmed enemy agents. The gray list was made up of suspected enemy personnel, and the white list was comprised of those personnel who could be trusted to assist us. Sergeant Williams was always busy, and his files were always locked up in the radio shack. An armed radio operator was always present to guard them.

The Communist used terrorism to demonstrate the government's lack of control and protection of their citizens, and to create panic and terror among them. The targets were village chiefs, schoolteachers, district officials, plantation workers and owners, village guards, police and soldiers. After the underground branch leader identified a target for assassination, the regular members of one of the compartmentalized intelligence cells in their organization collected the "who," "what," "where," and "when." The underground's job was to be recruited into the CIDG forces and subvert it.

The Outdoor Market at Khe Sanh

Passing through the town was always an aromatic treat. The smell was overpowering but not at all unpleasant, exotic spices mixed with the more familiar odors of animals and humanity. Some days the district headquarters required our coordination. I periodically found myself going along into town, and it was during these trips that I became acquainted with the market area. While we made good use of the local market and native foods, SFC Williams' covert agent net was active in the market. Here our agents listened to the conversations of the crowd for possible agitators. Customers were watched: who bought what and how much.

The town was fed supplies by great numbers of barefoot peasant women who walked the narrow Route 9 from the market in the coastal area to the market in Khe Sanh. The bridge abutments had been systematically taken out, closing the highway to vehicular traffic. However, the road itself could still be negotiated by walking. Banditry and seemingly mindless violence went with the territory. The bandits and soldiers exacted tolls from those scurrying from the coast to the market at Khe Sanh but still they came, carrying poles of heavily balanced basket loads of canned goods, chicken and duck eggs, onions, and all types of supplies on their backs, pushing bicycles and horse carts with farming implements. A quarter-mile from town, my sense of smell was already stimulated. The plentiful and wide-ranging aromatic blend of smells of firewood smoke and cooking fragrances mixed with those of the market ahead were a delight.

My eyes took in the sights of the different kinds of people and their dress and colors, and the sounds of people bartering. So much humanity was crammed into a small area. Small boys could be seen running around, peering through the legs of the grown ups while munching on sugarcane. The market was a place for finding out all the local and national news. The smell of women distilling syrup from sugar cane excited my senses. The young women wore beautiful wide-woven conical bamboo hats with their long black hair shimmering in the light, and they wore black trousers with white blouses. Almost everywhere you looked, peasant women crisscrossed gracefully beneath shoulder poles slung heavily with baskets of all types of goods. The fitted, bamboo-shoulder carrying poles were loaded with heavy, woven, rounded cages, loaded with trussed monkeys and ducks. Hapless ducks shivered violently in wide, open flat baskets, their feet tied together with rushes. Pigs were confined in conical baskets. From a quarter-mile away the Vietnamese potbellied pig could be heard squealing to be freed. Chickens were sitting docile and clucking. The small animals, fish and poultry were kept alive to be sold. Due to the lack of refrigeration, only as much meat, fish and poultry was slaughtered as was likely to be sold that same day. Other flat woven baskets were heavily laden and balanced with tubers, herbs of all kinds-particularly mint, and with duck and chicken eggs for the throngs of shoppers. Medicinal herbs and spices collected in the surrounding hills were sold, and were used in most Vietnamese dishes.

I saw many old shriveled faces. They were thin, bent hump-backed women with sunken, tired and rheumy eyes that time had left with little dignity. Their hair was pulled back, tightly sucking their lips over toothless gums. Many of these older women squatting on the crowded floor, together with their married daughters lining the walls, were working at food preparation. I watched them cough up phlegm and spit it to the side. The red splatter was everywhere as they went right on working, chopping, slicing and gently tapping, or preparing one thing or another, animatedly talking and laughing while watching the crowd.

Betel Nut

The egg-size betel nut grew in clusters high up, under the arching, elegantly feathered betel palms in most of the populated areas of Vietnam. An agricultural product, the half-ripe nut harvested with long spears from the smooth-trunked betel palm was a major item of trade. It has a bitter taste and delivers a mild high when mixed with the right herbs. Many of the married women, their teeth lacquered black to preserve them, showed orange-stained mouths, from habitually chewing the mildly narcotic betel nut. The fibrous layer under the smooth, yellow-orange ripe skin was used to dull the pain caused by diseased teeth and gums. For chewing, a dried brown-black slice of betel nut was used. It was sliced up and mixed with white lime paste, with a small amount of aromatic cardamom and turmeric mixed in to help release the stimulating alkaloids. It was then wrapped in the pungent peppery leaf of the betel pepper plant vine and used in much the same manner as chewing tobacco in the United States. It turned the chewer's saliva, mouth and lips an orange-brown color. The evidence of their spitting streams of it was everywhere.

All around, vendors cleaned and chopped, washed and peeled. Older married women were hunkered down, selling their homegrown scallions and peppers. Women, old and young, trimmed and minced lemon grass. For thousands of years, in hot countries such as Indochina, spices such as onions, garlic, ginger, black pepper and fresh and dried chili peppers have been used to heavily season food to prevent bacteria from causing food spoilage, improving the taste and making the food safer to eat. Spices commonly displayed in this market, and others like it throughout the country, have played a major role in Vietnam's ancient political and economic history.

Another source of nutrition were the baskets and bags containing crickets for sale. The Montagnard people slowly roasted and ate the crickets whole or with a rice dish. Pound for pound, there is more protein in the bugs than in a steak. The Montagnards simply removed the distal portion of the legs and wings and removed the heads. Since grasshoppers and crickets contain nematodes, they had to be cooked well. Unless fully cooked, the threadlike, nematodes, "roundworms" will take up residence in the intestinal track and all the organs of the human body.

Small and large fresh and dried fish, and chunks of meat dispersed throughout filled the interior with its pungent odor. The people of Indochina have been cultivating fish as food for a long time. There were many types of carp. The common carp was found in the canals and streams of Vietnam. The carp ate plant and animal food, and was the hardest to raise. However, there were grass, black, silver and bighead carp that were easier to grow in the ponds and rice fields. The grass carp ate aquatic plants, the black carp ate the small-shelled animals found in the paddies and ponds, the silver and bighead carp ate phytoplankton. The fish farmers made the best use of whatever they had locally. They could catch them by hand, nets or simply drain the paddy. Our cook fed us a lot of carp.

After walking only a few steps in the market the change of wind told my nose of more pleasant fragrances like cinnamon bark, cardamom and vanilla bean. The fragrant cinnamon bark, containing oil, once more valuable than gold, was found and harvested when the sap flowed, permitting easy peeling from the shrub-like tree in the surrounding forest to be used as an antiseptic. A large diet staple, dogs and puppies on a string were bought and sold.

Even a fortune-teller or mystic could be found in the marketplace. Fortune telling is an established part of Vietnamese culture. They believe that mystics have the power to visit the world of the dead, and they are consulted before any important major decision is made, such as parents planning their children's weddings or merchants seeking the best location for a shop. A shaman could be found anywhere with his magic potions and elixirs. One section that did a brisk business was native medicine. Chinese medicine came in all forms. One such medicine that I tried was powdered snake's blood. For the tired and weak, the powder could be mixed with warm water and drunk from a glass. I noticed no ill effects from the powder, and I actually felt better after drinking the mixture. A Chinese anti-malarial medicine from a plant cultivated in China known as ching hao su was widely used by the Vietnamese people for fevers and was in great demand. The powder compound reportedly attacked the malaria parasite; a single-celled animal classified as a protozoan, and killed it in the mosquito's intestine and salivary glands.

The humid air smelled of the odor of oily wood smoke and spiced foods, of the sweet pungency of tobacco and the antiseptic smell of kerosene. The large covered outdoor market was shaded inside where the harried sellers worked their magic, squatting on their haunches bartering in their high pitched haggling, cajoling cash from pockets for snake oil and powdered snake blood for whatever ailed a person. It was a magic place for many people of the surrounding mountains, where they packed their bundles and hopes on horses, bikes, buffalo, back or head, suffering their burdens to get here. My senses were intoxicated, my mind delighted.

Monkey for Lunch

The unpleasant fragrances were from a medieval level of sanitation. As I was to find out in the years ahead, these were common to this entire country. There were no latrines and women urinated by simply hiking up one pant leg while squatting and using one finger to hold their baggy pants to one side. No one paid any attention to sanitation problems. It happened everywhere I went, and in the years ahead, I would continually be reminded of the poverty in which the Vietnamese lived. The homes had no plumbing. Waste went right into the ground, the same source as the drinking water. Where there were latrines, the health hazard increased, because they were filthy breeding grounds for parasites and insects that carried disease.

The market left me hungry for fresh air. It was during a short trip to the district headquarters that I observed with a mixture of terror and awe, some Vietnamese soldiers eating a small skull the size of a baby's. A closer look at the soldiers' lunch revealed it to be the skull of a large monkey. While I waited on the captain, the soldiers offered me a small bowl of food containing rice with some fish sauce, meat and cooked sliced pepper. I could see the approval in each of their eyes as they watched my use of the chopsticks. The meat I was offered was monkey meat. It had a good taste, but it was somewhat dry, stringy and tough. It had no fat. The pepper is still stinging my mouth.

MSG Thomas Barrett with Survival Food

Our Team Mission

The first two months the weather was bad with considerable rain. We could drive much of the distance to the airstrip on Highway 9, but when we turned north onto the dirt road it was hard going. Our daily traffic had turned the dirt road into ruts of mud that literally sucked at our large tires. Early in our assignment, we had two U.S. Marines attached to our team, along with some Australian soldiers and a few New Zealanders. We had to recruit, train, equip and lead the local indigenous Civilian Irregular Defense Group (CIDG) forces on combat operations against the PAVN. The CIDG was comprised of locally recruited Montagnard tribesmen and was created to help establish government control over our area of operations in order to drive out the Communists. Our team was funded for Civic Action and Psychological Operations and for local purchases to stimulate the local economy. We were also funded for payment of covert intelligence operations, and for providing medical care for the Montagnard population in our area of responsibility. Additionally, we provided security for the villages in our area, conducted border surveillance and scouted our entire operational area, while building the new camp at the same time.

The border surveillance effort with the Montagnards had been initiated by the CIA. From our camp we conducted wide-ranging patrols to obtain prisoners for information, while checking the enemy's routes of communication and supply. At times we had sporadic clashes with the enemy at various locations in our area. I think I got more sleep on combat patrols than I did in camp, where we were always working, day and night.

We worked around the clock, building the hardened camp with its concrete underground bunker and corner-bunkers that were as much underground as they were above. Each corner bunker had five machine-gun positions and an ammo storage area. All mortar positions were hardened with concrete underground ammunition storage areas. A communications trench ran around the entire perimeter of the camp linking all fighting positions. The work was hard and steady.

The Chinese Interpreter

In addition to building a new camp, we had troops to train, and to accomplish our task we required Vietnamese, Chinese and Montagnard interpreters. Most were likable and willing workers. Shortly after our arrival, a new Chinese interpreter arrived at our camp. When I was finally introduced to him, all my wisdom and senses were galvanized. I can remember my immediate dislike for him upon looking into his face. It was his black, hostile eyes that I mainly didn't like. When I looked into the depth of them, I saw deceit and treacherous undercurrents, and although his ever-present smile pretended otherwise. His smile never reached his eyes and was more like a leer of contempt and loathing. *A smile is not altogether a reassuring thing.* His look was both invasive and evasive. He always seemed to be looking everywhere, but never at anything. From the first day I met him, he always seemed to show up like a bad penny and talk about things that were none of his business. He had a habit of asking personal information. I remember looking at him and thinking to myself, "Here is the enemy." To him, I must have appeared to be the most naive of the twelve members on the A-team. I didn't want to talk to him or even have him near me. I told SFC Williams about my feelings. Although he heard me out, he never gave me his take on the Chinese man, but only thanked me for my opinion.

The Superpower Challenged

Shortly after we settled in at Khe Sanh, we learned that in the very early morning hours of 1 November 1964, specialized units of sappers (Doi Dac Cong) of the PAVN conducted a successful ground attack on the well-protected American air base at Bien Hoa. The sapper units had boldly swept across the airbase from one side to the other, placing their charges by or on the aircraft, and in the American bivouac area, while eluding the Vietnamese and American security forces. All newsmen had been prohibited from visiting the air base since 1960 and it went out to the media that a mortar attack had taken place, when in reality it was a ground attack on the hanger and parking areas in the very early morning hours. Bien Hoa is located twelve miles northeast of Saigon. During the early morning hours of the attack, six United States Air Force B-57 jet bombers were destroyed, and eight others were damaged. Some twenty other aircraft and helicopters were destroyed. Five Americans were killed defending the base and 29 others were wounded. As a result of the attack on Bien Hoa, we knew that the dedicated Marxists governing North Vietnam with its army fully intended to challenge the might of the United States military.

Nungs

Our camp had a platoon of Chinese Nung mercenaries who served as our personal bodyguards. They were outstanding fighters whose Special Forces pay scale was higher than the members of the paramilitary CIDG troops and the troops of the Army of the Republic of Vietnam (ARVN). On patrol, a small squad of Nungs would accompany us in case there was an assassin among the ranks of the CIDG or Vietnamese. This ethnic minority had originally migrated to Vietnam from China's southeastern autonomous region of Kwangsi Chuang, which borders Vietnam, after the Communists took over the country. After the First Indochina War, the Nungs again migrated into South Vietnam. Both the Chinese Nungs and Montagnards were distrustful of the Vietnamese.

The Khe Sanh area had a high native recruitment potential from among the forest-dwelling Bru tribe located there, which was one of the reasons we were there. Starting in 1961, the ancient hill tribe, the Bru, with their intimate knowledge of the mountain jungle, were recruited by Special Forces to be guerrilla fighters against the PAVN. The Bru lived simply and in almost total isolation in the mountains between Laos and Vietnam and on up into North Vietnam.

Mass Execution

One day, shortly before departing on patrol we were informed of a mass execution. We went to investigate. The village of Houng Hoa was located southeast of our camp at grid coordinates XD 865375. This entire area was overlooked by the Co Roc Mountains in Laos. Co Roc Mountain, itself, was 845 meter (2772 feet) peak, located at grid coordinates XD 741316, dominated the entire operational area. The east slope of the Co Roc Mountains was where the PAVN had already dug in and fortified themselves. They had merely improved upon the cave systems, fortifications and airfields built by the Japanese during World War II. In the past, they'd only demanded money, livestock and rice from the village in return for being left alone.

I smelled the corpses lying in the open streambed before I saw them. The stench of putrefied flesh was strong. The smell traps itself in the back of my throat and deep in my sinuses. The odors emitted by the human body are uniquely unpleasant, different than decomposing animals. It is a putrid and foul smell that I would become quite familiar with during the course of the war. Tormented looks in the eyes of the villagers told us what had happened. Walking up to the creek, we froze in place. I felt my chest heave as the blood rushed hot in the veins of my throat and face--my hand twitched as my eyes surveyed the carnage. Agitated, I started to breathe deeply; although it was a cool day, I now felt hot. I stood surrounded by the thick, sticky-sweet smell of the rotting dead, that stuck in my nose and made breathing difficult. This experience had a profound affect on me. I felt anger. The sight and smell soaked into me. My eyes began to water. Now, in a state of physiological arousal, I felt the hatred hardening in me. The Malayan's use the word "amok," for this type of savagery. Now, I know how it got into our vocabulary. The word fits.

The large, noisy blue-green blowflies, having picked up the scent of gas accompanying decomposition, were everywhere. Flies were busy swarming over the nostrils and glazed eyes laying their tiny, grains of egg clusters. The flies had laid their eggs in every wound and orifice of the bodies. The fly-covered bodies appeared to have been there for a day, because I could already see small maggots feeding on the decomposing flesh. I noticed the uncertain and wobbling flight of butterflies that came and settled in search of salt and other nutrients. The iridescent flutter of beautifully rainbow-hued butterflies sparkled in the sunlight and had already infiltrated the open wounds. I watched as their tiny tendrils of their tongues uncurled and dabbed at the wounds, feeding on the dead. I felt a muscle pulse high at my temple. Numb, I stood still for a long time. Trembling, the emotion rising, I felt the sudden despairing amalgam of fear, then anger and rage. The demons of the present had been there. With faces grown hard, our dark, brooding eyes barely visible between the slits, we fixed our furious stares upon the scene before us. The villagers' only crime seemed to have been to want to continue following the seasons: planting, harvesting and tending their livestock. But now, this was one of the sites where the bestiality of the war had emerged. We stood for right, and now what I was looking at was wrong. Here was a loss of humanity and the glorification of madness, spreading terror to intimidate a simple people.

I never knew whether the District Chief was demonstrating his control over the area through terror by executing so many villagers, or if he had ordered the execution

to eliminate a particular segment of the population. I also realized that the massacre could have been carried out in retribution for a failed attempt by the communists to recruit Montagnards to join the 559th Rear Services Group's labor force. Then there was our I Corps commander, General Nguyen Chanh Thi, a very dangerous man.[4] A devout Buddhist who resented Catholics, he was appointed commanding officer of I Corps on 14 November and remained so for the duration of our tour of duty. He commanded the five northern provinces of Quang Tri, Thua Thien, Quang Nam, Quang Tin and Quang Ngai. These provinces included the cities of Quang Tri, Hue, and Danang. In November 1960, as a colonel commanding the Vietnamese Airborne Brigade, he attempted an abortive coup against President Ngo Dinh Diem. He wanted to establish a government acceptable to the communists--a federation with North Vietnam. After the coup attempt he fled to Cambodia. If anyone knew the real story behind the massacre, it was Sergeant Williams, but he would not discuss intelligence operations with anyone, unless they had a need to know. This massacre would serve as his inducement to obtain informants to protect them from future reprisals. Now I saw that there were no neutrals in this war. I was shocked to see all the dead, and suffered my first spiritual sickness, smelling the stench of death that filled the air.

    It was a forlorn scene: the site of a mass execution. These men did not merely die, they were slaughtered. Parts of their bodies were embedded in the creek bank and on the surface of the sandy ground everywhere. A syrup of bloody body fluids from every kind of wound had spilled into the soil beneath them. I could almost hear the now silent cries of agony that must have been uttered when they realized the intent of their executioners. Most were seen sleeping the sleep of the dead. However, the sightless eyes were wide open, stamped with death and an incommunicable horror. Lips were beginning to draw back over the teeth and eyes were sunk back into the heads, turning hard and dull and the hair began to slip. These were Vietnamese whose only crime was to anger the District Chief in Khe Sanh. They had been executed with grenades, and some with M-79 Grenade Launchers. The small craters were everywhere. Now, their corpses were lying in grotesquely twisted attitudes on the blood-soaked sand of this small creek, mutilated beyond description. Few were in one piece. Their mangled bodies were in jagged patterns of flesh, voided of their blue-gray, rope-like coils of entrails and limbs separated from their bodies. The now-rigid limbs of the bodies would have to be broken to fit them into coffins. Fleshy fragments were strewn about everywhere.

These mind-numbing images were to remain with me the rest of my life. I silently promised myself that no matter how long I served in this war, never would I let myself become anyone's prisoner. This visceral picture and its putrid smell, the odor of decay, would remain in my mind, at the back of my throat and in my nose throughout the war. I felt the anger, but rather than express it, I knew I had to walk away. I needed an alternative, to go back to work. Hard work. Turning to go and looking at the other team members, only their ears, red with emotion, eyes bright with anger, gave away their thoughts. Most of the native faces were blank. Already, this early in the war, a canker of bitterness, cynicism and disillusionment had started to grow within me. The years ahead in this beautiful country were destined to get darker.

The central authority person who enforced this harsh discipline and intimidation was the local District Chief of the district. The District Chief, with both civilian and military staff, was the lowest civil servant at the local level and was appointed by the Province Chief. Vietnam was truly in a state of continuing violence, political feuds, corruption and social fragility. It was the District Chief in the Khe Sanh area who frightened the tribesmen with tales of Communist reprisals. He also participated in the selection of villagers to be arrested, interrogated and killed. The villagers were so terrified that they asked to turn their weapons back in. I wondered if Communist agents had identified these people and decided that this specific act of terror, this spectacle of butchered deaths, should serve as an example to others and of what could befall those who failed to cooperate with the District Chief. It would produce fear and compliance among the population. Their deaths, without remorse, had been fast in some cases and deliberately slow and ferocious in others. I never read that anyone, anywhere, protested this massacre.

The PAVN was known for this type of intimidation toward those who failed to cooperate or volunteer to serve as fighters, laborers, or porters along the Ho Chi Minh trail. From the brutality of what I had witnessed, I surmised that the PAVN had Chinese advisors with them. Amid such beauty, aware of my own mortality, this massacre sent chills up my spine. The guerrilla's, major weapon was horror and fear, and superstitious people frighten easily. Aware of all the evil around us, I now tried thinking about all the wonderful things as well.

Footnotes:

1. There are over seventy-two military cemeteries along the Ho Chi Minh Trail.

2. The IL-4 was a World War II, twin-engine, high speed, long-range aircraft that could carry the same amount of cargo as our Caribou, with a range of 2,400 miles. The IL-12 was a later developed World War II paratroop or cargo transport with a range of 1,800 miles.

3. The French-made Peugeot and the Czech-built bicycles were favored. The pack bicycles called *xe tho*, each carried over 400 pounds of supplies, 25 miles a day. The North Vietnamese called their fleet of bicycles, steel horses.

4. Gen. Nguyen Chanh Thi was born on 23 February 1923, in Hue and died 23 June 2007, in Lancaster, Pennsylvania. In 1966, President Lyndon B. Johnson support of Premier Ky in their meeting in Honolulu gave license to dismiss Gen. Thi from the army and send him to the United States where he remained permanently.

Nothing is ever done in this world until men are prepared to kill each other if it is not done.

George Bernard Shaw (1856-1950)

CHAPTER 6

CAMP IN THE CLOUDS

We continued to work night and day on the new camp at the airfield as well as keeping up our surveillance patrols along the Laotian border. The most unique thing about being in Special Forces, besides knowing how to teach and fight, was knowing how to build. Our A-team of twelve men was responsible for feeding, housing and caring for an indigenous battalion along with building the camp. We had six months to do it, in addition to carrying out our normal combat and intelligence missions. In accomplishing this mission, we not only saved our Government money, but we brought civilization and security to this primitive area.

Each morning, long before light, we were up and getting ready for the trip to the airstrip. We took a right turn from our front gate, went east from our old French Foreign Legion fort, and traveled about a mile on Highway 9 to the left turnoff where we went north to the plateau. In addition to maintaining our own equipment and that of our troops, we provided medical care for those in our operational area.

Camp Construction

The weather changed constantly. We toiled first in the cold rain that would last for hours or days, and then in the dank heat. We transported our supplies and equipment to the proper work site to prepare our defensive position on the plateau. Our never-ending work kept us from becoming depressed by the constant rain. Rain or shine, it was work, work, work. When the intermittent good weather changed for the worse, as it often did, the flies inside our fortifications became prolific, noisy, agitated and troublesome. We were worn out by the unconscionably long hours and the intensity of the work, which began in the early morning and went on until after last light in a place where it seemed the rain would never stop.

At night, I had only to allow myself to relax and I was sound asleep. Sometimes this task was a little difficult, because my back was sore from all the lifting, loading and unloading of equipment we used each day; as well as my hands, covered with blisters from using the maul on the post drivers, and my muscles strained from the laying of wire and the making of ties. Our team of 12 men ate and slept in one location and worked in another. Each morning we were once again gently woken in the dark and then we turned, still heavy with sleep, and put our feet on the floor. We waited a minute for reality, then stretched our tired limbs from the preceding day and put on our clothes. The cold, wet weather had us struggling to dress to warm ourselves.

Meals

I vaguely remember breakfast, and I ate with no real desire to begin a new day's work, but I know my appetite was good. We had ample food and a wonderful, fat Chinese lady for a cook. Most of what she prepared was what we were already used to, with the exception of the eggs. The eggs were duck eggs and they were not only much larger, but much tastier also. Thanks to our medic, Froetschel, who had been a baker by trade before army life, our cook was able to perfect her technique at bread baking. We always had fresh baked bread. Our meals were not hurried. We let them settle, as we had an entire day of work ahead of us and we had to have the energy. We exchanged a few comments on work-related duties for the day. Then in the foul weather and wind we were on our way, faced with another long, hard day. While the work progressed at the new site, there was also always plenty of work at the old site for those remaining at the French fort. A lot of the retaining wall type revetments utilized burlap sandbags which constantly needed replacement because they rotted in the damp weather and the rats were continually eating holes in the newer plastic bags. Our meals at the end of the day were good and healthy. They consisted of rice and boned chicken, noodles and boned chicken, rice and beef, noodles and beef, rice and buffalo, or noodles and buffalo. The water buffalo was tough to chew and stuck in your teeth. The produce was purchased from the local market daily.

Labor Recruitment

Luckily, we had a plentiful source of labor in the Khe Sanh area and we recruited it. Those who wanted to work were always at the airstrip shortly after we were. Under good supervision, we used the indigenous personnel (native labor) to rebuild the strip. The Bru were paid in rice and the Vietnamese in their national currency. (Although the United States produced, supplied and fed most of the world with its rice, the Vietnamese did not like our brownish American-grown, long-grained rice. Most of this rice was grown in my home state of California, in the Sacramento Valley. (We in the U.S. planted it by aircraft, not by hand.) Each day, those arriving at the camp waited to be selected to work. Regardless of the weather conditions, they were standing or sitting silently.

During each day's labor recruitment we were alert and paid attention to the potential workers' general overall appearance and to physical reactions to our presence. Overt signs of nervousness, anger, lack of eye contact, and shuffling of their hands and feet--all these made them suspect and they were interviewed by our intelligence sergeant. Since the bodily functions of a person are influenced by his mental state, there were always some who looked nervous and worried with twitching eyes. Those who were worried had their eyes always flitting to the soldiers about them or were looking away when eye-to-eye contact was trying to be made. We would study those waiting to work and when we identified those taller than the Montagnards and with good close-cut hair, we checked them closer. They were always Vietnamese. I would walk up to them and take their hand in mine and examine them. Often I found clean, uncalloused hands and sometimes well-manicured nails. Occasionally, someone with a long pinkie nail was observed, denoting someone who considered himself upper class Vietnamese. He was more than likely a PAVN officer. If they were really nervous, you would observe redness from where they'd scratched their palms with their nails, or you would see fingernail indentations. Most of our recruited laborers, however, had hands coarsened by hard work in all seasons. Later in the war, we checked their trigger fingers for calluses, checked their shoulders for marks of their rifle slings and checked for bruises from the recoil of their weapons. The general consensus among us was that the PAVN were working and helping to build our camp for us while collecting their specific information on the locations and dimensions of the new camp and its facilities.

Main Camp

For the indigenous troops, we built permanent barracks and an indigenous messhall, separate team houses for the Vietnamese Special Forces and the American Special Forces were built, along with barracks for the Chinese Nungs. Defensive positions and a 15-bed hospital with shower facilities were also erected. The largest structure in camp was the underground communications bunker.

Airstrip

One thing I can say for the Khe Sanh area is that it could really rain. First the wind would increase, and then a low scudding dark mass of clouds would obscure the tops of the mountains. When you saw the first giant squall line advancing, it would be only a short while before the mighty wind would begin whipping the treetops. You could smell the rain. It began to cool the air. The wind usually was piercingly cold. The giant treetops would tremble to their very roots. The wind would bow the forest under its tremendous pressure. Then the huge black pall would bore down from the mountain and bring the rain. It could be seen falling in sheets, like a giant wall advancing. The lively thunderstorm could last for an hour or for days. When the downpour passed, a cold, fine misty gray rain would be left with the dripping trees. If a second storm came, the clouds would again close and darken for another onslaught. The air was always fresh and clean. We often wore our wool sweaters under the jackets of our jungle uniforms.

During this weather, the airstrip remained wet and slick, causing the aircraft to slide, and on occasion to dangerously slide off the strip. Not only would the Perforated-Steel-Plate (PSP) be wet much of the time, but when the water covering the strip was gone, it left a thin layer of red mud, making it very dangerous to land on. We had to continually work on the airstrip at the same time we built the camp. We removed the matting in the most dangerous areas first and filled them with crushed rock. That accomplished, we then went about doing the same for the whole airstrip, doing a large section at a time and tamping lots of crushed rock under the PSP. The rock was obtained from the old French engineer quarry near the old French Foreign Legion camp at Lang Vei. The PSP airfield would accommodate aircraft from the size of L-19s to C-130s. We had a lot of air traffic while building the new camp and therefore many dangerous takeoffs and landings due to the runway conditions. Many of the landing aircraft's tires would ride on a cushion of water, hydroplaning. The craft's brakes at these times were useless. Twice I saw an aircraft slide into the mud, once at the end of the strip and once along the side of the strip. Both were able to eventually get themselves out.

Once, during a period of heavy winds that were blowing from north to south across the strip, I watched an Australian CV-2 Caribou on the parking ramp take off the width of the runway from the parking ramp. On this particular day, it had been raining very hard, but had stopped briefly and the Caribou had landed. Just then the wind began to blow very hard from the north. The airstrip was surrounded by a sea of mud. The pilot was afraid to take off from either end of the strip, facing east or west. The wind would slide the aircraft off the strip and crash it or strand it in the mud. The pilot decided to take off the width of the runway from the ramp on the side. Not being an aviator, I felt a disaster in the making. The pilot backed his aircraft up on the ramp as far as he could and sat there with his engines running, faster and faster, until at last he released his brakes and roared off across the ramp and across the width of the strip and at the last moment lifted into the air. I couldn't believe it.

      Aircraft were always bringing in supplies that we could not obtain locally, and we worked hard at unloading the aircraft quickly--allowing them to quickly depart. From our airfield, we provided logistical support for the Royal Lao 33rd Battalion also known as BV-33 (Volunteer Battalion). It was positioned across the border at the airfield at Ban Houei Sane on the south side of Highway 9 in Laos. This unit was made up of Kha tribesmen, who had been mainly responsible for the clearing of the Bolovens Plateau in Laos. However, in 1964 the NVA and Pathet Lao had been in control of the Bolovens Plateau for some time. Our busy strip also provided emergency fuel for smaller reconnaissance aircraft. The right-wing Royal Laotian Army supported Prince Souvanna Phouma. On the other side, the Communist Pathet Lao and North Vietnamese Army supported the Laotian leftist Souphanouvong, known as "The Red Prince," One day, a company-sized Vietnamese unit showed up at the airstrip with orders to fly to Danang Air Base. The request was granted by the team commander and they were flown out of Khe Sanh. A belated radio check revealed no such orders had been given by the Vietnamese or Americans. We had given the North Vietnamese soldiers a free ride onto the Danang Air Base, where they promptly disappeared. Although we laughed about it, it made everyone nervous.

The Giant Stump

      Level ground surrounded our camp on the plateau, except for an old hardwood stump of immense size that stuck up at a grotesque angle. It stuck out like an old scarred sore in the open area—a giant old stump, the legacy of some great tree that had resisted all earlier efforts of removal. Half of its roots pointed to the sky, humped out in every direction, and twisting down into the ground like they would hold there to eternity, effectively blocking one of our fields of fire. It was huge. The wood was so hard that I could not sink an ax blade more than a quarter inch at a time. It had to be removed. Being the team's junior demolitionist, it became my assigned personal responsibility. A walk-around inspection revealed that a lot of it was still in the ground. I estimated the type of explosive I would use and where the smallest dimension of the stump was so I could put a set number of untamped charges around it.

Being young and relatively inexperienced, and not knowing the type of wood or how strong it was, I went to the messhall and sat down and calculated by the school formula for an external and untamped timber-cutting charge of TNT. The formula used was the diameter squared, over a constant of 40, that equaled pounds of TNT required (P). Now, armed with the answer of how much TNT was needed and thinking I would make quick work of that stump, I happily set about the job of its destruction.

Camp Khe Sanh 1964
Being Built by Special Forces "A" Team-323 out of Okinawa

I assembled all my demolition accessories and rigged blocks of TNT and equipment for an electrical firing system. With my blasting caps, firing wire, and my 10-cap blasting machine secured and stowed, I drove out to the stump and rigged my charges. With a feeling of great satisfaction I turned the handle setting off the charge. I peered through the blast and dust of the explosion. The stump had merely quivered and swayed a little and remained intact. My ego was somewhat deflated. Unbeknownst to me, the whole team had been keeping track of my progress from a distance, watching and listening and laughing.

I went back to the messhall, sat down with a cup of strong French coffee heavily mixed with sweetened condensed milk, and worked out the formula again. There was only the clinking of dishes from our Chinese cook working as I calculated with Composition C-4. Then, armed with an ax and charges of a higher velocity and a greater determination of my own, I was again on my way to blow the hell out of that huge stump. Using the ax, I notched the stump the best I could and placed the charges. It took some time to make the notches. The wood was extremely hard. Again, doubt was already creeping in. The charges effectively placed, I hopefully turned the handle on the charger. This time the great explosion could be heard for miles. When the smoke and dust settled, I saw that a few chunks had been blown off and the angle was a little different, but the tree stump remained.

Of the eleven other team members, I saw not one when I returned inside the camp to the messhall for another cup of coffee. I knew they could hear, but they remained elsewhere and said nothing. As I was to learn later, they had already split up and again gone about their duties. This stump was providing the team with some much needed laughter and relaxation at my expense. Now, bewildered, I decided to cheat and add more to the charge than what was called for by the formula. I was learning, but not quickly enough. The third try was the same. As I turned to the vehicle, my senior engineer was standing there looking at me with a smile on his face and as always his sad eyes looking into me. He was feeling for me what I was feeling for myself. He walked up to me and said, "Mac, do you want some help?" I said, "Yes." Borgardts said, "Let's go have a cup of coffee." Still, I saw no other team members, but by now they were beside themselves with the hilarity of it all. Sitting down and drinking coffee, Borgardts asked me to show him my calculations. He looked at them and said they were fine. Now, he said, "Take this formula and shove it up your ass." Going on, he said that there was only one formula to remember. Ever. That was "P," P for plenty.

After finishing our coffee, we loaded our 3/4-ton truck and went back with a load of demolitions. I worked hard with a D-handled shovel digging under one side of the giant stump, as directed by Borgardts. I was digging and sweating while bringing out the dirt between the roots. In this way, we would increase the pressure on it. With satisfactory holes in place, we set our charges and tamped them in place under the stump and again rigged the stump like a Christmas tree. Now, standing upright on shaky legs from the heavy exertion, with sweat rivulets running down our dirty faces and soaking through our uniforms, we looked at each other, smiling and certain at last. When the massive charges were blown, the dust, smoke and splinters went everywhere, and when all was clear again, there was nothing left of the stump. It was gone. I had learned my best lesson about the book and its formulas: it was merely a guide. When I returned to the inside of the camp and the mess hall again, the whole team was there and smiling. It took a team that worked together to accomplish a mission. I had accepted help and I was learning.

More typically, the extent of my demolition duties consisted of smoothly blowing one end off any number of 55-gallon drums so they could be used around the camp as water or garbage containers. I also blew up dud ammunition, mostly white phosphorus ammunition for the 57 Recoilless Rifle that had been exposed to moisture, and also dud 81mm ammunition. The hole for the underground concrete bunker built at Khe Sanh, utilized at a later time by the Marines, was initially blown with demolitions by Borgardts and myself. Several times we rigged and detonated charges in series. The dirt was excavated by the use of many laborers.

Unwanted Visitors

Whenever we were notified that there was the promise of unwanted visitors coming into our camp, Captain Allen would instruct me to go set off some dud white-phosphorus and 81mm illumination-flare ammunition with some charges at the approach end of the airstrip. I would blow up several rounds on top of the ground, which generally sent several crazily zigzagging rounds flipping end over end up into the air, along with a great mushroom cloud of white smoke. The aircraft, upon observing this still in the distant approach pattern, would always ask what the situation was. We would respond that it was just a little incoming. The aircraft would then turn around and head back in the direction from which they came. I routinely made trips down to an isolated area off the approach end of our airstrip, in an area of high grass near the forest and overlooking the canyon. I always watched my back and constantly scanned the area, for at times, I had an uneasy feeling that something watched my every move. When alone, and away from the camp, I was more afraid of a tiger than the enemy we had been sent to fight.

The Bees

One day, while performing the task of blowing up dud ammunition, I looked to the southern skyline, noticing what I thought was a dark squall line. Each time I looked up it seemed to be higher on the skyline and closer. Eventually I realized that it was probably birds of some kind. Then it dawned on me what it was when I heard the menacing drone of bees. I could see their crazy flight of shooting in, out and around and felt the fanned air of their little wings all around me. Normally, I have no fear of bees, not being allergic to them, but these were of an immense size. It was a mass northward migration of big, black bees. The mass was passing directly over the camp. Bees, sensing nervousness or fear, will sting. At this particular time, I was afraid, because the sky was turning dark with them and I was exposed out in the open. I jumped in my 3/4 ton truck and drove toward the opposite end of the airstrip as quickly as I could, one hand on the steering wheel and the other swatting them from my head. I was stung on the scalp about four or five times, and for a while I didn't feel very well. Then just as quickly as they came, they were gone, disappearing on the northern horizon.

Barbed Wire

Our team Captain never had to worry about us being unoccupied because we understood the urgency with which this camp had to be finished. There was always plenty of work, and our hands were never empty. Among our first priorities in building the new camp was erecting wire. We used the four-and-two pace method. We used 8-foot, U-shaped pickets placed four paces apart, with anchor pickets two paces out at mid-point between the long pickets. Usually the weather was cool, but it seemed the days were nice and sunny while building the barrier. The heat of the sun beating down on our backs was overpowering as we toiled in the dank heat until our tunics were rimmed with salt from our sweat. Against orders, we often removed our jackets and soaked up some of the sun.

We were young and hard. We surrounded the campsite with three double-apron fences, each with triple concertina and three more in front and behind the double apron, barriers sufficiently wide enough to keep any attacker outside of grenade throwing range. The concertina fences were reinforced with wide breaches covered with tangle-foot wire between each of the three apron fences. We did not trust the building of these double-apron fences to native labor.

I spent many hours driving the long stakes with a maul and a post-driver. It was hard work and we were always in need of a drink. One day, stripped to the waist and sweating, two Montagnards stopped by to sell us a drink of Montagnard whiskey. The policy was no drinking on the job. However, SFC Dennis was working with me this day and said, "To hell with it." We bought ourselves a jar of this slightly yellowed, clear liquid. I looked at Dennis saying, "I suppose I'll just have to gag this jungle piss down for God and country," and drank. The first sip over my tongue was not unpleasant. I took a large drink and felt it scorch a path of fire all the way to my stomach. The heat rose in my throat and my forehead felt feverish. I'm not a drinker, and I felt this one potent drink for the rest of the day.

Our barbed wire reels weighed 50 pounds; just loading them and getting them where they were needed was a tiring job in itself. I hated those reels. Our wire was standard barbed wire, 2-strand with 4-point bars. I used heavy engineer gloves of pigskin. The depth zone of wire entanglements consisted of two fixed bands of double-apron fences with accompanying concertina wire for barriers running parallel around the camp. Inside of all this was a channeling zone and tangle foot. I wore out a lot of engineer gloves erecting this barrier. Normally in the infantry, it would take a platoon of men only an hour and a half to complete a 300-meter section. We did not have this trained manpower, so our days were long and hard.

Mines

Our M-18 Claymore antipersonnel mines with their 800 steel pellets were concealed below ground, attached to the inside lid of ammo boxes placed in the ground. This way they were not visible or exposed to weather. When the lids were raised from the bunkers, they were so positioned to be effectively fired electrically, and sprayed outward. The steel pellets were blown out in a fan-shaped killing pattern of sixty degrees. The firing device's hand detonator called the clacker or a 10-cap blasting machine, were controlled in the command and control positions of the hardened machine-gun bunkers. The directional Claymore mines were checked daily with a galvanometer to insure a complete circuit to the electric blasting caps. During electrical storms we had to make sure that the mines were not primed, so we removed the detonating caps.

Bare-Breasted Tribal Women

Sometimes while making a solitary run back to our quarters at the French fort, I had opportunities to take pictures of the bare-breasted married women of the Bru while they carried their loads back to their village. Many of these tribal women had enormously flaccid breasts with large brown nipples and I usually took the opportunity to stop and get them to pose for a picture.

Politics

At the end of each hard day's labor in the camp, after our last meal, we had the opportunity to read and talk: to relax. The letters from home did not always bring good personal news and the newspaper received in the mail told of what we thought was criminal bureaucratic interference with the course of the war. Early on, it was evident that President Johnson had no policy for the war. Further, the top military leadership in the Pentagon and the commander in Vietnam, Gen. Westmoreland, did not understand unconventional warfare or the use of Special Forces. Therefore there was no integrated strategy. At Khe Sanh, we planned our own operations. All through the war years, we in the military read the newspapers and were astounded by "the suits" in Washington who thought they knew how to conduct a war in Asia better than the military. Cutting off the PAVN supply line in Laos, which should have had top priority and could have won the war, was off limits.

The Chinese Interpreter

One day in the midst of my labor, Sergeant Williams dropped by and told me that our Chinese interpreter had been found murdered. His swollen and decomposing body had been found in a large pool of the Rao Quan River where he allegedly drowned, but the marks on him and specifically the one around his neck told a different story. After such a long time in the water, I really couldn't tell that it was him, except for being told that it was. Dead, he seemed one less problem that we had to worry about. Unknown to us, he had already done his damage.

Hue

We were watched closely during our six-month Temporary Duty (TDY) tour at Khe Sanh. When the team captain determined that we individually had developed a bad mood, were overly tired or our mind was agitated, we were sent to town for rest and relaxation with more money than we needed. We were always told that when our money was gone, we were to return to site and not to borrow more. The closest large town on the coast, immediately to the east, was Quang Tri. Further south along the coast was Hue, then Danang. During one of these brief trips to the C-detachment compound at Danang, I caught a helicopter leaving Danang airfield for Hue and made a brief visit there. I wanted to see the city, and more importantly the inside walled Citadel of Hue. Although it was the time of the winter monsoons, the weather was fine. I landed on the southwest side of the city, near Highway 1 and the railroad, near the Linh Quang Pagoda. I saw a bicycle with good tires and bought the bike off of a grinning Vietnamese soldier. He had good reason to grin because I paid too much for it, but at the time I needed it. I crossed over the Phu Cam Canal into the city. I could see from the chopper that the thick and high inside wall was surrounded by a moat. I wanted very much to see the columned throne hall of the building known as the Palace of Supreme Harmony, where the Nguyen emperors received their subjects.

Vietnam's third largest city, Hue, embodied Vietnam's national identity. Located in Thua Thien Province, in Central Vietnam, about 400 miles south of Hanoi, it is the old and last imperial capital of Vietnam. The Citadel on the north bank of the Perfume River is surrounded by a deep-water moat and the Imperial City is located inside. I first rode the bike around the former high-walled Imperial City. That was my first mistake; it was immense in size. Traveling the roads around the outside of the walls was a long trip. One wall was something like 2,000 meters. It had not looked that far from the air. I noticed it was situated on the old Mandarin Road, now Highway 1, running along the western and southeastern side of the Citadel and crosses over the river on the Trang Tien Bridge. I felt badly that the ancient archways were left to crumble with neglect because of the war. This had been Vietnam's capital from 1802 to 1945, where the 13 Nguyen emperors ruled. The Imperial City was an ancient cultural center and a center of Buddhism and education, where music and literature flourished under the Mandarin scholars.

It was here that Nguyen Anh proclaimed himself Emperor Gia Long (1759-1820) and reorganized the country, creating a centralized state and the Nguyen dynasty. He united the three areas that the French had divided the country into. The northernmost part of the country was known as Tonkin, and its capital Hanoi had originally been the capital of all Indochina. The central part of the country was known as Annam, and its capital was Hue. The south was known as Cochin, and its capital was Sai Gon. Hanoi and Sai Gon were relegated to regional capitals. Emperor Gia Long now called the country "Vietnam."

Vietnam has only one north-south road the length of the country, and each year travelers using National Highway 1 are routinely stranded because of flooding during the monsoon season. Hue is split by the shallow Huong River, or as the River of Perfumes. The old French colonial city and mostly residences were on the south side of the river and the Citadel was on the north. In the old days, the dizzying scent of the surrounding forests and wildflowers gave the Perfume River its name, but much had changed since then. The river had always been Hue's major highway. Most of the old imperial tombs were located outside the city, along the river, so seeing them was out of the question. It wasn't too safe in the city, much less outside the city. On the northeast side, a ripe pungency marked the location of the Dong Ba farmers' market. Despite my strength of habit, I found myself stifling the urge to shoot a glance backward, choosing instead to be curious about everything displayed around me. I chose to naturally turn to look at one thing or another, while constantly checking my back without lifting my head.

Amid all the bartering, I focused on the unrelenting bargaining and haggling of one old woman, which was plenty of entertainment. Without staring, I watched her lean close and check the fish for clear eyes, not murky eyes. She smelled the gills for the off-putting smell, the telltale signs of spoilage. And then she gently lifted the fish itself, checking if it was stiff. Then she talked rapidly to the merchant, who seemed to have a humored but exasperated look, probably about the outrageous price. I imagined that she was an old and valued customer, who bought her fish and produce in the same places every day with the same complaints and comments.

For some reason, no one was allowed inside the Forbidden Purple City inside the Citadel. The Forbidden City was where the emperor stayed. I would learn later that there were anti-American Buddhist demonstrations in Hue and Saigon in late January 1965. I talked to a helicopter pilot who was to make a short flight to check something or other, asking him to take me with him and fly over the Citadel to get a closer look. He agreed, so I got to see the inside area from the air. Though I was disappointed at not getting to see it all up close, I could tell it was elaborately decorated with imposing dragons on the roof. The dragons were a symbol of nobility and power.

I crossed over the Trang Tien Bridge to the south side of the river and went to the MACV compound to look around the old French colonial part of the city. I knew I wouldn't go hungry because I could see there were many places to eat. I could see and hear the whirring of many sewing machines of people hard at work. People were slurping noodle soup at little sidewalk shops everywhere. The eyes of the old people held a rheumy indifference to my stare. The eyes of the young men near my age on the street held a hint of belligerence. Now and then I caught a glimpse of a young woman's deft eye deflection as she caught a glimpse of me. A slight breeze carried the smell of fish, and odor of people pissing on the walls. I found a small hotel and decided to spend the night.

The Kindly Old Woman

Heavy-lidded and sleepy, I stood before a haggard, time-scarred and withered old woman with smoke-reddened, rheumy eyes and a mouth that pressed against her time worn teeth. She took care of me without saying a word, only nodding her head. Thin and gray and now infirm, she had an honest, loving smile, and hardly any teeth. Her face was like the ghost of a long-lost beauty that still lingered. Her hair was dry and brittle from her bending over many cooking fires. She was as long-legged as a heron, and I wished I could have known her and her life's story. With one hand on my arm, she led me to a room where I immediately went to bed. I drifted off to the scent of the old woman's cooking, the sickly smell of incense burning (a part of the Buddhist ritual), and the loud chirp of crickets. The crickets were a comfort, a sign that all was well on the dark streets. The incense always covered up the more pungent smells. Two geckos skittered about hunting mosquitoes, the same grey color as the walls.

The next morning I was up early, roused by the soft call of the old woman and the smell of the cooking fires. The early risers were grilling meat for the early shoppers. I noticed the veins in the smiling old woman's hands, as she offered me a hot bowl of noodles and a fiercely potent cup of coffee with sweetened condensed milk. I ate, dressed and said my good-byes, paying my bill. As the old lady put away the money, I noticed she had much more than I did. I came to learn that many Vietnamese hoard their money to avoid income taxes. Then, too, they do not trust banks. On the street, my nose was greeted with the now familiar smoke carried on the wind.

Believe it or not, just walking down the street, I could find a whorehouse just by their exotic smell, the smell of bodies, sweat, heavy perfume, urine, sperm and heavy tobacco. I could stop and watch and soon I would see the usual slow direction of male traffic coming and going. The women had eyes with that shiny look being fresh from the love bed. One merchant shop that I entered had tiger bones and skins for sale. In some jars, there appeared to be organs. Both of these items in Southeast Asia are prized for their potency as medicines and as aphrodisiacs. Late in the afternoon I stopped in a small Vietnamese restaurant and ordered com co dau, a rice dish steamed in lotus leaves, and com cao lau, a dish of mussels, mixed with garlic, fish sauce, peanut sauce, banana flowers and rice. Both of these dishes were a specialty of Hue. As I ate, I listened to the unceasing, dull hum of motors on the streets and the subdued, musical murmur of many people. By this time, I had found the Vietnamese people in general to be inquisitive, generous and warm. However, a few hard-eyed civilian-garbed individuals glared at me now and then. I held their steady stare, locked in challenge. I resolved to myself that I had to always watch my back and never let these hard-eyed men remain there. I would always make sure that there were other people around and that I paid attention to my surroundings and possible avenues of escape, if I should find myself in a tight spot. I knew that if the end were to come, no matter what the situation, I would find myself alone.

Fogged In

All too soon I had to hitch another helicopter ride, return to Danang and go back to the mountains. I stopped briefly at a Chinese restaurant and bought myself some delicious steamed buns filled with pork and cilantro to munch on during the flight back. Eventually, I found myself back in Danang, hitching a ride on the familiar C-123 workhorse. It was a short ride. The aircraft buffeted and kicked around, bringing me back to reality. I had no sooner quit my daydreaming than we flew up the valley. We should have been at the escarpment at the end of the strip of Khe Sanh, but when I looked out one of the windows I could not see anything. We were in the clouds. I was already disoriented and scared as hell. I went forward into the cockpit area and the navigator was as close as he could get to the pilots. We had already circled the area once. There was nothing outside that they could see, except solid fog. These two particular pilots were on their first milkrun into Khe Sanh and were unfamiliar with the area. The navigator's experience and instinct was supervising their banking turn. I told them they were circling in between the mountains. The pilot told me the navigator had made this run many times and had the situation in hand. Our camp radio operator told them the ceiling was very low. I watched the fog whisk past the porthole window. It was still solid. The navigator told me to buckle up, and as I did so, the aircraft banked into one more circling turn and started its approach to the strip. I was the only passenger. Anesthetized by fear, I sat, calm and deliberate, in the eerie silence. I just knew that we were going to splatter all over the mountain. We were making a dizzying descent. I watched through the porthole as the aircraft slowly descended and soon we were in the open, below the ceiling. I could see we were approaching the escarpment at the end of the airstrip. The ceiling was very low. Then euphoric relief flooded over me as we plunged out of the fog. At the parking ramp, I had to tell the navigator he did a good job. The aircraft was quickly gone again. The clouds' tendrils were now approaching ground level. Soon the camp was cold and wet, and dripping everywhere. We were fogged in. If only the fog had settled in before I got back, I would still be in the Riverside Motel in Danang, suffering with the lovelies.

Making Bricks

Upon my return, I was put back to heavy labor, helping to build our new camp's defensive positions. Daily I took a convoy of vehicles from the airstrip up Route 608, a dirt road running northwest of our new camp following parallel to the Rao Quan River below the road. Along this route I always took a long hard look at Hill 558, which overlooked the road, and the one behind it to the southeast, Hill 861 at XD 803442, approximately 1300 meters west of us. Hill 861 would later be highly contested and fought for by the Marines in the defense of Khe Sanh in 1968. We made maximum use of local resources, running patrols out along the streams until we found the right aggregate materials for making bricks consolidated in the same general area. We did this right under the noses of the NVA. We were ambushed only once, while hauling this material back in trucks to our camp.

Building the Bunkers

The underground command bunker was located approximately in the center of the camp. Naturally it had to be closer to our team house than anything else. To build this underground bunker required a lot of manpower along with wheelbarrows, pick and shovels, and a lot of demolitions to make everyone's work easier. The underground bunker, the four corner bunkers and all mortar positions were hardened and their ammunition storage areas were built underground. Men were able to sleep in all of these positions if needed. All four corner bunkers, contained positions for five pedestal-mounted machine guns, which had clear fields of fire, ammo storage areas and built-in bullet deflectors. Our mortar system was unique. In the center of the pit we marked the area needed for a truck tire to be dug, then measured an area of two-feet wide and laid in cement to contain the tire, while leaving a five-inch slot for a wooden runner. The mortar bipod legs were attached to the wooden runner, so they could be slid around in the slot in a complete circle. We fit the 81mm mortar base-plate into the tire, and where the three flanges on the underside of the plate marked the rubber tire, we cut through these places and the steel belt so that the base-plate would fit snugly into the rubber tire. We then packed the inside of the tire with sandbags filled with clay. The result was a base plate that did not move or shift its position. It remained completely stable, no matter how many times it was fired. This resulted in only one initial registration for all four sides of the camp. From then on, it was merely shifting fire from a known point to the location of a target, which the observer identified on the ground. All concentrations were painted right on the wall and marked on our radios for each position, with the elevation and charge setting noted, so that immediate fire could be placed on the target indicated. When our commander called for a certain concentration on the north, east, south or west wall, we merely grabbed one leg and slid the legs around to the required wall. The bipod legs were permanently set on the sliding wooden runner. We never needed to use the sight. Without the sight on the mortar, we merely eyeballed the alignment of the dovetailed slot for the sight with the necessary line on the wall for direction. We would fire one round at a designated area. An observer noted the burst in relation to the observer-target line and gave us an adjustment. The deviation was given as "right" or "left" in meters and the range as "over" or "short" in meters. If no correction was needed to burst location, the word "repeat" was given. How much of a shift we needed from an indicated registered concentration resulted in how much of a pull on the legs we gave. This gave us our direction. We leveled the elevation bubble and cut the charge on the round itself by removing a set number of powderbags, and dropped the round down the tube. Our system only required one initial registration in the beginning when we selected concentrations. This had required only one evening of work. Thereafter, we could hit any target and shift from any known concentration to a brand new target and immediately hit it. It took no time. Those who came to our camp never knew how we did this. Inspectors always called the targets. After the test, they would always just walk back to the team house for coffee shaking their heads. They didn't understand how we not only hit the targets they picked, but how fast we did it. Their confusion was always a great source of amusement to us. But then, we were good.

The Marines Landing

During our breaks of hard labor building the camp, we listened to the news on the radio and read the newspapers to supplement what we learned from the intelligence reports. On the night of 7 February 1965, about two hours after a seven-day ceasefire had been declared for the Lunar New Year celebration, the II Corps advisory compound and air base at Pleiku in the central highlands, was attacked by 30 North Vietnamese Army commandos using mortars and 57mm recoilless rifles. At the same time, the nearby airfield at Camp Hollaway was attacked, damaging 15 aircraft. A total of nine Americans were reported killed and 128 wounded. During this time, the strength of our armed forces in South Vietnam was listed as 23,590 men. The North Vietnamese forces were on the offensive. On 8 March 1965, we knew without a doubt that something was going drastically wrong in Washington because there was the landing of the 9th Marines Expeditionary Force at Danang, backed up by two platoons from the 3rd Marine Tank Battalion. Reportedly, they were to insure the security of the airfield there. But Special Forces and Air Force reconnaissance had forewarned of the large numbers of PAVN units infiltrating the Western Highlands. On 18 August 1965, American Marines conducted the first, large major ground operation of the Vietnam War in Quang Tri Province, south of Chu Lai. During Operation Starlight, the Marines conducted the first preemptive "spoiling attack" of the war to prevent an attack on the Marine base at Chu Lai. Operation Starlight was supported by a helicopter insertion to the west. A company of the 2nd Battalion, 4th Marines immediately confronted the dug-in Viet Cong 60th Battalion, holding the high ground. The Marines had 45 men killed and the 1st Viet Cong Regiment was rendered combat ineffective in this operation. Six other amphibious vehicles would be heavily damaged in heavy fighting on the Van Tuong Peninsula, south of Chu Lai. The small covert operation in Vietnam was now growing into a huge military operation. Now I understood why the Marine officers had been attached to our team, because a much wider involvement had been planned from the beginning. The nature of the war had just changed and Army commanders would be slow to pick up on this. By the end of the Vietnam War, the U.S. Marines would suffer 13,065 men killed-in-action and 88,633 wounded in action.

The 9 February 1965 battle of Binh Gia in Phuoc Tuy Province, where the well organized and well led 33rd South Vietnamese Ranger Battalion was surrounded and destroyed. My friend, Ranger advisor Sergeant Harold G. Bennett, was taken prisoner. The communists took a unit three to four times their size, in this case a reinforced regiment, and sucked them into an open U formation and then slowly closed in on them until there was no way out. The North Vietnamese then slaughtered them. Slowly over time, the loss of these well-trained professionals and units would take its toll on the army of South Vietnam and the United States because of this piecemeal use of elite units. We were killing and wounding 1,000 noncombatants a week later in this war. This was the fault of those military officers sitting behind desks or in the field who had no real experience in warfare, having served and earned their ranks in a peacetime United States Army. It was also the fault of the civilians who maintained control of the American Army in Southeast Asia, misusing the military and risking our lives with no clear intention of winning. It was evident to all of the professional soldiers that a war cannot be run from Washington. The professional commanders in the field had to have freedom of movement. If General William C. Westmoreland, one of America's greatest generals ever, had been allowed to use our training assistance and leadership in the field and logistical support to invade Laos and North Vietnam, to choke off the PAVN infiltration and resupply effort, things may have been very different.

Medical

We built large, covered, screen-enclosed latrines for our native troops that would accommodate a squad of men at one time. We actually had to instruct the troops how to use the latrine. Their way was to squat on the ground, while taking a dump naturally. However, they considered it dirty and nasty to sit on a toilet seat while performing the same task. We had water and cleaning material right on hand in the latrine before each seat, but they were unaware of what it was for. Although we had our own latrine inside the team house, the entire team was instructed by the Team Captain to use the indigenous troop latrine for a period of time so that they could see how it was done. Instead of going to our own latrine in our underwear and shower shoes at night, we had to partially dress and strap our .45 cal pistol on and leave the team house to use the latrine. We found that old habits persist, because at night, groggy with sleep, we would invariably sit on a seat where someone had squatted with his feet on the seat leaving everything the boot soles had picked up. That wasn't the worst of it, but you can use your imagination for the rest. We learned. At night we had to carry a flashlight to check the seat before using. We were all very happy when the Team Captain no longer required us to use their latrine.

Flies

We had to teach our troops everything, and one was how to deal with their own waste, as it bred flies. One job that I particularly did not like was dealing with our human waste. Under each toilet seat was a half-barrel. To access these barrels we had hinged doors on the outside of the latrine. We had a hook that we dragged the barrels out with daily. We used a mixture of gasoline and diesel fuel, a longer burning mixture, to incinerate the contents. I used a metal stake to stir the raw sewage while it was burning. Naturally, I learned to stand upwind to avoid the smell of burning feces the best I could, but I had this very brief job just on the few days when the air was hot and humid and most oppressive. To stir, I naturally had to be right there in the black smoke. It reminded me of lumpy molasses. After it burned a while, a layer of ash accumulated on the surface and then I had to mix it up well again. I did this over and over; all the while the level was dropping until there was nothing left. I was very happy when our indigenous troops understood how this was done and I no longer had to demonstrate how to burn feces.

Water

At minimum, people need about half a gallon of water a day for drinking and a total of 1.3 gallons to enable them to wash. Our covered water cistern in the old French fort we lived in while building the new camp depended upon harvesting rainwater. We used the runoff from the constant rain to keep our cistern filled. It had to be inspected frequently because rats often were drowned in it. And someone was always putting a dead rat in it. Nothing turns you off quicker than to inspect your cistern and find a bloated rat's body breaking the surface of the water level. We would periodically clean it. Because of the rats, we had to use chlorine to disinfect the water, a dangerous practice.

Water was also one of our first problems as we started building the camp. We were particularly worried about cholera, a waterborne bacterial disease that is likely to spread in warm weather. Cholera is a natural part of our ecology; it is in every country's environment. Vietnam was a coastal country, and because of a lack of sanitation services, acute diarrhea, severe dehydration, and death, were a common occurrence, throughout the entire country. During the October and November rainy season, the bacteria in the ocean is carried up the rivers during the high tides and contaminates the water supply. After the people get sick, the sewage flows back into the ocean. This cycle is continuously repeated.

Poor water quality and cholera were intertwined and symptomatic of a larger problem foreshadowing other health threats. Tainted water and uncooked food were the cause of cholera. When people become sick with the bacterium causing cholera, they cannot take in water and they go into shock. They become very sick and die if they do not receive medical help. Infected people's muscles and sinews would cramp, causing vomit and excrement to shoot out of their body, as they turned skeletal with a skull-like head. Special Forces medics had a hard time weaning superstitious villagers and small rice and sugar cane farmers away from disease-carrying pond water that were often shared by village people and livestock, such as ducks, and water buffalo. Cholera and diarrheal diseases flourished in these waters and made many people sick. One trip to their latrine areas provided ample visual evidence of this. These bacteria could be deadly, one-celled microorganisms. Many of the villagers, especially the old and infirm, drank polluted water. Cholera can be averted with clean water and good hygiene. Hepatitis, upper respiratory infections and acute intestinal diseases like dysentery were all around. Water was sold in Vietnam. It was considered safe if it smelled of woodsmoke, meaning that it had been boiled a full half-hour.

Medcaps Among the Bru

Three of us usually escorted the medic on his rounds of the villages along Highway 9. Only once did I escort the medic below the escarpment, near the limit of our operational area. However, I went several times in our immediate operational area to the different villages, made up of small and large communal long houses. In the villages, the practice of using the streams from which they took their drinking water was the reason so many people had worms. For the mountain tribes, you had to convince the shaman and village chief that the spirit of well water from an underground aquifer was better than the spirit of the stream or river water. I noticed on these trips that there were many children. The reason that there were so many children was that among the Bru tribe, it was common for a young girl to marry at age 12 or 13 and start bearing children. Here, young girls going through puberty start developing breasts just past nine years of age. Typically, girls begin breast development about a year before their first period, when their reproductive organs become functionally active. The Bru, knowing that human development is unpredictable, waited until the time when the females had their first period around age twelve, and then they were considered ready to marry and start raising their own children. Once married, it was just a matter of hitting the fertile time of twelve to fifteen days after their menstrual cycle.

Among the Bru, an agrarian and hunting society like early Americans, the belief was that the more children they had the more hands there were to work and hunt their subsistence. These poverty-stricken Bru families would have up to 10 children. Infant mortality was high among the Bru and animal sacrifice was common to cure children's physical ailments. For instance, children with epilepsy were thought to be gifted, not ill, and therefore received no medical help. The children did not attend schools. They had no written language until 1963 when a missionary couple by the name of Miller organized and put to print their language. The Millers lived and worked in a Bru Village. I saw a copy of the book at the language school library at the Presidio in California.

In all the villages the most common ailment to be seen during a MEDCAP mission would be foamy white patches on the whites of the eyes, which show that the eyeballs are starting to deteriorate. Symptoms of malnutrition are common in this part of the world. Where there is a lack of vitamin A and clean water, trachoma will be common. The cornea of the eye suffers most. Blindness and night blindness are also common among men where fresh vegetables or fruit were not provided for long periods of time. The lack of vitamin A dries out the body's mucous membranes, increasing vulnerability to diarrhea, pneumonia and other diseases.

The Working Elephant

It was during one of these medical trips to a nearby village that I saw my first working elephant. As I approached the elephant it stiffened and stood more erect, raising its ears and head high. It swayed and huffed, sensing my different smell and color. Its ears twitched. It shook its head slightly. I stood nearby watching and taking pictures, detecting an almost imperceptible rumble or slight humming sound. The handler asked me if I heard the sound. The sound was the elephant's means of talking or communicating. However, there was no real audible sound, only the humming. The elephant's means of talking is beyond our threshold of hearing, which accounts for never hearing them on patrol. They are supposed to be able to communicate with each other over several miles' distance.

One of the most notable things I saw in these Bru villages was the belligerent Vietnamese potbellied pigs, which were allowed to roam around at will. They were often seen rooting in and around the villages acting as the village scavengers. They were an earth gray color with large bristling black hair that started at the top of their head and thinned as it ran down the top of their back. Most notable were their swayed back and large stomachs. Large, unneutered male pigs would grow tusks and were considered dangerous. Much to a roaming tiger's delight, they were easily located by smell and noted for their poor eyesight. All we had to do was keep our distance from the pigs and not smell like food, because their sense of smell was very good. Those pigs that had plenty to eat came to be a very large size. They were an important cash item, but had to be eaten immediately, because pork is quick to spoil.

Early in my first tour of guard duty, I noticed that the tribesmen and Vietnamese always used lights to go any place at night. It was rare for me to see someone moving without a light. They also depended heavily on their sense of hearing. During guard duty, I learned to walk softly and found I could approach them in the dark easily. I would stop at a little distance and then watch and then speak to identify myself. They were always startled. I spent a lot of my time on guard, sitting in the dark where I could watch for anyone approaching our team house, and listening for the little musical pinging sounds of strands of barbed wire parting, announcing bad guys coming to visit. I watched everything these people did, and tried to understand why they did what they did. I did this to try to understand what their advantages and disadvantages were to themselves and myself.

Pay Day

Our camp had a lot of ghosts. According to a time-honored custom, the Vietnamese camp commandant had been defrauding the military treasury by collecting the pay of dead men, deserters, and ghost recruits. To avoid this practice, our team commander had to insure that at each muster an accurate count of personnel was made and that the camp roster was accurate and always up to date. He was present each payday to see each individual paid. Our team Captain always checked the troop rosters and found where the officers were defrauding their military. The captain kept an original list of the men who were present when we arrived and found where soldiers that had been killed or transferred were kept on the books. Captain Allen made up rosters and made the men sign for their pay after their name. When recruits were called for, invented names were entered on the rosters. The imaginary recruits and the dead are sent on "detached duty," to places that were made up. Their pay was still being drawn and kept by the Vietnamese camp commander and the company commanders. They failed to create savings for the imaginary soldiers kept on the books.

Troop Entertainment

At night after we moved into the new camp, we rigged a screen in the mess hall of our team house for showing films to entertain our troops. We would show western movies, such as John Ford's glittering production of "She Wore A Yellow Ribbon." It was a favorite of our Chinese mercenaries (Nungs) and of Bru tribesmen, who always cheered the Indians in the film. Among the tribesmen you heard a clucking of tongues and saw their glittering eyes as they watched the Indians. Looking around the darkened room, the glitter of eyes revealed the screen had their full attention. Most of these warriors had never seen a movie in their lives, and their childlike delight was readily apparent. We served cold refreshments and a good supply of low-grade twist tobacco leaf and Vietnamese Ruby Queen cigarettes to the troops, which they always enjoyed with the film. The air was always thick with old gray smoke. When we turned the lights on to change the reel, you would see their smiling faces, puffing at their small wooden pipes. Blue threads of smoke were woven all through the mess hall. We could smell the twist tobacco everywhere.

**Warriors, proud and strong are
too soon gone--Their rain
wind and thunder moves to
silence in the Highlands**

Author

CHAPTER 7

BORDER SURVEILLANCE

Tribal Village
During the 20th century, the Bru tribe trekked into Southeast Asia, having been driven out of China by the Communists. Their area was located in northwestern South Vietnam and in the contiguous areas of Laos: the Kha Leung plateau west of the Laotian Annamite Mountains and across the 17th Parallel into North Vietnam.

Bru Characteristics
These were a people who carved their homes from a mountain forest, which knows no mercy. The Bru built their communal long houses on the south side of the Khe Sanh mountain plateau, exposed to the warm sun and protected from the winds. These houses were made of solid wood teak logs on top of 8 to 10 upright log poles with bamboo or small sapling floors and grass thatch roofs. They served several couples, their children, and assorted relatives. Entrance was made by a

notched-pole log or more conventional type ladder to an open-air platform well above the ground. They also offered protection from panthers, bears and cobras. The panther, different than the tiger, fears man and therefore hunts man at night, in and around villages. This man-eating animal is very difficult to kill. The Bru warriors were shaped and tempered in a harsh environment. Unlike the Vietnamese, they were reclusive and secretive, and had their own dialect and tradition of oral speech derived from Chinese. They spoke a non-tonal language full of vowel, consonant and diphthong sounds. At the time of our insertion into the area, a local missionary family was working on the first permanent written language for the Bru.

Among the patriarchal Bru, the social structure was simple. The head of the family was the oldest male member, responsible to the head of the clan. The clan leaders were responsible for the welfare of all the members of the clan. The leaders were subordinate to the village chief. Within each clan, one member was responsible for traditional behavior patterns. One example was reverence for the spirits. The tribe never questioned the authority of the village chief, himself subordinate to the Vietnamese district chief. The tribe's economy was dependent upon raising cattle, some farming of wild brown rice, hunting with crossbows and spears, and the gathering of wild fruits and tubers.

The Shaman

A village chief controls the tribe. He is in turn controlled by the shaman. Fears that the tribesmen experience in their daily lives are present in their sleep. Many young men reportedly died in terror in their sleep. According to their relatives, they died with terror on their face, fighting for their breath. These incidents made their spirit world an everyday reality. The Shaman brightens and clarifies the dark world of spirits for the Montagnard tribes. The Shaman and his magic, stands between the people and the spirit world. They included among their practices traditional Chinese acupuncture. It was used to relieve physical pain and those health problems resulting from functional ailments of the body. I was always amazed when I saw it put to use. The Shaman first used the tips of his fingers to find and apply point pressure (acupressure) to various parts of the body that would relieve symptoms in other parts of the body. Usually I would see the aging medicine man use his steady fingers to find the centers of pain and nerves, while talking to the individual. He would then draw an elaborate colored design on the back that ended in circular designs of the pain and nerve centers. Then, into the center of these circles, his nimble fingers twirled the needles, inserting them into the body. I watched as mostly older people endured the short-term discomfort of the long protruding needles to treat the nerve and muscle-related illnesses. This practice was used as an anesthetic to kill pain and to perform other minor operations that required cutting. It was also used to rest the patient comfortably. The needles triggered the release of endorphins, the body's natural pain relievers. Prior to use, the needles were tipped with the medicinal mugwort and sterilized over a flame. The mugwort would be lit with a match, and its slow, barely noticeable burning would warm the needle and its heat would be transferred into the nerves. Thereby the tension was relieved. In all the cases I witnessed, the patient, being relieved of the pain, was soon asleep. Usually the needles, contained in small pieces of bamboo, were encased in a small box. Always, I came away thinking that Western medicine left a lot to be desired, because we relied strictly upon chemicals to induce the same effects.

The Interrogation

Since prisoners of war were valuable sources of information on our area of operations, I was invited to watch an interrogation. The prisoner was captured on one of our patrols. The interrogator had a half-smile on his face. However, under hooded lids, his deep-set, small and cold eyes reflected something more ominous: the hard edge of cruelty. He had started confidently and aggressively with his questioning. The prisoner was largely silent. As I watched the cruel interrogation, I noticed that a subtle change had taken place in the interrogator as he went to work, landing a blow to the head and shoulder. When the standing man refused to answer, the interrogator would strike him with a short stout hardwood club. I felt the bile rise in my throat and swallowed nervously. The prisoner did not flinch once while being struck. He would stagger slightly and then again stand upright, shaken and sober. I moved around where I could see the prisoner's face, as he stared at a place just above the interrogator's head. Exposure to the elements had given his smooth-skinned face the color of mahogany. I now watched very closely. He stood erect, his facial expression determined and dignified, sort of insolent. He was relaxed with arms folded at his chest. I saw the sudden hardening of his expression. Still showing no fear of pain, his eyelids hardened. Only his eyes had gone small and sharp in defiance, and a kind of angry resolve showed in his lips. I could see that he knew if he must die or be beaten, he would do it with dignity. He refused to give them the satisfaction of losing his dignity.

What I saw was unnerving, not only to me but to the interrogator. There in the steady eyes of the prisoner was the look of the wild and unconquered: the look of a wild beast of prey, eyes unafraid, staring back. He showed no weakness. In the beginning I had felt sorry for the prisoner. I now felt proud to know that there were such men, even if they were our enemy. He never once flinched at being struck so hard, but there is a limit to endurance. I knew that I never wanted to be in the prisoner's place. It was a sickening display of violence, but it was necessary.

The Field Telephone

There was a field telephone whose wires were wrapped onto a finger and toe of the well-secured prisoner seated in a sturdy chair. Cranking it generated a direct current. The prisoner's unsophisticated mind did not understand that the cranking would not kill him, but merely help him lose his control, if possible. A little water was used to help the contacts. The telephone was cranked, arching his body in the chair as the low electrical charge raced through his body. I could see the prisoner was now visibly unnerved and distressed, fear shone in his dark eyes. He reached his limit. Again, a current raced through his body, jarring his nerve centers, making him gasp as if in a pained spasm. A noticeable tic now appeared at the corner of his mouth. He now exhibited fear of this slight pain. I could now detect that his fear of this strange pain was worse than the pain itself. He was now rigid and anxious, clinging to the chair with his whole body, in anticipation of the electrical charge; he had reached the point at which there was no reserve of heart or nerve left. The charge became more intense because he could not relax. I could see that he felt terribly threatened. Fear never left him. His breathing became harder and his eyes were wide and panicked. The interrogator made a visible show of the moment he would crank the electricity, while watching the prisoner contort his body to try to avoid the pain. This went on for half an hour. As each charge sent his body rising in a taut arch, he emitted a low moan after each charge. His entire body began to tremble.

The interrogator allowed a rest break. The prisoner sat rigidly in the chair. As he was allowed to relax for questioning, his body slumped. He sweated. I could see he was defeated by a simple interrogation technique that was beyond his comprehension. I had this technique used on me many times in training, and was well aware that it was harmless but very uncomfortable. It had not been used sadistically, such as on his penis or rectum. When he finally began to talk to the interrogator, they had to listen carefully because his mouth barely moved and he talked so low from exhaustion. What I learned during this interrogation was that the fear of pain was worse than the pain itself.

Aerial Reconnaissance

Shortly after the interrogation, I was told that I was again scheduled for patrol, and that the next day an O-1 Bird Dog (L-19) aircraft would be available at the airfield for an aerial reconnaissance and observation of our planned route. I looked forward to it; this aircraft had proven to me it was nimble and versatile. This flight was a great diversion from my normal workday. We checked the trails leading south along the border and inland. I watched for the bright little flashes that meant someone was shooting at us. Through the low scrub, I got a brief glimpse of a large running tiger. The beautiful, orange-black color stuck in my mind.

We saw no activity at all except for one incident in the mountains away from the border. *A pathway!* Looking closer, I saw there was a hidden structure under the trees cunningly concealed. If we had not been flying low, we would not have seen it. We attempted to get a better look under the trees in one place. I watched carefully as we approached, but saw nothing. As we flew over at two hundred feet, still nothing. As I looked back, I saw the silent flashes from the ground and heard the nearby popping sounds of small-arms fire. Only after we had passed by did they fire at us. I informed the pilot and he turned, gaining altitude. He marked the area, and requested any strike aircraft available and flew on. Evidently no one was available for a strike, or it would take too long.

As we flew north of the airfield at Khe Sanh, I saw a solitary bull elephant high up on the mountain in the tall waving grass. He was just standing there. I looked for others of his kind nearby, but there were none. Evidently he was large enough to have already left the family unit. After adolescence, the males leave and live a solitary life, except for brief periods when they breed. This was the only wild elephant I was ever to see. One of the other team members, SFC Dennis, I believe, reported seeing a large bull at close quarters on patrol. He had come into a small clearing, just when the elephant had done the same from the opposite direction. They had just stared at each other across the clearing. Then the elephant stiffened and his ears and trunk came up snorting loudly, a clear warning that an intruder was dangerously close to invading that most sacred domain: a bull elephant's personal space. Dennis quickly turned the patrol and went another way around.

The Substance of Nightmares

A new day found me up bright and early, well before dawn, making a last check of my equipment. *Another long patrol!* In the dark, I saw several other men moving silently through the fort to our assembly area. I had an ample amount of insect repellent. Men formed ranks and their packs were deposited on the ground to their front, with rifles on top.

Everyone made a last-minute adjustment of clothing and web gear. On a low command, each shouldered his pack, turned and was moving out through the darkened fort enveloped by a low hanging mist.

Beginning of Patrol

I remembered hearing on Radio Hanoi, Hanoi Hannah saying, "We will be seeing you." It was November, and the weather was good. Ahead stretched forbidding and impenetrable wilderness of shadowy paths. They were established by generations of Bru tribesmen, following the natural contours of the land through the steep, dark, hardwood forest-covered mountains. To patrol our area was to experience a pure feeling of isolation, a twilight world of dense stands of tall and mighty virgin forest, where the play of light and shade were music without sound. Many miles of incredibly dense low ridges below the thick forest were still dominated by beasts and primitive men.

Wildlife

We would often come across undulating herds of wild buffalo grazing, lowing among the shoulder-high, mineral-rich grass in the afternoons. The air was thick with the familiar rank, musty, acrid smells of a large herd. They were not easily forgotten. When our presence became known, buffalo were quickly on their feet, staring at us belligerently. They didn't move. At first, they were startled and frightened. I watched as their slobbering nostrils dilated. Some would huff and bellow. They drew in our scent to define it, shook their heads, pawing the landscape; then most of them relaxed, cropping the grass. Now and then, however, it was not uncommon that a bull would act differently--blowing enraged snorts of air, while pawing and kicking dirt, grass flying, and taking quick several steps in our direction before calming down. You could feel the earth tremble beneath the weight of their hooves. They were unafraid, and they let us know it by a shake of their head and posturing. Up close, the shoulders of the massive dull black body of the animals stood as high as my shoulders. The horns of many spread outward to a span of six feet. The tips of the horns curved wickedly upward. We were very careful to be quiet and keep moving slowly. Our rifles were always ready. They had been known to charge intruders. One thing was sure: if they did charge, you had to be prepared to shoot. I had seen soldiers try to kill domestic buffalo, and knew they were very difficult to kill. Like a soft breeze, our patrol slowly moved down out of the high country toward the river border and the sharp and thorny bramble patches common in the hot low areas.

The trail ran parallel to the river, overlooking grasslands and open forest. Mountainsides looming over the Se Pone's winding path. It had been used by generations of bare feet, and then by the boots of the Japanese and French.

There was little room for humor on patrol, but one day we managed to find it at a stream crossing. Our near side of the bank was low while the immediate opposite side was high. It became higher as it went upstream. After setting up security on our side to cover the opposite side, we sent one scout to wade cross the stream, climb the high bank and look around. He had no apparent trouble climbing the bank. As he reached the top with his head looking over the top, a swaggering giant gray-colored monitor lizard ran up to the edge of the bank; he was holding his fat, heavily-built body erect off the ground by strong thick limbs and large claws, looking for a weak, small, easy meal. I couldn't believe my eyes. It had to have been eight-foot long. Apparently it heard the muffled noise or felt the vibration of the climber who chose that time to approach the top. A nimble, magnificent giant lizard with its monstrous head held high, met the scout face to face and with its unblinking black eyes, glared at him. Luckily, the startled scout avoided being bitten. He emitted a scream and immediately tumbled backward, down the high bank, and fell into the deep pool of the stream immediately below him. Everyone broke into laughter. The war was forgotten for just the moment. I say the scout was "lucky" because this large lizard with such a large head could have inflicted a painful wound with its large teeth and strong jaws. These great lizards were tree climbers. I only saw two monitors in Vietnam, the other in a tree, looking like a part of the giant limb.

We sent our scouts and a security team across the stream. After the opposite bank was scouted and secured, we crossed. The only hostile movement observed was in the slow-moving stream, kicked up from the detritus-littered bottom. The leeches swam smoothly and rhythmically, making a slow undulating movement through the water that was easily seen. They swam by, contracting the muscles along their back and bellies.

Unless our scouts came to a natural obstacle to our line of movement, they would be almost a half-day ahead of us. They were experienced and skillful. We had been hunted for days on our last patrol. Remembering the fear, we knew that there was no longer any such feeling among us, as "safe." The day we began our patrol, the river water was high and murky from recent rains. Often in the lower country, we would be traveling on hands and knees, bending and stooping to get under and through an endless maze of vines and creepers. The pace was slow. The physical exertion was nothing compared to the mental exercise of staying alert, which was extremely difficult. In the beginning, the heat sucked the vegetation dry and the high brushy areas were noisy. Always our bodies were covered with long sleeves and trousers because of the biting ants. We would be operating out of communication's range down along the border some twenty klicks through an area known as part of the infiltration corridor of the Troung Son Mountain Trail (Ho Chi Minh Trail). Though we had our standard platoon issue PRC-10 radio, it was useless. We also had the small black HT-1's for ground-to-air communications. A small utility transport, U-1 Otter made a daily courier flight into Laos so that we could communicate and relay a message through when he passed overhead.

As the days went by, we followed another higher trail. The land began to lead us up from the lowland into the dark veritable heart of the mountains. I took a last look at the high, thin clouds in the eastern sky, warning of yet another storm. Our patrol entered an area of primordial monsoon forest of 90-feet tall, where serpentine liana vines connected the unbroken leafy canopy of the forest. Little sunlight ever penetrated beneath the trees. It was forever dark and gloomy here. We were hidden among the shadows of green foliage above the river. I found myself at home in this unimaginable world. The sounds of the forest were hypnotic. I relaxed while listening and watching the incredible variety of singing birds that had begun to flutter and dart through the giant trees overhead, ecstatic with the morning light in their normal activity. Occasionally, a mechanical "*creeek* " was heard skyward. Quickly looking upward, we would see the noise was created by the feathers of a passing prehistoric-looking bird called the hornbill, as we swallowed down the sour taste of our empty bellies. Always, we suspiciously listened to the muted sounds of the smaller birds, the cackling and clucking of browsing jungle chickens[1] and the loud scolding calls of larger birds-- nature's sentinels. Noise in the mountain forest always meant the warning of unwanted guests: leopards, tigers or man. The birds were a vivid, colorful reflection of life itself. I never became tired of watching them. In other areas, as we continued to move, there were a variety of langurs, the common graceful vegetarian Asian monkeys whose digestive tract was compartmentalized like a deer's. The langurs lived on leaves and shrubs. The other kinds of monkeys with a digestive system like man had to pick around to find enough to eat, making their living on fruit and smaller creatures. They were commonly seen in the deep deciduous forest in Vietnam. They had a lanky body, with long, slender limbs and tail, and a well-developed thumb. They were usually active in the morning daylight, moving in large groups in search of food, often seen leaping from limb to limb in their travels in the deep deciduous forest.

As the thick forest again began to thin, groves of bamboo and liana vines began to thicken in trees, sprinkled with only a few bright spots of light across the forest floor. As we moved deeper into the forest, it became dark and gray. An impenetrable, perpetual dankness followed. Our tribesmen searched for the acrid hint of smoke in the slight breeze. We could smell each others unwashed body because of the heat contained by the large trees. The forest closed around us, and the daytime darkness and loud chatter of monkeys and birds overhead reinforced a suffocating sense of closeness, like a door slamming shut behind us. No matter how many times I traveled these main trails, I always had the same impression of them: that they always looked swept. They were too clean.

Watching and Listening for an Omen

In these mountains, our physical well-being was entirely dependent on cooperation between the Bru and ourselves. The tribesmen were great hunters with a reverent attitude toward their environment. The Bru were an intelligent people, and great trackers. They detected animal odors held in a state of suspension. At night, listening further to the wind-stirred forest's moaning, a falling tree, the nearby brook's murmur, night birds and some animals, you could almost see and feel a shape emerging out of the mist in the darkness. According to their beliefs, Mr. Tiger or "Bok-Klia" knew how to imitate other animals' cries, as well as the speech of man. The first time I smelled a tiger that had just crossed the trail ahead of us, I had to be told what it was by one of the tribesmen and I never forgot the rank odor. To maintain my own survival instincts, I paid close attention to their expertise in jungle lore. I would try to emulate their cunning, craft and stealth. They were careful about listening and knew how to distinguish the sounds of the forest. The nocturnal noises of these vast mountains were weird and strange. The Bru would constantly stand their heads cocked, waiting, always listening for something. Our greatest enemy always arrived at sunset. As the sun would slip below the horizon, I would hear Ratchford's low voice say, "Here they come." As always, I heard the high-voltage "hummmm" of mosquitoes. It was sometime during these early days that I became infected. We again moved cautiously down near the river.

Sniper Attack

Across the river, hidden somewhere behind the palm trees, high grass, vines and creepers that grew in profusion down and over the bank, a sniper sought a target. There was one clear area on that same side the embankment, covered with thick sun-cured hummocks of long grass. My experienced patrol partner SSG. Haynes had told me to let the tribesmen get the water because if whoever might be watching the river was a Montagnard, he would not shoot one of his kind. I didn't feel like drinking from a canteen that might have a leech in it, so I had decided to go for my own water. I sat above the river on the high bank inside the brush watching before moving down to the water. While I was searching the foliage of the high, opposite bank, my eye caught vigorous motion on the water. I watched the visually beautiful ripples created by the motion. The only thing moving was a large snake gliding through the water, leaving in its wake the ever-widening semi-circular ripples.

Somewhere on the far bank a bird chattered, and then I felt it. I felt the eyes of something watching. I shrugged it off, telling myself it was nothing. I was nervous. I quickly moved down the steep bank to the water's edge. Dry-mouthed, I prostrated myself belly down on my hands and toes to drink. I pushed back and up into a squat and filled my canteens. The flap of a bird taking flight noisily in alarm on the far bank alarmed me. I experienced a numbing intense sensation. *Something---or someone?* I had just finished filling my canteen and felt the hair on my neck stiffen. The sudden unnatural quiet was unsettling. There was only the sound of the water, faintly lapping at the shore. As I put the canteen back in its pouch, I had the sensation of being watched. Then like a light in my head being turned on there was a feeling of a watching presence. I felt panicked and tried to remain calm, feeling the faint rush of blood to my temples, panic now screamed at me. Barely breathing, I fought to control myself and remain calm, to relax the pounding rhythm of my heart. Overwhelmed by a brute fear, I tasted the aluminum rush of adrenaline at the back of my throat. My eyes quickly focused across to the high stream bank to the tall grasses there and searched the cover of the opposite bank. I now feared what I could not see. I was too far from any cover. As I jerked up in turning to run, the sonic sounds of two bullets cracking close over my head startled me. Now my blood was pounding through my veins.

A shooter was firing from a relatively close range and instead of concentrating on just one of us, he was switching from one to the other of us in the open. Another burst sent tall, liquid shafts exploding up from the river's edge where I had just been squatting. I sprinted about twenty feet up the steep bank and went down behind a small log lying in the open. The bullets were cracking viciously all around. Suddenly I was afraid. The log was not only small, but it was also rotten. Two more bullets whistled past my ears like the fine whisper of hissing death, spraying a stinging cloud of fine sand over me. I heard a "whop." There was the sound of lead smacking against flesh and cracking bone, and one tribesman lay wounded. He cried out. I turned my head and peered up the slope.

I saw men quickly run out, snatch up an arm and a leg, and lift the wounded man. His head was slung back and wagging in semi consciousness, as they lumbered up and into the cover of the brush. For a moment, I was glad, so glad that it wasn't me that had been shot. I could hear Haynes yelling at me, but I couldn't hear a thing except the sonic cracks over my head and the pounding of blood in my ears. Confusion and doubt momentarily struck me. Then I leaped up and again sprinted for the top of the embankment and cover, as bullets kicked up spouts of earth. The air rang with a loud explosion behind me. A second explosion shook the air. As I entered the brush, there was SSG Haynes laughing at my enormous eyes and stupefied expression. He had covered me the whole time and had used the M-79 on the only visible target across the river--a hut that was now in shattered pieces and still in the air along with plumes of smoke. Haynes had disintegrated it and other likely areas. Luckily for me, the shooter firing at us was not concentrating on just one of us at a time and therefore was not as effective as if he had concentrated on just one. The NVA now knew we were here. Getting a medical evacuation for the tribesmen who were lightly wounded would now complicate our problem. We checked on the wounded. One died while we attended to him, I saw his head go back and his fixed eyes bulge. Then his pupils contracted and suddenly went wide. I had my first of many lessons in warfare. I had been too rash.

Our bodies and minds were now alert. We now knew they were aware of our presence and that they would make best use of their bamboo telegraph. They would be after our patrol, and we were now slowed, carrying wounded personnel. This incident taught me that I had not followed good advice and that my enthusiasm was a positive handicap. I had taken a foolish risk, failing to think about the possible outcome. I would have to model myself after SSG Haynes and develop a more patient and stable character if I wanted to develop the capacity for survival. Now I was determined never again to ignore my instincts. We were now going to be the hunted. We followed a dry, rocky runoff, which would only have water when it rained again. We used the rocks to hide our trail. Periodically, the rear security would drop off one side of the trail and watch our back trail.

We moved away from the vicinity of the river in a zigzagging route, trying to lose any tracker following, as the western mountains were backlit by the setting sun. Our wounded would have to endure for the time being. After stopping for the night, I checked the area for snake holes and nests, and ant or termite colonies, and then watched our back trail for a long time. As night deepened, the smell of damp earth, and a sweet, tangy, soothing scent grew stronger. With the moon behind me, I stood in deep shadows close to the trunk of a tree on the shadow side. My eyes swept from side to side, concentrating on the better-lighted patches to my front. The more I watched, the more I became aware of the shadows and the tricks of the moonlight and their effect on my mind. Finally, I forced myself to sleep. No one had been observed following us, but that didn't mean a thing. They would be looking and planning.

The sharing of food tightened the bond between the tribesmen and us. I got used to the pungent aura of nuoc mam, a fish sauce used on our rice. Before long I would become addicted to it. All of these indigenous people drank the blood of birds or consumed it jelled for extra energy. The blood of birds has about twice as much sugar as the blood of mammals. Our Vietnamese counterparts shared their sweet potatoes, and balls of sticky rice mixed with salt and crushed peanuts, or alternately with a mixture of minced meat, red chilies, maize and corn. They all were quite good. I always carried and shared cans of boned chicken with them. During our close contact with each other, there were always the broad, smiling, scarred faces looking into our light-colored eyes. They wondered greatly about our different complexions, eye color, hair color and features. Our light skin color was always a source of amusement to the tribesmen. They frequently rubbed my skin on my exposed forearm, pulling at the light-colored hair, then rubbing the skin in the vicinity of freckles and silently laughing.

    Later, while I was performing my nightly vigil, standing motionless, watching and listening, I happened to notice a winged hunter. My attention was drawn to the sound of rapid wing beats. A large, almost black hawk caught a bat in flight. Later, still awake, I watched patches of ground fog develop and move like ghosts among the trees. Stars began to cross the black arc of sky. The only sound's, were from shrilling insects, croaking tree frogs and toads, and some anonymous night bird uttering a hauntingly plaintive call, occasionally joined by passing swoop of a bat. I had resolved to myself to silently listen late every night and early each morning, to expand my senses and awareness so that I could pick up on any disturbance or possible intrusion. I had no idea how long this war would last, but I wanted to be one of its survivors. The fiery arrogance that I had when I left Okinawa was now gone. In its place, were new skills, an acute awareness of all sounds and movement in the mountain forest. They would provide me with the confidence and security to be a survivor.

The Tiger

    Once I awoke to a nocturnal chorus punctuated by a tiger's distant, deep-throated, echoing cough resounding through the forest. It was a long, drawn-out *Aaaaoooommmmnnn* echoing through the forest. I was not certain that I had heard a tiger. Paralyzed, I listened more intently in awe and with a renewed passion for life. There it was again. *Aaaaoooommmmnnn!* It was a large tiger. Tigers are solitary, and come together only to mate. Its roar seemed to echo within its chest. He was prowling for prey, calling for a female, or warning us to stay out of his territory. The tiger was not impressed by our presence. We must have been close to an established scent post that identifies the animal and announces his presence to intruders. Upon finding a female's urine-sprayed tree, a male tiger would emit a thunder-like roaring, then lie down and wait. The low resonant, echoing sound was a deep-chested "*EE-o-ungh! OOoo-oo-ongh!*" that roared through the night. It was a rising, isolated sound that fell back into silence. None of us slept too soundly, but I was happy that I had been able to hear the sound. I lay down again. I slept with my rifle cradled in my arms, the receiver protected between my legs, always listening to the forest around me. I could hear those near me. Their breathing was deepening and becoming rhythmic, and I knew they were sleeping. A lone man at night in these mountains could not afford to sleep. Many days passed without incident. The lesson we learn from the tiger is that we must hunt slowly and silently at all times. He is the symbol of darkness and the new and full moon.

Living off the Land

The gnawing pit of my stomach was rumbling. We had shared all our food, and now after two weeks we shared the hunger. I tried to swallow down the sour taste of my empty stomach. After the many days on our long patrol, we were again without rations. Here in this wilderness, there were no fantasies, only the absolute truth of survival. Largely our diet now was tubers, dug from below the ground. Staying alive while being hunted by human hunters, these were facts modified only by time. I went hungry a lot and my stomach had shrunk. My mouth and throat felt dry. I began to feel light-headed from an empty belly. Spasmodic rumbling and general discomfort of the stomach followed our hunger pangs. Sleep was one way to relieve the painful feeling of an empty stomach. I also knew that if I kept my stomach filled with water, it wouldn't complain as loudly. But the soothing caress of the water was soon gone, and the squeezing ache of gnawing hunger returned. Eventually, we reached a point in our hunger, past the pain, where it became insignificant. I felt flaccidity spread through my body. We now had to live off the land.

Bamboo

Feathery bamboo groves were often seen waving in the wind in the distance and encountered on the low areas of the river. The wild and extremely hardy groves thrived best in loam-type soil where sheltered from the wind. Bamboo is an important food source for the tribesmen. It is eaten for good digestion: the tea is used for peptic ulcers and bamboo broth or soup for hiatal hernia. Bamboo also acts as a stabilizer of the soil and prevents water runoff. The shoots are best harvested during the wet season, because then they are especially abundant. The young bamboo shoots protruding from the ground, if obtained before leafing out, serve as vegetables. We avoided the risk of cyanogen poisoning by boiling the shoots, then there was no risk involved. When the fibrous bamboo shoots first start poking out of the ground to about six inches, they are best for consumption. The shoots can be dug up and saved for a later meal. They are highly prized for their flavor and crunchy texture. We cut off the tip, washed it thoroughly, then boiled it in a helmet for two minutes and sliced it up, ready to eat. Bamboo groves are difficult to move in without making noise. We avoided them when moving.

Death Comes Courting

It was late afternoon, the kind of day when the fetid smells of the sun-heated foliage made the act of breathing a labored one. We were slipping up the trail, stopping and searching each new bend that followed a semi-dry rocky creek bed in a section of low terrain. The trees and other vegetation grew so tightly, thwarting our line of sight. Our heads were always turning slightly to catch sounds more clearly or to pick up the faintest sound of human activity. We were always sniffing the air for the mere trace of smoke or smoke-saturated uniforms of the NVA.

The afternoon's spectral and sonic cacophony of light and bird sounds that resounded through the trees and brush told us we were secure. The returning of one of our three scouts up ahead stopped our advance. After a much-whispered conversation, it was determined that the lead scout had come across a smooth-bottomed sandal track still filling with water at a wet place in the creek. Whoever had made it must have been in a hurry. The deeper part of the track had been at the ball of the foot. In a shared awareness, our imaginations ran rampant with speculation: An ambush might lie somewhere ahead around one of the bends. The possibility registered with pain in our heads, guts, nerve endings, and adrenal glands.

The other scouts had watched water fill a track the NVA had made. They were trying to determine how recently it had been made. In minutes, another scout returned. More whispered conversations. The two scouts had conducted a stationary visual search of that immediate area and determined that there were no other tracks, only the transfer of a little mud from his sandal on the smooth rocks. Some pebbles were pushed below their natural bed in the creek. A few stones' dark coloration change was evident from being turned from their bed. Some scuffmarks were made where he had gone hurriedly up the bank.

Understandably, fear may have kept the scouts from searching too far or too hard. The small bits of mud were flattened and smooth, except for that which fell from the side of his sandal. The extended stride was from east to west, moving toward the higher ground. The natives, indigenous to the area, didn't wear sandals. However, the NVA did. The lead scout had determined that the man was a soldier, alone, in a hurry, and traveling light. After making a comparison with his own track, he determined that the lone track had been made only minutes ahead of us. We reasoned that we had been shadowed and that the tracker following parallel to us had possibly determined our present direction of travel, and had now hurried ahead and cut across our trail ahead of us, "cutting for sign." Judging from the clean trail in both directions, it was possible that he was aware that he was ahead of us. Only one scout remained ahead, watching the area and listening.

Time now seemed to be standing still. The NVA tracker must have quickly crossed the trail, scanned it, and made the connection with what he didn't find. We decided to move on the way we had been going. A deep foreboding loomed within me, for somewhere in the deep shadows our greatest fear waited. Every man's nerves were tightly strung. Abruptly, the silence was broken by a single, ominous crack-thump of incoming fire. I winced. The rifle shot, fired well ahead of us, came from a vantage point. There was only the whisper of the wind, as the echoing boom of the shot trailed off through the small valley. Tingling with alarm, we all knew a warning shot had been fired. We knew that whoever had followed and scouted us had done it by traveling parallel to our formation. He knew the terrain well.

    Waiting long minutes with bated breath, we were filled with gut-wrenching uncertainty and anticipation. I could now feel the silence around me, raising bumps on my flesh. My chest felt tight, as if it were being squeezed. A high level of adrenaline was pumping into our blood streams. I could smell the acrid cold sweat on the men around me. It was the sickly-sweet odor of fear. The skin on the back of my neck began to crawl, my hair stood on end, and my heart raced. I could see the emotional experiences occurring from the sweat-beaded expressions on all the faces around me, the looks of anxiety. A troubled silence fell, heavy and expectant. Palms were sweating, as all the men prepared themselves mentally and physically to fight the unknown, the unseen. It was now very quiet. We had to be very careful.

    The point element was under the leadership of Haynes, our most experienced veteran. I saw him coming back down the file formation. His eyes were roving, a look of intense expectancy and awareness written all over him. He informed me that we were going to be ambushed. They were aware of our timely arrival and were now waiting on us with great expectations. Our immediate future course of action was now riddled with uncertainty. He had made a decision based upon previous situations, and his intuition and gut feelings. We were not going to be rash and be drawn into the area from which the shot was fired; rather, we would choose another direction, hoping that the NVA had not had enough time or personnel to completely ambush the whole area. This was a ruse using the shooter to decoy us into a large ambush. He then left immediately. From his manner and eyes, I could see that he was calm and relaxed. I had, however, observed the tension in his back. His palms had been sweating and his face was pale, as I am sure mine was.

Knowing that death was waiting, I let my thoughts leap to what lay ahead. I fought to remain calm. Panic would be my worst enemy. The fear made everything seem brighter and closer. The quiet seemed excessive. Reasonably relaxed and in stoic silence, we began to move slowly forward with caution, almost unwillingly, along the now treacherous scar of a trail. Our point element moved in a balanced control like the large striped cat, in a methodical, slow and deliberate harmony, in a concentrated meditation, which would hopefully help them see and hear all. No move was wasted. Fear and instinct now brought that familiar sick feeling to my stomach. It was unsettling to move calmly, given the sensation that we were now being watched by eyes of unseen soldiers, the certainty that violent death was waiting along the trail. You could sense the menace heavy in the air.

I would live or die. Like Haynes, I had to face my fear. I emptied my mind and concentrated on seeing everything around me. It was completely quiet; no birds called. Again, I felt the fear of what I could not see, and knew that my life might be lost already. But with my heart racing and the blood pounding in my veins, I felt more alive than ever. Our senses were now perfectly attuned to our environment. As the adrenaline began to stir in my limbs, my temples were pulsing. Glancing uneasily to each side, we now chose each step with great care, moving slowly. Our long file formation was now turning northwest on the trail and moving up a long slow grade of a hill that rose sharply on our left. This portion of the trail was now paralleling the direction along which the NVA tracker had earlier cut our unmarked trail. The lone shot was distracting suspicion from our immediate area for most of our troops. The trail now narrowed to pass over a low place in the hill, surrounded by trees and rough brush on both sides. Just below the slope was an ideal area to conceal an ambush. All were intent on their surroundings.

Sweat beaded Haynes' hardened face and trickled down his chest. There was a smooth flow to his movement. He moved, each step careful, eyes searching for danger. He was alert and alive, with a tightness around his mouth. His low and scanning eyes, hidden deep in the shadow of the hat's brim, searched from side to side and forward, constantly scrutinizing the silent maze of trees and light-starved saplings. The ground here was covered with dense undergrowth and single-canopy trees interlaced with creepers. He looked for the shine reflected from a watching face, movement, and the earth-tone colors of tan or black uniforms of the enemy. The patterns of trunks and limbs became wavering green and brown shadows, all casting a chaotic pattern on the forest floor through the first line of foliage. He searched his immediate shadow-dappled surroundings, knowing what would appear at the side of his vision. He watched for any odd angle or alterations, a sign of a shooting window, which would allow a clear shot through the thick latticework of ropy masses of vines and saplings. He studied the interlocked branches and tree trunks for a shade of color or low-silhouette shape out of place. His educated thumb intimately caressing the selector switch on his rifle, Haynes was sure-footed and steady as he approached the top of the hill. A faint breeze stirred the leaves as he tried to focus his eyes on something farther back in the cover. Then as a warning came the sudden manifestation of sour sweat and clothes saturated with wood smoke. Too late, he realized they were there, despite the fact that they were well concealed. The angry, staccato sound of a dozen bunched shots cracked against the hill. The sudden attack was followed by the methodical popping of AK-47's, then a ragged volley of answering fire. The echoes curled around the hill, slapping it again.

The Berserker
There was no holding back. A rapacious ugliness transformed Haynes' face. A fierce concentration showed. The point element moved quickly, led by the resolute staff sergeant. Like the berserker of old Viking legends, he immediately took the fight to the enemy. Fear had turned to anger, then fury. Finally, possessed by an ungovernable, maniacal rage, he

became strong. Rage steadied his nerves. With an abnormally heightened clarity of mind and an uncompromising courage, he immediately charged into the ambush. His finger on the trigger, he was unleashing an automatic burst to cover his advance.

Our assault element stopped their advance at the now-empty prepared positions. Some were stopped by more heavy brush. Haynes' mind registered the bullets whining and exploding bark off the trees and brush around him. Other members of the point were wounded in this assault. The ambushers had rapidly fled their positions. Haynes knew too late that he had already tripped a booby trap wire that had failed to explode in his headlong rush to attack. The Chicom grenade was now somewhere behind him. Just ahead of him was another long, yellowed bamboo handle with its dark serrated head sitting upright on the ground. It was easily seen amidst the brown leaves that covered the ground. Haynes commanded the warriors to stop. He had heard them leave their positions. Nervously, he swung through a complete 360-degree-circle, quickly searching his immediate surroundings. Satisfied that there was no immediate danger from his rear, he again faced forward and quickly located a tripwire ahead. He turned in place once more and searched for more trip wires and vines that would detonate any other booby-traps on his way back to the trail. He saw another booby-trap immediately to his front, the short hairs rose on his neck. He slowly started making his way back to the trail, avoiding the booby trap.

Two men ahead of me were down, falling silently. Only one body was kicking feebly. I knew from their color that they were already dead. One was on his back, arms at his sides, and the other, face down, lay with one arm sprawled out, the other under his body. I checked one and saw he had been shot in the head. The back of his head had a huge gaping hole and a gray fluid was draining from it. The other was lying face up, his eyes wide open, staring up at the bright sky. I checked for wounds and found nothing. When I rolled him half over, I found the back of his head gone. The two men had never heard the sharp crack that ended their lives. Both were shot in the brain and killed instantly. Their vacant eyes were dilated and glazed over in death, half rolled back into their heads. The sharp odor of cordite was strong.

I was sweating with excitement, when a small inconspicuous shuffling sound caught my attention up ahead and off the trail to the left. I heard the rustle of actual hurried movement: a slight sound of brush grating against uniforms, the scuffling of crunchy leaves and the snapping of small brittle twigs as someone ran. Not discounting the slightest sound, I moved off the trail into the brush, scrutinizing my way ahead and back-and-forth for booby traps. Then there was again the scuffling of leaves followed by quick, racing footsteps, and the fast snapping of broken twigs as men moved through the brush ahead, causing me to turn suddenly. The NVA, fearing they were going to be flanked, were now bailing out. I saw two khaki-clad, fast-moving armed men disappear over the hill to my right further up the hill. I switched the selector to automatic, but before I could fire on them, they disappeared against the backdrop of broken terrain, becoming part of the shadows. Then silence prevailed. Just a few men with rifles could raise hell with a larger force, with hit-and-run tactics. It was the simplest kind of warfare, where they killed a few, then escaped to launch a new attack. Soaking in sweat, I felt tired, physically and mentally.

Antipersonnel Mine

An examination of the ambush area revealed the spot had been chosen with considerable thought. Their fighting positions and aiming stakes had been employed for their rifles as the NVA had lain in wait in the protective foliage, and mines had been employed to channelize and restrict movement. Ratch pointed out a well concealed, cast-iron, cylindrical mine on a wooden stake in a well-shaded area, which had failed to detonate. A trip wire was attached in such a way that if pulled by someone moving through the brush, it would activate the mechanism. Taking a good look at the segmented cast-iron body of the antipersonnel mine, I then photographed it. It was a common communist bloc type, known as the POM-Z, which had an effective casualty radius of 30 feet. It was placed very close to their occupied ambush positions, but on higher ground with a slight rise between the mine and their positions in some dead space, which allowed them to retreat without being hit by the blast. This particular mine was known as the "chocolate box mine."

The fighting position was furthered prepared with punji stakes, and with narrow cut windows through the brush. You could recognize the shooting windows easily after seeing the positions and looking down the tunnel into the trail. From the trail, they were difficult to detect. The fast and violent counterattack led by Haynes had saved more men from being killed and wounded this time. I was beginning to realize that Haynes was endlessly patient, quiet and deadly.

Our radios were well out of range to contact Khe Sanh. Our only hope was to communicate with our HT-1 radio used as a ground-to-air system. Aircraft usually passed overhead on daily runs into Laos, and they would relay the message for a helicopter to make a medical extraction of our wounded. At times they did not respond, but always relayed the message.

After the ambush, we regrouped and selected our point element for movement. Our sinewy, hawk-faced tribesmen, designated to be on point, were visibly frightened. Their eyes looked wild. I could see the tremor that came from deep in the thigh, above the knee, causing their knees to knock uncontrollably and hands to spasm. As we prepared again to move forward, I looked around and saw everyone was as scared as I was. The point element was silently and bravely fighting to remain functional under the immense pressure and now cautiously moved forward up the trail. Many others were betrayed by a slight shivering as their legs revealed their emotions. Again, I could taste the sweet, sickening taste of fear filling my mouth. My heart hammered in my throat. I remembered our earlier successful ambush of the NVA along the Se Pone River. Now, I was living a part of the terror that they had felt.

Our motions were slow and deliberate as we attempted to get into the rhythm of moving through the area as quietly and unobtrusively as possible. Our disciplined eyes were constantly swinging, searching, and analyzing, trying to break down the form of a hidden man: alert to seeing before being seen. The main lesson I learned in these early years was that your body, mind, and senses have to work in a tight intuitive union or you will not survive. Patrolling is an intellectual and sensual activity on which everyone's life depends. We came to a large, dead-flat open bottomland area with a stream running through it. The point element caught the reflective shine from the flattening of dirt in the trail of a smooth sandal print. We stopped and crouched next to some small trees and a large bush in order to break up the body's outline. We systematically searched ahead with our eyes, looking to the left and right to the limit of the range of vision. We tried looking into the cover with binoculars, using our eyes to search our area of projected forward movement. We noticed a large grapefruit tree, in the middle of this area filled with enormous yellow-skinned grapefruits the size of cannonballs. Starving, we now had a plan.

Three of us approached the tree. Because of the size of the tree, we had to assist one man to climb the huge trunk of the uncultivated, forty-feet tall tree. Picking and shaking out the fruit was difficult for the climber. Then the two of us who remained on the ground caught the fruit. We hurriedly distributed the fruit to the troops. We quickly peeled the rind, which was covered with a light coat of wax. The fruit was tart and very sweet. I rubbed the wax from the rind with one finger and rubbed it on my dry lips. Almost immediately I felt stronger and better.

The warm moderate breeze coming through the tall trees had only a good forest smell to it. I stared momentarily through the high canopy, trying to assess the passage of time. We moved in a perpetual gloom of twilight, beneath the wide-spreading branches overhead. The air was warm. I took several small sniffs with my mouth open to give that extra dimension to smell, I still could not scent anything out of the ordinary; no scent of a cooking fire, animals or people. There were only the pungent odors of the stream, moist earth, plants and forest.

As we continued to move, I began to notice that there was none of the thin piping of birdcalls, none of their fluttering from branch-to-branch. There were none of their territorial warning messages to each other and to every other living thing in sight, saying, "This is mine. Stay away." There was something hypnotic and frightening about the utter completeness of their disappearance. We stopped and listened frequently. After ten minutes, hearing nothing unusual, we continued on. My head now ached, and so did the lower part of the back of my neck. I felt as if a rock was sitting high in my stomach and the strain was exhausting. Forgotten was the ache of my shoulder and neck muscles from the weight of my rucksack. The atmosphere was tense. Again Haynes ordered me further back in the formation. Much later, after the patrol, he explained that he was trying to keep me from getting shot.

Ambushed Again

We were again moving slowly and cautiously. Once more came the sounds of the Kalashnikov assault rifle. I saw the disturbing future possibility of my own mortality looming stronger before me, as men flinched and ducked aside at the sound of more staccato chatter of automatic weapons coming from within the thick undergrowth. I grabbed a nearby M-79 grenade launcher and fired three of the 40mm rounds in a high arching loop to the rear of the place from which the initial Kalashnikov fire had come. Bullets again cracked overhead, thudding into the ground. Some ricocheted with a whine past our ears or exploded against the trees, throwing bark. Fire was returned and then it was quickly over. It became quiet again. After a brief period, we started our classic infantry advance-- fire and movement toward the area of fire.

Again everyone was ducking low in reflex at the sudden burst of automatic fire from a lone Kalashnikov. Our point, supported by a base of fire, moved forward. The area was empty. A brief check of our condition revealed that no one had been wounded, but our point man had been knocked to the ground during the initial firing. The impact of the bullet had shattered everything in the pack. SSG Haynes directed the point quickly out of the area. We moved rapidly until dark. Then we organized a night defense and waited. It was a long wait, a long night. The PAVN had not found us by the following morning, but we had made contact with an aircraft passing overhead into Laos. We moved toward the higher terrain while searching for an open area large enough to serve as a helicopter-landing zone. We knew that we had to move on, because any radio transmission would give our position away. But we had to wait patiently. The NVA had broken their hunt for us down into smaller groups of men, each scouting an ambushing of our likely routes through the hills. We knew that once we were found, they would consolidate into a larger, single force to surround and kill us. It was the simplest kind of warfare: hurt us as much as possible, then withdraw and prepare to launch a new attack at some other unexpected place on the map.

Medical Evacuation and Re-Supply

We made every effort to get our badly wounded quickly evacuated so that they knew they had a chance when operating in these extremely remote areas. The Bru tribesmen and the Vietnamese are superstitious about being left in a strange place. To them it means an unmarked grave. They feel that without a proper burial ceremony, the remains of the dead will roam the world unhappily as lost souls. The Montgnards believe that fireflies are the spirits of their departed heroes. At twilight, the glow of bright yellow green from the dozens of fireflies lighting up the growing darkness, reminded them of this.

Aerial Re-Supply 1964 Laotian Border

At dawn the next day, we waited nervously, ears straining for the first faint clamor of the helicopter. Finally, the intense and overpowering silence of the wilderness terrain was broken, by the faint whirring of the chopper. A quick check of the wounded was made to be sure that they were ready. One man's breath was hissing sharply through his teeth from the pain. He had assumed an unnatural position created by the terrible paroxysms of pain. After looking at another man, I knelt and felt his brow and the lower back of his neck. I recognized significant fever shining brightly from his eyes. I could smell the dull metallic odor of fresh blood. I could see the flushed, dry, and hot skin. I knew that his heartbeat would probably stabilize as soon as the helicopter got him into the windy and cool atmosphere of high altitude. Hearing the rotor blades of the chopper in the distance, about two miles away, we conducted a long count. While depressing the handset, we transmitted a steady radio beam to guide the chopper within sight of our location. The buffeting sounds of the chopper were now unmistakably closer. We then directed him by voice toward our exact location, using the clock system. Finally, in the distance, we saw the glinting rotor blades.

Popping Smoke

We informed the aircraft that we had dropped a smoke grenade to visually establish our location and the wind direction. The pilot also confirmed the color, just in case the NVA were also playing with smoke. It was standard procedure for the pilot to make a radio confirmation of color before approaching a smoke marker to avoid being shot down or being captured on the ground. When the Sikorsky H-34 Choctaw flew over us, we repeated the word "spot," at which time the chopper continued to fly on and around us in a wide circle. Again on our direct heading he gradually lost altitude, building up air speed on his approach. He descended quickly and changed pitch giving him sufficient lift to halt his descent, and then he landed on the LZ. We hurriedly loaded our wounded in the wash of the rotor blades. I could see their blood-shot eyes and twisted faces filled with pain. There were nasty-looking flesh wounds, but they weren't dangerous. Air evacuation provided a great morale factor and helped overcome any psychological burden, among our Chinese, Montagnard and Vietnamese ground troops. For these people, tending the remains of the dead is a task taken most seriously, and every effort would be made on our part for their recovery for continued good relations.

The tall grass waved violently. The chopper rotor continued to turn slowly, the sound deafening. The helicopter shuddered and lifted off, straight up out of the LZ. Then it turned, nose slightly down, swinging low over the forest building up speed and clearing the treetops. It quickly climbed high and left the area. They had not brought us any rations.

We heard the Otter droning north of us. After Haynes communicated with the aircraft, it turned and we could hear it headed for us. And then, suddenly, it was there. We saw it snaking along the ridge just above the trees of the unfamiliar landscape. A face peered out the open door of the aircraft, checking the recognition panels. The Otter reduced power. A moment later it started the drop. Our supplies were pushed out the door, into the rushing air by the kicker. A static line secured to the floor of the aircraft automatically opened the small pack parachute after it cleared the aircraft. The last of the small wooden palettes of white G-13 cargo parachutes blossomed overhead. I watched as the supplies wafted down to be sure of their location, as I moved toward their drift to pick them up with a detail of men. The Otter aircraft droned on over the horizon and vanished, and then the faint sound of the engine was gone.

Going Home

We headed back to Khe Sanh. Being flexible, we took a different route in order to forestall another easy ambush. Amid the fog of uncertainty, we would again take the hard way home, off the trails, along dry creek beds, through the mountains further east. I tried not to think of how long we had been on patrol or how far from Khe Sanh we had come. For now, our camp existed in another world, another dimension of life. We had more immediate concerns, like preventing the occurrence of the inevitable. The predatory shadow of the

NVA hung over us. We now had to trade space for time. The pace was hurried, and it took a while to adapt to it.

We had been pushing hard since the first gray stain of predawn, squeezing every mile we could out of the day and following a tortuous path cross-country until near dark. The blue sky had looked like a mirror to heaven. It had been hot and humid. Rising water vapor mixed with the volatile gases from the earth, lifting it to the clouds now above. The heat of the sun was continually fueling the clouds. Now, watching the sunset, I noticed it was yellow. Being weather wise, I knew it foretold that strong winds would come sometime the next day. The weather was deteriorating as we headed for the distant undulating tree line. The walls of the mountain forest closed in. I hoped that the NVA patrols would confine their searches for us to the easy and quick flat low areas along the river. We slipped silently and swiftly through the distant mountains, taking the long way home.

We were headed into the high mountain ridge, into the continuous canopy of the rain forest. Thrusting through the leaf mat, fat tree trunks of 90-feet tall trees covered the mountain ridge. The area was strewn with giant-sized, rounded, four-feet-high, moss-furred rocks. Enormous gnarly roots also energetically burst through the surface of the ground everywhere, making the trail difficult. The rain forest here received some 150 inches of rain in a year.

Our back trail was closely watched. We would follow along the high mountain ridge. The old, thick timber was dark at the top of the ridge because the branches were intertwined overhead. Birdsong rose endlessly, assuring us that the area was undisturbed. Haynes and I, both hill-country deer hunters, were able to avoid walking and climbing injury because we used the same style of walking as our Bru tribesmen. With our heavy packs, weapons and ammunition, leaning into the hill, we climbed upward careful to remain quiet while watching the man ahead of us, maintaining the same pace. Placing each foot flat on the ground, using our thigh muscles and taking several steps along the side of the hill, we gradually ascended. We switched back in the opposite direction in the same manner. This method kept us from straining tendons in our heels and injuring them. At the top of each hill, we balanced our downward movement by leaning backward and switching back and forth, thereby keeping the shock of some of the steeper parts of the hill in our knees and thighs and holding onto solid saplings to maintain balance. Again the seemingly slow pace kept everyone together and quiet, but it was in actuality rather fast. This avoided injuring the toes and toenails, which would result in blacktoe that would eventually cause you to lose the toenail. Once the toenails turned red and sore, you were bound to lose a nail and begin limping. We could not afford to have this happen. We learned to be very careful of what we grabbed, quickly looking when we reached out, because many of these trunks had thick thorns covering the sides. Weak and limber trees would shake, their limbs and leaves rattling, creating noise. To move quietly and unobserved, each man had to be slow and patient.

At one point during a short break, I leaned back on my pack and looked up through the heavy shadows of the trees at the sky. Closing together at the top, they shut out the light so that the weird and funereal aspect of the place was perfect. It represented a forbidding appearance, which would appall most Americans. My eyes searched for the incessant sharp calls of many small black birds feeding above us. Several were perched on limbs in a small shaft of light penetrating the canopy. They were illuminated and were not black but a brilliant sapphire color with black wings. Others were a beautiful green. I was very tired, and realized I was allowing my mind to wander because of the great beauty of the trees and the birds. As far as we could tell, we were not being followed yet. This only meant that they were well spread out, looking for our trail. It would be only a matter of time before they found it. We counted on covering a lot of distance before the storm. Hopefully our trail would be washed away before they found it.

Leeches

The terrestrial leeches were a constant threat. They were about an inch long, but some were much longer. They wait on leaves, sensing the approaching vibrations of a warm-blooded victim about to pass by, and quickly attach themselves. During any rest break, you could see them congregated. As if on command from our body heat and odor, they would make their way toward us, using their terminal sucker. We watched their strange looping motion as they moved. When you reached down to pull one off with your fingers, they would contract their muscles and flatten themselves out, which makes it nearly impossible to grab them. While crossing a stream, we would pick up the larger aquatic leeches. We used fire from a match, salt or our standard issue repellent, which worked nicely. If you pulled them off, a part of the head remained lodged in the flesh and caused an infection and scar. They weren't a problem in our operational area at Khe Sanh, because it was really cold. Finally, we found a good place and settled in for the night. During the night on watch, I noticed the stars appeared blue: an omen of a storm. It always grew cold not long after moonrise.

The next morning, we moved softly along, backs bent from the weight of our packs. Our environment made good theater, for all around were the murmurs of nature--small birds' noisy calls, whistling and growling of monkeys further back in the forest and every now and then the loud cry of a peacock. The small birds roosted close to the tree trunks and fluffed their feathers, signaling the storm. I noticed the surrounding vegetation was dry and that the leaves were turned up. As I watched the sky, the wind had picked up and the air had become more humid. I felt as if my back would never again be straight. Frogs and crickets were replaced by rhythmically droning cicadas as the sun climbed directly overhead, seeming to welcome us. We had to keep a close check on our clothes and bodies for small, lean and mean leeches at all times along the trails, through the bushes and trees.

My legs ached. The sky was a bright blue, but in the distance I watched the rapid growth of towering black columns of clouds massing. Soon came the sighing of the wind in the trees, the birds flying low to the ground and only for short distances. The insects were now silent. The forest too became silent. A sense of something about to happen hung over our patrol, a period of unnatural calm before a tempest.

Patches of clouds came rushing over the mountains. White cirrus clouds were morphing into dark clouds. They mustered vertically into towering black masses. The structure of a storm was building, and coming closer. On patrol, it always seemed to be our lot to be cold, wet and miserable. There was flickering of light beyond the trees, followed by a faraway rumble. A fast-moving storm was coming closer. The sun became obscured and a definite chill pervaded, as wisps of cold gray clouds scurried and caught on the hilltops. We could see lightning, but dismissed concern because it seemed so far away. But now it grew stronger and closer by the minute. Then came a small sweet-smelling gust of wind. The treetops begin to wave. I felt a sense of renewal from this enormous force of life. Tall dark clouds continued to build.

Mother Nature was about to unveil herself, and reveal her extraordinary primal strength and savagery. A cool breeze quickened. The wind had gotten stronger. I could smell the odor of rain on the wind and the pungent vegetation and decay of damp earth. I could also hear the echo of distant thunder; it was far away, but active. The wind gusted. The treetops were now waving violently. We moved into a low area of the forest for the thermal cover that offered refuge from the high winds and chilly temperature. Twigs and leaves tumbled down through the foliage. I settled down and sheltered myself next to a large, thick-trunked tree. We crouched motionless, listening and watching as it became still. Then the wind picked up with the added heaviness of increasing humidity. I could hear a low-pitched, ululating moaning. Another series of gusts developed. Anticipating rain, I noticed that the air had grown still and saw that the towering anvil-shaped clouds had darkened.

The distinctive pre-rain smell had materialized, enhanced and fully saturated with a fresh and soothing earthy aroma of the trees of the mountain rain forest and vegetation within smelling distance. There was a flash of lightning in the distance. Then there came a pungent whiff--the electrifying stink of ozone. I saw the different beautiful colors of vapor in the sky, as the storm seemed to laugh at us. Rain patterned a soft staccato on the leaves overhead. The sky had turned ominous.

The storm mass was expanding. There came the solid thud of raindrops on the leaves above. Soon water dripped to spatter the ground around us, bringing renewed life to the forest. I was fascinated with the creative force of the black monsoon skies, as I looked at what appeared to be the center of the storm and saw the colossal downdraft of heavy gusts of wind and rain bearing down on us. I listened to the howling song of the wind, feeling a chill at the back of my neck. My skin tingled. Then like the wrath of God, it came, like a fog creeping over the mountain. The sheer force of the wind rocked the hilltop as it became dark. We were now in the grip of the monsoon. I felt the hair on my arms and neck stand on end. I listened to the forest shiver and sway in the onslaught of the storm. I wasn't prepared for the extent of sounds that followed. Slumped down in my saturated uniform, I listened and watched as trees moaned and creaked. I saw flying debris and branches blowing in the wind. I heard the patter of falling rain and leaves, and then felt the stinging bite of the rain. My ears began to pop.

There was a searing flash of lightning, jagged tendrils zigzagging across the sky. The first volley of deafening thunder was followed by a crack-boom of a thunderclap that shook the ground. A long streak of lightning flashed so close that the thunder was almost simultaneous. It felt its way to the ground, whitening the surrounding swaying forest. I jumped. I saw the yellow, green, blue, gray and black in the lighted sky as the fury of the storm broke above us. The forest was now dancing. It was beautiful and electrifying. I could smell it. The air turned crispy cracklely with electricity. I could feel its power tingling in the air all around me, and its effect on my body. The giant rain-bearing thunderclouds burst.

There were lulls in the whispering and drumming of the wind and the rain, darkness between the thunderclaps. Then came the sound of driving rain falling on the canopy above. We were protected from it for a while. Thunder echoed through the canyons and bathed the mountains. It sounded like the roll of drums. It was slow at first, but became heavier and heavier. The hard, battering rain drenched and stung us. It came in slashing gray sheets of lead. It fell with a force I had never experienced before. We were waterlogged. It was as if the sky had burst. It lasted hour onto hour. I could no longer see around me with my squinted eyes, except when the overhead lightening illuminated the area or the wind became strong.

My feet were submerged in the water that was running under me, but I was already so wet that it made no difference now. I prayed that the water around us would not become a conductor of ground current from the lightning. It was phenomenal. The savagery of Mother Nature sounded like the end of the world, respecting nothing. The wind seemed to redouble in its shrieking violence suddenly as the storm reached a demonic intensity. Then, after a while, it had passed overhead, moving away to the southwest. Only a steady, light rainfall remained. Moisture had darkened the bark on the trunks of the trees.

A nervous distant wind coming up, then the surprising mutter of another rain. The first fat drops from a shower again spattered the trees overhead. The intense cold rain was piercing us through and through. We were again famished. Water dripped through the spectacular emerald greenery of 100-feet-high triple canopy of the forest. Then solid sheets of water descended through the trees, in a cold and mournful downpour. The hard and chilling wind danced around. We could see only a few paces ahead. We were cold and wet. The rain, never stopping, again came in bursts. The howling, capricious wind blew harder and harder, rampaging terribly among the trees. Periodically, there would be the smashing sound of some great tree or limb falling to the ground. Finally, the rain again slowed. The cold wet air smelled good. Our ragged camouflage uniforms were plastered to our bodies. A way past midnight, it seemed like the rain was slackening. We waited, crouched throughout the long, dark night and shivered in the dribbling, miserable darkness. Hidden from our enemy and from each other, we listened to the wind roar through the night.

Finally, it was dawn. Now thoroughly chilled, stiff from the wet and cold, we continued to move. We crossed over shallow, giant tree roots crisscrossing the trail like gnarled fingers, and past bamboo groves. We baby-stepped our way up the rock-studded, narrow trail that had turned into a treacherous mudslide in places. The forest turned dark gray and glistened unnaturally. A slow, cold drizzle fell from the pewter sky. Gauzy tendrils of an eerie fog rose among the mossy giant trees and crept forward as if on the great cat's feet. It was like another world. We were exhausted and soaked to the skin. I now had a deep respect for these storms. And I was grateful. The weather would wash away sign of our trail. But we knew they would soon find it again.

Dreary, bone-chilling days were to follow, with clouds so low as to obscure the mountains. Hard rain came, and winds whipped branches overhead out of a gunmetal gray sky. Heavy clouds darkened the nights. Our gray faces, haggard and drawn, unshaven, took on bluish shadows under our eyes and mouths, signs of our weariness. The rain was the worst, bringing gloom and discomfort, as if the world were weeping. About the time that our body heat was to dry our uniforms after a lull, a strong breeze would shake the tree branches above, sending a cold shower of water down upon us. We moved on into the mists and shadows. Now we would be leaving a trail that any city boy could follow. Tall grass in the few high, open areas would take a long time to stand back up. The uniform color of the wet, silvery grass would show a clear dark trail where we'd knocked off the dew. Mud from the bottoms of our boots would scrape off onto the vegetation and rocks. There was no hiding our trail. We had to hurry. Substance was replaced with phantoms; when it wasn't raining, thick concentrations of mist took on humanoid forms in the still dark shadows deep among the trees, rousing suspicion, apprehension and fears. Now, I was beginning to understand the Bru. At times it felt as if the ground had sucked at our feet, while our bodies shuddered in uncontrollable spasms, as above us, the wind tossed and gusted through the trees. Our legs ached and trembled.

The leeches would gorge themselves by sucking our blood. Once they bloated, they would fall off. They swell to the size of a pencil in an hour and drop off unnoticed. If by chance it was to get into your ear, nose and sometimes the sinuses, or any other of the body's orifices where it becomes distended with blood, then we were in real trouble. When we drank unfiltered water, they could enter the mouth and lodge in our throats or noses, causing bleeding, obstructions, and excruciating pain. Internal infestation would require a surgeon. During any stop, I not only had to be aware of the forest around me, but the ground I stood upon.

If the weather was dry, the leeches would hide under the leaves. The drier it was, the deeper down they could go. When the weather was wet, they were everywhere. Sooner or later, they would gather to help drain the blood of any wounded person who was lying helpless. It was a long, dreary night, with the rain coming down on us in a cold drizzle. Always we were hoping for the rain to let up. Finally the day came.

Mourning

At last there was a glint of sun through the trees. We were coming to an open area. The fetid odor of death was strong now. It saturated my lungs and mingled with the stink and heat of my own sweat. The corpses of our members were in various stages of decay, and the stirring of air carried the heavy, powerful smell of rotting human flesh. Shivering, we emerged from the shadows of dark, brooding, dripping trees of the mist-shrouded mountaintop forest into the sunshine. We halted at the edge of the forest. All that was before us was a long, downward-sloping open spur of nothing but kunai grass. One of the things that made me proud of the Bru was that when we stopped or took a break, they never bunched up and lost their vigilance.

The sun had already burned through the last remnants of the storm. A splashing, waving sea of tall *kunai* grass formed a moving mosaic of light as far as the eye could see. This was the last high point of the ridge. We now had a direct line of sight for the operation of our radio in the event of trouble. We felt a little more comfortable in this knowledge. We could see the blue skeins of smoke rising from a thousand cooking fires far ahead. Although we could not see the town of Khe Sanh, a thin, grayish-brown blanket of smog trapped in the cold sky blanketed the entire town area.

The sun illuminated all the other blue-tinted peaks. I searched the surrounding terrain barely visible over the top of the vast plain of coarse *Kunai* grass. Then my eyes followed a distant treeline. In the open, near a large grove of bamboo, I saw several large black blurs on the horizon. They looked too tall to be water buffalo. I took out my binoculars and got my first and last look at a small number of Gaur, the largest wild cattle on earth. I could see the white-stocking legs, the distinctive ridge on the withers and the short forward-curved, horns. That was the only direction from which I felt we were safe that day.

Soon the area ahead smelled of wood smoke, cooked food, village livestock, decaying vegetation and the flower of betel nut palm. We were greeted by great numbers of silent women and children who stood staring at us. When told of the deaths of their men, some young tribal women briefly laughed hysterically at the prospect of facing the unknown without them. Their oval faces went pale, contorted with anguish and shock, staring blankly through enormous eyes.

In the dimness, an old woman released her grief in an ancient, echoing song of her people. There was a troubling silence among the younger women. Then, as the shadows grew longer, the heads of the Bru women went back, and a wild, powerful sound exploded, pouring out their hearts in a mournful, keening sound on the wind. The sun had fallen to the horizon. Then again came a plaintive, wailing, melancholy mourning song that supplicated their god and allowed the release of pain. The sound echoed to the surrounding hills. It was vacant at first and then full of an awful, furious sadness. It rose and fell in octaves in the eerie dark twilight across the camp as the age-old wails erupted from the trembling women gathered at the sides of their dead warriors. Some leaned their heads forward and sobbed, drowning in anguish.

A babbling squall of crying came from the babies and frightened children hugging the legs of their mothers. Now, for the Bru, began those rites that dealt with the ancient fear and appeasement of the restless spirits of the dead. The clan would join the surviving families in their prolonged mourning, chanting and dancing until the clan head decided the time was right for the ceremony. Depending upon their status within the tribe, some of the dead would be wrapped in a cloth and mat, or sealed inside of a hollowed log, and then be buried in the ground.

As I walked away with my Vietnamese Special Forces (LLDB) counterpart, the blustering winds carried away the lamentations. I had a new appreciation for life. Each sunrise and sunset gave me hope. In the years ahead, however, the nights were to get much longer and more terrifying. Our long days of patrolling and hard labor were over. Our time at Khe Sanh had come to an end.

Footnote:
1. The domesticated chicken's wild progenitor *Gallus gallus*. The Fire Pheasant, earthly cousin of the divine mythological Dragon-Phoenix of the Vietnamese people.

Charles A. McDonald

Here on earth, God's work must be our own.

John F. Kennedy

CHAPTER 8

RETURN TO OKINAWA

It was now the latter half of April 1965. Our Temporary Duty Assignment (TDY) was over and our Special Forces replacement team was on hand. Before our team's return to Okinawa, I became unusually tired. A fever came upon me and I became very sick with violent headaches, constant body pain, spiking fever and delirium. After our return to Okinawa, I went to bed in the local village and remained there for a length of time, and was quite miserable. I was so sick that a bucket had to be left beside the bed for me to periodically puke and defecate into. Even at these times, I had to be helped. My stools were covered with a white mucous that frightened me. Although close to medical help, and knowing I should go on sick call, I was too sick to help myself. A blood smear would have to wait.

When I reported back to the company and stood in formation at roll call one morning, I thought I had been AWOL and was in serious trouble. But the only thing the commander, Colonel Elmer E. Monger, said to me was, "Do you feel better?" I replied with an amazed "Yes, Sir" and that was the end of that. Our 12-man team, A-323, ran one class of men through a jump school in the Sukiran area. I was given the choice of an assignment in Korea or of returning to Fort Bragg to be promoted. I chose to return to Fort Bragg.

Indo China
During this time, Russian and Chinese Air Defense troops had begun manning the anti-aircraft and surface-to-air missile sites in North Vietnam. A number of Chinese Divisions were now in Laos and North Vietnam. North Korean combat pilots were flying for the North Vietnamese Air Force. The North Vietnamese Army was heading south. Russian and Chinese pilots were now actively engaging the American Air Force over North Vietnam and the surrounding areas. The war was building.

Fort Bragg
By 20 July 1965, I had returned to Ft. Bragg, North Carolina, and my very brief stateside assignment to the 7th Special Forces. Camp Bragg came into existence on 4 September 1918, named after West Point graduate, General Braxton Bragg. Bragg was a native North Carolinian from Warrenton, who was a brave and skillful Confederate officer. The Fort Bragg military reservation is located at the western edge of the Fall Line of North Carolina's Coastal Plain, 10 miles northwest of the nearest large town of Fayetteville. The team and training rooms of Company E, 7th Special Forces were now in the old wooden barracks, but the men slept in new brick barracks and ate in beautiful new concrete mess halls. The years ahead would see an even larger barracks construction program for America's elite soldiers. With its 140,618 acres of swamps, sand and pine-covered hills, it makes an excellent training area. Its vast and magnificent longleaf pine forests are filled with many trees 100-feet tall, and wire grass and oak brush cushion the wide spaces between its pine and oak forest.

Troop carrier training for the Airforce is conducted from Pope Army Air Field sited on Fort Bragg, named after Lt.

Harley H. Pope. Earlier, I had spent almost a year in Special Forces Training Group here, qualifying to become a member. I remember Training Group well.

Training Group

I had been recruited from the 101st Airborne Division by a Special Forces recruiter, Sgt. Spanio. He had recruited so many of the best conventional soldiers at Ft. Campbell that he eventually had been told to leave the post. I arrived at Ft. Bragg in June 1963. This was shortly before my old division commander, Major General William C. Westmoreland, had arrived to take command of the base. He was assigned to Special Forces, which had a mission of such tremendous significance that it had specially recruited young men with good minds and physiques to withstand the rigors of service. Special Forces Training Group was made up of World War II-vintage, two-story wooden buildings. It was here that I would spend nearly a year in a very demanding outdoor and indoor classroom training area to qualify for that more interesting job assignment.

Living in the barracks, one of the first things I noticed was that Special Forces Training Group was made up of men from rural backgrounds in the United States, from the various Spanish-speaking areas of the world, and from Europe. Most of the countries of Eastern Europe were represented. The professional soldiers represented the cream of the crop of the best American army units. There were veterans from many of the world's armies. A number had served during World War II in the German Army. Some of the instructors had been members of the OSS. One instructor I remember, Sgt. Roger Ballenger, had been an adviser to a Royal Laotian infantry battalion in April 1961. He was captured in an ambush and held prisoner by the Communist Pathet Lao in Laos. Eventually, he was flown in a Russian aircraft to Vientiane and released in April 1962. All of the recruits were men who knew what it meant to be an American, who would be true to their oath of enlistment in the service of this country. They had put aside their present and future dreams, their doubts and fears, for the privilege of earning the right to fight communism as a member of Special Forces.

In 1963, the U.S. Army led the way in changing the armed forces from being dependent upon an industrialized system of warfare, to training and fielding a true warrior society, embodied by Special Forces with its "Green Berets." In the Special Forces Training Group, we were expected to willingly work and study, preparing for greater responsibilities to come. We had been informed early in training that those of us who did extremely well would receive overseas orders for Okinawa. We were to spend nine to twelve months in training. Those of us who were left to graduate would qualify for eventual service in the A-teams. Operational A-teams were self-contained, operating independently in isolated areas of the world.

I had attended the Special Forces Qualifications Course, starting with Methods of Instruction (MOI). MOI consisted of demonstrating your teaching ability by teaching an unknown subject to the other students. Our performance was graded by demanding instructors. The next phase of our training covered common skills, which consisted of many subjects. The training and test on map and compass, which included the use of geographic coordinates, was the easiest for me. I had already had many years of map and compass training, with accompanying terrain walks. I could understand where I was at all times. My Military Occupational Specialty (MOS) training was in weapons. We were trained to be proficient in all infantry weapons, both in order to train others, and in order to be ready in the event we needed to pick up other weapons for use in our tactical operations. This included all known weapons in use by the communist forces in Indochina. I did so well in the heavy weapons portion that I was assigned a Heavy Weapons MOS of 112.73, or indirect fire crewman. We were then deployed to the great outdoor classroom of the Uwharrie National Forest, forty miles west to central North Carolina, for the final phase of our training. There we were closely observed in order to evaluate how well we worked together. Those students previously judged mentally or temperamentally unsuited for Special

Forces teamwork had already been dropped from the training program.

It was late at night when we passed through the small town of Uwharrie, south of Asheboro, on Route 109. It was here that we began our unconventional warfare training, our guerrilla and counter-guerrilla training. It was here in the Uwharrie National Forest that we were evaluated in all of our skills. Most of the men who failed the course failed here for poor teamwork. I spent many nights performing reconnaissance work. I loved the independence of working as a small team. I loved the night movement. Graduation from Special Forces Training Group had found me on my way to Okinawa, but now I was back at Fort Bragg again.

While stationed at Fort Bragg, we constantly found ourselves training in the field at Camp McCall, North Carolina, located 35 miles away, near Aberdeen and Pinebluff, North Carolina. Another training area we used frequently was the Green Swamp in Brunswick County, southwest of Wilmington, North Carolina. We made our day and night tactical parachute jumps from the older C-47s (Douglas DC-3), the Curtiss C-46 Commando, and various types of helicopters.

On 13 November 1965, I was again leaving Ft. Bragg. This trip, I was assigned to the Delta Project (B-52). But first, I had a 30-day leave. Before heading back to Vietnam, I drove across the United States to my parents' home in Sacramento, California.

I spent most of my time there doing absolutely nothing but resting and visiting family. Eventually, I found myself at the local college library. There I spotted a young woman clad in a colorful Japanese kimono, intently and busily searching the many volumes back among the bookshelves. I wandered back, searching for a nonexistent book, and very innocently engaged her in conversation. Pretending to be busy with my search, I pulled at random an unknown book from the shelf, and while paging through it, kept talking. When our eyes finally locked, I invited her to get coffee.

Her name was Keiko Iwai. She was a very traditional Japanese woman from Nara, Japan. I learned that she had never worn Western clothes in her life, and had no intention of ever doing so. I invited her to my home for dinner and to meet my parents. Three days later, with time growing very short, I asked her to marry me. She said "no." Naturally, I was deflated, but it was just as well, I thought. My future didn't look too bright. All too soon I found myself again departing. I headed to nearby Travis Air Force Base, and then to Vietnam.

Nha Trang

On 20 December 1965, I arrived back in South Vietnam. According to the Chinese lunar year, it was the year of the Snake. My orders took me to Nha Trang on the central Vietnamese coast. The 5th Special Forces Group (Airborne) was headquartered at the beautiful beach resort town of Nha Trang on the South China Sea. Due to the offshore breezes, Nha Trang was generally cool. Large trees along the long beach front shaded the French colonial-style buildings. Hon Tre Island could be seen far in the distance. The streets were cobblestone. Barges were busy along the coast of Nha Trang unloading large cargo vessels of their supplies. Anyone could see that a buildup of American forces was underway.

After checking in at the Headquarters for the 5th Special Forces Group and being processed in, I was unceremoniously told that the Project DELTA compound was located up the dirt road to the northwest from the main gate. The sergeant major told me that I could make my own way up there. The compound was on the west side of the end of the airstrip. I picked up my gear and walked there.

I knew a number of the men personally, having served with them in "Charlie Company" on Okinawa. The men of Project DELTA thrived in ambiguous situations. They were the type of men who like intense experiences. They were inner directed. Everyone believed they could control their fate. Their senses, finely honed in previous operations, were now instinctual and they believed that whatever situation developed, they could handle it. These beliefs in the future would merely demonstrate our lack of prudent judgment. I soon found myself with another sergeant picking a training site on Hon Tre Island.

Hon Tre Island

It was a windy, early morning. The musky smell of the ocean was strong as I stopped to observe and listen. The bay's warm, damp, heavy air smelled of salt, fish and seaweed and was heavy in my nostrils. Nothing moved and I could hear only the slapping of the sea against the wharf. The water was quietest before sunrise. There was no light reflection on the clouds, and the entire Nha Trang area was dark. I could smell some wood smoke from other early morning risers preparing food for the new day. The small narrow wharf was empty. The boat could hardly be seen in the dim gloom of the shadowed blackness. The dull light of a single small bulb glowed at the end of the pier. I listened to the smack of water against the low-silhouetted Boston whaler moored alongside the quay.

We cast off from the black, barnacled dock pilings shortly before dawn. The smell of the dock area was lost in the fuel vapors. We paused, rocking in the gentle sway of Nha Trang Bay just before the dark channel, and then passed into the open black sea. Away from the wharf, our night vision was good. We could see the dark ocean and the sky, which was only a little lighter. Our engine groaned to life, gradually picking up speed. We plunged through a quartering current, across the rolling and heaving whitecaps, now far from shore, yawing wildly from the battering shocks of wind and rough, shifting current.

Our destination, Hon Tre Island, was due east and low on the horizon. Hon Tre Island was very large. It was located thirty-five kilometers north of Cam Ranh Bay. It was used by Project Delta as a training ground, as were the coastal mountains surrounding Nha Trang. We were going out to the island to check the low-lying area for a shooting range. Near land, the water had been rough, but now, out in the open water of the channel, the contrary trade winds made the waves so rough and boisterous that they became life threatening. As we stared ahead, the high swells of the South China Sea sent us rolling, pitching and diving from the towering crests of battering black waves. The crests were taller than two men. We tried to maintain our heading to the landing site. I could smell the heady, salt tang of the South China Sea. It smelled good.

Our slow passage went on for a good while. The night was making its transition from gray to yellow and rose, as dawn crept out of the east. We saw the hazy silhouette of the remote and strangely threatening rugged mountains, rising from the ocean ahead. The gray fog mist that covered the island and ocean was slowly dissipating. The pink blush of sunrise came over the sea, and finally, we were tilting our hats against the first rays of the rising sun. Ahead stood the island's dark mountains, still covered with mist at the top. Across the westernmost mountain ridge laid a natural, hidden bay. It was toward this destination that we turned, heading north and making our way around the point to the cove heading east again. The land was close now, and soon I could hear the low, sullen, booming sound of the surf over the wind, and the raucous, kibitzing seagulls were whirling overhead, as we turned south and crept forward toward the looming towering rocky cliffs. I watched and listened with rapt attention to the white surge and break of the waves battering the rocks of the reef at the entrance to the channel, sweeping over them and sucking back and gathering and rushing forward again as we found ourselves caught up in a headlong rush in the current.

We shot through the threatening shapes of rocks, low breakers and wind that marked the edge of the furious wild sea. With the roar of the ocean in our ears, and flecked with wind spume, the waves became smaller, and then disappeared entirely, as we entered light blue-green water on the leeside of the island entering the easy swells, then a calm sheltered area. We made our way into the cove, to the gentle sighing of the wind, where the water turned a light green. I looked down into the clear water below as a shadow passed moving darkly across the sandy bottom, its tail swinging rapidly from side to side. *"Shark!"* I said to myself. Ahead in the distance, I saw long-legged wading birds take flight and depart, and a tiny rind of white beach.

For training we used the two islands that had formerly been occupied by the Vietminh. Both islands, dominated by tall, multi-hued green rain forests, loomed straight up out of the South China Sea. Smaller, wind-sculpted scrub trees crowded the shore. The main island, Hon Tre, contained one coastal hamlet on the west side of the island. Between the island's two mountains, there was a French planter's coca plantation. The smaller, eastern island, Hon Meo, had a reef-protected bay where the French plantation owner lived. These islands were the largest of a chain of islands. The rocky granite palisades of the Hon Tre Islands were quiet and restful-looking with the most beautiful blue-green water lapping the water-worn stones and the narrow deserted white coral sand beaches.

The Cove

We could see as we entered the cove, the individual branches of leathery, waxy light-green leaves and twisted branches of the gnarled trunks of a mangrove swamp to our left, contrasting with the gray rocks and darker forest foliage. Gulls on the beach squabbled noisily. Beneath the mangroves, the waters were a brilliant, iridescent light green. We moved a little faster, until we were in the calm water of the sheltered natural bay. We could now see the bright white sandy bottom and its large weed bed. The light came off the water as if off glass. Its clear, tepid waters had a large weed bed on the bottom, a natural fishery teeming with fish. Fish could often be seen breaking the surface, driven upwards by the sharks swiftly gliding beneath them.

The Boston whaler grated on the shore, and we jumped out and dragged it up on the sand. Our eyes quickly scanned both directions of the long white beach for anything suspicious, but it was unmarked by boat or foot tracks. Then we made our way up the sand of the sloping, thin white beach. Paralleling the beach was a typical Asian graveyard, with its cement tombs built to resemble the woman's womb, the womb from which all men come. These concrete tombs were similar to the structure of the Japanese "*turtleback*" tombs on Okinawa. The Japanese call them *kofun*. Here, as everywhere throughout Asia, the air was thick with the living spirits of the dead. The people are Buddhist, and unlike most Westerners, they live their religion. Behind this tomb was a long, low ridge. The forest and impenetrable scrub crowded down to the water's edge. We saw that the area in back of the beach would serve as a weapons testing range, and we found a suitable helicopter-landing zone on the ridge overlooking the beach area. We returned to the mainland.

Patrolling Mission

Our days were spent on early morning training marches and runs with all our equipment. Afternoons were spent climbing rope ladders and rappelling from helicopters. Nighttime was playtime. Days later, our commander, Colonel Beckwith, told us all to pack our gear; we were conducting a training exercise. Our skill and aggressiveness would be evaluated by a number of two-man patrols. We saturated Hon Tre Island and the mountains surrounding Nha Trang. Two-man patrols better utilized stealth and concealment, and enabled us to move faster and safer. My partner, Sgt. Dupris, and I drew Hon Tre Island. We were to perform a series of reconnaissance missions on half of the large island.

First, we would perform a *Point Reconnaissance* on a specific location, maintaining surveillance of the ocean activity near the beaches and of the French planter's plantation located between the two islands. This would be performed during both day and night time. We selected a nice high point nearby, where we could keep surveillance on both the beaches and the approaches to the house at the same time, without having to move closer at night. Before leaving, we would conduct a beach recon: checking the depth and slope of a beach, identifying obstacles, and determining the best possible route from the beach to the top of the island. After our Point Reconnaissance, we would conduct an Area Reconnaissance, during which we were to select the highest point of the island. We would then pick the largest tree at that point, climb the tree, and stick a red cloth in its uppermost branches, where it could be seen and photographed by the Air Force.

The Island Insertion

We were inserted by a Huey helicopter on the windless side of the island. The very first things we noticed were the heat and the thick brush through which we had to move. The water-smoothed rocks were too hot to touch, and the surrounding brush offered little shade or comfort. The small, short leaves were curled and almost dry. Our thirst and the heat made us extremely weary. On a hot day such as this, our bodies could lose up to two quarts of water. We knew that we would soon have to find a source to replace that water.

On the southwest side of the island, there was no real beach area. Instead, a cliff area rose well above the ocean. The waters around these small islands were crystal clear. They were part of a perfect marine nursery, a favorite haunt for whales and sharks. The latter could be frequently seen from the cliff areas.

We performed our point reconnaissance without seeing any boats come near the beaches, day or night. After dark, there were no lights or blinking lights to be seen. It was cold and windy, with a scattered light rain that fell periodically throughout the night. I enjoyed watching the sun come up from the South China Sea. During the day, there were only three indigenous workers to be seen. They worked around the house.

In addition to these tasks, we were to determine the declivity of a small beach area, take measurements, and determining a possible route off the beach and up the mountain. On Okinawa, in the diving school, beach reconnaissance had been part of my curriculum, making this task easy. The small beach proved large enough for a large landing craft, because it dropped off quickly into deep water with no soundings required. The only two possible underwater obstacles that were present were deep. I paced off the dimensions of the beach and tested the depth of the water. There was only one, shallower underwater obstacle, a large rock, and it was deep. I made my drawing for the commander, stashed it, and then we took off up the mountain ridge, following the route most likely to be used as a future road site.

As we slowly moved up toward the top of the mountain, we encountered the ominous buzz of mosquitoes, the real danger of the forest setting. They began to track us as it grew dark, and caught up while we were taking a break. I was paying special attention to the seemingly untrodden leaves of the forest floor when the first sylvan hunter, following our trail of carbon dioxide and body sweat, caught up with us. We were their source of a free meal. She had tracked us from a long distance, and as she got closer, my body heat had given me away. I could tell right away that she liked me. I watched with great interest as the small, elegant female alighted on my arm and started to probe for a blood vessel. I watched her insert and pull her probe out and shift position several times. I knew that when she found the right place, her butt would lift. It lifted. With great feeling, I socked it to her, gently.

Not even the birds and animals were safe from this insect. They transmitted whatever disease was in their system, or whatever disease the previous host had, to you. In addition, to a weekly chloroquine-primaquine tablet for malaria, we were required to take one Dapsone (DDS) tablet daily, serving as a leprosy suppressant. I didn't take them for fear of losing contact with reality or becoming psychotic. Continuing on up the mountain, I thanked our lucky stars; we had found water. There was a soundless trickle that would soon disappear again. It would be enough. We spent the night on the side of the mountain, near a dry creek bed for cover and concealment if needed.

Finding the Highest Point

It wasn't hard to find what we were looking for; we were in open forest, without any understory of brush or smaller trees. All the trees were mature and quite large. The only noticeable disturbance that I observed in the leaves of the forest, were the small, fresh imprints made by the sharp hoofs of a deer in a hurry. The small surface area of the tracks, were made through several layers of leaves. The deer had been trotting from south to north along the top of the ridge. Wondering if the deer was in a hurry to get somewhere or if someone had alarmed him, I climbed the tallest tree at the highest point of the mountain. I managed to put the cloth marker in the top of the tree, where it could be seen from the air. The Air Force would later confirm the marker.

During the night, the islands' massive trees allowed little light to filter down from the treetops. The moon came up strong, and shafts of light dappled the forest floor. We had seated ourselves under the tree-clad summit and determined the highest point and tree. The heat was heavy even in the shade, and I pulled out my small round pebble to suck on. In the morning, we were told to prepare for an extraction. Upon our arrival back on the mainland, we were then told to prepare our gear for movement. I had only to clean my weapon and myself.

Alerted for 1st Infantry Mission

As we were preparing for our mission, we learned of the mortar attack at camp Khe Sanh. They received some sixty rounds from 120mm mortars in the attack, at the beginning of the New Year, on 4 January 1966. The blistering concentration of fire walked carefully over the above ground facilities, destroying everything. The important hardened positions such as the underground bunker and fighting positions were left intact, however. When the NVA firing site was located, it was found that the computed firing data was in Chinese. Our Chinese interpreter had already paid the price for this, but there must have been workers hired in building the camp that paced off and measured the specific targets.

This attack was significant in that it required a major logistical effort. The standard motorized regimental 120mm mortar has a wheeled carriage, and a maximum range of 5,700 meters. It is capable of only small angle shifts of 6 degrees without shifting the bipod. It was reported later that the body of a Chinese officer was also found. I remembered hearing Hanoi Hannah broadcasting earlier, while our team, A-323, built the camp at Khe Sanh, saying, "We will be seeing you." As of 21 December 1966, the newly activated Lang Vei Special Forces camp became operational on the Lao border, on Highway 9. When the Marines were inserted into Camp Khe Sanh to take over this Special Forces camp, our Bru tribesmen were moved from Camp Khe Sanh to Lang Vei.

SGT RONALD TERRY (Project Delta) BEING DECORATED BY THE LLDB

> Bred by nature's drive
> for balance, they are strong
> in mind and heart. They go
> where few return, or none.
> Only one will see them
> go, and know.
>
> *Author*

CHAPTER 9

PROJECT DELTA & OPERATION MALLET

Run For Life

As of 1965, there were already considerable numbers of PAVN troops present in South Vietnam, and the personnel in the People's Liberation Army (VC) were mainly North Vietnamese. Phuoc Tuy Province was the operational area of the newly formed People's Liberation Army (PLAF or Viet Cong) 5th Infantry Division, which was commanded by Senior Colonel Nguyen Hoa. The 5th division had been formed on 23 November 1965, in the dense mountain forest of the May Tao

Mountains, and formed from the local 274th Mobile Regiment, 275th Mobile Regiment, and the D445 Provincial Mobile Battalion.

By November 1965, General Vo Nguyen Giap's regular North Vietnamese Army divisions had begun a bloody testing of the American divisions on the battlefield. Large numbers of American troops were becoming casualties. In December 1965, my home was the 5th Special Forces Group long-range reconnaissance unit, known as the Delta Project or B-52. The 5th Special Forces Group Long Range Reconnaissance Patrols were made up of personnel specially trained to gather intelligence and conduct ambushes, sabotage, or assassinations. Our commander, Colonel Charlie A. Beckwith, a veteran of Mobile Training Team "White Star" in Laos, had been serving in Special Forces since 1958. On 29 December, he was alerted for a reconnaissance mission to support the 1st US Infantry Division in "Operation Crimp." One company of ethnic Chinese troops guarded our compound in Nha Trang. Our assigned reaction force was the 91st South Vietnamese Airborne Ranger Battalion.

"Operation Crimp" was the beginning of our second large-scale search-and-destroy missions and our first helicopter war, a war for which our conventional minded military leaders were unprepared. Our enemy would launch hit-and-run attacks and then disappear back into their vast system of underground tunnel complexes. Major unit commanders needed to know what was outside the range of influence of their heaviest guns. As in every war, secret long-range patrols were the answer.

On 2 January, our three reconnaissance teams, Delta's 145th Aviation Platoon and Delta's two assigned US Air Force Forward Air Controllers, departed Nha Trang for the III Corps Tactical Zone. On 4 January, three additional Project Delta teams arrived in support of this mission. Upon our arrival, however, we found that our unit's mission in DELTA Operation 1-66 had been changed: we were now supporting "Operation Mallet." The 1st Infantry Division in "Operation Mallet" was to clear 78 miles of Highway 15 southeast from Bien Hoa, south to the lowland forest of Long Than district.

DELTA's mission had been stated simply: to conduct an area reconnaissance on the fringe of the Rung Sat Special Zone (RSSZ) for any sign of activity. Our tactical area of responsibility (TAOR) was west of Highway 15, an area cradled by the Rung Sat mangrove swamp to the south and to our west by the large Nha Be River. The large Phu Hoi village was to our north and five large contiguous villages to our east, spread out along route 319 from north to south. Twenty-five hundred meters to our south was the four-hundred-square-mile area of the Rung Sat (Forest of Assassins). This area, located southeast of Bien Hoa and Saigon, was within striking distance of both cities for the PAVN forces. Since the mid-1950s, it had been an operational sanctuary for the Viet Cong and PAVN forces since the days of the Binh Xuyen bandits, who managed the opium traffic for the French Intelligence Service. No reliable up-to-date information was available concerning the NVA and VC Main Force battalions' activity in on our target area. At this point in the war, no American unit had ever operated in this area. What information that was known came from agent nets, aerial photos and enemy actions conducted along the highway. We would conduct surveillance on suspected and known activities and installations to acquire targets for air, artillery and infantry exploitation.

We were issued our map, Nhon Trach, Sheet 6330 II, and our team made its map and aerial photo study. The team leader had earlier conducted the visual aerial reconnaissance and planned his patrol route. The general plan was that the chopper would fly over the forest to the south, make a dummy insertion, turn around, fly slowly back to the north and drop the team short of the forest. It was a period of good flying weather. We would then run into the forest after the insertion, find our remain-over-night position, and make a radio check. The next morning we would patrol to the north through solid forest, checking the area.

Our operational area was in the Nhon Trach District of Bien Hoa Province. This area was covered with a dense monsoon type of tropical deciduous forest that was located on low rolling land 25 meters above sea level, but was well drained. Our operational area was surrounded by roads. To the east of our insertion point was Communal Route 319. Across this road to the east and south were the mangrove swamps of the Rung Sat. 8,000 meters farther east was National Highway 15, leading south to Vung Tau. To our west was Communal Route 357 and beyond, the rubber plantations. The area was heavily populated, as villages were all along these roads. Large swamp and multiple river systems surrounded us everywhere in the distance, except to the northeast.

Late in the afternoon on 8 January 1966, I sat on the ground, leaning back on my pack, trying to relax. I had been watching the mechanic trace the fuel line with his hand and eye from the fuel filter to the fuel transducer, checking for a possible problem. I was on Team number 3, made up of four men, the Team leader SSG Brooke A. Bell, Lt. Guy H. Holland II, myself, and one Chinese Nung whose name is now forgotten. I could see the clouds were breaking up, but it was another gray day for me. The highest form of egotism is fear. The loneliness of my fear was without mercy. There was no sympathy. The pilot had been given the word to crank and had pulled the "starter ignition switch" just after we arrived at the launch area. The Huey was cranked up and the rotor system slowly began to turn and whine, coming up to speed. The pilot concentrated on his instruments. As the ship's main rotor began to build up to its operating RPM's, the noise of the rotor became deafening, and the helicopter began to vibrate. The door gunner motioned for us to load. Our brief silent mental preparation had come to an end. Our four-man team climbed into the ship and we seated ourselves--one man in each doorway, two on the seats. The engine run-up procedures were completed.

The Huey lifted six feet off the ground, hovered, turned and pointed its lowered nose northward. As it moved forward, accelerating to its maximum forward speed, it gained altitude. We then turned southeast and left our loading area behind. The projected weather outlook was for a dry, clear, bright day with high visibility. If anyone was in the area at insertion time, we could be seen. There would be no rain to limit visibility or muffle the noise of the helicopter on its low approach. The humidity would not be high enough to muffle sound either. As

I looked at the light-blue colored sky, it foretold of lasting good weather.

My feet hung above the helicopter's landing strut. As the helicopter gained altitude and speed, I moved my head back slightly in the doorway to avoid the slipstream of cold air rushing by. I could feel the helicopter begin its steep climb. With the wind whipping my scarf and headband, I sat in the door behind the pilot holding on with my right hand, with my left hand holding my weapon and my feet dangling. We rose to about 3,000 feet. Everything looked clean and beautiful. I watched as we flew across miles of forest. The sea of green was below. I was struck by the tranquility of the green mountains and patchwork of fields. Yet I also felt tense and uneasy, contemplating the sinking orange sun's last slanting rays as the dark shadows lengthened.

On the Ground

The ride had been smooth all the way. Far to the north, east and west, we could see cultivated areas and plantations. We orbited high to the north of our area until just before insertion time. Then the chopper, still high in the sunlight, banked steeply and began its run into the area, gradually losing altitude until it banked south and ran in low and fast for the insertion. I saw the last available sunlight glinting off the roofs of the nearest hamlet to our east. It was Dong Lan Hamlet (YS 146807) sitting astride Communal Route 319. We skimmed low-level over the field of grass at 120 miles per hour, with the pilot contour-flying, adjusting the slicks altitude to the level of the terrain. The sound of the Huey was loud. There was one thing that we could count on: the enemy was always highly disciplined and capable of maintaining excellent regional communications and intelligence. If they spotted us, they would do their best to capture or kill us. We would have to use our heads to remain unseen from now on.

The amber setting of the sun, already eclipsed behind the mountains, slowly changed the blue western horizon to a blood-red color. This was an omen of good weather; the red evening sky was an indication that the following day should be relatively calm and sunny. The far-off ridges were set in violet light, which rapidly grew somber as darkness fell. Wisps of orange could still be seen across the sky. The chopper's fast approach slowed abruptly: its nose lifted and its tail dropped to lose speed, then, settling in its descent, it dropped closer and closer to the ground, whipping the tall golden-brown grass furiously in the downdraft. As the team sat in the doorways on both sides of the chopper, we watched the ground rushing up at us with finality. Fifteen minutes until it was completely dark. The chopper had flared and hovered too far out in the field. We were too far from the forest. We jumped the last four feet together. The aircraft yawed abruptly the instant we departed, stabilized, then tilted its nose and was gone from the area. It was 1855 hours.

Ignoring the departing helicopter, we focused our attention on disappearing as quickly as possible into the thick forest ahead. We lined out into a dead run. We were now quite alone in a large open area. The long blades of grass whispered around our legs pulling at our feet. We watched for movement along the tree line. A few small birds rose startled, dipped, shrilled and flew low over the grass and away. I heard the sawing of grasshopper wings in our wake. We had to get as far as we could, as fast as we could, before it was completely dark. Although the NVA would not be able to find our trail in the open field the next day, because the wind and moisture of dew at night would cause the grass to expand to its normal upright position and cover our backtrail, the chances that our insertion had been observed were better than good.

The tall trees cast dark shadows as dusk gradually turned to evening. We came to a slick; wide and well worn trail skirting the outside edge of the treeline. We waited on line in the prone position, watching and listening. The team leaders signaled. Our communication was effortless, without words. The entire team ran across the trail as one, careful to leap as far over the trail as possible, to leave no sign of our presence. I scanned the trail for tracks as I went over it. Nothing. Night closed in behind us as we disappeared into the trees. There was absolute silence in the forest. Without disturbing the leaf-matted floor or foliage, we crawled into a thicket on our hands and knees until the canopy of brush opened up inside. We had found a well-drained and level place where old dry and brittle leaves had drifted over damp leaves. As soon as we had stopped moving and were in our remain-over-night (RON) position, the team leader contacted the command and control chopper and whispered our all clear.

We were on our own until 0730 hours when our situation report was due the next morning, unless trouble developed first. We cleared an area for ourselves quickly, so that we could move without any noise if we had to. We would not eat: to do so would deaden our senses. We sat quietly and patiently, watching our backtrail. The trail had already merged into the deep shadows. An awesome, tense silence rang in our ears. Our survival depended on instant alertness. It was night--a time for listening.

The Search

We would watch and listen attentively in case the NVA came searching for us. There were many larger trees whose canopies stretched over our brush hideaway. This offered us the concealment we needed until morning. There was just enough room for the four of us to sit up and relax until we had to move again. The darkness was our best friend now--we embraced it. The forest was stygian. There wouldn't be a moon until later, and the forest had acquired a stillness that was overpowering. A gentle breeze was blowing. I closed my eyes, lifted my head and took a deep breath, flaring my nostrils. I could only smell the slightly damp soil, rotting wood and leaf mold. Scent carries well on a warm breeze. I have always picked up on scent well, because I have never smoked. The only sounds to be heard were the wind sighing in the trees and the Nightjar bird's harsh metallic ringing "cry--teeok--teeok--teeoker." There had been no large flying foxes leaving the forest to raid the fruit-producing areas for their nightly meal. There had not been the hoot of any disturbed gibbons, thank God. Disturb them, and everyone would know where you were for a long time. The stillness extended itself.

We had been listening for two hours, holed up in the thick deep brush which had sheltered us since our insertion, only about three hundred meters from our insertion location.

Until the moon came up we would remain in place, listening. Until then, we would be engulfed in the brooding dark of the forest night. We wondered if a trail watcher was in the area. The rotting leaves gave off a phosphorescent light. As time passed, I heard a faint barking from a solitary animal to the east. A little later, I heard several animals barking wildly. Within a half-hour, I realized that I had been listening to barking dogs far in the distance, not deer. I had a vague feeling that all was not well. The moon was up and was almost full, with not a cloud in the sky, but we had decided not to travel with it. Our eyes, with the pale reflection of moonlight, glistened brightly in our shadowed faces.

 I reached out and firmly but gently took hold of Bell's shoulder, leaned over to his ear and whispered very softly that before long we would have company; that those dogs barking in the distance meant that men were up and moving around in the distant village. One dog barking didn't mean much--that someone had to take a leak. But all the dogs in the whole village were now barking, which meant a great number of people were moving around. Perhaps the helicopter had been either heard or seen; they would probably search the area before much longer. Bell listened and was momentarily still and silent. Slowly, he leaned over and put his lips to my ear and whispered, "I don't like the sound of that and I hope you're wrong."

 It was past 10 o'clock at night, and the moon had risen over the forest, silvering the treetops and the area near the trail. It was beautiful. We were able to make out definition of form in the darkness. We could still detect nothing suspicious. I was thankful for the moonlit night sky, which was so clear that little patches of stars in the heaven could be seen.

 It had been some time since we last heard the dogs barking, quiet long enough that we were becoming anxious and very tense. Almost an hour later, I began to get a vague feeling of dread about the silence. Our suspicions were confirmed when we detected a faint sound from the direction of the trail. Like all true horrors, the sound we dreaded came in the night.

 The soft swish of feet. Our fear was beginning to grow. The echo was sharp, due to the hard ground. Our heads pivoted toward the noise. It grew louder. It was coming from the direction of the village to our west. We observed a pinpoint of light sweeping back and forth across the trail. They were looking for an indication of earlier movement, such as the distinctive type of track left by the American-issued jungle boot, or the grass pushed down. Thank God, there had been no rain and there was no dew on the grass to cause us to leave evidence of our passing. We strained our ears to hear the faint sound of men briskly walking along the trail. We caught the far-off murmur of voices. Men were talking low. Voices carry well at night. Then there was a metallic sound followed by the tread of walking soldiers. We knew the enemy had heard or observed our helicopter insertion, or both. Now our complete silence was imperative. I felt a cold, gut-wrenching fear.

Bell had reached out and touched each of his men to alert them as they sought each other's hand for comfort-- reassurance that all would be well as long as they had each other. We were in the close proximity to the enemy and able to conveniently observe them. They could not easily surprise us. We had to calmly remain patient and control our nerves. Bell also wanted to prevent any of us from sudden panic, since we were new to him and, as far as he was concerned, untested. Our eyes and ears were riveted toward the direction of the trail to the muffled sound of equipment and a man's voice. We listened and waited in breathless silence. We had become the hunted. I felt a sudden desolate sense of loneliness.

The Forward Air Controller (FAC) aircraft would not again be on station until after light in the morning, but would remain on standby even when not in the air. During the daylight hours he would make a large orbit just out of hearing range, though sometimes if conditions were right we would be able to hear him. This was to preclude the North Vietnamese from pinpointing our patrol. It was now 2300 hours.

Found

Again we heard the heavy and clumsy tread of many men and equipment on the trail we had crossed earlier. Again came the soft swish of men walking through grass. In the darkness, muzzles flashed for 15-seconds, as they randomly shot into the brush. Swaying my head like a snake to catch all possible light from the sky among the branches, I made out the black shadows of moving khaki uniforms and metal through the dark brush. The flash of their weapons reflected from the lighter patches of earth in a few cleared areas along the trail. I caught the quick reflected red gleam of the large eye of the nocturnal Nightjar bird, during his noiseless erratic flight searching for a flying moth. The Nightjar had possibly been drawn to the pinpoint of light in the vicinity of the trail. Bell leaned close to my ear: "They are trying to make us give our position away." The only thing they were really accomplishing was losing their night vision, since they didn't have flash-hiders to shield the flash. Movement on the trail had been steady for about a half-hour before it became completely quiet again. The murmur of talking men took a long time in passing. There had to be at least a platoon-sized element in our general area now, searching. We decided to remain in place. I was now worried and afraid of what first light would bring, if we lived until then. I dimly imagined what would happen if captured.

The Night Before

I strained to hear and suddenly my body went tense. I knew I had not heard anything distinct, but the darkness of the night had sent me a message of silent warning. I sensed something was going to happen. My hands reassured me of the magazine in my rifle and my knife. My educated thumb unconsciously sought out the selector switch on the receiver of my rifle. We strained our eyes into the dark to see the outline that didn't belong out there but we could see nothing out of the ordinary. Then I heard the sound of a branch hitting wood that I knew to be a wooden rifle stock. I tried to control my breathing, and fight back the rising sudden fear. I sensed Bell stiffen, I placed my hand firmly on his leg and squeezed asking, "You awake?" "I know," Bell answered before I went on. "I heard it, too." "We got visitors again on the trail." More men were moving on the trail. I felt sick.

Time to Move

The stars had gradually faded. The darkest hour had come and gone. It was now Before Morning Nautical Twilight (BMNT), when we were first able to see to our front. The time that we had dreaded all night had arrived. There was just a hint of the gray pre-dawn light coming from the east. The forest was emerging from the darkness. We knew that the enemy had not gone back the way they had come; therefore, it was reasonable to assume that they had checkerboarded the area and were now waiting for the team to move. If the team didn't move, they sooner or later would make a sweep of the area and find us. I could already see the first dark gray stains spreading across the sky overhead as the sun came closer and closer to the horizon. It was a primeval morning, as the dim outline of trees took shape. We knew there were now many men positioned and waiting for us to move. We would soon be discovered. We didn't feel good about what we were about to face. Sunrise came. Our biological clock was set. We had lived through the first night.

It was suddenly morning as the gray of the dawn faded to yellow, gold and brilliant orange spreading across the eastern sky broadening to daylight. The miraculous birth of a new day dawned bright and clear. But there was none of the usual deafening and musical sunrise sounds of gibbon troops hooting. The quiet seemed excessive. An omen. My mouth was dry from fear and my gloved hands were sweaty. I took two salt tablets, and carefully and quietly tipped the plastic canteen and drank some of my water, so I wouldn't dehydrate if we got the chance to run for it. I didn't want to get killed because of cramps, exhaustion or heat stroke. With our fingertips we brushed leaves back over our remain-over-night site. Satisfied that it looked natural again, we prepared to move.

With a half-hour to radio contact, Bell directed me to take point and move almost directly west, crosswind on an 80-degree azimuth for 100 yards, then turn directly north into the wind and maintain that direction. With dread, I tightened the carrying strap on my rifle over my head, so it wouldn't drag. I made my night setting on the compass. I noticed Bell watching me do this. I had always used a night setting even for daylight, which made it easy to use while running and maintain a known direction. *Your life depends upon it, especially if it grows dark on you while running.* We rose quietly and moved in ghostlike silence, slowly like a snake emerging from its den. The team moved, maintaining a staggered five-yard interval to avoid creating an easily observed trail. Our weapons ready, each man faced his area of responsibility. The rear security, the fourth man, would observe to the rear in an arc of 180 degrees for anyone following us. The team leader and the third man observed flank security, mainly to the sides, while I covered to the front. My eyes were fixed on the horizon to look for changes in our surroundings. This way no one man had to turn his head too much. Movement, no matter how small, is easily observed in the forest. We would change directions frequently the way animals do.

The Ambush

I was on my hands and knees so that I could prevent outlining myself and see under the brush, watching for color contrast: contrast between the mottled light and shadow, anything that was brighter or duller than its surroundings, motion or well-placed booby traps. Crouched, the whole team began to move with great stealth. We were careful not to rustle the few dried leaves on the ground, snare our uniforms or make a noise by brushing against branches. Most of the leaf mat was still slightly damp and silent underfoot. I could smell the damp soil and the slight rotten odor of decomposing leaves. If it had been drier, it would have crackled with the shifting of our weight. It had not been too long since the last rain and the soil was still rather soft beneath the fallen leaves.

Even now, however, every now and then there'd be the slightest, faintest crunching of leaves as we moved over a patch of drying ground. To me, it sounded like an avalanche. We now had to take great care; a fresh green leaf knocked to the ground would strongly suggest our presence, or a broken twig above the ground would indicate our direction of movement if we were to be trailed. Bell was following me in a low crouch, his eyes at a level just above mine. We stopped every few yards to watch and listen. We heard nothing at all. There was

In This Valley There Are Tigers

no chirping of insects. The trees stood in unmoving silence in the gloom. There was limited visibility, due to their great size. No birds sang. No monkeys whistled or howled as they usually do in the morning. We were near a large field, and there was no buzzing of grasshoppers or crackling sound of their flight. There were none of the usual day sounds of the critters that we were used to hearing, no sound at all, save the overhead whisper of the leaves. It provided no sense of security. There was no whispered communication, only the felt presence of each other. The branches of the trees met and mingled overhead, producing a deep, dark gloom further into the forest. Where we were, close to the edge of the forest, there were still patches of sunlight. In several places the canopy opened in glistening patches, letting in the sun through a luminous curtain of leafy green. Lingering, billowy, oval-shaped clouds in the blue sky peeped through, giving a tranquil, silent assurance of well being for the moment, but an inner awareness was screaming at me.

The silence was an indication that the critters had been very recently disturbed. The Vietnamese were waiting for us. Bell indicated that we should stop and listen. I studied the way ahead, so that I wouldn't have to look at the ground so much. I would move very slowly, staying in the shadows, keeping myself, and the team balanced, so that we were not so awkward and noisy in movement. It was time to make our situation report and inform the FAC of the contact made during the night. Our operations center would be listening and have the helicopter crews prepared to launch if needed. We broke out our long antenna for our AN/PRC-25 field radio. Our radio had a line-of-sight transmission of 25 miles.

At the end of transmission, the long antenna was unscrewed, folded and put into its carrier, when Bell lightly tapped his rifle, indicating it was time for me to move. I froze in place, stopped dead in my tracks, listening, attuned to an inner warning that caused my adrenaline to run red hot. All my senses screamed: *Danger!* Staring ahead under the brush, my senses keen and attuned, my eye caught a flash of motion and faint stirrings. One of nature's miracles, a miraculous warning came of the presence of others. *Our enemy!*

Nature's Sentinels

A coalesced flock of about ten, small jittery birds, of different descriptions, wary and watchful, were flitting and skittering through the brush with an undulating flight, chattering angrily as if they had been disturbed ahead. The birds stopped, cocked their heads, their beady eyes observing our unmoving figures with clear suspicion. My heart thudded like a trapped beast. Time dragged on. *Where are they?* The only sound was the beating and whiffing of wings fluttering forward five or six feet at a time, during their restless arrival and departure, as they broke around us. They darted everywhere. Branches bent and whipped as they came and went so close, whistling an alarm across our path from shrub to shrub, alerting us to danger. All flying at the same time meant they must have been disturbed by a large number of men. As quickly as they had appeared, they were gone without a sound. I was scared of what could happen in the next few moments. My sphincter was tight. On a higher consciousness, birds serve as signs, protectors, and teachers.

I struggled with deepened respiration and quickened circulation. We remained perfectly still. My mind was full of dread. My heart was racing. The birds moved past the team on both sides as if we were just part of the forest. I had a bad feeling about this. Danger was very close ahead. I flattened myself onto the forest floor to peer ahead so that any object to the front of my vision would be silhouetted. I scanned the area, looking for any spot from which a hidden enemy could watch us, unobserved, and saw nothing. I scanned and tuned my ears in for that little displaced something, that half-hidden motion, that unnatural shadow, an unlikely sound. Nothing. Everything was too silent. We waited and listened. The back of my neck was crawling. Bell leaned over to my ear and whispered: "What do you think?" I stared at Bell for only a moment: "I think that we had better change direction right now." Mother nature had given us a warning, and we had paid attention.

Bell pointed the change to the prearranged direction of south. I made my night setting change on my compass. We were all thinking the same thing at the same time--that a large number of men were scattered throughout the area waiting and watching, all hoping to be the ones to ambush our team.

From sheer habit, my right thumb constantly felt out the location of the weapon's fire selector switch. My thumb would do its job without being told. I listened and watched for sound and movement, and tried to see into all available cover. As I moved, I kept asking myself: "If I was shot at right now, where would I take cover?" Now in a low crouch, head and body held upright, elbows in to my sides to maintain body control, I turned my foot in the air, keeping my balance, so that it came down pointed in the direction I wanted to go. This way I avoided any scraping noise and then turned my body to align my step. I placed the outer edge of my foot down and rolled it inward, feeling for whatever was under it, and allowed my weight to settle while scanning the area intently. We remained in the shadows to blend with our surroundings.

An ambush would have to be close up. If we were able to detect them first, it would at least give us a good chance to defend ourselves if need be. However, we would break contact without fighting, and run, if at all possible.

The further we moved, the more anxious I grew. The trees grew close together overhead, shutting out most of the light. The vegetation was thin at ground level. We had not yet detected any movement. We could now see only about 30 yards ahead. The ground was slightly soft and dank. We moved cautiously, but as the uppermost layer of dead leaves settled softly under the weight of our feet and bodies the slight crackling and crunch sound echoed and magnified in my ears. My heart beat quickly. Nothing moved. The sun had risen well above the horizon and the air was turning hot. The tops of the trees swayed gently with the wind, which seemed to be blowing from the east. I momentarily thought about rain possibly coming, but hoped not. Rain would only mean one thing--that a trail would be left wherever we would go. Although flat terrain made it easier to detect someone, with my head just above ground level, I still saw nothing to hide anyone. I saw the high termite mounds and disregarded them. It would be the last time during the war that I would do that.

Minutes later I thought I smelled something different in the air. My head ached, and the pain in the lower part of the back of my neck was intense. I felt as if a rock were sitting high in the pit of my stomach. My throat felt thick from the pressure. I was alert, but suddenly frightened. An aura of threat prevailed. My sixth sense was screaming at me now that the NVA were close by, lurking somewhere behind the cover of the forest. I felt death staring at me with invisible eyes. A light breeze working our way caused me to tilt my nostrils and take in a deep lungful of air. A slight odor had aroused my nose. That ancient sense, the hoariest of them all, fired a continuous signaling cry of warning to my brain. Mouth open, I breathed in slowly in short breaths, expanding my nostrils as I did so. I smelled something different, the salty, pungent smell of urine. My eyes searched frantically, left and right. *Nothing!* The air was warm enough now to identify the unmistakable smell of sour acidic sweat; body odor and clothes saturated with wood smoke and incense, rifle oil, and the unwashed smell of those who eat a lot of fish oil. The aroma just hung there.

A cool, persistent wind began to blow through the trees, causing the leaves to flutter as others began to fall. *A slight smell of mothballs!* The Vietnamese were manning a position located in the base of three old red dirt termite hills sticking up from the forest floor. A silent signal must have been given because several mines went off at the same time. The surrounding forest silence was shaken by the loud explosions. I felt a rushing in my ears. The sudden sound found us already face down in the dirt. The communists were rapidly shooting at where we had been standing, now empty space. High-velocity rounds tore through the quiet solitude of dawn's early light over our heads. I could smell the acrid stench of cordite in my nostrils. There was no time to think. I felt my lower lip quiver. They were well camouflaged and positioned below ground level, watching in the undergrowth behind the termite hills. Evidently there was a tunnel system at the rear side.

We had reacted to the threat instinctively, simultaneously, effectively. Dropped to the ground together, facing the enemy. We recovered from the shock quickly. There was no cover between our team and the NVA. Bell whispered loudly for grenades. We pulled the pins together and on command lobbed them the very short distance to their positions. Our team was gone in the blinding flash, smoke and flying dirt. The grenades were almost perfectly on target. In seconds it was over. I was last up and running at the sound of the explosions from their chosen killing ground. The ambush had lent wings to our fear-driven feet as we attempted to vanish. The shooting had stopped. I heard a nervous chatter of Vietnamese behind me. They realized we were already gone. Only the smoke and drifting debris was left wafting away on the breeze. We knew the value of time and opportunity and had to put a lot of daylight between them and us. Our feet drove into the soft, mulched soil. We ran. We could not sustain the pace for any length of time. Now, our success would depend on how we used our time and the terrain.

On the Run

I was well behind and had to catch up. I ran blindly, fearfully and with utter determination into the darkness of the black forest. This would be a long-distance showdown, and all we had in front of us was the wild vastness of solid forest. We had to shake them somehow. A bullet narrowly missed me, making me stagger in the wind of its passage. My muscled legs exploded into action, elbows pumping in time to my fear-driven feet. Filled with terror, my head went down and I dug in as hard as I could. My brain slowed down the passage of time so that I seemed to run forever, blindly eating ground in huge springing strides, to catch up. Panic time! I almost lost sight of them, hugging the deep dark shadows ahead of me. I was running as hard as I could and had gotten into top speed within just a few full strides. We had stretched out into a strenuous long running stride, working our upper bodies as much as our legs. My arms rose and thrust like living pistons. I soon realized I was wasting precious energy using my arms and would pay for it later. As I fought for my breath, I could hear the dreaded sound of sporadic gunfire behind me. Right now, I had to get out of their line-of-sight. Again I heard the distinctive chatter of 7.62 caliber rounds from Mr. Mikhail Kalashnikov's assault rifle cracking and popping in the air over and close around me. The leaden messengers splashed the trees around us, ricocheting off into the thickening forest in whining tangent to our flight. I instantly thought that I was being fired on from another direction, but realized that a high-velocity round passing a large solid object like these large trees will make a sonic crack. Bark flew off the tree next to me. My cheek and arm were stung hard by flying chips of bark. Bullets pattered the tree directly ahead of me. Some fragmented themselves, hurling bits of lead in all directions. Leaf litter was dancing by and ahead of me as bullets tore little furrows in the ground. I ran right to put a large tree to my back as I continued to run.

    I saw the team leader running. His pack blew up. The combined force of his running and the bullet that had found him center mass drove him into a tree, knocking him down. Then Bell was up and still running. The inside contents of the pack had stopped the bullet. I expected that every step I made would be my last. We ran at an amazing pace, penetrating deeper into the verdant forest, trying to lose them in the shadows to blend in, to become an indistinguishable part of the background. The idea was to let our bold and natural, broken striped camouflage color pattern that ranged from light to dark "blend in" breaking up our form and work for us. My last glimpse revealed the NVA doggedly pursuing at a distance. We ran, seeking the sanctuary of the dark timber, our feet pattering on the damp leaf mat. Running at angles from the cover of trees into the darkest shadows, hoping their eyes could not follow our line of flight and momentarily lose us. A high-velocity round cracked over my head. Camouflage could not hide our movement. Once discovered, I knew our trail was easier for an expert tracker.

    I heard the distinctive popping sound of many weapons being fired simultaneously behind me. Death whispered through the air. Suddenly I saw the team leader, ahead of everyone, run straight into a tree. He bounced backward, smashing flat onto his back on the ground. Bell got up just as quickly as he went down and continued running. My head jerked forward and my eyes and mouth opened wide as bullets being fired from an automatic weapon began to hit the tree directly in front of me, showering me with bark and spewing clumps of earth around me. We ran like the wind. I was running scared as the gaps between us widened. I felt the challenge. I was well conditioned and ready. I felt the fire in my spirit rising to the test.

We moved in unison. We had to stay together. The three other team members ahead of me were running fast. We had to put as much distance as possible between us and those following. My breathing became labored, as my aching lungs struggled to meet the demands of my body. I was wheezing and could hear the blood pounding in my ears and feel the violent coursing in my veins. My chest was beginning to feel painfully tight. My heart felt like it was up in my throat, my legs a little heavy from starting too quick a pace. I was worried. I was feeling the effect of fatigue early. We were slowly settling into a slower pace; we were measuring our stride, so that we could run effortlessly and maintain it over the long distance. Everyone knew that we had to regulate our breathing before pain hit our sides. We could run a long time that way. My lungs hurt. We didn't know how far we had to go yet. As far as the map showed earlier, we were in solid forest with no landing areas close by. So, with our feet rising well above the ground, we maintained a pace that only the hardiest of Vietnamese would be able to follow. Breathing rapidly and heavily from fear and hard running, I knew I now had to fight hard to control my fear as sweat formed rivulets down my face. I tried to keep the larger trees to my back for cover as I ran and endeavored to remain in their shadows.

The Air Force

Finally I saw the team stopping to make our first check with the Forward Air Controller (FAC). The pilot was flying the low-altitude, slow-flying O-1 Bird Dog, our on-duty observation aircraft. The team leader would inform him that we were in contact and trying to evade. Since larger aircraft had trouble picking out ground targets, the FAC in his small O-1 acted as a "spotter," marking targets with white phosphorus (WP) smoke rockets. He could direct aircraft right in on top of a fast moving ground force or a well camouflaged, hidden enemy. As I stopped, I briefly saw their frantic faces stare as I caught up; the anxious facial expressions were of worry and terror. I quickly set my rifle butt down as I kneeled on one knee behind a large tree and held onto the barrel with both hands, high up, and laid my weight onto my arms. I rested, leaning on them, getting my breath. In the shadow of the great tree, I took three deep breaths to try and clear my mind. The hairs on the back of my neck prickled, my whole body was soaked in sweat. My tunic, black-wet, was plastered to me. My mouth open, panting, I leaned the barrel to my shoulder and unbuttoned the top three buttons of my shirt to help cool myself.

Easy Visual Tracking

My throat burned and I could feel my hammering pulse there. My chest was heaving in breathless agony, as my throat and burning lungs rasped for air. Contact with the short antenna on the radio couldn't be made. The radio required the use of the long field antenna; therefore, our first attempt to establish communication with the FAC was not successful. For some reason, he wasn't there. He may have been flying just a little too far away. I was watching our backtrail. I neither heard nor saw anything, but felt a presence, eyes watching me, as though they were arrows, probing, searching. I was nervous, mouth dry, heart thumping wildly. I studied the patterns of light and dark and finally distinguished an outline. Then I saw the strange surreal shadow, long and black, shift. It seemed as though something dark stood there. I trembled. He was standing with his back to a large tree, making it difficult to see him. I knew he could see our trail. He could see us. I could see our back trail and the unmistakable scratch marks made in the leaf duff from our vibram boot soles. I turned my head and eyes ever so slightly and slowly to catch the light and scan to see if there were others following behind him. My breathing still labored, the intervals quick and short, I tapped my rifle. Movement in the shadows beyond the tracker. A number of moving shapes in a low crouch followed the tracker. A shiver climbed my spine like a lightning bolt. They were coming; they were trailing us. The pressure was building. The stress--both emotional and physical--was there. I shifted my feet and eased slowly toward a standing position, as I heard the team jump up and move off, continuing to run again. I turned and was off again, keeping the large trees to my back. Flying bark peppered my back, as rounds struck the tree. My starving lungs still gasped for more air. As I ran, my senses searched the isolation of the forest surroundings concealed largely by darkness. Tension and anxiety were building in me, but I knew I could outrun them. I just had to focus my concentration to help my body work better. By this time, I had forgotten that I had a pack on my back, four grenades, three hundred rounds of ammunition, rifle and a harness with all the tools of survival attached and a completely wet uniform. My will to survive gave me strength. They were following close behind, but they couldn't shoot accurately and run.

    We had been running easily now for sometime, trying to melt into the forest. We were still hanging tightly together, not stretching the distance out between ourselves during the run, except to keep enough distance that a single round would not get us all. We settled into a fast pace. We lifted our feet just enough to clear the ground and slide them forward, keeping our arms down in a relaxed position. We were slowly lengthening our running stride and applying a little more force to cover the ground more quickly. Our stride changed periodically as we adapted to the changing surface of the forest floor, but it remained just short enough that it wouldn't tire us too quickly or cause us to trip. Our gait developed into a fluid grace. The flat, deep carpet of the leaf-littered forest floor was firm and a little springy. It was easy to run on, and retained little impress of our boots except for the few disturbed, topmost leaves lying faded, dry and crisp that betrayed our passage. At this point, there was nothing I could do about that. The litter of leaves, deceptively beautiful, made our footing treacherous, hiding leaf-covered rocks, roots, holes and branches. We didn't have enough of a lead over our pursuers, and could not afford to fall and hurt ourselves. If I stumbled on a rock or a dead stick buried in old leaves, they would have me. I felt a heightened sense of life. The landform gradually rose, and wide, shallow depressions created by rain runoff appeared, not noticeable to the eye at a distance. I feared we would run up on the enemy lying in wait.

I could feel the sweat running down my face and legs. We didn't have a lot of obstacles to overcome while running, except for ducking under the occasional branch and vaulting large fallen branches. I knew we could be trailed more quickly. As we twisted and turned, running between the trees, we had to watch for shadow-shrouded holes wherever our feet were landing to keep from injuring a muscle or tendon in our legs. I stopped momentarily behind a large tree. My body, now use to being in motion, had not wanted to stop. Peering back into the depths of the shadows, I again saw a slight movement. With the silence of smoke, he was no more than a lone shadow in the gloom. I would remain conscious of him now, every second of this run. The tracker was well trained and wasted little valuable time determining our direction. I ran on.

I tried to search for any hint of movement in the wider area of my peripheral vision, trying to take in a 180-degree arc in case they were ahead of us, waiting. I had to concentrate on not looking at the obvious or restricting my focus to a zone of 10 degrees, which is what most people do; I had to see the wider field of view around us. We ran and ran, beginning to feel, more than see, that our pursuers were closing in. The sun was high and the heat of the day had begun. The amount of sweat coming off my head was blinding. As we navigated our way through the forest, I tried to keep focused ahead of me and to the sides as much as possible, though fatigue set in too quickly from running.

The Forward Air Controller

We finally stopped again and made our second attempt at establishing communications with the FAC. As I tried to relax, I sucked in air to recharge myself with oxygen. We made contact; I could see Bell talking. On subsequent radio checks we could now use the short antenna because the FAC would be coming within closer range. Those checks would be quick. The team leader quickly informed us that there was nowhere close by to use as a landing area, but gave us the general direction in which to run that would eventually take us to one. We had a long way to go. The good news was that a flight of Air Force A1-E Skyraiders were already close by, flying in orbit, waiting. We were in trouble. Deep trouble! We now began serious evasive action by changing directions and dropping our first smoke grenade. We would continue to do this after each radio check. Now we were really going to have to run. The Air Force would immediately strike between two smoke grenades. The FAC was now at a high altitude over our position and would hold an extremely tight corkscrew turn as he descended, studying the terrain for a sustained period of time.

Our zigzagging would consist of sixty-degree changes, while maintaining a general direction of travel to a pick-up point. These changes in direction would briefly delay the tracker and hopefully give us time and a distance gap. As rear security, I would tap my rifle to warn the team on the radio when I first saw the enemy trailing and catching up to us. A shadow moved and melted into the dark again. Then I saw him. I tapped my rifle. It was hard to say how long he had been standing there. It seems that the same man always appeared first. He had to be the tracker. The tracker had that earnest single-mindedness, the ability to observe and interpret the faint distinguishable trail we left on the springy leaf-covered ground. Each time I saw him, he was either moving at a steady pace or was a motionless hovering shadow, standing or in a crouch, head near the ground, always looking up.

The tracker was using the oblique light angle to look ahead to see and read the visible line of disturbance we had made in the leaves while running. Wherever our fast-running trail deviated from a straight line, the leaves were flattened and depressed and reflected more light. Other leaves were violently pushed outward from our feet and upturned to the side; these leaves pushed up by our downward foot pressure appeared darker for the tracker to see. The available light revealed a color difference. I could feel his brown eyes probing the shadows, circling, seeking, and always picking up the trail again, because he knew where it would go. I just hoped he didn't already know where the nearest LZ was. I wanted to kill him. I tried to get him in my sights, but I was breathing too hard. I braced the rifle against the tree. I had too much sweat in my eyes and still could not steady the rifle. I wasn't supposed to fight anyway, unless I had to. They finally broke the long antenna down and the radio pack was slung onto the operator's back and we ran, knowing we were no longer truly alone. Our stride lengthened through the dim half-light and dark shadows of the massive trees.

While running, I was beginning to feel the effects of the rising temperature. I saw a large tree ahead of me. When I got to it, I stopped behind it and looked back. I could see nothing. I could feel him there. I had to run hard to catch up and I was laboring. My mind's self-discipline was willing my body to continue. I had to ignore my own discomfort. I needed to catch my second wind. My body was producing a tremendous amount of heat. Sweat clouded my eyes. The team stopped again to make commo. I slowed, stopped, turned and stared. Nothing. After a few minutes, in the distance I could make out flitting shadows. In warning, I tapped my rifle. Sweat ran down my nose, falling in a steady stream to the ground. The FAC had again been informed of our changing azimuth on which we were going to run. We took off running again, dropping another smoke. As soon as the FAC observed the second smoke, he notified the fighter aircraft and flew off to one side of the area.

While running, I unbuttoned my shirt and opened it the best I could to help cool my body. I unwrapped my camouflage scarf and put it in the side pocket of my pants. I was feeling sluggish, and had to be more careful of the many fallen limbs and holes. I was losing track of time. I knew I had to keep thinking. I had to keep running. I saw that the team leader had again stopped and was on the radio. I stopped and took a position behind a large tree. I watched our back trail. There was nothing--only the silence and the shadows. I quickly took another drink of water. I thanked God for the sugar in my canteen. My water was mixed with "Bugs Bunny Kool-Aid." Again there was no time to rest.

I caught a slight movement through the screen of trees. Inevitable as destiny they loomed. It was like a terrible primal nightmare that was reaching out to grab me. Then I saw them coming again, gliding like shadows from tree to tree. I stared:

one, two, three small dark forms moving quickly, coming nearer and nearer. I didn't wait to count more. There were many more. I tapped the rifle and waited for the team leader to start the run again. I wanted to shoot that tracker so badly but I was still breathing too hard to be accurate. We were off running again before the color could return to our faces. The FAC was now informed of the azimuth and distance we were running, and that we had dropped a smoke grenade. My body was beginning to struggle during the run. My heart rate was so high that I felt like it was going to burst. I was using too much energy too fast. I knew that I had to gain control of my body. I was gutting it out. I was tired. I was feeling a little pain. It was crucial that I will myself to concentrate to keep my mind clear. I had to fight to control my breathing to let my body recover, or my legs would turn to cement. I knew if I didn't, sooner or later I would run out of energy and fall on my face. I counted on my tiger suit to blend in. Now that we were deep in the dark forest with these big trees I wasn't so afraid they would hit me, as I have always run faster in the dark. The popping sound of the automatic weapons behind me was brief and frightening. Several rounds exploded into the ground nearby, sending up geysers of dirt and leaf litter. Another burst of automatic fire barked the tree closest to me. They could still see me.

I dropped my arms down and carried my slung rifle low at my waist, my right hand on the weapon. It had to be carried slung because if a bullet hit me, the impact could be great enough to cause me to drop the rifle while running, which could mean a considerable distance between the rifle and me. I kept my stride long while watching for an ambush to the sides. I gradually began to push myself mentally. I didn't know how far we had yet to go. Growing weak now would mean only one thing--dehydration.

Napalm

I could see the team stop and the team leader operating the radio again, which was still on the other man's back. I went down behind a tree in an instant. I took up a watchful position behind a thick tree trunk, waiting for the Vietnamese to appear on our back trail. I tapped my rifle as I saw the evil little buggers cautiously coming through the trees like shadows. They were moving fast. At the same moment the team leader finished his transmission, we dropped a smoke and were running quickly. I could hear the loud, gigantic piston engine of a Skyraider swell, coming in extremely low and slow. I saw and heard the thunder of an A-1E go over just above the trees. He was momentarily framed against the sky. The thundering noise of the Skyraider's big piston engine washed over me then retreated rapidly in the opposite direction we were running. I caught a glimpse of the shiny six-foot-long napalm canister dropping free and tumbling end over end. The napalm tanks were designed to tumble when released to increase its gooey spread. If anyone had any doubt about where we were, they didn't now. I only slightly turned my head, and saw out of my peripheral vision the TNT and white phosphorus initiator explode. The jellied orange fire covered a large area and created a large fire and black smoke immediately behind us, further advertising our location. Inside the aluminum canisters of jellied napalm was a honey-like mix of 33 percent gasoline, 46 percent polystyrene thickener and 21 percent benzene. The flammable substance was the color of wheat and had the consistency of honey. Whatever the napalm hit, it would cling, and because of its consistency it would stick and cause more damage. Those caught in the open area of coverage would die from burning or carbon monoxide asphyxiation.

    The ground shook again and again. It scared me so badly that I rolled in the leaves and then was up running, looking for the last man ahead of me. Again I heard the sound of the fast, low-approach of the propeller-driven A-1E. Our pace picked up. The fixed-wing Skyraider aircraft would now be dropping their 250-pound bombs. There were popping white flashes and concussion waves from the explosions that felt like they were right behind me. The bombs and the enemy were close behind. Black smoke and debris were everywhere behind me. I knew that the impetus of the bombs at impact would throw most of the shrapnel in the same direction the aircraft was flying. Pieces were flying overhead everywhere.

    Now we would run approximately 100 yards as fast as we could to put as much distance between us and them, in order to stop again and make another transmission. The Vietnamese would now pursue us at a faster rate. They knew now for certain that their only safety was in staying as close to us as possible. Otherwise, the A1-E's would turn them into dog meat. The Skyraiders would do the same to us if we didn't run like hell as soon as we dropped a smoke grenade. The Skyraider was always precise with its ordinance.[1]

If the NVA were running as hard as we were, they wouldn't be able to shoot very accurately either. Then several bullets hit the tree next to me, blowing bark off like minor explosions. The NVA weren't being diverted from their attempt to catch us. The AK-47 assault rifle round rarely deflected on hitting anything in its way. As soon as I ran by a large tree, bits of bark were flicking off and hitting me. After passing the large tree, I put it to my back and ran directly away from it so that it hopefully covered my back. As my distance increased from the tree, I would pick another tree on the opposite side. Every now and then I had to run around a patch of sunlight. If I ran through the light, it could be momentarily blinding. I would not even look at the occasional patches of bright light so as to keep from ruining my light-sensitive peripheral vision. No matter how fast I ran, my legs still couldn't keep pace with my despair. I had to block it out. *"It's just a state of mind,"* I reminded myself. "Concentrate--I will make it." I started to pray and slowly felt a surge of energy. Sweat and fatigue blurred my vision.

At our next stop, torrents of sweat streamed down our noses from our weary faces. Our uniforms were much darker now, completely soaked from sweat. We informed the FAC that we were changing direction again. He was just low enough over us that he could see the smoke in the trees. We gave the FAC the azimuth and distance we were going to run on and dropped another smoke. We ran like animals, zigzagging through the forest. The bitter realization I had was that we would not elude the tracker on our trail. One leg we would zig and the next we would zag, as we were aware that the A-1E's were going to immediately strike between the last two smoke grenades. In the distance I could hear the sound of the aircraft and its cannons firing.

Bbbbrrrrrbbrrrrrrrrrbbb!

They came in extremely low, strafing, sending me rolling again at the sound of expended cartridge shell casings falling around me in the trees. The aircraft expended a hundred shells a second. The big, thumb-size bullets that would blow a man up were tearing into and through trees and ricocheting behind us. I was continuing to sweat--a good sign. I knew if I got too hot I was in trouble, but as long as I concentrated on my breathing and kept it regulated, I was safe. All my senses were heightened. I now felt energized psychologically and physically. While I watched for the Vietnamese to catch up to us, the wet uniform kept me cool. It would have dried quickly but we didn't stop that long.

I had only one real problem--to conquer my fear and keep a sharp watch while running through the forest. I heard and felt the wind from several bullets go by me. For one brief second I thought that I needed a miracle. I realized that my second wind had just come unexpectedly and that my body was capable of a lot more. I felt comfortable and warmly relaxed. I felt the deep places in my thigh muscles pumping, sliding, expanding and contracting. I no longer felt heavy. There was strength in my stride. My leg muscles were humming. I couldn't remember when the piercing pain had passed out of my lungs. There was no sign of cramping or dizziness. Sweating rivulets, my breath was now becoming a rhythmic flow. The whole team was still running strong.

Extraction

We had stopped for commo again. After talking to the FAC, Bell said that we were just a short distance away from our pickup point. The command and control ship, pickup ship, and gunships were already in orbit, waiting for us to arrive. I suddenly realized that I had the ability to make it through this ordeal. The miracle I thought I needed had just been received. I felt we could outlast those trailing us. My mind was now convinced it could push to other limits. I prayed a bullet wouldn't hit me. I prayed that I wouldn't turn my ankle. Now, all those years of running and working out would hopefully pay me back. I had not yet seen the Vietnamese trailing us. We dropped our smoke grenade. They had not caught up to us, and we were off, running with hope in our hearts. We could hear the A1-E's coming in again.

BBBrrrrrrbbrrrrrrrrrbbb!

My mind registered the sick tenseness of my adrenaline-filled body, hearing the sound of the fighter strafing the jungle behind us. Tree trunks exploded around me. We ran harder as the A1-E's roared over. The large 20mm cartridges, which were being kicked out of the wings, fell all around me briefly as the aircraft passed directly overhead. I was still sweating. My mouth was still wet. Both good signs. If they were to become dry, then I would be in trouble.

Running in the rear through the dark-green gloom, I could now see a bright view ahead, directly across our front. We were approaching a clearing. I caught up to the team and threw myself down on the ground. I paused, looked up, my eyes sweeping around at the members of the team. Strong-spirited, piercing eyes looked back. I could hear them sucking in their breath. Bell turned the radio on. Bell said, "McDonald, get out there a hundred yards in the open and get your panel ready." I thought to myself: "Out in the open, with all these men trying to kill us!" Finally, out of the dark and into the light. Crouching low, I started running for the open, beyond the trees. Just as I reached the tree line, I dove forward, seeking the concealment of the thigh-level, tall grass, quickly low-crawling on the flat of my belly. The tall grass was waving as I parted it in a fast, low crawl out into the field. I looked back at the trees and knew I was far enough out.

I had just removed my international red/orange panel when Bell yelled, "Stick it up." There was the faint heart-stopping sound of rotor blades coming from the south. I could now hear the heavy whopping sound of the rotor blades of the approaching chopper in the distance, coming fast. I rolled over and stuck my arms straight up and pointed the panel at the chopper. It roared over my head and kept going. If I had failed in getting the panel up in time and getting an acknowledgment of our team's position, the Vietnamese trailing us would try their best to send us to hell. The lead helicopter had seen the panel and acknowledged our position. Then, I heard the menacing throb of approaching gunships. For me, the sight of these helicopters would become the most enduring image of this war.

I heard the roar of gunships firing, lifted my head and glimpsed their glinting rotor-blades. I saw the two gunships hovering just above the far tree line. They were covering the rest of the team as they broke from the cover at the edge of the forest. I watched the Huey coming in fast. The recon team, anticipating the Huey's touchdown spot, was running full stride for the pickup ship. It came in fast, flared violently while decelerating, lifting its nose and dropping its tail, leveled and landed quickly. I looked up as Bell ran past me yelling "You coming?" I was up and running. The gunships were continuing to fire on the forest edge. I was into the prop wash and then the helicopter. I had beaten the team leader to the helicopter. I was running for everything I was worth.

My forward momentum was so great entering the helicopter that I had to be grabbed by the door gunner to keep from going out the other side. The crew chief had grabbed my harness and held on. Chest heaving, and rasping for air, I listened for the sound of rounds popping above the whine of the Huey's turbine. I didn't hear any. The tempo of the blades increased and the pickup ship lifted, tilted its nose, and ran forward toward the forest, then lifted up, with the aircraft's skids barely over the trees, nosed the Huey over and accelerated away. Sitting in the door, I looked down. Below, inside the tree line under the trees, the area was full of troops. Little yellow muzzle flashes were twinkling from AK-47s everywhere. They were clearly visible as they shot their last rounds at us. Then I felt the cool air as we ascended upward to a safer altitude, above the range of small-arms fire. As I looked at the spectacular landscape, I realized that I had just competed in the ultimate experience and had won. I had survived. We were alive, through some miracle. I started to shake from an adrenaline rush. It was now 1030 hours on 9 January. Our pickup area was just north of route 319, in the least populated area of the road system. Beyond it was 300 meters of open rice fields and then the mangrove swamp.

We were overheated and drenched in sweat, it poured from our pallid faces. I looked around behind me, as I sat in the door and looked at the others. I saw eyes glazed with exhaustion and strain. Our chests still heaved. The muscles in my legs were trembling, almost cramped. The wind in the open doorways of the chopper cooled us. When we got back to our base, the black door gunner smiled at me and told me that we had looked like wild animals running out of the forest. I had felt like one. Team's 1 and 2 were still in their operational area. We had been the only team chased out of our operational area, so far. After the general staff debriefing, my Commander, Colonel Beckwith, asked me how I felt. I said "O.K." The Colonel said: "Good. You're going back in tomorrow." This time it was a suspected truck park.

That night I jerked awake from a bad dream, filled with a terrifying vision. It was the kind of dream from which you awake with your heart in your throat. Bathed in sweat, I laid immobile. For a long time I remained almost paralyzed, struggling to breathe with an accelerated heart rate. My eyes were wide open, staring into the darkness. My neck and shoulder muscles were tight. I feared where I might be and what situation I might be in.

My dream was that of a lone helicopter insertion into a small landing zone encircled by tall trees. I could hear and feel the wind and the rotor turning. I could see the forest clearly and smell it too. There were tall trees with their rotor-whipped branches waving as we descended. I also saw the individual faces of the PAVN standing inside the tree line watching. At this point I felt a strange paralysis, knowing what was about to happen.

Then, I awoke. I lay there, my chest rising and falling convulsively, still feeling the immobility and fear, I was confused as to where I was, until I became aware of my real surroundings and realized I was safe for the time being. I got up and started preparing for the new day's mission. The dream clung to me as I took a shower and afterward as I ate breakfast.

Everyone else was strangely silent. I wondered if anyone else was experiencing their own demons. Was this my destiny? Now, for the first time in my life, I was really frightened.

2nd Recon Mission/Operation 1-66

The day had arrived all too quickly for me. It was 10 January 1966. I was tired and shaken from my dream. Everyone went about their own business silently. We were all up for breakfast and would spend the greater part of the day preparing ourselves and our equipment for a last-light insertion.

Briefing

Our team assignment was given. I was now on team number 6, a three-man team that included SSG Frank N. Badolati, SSG Ronald T. Terry and myself. Frank was the team leader. I was low man on the totem pole. Air Force aerial reconnaissance photos revealed a suspected truck park. We all accepted our next patrol assignment with our characteristic stoicism, and as usual our inner feelings were anything but calm.

In Flight

I sat in the door looking into the onrushing air, staring at the landscape. My feet dangled above the skids. There was not a cloud in the blue sky. The sun was setting on the western horizon. Our Huey would fly at 2,000 feet until approaching our operational area. About a mile out, the helicopter descended to treetop level. The Huey now hugged the contour of the treetops and ran straight into our insertion point, shuddering as he reduced air speed. I knew the whopping of the rotor blades could be heard two miles away by anyone on the ground.

On the Ground

Our insertion point was just a small break in solid forest. A very small clearing was all that there was. The hole was just large enough to lower into. The pilot was experienced. He had to be. He had to hover the Huey, and then start a slow vertical descent. I listened to the loud hum of the turbine engine and felt the vibration of the rotor system as we descended through the trees. I prayed no one was around to hear or see us. The rotor wash wildly agitated the foliage. Through half-shut eyes, I watched the down draft of the rotor blades. Branches, leaves and twigs danced all about in unison, some breaking off and flying everywhere. The down draft was flattening the tall grass. We jumped the last seven feet, freeing the chopper of our weight. The chopper yawed briefly and immediately lifted back up with the increase of engine power felt by our departure. The aircraft soared up into the sky and was soon gone. We were alone. The silence was total.

After the insertion, working with a long stick and my rifle as quickly as possible, I meticulously closed and poked up grass and weeds. I brushed it upright smoothing away the obvious signs from the wash of the helicopter's rotor blades. I then worked at closing our narrow, flattened passage through the grass as I brought up the rear to disguise our passing from any casual observer. The formation for antitracking is the Indian file. Everyone stepped in the footprints of the man in front of him. The humidity was high and there was enough of a wind to allow the grass to return to its upright position after six hours. With my help, our trail would be hidden by morning. The forest was too open for good concealment, but the grass beneath the trees was above our waists. Badolati and Terry led off with long, steady, noisy strides. I followed as rear security, stroking the blades of grass back into their original position from where our feet had trodden. We moved under the gloomy and seemingly unending stretch of forest. After we put some distance in from the insertion point, we slowed down to a quiet pace more suitable to seeing what was around us. Now our eyes were doing most of the walking, as we placed our feet before committing our crouched weight. Our arms were held close to the body. It was now easier to keep up and pull the grass back in to hide our trail. I didn't have to hurry.

The 1st Night

We skulked along very slowly from tree to tree through the tall grass, blending ourselves to better advantage. Stopping at each tree, we pressed closely. Our roving eyes watched for any movement. Nothing other than natural sounds pervaded the silence. There was now only a murmur of a rising breeze.

My ears attuned to all the sounds of the forest, caught them and arranged them to my knowledge of this country. There was only the low hum of insects pervading the air. Suddenly my head was up and alert, lifted by a tremendous sound. There it was again. It was the sound of bats leaving their hanging perch. They flew with a near-silent force into the empty blackness, some distance away--all were real to my senses. We had to stop for the night. Like a black mantle, the darkness settled over us. Standing and listening, I could hear only the whispering wind, my mind filtering sounds. The dark sky above the trees was studded with white, cold stars. In order to keep my edge, I finally slept.

The 1st Day

With the sun rising behind us, we moved slowly toward the mountain with our eyes on the grass horizon. I had the point. The air had cooled during the night to dew point and left us in a dangerous situation. There was heavy dew on the grass, and we were leaving a well-defined trail. Hopefully, no one would stumble upon it; the heat and humidity burned the dew off, healing our back-trail. I had learned early in the war that grass usually returns to its original position, especially after a good rain. One of the best anti-tracker traits is to remain patient, moving slowly and carefully. We made a lot of stops, to watch and listen. Once a tracker has hunted you, you learn to move more carefully, remembering the fear and terror. We had all been tracked and hunted, and had no wish for this to happen again. We knew we were never safe.

The Jungle Chicken

We quickly ducked low within a dry, sandy depression of a streambed. While whispering and trying to decide which direction was the best direction to travel safely and unobserved, we watched in rapt attention as a jungle chicken unhurriedly worked his way down the slope and into the dry creek bed with us. It is said by shaman that among the deities that if chickens are listless in their eating, the gods are angry. The chicken is the enemy of ghosts and evil spirits, which roam free at night and are bound during the day. All three of us looked at each other and smiled. *The gods are not angry.* It served as a reminder to remain vigilant. Nothing was said, but the decision was unanimous. Our subconscious at work and listening to our instincts, we decided on the direction that the unalarmed jungle chicken had come from. Our brains and intuition took over.

We started working our way up the mountain. A large bamboo grove blocked our ascent up the steep mountain. Bamboo is to be avoided because it is specifically noisy. Just one man attempting to walk in a bamboo groove is noisy, much less three men. We made a detour around it and moved up the mountain.

At the top, we took a break. We could never relax our alertness for a moment, trying to keep a constant vigilance. Our bodies cried for rest, but our instincts would not let us. Periodically we dozed and woke, dozed and woke, always conscious that someone may be searching for us--watching us.

The Monkeys

We were taking a break on top of the mountain, sitting apart. I felt an unseen presence around me. Then came the sound of branches rustling, scratching and chafing against one another. There was also the sound as if someone were walking in the leaves and scratching. It made me turn my head. Badolati stared at me with his finger to his mouth. He wanted silence. A large band of gray-colored, muscular macaque monkeys had moved into the midst of us. They had been moving through the terrain on the ground and in the trees in search of food, gathering and eating vegetation, smaller animals and insects, when the large males made contact with us. We froze in place. The troop smelled us and then I could see that they saw us. We avoided staring them in the face, a perilous faux pas in simian society. The soft movement of man-like walking in the brittle dry leaves drew my attention to the two larger figures on the ground. The troop watched two large, older males from the smaller trees around us, while keeping a close watch on the sky. They checked every bush and every tree they walked under for winged or ground predators. I watched the nearest large, aggressive male with his chilling glare. The old male cocked his head while looking at me, and with a barely audible growl, he warned the others of the troop to go back. The longer hair on the back of his shoulders was standing on end. They were only slightly excited by our scent. Another large male exhaled a series of deep, quick huffs and swayed on its hind limbs. We just watched, barely daring to breathe, our necks muscles tight with waiting. The shoulder hair went down. He didn't perceive a threat. They were now mainly curious about us, but with any sudden movement the entire troop would be screaming at us. Everything in the mountain and surrounding forest would then know we were here and where. We now had to sit very still for fear of alarming the troop. Knowing that a direct stare from a monkey is a threat, we kept them under observation only in our peripheral vision. We didn't dare move. I watched several large males in different trees come down the tree trunks head first, watching us closely. When they were all aware of our location, some sat upright on the ground and stared. Others stood erect. Most of those on the ground had gone into the trees. Then as if some silent signal had been given, they quietly left the area just as they had entered.

Finding Water

The cave was located on the north side of the mountain, at the head of an open draw, above a dry creek bed that was surrounded by tall trees and large boulders. Because of the path of the sun, only a little colorless light flooded into the cave. It was not so deep or wide, but it was cool and moist. At first it was completely dark inside the cave until our eyes adjusted. From the entrance, we could hear water dripping and pooling within. Terry and I lay on the broad bench to the cave and watched the surrounding area while Frank checked the cave. Further back inside, there was a slow dripping sound. A check with a flashlight inside revealed a thin, soundless trickle staining a rock face. Badolati had found water. When he came out, he said, "Drink and fill your canteens." Water also ran down from the ceiling on the wall of the cave into the same pool of water. The pool would allow us to fill our canteens a little faster. I smelled it, and then tasted it; we had good water. It was a cool place. While filling my plastic canteen, I studied the dark void surrounding the cave entrance. I didn't like the cave, I felt trapped within it. On the ledge outside we rested, and just quietly watched and listened a while to the buzz and drone of insects.

A deer sprang into the clearing below us. Then with long, graceful strides, head erect and pointed forward, it came bounding up the hill. It stopped and stood motionless just below us to our right and quickly turned its head, staring back down the hill, nervous and alert. Its cupped ears pointed downward and rotated slightly. We were all eyes and ears, trying to see and hear what had frightened the deer. It lifted its nose slightly to the steady uphill breeze, scenting for odor. With one stamp of its hoof, it moved quickly into the timber and out of our sight. We immediately ascribed its behavior to human intruders. Peeking over the ledge and without moving our heads, we scanned the area. We detected nothing upright below us in the shadows. It had to be a big striped cat. Thank God. But still we waited and watched for something to move. We saw nothing. As we continued to move further down, we could see that there was definitely a good dirt road at the bottom.

The Road

We had to check the road for signs of use in daylight. We knew that the low, flat area would be kept under observation, and dangerous to cross if anyone were around. We approached the road and crouched down, watching both directions, while listening and examining the dirt roadway from different angles.

Alert and cautious, we observed a shallow depression and moved to it along the side of the road. Using the low area in the roadway, we spread out, walked out and checked it for tracks. The sand and clay-like silt of the road was fresh and clean since the last rain. Whatever sign had existed had been washed away, and the ground was still clean. All the grass areas were standing upright. It had definitely been well used, but not recently. No vehicle or foot tracks were found, not even a partial track.

Terry checked about a half-mile of the roadbed for tire and foot tracks. Badolati and I waited, checking inside the brush and woodline, on opposites sides of the road. The ground, grass and leaves in these areas were also undisturbed. No old or fresh broken twigs or branches were to be found. We found nothing except the easily distinguished animal trails. The area was clean, except for what sign we may have left. I had brushed out our tracks in the road with a leafy branch.

The Second Night

We found ourselves a position just off the road to remain over night to listen and observe for any night movement. During the night, Sgt. Ronald Terry slept too close to a nearby termite colony. They followed the odor of carbon dioxide exhaled through his normal breathing to his location and completely ate up his ground sheet. The immense soil-dwelling colonies have elaborately structured mounds with over a million individuals. They smelled like mothballs. They marched in columns along exposed odor trails or underground constructed humus trails along the surface of the ground. They would eat rubber, wood, electrical cables and living trees. We always carried a thin, noiseless and pliable ground sheet to sit or lay on during the night.

Extraction

Early the next morning, we made radio contact and were ordered to prepare for an emergency extraction. The only LZ available was near some betel nut trees. The area wasn't big enough, so we attacked the trees with our large knives. Before we could finish clearing the LZ, the helicopter had arrived. The pilot informed us that he would finish the job. I could see that the main rotor blades visibly slowed with the impact of the trees. Blocks of the trees flew as the aircraft descended. The imbalance of the blades made for a shuddering ride home. A set of blades was ruined, but we were out. It was now 0825 hours on 14 January 1966.

As soon as we returned, we learned that all teams and their personnel had returned safely. We were standing down. Our reconnaissance missions for the 1st Infantry Division were over. As we prepared to leave and during the trip to Saigon, we listened to the accounts of the other team missions.

Team One

Team number 1, made up of SFC Marcus L. Huston (Team leader), SFC Robert K. Price, SFC Robert P. Whitis, and two nungs, on 8 January, had also made their last light insertion at 1855 hours. At the time of insertion, they went into the wrong landing zone at grid coordinates YS 078861. The Team leader decided to exit the helicopter onto the ground. After the helicopter left, it was too late to do anything about it. The team made quick radio contact with the FAC and then shut the radio down. After an uneventful night and a little early morning map work they realized that they were now located 2500 meters from their intended landing zone, and were presently in a populated area crisscrossed with many trails. The team was located just south of Bau Ca Hamlet, putting them between a populated area and swamps to their immediate south. SFC Huston realized that they would only remain unseen by using their heads. He thought that being too close to the populated area would increase the chance of discovery by anybody--an enemy patrol, a native worker, a boy accompanying livestock or even a stray dog.

The terrain between the team's location and their assigned area of operation was very sparse, running between an open rubber plantation to their north and another to their south. During World War II, this area of old Cochin China was controlled by Japan and accounted for much of the world's natural rubber supplies. The specimens of Hevea, the tree family that produced the milk-like latex, from which rubber is made, dominated this area.

After making a radio check with the distant FAC and reporting negative enemy contact, they gave him their direction of movement on an azimuth of 123 degrees and shut the radio down. A good look at the map and the terrain revealed that the low areas would permit their movement across the open, flat terrain to remain hidden from distant observers if they kept a low profile and a good interval. The ground sloped slightly higher to their north and lower to their south and east. Keeping to their route moving cross-country was easy; in the distance to the left was the forest and to their right, it was open and brushy. They traveled on the hardest ground they could find in order to leave as little evidence as possible of their passing. The sun in the first hours was in their eyes; a slight wind was in their faces. They used the long shadows of the small trees and brush thrown in their direction. Soon the sun would be overhead and at their backs, and they would have to cross this dangerous area by using the natural depressions in the terrain. They moved without incident. Later in the day, the sun, now at their back, acted as a rough guide for their direction of movement. There were few clouds in the early evening sky, promising fair weather for the next day.

At last light on 9 January, the team leader reported negative contact to the FAC. The team spent the night in a little hollow in the open, huddled close together in tall grass that hid them from view. They sat with the dark shadows of the surrounding brush at their backs to disguise their own shadows in the lighter colored grass. As their eyes searched during the day, their sharp ears frequently turned to the light breeze to listen, suspicious of every sound. The night slowly passed, uneventfully.

Tracks

Early in the morning, still using the cover of darkness and the terrain to their advantage, they again moved slowly. Their first stop was to make a successful commo check. Without making any noise to betray their movement, they stopped frequently to study the ground and listen and watch for movement. They crouched below the skyline and their background, moving only in the natural folds of the ground, letting their eyes do most of the walking and alert to any sound.

They arrived in their tactical area of responsibility (TAOR) at last light on 10 January, and reported this in their commo check to the FAC. With the cloaking darkness finally came the twinkle of stars. When the moon came up, it gave an eerie glow to their surroundings. Only the natural sounds were heard, the wind, the chirping of birds and insects. This night, too, passed uneventfully. During the early morning hours of 11 January, the team moved until the point man halted the team and moved ahead. He came upon a clean and smooth, high-speed trail, well concealed from above. The point man, in a crouch, dropped to one knee in order to examine the trail more closely and scrutinize the faint, fresh prints. The prints were on the opposite side of the trail from the sun, and the shadows from the ground disturbance showed up better against the sun. The sandal tracks were easily seen, telling him what he needed to know. He pointed for the team leader. There were distinguishable tracks to be seen. Men had recently passed this way, moving northwest. The Team leader, now excited, decided to watch this trail that ran from the northwest to the southeast. The team backed off and sat, keeping the dense shadows behind them so they could not be seen, and observed the trail from a distance. SFC Huston checked his grid coordinates (YS 103844), then made his commo check, making the FAC aware of their position and the nearby trail. The quiet team listened to the whispering of the trees and the calls of the tiny birds.

At 1140 hours, his eye and ear caught the flutter and quick flight followed by a plaintive twitter of a bird down the trail. Perceiving something suspicious, SFC Huston lightly tapped his rifle stock, signaling for attention. He silently alerted everyone. They waited and watched in the direction of his line of sight. Soon, because of the hard dirt nature of the trail, Huston detected a sharp echoing sound and vibration emanating from down the path on the light breeze. Someone was coming; there was faint movement, approaching from the southeast. They now stared intently down the trail. Soon, three armed and alert NVA came into view. The NVA were easy to see against the light surface of the trail and the dark green foliage. The eyes of Delta worked feverishly. The weapons of the NVA could not be identified because the team remained hidden too far back in the brush. After the enemy walked out of the area, the quiet was again oppressive. Patiently, the team continued to wait and watch. Later, at 1545 hours, another three-armed NVA were observed moving in the same direction. The enemy was dressed in black, except for one individual, who wore a khaki shirt and tan helmet. SFC Huston now eased his team through the shadows of the thick scrubwood, 1,000 meters to the south, to grid coordinates YS 104834. Then he settled into the brush, watching another high-speed trail exiting the rubber plantation. The trail to their front ran from the northwest to southeast, to the side of route 357.

Again at 1800 hours, a team of two-armed NVA was seen approaching from the southeast. One soldier was wearing all black and was armed with a 1903 Springfield rifle, or possibly a Mauser; the other soldier, wearing a blue shirt, was carrying an unidentified automatic weapon that had bipods.[2] To SFC Houston, there were three possible answers as to who and what these men were doing, in keeping with the timing of their sightings: (a) these patrols were commo liaison personnel carrying messages and mail or guiding a replacement to his destination; (b) this activity indicated a camp somewhere to the northwest; (c) because of their concentration, they could also have been checking the trail for sign of tracks crossing the trail or in the trail. After the team reported the enemy activity to the FAC, they remained in position overnight, listening for traffic on the trail; however, this night too passed uneventfully. The next morning, SFC Huston, after making commo, warily eased the team northwest on a general azimuth of 338 degrees to grid coordinates YS 101843, where the team exfiltrated during the morning of 12 January at 0830 hours without incident.

Team Two

Team number 2 was made up of SFC David W. Disharoon (Team leader) SSG Billy A. McKeithe, SSG Norman C. Dupuis and two nungs. On 8 January, their helicopter skimmed in over the treetops, dipped toward the ground, flared and before settling to the ground, dispatched the team. The team had inserted at grid coordinates YS121839, 300 meters east of communal route 357 without incident. Some 2 kilometers further east was the all-weather communal route 319, which was heavily populated all along its distance. One high-speed trail was just to their north and another a kilometer to the south. After moving quickly away from the insertion point, the team moved into an overnight position. During the dead of the night, the team listened attentively: there was little wind. No unusual sounds were heard.

On the morning of 9 January, after sending their situation report to the FAC, the team moved slowly and carefully southeast. Their direction of movement was easy, using the rising sun seen through the treetop as a guide, keeping it on their left shoulder. The area was heavily populated, so the teams movement was slow and cautious, easing forward only a few steps at a time, keeping to the available cover and concealment, spending most of their time at a halt. They patiently watched and listened while resting, noting that the multitude of birds all acted normally. There was no need to look at watches. When the sun was overhead, it would be noon. Traditionally, few natives moved about during this hotter part of the day. There was little wind, the sky was clear and the air was warm and humid. They memorized their location with their reference system in their heads in the event of trouble. After moving about 100 meters, the sun by now was setting in the last quadrant of the sky. The team leader, watching flights of birds going to roost, selected a remain-overnight position. Another night passed without incident.

In the small hours of the morning, on 10 January, as the stars had begun to recede, the team was alert and prepared to move. At a signal from the team leader, they rose silently and started moving. Again, they cautiously moved a few steps at a time. The team had been moving off and on for over two hours in this manner, stopping frequently to watch and listen. All of a sudden, Disharoon woke up, he didn't realize when the change had taken place, but there was an abrupt silence, the birds were no longer active and noisy. It was too quiet. Too still. They had moved approximately 50 meters during all this time. Now, nervously alert, they first observed a deep shadow within the shadows. The team stopped to prevent any betraying movement and went to ground. There was a faint movement, then the shadow became shadows, then forms. As his eyes searched left and right, he realized he was observing an enemy platoon 50 meters to his front taking a break on the trail. Most of them were lying back on their packs. Their slight upright stationary movements had given the PAVN away. SFC Disharoon slowly crabbed his way back a couple of feet to the radio behind him and, checking his watch and radio. He knew exactly what to do.

Now came the repulsive primal moment of truth: he was going to be responsible for killing these men. Cautiously and quickly, SFC Disharoon turned the volume down before turning the radio on and preparing to transmit, hoping the FAC was not too far away. The time was 1230 hours. He whispered into the handset. Contact with the FAC was immediate. He gave the enemy location at grid coordinates YS121835. The team now waited and watched, as they listened to the distant FAC orbit in a very wide circle marking the area in his mind and on the map. Waiting on the A1-E's to arrive; the FAC then flew further out of the area, for the unsuspecting enemy was sure to be listening.

Each aircraft carried 8,000 pounds of mixed weapons, including napalm, bombs, CBU-14s (bomblets) and four 20mm cannons with which to strafe. The team waited. Finally, after three-quarters of an hour, the FAC informed the team that they were ready. SFC Disharoon's trained ear could hear the slow, reliable old A1-E Skyraiders, rolling in and lining up for their approach run. As they watched, the sitting, quiet and unseen birds in the trees now began to scatter in flight. Disharoon knew that this aircraft was very precise in dropping ordinance. He saw the enemy soldiers frozen, listening in breathless silence. Too late, the ultimate terror; they realized they were the target. Shrill voices revealed their sudden panic as they started trying to run into the shadows in every direction. Disharoon could sense their fear.

The air strike was quick and sudden. The low flying aircraft jettisoned the silver canisters. They tumbled end over end. The six-foot-long canisters struck the tops of the trees. The flames burst. A splashing, burning wall of fire rained down onto the ground, enveloping those frozen in disbelief and too slow to react. A symphony of nightmare screams followed the roar of burning as clouds of black smoke rose. The screams pierced each recon team member and made their blood run cold. The noise level became unbelievable. The team lost all sense of time as, with dry mouths, they watched this emotional spectacle of their making. Disharoon informed the FAC that they were on target, and should widen their target area a little bit. The next aircraft roared over. The wall of flames was now closer. The intense heat could be felt. While the area burned, the Skyraiders were dropping their bombs. The heavy percussion's shook the ground under the watching team, lifting them slightly. The noise was terrific. They felt the shock waves beat against their watching faces. The aircraft banked in a climbing turn, circled and again rolled in to continue the attack, slowing their speed as they started their blazing strafing runs. Their guns chewed the trees and ground as the debris of leaves, bark and branches exploded everywhere. The team watched the explosive impact of the 20mm cannon rounds. Debris and limbs flew everywhere. Then it was over and the sound of the aircraft engines faded into the distance.

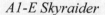

A1-E Skyraider

Again it was quiet in the forest. Very quiet! The team lay close to the ground, watching and listening. Then SFC Disharoon had to check the area. Now came the hard part, making the bomb damage assessment (BDA), the acceptance of those he killed, looking at them, seeing their faces close up and personal. Smoke and dust hung over the horrible napalm and bomb-blasted debris of death and destruction in this section of forest, as the team searched the target area, finding numerous body fragments. The area smelled of blood, burned flesh and feces, and the stench of death. The scene was imprinted on their minds. There were fifteen bodies scattered about the area. The team now ran through the target area and moved on a short distance to the southwest.

As the afternoon and early evening quickly passed, SFC Disharoon stopped the team to prepare his situation report. After sending the report to the FAC, and with darkness quickly approaching, the team cautiously continued in a southwesterly direction toward a possible extraction point. They found a place to remain over night. Disharoon's flesh crawled knowing that many of the enemy had gotten away and that by morning they would have to move carefully. It would be a long night. . .

During the night, the team remained absolutely quiet, and the night sounds echoing around them were normal ones. The night passed without any unusual occurrence, and the first streaks of daylight were now appearing in the sky to the east. The scent of the air was clean and sweet. The team studied the surrounding forest as the sun rose slowly. After sending their scheduled morning situation report on 11 January, the team again continued their move to the southwest. The team had taken several breaks during the morning to listen and watch before moving on again. The sun was now high overhead, helping the team to see into the shadows. Disharoon's eye caught the sudden flight of a bird. Then the point man heard movement and saw a faint gleam ahead. It was coming directly toward them. With pounding hearts and fingers on triggers, the whole team stopped at the direction of the point man. Each man took cover behind the nearest tree trunk, dropping to one knee. A faint but fast-approaching dark, bulky blur of form ahead moved on a collision course with them. Suddenly, the team encountered six well-armed enemy soldiers at point blank range, face to face. Looking into their eyes, the team's instant reflexes reacted to the Vietnamese before their startled response and shock allowed their minds to react. Forced to open fire, some of the men fired from their kneeling position; two men moved up on either side of the three men forming a line, and remained upright as they fired. The bodies of the Vietnamese bucked, shuddered and twisted in pain from the impact of lead from the automatic fire as blood spurted everywhere. The team killed five, wounding the sixth. The wounded man didn't last long. This encounter had been close and personal. Luckily, none of the team was wounded. Now utterly terrified, they realized that the PAVN would know where they were from the sound of the gunfight. The PAVN would instantly recognize the sound signature of the M-16 rifle, know an American reconnaissance team was in the area and know their general location. They were compromised and in big trouble. Time was running out for them.

Looking at their map, the team leader plotted his location at YS121835, then picked a place on the map where he hoped there was a space large enough for a landing zone. They now had to move southwest on an azimuth heading of 213 degrees as quickly as possible to the landing zone approximately 1,000 meters away. SFC Disharoon made immediate contact with the FAC and told him of their situation, present location, direction of movement and the coordinates of their landing zone. Now they could count on being tracked wherever they went. SFC Disharoon had decided to forego the closest area, only 200 meters away to their west, in hopes that the NVA would be delayed in searching this immediate area. He realized that the quicker the team moved, the more they would scuff the surface of the ground, making it easier for the PAVN to track the team. He had to avoid the panic of moving too fast.

The PAVN already knew where to start looking for positive proof of an existing trail of someone that didn't belong in the area: somewhere near the bomb-site, and when they found their dead patrol they would by then know their direction and number of people involved. Once the PAVN found where their trail started, they would visually track and follow their trail. The team would travel southwest on a general azimuth of 212 degrees. Being careful to avoid ground disturbances and making periodic abrupt changes in direction of 90 degrees for short distances would help increase the time and distance gap between the team and their pursuers, and would make it more difficult to track the team. Hopefully, it would take the PAVN a long enough period of time to find their trail and work out their sudden turns and again reestablish their trail. However, Disharoon realized that the PAVN would soon reason their true direction of travel. It was possible that they would sense the intended route and know where it would end. Hopefully they wouldn't guess the extraction point before the team got there, wouldn't be waiting for them. Any clearing in a forest area was a danger area. Their route of travel paralleled communal route 357.

The team, tired but elated, found the landing zone at grid coordinates YS116826. Their eyes observed a grown-up field surrounded by a line of trees. Reassuringly, they could hear the FAC in the distance. The team leader quickly made contact with the FAC, who told him that the pickup ship was inbound and that tactical air support was now in orbit. The team leader directed the point man well out into the field. Concealed in the brush and grass, the point man ripped the international orange-red panel from his pack and readied it. The rest of the team laid flat in the grass for concealment outside the woodline with the last trees for cover, watching back toward the forest and listening for their pursuers. The team leader knew the PAVN were aware of their location and were now spread out on line coming through the timber. Then the team heard the distant incoming sound of the engines behind them. The first helicopter roared low over the distant treetops, flew directly overhead and kept going, verifying their position and panel. The team could hear the NVA, now close behind firing at the helicopter. Then it appeared just over the tree tops and settled, flared and touched quickly down, as two gunships rose above the distant tree line and provided covering fire into the edge of the forest, providing the distraction needed to allow the team time to load and be extracted. The recon team broke from their concealment and sprinted some fifty meters through the tall grass and brush of the clearing to the pickup ship and leaped aboard. The pursuing PAVN had all arrived at the edge of the forest by now. Even under the covering fire of the gunships, the extraction ship and the gunships were taking enemy fire. Then the pilot was pulling back on the collective. The ship lowered its nose, running forward and picking up airspeed, rose over the forest and departed. Shortly after the sun had passed meridian, the A1-Es rolled in with successive strikes of napalm canisters, then eight general purpose, 750-pound bombs and twenty 100-pound bombs circled the landing zone with a curtain of steel, killing some twenty-five personnel.

Saigon

We were trucked into Saigon in the M35, 2 1/2-ton Cargo truck. I passed the time during the trip watching the villages I passed, where young women winnowed rice by tossing it on a flat basket in the fields, while farmers bent and straightened under their conical hats. Small children herded flocks of ducks. As far as you could see people were working the land. Finally, we arrived at our destination. Saigon was known as the Paris of the Orient because of its lovely, tree-lined boulevards. The city has had many other names in its distant past, but the original name of Saigon had been Prei Nokor, "settlement in the forest."

Fascinated, I watched the streets clogged with a torrent of three-wheeled trucks, old cars, taxis, noisy motorcycles, scooters, military vehicles and the quieter whir of thousands of bicycles weaving through the streets. The city had 1.5 million people. All the traffic moved without the use of streetlights. I was amazed at the amount of blue exhaust smoke in the city. There were clouds of it.

Saigon was Vietnam's largest city, located in Gia Dinh Province, 45 miles from the South China Sea on the Sai Gon River. It was also a major port of entry for sea cargo for the war. It was a beautiful, decadent and very dangerous city. A city where you were never safe, but it swarmed with beautiful Annamite women in the traditional ao dai, the high-necked split tunic over full, loose cotton trousers. At night, there was little traffic on the streets and the torpid air was filled with the cool smell of camphor. Naturally, we found ourselves sitting in a bar on what the French called the *rue Catinat*. To the Vietnamese it was "Tu Do," or "Freedom Street." Saigon was a place to relax and enjoy the pleasures of life; for no one knew how much longer he would be able to. Life in Vietnam could be very short. It was easy to recognize our behavior. We were in a state of depression. Each of us was undergoing our own individual, distressing internal conflict, a crushing weight that came into focus on the realization that there was no escape from the realities of the war, that we were expendable. And so we physically fought with others at the drop of a hat, isolated ourselves from friends, spent all our money self-medicating through drinking and womanizing. I came to realize that I had to break out of this state of being. I had to leave. My decision was made.

I left the bar and spent the rest of my time walking almost everywhere, looking and watching. I didn't want to think. At night, in the heart of the city, the neon signs of bars and nightclubs lit up the area everywhere. We were soon on our way back to our base in Nha Trang.

Going Home

After our assignment to the 1st Infantry Division, DELTA was officially on a 15-day stand down. Upon our return to our camp, a letter waited for me--the answer to my dreams. It was the girl in the kimono in the Sacramento library. At first sight of the brown-eyed, black-haired girl, I had fallen in love. She had turned down my marriage proposal. But after I had left for Southeast Asia, she had relented and decided that she would marry me. I was granted a 15-day leave. On 20 January 1966, I returned to California. A week later, I married Keiko Iwai in Reno, Nevada.

Wife

My beautiful wife Dr. Keiko Iwai McDonald was Buddhist-Shinto. She was born 1 January 1940, in Nara, Japan, where Buddhism was established in 749 with the dedication of the Great Buddha at Nara. In Japan, Buddhism vies with the national cult of Shinto. Keiko was a World War II war veteran, having survived the bombing of Japan. She had a medium complexion, black hair, brown eyes, stood 5 feet 2 inches tall and weighted 100 pounds. I had met my wife in my hometown of Sacramento, California in 1965. She was educated in both Japan and the United States, receiving her undergraduate education in Japan and her graduate education in the United States. Keiko became a naturalized citizen on 1 May 1970, in the Lane County Courthouse in Eugene, Oregon. Her naturalization number was 9413637.

Unbeknownst to myself, the worst disaster in the Vietnam War was about to occur to Project Delta while I was on leave. Still, during the days and nights to follow, severe anxiety caused an uneasy feeling. Call it my gut feeling, premonition, my intuition, a sub-conscious warning, whatever. It was very real to me. I came to believe that I was being given a glimpse of my fate. I believed that the dire force of the dream was warning me of a future reality. Between my premonitions and suffering the break-bone pains of dengue fever, I found no relief in sleep. I was actually afraid to go to sleep.

My wife, Keiko, would remain my guiding star in all the lonely, dark nights and years ahead. For all too soon, I would be on my way back to the war. Amid the brutalizing violence, my heart and mind would be full of love. I would remember her presence, her beauty, her intense brown eyes, which would always be with me. If it had not been for her, the brutalizing dream would have swallowed me.

Footnotes:

1. The versatile Douglas A-1 Skyraider (SPAD), recognized by its throbbing eighteen-cylinder piston-engine roar, was first deployed in the Korean War. The A1-E had the endurance to carry a lot of ordinance and stay aloft for hours. When fully loaded, it had 8,000 pounds of mixed weapons, and was the best counterinsurgency aircraft at the time. It was

armed with four 20 mm cannons in the wings, napalm, bombs and CBUs (Cluster Bomb Units). Anyone who has ever been in serious trouble in country with the NVA knows that the A-1s were some of the best help you could get. When jet aircraft were grounded due to weather, you could count on the A-1 to be flying and loiter aloft for hours. This heavily armored aircraft could sustain heavy damage and continue to fly. From 1962 to 1973, there were 153 Skyraiders lost in combat in Vietnam, 147 to enemy ground fire; two were lost to communist MiG's; two were lost to Surface-to-Air missiles, and two were lost by attacking communist airfields. The Skyraider was known by its call sign of "Sandy" in its rescue helicopter escort role and SPAD in its support of ground combat operations. Many of these aircraft were operated by the Navy and flew from aircraft carriers in the Gulf of Tonkin. In this role they escorted the Jolly Green Giants looking for down pilots. The Sandies would patrol at a height trolling for fire until the pilot was located. Over 3,000 pilots were rescued in this manner during missions in Southeast Asia.

    2. The blue shirt came from the cloth furnished by China to the PAVN for uniforms.

> Flying beneath charcoal clouds, men
> stare into the jaws of the An Lao Valley.
> Their hearts, resolute, delta's teams
> approach the storm.
>
> Author

CHAPTER 10

PROJECT DELTA (B-52) & OPERATION MASHER

I was home on leave in California to get married. A few days later, my new bride, my parents and I were sitting in the family room and watching television. The news came that two teams of Special Forces personnel had been killed in action. That was it. No other details had been given. My family's quick shocked reaction soon gave way to a change of subject. For the remaining few days of my leave, I was haunted and felt uneasy over this announcement. Subsequently, upon my return to Vietnam, I learned the following detailed accounts from the After Action Reports and the surviving members of B-52.

1st Cavalry Division

On 24 January 1966, the 1st Cavalry Division's Third Brigade (the Garry Owen Brigade) launched the Bong Son Campaign in eastern Binh Dinh Province of II Corps area. The 1st Air Cavalry Division (Airmobile), commanded by Major General Harry W.O. Kinnard, was located at An Khe, about 40 miles southwest of Hoai Nhon (Bong Son) in the Central Highlands. They had requested long-range reconnaissance assistance from Field Force Vietnam (FFV), an army corps headquarters which exercised operational control over U.S. and allied forces in the I and II Corps Tactical Zone. On the same date, the Commander of FFV, Lt. Gen. Stanley "Swede" Larson, assigned to the 5th Special Forces Project Delta the mission of supporting the 3rd Brigade, 1st Air Cavalry Division, with reconnaissance teams.

Initially, the operation was officially known as Operation Masher. The Vietnamese would call it Operation Thang Phong. But so many Americans were killed in its first phase that, from the second phase on, the name of the operation was changed to Operation White Wing. During the first week, fifteen hamlets had been destroyed. It began with an air assault into the Cay Giep Mountains, then moved down into the Bong Son Plains and north into the coastal plain. The Masher/White Wing Operation consisted of four phases and was to last 41 days.

On 28 January 1966, the 3rd Brigade of the 1st Cav began Phase I of the operation. It was supported by the aviation assets of the 133rd Assault Support Helicopter Company and the 228th Assault Support Helicopter Battalion, both equipped with CH-47 Chinook helicopters. These two units were initially responsible for the night movement of the 3rd Brigade's supporting artillery units. Cargo helicopters flew into the perilous mountain positions after infantry and engineer troops had cleared enemy personnel and immediate timber. CH-54 helicopters then carried 155mm howitzers in newly fitted, special slings. They displaced the guns to inaccessible mountaintop firing positions. Ammunition and supplies were then delivered under heavy fire despite the adverse weather conditions of low ceilings and poor visibility. Ten of the

Chinook pilots had already been killed. Echo Battery 82nd Artillery (Aviation) with its OH-13 observation helicopters, "Huey" UH-1B helicopters and O-1 Bird Dog aircraft, served as the eyes of the artillery providing aerial observation and reconnaissance. In addition, it provided aerial rocket artillery, adjustment of artillery fire and medical evacuation. The Huey slicks of the 227th and 229th Assault Helicopter Battalions had a reduced load limit due to flying in the mountains. However, they were extremely busy, ferrying troops and supplies to the infantry and artillery units from their distant base at An Khe.

Bong Son Terrain

The Americans and South Vietnamese called the rural district town of Hoai Nhon, "Bong Son." The town was located in Binh Dinh Province, on the north side of the Lai Giang River. Binh Dinh Province was considered by the Vietnamese to be a hot bed of revolution. In 1771, in the Tay Son hamlet of Binh Dinh's Binh Khe district, a young upstart named Nguyen Hue began a rebellion against the Nguyen Emperor. This event, famous in Vietnamese history, became known as the "Tay Son Rebellion."

On 26 January, after initial coordination with personnel representing the 1st Cavalry, Detachment B-52 DELTA Project left the airfield at the coastal town of Nha Trang and flew by C-123 to the Bong Son airfield. The last elements of Delta that departed from Nha Trang arrived at Bong Son by 1700 hours. The 145th Aviation Platoon, assigned to Delta with its 6 HU-1B Iroquois infiltration slicks and 2 HU-1B Iroquois, was on site, serving as aerial weapons platforms (gunships). On the flight in from Nha Trang, the teams had noticed the abrupt, dark forested mountain range to the northwest of Phu My District, which walled off the long, green coastal plains from the interior. The dark ridges of the nearby mountains, ominous and threatening, floated above a heavy ground mist, a rugged terrain made up of craggy, jungle-covered peaks with deep gullies and draws. The airfield was located about a mile and a half to the west of the town of Bong Son, between road 514 and the Lai Giang River, on the northwest side of the Cay Giep Mountains.

Both the Forward Operating Base (FOB) headquarters of the 1st Cavalry's 3rd Brigade and the nearby Delta Project combined command post and logistical site were positioned in an open, level area near the ocean at coordinates BR 865965. The village-studded Bong Son coastal plain bordered the South China Sea, a series of low, flat hills, crisscrossed with a fertile mosaic of silvered streams. The villages were heavily populated, surrounded by tall palm trees, rice and sugarcane fields, and murky swamps extending up to Tam Quan in Northeastern Binh Dinh Province. The immediate area sat astride both the old Mandarin Road, now called Highway 1, and the coastal railroad, the backbone of South Vietnam's north-south transportation system.

The Briefing

The day they arrived, Major Charles "Charging' Charlie" Beckwith was gritting his teeth, heading for his briefing with Col. Moore. He had previously worked with the Cav's 1st Brigade at Plei Me in Pleiku Province during Operation SILVER BAYONET and had a bad experience with Col. Stockton, the commander of the 1st Squadron, 9th Cavalry. Stockton had exhibited a lack of cooperation and grudging use of air assets. The 3rd Brigade operations and intelligence staff quickly briefed Major Beckwith and his Project Delta staff. Project Delta would operate in the northern end of the An Lao Valley, which was the operational area of the PAVN 22nd Infantry Regiment. Its mission was to conduct surveillance on the main routes leading into the northern end of the long and narrow An Lao Valley, and to determine whether the North Vietnamese Army was using the routes either to reinforce their positions or to withdraw. Col. Moore's famous last words to Charlie during the briefing were, "You find them. I'll kill them."

The ground operation looked good on the map: a U.S. Marine force to the north was pushing south toward the An Lao Valley, while to the south the 1st Cavalry and a Vietnamese Airborne Brigade was pushing north forming a hammer and anvil operation.

However, intelligence was limited on the An Lao Valley; since 1958, no friendly units had operated in the area. In addition, many of the old people were former Viet Minh who had never returned to the North in 1954, after the war with the French was over. ARVN personnel at the 22nd Division Headquarters in Qui Nhon felt that at least two regiments would have to be deployed to enter the An Lao Valley.

It had been raining steadily, and the rice paddies were flooded, greatly restricting movement for the U.S. infantry. None of the area north of Bong Son was under government control, and the rice harvest belonged to the enemy. According to the briefing, the total population of the area was about 500,000. The 3rd NVA Division controlled the lives of these people. It also kept National Highway #1 closed in the Binh Dinh Province. Indigenous people in the area, readily supplied food and supplies, as well as intelligence, to the PAVN.

This province and its inhabitants were an ever-present problem. The enemy's regional and local militia had traditionally employed guerrilla tactics. The PAVN had adequate intelligence to ambush and raid government forces and then quickly withdraw. The ambushes brought them weapons and demoralized the government forces, while the raids destroyed supplies, equipment and installations. Main force units were organized along conventional military lines, such as platoons and companies. They shared responsibility for the province's security. When these units had adequate strength, they would conduct positional warfare as well. At the time of the mission, they had recently done so.

South Vietnamese control of Binh Dinh Province was further threatened because the people were sympathetic to the Communists. Even more of a worry for Project Delta was the fact that the weather would keep the U.S. Air Force from flying a type of reconnaissance mission known as "Red Haze." "Red Haze" missions detected heat emissions from the ground, showing the presence of large numbers of troops, generators, vehicles, field kitchens and cooking fires, and so on. It also revealed the freshly cut vegetation used to camouflage positions. This would have given eyes to the Delta Project, allowing them to work around these spots instead of going into them blindly.

An additional point of worry was the fact that air support and communications would be severely limited due to the weather. The AN/PRC-25 FM field radio, to be carried by the recon teams, had a line-of-sight transmission range of 1-3 miles with the 3-feet-long, antenna. With the 10-foot-long whip antenna, the range was 5 miles, depending on various conditions. On level ground, with a minimum of ground foliage, the 5-mile range could be reached, but the teams' area of operations (AO) would be deep in the mountains. The teams would have to rely on the FAC to act as their radio relay. If the weather turned for the worse, there would be no communications. The men of Delta were aware that they constantly needed to avoid compromise. If compromised, they absolutely had to be extracted from their mission.

PAVN Order of Battle

Binh Dinh Province was located within the boundary of Inter-region 5 (Inter-regions were the regions linking North Vietnam's High Command and Politburo with the Central Office for South Vietnam (COSVN) in the south). COSVN, an American acronym for the highest political leadership element in the South, was established in June 1961. It remained mobile throughout the war, and had no fixed headquarters. During the war against the French, MR-5 had included some 10 provinces. During 1964-65, however, as newly infiltrated PAVN units were incorporated into the extant structure, it was recognized to include only the provinces of Quang Nam, Quang Tin, Quang Ngai and Binh Dinh. MR-5 was bordered on the south by the "Southern Extremity" (Cuc nam) Military Region, which consisted of the provinces of Khanh Hoa and Phu Yen. On the west it was bordered by the Western Highlands Front (Mat Tran Tay Nguyen): the provinces of Kontum, Pleiku, Phu Bon and Dar Lac. To the north, it was bordered by the Tri-Thien-Hue Military Region, which included the provinces of Quang Tri and Thua Thien, as well as the ancient imperial capital of Hue. MR-5 controlled the Central Highlands, linking the Ho Chi Minh trail (Duong Truong Son) to the roads in South

Vietnam, and thus increased PAVN offensive operations in the lowlands. At that time, Major General Chu Huy Man, 52, an ethnic minority member who served concurrently as Political Commissar, commanded MR-5. He was a hill tribesman (Montagnard) and veteran soldier. He joined the People's Army in August 1945 and served as a regimental commander at Dien Bien Phu.

As of 1965, the principal military force within Binh Dinh province was the 3rd PAVN Division, aka Yellow Star Division (Su Doan Sao Vang) or the 610th. The Binh Dinh Front controlled the eastern portion of Vietnam, which included the An Lao Valley and coastal plain. The 3rd Division was formed in Hoai Nhon district of Binh Dinh on 2 September 1965. The North Vietnamese Army's 3rd Division commander was Senior Colonel Giap Van Cuong and the Political Commissar was Dang Hoa. Regiments of the 3rd Division included the Quyet Chien Regiment of MR-5, and the recently infiltrated Quyet Thang and Quyet Tam NVA Regiments from North Vietnam. The 3rd PAVN Division, as all other military units in Binh Dinh, operated under the control of the Binh Dinh Front, established in 1966. They controlled Binh Dinh Province's An Lao Valley and coastal plain. Senior Colonel Giap Van Cuong concurrently commanded the Binh Dinh Front. The Front's Political Commissar was Tran Quang Khanh, who also served as the secretary of the Binh Dinh Province Party Committee. All three regiments now occupied the An Lao Valley in Binh Dinh province.

Project Delta was tasked to support the 1st Air Cavalry Division by locating the NVA forces, which had largely disengaged themselves after the initial large battle with the 1st Cavalry. The recon teams were also assured support if they got into trouble with the PAVN. A company-sized reaction force was to be provided by the 3rd Brigade, in order to both exploit suitable targets and help any team having to exfiltrate under enemy pressure. This was not to be the case.

The Enemy Units

During the rainy season from May to November, the PAVN spent their time in the mountains, conducting reconnaissance, rebuilding their units, training personnel, maintaining their uniforms and gear and building up the strength of the individual soldier. The PAVN troops often wore mix-matched attire, because the units only received enough material to make two uniforms per year for each individual soldier. The standard uniform of the NVA was either khaki or green. Frequent washings on rocks along the stream beds often caused the Chinese-issued green cotton material to fade, leaving the cloth a murky color which many Americans described as "gray." Once the rains subsided and movement became possible during the dry season, the PAVN could usually be counted upon to reappear and conduct their Winter-Spring Campaign from December to April.

From 1966 on, the construction of the Truong Son Trail, aka the Ho Chi Minh Trail, fell under the supervision of Lt. Gen. Dong Sy Nguyen, the commander of Logistics Group 559. Logistics Group 559 was a special transportation unit established in May 1959 to move supplies down the Ho Chi Minh trail for newly arrived PAVN units in the South. At about that same time, three regiments of infantry and two battalions of artillery were reportedly moving into the Western Highlands of the Tay Nguyen Front from the Truong Son Trail. In January of that year, Delta was alerted for an operation in the remote mountains of the upper An Lao Valley.

This operational area covered some 1700 square kilometers, and the NVA were always widely dispersed within it. The objective was to locate the 3rd PAVN Division and its supporting units, and to report on any enemy troop movement in the surrounding mountains. The Third Division had the combat initiative in this area, with its ability to appear and engage whenever it was advantageous and then disappear at will.

The PAVN 12th Infantry Regiment (Quyet Thang Regiment), formally the 18th Infantry Regiment of the PAVN 312th Division, was commanded by Lt. Col. Xoan, and was deployed in Hoa Hoi District. Its subordinate 7th, 8th and 9th battalions occupied the area from the Cay Giep Mountains, just south of Bong Son, to an area further south in and around the Mieu Mountains, and from Hill 82, south of Phu Ninh (BR

973789), to the well-fortified village of Hoa Hoi at grid coordinates BR 031699. The village of Hoa Hoi is located in the fertile coastal region on Road 505, east of the Mieu Mountains and Highway 1. This area was crisscrossed with fortified enemy bunker systems. The 12th Regiment controlled the use of the national railroad, Highway 1 and Road 505 by interdicting and harassing the military and civilian operations and traffic that traveled upon them.

PAVN Major Khanh's Viet Cong 2nd Main Force Regiment (Quyet Chien Regiment) was deployed in the Kim Son Valley at BR 738801. The 38th, 93rd and 97th Main Force Battalions were the identified units in this regiment. The 93rd Regiment was commanded by Lt. Col. Dong Doan. Whenever the area south of Bong Son was void of US troops, the 2nd Regiment would move back in to occupy the coastal Cay Giep mountain range at BR 931902. Main Force units were usually organized along conventional military lines, moving from region to region. Guerrilla forces at the regional or local level supported them all.

The Kim Son River that flowed in the direction of Bong Son divided the valley, with its dense civilian population. This operational area was located due south of the An Lao Valley and southwest of the village of Bong Son. Eight twisting ridgelines compressed the low ground of seven small valleys, giving it the appearance of a bird's foot moving south. The Cavalry called it the "Crow's Foot." The abundant streams supported the heavy population and the many productive rice fields surrounded by thick brush and forest, making it an ideal area for a base camp. The Kim Son Valley was to the northwest of Hon Giang Mountain at grid coordinates BR 8177, and was well fortified with bunkers and underground-interconnected tunnel systems. The PAVN units all had indirect fire support and anti-aircraft defense. In addition, an unidentified transport unit and eleven local force companies were all located in the high-ground of the four main stream branches, in the headwaters of the An Lao River Valley just below the province of Quang Ngai.

The PAVN 22nd Infantry Regiment (Quyet Tam Regiment) was commanded by Major Tin Phuong. The

Regimental Political Officer was Major Loc. This regiment was supported by the 48th Engineer Company. The An Lao Valley, with its craggy, jungle-covered peaks, was located 19 miles northwest of Bong Son (Hoai Nhon) and 12 miles west of the town of Tam Quan. Both towns were on Highway 1. The peaks in the foothills rose to 1,600 feet or more. Thousands of civilians resided in the valley. It was split by the An Lao River. Road 514, branching off of Highway 1 at Hoai Nhon, ran along the eastern side of the river. The town of An Lao (BS 7409) was located in the valley 3 miles to the south of Hung Nhon (BS 7414).

Major Beckwith returned to his unit area and briefed his men, warning that this was an extremely hazardous mission, and would be difficult to accomplish. He also revealed that each of the Project Delta teams would be infiltrated into their operational areas by a single helicopter at last light the following day, 27 January 1966. Due to the hazardous nature of the assignment, Major Beckwith requested only volunteers. Seventeen brave men stepped forward. They were formed into three teams and team leaders were assigned. The Vietnamese mercenaries with Project Delta refused to go out on this operation. The Delta team leaders conducted their aerial reconnaissance of their respective operational areas. Things were moving altogether too quickly.

Situation

Their 1:50,000 scaled maps of the An Lao operational area were issued and studied. The three teams' individual tactical areas of responsibility (TAOR) were assigned during their briefing. Their brevity codes were issued, and the teams' radio reporting times were established with the Forward Air Controller (FAC), who would be in the air nearby acting as their aerial relay. Trying to communicate with the Forward Operational Base (FOB) at Bong Son was out of the question due to the distance, mountains, and triple canopy. The FAC would remain in the operational area if the teams got into trouble. With no "Red Haze" mission flown for up-to-date intelligence, the teams would go into the PAVN's safe area blindly.

Team #1's (Eskimo) operational area was at the apex of the north end of the An Lao Valley. At the head of the valley, a large ridge came down to the valley floor. On the east side of the ridge, a stream, the Nuoc Dinh, flowed into the river Song An Lao. After a map study and aerial recon, the team leader chose to land to the east side of route 514, between the villages of Nuoc Dinh to the south and Thang Xin to the north. Team #2 (Capital) had the eastern side of the TAOR, with the stream Nuoc Tre bordering on the east side of their operational area. Team #3 (Roadrunner) had the operational area on the west side of the An Lao Valley, above the stream Song Gio.

They'd been promised support from a 1st Cavalry infantry reaction force if any trouble was encountered. The UH-1B's of the 2nd Battalion (Aerial Artillery), 20th Artillery, would provide the extreme close air support. The UH-1D Huey personnel transport aircraft from the 1st Air Cavalry's 227th or 229th Assault Helicopter Battalions would insert them into their operational areas. The Delta Project had no reason to suspect that the operation would encounter support difficulty. After all, Delta was providing their intelligence, and there were two Battalions of helicopters ready to respond.

Operation 2-66, Team Composition

Team #1 (Eskimo). This five-man team, led by SFC Henry A. Keating, was composed of SFC Robert P. Whitus, SSG Norman C. Dupuis, SSG Agostino Chiariello, and SSG Brooke Bell. This team would be inserted just to the east of road 514.

Team #2 (Capital). SFC Frank R. Webber Jr. led this six-man team, with team members consisting of SFC Marlin C. Cook, SSG Donald L. Dotson, SSG George A. Hoagland, SFC Jesse L. Hancock, and SSG Charles F. Hiner. It would be inserted far into the interior of the mountains on the east side of the An Lao Valley.

Team #3 (Roadrunner). SFC Marcus L. Huston led this six-man team, with SSG Billy A. McKeithe, MSG Wiley W. Gray, SSG Ronald Terrance Terry, SFC Cecil Joe Hodgson, and SSG Frank Neil Badolati. It was to be inserted into the western foothills, within sight of the upper end of the An Lao Valley.

Team #2 (Capital)
(L to R) SSG Dotson, SSG Hoagland, SFC Cook, SFC Hancock and SSG Hiner.

Team #3 (Roadrunner)
(L to R) MSG Gray, SFC Hodgson, SSG McKeithe, SSG Badolati and SSG Terry.

Chopper Pad

As the teams waited at the launch site to load, no one spoke. The pilots were making their preflight walk-around. There was a quiet resolve as the reconnaissance teams silently made their last-minute checks of their gear. Nervous, they avoided eye contact with each other as they prepared to set their lives adrift again upon the winds of fate. All were aware that small patrols in an enemy-controlled territory always faced the risk of encountering a numerically superior force. They had come to accept the whims of fortune. The weather report for flying was considered marginal--temporarily poor with periods of driving rain. The emerging ground fog would also make for poor visibility. The sky was mostly covered with an extremely low ceiling of heavy black, puffy cumulus clouds hugging the mountaintops.

The reconnaissance teams knew that the rain and humidity would help to muffle the sound of a helicopter on its low approach, but the low hanging cloud ceiling would amplify the noise. The possible devastating effects of bad weather made everyone a little tense. The air seemed to carry a stench. The barometric pressure was dropping, releasing the methane trapped below ground in the surrounding low swampy areas. It would rain soon. The problem of air support and extraction, not to mention the lack of a reaction force from the 1st Cavalry due to bad weather, weighed on everyone's mind. But they were confident that Maj. Beckwith would move heaven and earth to get them out in the event of a worst-case scenario. As the shadows grew longer, Team Capital paused for a last picture in their faded "Tiger" camouflage. The flight crew gets in and conducts another preflight, checking overhead switches, going down their plastic-laminated list.

The spell of the recon teams was broken by a start switch. The main rotor blade begins to turn. The whine of the turbines and a perceptible vibration, as the long rotor blades began to turn slowly. They listened as the engines built up torque, thudding faster like a heart beat. Soon there was a strong pulsing sound from the big engines, which drowned out any conversation as the blades rapidly beat the air. Now, only their eyes spoke. The helicopters shook, then the pilots brought them down to an idle. They signaled the teams to board. The three groups of men boarded their respective choppers. A quick, last photo was taken of the smiling Badolati and Terry of Team Roadrunner, already seated together inside the helicopter. Once again the engines built up torque, until the sound became deafening. The door gunners watched the rear of their helicopters and gave the pilots the "clear" to take off. Then the first pilot pulled pitch to lift off, bringing the Huey to a five-foot hover. The pilots checked their gauges as they stabilized. The Huey dipped its nose and moved slowly forward. Soon it was rapidly accelerating, then shuddering as it raised its nose into a gentle climb. The chopper made its slow, climbing run, lifting higher and higher and leveling off at 200 feet. The second helicopter easily lifted higher, dipped its nose and moved forward. Finally, the third ship followed in turn.

The choppers banked south, flying over the Lai Giang River to the south side and turned, following the winding river westward. The pilots obsessively watched their instruments and the sky and terrain outside their cockpits along with the deteriorating visibility. All wondered if they would outrun this mess in the weather. The far mountains appeared closer, in sharp focus due to the changing weather. The secondary road 514 on the north side of the river could be seen clearly. All too soon, they abruptly turned northwest, each chopper breaking formation, initially following the An Lao River and road 514. With daylight waning, they headed to their respective insertion points. The nearest was eighteen kilometers, while the farthest was twenty kilometers away. They were on their way. Before them was the verdant, vine-tangled mountainous terrain surrounding the brutal land of the An Lao Valley, with its usual low rain-swollen cloud cover. The team members watched the heavy overcast sky, the lighter-colored thick groves of bamboo, and the lush, dark, solid forested slopes below. The landscape was transformed by variations of changing light, wind, color, shifting stormy winds, and the rolling clouds of the gray sky. It made a wild, primal sight. The clouds hung ominously gray overhead and clung to the tops of the ridges to the west, low and thick like a blanket, as the sun sank behind them. The cold and dreary weather settled over the landscape, making low-level flying necessary, as the purple shadows deepened in the menacing, thick mountain forest below.

  The valley had already grown dark in the twilight, made darker by the clouds. The silver threads of streams betrayed the deep shadowed rifts through the dreaded, beautiful expanse of forest. Overhead, clouds melted into a velvety blackness. In the distance, open areas of tall grass took on a bluish cast. Two men sat in each open door, their legs dangling, to facilitate a quick exit. They gripped the aluminum piping of the canvas seats, folded down from the bare wall of the backside of the fuselage, where the rest of the team sat. Only the lonely whine of the helicopter's turbine and the cold whipping wind sounded in the silence as each man sat mute, lost in his own thoughts of the trial and hardship they faced ahead. Some frightened and praying to their God, felt a sensation of dread in the pits of their stomachs, knowing the absolute and veritable truth, that in the blink of an eye, this could be the end. The stunning deep green backdrop of imposing mountain forest mesmerized others. Each helicopter would abruptly lose altitude, make a false insertion and run into its selected landing zone in the foothill areas below the main ridgelines. The teams would land in areas that were from 1,500 feet high, below the ridgelines and mountains, and would climb behind them into the swirling, mist-shrouded interior to a height of almost 3,000 feet high. Here was the dense double-and triple-canopied mountain forest. All to soon, the pilots increasingly preoccupied were lowering their collectives, losing altitude and bleeding off speed as angry gusts of wind buffeted them. The three teams were descending to their small respective clearings below, into the depths of reality. Now standing on the struts, as the door gunners leaned forward to check the tail rotor clearance and give their "clear," they jumped the last six feet into the sawtoothed, man-high elephant grass. All were worried and unsettled about the changing weather and NVA trackers. *Grass stems that would normally return to their upright position six hours after being lightly stepped on, may still be lying flat two days later with low humidity and no wind. However, if rain fell after the grass was stepped on, it would be standing upright more swiftly, maybe in a matter of minutes and return to its original round shape and uniform color. Moving after a rainstorm gives the tracker the advantage.*

Team Eskimo

Team Eskimo was on the ground at 6:58 p.m. During their last-light insertion at coordinates BS 746197, they had quickly moved into the timber off the side of a ridge above the road. They had had their look at the vast black sweep of invisible land. The team leader, SFC Keating, had his men wait, listen and watch. Everything appeared normal. There was only the sharp, clear sound of birds calling. The birds were flying low to the ground due to the thinning air. Bad weather would soon be upon them. He hoped that the weather had covered the sound of their insertion. Keating wanted to check the road for tracks. The air was dense, and with the developing ground fog, there was little chance of their being seen from any distance. Keating knew that any tracks they came across would be fresh: the rain would have washed the roadbed clean of all old tracks. He quickly moved his team to the west, across the road that ran inside the woodline. Everything seemed ominous, as if sinister forces had already surrounded them, as if being warned.

The team detected the faint traces of many man-made tracks in the wet soil of the small roadbed. The soil was damp, and the small, flat, plain, rounded-sole imprints were eye-catching. The well-defined heel and toe marks of the deep, widely spaced prints, with the scuffing of the toe, indicated that they were traveling south in a hurry. The coming rain would soon erase all traces of ground movement, including their own tracks.

They studied the far bank of a stream, the Nuoc Dinh, up and downstream, listening for any sound. They ran right through the water, high-stepping across as quickly as possible, barely wetting their feet. The team had crossed the Nuoc Dinh where it gradually curved around to the right, at a point where there was little chance of being observed. The banks were not steep and would allow them to cross without leaving any scuffmarks in passing. The gradual, rocky slope favored their crossing. They could use the hard surface on both sides. Careful not to dislodge any rocks, they made their crossing.

They continued moving north three hundred more meters to grid coordinates BS 746200 and then crawled into the thick brush to remain-over-night (RON) and wait out the weather. They listened and watched for signs of any communist troop movement along the road they had just crossed. In the darkness, only the sound of rushing water reached their ears. The air was rich and alive with the smell of all of the pungent odors rising from the live brush and trees of the mountain forest. The vague scents from the nearby stream, the earth and damp mud were easily detectable. They knew from the random air currents that rain was coming. It was now abysmally dark. They were aware of the small night creatures, skittering silently around them in the undergrowth. A drizzling rain began after dark. No one slept. Holding their bladders in check kept them awake. Team Eskimo spent a miserable, wet and uneventful night.

Dawn came, but the cold gray tones of the early morning mist, fog, drizzle, and low-hanging clouds were the only hint that the sun had emerged from the east. The air felt heavy to breathe. The team's eyes slowly crawled across the forest. Then they got up stiffly from the ground, preparing to move. There was only the faint hissing sound of hot urine splattering the tree trunks. Each man could smell the sour stench. At 0650 Hours, SFC Keating directed his point man, SSG Dupuis, to move in a northwesterly direction. In the early morning light, the heavy moisture-laden atmosphere impaired visibility and the sense of smell, but the rich odor of rotting humus was still strong. An early morning gauze of thick mist that hugged the ground was strangely calming. The members of the team could smell smoke, the faint fragrance of wood smoke drifting on the wind, moving down the stream with the morning thermals. Looking upstream, they could see a faint blue haze. There was no one to be seen, but they knew people were there.

Dupuis moved the team slowly and quietly through the low-lying brushwood and forest, searching for the firmest possible footing in the hard-packed sand. Visibility was only about 25 yards or so. With the leaves wet, their footsteps were muffled. They avoided the patches of shiny mud that would reveal their tracks and stick to their boots. They entered an area of thick brush and bamboo and then the forest, moving uphill through the timber. Now they could no longer see the valley, their view blocked by the heavy foliage. They were able to move quietly because the light-drizzling rain covered any slight sound they made. Tree by tree they crept, listening and waiting for minutes. Then they slipped another few yards through the large trees and boulders. The team moved slowly, weapons at the ready, constantly searching the shadows far ahead and glancing from side to side and to the ground around them as well. Dupuis noticed spiders anchored in the apexes of tight webs, silvered by early morning dew. He moved around them so as not to leave any evidence of their passage. The team slowly climbed a small, gradually sloping finger ridge and stopped at 0850 hours. After moving for two hours, the men needed a break.

SFC Keating climbed a tree to observe and listen to the valley below. He plotted his present position at grid coordinates BS 737204. Disappointedly, he was only able to see a 700-meter section of the valley. Within his field of vision, to the east, was the bend of the Nuoc Dinh. Further on, across the other side of the stream, he could see rice fields, Thang Xin village, and portions of the trail that ran before it. Part of communal route 514 could be seen south of the village. The team remained there for a half-hour, while the team leader observed the valley. After climbing down from the tree, Keating informed them that he had observed no activity in the valley, but that all the rice paddies were under cultivation, and all the trails below were easily seen and well used. Because fog developing in the valley was obscuring his observation, he had decided to move northeast to lower ground again to be close enough to the trails and route 514. There they would be able to better see and hear any enemy movement.

As the team prepared to move, SSG Dupuis faced uphill. He sensed close movement to his left front, near a well-used trail. Then SFC Keating sensed something. Now both men's eyes and ears were alert for any sound emanating from the darkness. Again, they both heard men coming. There was a shifting movement in the shadows. Stopping, they simultaneously saw movement in their peripheral vision and heard a rustling sound quickly emerging through the foggy mist. More footsteps were coming. Then they saw them. At a distance of fifteen meters, the three fast-moving, black-clad figures quickly appeared, moving in their direction from the cloudy gloom of fog on the trail. The PAVN immediately observed the recon team. Only one PAVN was armed with a weapon.

They reacted slower than Team Eskimo. The two unarmed PAVN took cover as the one who was armed raised his weapon, a U.S. M-1 Carbine, to fire. Dupuis and Keating, who had reacted and fired instinctively, immediately wounded the North Vietnamese soldier. The sound of high-velocity gunfire had broken the stillness of the mountains. Without hesitation Dupuis and Keating both reached for hand grenades, as one of the black-clad PAVN broke cover, quickly recovered the weapon from his dead comrade and fired two rounds.

Dupuis threw first. The M-26 Fragmentation hand grenade was swiftly followed by another from Keating. The firing had stopped, followed by the blast waves of the explosions. The two explosions killed the wounded man in the brush and blew him out into the trail. Dupuis was startled at the impact of a red-hot stinging blow to the side of his head. A large fragment of shrapnel had hit him in the head, tearing a gaping hole and stunning him.

Then the forest was silent. Keating motioned for the two men behind him to flank the enemy position to the right. As the two men closed in on the quiet enemy position, the three remaining recon members simultaneously closed in as well. SSG Dupuis, although wounded in the head and still dazed with pain, was able to follow the team leader quickly in the direction of contact. All that was found were two separate, bright red blood trails leading away from the area. Judging from the amount of blood, both enemy soldiers were badly wounded. Keating checked the soldier laying in the trail. He was dead. The impact of the grenade fragments crushed and tore tissue of the hollow internal organs, such as the bowels, lungs, and nonelastic tissue, such as the liver and kidneys. The pulmonary hemorrhage caused blood to drain out the nose and mouth of the dead NVA. A search of the body revealed nothing. The team had been compromised.

Changing Direction

The team leader was now aware that his men's lives were at stake. But, sticking to his original plan, he unhesitatingly initiated a quick briefing for their movement out of the area in a northeasterly direction. Dupuis, still on his feet, informed the team leader he had been hit in the head. Keating quickly checked him and found that a piece of shrapnel had hit him above his left ear. Dupuis told Keating that he felt dizzy. Keating appointed SSG Bell to take the point, while Dupuis now brought up the rear. Dupuis managed to keep up, trying to wipe away the blood streaming down his face, and stem the flow with pressure to the wound. They moved lower, down toward the stream, and crossed to the other side at the head of a deep pool in the stream to reach grid coordinates BS 744207.

It was an extremely demanding effort for Dupuis. After a distance of 500 meters, Keating, worried about Dupuis' condition, stopped the team. They took up defensive positions, listening and watching for movement from their rear. Here, SFC Keating decided to transmit a quick spot report. A brevity code was utilized to keep the information short and secure. The spot report consisted of the team's location in coordinates, direction of movement, any important information that the team was sent to collect, enemy activity and friendly casualties. The transmission had to be quick and short, so that it could not be monitored and their location determined by an enemy direction-finding specialist.

While the team listened and watched for movement to their rear, Keating immediately unknotted the olive-drab triangular bandage worn around Dupuis neck as a bandana, and applied it to his shrapnel wound. He continued to feel nauseated and weak. The middle portion of the triangular bandage was placed over the dressing and tied off, causing the pain in his head to throb even more. The only wounded member had been cared for quickly. The team leader heard no aircraft nearby, so he had the long whip antenna broken out and he attempted to send a spot report to the Forward Air Controller (FAC). The FAC, in turn, would forward their message to the Forward Operational Base (FOB). There was no response. He stared up at the hills surrounding the team and knew why: the high ground and weather were blocking the transmission. Quickly, he ordered the long antenna broken down, and moved the team further north.

The team began to encounter a number of well-used trails, all running generally from the northeast to the southwest. Keating decided to move back west, across the stream and up the high ridge. They carefully changed their direction in their uphill movement. Stopping and moving off their trail a short distance, they held back and watched for movement behind them.

Dupuis teetered, hovering on the verge of collapse as the team climbed higher. The woods-wise team leader knew that any tracks or sign they left moving uphill would be harder to follow. Careful in the placement of their feet, the team avoided leaving any minor disturbance or spiral twist against the spongy leaf-mat that might indicate a change in direction. The team was headed in the direction from which they had come, but from above their back trail, finally halting in the dark shadows. Their eyes roamed the mature trees that rose from the slope, as they watched and listened to their back trail for the possibility of a fast-moving PAVN tracking team. There were only the normal sounds of the forest. Keating cautioned his men to walk slowly and carefully so that they would not scuff the humus and leave any unusual disturbance. They now moved for the saddle at the top of the ridge. The slower their movement, the harder it would be to track them. Dupuis, his head aching and bleeding due to the exertion, still maintained his strength as he reached the top of the ridge.

No Radio Contact

The team arrived at the top of the ridge and stopped on the south side of a saddle at grid coordinates BS 733206. They overlooked another narrow watershed that led into the An Lao Valley. Through a few openings in the trees, they could see the rice fields between the existing villages of Nuoc Trong Thuong to the north and Nuoc Trong Ha to the south. The area looked as it should on the map, but still the team could observe no people in the village or working in the fields. There was not even any smoke haze above the village to indicate cooking fires. They moved over the crest of the hill to grid coordinates BS 730206, well below the ridge, near the bottom and out of sight of anyone moving along the top of the ridge. Again they stopped and broke out the long antenna to make contact with the FAC. Still there was no radio contact. The team leader was worried. Soon the PAVN would be searching for them, and now he had to worry about his wounded man. Adding to everyone's nervousness and anxiety was the fact that, as of yet, there had been no communications. Their worst nightmare was coming true. Their rear security would now have to have "eyes in the back of his head."

    The team leader again studied the map. He would move the team north, a little higher to a south-facing slope, and attempt to make commo again. The team moved a little lower to observe the valley at grid coordinates BS 725208. There was still no sight of people, either in the rice paddies around the village of Nuoc Trong Thuong or on the trails nearby. The team moved again, contouring along the side of the ridge a little to the east, then north a short distance until the ridge turned west again. They slipped quietly along the edge of a small clearing next to the woodline. Despite the stress, Keating noticed that the surrounding tall grass was not beaded with water, as it should have been due to the wind and quick evaporation.

    Their destination was the south-facing slope at grid coordinates BS 729208. They arrived and found a small clearing. Keating thought that they had little chance of being observed if they entered it for a short distance and crouched down. Certainly they could hear anyone moving by in the tree line and remain hidden. The team carefully parted the grass to avoid twisted or broken stems, and then hunkered down out of sight in the tall grass near the woodline, in a defensible hollow. The rain would soon cover the presence of a trail through the grass, and if they advanced slowly, the vegetation in the tall grass would cushion each step and obscure any impression. The entire team was now extremely worried. The weather was getting worse.

Keating called the FAC. The others' periodic glances were rewarded when they saw relief on his face: he was finally talking to someone. He had been immediately answered by the FAC, who would relay their message to the FOB. Team Eskimo made the Forward Air Controller (FAC), Air Force Captain Kenneth L. Kerr, aware of their situation. The team was notified that he was busy elsewhere, but a helicopter was being dispatched to their location. Keating knew it would take some time for the PAVN to move enough troops into the area to organize a search and find them. Still, they had to remain hidden from those scouting the area until the helicopter was close enough to signal it. The team waited patiently. They grew nervous as the time passed, not knowing how long it would be before they were found.

Finally, the familiar sound of the helicopter came from the far distance. They all knew that if they couldn't hail the passing helicopter with the radio, they would be on their own for some time. They radioed and made contact, but as luck would have it, the helicopter had already spent two hours searching in the extremely bad weather without spotting or hearing from the team. The pilot, with the helicopter now low on fuel, notified the team that they were returning to base and would be back in the area in 45 minutes. Spirits dropped as the team listened to the sound of it fading blocked by the far ridges of the mountains. They were alone once more.

Suddenly, there was the familiar faint sound they had been waiting for--a dull rhythmic thumping. As they listened the sound continued to grow louder. The distinctive *whop. .whop. .whop* reverberated in the valley. The team leader grabbed the radio as soon as he heard it. Upon re-entering the area, it spotted the team leader's panel almost immediately. Seeing that the landing zone was too small and had too much slope, the pilot directed them to move 400 meters south, to a clearing shown on the map. The team picked up and moved. About an hour later, they again heard the sweet music of the helicopter. It appeared on the horizon. When the pilot answered, the team felt relief. They found the open ground thick with eight-foot tall elephant grass covering a steep hillside. Keating notified the pilot that he would have to move Team Eskimo to the top of the ridge, where it was flatter but still covered with tall grass. He also requested a rope ladder.

It was now getting late in the day. The worried team arrived at grid coordinates BS 728204. Much to their relief, they found that the elephant grass in the area was silvered with beaded water. No one had been searching the area. Hovering overhead, the extraction chopper notified Keating that only four members would be extracted on the first run. The chopper dropped rope ladders to the waiting team and successfully loaded four members of the team. The team leader waited alone for 10 minutes on the ground for another chopper. At 1620 hours, he was extracted.

Team Capital

At last-light on the evening of 27 January, at 1850 hours, Team Capital, led by SFC Webber, was inserted 1900 meters to the east of team Eskimo, on the high ridge line above them at grid coordinates BS 766198. The insertion point was in 8-foot-high elephant grass surrounded by tall timber. They were above a well-timbered watershed between two main trails, one below them to the west, and the other below them to the east. Their primary objective was observation of the trail to their immediate west, which ran southwest to northeast. The team quickly moved four hundred meters away from their helicopter insertion point, heading west-northwest. As the team moved back into the trees, the forest closed in around them. They passed over the crest of the ridge, following a gentle sloped finger ridge, and made their way down the mountain under the verdant, three-tier jungle canopy to a place above the trail. They came up a draw. At this point, the team stopped to observe the trail. They found a defensible hollow in a thicket and crouched there, alert, to remain overnight.

The trail was only 75 meters away, slightly below them. During the very early morning hours, a light rain had fallen. It was cold and damp, but they were sheltered from the now-dying wind, and were not altogether too miserable. Visibility was poor. Later, a shroud of fog, and total ominous silence surrounded the team. There were none of the usual sounds of the night creatures. No one slept. They all watched and listened. With their ears constantly alert for any sound emanating from the night, they kept themselves awake by thinking of their wives, lovers, and home. The rocks and damp leaves radiated the coldness. The long dark hours dragged by, and at last the night passed on. On 28 January, as the early morning black turned to gray, the team still watched and listened, dreading the coming day.

At first light, they silently prepared to move. The long night had been uneventful, but the night's innocent silence had not allayed their fears. In the first faint, chilled gray minutes of dawn, the light outlined the hills above them. At 0730 hours, the FAC was on station overhead somewhere nearby, and the team leader made radio contact, reporting negative traffic. At last, the blackness paled as dawn stole out of the east. The morning was quickening, and gradually filtering through the trees. It was lightly raining. In a state of constant tension, the six-man team was ready, watching the forest shadows and listening for any sign of movement or sound. But as they sat there in that early morning light of late January, the only movement and sounds they detected were natural.

Fresh PAVN Trail Sign

On 28 January, as the light fog bathed the tree-covered hilltops, the team cautiously crept from their RON site and began moving directly toward the trail marked on their map. Completely focused, they moved past the massive bases of the trunks of gigantic and mature trees, whose widely-stretched canopy of foliage interlocked far above them, denying almost all light to the forest floor. They paid close attention to foot placement, so as not to leave a distinguishable trail on the spongy ground. They avoided leaf-covered rocks, wet slick areas, roots and holes that were a hazard to their movement. All objects except for those at close range were almost indistinguishable in the dark-gray obscurity.

The point man stopped, and the team quickly froze and dropped down, crouching low, weapons at the ready as they smelled, listened and watched. The breeze brought to their nostrils only the feral innocence of the landscape. Ahead of them, in the shadows, was a meter wide trail. The trail appeared to have been well traveled during the previous night.

The point man, SSG Hiner, carefully approached and quickly looked both ways. Nothing. He spotted tracks, confirming that the trail had been used during the night. Hiner went down on his knee, studying the tracks, noting that they contained no standing water. Furthermore, the moisture had not yet blunted the tracks, indicating that they were only hours old, and had been made after the rain had fallen. The tracks were not spotted with raindrops. The shallow, plain prints of the PAVN were clear in the damp soil. *They were fresh!*

Webber decided to move on. The team crossed the trail, following it in a southeasterly direction. They continued to move cautiously back up the mountain for another 400 meters to the top of the ridge, using the large tree trunks for cover and concealment as they went. The slope was covered with large hardwoods, massive boulders and very little undergrowth. Slowly and silently they worked across the level top, crossing back over the trail and continuing down for another 200 meters.

Back Over the Top of the Ridge

Team Capital was now just below the crest of the mountain ridge. Again they slowly moved down a narrow finger ridge, through large, old growth open timber along the side of the mountain, their eyes sweeping the landscape as they went. The well-used trail was below them, on their right, in a draw. The forest canopy was 150 feet high. The team's position now overlooked the head of a small finger valley, cradling a tiny village. The village was surrounded by cultivated rice fields, and dwarfed by the bulk of the mountain that lay behind it. In the dark space beneath the canopy, there was little growth, and as the team moved from tree to tree, the men felt tense. The area was just too open. The team decided to move southwest into thicker undergrowth, after coming across an area crisscrossed with well-used trails. Fresh tracks were again visible, but they were somewhat older than the earlier ones, leading to the ridge back above them from the valley floor. The rain had had its effect on the smooth, shallow sole imprints of the PAVN. Raindrops marked the tracks located on the higher elevated ground of the trail and water sat in the tracks of those in the lower part of the trail. The team leader determined that they had been made in the last twenty-four hours. The wet, pushed-up sides of the tracks in the soft ground were almost rounded out. A lot of men had moved through the area, off the top of the ridge. The wet, but still hard-packed, well-used, high-speed trails were scouted for a short distance.

More Trails

The team came upon a trail with an unused, half-collapsed hut, black with rot and furred with green moss and rusty fungus. It had not been occupied for a long time. The team continued following this same trail, moving in parallel with it down the mountain, until they reached a point 300 meters above the stream at grid coordinates BS 763187, where they stopped to eat. In Vietnam, a well-trodden forest trail invariably follows a stream course below the trail. There a trail forks off, usually traveling, with a straight-line directness further into the interior. While the team was eating, the birds were active and noisy. Afterwards, the team broke out the long antenna and made radio contact with the FAC. Quickly collapsing the antenna, the team continued down the mountain.

They continued moving in parallel with the trail, but from a good distance, so that the team could observe anything moving their way along the trail without being seen. They quietly moved through the trees, boulders and the leafy humus, cautiously inching around and over obstacles in the path of least resistance. Paying close attention to his surroundings, Hiner told Webber that the forest around him was changing. The trees were smaller. After another twenty minutes, the understory started thinning out. Hiner noticed that the birds were no longer active and noisy. He slowed the team's movement now as his senses awakened a warning within him. The team had reached the level above the village, where the people had been cutting wood for fuel.

The Woodcutters

Hiner caught the vague, unmistakable whiff of familiar odors. Collective body sweat, tobacco and a sweet-sour stench came to him in an overpowering wave. He signaled a halt. He saw nothing in the dim light, but his instincts told him they were there. And that, he knew, was trouble. Each member of Team Capital had already stepped to the darkest side of the nearest tree for cover. They were craning their necks forward, letting one eye peek ahead while observing their respective areas to the sides and rear. The air was tense.

They had that foreboding feeling that something bad was about to happen. It was a feeling often experienced by combat soldiers. Ahead of the point man, something in the shadows was not right; they heard a slight squeak and a rattle. He made out a cart with two water buffalo hitched to it, staring at him. He smelled the sweet-sour smell of livestock. They were almost invisible in the darkness. The buffalo had given them away. Something dark stood in shadows. There was again a flicker of motion so slight that Hiner's eyes scarcely detected it. Then he saw them. A shadow separated itself from the trunk of a tree. In a blink of the eye, it was joined by other shadows, all wearing black. Observing them from a short distance away, in the thin ground fog, a band of woodcutters stood motionless. The team was compromised.

Hiner realized the woodcutters had paused in their work, and after a moment resumed working. Hiner knew that the team had been seen and signaled for them to fade back into the forest. He alerted Webber, who was behind him, to the Vietnamese presence. As Hiner observed the area ahead, the team leader agonized over whether or not to kill the poor, innocent and unarmed woodchoppers. He decided not to kill them. The woodcutters had already worked up the mountainside until they were out of sight.

The Wallow

A mistake in judgment had just been made. Woodcutters often served as informants for PAVN Special Forces units. As Hiner watched, the further away they were, the more quickly the woodcutters moved. All the team members knew that it was just a matter of time before trackers and infantrymen of the 22nd Regiment converged on the area. SFC Webber collected his team and led them from the low area into thick brush of higher ground. Hitting heavy cover, they were quickly crawling through the thick growth. Hiner, on point, stopped momentarily, sniffing, thinking about what he was smelling. They moved more carefully now. There was a faint smell of methane gas permeating the air. It grew stronger as they moved. They encountered a haze of mosquitoes and flies. A growing, strong, sweet-sour aroma of decomposing manure and the musky, earthy stench of livestock now made them more wary. With it came the sharp stench of urine and feces hung in the thick air, as they moved forward on their hands and knees. When they broke out of the brush, a buffalo wallow was immediately in front of them, with trails running in all directions. The wet and deep black dirt topsoil was hoof-pocked with buffalo tracks, and ripe cow manure was visible everywhere. This was where the large animals rolled around and around, kicking mud and filthy dark water in all directions, cooling themselves with a coating of mud. There were no large trees, just ten-foot scrub trees. Seeking the thicker forest, the team now ran through the area into a cultivated area of banana trees.

At this point, they heard a dog barking from the village below, about 200 meters down the mountain. It meant only one thing: people moving around unnaturally fast--fast enough to excite the barking dog. People were being alerted and getting ready. Almost after these thoughts registered in the minds of Team Capital, they heard someone banging an alert on metal. The banging had a pattern to it. It wasn't hard to guess what it conveyed. The person banging the metal would bang for about a minute, pause and then start again. All other noises were drowned by the metal banging.

The team, bent at the waist and knees, ran northwest until they could not hear the banging anymore. Webber stopped the team to check his grid coordinates. They were now located at BS 755185, some 600 meters north of the village. Quickly, they started moving again, and came across freshly cut trails. Two to three meters wide, the trails ran from north to south, coming up from the valley floor. The unwilted leaves on the cuttings from the brush were still green and fresh. The men cutting this brush were somewhere nearby. Plain-soled tracks were everywhere. The team leader stopped his patrol here to look at the area and check his watch. It was now 1600 hours, getting late in the day. The team huddled closely, discussing their situation and decided to look for a place to remain-overnight (RON), with good cover and concealment. Webber switched on the radio and reported their situation.

Worries

The electricity in the dry BA-386 battery would drain quickly depending upon the number of transmissions, temperature and humidity. The battery life was 60 hours. Radio transmission was short and sweet. Each member of the team individually prayed to see the next day's light. After setting up for the night, they quietly discussed their situation again, and decided to re-cross the largest main trail that ran north to south, and to come back again to a point above the village. Hopefully, the PAVN would have already checked it and moved on.

That night, they didn't have to worry about their scent traveling. The rain would take it to the ground. It was a long night's vigil. Hidden in the brush, the team listened to the sounds of the pattering rain on the trees. Their eyes and ears searched and probed the source of each new noise. They listened to the shrilling of the tree frogs, and smelled the clean, fresh air that came before a rain, and the small *plit . . . plit . . . plit* of the drops hitting the leaves around them. The tree limbs overhead shivered in the rising wind as the rain began to fall. The night passed uneventfully. Unknown to the team, elements of the PAVN 22nd Infantry Regiment were hard at work, establishing area ambushes for the team, and trackers were even now searching for their trail.

Early in the morning on 29 January, the weather had turned for the worse. At first light, there was heavy rain. The mountain was covered with a heavy fog that hung low over the ground. The team waited, watched and listened without eating, until it was time to make radio contact at 0730 hours. They reported negative traffic. The only sound was a bird calling somewhere close at hand. An answer came from nearby. A twitter of movement, then silence. Finally satisfied that all was well, the team slowly and silently slipped out of their RON position and began moving, with SSG Hiner as point man. He was followed by SFC Hancock, SFC Webber, SFC Cook, then SSG Dotson. Rear security was SSG Hoagland. The shadows loomed large in the coming faint light of morning.

Hiner led the team into heavy undergrowth and rocks to avoid detection. They halted more often, and listened for longer periods. They wondered about their tracks being found and followed. They moved back to the east, contouring along the side of the mountain. At 1000 hours they stopped and ate, 30 meters from the main upland trail. Although they could not see the trail, they would hear if someone were using it. The point man slowly emerged from the heavy brush at the side of the trail, looking in both directions. Here the main trail was two to four feet in width. It had been used by a lot of soldiers since the early morning rain. The team quickly hopped across it and turned their direction south, down the mountain. They now concentrated hard on choosing their footing in the rocky area by stepping a little higher, to keep from twisting an ankle on the slick rocks.

Slowly, they emerged at the top of a rocky cliff. Finding a suitable route, the team now moved west again, forced by the terrain and very heavy brush to close up into a tight, single-file formation. They were in the claustrophobic grip of the terrain, moving almost blindly on hands and knees, pushing through crevices among a snarl of interlacing branches. There was no way to stand up. They noticed that many of the plants folded their leaves, and that the insects were bothersome and noisy, forecasting rain. The team carefully threaded their way through the thick, rugged undergrowth.

The weather continued to be poor. Soon, the drumming of the rain on the brush and rocks interfered with their hearing. They moved more guardedly than ever. Gradually the point man, Hiner, saw what appeared to be an open area up ahead, and headed the team for it. A quick check of the map determined that they were at grid coordinates BS 752183. Team Capital stopped.

Hiner now scrutinized the clearing from inside the heavy brush. The small, gently sloping hillside clearing was fairly clean of underbrush, but it did contain a jumble of large, three-to four-foot-long rocks, which stood just as high above the ground. The low side of the clearing was to their left, the high side to their right. It was about 20 meters long and 10 meters wide. Webber checked his watch. It was 1040 hours. The team remained still, watching and listening for five minutes. With a spine-tingling awareness, hearts thumping against their ribs and adrenaline pumping, they could not help but notice the unnatural silence that had fallen over the mountain forest. Nothing moved. They held their breath and for the longest time they listened, straining their eyes, searching. Always, as the team moved, they mixed caution with courage. Wariness had been their constant companion, alerted to the cry of every bird, or the snap of a twig. Nothing escaped their notice. Now, the unnatural stillness foretold a deadly presence. No birds chirped. There was a funeral silence. They heard only the sigh of the wind.

The team broke out of the thick undergrowth into the small clearing. Although there was a chill in the air, their palms were damp with sweat. Their eyes were trained constantly on the trees and undergrowth that lined the clearing. They tried to see into the surrounding brush and its shifting leaf-light. Hearts thundering, they stopped. They dropped into defensive positions, facing outward, sweaty palms clutching their rifles, and again held their breath to listen. Hiner suddenly had that odd feeling, a sense of not being alone, of being watched. A small gust of wind brought them something else: a distinct pungent smell, of unwashed bodies mixed with the faint odor of fish sauce, of uniforms long exposed to wood smoke. A chill went down each man's neck. It was too damned quiet and now, too late.

The PAVN were watching through tiny openings in the thick wall of brush, through carefully pruned shooting lanes which enabled them to see and remain undetected. In that next instant, the air was rent with the explosive and characteristic popping-rattling sound of the Kalashnikovs' AK-47's, coming in from the team's left rear flank. It seemed unreal, as if coming from everywhere at once. The 7.62mm assault rifle rounds smacked bodies, branches and rocks. The automatic fire was intense and sustained, but brief. Hancock, Hoagland, Webber and Cook were wounded. SFC Jesse Hancock's head popped back violently, following a hollow smacking sound. His body lurched forward convulsively and was slammed to the ground in a heap. He was killed instantly. SSG Hoagland, as rear security, had been the closest to the NVA. He collapsed backward, hit high and low in the back. Unable to move, he still retained his rifle. Again came the distinctive slow, deep popping sound of AK-47 fire.

    The team searched for targets, but saw nothing. They returned fire in the direction from which the most firing came. The brush was too thick to see anything. The sound of heavy automatic fire told the team that at least a platoon-size element was involved, but the sonic crack of rounds passing near the rocks confused the true direction of the rounds. The team could not see through the screening brush into the shadows. However, the PAVN had no trouble seeing them. They were looking from the dark into the light, the ideal ambush situation.

    Webber looked down to see his bloodied sleeve. His wound left him with one useless forearm, bones were shattered from the elbow down and muscles were damaged. He could not manipulate his fingers or move his forearm. It would take a short while for the pain to begin. He used his wounded arm as a prop to fire and load. There was no time to examine the wound. Cook had been hit twice by several bursts of AK-47 fire, both in the back and the stomach. He fell loosely, heavily onto his stomach beside a small tree. He was writhing on the ground in pain, but still had hold of his rifle. Unable to move, his eyes wide and staring, Cook looked down at the dark stain spreading and soaking into the ground. He called out to the team that he couldn't move from the waist down. He told them not to bother because he couldn't travel and that they would be killed if they helped him. Then he coughed up a pink froth with small pieces of pink lung. His eyes, filled with pain, were now dark and dangerous. This was his final stand against the inevitable. Fighting the terrible pain, Cook began returning fire into the surrounding brush, where muzzle flames flickered in the shadows.

Dotson and Hiner were the only two not wounded. Hiner low-crawled as fast as he could, up the hill to the north side of their defensive area, to provide covering fire in that direction. After settling into place at the top of the clearing, Hiner heard Cook calling out to him, telling him to get the radio out of his pack. Hiner yelled to the wounded Webber to cover him with fire as he took his bearing on the tree where Cook was located and moved back down the hillside. He quickly started a fast low-crawl down to Cook, who still lay exactly where he had fallen--beside the tree on his stomach--firing along with Webber. Both men put out a heavy volume of covering fire. Hiner quickly looked at him as he removed the radio from his pack. Cook's face looked terrible, and was wet with sweat. Hiner could hear his hoarse breathing. The radio secured, he quickly low-crawled over to Webber's position behind a large rock.

Hiner started transmitting, requesting any station that could hear him to respond. Looking at the low clouds just above, he worried about establishing commo. And even if he could be heard, could anyone help him? Webber now moved to the southern edge of the brush of the clearing. He felt a searing hot pain. His stomach began revolting, as he swallowed it down. Hiner called the FOB and got no response. He then called any station that could hear the sound of his transmission. He was immediately answered by an unidentified aircraft, which later turned out to have been a not-too-distant C-47. Hiner identified himself and gave the aircraft his grid coordinates and situation in the clear over the radio to relay. The C-47 relayed his message to Delta's FOB, mobilizing the headquarters. At 1040 hours, Capt. Kenneth L. Kerr USAF, the on-call Forward Air Controller (FAC), told him Robin One was standing by and alerted. In this weather, the FAC made his own judgment about flying.

The Scramble

The FAC immediately grabbed his map, survival vest and flak jacket and left for the airfield. At the aircraft, a little two-seater, high-wing monoplane, he threw his flak jacket on the seat. He would not wear it. Capt. Kerr's well-trained hands and eyes made a quick pre-flight inspection. He checked the gas and oil. Moving clockwise, he inspected the four rockets under one wing to insure that the safety pins were pulled. His hands and eyes roamed the control surfaces for free movement, and then moved toward the tail of the aircraft to repeat the process. Satisfied that his rockets were all armed, he climbed into the aircraft. Using his grease pencil, he wrote the frequencies and call signs on the left window, above the radios. With his crew chief standing by, he turned on the ignition switch, yelled clear and started the engine. It coughed as the propeller whirled to life. After a moment, he began to taxi, turning on the radios as he went. He built up his airspeed to 45 knots and lifted into the sky. It had taken the veteran pilot all of five minutes to scramble and become airborne.

As he rose above the airfield in his Cessna O-1 Bird Dog (L-19), west of Bong Son, he called the TOC. The FAC notified them that he was in transit to the area. Capt. Kerr's aircraft was equipped with a multi-channel UHF radio to communicate with fighter aircraft, a VHF radio to talk to the command post (CP), and an FM radio, located to his left above him to communicate with troops on the ground. He now turned on his FM radio as he flew up the An Lao Valley and began attempting to communicate with the patrol on the ground. He flew the aircraft into Team Capital's transmission range at 95 knots, while his eyes scanned the area.

Seeing that Webber was now in a good defensive position, Hiner yelled for Dotson to move to where he had previously been, at the top of the clearing. Hiner, still listening to the radio for the FAC, saw in his peripheral vision SFC. Donald L. Dotson rising from the ground and attempting to move his position across the clearing to secure Hiner's place. He got only 10 feet. Dotson fired only one round off as he moved, before he was knocked backwards with the explosive impact of solid hits. Several bullets had ripped high into his chest, and all passed out his back, that would have caused blood to drain out of his nose and mouth. In mid-stride, he flopped to the ground without a word, didn't even stumble or try to break his fall. Eyes glazed, he weakly attempted to rise. His breathing became labored, then, he closed his eyes. His breathing now came in shallow gasps. He slowly slumped forward as his final breath wheezed out. The ground darkened below him as he sank into oblivion.

Robin One

The weather was very poor. The FAC, still flying low and slow, was worried about both the team and himself. Hiner's ear remained riveted to the radio and finally heard the FAC calling. Team Capital had just established radio contact, but Hiner was still unable to hear or see him. Robin One requested Team Capital's immediate location. The weather seemed to close in behind Capt. Kerr as he flew north. Hiner immediately complied with a six-digit grid coordinate and situation report, telling him that they were now completely surrounded by a platoon-size element. Robin One informed Hiner that due to the bad weather, he could not call in any Air Force tactical aircraft. The cloud ceiling now varied at only 300-500 feet, and flying extremely low in the reduced visibility of foul weather increased the chances of being hit by small arms fire. Finding one little open patch in the valley, Robin One was now flying at 60 knots (about 69 mph). He entered into the patrol's area and, banking in a wide orbit at an airspeed of 60 knots, he started watching and communicating. Hiner threw a red smoke grenade. As Capt. Kerr banked the aircraft, its nose now slicing through the horizon at an idle and maintaining a speed of 45 knots (about 52 mph), he flew over and pinpointed the team's exact position by a panel marker.

Kerr informed Hiner that he had to leave the immediate area to escort the gunships to Hiner's location. A pair of aerial rocket artillery UH-1B Huey gun ships, armed with 2.75-inch rockets, was on the way. They would provide the artillery fire support that was beyond the range of conventional tube artillery. These were commonly used on obscured targets, in mountains and jungle, where suppressive fire had to be accurately controlled. Each helicopter carried 48 rockets. Dense clouds over the mountain ranges were causing the delay, but as soon as he arrived back with the gunships Hiner would mark his position with smoke again. They would have to find holes through the cloud layers.

As the FAC exited the valley, the Iroquois aircraft were pulling pitch and gaining rpm's, straining toward lift-off. The pilots scanned the gauges, stabilizing in a hover. Now the choppers lowered their noses to build air speed and make their forward run. They climbed for altitude; scattering multitudes of birds that were trying to sit out the storm. Quickly, they rendezvoused with the FAC, who had just exited the valley and was now banking to the left, arcing around to lead the choppers. They followed him up the wild-looking An Lao River, flying through rain and fog in the treacherous mountain terrain.

A half hour later, Hiner heard a distant whining sound, like a far off mosquito: the drone of the low-flying, single-engine aircraft. Robin One requested smoke now. Hiner pulled the tape off his yellow smoke grenade and straightened the pin.

The Gunships' First Run

Responding to the now transmitting FAC, Hiner informed him that the Team had suffered two killed-in-action (KIA) and two wounded-in-action (WIA). He also requested that the gunships make their runs to the south and east of his position. The PAVN were keeping up sporadic gunfire throughout his transmissions. Frantically, the team fought back during the short time it took for the FAC to arrive in the immediate area. Hiner informed the FAC that he was popping another smoke. He popped the smoke grenade and threw it into the center of the clearing.

Unfortunately, due to the low pressure, the yellow smoke could not be seen. It hung sluggishly and drifted slowly along the ground, curling upward serpentinely in the slight breeze. Hiner was informed over the radio that the smoke could not be seen. This sent him into a frantic search for another smoke grenade. Hiner quickly popped another, and told the FAC to conduct their strike in a radius of 50 yards from the smoke. The FAC identified the correct color. Red. Flying at low altitude, the FAC turned, sliced the nose through the horizon at an idle, then flew at 60 knots, in a slant. He used the

3rd nut on the windshield as an aiming point. There was a loud whoosh as he fired the white phosphorous (WP) smoke marking rounds, to identify the target areas for the gunships.

Hiner looked at Team Leader Webber and saw him struggling to reload his weapon with only one arm while returning fire. Overhead, the gunships, flying extremely low on a gentle glide slope and at a reduced speed, were vulnerable. They made their first run. The remaining members of Team Capital listened to the distant rhythmic thumping of the gunships coming in to attack, their turbines gradually growing louder. They were frightened. Hiner and Webber heard the sudden, explosive impact of ripple-firing, and the whooshing sound of the rockets. The ground shook in successive waves as rock and dirt geysers erupted.

The PAVN had held fast, hugging the American position. There was no longer any incoming fire from their positions around the clearing. The Team was beginning to have hope that the PAVN had withdrawn. But after three minutes, it started again. The incoming fire was now the heaviest from the south, west and eastern portions of the perimeter. The PAVN had a hard time seeing from the northern uphill side unless they exposed themselves. Rock chips were flying everywhere. The gunships were being cautious about firing their rockets too close to the team. Hiner informed the FAC that the PAVN were between the strike zone of the helicopters' first run and the edge of the clearing. Hiner told the FAC to have the gunships make a strike right over their position.

The Gunships' Second Run

The gunships complied, attacking and chewing up the clearing very precisely. Having expended all their ordnance, they now had to leave. The aggressive and well-camouflaged PAVN force recognized that it had isolated the six-man reconnaissance team. They began their "hugging" tactics around the perimeter and started attacking by fire. After the gunship ran down the center of their position, Hiner exposed himself by scanning the perimeter. There was a blinding flash followed by a searing pain. Hiner received a glancing blow from a 7.62 mm round that parted his hair. His head seemed to explode, as he felt himself hit the ground. Blood was fountaining and running down his face and chest, dripping from his face pooling on the ground beneath him, as he lost consciousness for a few moments. When he came to, he was nauseated, weak and dizzy. A sudden momentary blackness came upon him whenever he attempted to lift himself upward. Lying on his back, he attempted to raise himself on his elbows, but the pain in his head was too intense. After a few moments passed, he gave up the effort. He flinched from the pain and pressed a cautious hand over his head to test whether the bone grated. As far as he could tell, it did not. With his ears ringing, he tried to focus his eyes on the radio, hearing the voice of the FAC calling to him. His head was still pounding. Keeping his eyes closed, trying to help his eyes focus, he felt for and found the radio handset. It was important now to keep talking, to stay in contact, to keep the FAC informed. He told the FAC that he was wounded.

Hiner requested an Air Force strike, using napalm to burn an LZ next to their position, and was told he could possibly receive more from B-57's nearby. But he was also told that the FAC was worried about collisions over the area. Hiner requested the 1st Cavalry reaction force. Unknown to Hiner, however, the Air Force fighter-bombers were being used to conduct low-level missions for the 1st Cavalry. Extremely worried about the time delay in the return of the gunships, he asked how long it would be before the gunships returned. He was told that the 1st Cavalry had none available at the present time and that the helicopters would be on their way back in a half hour. The captain informed Hiner that he would use his aircraft to buzz their position to intimidate the PAVN and hold them back, though his aircraft had no armor protection and lacked self-sealing fuel tanks. After several low, high-speed passes under automatic fire, the FAC informed Hiner that available gunships were again entering the valley, and that he now had to leave just long enough to intercept and guide the two gunships into this area.

The Gunships' Third and Fourth Runs

The gunships arrived and each immediately made two passes around the perimeter. His temples savagely throbbing from the pain, Hiner informed the FAC that the PAVN had once more stopped firing. Their ordnance expended, the second pair of gunships returned to Bong Son. As soon as the sound of the helicopters faded down the valley, Hiner called the FAC and said they were again receiving fire from the east, and that he could see glimpses of the PAVN moving in closer to his position. They were preparing to overrun his position. His head still throbbing, he requested the rockets be fired very closely in on the perimeter. The volume and din of enemy fire around the perimeter intensified. The FAC could hear the gunfire in his headset. Worried, he warned Hiner about such close supporting fire. Hiner's reply was to fire the rockets closer.

Webber sensed movement amidst the screening brush and trees. He focused. Movement again, flitting among the trees and brush in the dappled light and shadows. There was a brief, muffled, tonal conversation in Vietnamese. Then again, as if the wind had lightly blown a few leaves, the khaki uniform appeared. Webber's eyes blazed malevolently as he saw his enemy, a lone North Vietnamese Army regular, a "*bo doi*" with a red star on his khaki cap-rise up and throw a grenade. He fired and then yelled "grenade" to Hiner. He saw the Chicom stick, "potato-masher" grenade arching high through the air, flipping end over end into their position. The explosion of dirt, smoke, rock chips and shrapnel enveloped the area. The potato-masher was quickly followed by two more. Immediately after the three explosions, Webber pointed to Hiner in the direction from which the grenades had come. Both Webber and Hiner now laid down a magazine of ammunition in a crossfire in that direction.

Webber now felt exposed. He knew that he had to move his position. The watching eyes of the PAVN were too close. Before long he would be too weak to help himself, so he would have to join Hiner in his nest of boulders. The wound caused him to sweat. It had transformed from numbness to a blinding pain searing his arm. His trembling knees probably wouldn't hold him up if he tried to stand or run. He low-crawled now, and attempted to retrieve the mortally wounded SSG George A. Hoagland. Hoagland couldn't move, said he didn't feel anything from his mid-chest down. There was no longer any conscious movement, which indicated that his nervous system was disabled. Hoagland told Webber to leave him. He was dying, and faced his death with courage.

Webber quickly low-crawled to Cook, finding him still alive but unable to talk. Webber managed to drag him over to Hiner's position and laid him down on the opposite side of the large rock. Webber could see Cook's pulsing neck muscles throb as searing spasms of extreme pain pulsed through him. Webber administered morphine to Cook and himself then crawled around the rock and joined Hiner. Webber's face was white from the tremors of pain shooting through his arm. His energy was ebbing fast. His limb was useless, the forearm shattered. Hiner dressed Webber's wound and checked his watch. It was 1230 hours.

The Gunships' Fifth and Sixth Run

The FAC requested smoke again and Hiner told him to wait. He was out of smoke and had to search one of the dead bodies. Hancock, lying on his stomach, was the nearest and easiest to get to. His head pounding, he managed to sit up. As he got to his knees, his body swayed. He knew he would have trouble standing, much less running. Hiner ran spraddle-legged, staggering as fast as he could. The jolting movement intensified the pounding in his head. His feet felt sluggish and unresponsive. He kept expecting to be slammed to the ground. It was only a short distance but it seemed to take forever. His blurred vision and nausea threw off his balance, and he wove from side to side as he ran, staggering almost uncontrollably. Hiner flopped down beside Hancock and opened his pack.

The searing pain in Hiner's head continued to swell and rise, then slowly subside and dissipate in a rush of unconsciousness. Hiner revived momentarily. He was determined to choke back the brutal pain and doggedly endure it. The smoke grenades were there. He told the FAC to pull the rocket strikes out from the edge of the perimeter where the NVA had pulled back. The third pair of agile gunships made their first rocket run right over the edge of the perimeter. The explosions were deafening. They turned and came around, making their final run, exactly the same as the last. Back at Bong Son, Delta's FOB, was listening in. He asked the FAC to find out if Team Capital could move to a landing zone.

Special Forces Forward Operational Base at Bong Son

Maj. Beckwith alerted the 1st Cavalry's Third Brigade staff, he needed help. The staff replied that all their units had become heavily engaged elsewhere and all air support elements were already committed to their own men. By noon, Maj. Beckwith, still pleading with the 3rd Brigade staff for air assets, was notified that the third team had called for help and an emergency extraction.

1st Cavalry Engaged

The 1st Cavalry's main heavy contact with the NVA was north of Bong Son on 24 January. It was followed by only light, sporadic contact for several days. Then the brief lull in the fighting was over. On the 28th of January, with a low cloud ceiling and early morning fog, elements of the 3rd Brigade were ordered by the Division Commander to conduct a combat assault north at Landing Zone Dog, a well fortified village, between Tam Quan and Bong Son.

Units of the 2nd Battalion, 7th Cavalry under Lt. Col. Robert A. McDade came into heavy contact with the PAVN at the hamlets of Phung Du (1), on the national railroad and Highway 1. Four of the low-flying CH-47 Chinooks, braving the heavy anti-aircraft fire, had been shot down in one hour's time, and twelve UH1D helicopter troopships were badly damaged. They had carried the infantrymen into the low areas under PAVN observation, within their fields of fire, and had received heavily concentrated anti-aircraft fire. By mid afternoon, 28 helicopters were so badly shot up that they were grounded. In the 1st battalion, 7th Cavalry's area of operation, another CH-47 Chinook was shot down while carrying a 105mm howitzer later in the afternoon. The Americans secured the helicopter and howitzer, but had a highly contested fight with waves of attacking NVA in the open terrain. The Cavalry remained pinned down for two days in the macabre site of a graveyard, moving from tomb to tomb for cover. The enemy occupied a maze of zigzagging communication trenches in the small hamlet, with fighting bunkers, underground bunkers for protection against artillery and aircraft. These PAVN fortifications were well concealed by thickets of bamboo, cactus and tall palms, and were well protected by mines, booby-traps and punji stakes.

Maj. Beckwith's aura of self-assurance was momentarily shaken. A dark and terrible emotion showed briefly in his eyes as he listened to the 3rd Brigade staff explanation. He knew that resources that should be redirected immediately would not be. There would be no 1st Cavalry reaction team for Delta. They were on their own. Delta was now dying and Maj. Beckwith-tall, fierce and strongly built-was helplessly enraged. All present could feel the anger that flowed between Maj. Beckwith and the 3rd Brigade staff. His hard, square chin was set, his face grave and stern. His nostrils broadened. His mouth tightened. The vein behind his ears throbbed. A sudden poise of his head indicated thought and power. His eyebrows drawn down and tightened, with nostrils opened wide, he gave one last hostile glare. He turned and departed.

Returning to his area, he ordered all those recon and support personnel in Delta remaining behind to ready themselves and standby to go in on a moment's notice, to attempt to rescue at least one of their lost patrols when the situation allowed. He was again updated and briefed by his communications and operations personnel. Maj. Beckwith still had his Command and Control (C&C) helicopter, and went into the air to be ready in the event a situation presented itself. The commander of the Delta Project, like his lost teams on the ground, felt very much alone. He had been promised support, and there was none. He knew that he would get them out if he had to do it himself.

Team Capital

The FAC asked Hiner if the team could move to a landing zone (LZ). Hiner's voice was now fading and getting weaker. "Negative," he replied. Every member of the team was either dead or wounded and unable to move. He requested a reaction force, as the popping sound of a heavy volume of AK-47 fire started hitting the ground and rocks from the southeast portion of the perimeter. The FAC again requested the estimated strength of the NVA while he flew around the area to select a landing zone for the reaction force. Locating one, he marked it in his memory. Hiner replied to the FAC, "Platoon strength." The FAC now informed the Delta FOB that a reaction force of 15 men was needed to relieve Team Capital. The FAC started making treetop level passes over the Team's position to ensure he had their exact location, and to try to scare the PAVN and keep them away or down, hopefully taking the pressure off the two men. The FAC made three passes before the gunships had arrived, talking with Hiner as he did so to get an exact fix on the position for the next strike. Then he climbed, made a wide turn, and fired his two smoke rockets, marking the exact location of the PAVN forces, twenty meters from their position.

Four Gunships Arrived Overhead

Hiner tossed one of the grenades retrieved from Hancock's pack, and requested that the gunships fire their aerial rocket artillery 50 yards out from his position in a 360 degree circle. He asked where the reaction force was. The FAC called the FOB and asked about the estimated time of arrival (ETA). They were on the way to loading on the choppers now. The FAC relayed that information to the two men. It would be another thirty minutes. Hiner and Webber speculated and worried if they could last that long. His head throbbing in agony, Hiner was only dimly aware of the gunships in the distance: they were banking sharply and bearing in for their direct fire support mission. He continued to have trouble with his equilibrium and coordination. Then he passed out again. Webber's arm was throbbing and he was very weak. He could feel the grating sensation. But it didn't matter, for right now, he was still alive. He was more worried about Hiner, who didn't seem to be either conscious or moving.

Each helicopter made its run. Hiner regained consciousness and lay for a time, with eyes blank and empty. As they listened, they heard the whooshing roar of the 2.75-inch, high explosive rockets, and felt the violent explosive concussions while their eyes were clamped shut. The first gunship was striking the north side of the perimeter; the second, the west side; and the third, to the south. But all the smoke, dirt and rock debris from the explosion caused the last gunship coming in from the east to misjudge the target. His rockets came right down through the middle of the perimeter. The deafening shock waves of the explosions chewed up the area and spewed shrapnel and debris everywhere, hitting SFC Marlin C. Cook's position on the other side of the rock. His agony was over. Immediately after the rocket strike, the FAC informed Hiner that a reaction force was getting ready. Neither Webber nor Hiner noticed what happened on the other side of the rock. Later, the gunship pilots would report that they saw Cook's body lifted off the ground by the intensity of the strike, as the rockets swept dead center over Team Capital's position.

Reaction Force Under Fire

The choppers, loaded with the Delta reaction force, started inching their way up the An Lao valley. Forced to fly low and slow due to the weather, the reaction force almost immediately started receiving heavy ground fire. Now the PAVN's green tracers were everywhere. The PAVN had used their time wisely. The further the choppers went, the heavier the ground fire became. The force turned and started flying back to try an approach from the north. The pilot, Major Murphy, came on the air with the FAC and informed him that they were now in the air and that they were going to try to come in from the north. "Negative," the FAC responded. It was impossible that way due to the extremely poor weather to the north. The reaction force would have to come up the valley. Major Murphy informed Capt. Kerr that he had already tried that way and had received heavy ground fire. Capt. Kerr replied that he had been flying back and forth to guide the rocket ships in and that he could make it that way. The now doubtful Major Murphy turned the lead ship in the formation and started climbing above the clouds. Major Murphy called the FAC and said, "On the way."

The FAC told Hiner to hang on; the reaction force was still on the way and would be in the area shortly. Major Murphy called the FAC and now informed him that he was above the clouds at twenty-five hundred feet, trying to find a hole to lead his formation through. The FAC told Major Murphy to rendezvous with him at Bong Son, then informed Hiner once again that he had to leave the area to guide in the reaction force. The FAC again flew down the gauntlet of NVA fire, through the closing walls of the valley, and picked up the reaction force, leading the formation back through the green tracers of heavy ground fire. He told the choppers to standby while he marked the best and closest LZ he had previously selected with his last two smoke rockets.

The LZ was not close to Hiner and Webber, but it was their best bet. After Major Murphy dropped off the reaction force, the FAC told him to orbit around the southern end of their approach in the valley because a second reaction force from the 1st Cavalry was now on station just to the north side of the valley. Capt. Allen J. Carter, from Project Delta, was with the Cavalry reaction force. The reaction force, under Delta's Lt. Holland, had now secured the LZ for the 1st Cavalry. Holland threw a yellow smoke grenade to inform the FAC he was on the ground and not to let anyone fire on his area. The 1st Cavalry would remain behind to secure the LZ for evacuation or until they were called upon to help Lt. Holland move to Webber and Hiner's position. Hiner and Webber heard a helicopter approaching and threw a smoke. Hiner got back on the radio and gave a situation report, then started asking for a reaction force again. His headache caused him to speak more sharply than he had intended. He passed out briefly once more, and when he again became lucid, he heard the FAC say the reaction force was on the way. Hiner informed the FAC to have them use rope ladders so they could come right into the clearing. The FAC informed Hiner that the reaction force was already on the ground and working their way toward them.

Lt. Guy H. Holland's reaction force had landed in a distant area away from the two wounded men. Their LZ was south of Hiner and Webber's position on a gentle sloping part of the ridge. The reaction force now stared into the utter stillness of wavering and shifting shadows. They had a steep climb in front of them. Lt. Holland knew they had to hurry: the noise of the helicopters had provided the NVA with a good idea of their location.

Major Beckwith made the initial helicopter extraction attempt in the C & C ship. The major had made his decision. His helicopter was coming in above them, offering hope. The pilot had descended at maximum speed and was now slowing. He whizzed in, skimming over the tops of the trees. The situation looked good. But when it was well within range, the helicopter was met with intense anti-aircraft fire. Hearing the hits on his aircraft, the pilot immediately aborted. His helicopter was riddled with a hail of enemy fire. As it lurched, he swung it quickly around and away, trying desperately to evade the fire. The crew chief notified the aircraft commander that Maj. Beckwith was hit by a 12.7mm round in the stomach and was bleeding badly. The wound was below the rib cage.

An emergency call from the pilot notified Bong Son of an incoming wounded passenger. The pilot now raced his ship to the base, utilizing the increased speed of the newer and wider blades mounted on the aircraft. His passenger could smell the raw, overpowering odor of torn intestines, and immediately alerted the pilot. The major was forced to lie on the floor on his back. An inspection of the gaping wound revealed the balloon-like bulging intestine. Although the helicopter managed the return trip, it was shot up so badly that it could not again be moved under its own power. A Special Forces medic quickly treated the still unconscious Major Beckwith. He soon awoke, suffering from shock but feeling no pain. His men placed his litter upon an incoming helicopter belonging to the 85th Evacuation Hospital stationed at Qui Nhon.

End of the Line

Webber and Hiner felt that it was the end. They had been fighting to stay alive for two hours. Trying hard to focus his slow-to-move, bloodshot eyes, Hiner called Robin One

(FAC) asking for help. The FAC was desperately requesting help in the form of a reaction force from the FOB. Because of his condition, Hiner could only vaguely hear him on the radio, and didn't know to whom the FAC was talking. The area around the remaining two Delta Team members was quiet. Webber was very weak from the loss of blood. He worried about Hiner, whose head wound was still bleeding, and whose fainting spells were becoming more frequent. Hiner crawled around to each dead body, checking it. He collected their grenades and ammunition and returned to Webber's position. Both men figured that they were going to need all the ammunition they could get. The FAC was directing a chopper from the 1st Cavalry over the clearing, when Webber told Hiner to get out into the clearing and wave to the gunner. Hiner waved to the gunners, who in turn pointed down the ridge towards the reaction force.

    The FAC told Lt. Holland to take a compass bearing of 360 degrees, straight north towards Hiner's position. Immediately after the FAC's transmission, Hiner informed the FAC that he was now receiving fire from the southwest. The FAC again used his unarmed aircraft to buzz the NVA positions on Hiner's southwest side, trying to get them to stop firing or to scare them off. He flew his aircraft at top speed, hoping he didn't provide much of a target. The NVA were well aware that this small aircraft was responsible for bringing death and destruction, and had been trying to shoot it down. Banking in a large circle, the FAC now remained over Hiner's position. He attempted to raise Hiner on the radio, but Hiner had passed out again and Webber was now too weak from loss of blood to help himself.

    Lt. Holland contacted the FAC, asking how far they were from Webber and Hiner. The FAC requested that they pop a smoke grenade to mark their position. Seeing that they were located southwest of Hiner and Webber, he gave them a compass heading of 30 degrees. Lt. Holland's force was quickly moving again. The FAC called Capt. Carter and informed him that he had located a small LZ, approximately 150 meters to the north of his position, which would accommodate one helicopter at a time for evacuating the dead and wounded. Capt. Carter said he would move north and secure it. At this time Lt. Holland called the FAC and stated they were again marking their position with smoke. The FAC quickly found the drifting smoke and gave him a compass heading of 50 degrees. Hiner, once again lucid and desperate, came up on the radio and asked the FAC where the reaction force was and how soon it would reach him. They were approximately 100 meters southwest of his position, down slope. Hiner replied that they were not receiving any incoming fire at this time. Lt. Holland requested through the FAC for the two wounded men to throw smoke and fire three rounds into the air so the reaction force could get a quick fix on their location. Hiner threw the smoke and Webber fired the three rounds, slowly, methodically. Now everyone knew where they were.

The FAC could see Lt. Holland's force closing on the two men. Lt. Holland requested the FAC buzz the two wounded men and cut his engine when he was over their position. The FAC repeated this maneuver for five minutes and then called a gunship in to hover over their position as the reaction force stealthily approached. The helicopter complied and hovered for ten minutes fixing the location for the warily watching reaction force. The NVA had withdrawn. At 1530 hours, the reaction force broke through the clearing and found the stunned Webber and Hiner, both in a numbed state, covered in each other's blood and in the blood of their fallen comrades. The great loss of blood rendered both men a little insensible and also put an end to their pain. Webber's eyes struggled to focus on the faces of the men who had saved him. Hiner had a stinging headache behind his bandaged head. They had survived the carnage. Their souls had not.

The Ride Back in the Helicopter
A stunned silence followed as the members of the reaction force looked into the bloody, grimy faces of the two wounded men on the ground before them. Webber and Hiner, with tears stinging and clouding their eyes, looked back up and around the circle of men, one by one, and were overcome with such emotion that they could not speak. A helicopter flying up

the valley quickly materialized, its two gunners ready, their eyes searching the terrain. It quickly banked, and the pilot, lowering the collective, flew coolly and steadily into the area. The chopper flared, stabilized in a hover, and gently eased down to extract the wounded men. The pilot throttled back to keep the rotor wash from creating too much debris in the air. Webber and Hiner were now very weak, and needed to be physically assisted onto the chopper. Pain bolted through them. The Huey rose and flew out over the valley, turning south. The air cooled quickly with the altitude. On the ride back to the hospital, both Hiner and Webber, drifted in and out of consciousness. For the two wounded men, a peaceful somnolence settled over the chopper. Then sweet oblivion! Of the six Team Capital members, four were killed and only two survived.

Team Roadrunner

A lone helicopter passed over the small Gio River, its silver water already faded to a dull pewter. SFC Houston's six-man team was quickly inserted at last light, at 1900 hours on 27 January 1966. The door gunners were watching for the enemy, while keeping a close eye on the rear of the ship. They were standing by to communicate to the pilot if the tail rotor came too close to any object. When the whole reconnaissance team was out of the chopper, they gave the "clear," trying to avoid lingering near the ground too long.

The team landed in a clearing just below the crest of the mountain ridge at grid coordinates BS 711172. The pilot pulled back on the collective and nosed the chopper up and into a quick turning climb, away from the team's position. They hoped that no one had heard or observed their insertion. They immediately moved 200 meters northeast through the elephant grass, into the increasingly darkening cover of the trees, running two hundred meters below the crest of the finger ridge, above the nearest civilian populated area, the village of Hung Nhon, at grid coordinates BS 742144.

Tense, slightly sweating despite the cold, each man huddled closely by, keeping his distance, listening and watching with wide eyes. It was a high-up and lonely place, many miles from the nearest friendly face. Small wings buzzed at their ears. There would be no moon or starlight. Hopefully they would be safe for a while. Their weapons were at the ready. The men of the DELTA Project knew that if the PAVN were aware of them, they would already be using the terrain, darkness, and adverse weather as opportunities to set up their hasty ambush positions in every site where they were likely to encounter the American patrols. The PAVN commanders would checker-board every grid square of the map, completely enclosing the area. Their suspicions were well founded.

One small group of NVA was quickly closing in, scanning the horizon and ground ahead of them for any sign. The PAVN knew that reconnaissance forces were deployed well forward in the offensive, and that sooner or later the 1st Cavalry was also coming. It was therefore necessary to locate and kill the Americans as soon as possible, before they wandered too far and learned too much.

Their first day was a short one. The existing light dropped low over the western range of mountains as the team went into the thick brush to remain-over-night on the southern exposure of the mountain. The thick cloud cover obscured the moon. There were all sorts of rhythms to attune to-the play of the wind through the trees, the emergence of the area's resident insects, birds and animals-as the team settled into the business of holding still. It was an edgy experience to absorb everything as the light and cold air settled at twilight. The smell and feel of the air was changing. Only a few night insects had begun their incessant, low, monotonous song. The birds were largely silent, apparently nervous about the coming storm. The tree frogs had been calling with their sweet, melodious trilling in anticipation of the rain. The sound of small animals moving in the trees was almost undetectable. At night, the ground was the most dangerous place to be. Predators hunt best in total darkness. Fearful shapes took form and the smaller creatures, sensing the danger, went to the trees. Dull, glowing patches of phosphorous scattered throughout the forest gave depth to the darkness. Then, the mountain forest came alive with the drizzle of rain.

As the hours wore away, the team members' attention was attracted at intervals to the steps of some padded, soft-footed animal somewhere nearby, which soon stole away into obscurity. The solitude of the night passed uneventfully, with intermittent spells of light rain drumming on the canopy above. Periodically, they were soaked with sluicing sheets of rain. The men were uneasy and already so wet and wretchedly cold that it made no difference. It grew very black and still, save for the heavy pattering of water accumulated and dripping from the trees. They had spent a long night peering into the dark, listening. It was now that formidable hour before dawn, when even the life of the forest seemed at its lowest ebb. The last vestiges of the night seemed to pass at an incredibly slow pace, but finally the awakening chorus of the coming daylight commenced with sleepy chirps and the twittering of birds coming awake and beginning to move about. As the new light emerged out of the east, the chilly dawn mist hung in a ghostly, gauzy veil over the narrow creek below.

Dawn's Early Light

The short antenna was removed and the long one was hurriedly broken out and screwed into the radio. The team leader whispered into the handset, praying for an immediate response. Radio contact was quick and successful. The long antenna was now replaced by the short one. Its signal would radiate straight up when any aircraft showed up in the immediate area. Commo was made at 0720 hours, as the team reported their location, negative contact and direction of movement. Chilled, damp, and miserably cold from sitting too long in one position on the cold, wet ground, they stood slowly, working out the stiff muscles and pain in their joints. After urinating on the nearest surrounding tree trunks, they were ready.

At 0730 hours, the bleary-eyed team began to move slowly, contouring and winding around through the overgrown forest, across the head of a deep ravine. They were headed in a southeast direction, along and up the opposite, gentle-sloping finger ridge. They moved carefully to avoid disturbing the leaves. On the opposite side of the ridge, the team noticed freshly disturbed dirt. They moved until they came to the point above a stream, from which they could see the ravine below, and stopped to observe a trail running along side the stream. SFC Huston decided to confer with his men about checking the area where he had observed the disturbed dirt.

The PAVN Ambush Site

Huston selected a well-concealed position twenty meters further down the ridge to better observe the trail below. He posted SFC Hodgson there with the rest of the team. This was at grid coordinates BS 715170.

The small village of Hoc Khoan lay below them in the valley at the edge of the mountain. Voices could be heard in the valley. Not wanting to be surprised by any PAVN movement on the trail, SFC Huston went back up the ridge taking his second-in-command, SSG Badolati with him to check the area thoroughly. The team watched and waited in silence. The only sound was the murmur of the wind and the rush of the nearby creek.

Huston and Badolati moved about the ridge. They found it to be saturated with the fresh, raw dirt from a newly prepared, platoon-sized ambush position. These individual fighting positions were known as spider holes. They had been dug the previous day. The holes were two feet deep and a foot wide. Checking his watch, Huston noted the time. It was 0930 hours. Having seen enough, the team's two leaders headed back down the ridge to the rest of the team. As soon as they joined the team, SFC Huston noticed Hodgson's alert body movement, rapt attention and posturing behind his weapon. He was keyed up, his concentration focused forward, watching down the trail.

Huston reacted with a startled response to the single report of the rifle. Hodgson continued to fire. He fired several bursts, seeing the approaching PAVN legs buckle, twist and then fall. The team leader immediately withdrew Hodgson and the rest of his team back, away from their positions, as he and Badolati sprayed the area down trail with fire. Huston quickly conferred with Hodgson. Two PAVN killed, wounded a third coming up the trail. Huston heard muffled voices, barely audible but excited rising, broken and low-pitched, the tonal sounds of spoken Vietnamese. There was more sound of movement on the trail, well below their position. They were not going to go away. Huston told Badolati to lead the team down and across the trail and creek, and up the gentle-sloping hill on the other side of the draw. Badolati moved to the trail and briefly stopped to check the area. They watched and waited. Badolati approached and carefully checked both directions. Nothing. The team rapidly crossed the trail in one large stride, blending into the darkness. They moved a short distance away from the trail and stopped, waiting and listening to make certain their movement had gone undetected. The men crossed the creek and slowly and quietly contoured up along the side of the hill, until the time when the sun would normally have reached its zenith. There was no sun. The sky was still heavily overcast with drizzling rain. Huston knew now that they had been compromised.

He became the team's rear security, making sure they were not followed and attempted to sweep and cover their trail. He hoped that whoever followed would only quickly scan the area without seeing their trail. Huston was seriously considering an extraction. As the men moved up the hill, they observed more newly constructed ambush positions. Each of the many freshly dug fighting positions had two machine-gun positions, clothes and baskets for hauling away dirt and concealing it away from the site. The team leader warned his men to touch nothing. SSG Terry told the team leader that he had observed a platoon-sized force of khaki and dull-green uniformed PAVN moving up toward the hill. Voices could be heard, as if directing others in the valley below. Huston told the men that they were now going to move quickly and try to evade the quickly closing enemy force. They headed for the dim light of the cool deep green, running bent at the waist and knees. Soon they were pumping their arms and legs fast for a short distance, then stretching out into a long, slow stride. They would keep this pace for two hours.

It was 1200 hours, when Huston called a halt. They were breathing heavily from the run, their chests heaving, and their blood pounding in their temples. Their eyes smarted from the rivulets of sweat running into them and off the end of their nose, as they set up security to rest. The weary team would remain here to catch their breath and make commo before continuing to evade the PAVN soldiers. They were unaware that they were now being tracked through the mountains. The "bo doi" of the 22nd PAVN regiment, in their faded, Chinese-issued green uniforms, were following closely behind the small team of scouts who were trailing the American team. The trackers, by now, would have identified the number of personnel and confirmed that they were a reconnaissance team. The PAVN would harry the Americans through the mountains until they killed, captured or ran them out of the area.

The Tracker

Unbeknownst to the Americans, a vigilant and silently moving North Vietnamese Army regular "bo doi" tracker must have already picked up their sign. I'm sure his predatory eyes studied the ground while he squatted and gently brushed the impressioned leaf edges of a boot track with his fingertip. He would have a vivid awareness of everything around him. A team of six men in a hurry would leave an easy trail for any experienced tracker to find. The "*bo doi*" tracker would see where the Americans had made an attempt to lightly sweep their backtrail. Their tracks would still be visible to the trained eye. The American jungle boot was made for good foot protection. It was not made for stealth, however. The large vibram sole, while good for traction on any terrain, had a raised portion that would leave noticeable marks on bare ground and leaf carpet if the wearer moved too quickly. The tracker would know exactly who had been there. While the Americans left heel marks, the PAVN did not. The length and breadth of the distinctive, deep parallel bootprint impressions indicated tall, well-built, heavy men in good physical condition carrying equally heavy packs. The tracker would also know from the length of stride that the Americans were moving quickly.

The PAVN tracker would rise from the ground, and quickly and silently move to the point where the trail would be disappearing up ahead. Others would follow him patiently, at a distance. The trail would become easier to follow because the Americans would be running. The tracks, now a shorter distance apart and easier to see, ran down the hill. The trackers' sharp eyes would become aware of any movement, then, from the Americans, came the slightest sound. At that moment, the hunter must have found the hunted. The tracker would have moved back the way he had come to confer with the unit's commander, who would then issue instructions to a subordinate, who would in-turn wave a selected number of men forward for their instructions.

Attempting Commo

The team had now been stopped for about ten minutes, just below a hill. There was a constant awareness as they stopped to rest and relax. Huston could smell the acrid odor of sweat and fear. Each man was quietly facing outward in a small circle. At any given moment, they could come under observation of the PAVN. Only the low hum of insects pervaded the whispering wind. The team leader started to check and verify his location on the map. They were approximately eight kilometers northwest of An Lao, on the south side of a finger ridge above a deep draw and creek. Their position was located between two main trails that separated at the foot of the mountain and paralleled the finger they were on. Both came back together at the top of the mountain ridge that ran northwest/southwest. SFC Huston, by habit, glanced hopefully up for the position of the sun, though the weather was still marginal. A quick glance at his watch confirmed the time. It was just past noon. After catching his breath and getting his breathing regulated again, he prepared to make radio contact with a situation report and a request to be extracted. Suddenly all was quiet, the hum of the insects silenced.

Found

SSG Terry experienced an eerie sense of uneasiness, of another man's presence, of being observed. He raised his head, searching. His instinct, or the subconscious hearing of a sound, told him they were there, somewhere. The light erratic wind, combined with the mist and drizzling rain, made it extremely difficult to classify sound and scent. There was a slightly different sound and also a different scent that had caught Terry's attention on their back-trail. He had been lying back on his indigenous rucksack, but now slowly rose to an upright position, silently alerting the team. He had caught the quiet sound of an almost indiscernible smooth animal movement. Within seconds, Terry could make out the barely audible low whispering of voices. The slight breeze and creaking trees created a confusion of noise, overriding the sound of the trackers' approach. Then the nightmare began.

As he cautiously scrutinized the immediate area, Terry detected a subtle but harsher shadow in the brush, about twenty meters away on their uphill side. A small rounded silhouette. The distant image became discernible. A brown face stared at him. Shocked, he momentarily stared back, as the face blended so well with the shadows. Overcoming his initial shock and confusion, Terry lifted his rifle and made a smooth trigger squeeze. The man was down. Nearby, muzzle flames flickered from the brush. Badolati and Hodgson jumped to their feet, prepared for flight. There was the sound of a bullet striking bone, followed by a sharp, pained, wordless, agonized cry as Badolati was knocked past Huston by the impact. Badolati had been hit in the upper portion of his left arm. He remained on his feet, his back arched and he shuddered in pain. He moved past Huston through the forest. The 7.62mm round had nearly severed his arm.

The Firefight

Surprised, everyone hugged the ground and waited as the AK-47 fire fell to a lull. Now the team fired suppressive fire. Everyone knew Badolati had been hit, they could hear cries and see the arterial spraying of his blood in all directions as he moved. Hodgson twisted sharply with the impact of a bullet as it struck the receiver of his rifle just as he brought it up to fire. The impact threw the weapon from his hands, rendering it useless. Now unarmed, Hodgson followed and caught up with Badolati. Seeing Badolati's condition, he quickly applied a tourniquet to what was left of his upper arm. Badolati's arm hung by only some intact tissue and muscle. Most of the blood loss was stopped; there was now only seepage. His hand and forearm were placed inside his jacket between the buttons, and a triangular bandage was applied to help him carry it. He still had one good arm. The team leader, SFC Huston, pointed the way north for Hodgson and Badolati to move. Unarmed except for grenades, Hodgson asked Terry for the 9mm pistol that he carried as a backup. The packs were left in place. Hodgson helped Badolati, who was now suffering from shock. When Huston asked Hodgson if he had been hit, he answered, "No." But Huston saw fear in his eyes. Everyone returned fire in the direction of the PAVN, then moved out, one after the other, quickly, covering each other as they went. McKeithe remained behind the rest of the team, covering the team leader. They soon caught up with Hodgson and Badolati. SFC Huston led them approximately 30 meters at a run, then checked to see if everyone was together. Huston told Hodgson to stay with Badolati because he was unarmed. After the team had moved approximately 400 meters, Huston called a halt to attempt commo with the FAC or the FOB, and discovered the pack with the radio was now in the hands of the PAVN.

The Blood Trail

The PAVN would secure a perimeter well out from around the rest area that the Americans had occupied during their break. Now, the small "bo doi" tracker would enter the area and walk carefully over to where the American team had been when the shooting started. He would spend some time to thoroughly assess the scene. Blood was splattered everywhere. Its pungent, salty smell would be overpoweringly strong in his nostrils, and its copper metal taste would sit on the back of his tongue. From the direction in which the spray of blood hit the ground, and from the scuffmarks, he would determine where the wounded man had been when hit. He had been standing. The bright red blood splatter was of great volume, and irregular in pattern. Looking ahead, he would see bone fragments. A spattered blood pattern indicated the wounded man was moving off rapidly away from the point of impact. Establishing the flight line, the tracker would know the Americans trail would be easy to follow, for a short distance at least. The order would be given for the ditched American equipment to be gathered, put in one place, and quickly displayed, as he would continue to follow the blood trail. The tracker would follow as quickly as he dared in order to keep this man bleeding. He knew that the pursuit would eventually lead to the death of the wounded man.

The PAVN and "bo doi" tracker would look at the equipment left behind. The Americans had left six packs with their food, which the enemy could now use. The packs also contained extra ammunition. There were two M-16 rifles, one serviceable and the other useless, which would be cannibalized for parts. There was also a 6.35 pistol, three valuable lensatic compasses and four pairs of binoculars. The quality U.S. compass was a much-needed item by the PAVN. These valuable items, abandoned by the Americans, indicated their state of panic. They would discover the two radio sets, AN/PRC-25s and an HT-1. The highly prized radio sets would be sent to their Communications Intelligence units. The tracker would now lead the men quickly through the forest on the easy-to-follow trail. The Americans were running. The wounded one would leave a scuffed trail and fresh, oval-shaped blood drops on the leaf mat. Like the fingers of a hand, the splatter marks were pointing the way. The further they moved, the more blood they would encounter.

No Radio

Huston now halted briefly to have Badolati attended to. The only radio the team now had was the ground to air, HT-1. Badolati, in shock and pain, was now frightened. He felt faint, and his knees were wobbly and threatened to fold on him. He had managed to run only because of the increased adrenaline flow to his body. SFC Huston used the HT-1 to call their emergency code word, "Flaming Arrow," indicating to anyone listening that the team needed immediate help. It meant Americans in contact and in danger of being overrun--needing any available aircraft to provide air support. The only reply they heard was "Alpha Mike."

The team fought to calm their labored breathing. Huston gave the HT-1 to Gray to carry. Badolati was still losing blood; Hodgson put another tourniquet on quickly. Badolati was now in a lot of pain, and asked for morphine. It was administered. Huston told the others to keep running, and took off again. His plan was to lead his men north, out of their tactical area of responsibility (TAOR), and then west and finally south to reenter the TAOR at their emergency rendezvous point (RV).

The team ran. They quickly came upon an old, hand-made rock wall, where they stopped and took up a defensive position. The three-foot high, eighteen-inch thick wall ran for as far as they could see both ways through the forest. He knew they could now stop here and defend from this area long enough to attend to the exhausted Badolati. Crouched behind the temporary safety of the low wall, they peered over the top to scan the area. There was a brooding silence. Huston looked at each brave man, seeing the fear in their eyes. Badolati sensed that he was going to die and told Huston as much. Huston told him that they would make it out. Badolati wanted to be left behind so that the team would have a better chance of making it out. He continued to beg Huston to leave him. Huston hoped the NVA would run up on the wall, so that they could kill or hurt the PAVN badly enough to halt their pursuit. The team took up their positions.

What they dreaded most happened soon after. The 7.62 mm rounds of automatic AK-47 fire slapped into the trunks of the trees around them, hammered into the rock wall, and plowed into the ground in front of the rock wall, kicking up debris. The PAVN were already there. Rock dust, wood chips and bark were flying everywhere. Huston told Badolati to start moving north, adding that the rest of the team would catch up with him quickly. Badolati started running north by himself as Huston watched his direction, then turned back to firing over the wall. The team returned a heavy volume of fire. The khaki and faded green uniforms of the PAVN were now materializing out of the darkness of the forest, utilizing fire and movement. At the wall, SSG Terry and MSG Gray both returned fire, emptying a magazine apiece into the khaki ranks. Reloading, they saw Hodgson running to the west. Terry and Gray picked up and followed behind Hodgson. As soon as Terry and Gray caught up with Hodgson, it was apparent that they were alone and that the PAVN were now close behind them. The three men heard firing to the north.

Startled now, Huston saw that three of his men were gone. Huston moved up to the cover of the wall and started returning fire. Realizing that he and SSG Billy A. McKeithe were now alone, he started moving away from the wall to take up the run again. McKeithe, who was himself using the cover of a large tree, covered Huston from the rear. He asked McKeithe where the other three men were and he said they had already left. Huston gave McKeithe the chemical CS gas powder grenade. McKeithe threw it into the air.[1]

The CS would intensely and painfully irritate the eyes and skin, and radically sear the respiratory system and stomach, often causing temporary blindness and disorientation. Unidentifiable to the PAVN soldiers, it would cause enough fear among them to stop or slow them down. The lingering, noxious, crystallized gas would saturate the surrounding overhanging vegetation, helping to delay and confuse the enemy. The gas could last for days or until the heavy dew or rain, washed it away. Once human contact was made with the small powder crystals, they would stick to them.

No one was left to defend the wall but just the two of them. It was time to move. As Huston ran passed McKeithe, he said, "Let's go." The two men, their adrenaline pumping, put on a burst of speed turning corners around trees for cover, hoping that with their accelerated pace they would be lost from the enemy's view. They quickly caught up with Badolati.

The tracker would send a scout to circle the area. There were only three places beside the wall, where bright brass cartridges littered the ground. One spot to the rear with scattered cartridges would show where one man had been firing. Checking the immediate area, he would find where the wounded man sat against a tree, facing the wall. The leaves would be compressed from his weight and smeared with blood. A small pool of blood would show where his wounded left arm had been. There were round drops where the blood fell only a foot from the blood-soaked wrapping. The tracker would have picked up the small, empty gray tube and smelled it. It was the quarter-grain morphine ampule left behind. Other compressed points belonged to the man administering to the wounded man. They had stopped the bleeding; there was no blood trail leading away from the tree. The scout would have quickly returned, having found the ground disturbance of the Americans' trail. The tracker would follow his scout and find the scuffed surface in the spongy, matted dead leaves.

Terry, Gray and Hodgson moved west about one hundred yards and came across a trail junction with a trail watcher's hole located above it. The junction had a good view and a field of fire covering both trails. They selected a hide with a good light and dark background and positioned themselves in front of it, hiding in plain sight. The natural background tones were matched by their effective "Tiger suits" camouflage, blending with and breaking up their human outline. They remained motionless; only their eyes moved. At 1845 hours, they observed two black-clad scouts moving north on the trail. One was packing a lightweight "DELTA" poncho, instead of the normal blue plastic issue of their army. The three remained there another 15 minutes, until 1900 hours, then moved slowly south into lower ground. Hodgson, Terry and Gray successfully evaded the rest of the day of 28 January, moving downhill. Then like a black mantle, the deadly dark silence of night's solitude closed in around them, cloaking the hills. Just before stopping for the night, they changed direction and turned west. They were too close to the valley. The three frightened men would spend the long night huddled together, back to back for warmth. Suffering from extreme stress, a high level of adrenaline was discharged into their blood, which produced a strong scent. They could smell one another's fear. They listened to the sounds of the night, always wondering where and when the silence would be broken. Early in the night and for the rest of the night, Terry, Gray and Hodgson heard troops moving in the dark, up the trail to the northwest. The barking dogs in the villages below them indicated a lot of men were moving around.

SFC Huston, Badolati and McKeithe

After catching up with Badolati, Huston realized that their existing team was split. Their breath was coming in hoarse gasps, rasping their throats and their lungs, feeling tight and burning from their run. Badolati fought to stay conscious, the pain keeping his mind sharp and cold. He knew he had to endure. His arm was hurting fiercely in the wet climate. Huston realized that being in two three-man groups would help them to evade and confuse their nearby enemy. He and McKeithe had not seen or heard any movement behind them after the grenade was thrown. They ran a short distance for about 15 minutes, before coming to a stream. They took a quick look back. Nothing. It was all quiet along their backtrail. Huston decided to use the stream to cover their trail and try to lose the PAVN. Then they stopped, hearing, and feeling a familiar dim sound, increasing in volume.

It turned out to be the rotor blades of a Huey, quickly approaching up the valley. Remaining stock still, Huston and McKeithe observed approximately 40 well-equipped and armed PAVN move out into the open and fire on the low flying and exposed helicopter. All were wearing web gear and their small, soft "pork-pie" hats, with red stars at the center front. It had started to rain. Huston and McKeithe began to breathe easier again, knowing they didn't have to worry about making noise. Now was the time to move quickly. They went slipping and sliding through the water as the sound of the helicopter rapidly accelerated away.

Time passed. They left the stream. Badolati's initial jolt of adrenaline had long since dissipated. His breath was coming in gasps, rasping in his throat, and his lungs were on fire. He was now growing very weak and losing feeling in his limbs. He knew that if he stopped, they all would stop, and they could not afford to do this. He was now trudging wearily along and needed to be helped. Huston knew that their hurried trail in the rain could be easily followed.

Huston, Badolati and McKeithe stopped in the darkest shadow of a great tree, their eyes scanning the surrounding area. They heard the mellow murmuring of a small stream. When they came to it, they decided to move upstream in the water to hide their trail. They stopped as Huston studied the stream bank. He had to avoid leaving the darker sign of fresh scuffed dirt in the area where they would enter. It was about two feet deep. He saw what he was looking for about twenty feet away. They entered the stream, utilizing a low, hard rocky area without disturbing the stream bank. As before, Huston hoped the water route would throw off their trackers. Careful not to slip or slide, they walked in the stream away from the area as quickly as they dared. Huston and McKeithe could hear their own footsteps, and the water swishing as they moved. They knew they had to stop. Around 1500 hours at a fork in the stream, Badolati, white-faced and feeling cold, worrying that he was slowing the others down, told the team leader to leave him behind. He could not go on. It was obvious to the team leader that shock was setting in. Huston could see that his eyes were dilated. Huston and McKeithe told him that they would stay with him.

Badolati was bleeding to death. They helped him up onto the three-foot-high stream bank, then climbed among the boulders and shrubs lining the stream bank and laid him down in their cover and concealment. An abandoned hut was about 15 feet away. The two men lay on both sides of Badolati. Seeing that he was suffering greatly with the pain and loss of blood, they decided to give him all their morphine. They each gave him the last of it. His last anguished whisper was, "Save yourselves." They laid out extra magazines and hand grenades, determined to take a few PAVN with them if the NVA showed up before Badolati died. They knew they would be able to defend themselves from this covered and concealed position. They lay in the prone position, alert, listening and always watching their back trail. They could smell each other's acrid scent of fear. There was only the sound of the wind, the rustling of leaves, the drip of water from overhead, the drone of mosquitoes and the muted, babbling music of the stream. An awful weariness had enveloped the two men. They knew the PAVN were out there, close by, searching. Once the PAVN searched the forest ground area and found the jungle floor undisturbed, the next logical choice would be the stream. Huston and McKeithe knew that sooner or later the PAVN would come along the stream. They prayed it would be later. Both men prayed silently to God and for Frank Badolati.

While both men were comforting their wounded comrade, dewdrops worked their way down from the dense leafy cover slowly dripping on them. The atmosphere was heavy with dampness, but both men could detect the rank, sweet smell of blood. Badolati groaned. The dark shade was almost like twilight. Now, as they crouched and trembled, the full enormity of their predicament settled upon them. The team leader could see and feel that Badolati's breathing was now shallow, rapid and uneven. Periodically, he would open his eyes and speak. Then his loud, heavy breathing would be followed by a quiet lapse. He would come and go in his delirium. His strong heart fought to stay alive. They thought that he had died several times, between 1700 and 1715 hours, but he always came back. Huston felt for his pulse and could not find it. When he placed the palm of his hand on the chest, there was a faint sign of movement. It was now 1715 hours. Badolati was in an insensible state, the coma preceding death. Then grim reality. The end came.

His eyes opened wide and slowly fell with his last breath. They knew that the soldier had painlessly bled to death. The long, valiant fight to survive was over. His breath came loudly with a soft rattle. Then silence. Another sighing breath. Silence. The overwhelming odor told the silent truth to the team leader that the body had now lost all control of its functions. Badolati's head was turned and Huston could see that there was no throbbing in the large vein that ran down the side of his neck. Badolati's nails were blue. He again felt for a pulse at the neck and wrist. Nothing. He placed his palm down on the chest. There was no respiration. There was no eye reflex. They waited until both were sure that their comrade was dead. Then they took a good look around. It was now 1730 hours.

Huston and McKeithe had remained with Badolati for two-and-a-half hours. They now had only an hour-and-a-half until dark. Low-voiced, they discussed their plan. They decided against running for their rendezvous point (RP) to the south. Huston told McKeithe that they should go as high as they could, taking the most difficult route in the terrain. Stepping only on rocks, they reluctantly entered the stream and slowly continued to move uphill. Crouched in the depressed area of the stream, they moved slowly with a stealthy grace so that only a portion of their upper body could be seen, and then only from a close distance. Both men hoped that there had not been enough time for the PAVN to think out the situation and establish ambush sites upstream and downstream.

They were hoping that the stream sediment would quickly settle and that the flow of water would soon erase their tracks before the PAVN discovered their trail entering the stream. Their thoughts were now of survival. Finally, their eyes sweeping the landscape for movement or sign, they left the amber-colored stream and exited on rocks at a low place in the stream bank. Lifting their feet slowly, they allowed the water to clean the soles of their boots, so as not to leave any grit on the stepped-on rocks. They were careful not to break down the stream bank or step in soft soil. They stepped only on the rocks, moving cautiously around, between, over and under, along the path of least resistance, as the forest and obstacles dictated. Stealth was now their greatest asset. Always watching, listening and smelling with each step, both men were in touch with the feel of the mountain forest.

About an hour after Badolati's death, the PAVN trackers would have arrived at their last stop, following the still slightly disturbed sediment impressions and small-disturbed stones in the bottom of the stream. The PAVN would find Badolati's cold, pale body lying in the streambed, dead. There was a possibility that after the two members left, rigor mortis had caused the body to sit up and roll over and down into the creek. The trackers were being followed by a large number of the 22nd Regiment's infantrymen. NVA prisoners later stated that they had buried Badolati in a shallow grave next to the stream, with all the respect due to a brave warrior.

Huston and McKeithe consciously focused on maintaining an easy pace, trying to avoid nausea and headaches that would limit their ability to think. Their ears attuned to every sound, they moved carefully and silently, warily watching where they were going. Each fought his own battle, controlling a surge of panic. Studiously avoiding bare soft ground, they submerged themselves in the maze of night's darkest shadows. They stopped frequently, and remained hidden and motionless for long periods against the side of the nearest and largest tree trunk. Staying away from any trail, they made their way through the thickest cover and concealment they could find. Huston and McKeithe made many abrupt changes in direction, winding around large rocks, boulders and large serpentine tree roots that snaked back and forth, forming steps upward from the dark timber and choked gullies to a forested knob near the open, high grasslands. The ascent was steep. They traveled the straightest line in the dark, so that they could avoid the slipping and sliding of their feet disturbing the ground. They shortened their step as they moved uphill, climbing with a slow rhythm, to avoid disturbing the ground clutter. Heads up, they felt ahead carefully for debris that might make a noise and give them away. They moved until it got so dark that they could not see, and then halted for the night. It seemed like an unreal nightmare, with dreams of gloom and mournful whispers of the wind, the terrible solitude. They were not deceived by the calm, and held no illusion of safety, they spent the rest of the night wide-eyed, staring into the darkness and straining their senses for any trace of their pursuers. They shook involuntarily.

    The following morning remained cloudy, gray and chilly. At 0600 hours, on 29 January, they began to move quietly and patiently up the mountain, letting their eyes do most of the walking. They came to a point where the timber ended and the tall elephant grass covered the top of the mountain. They made their way slowly out onto the downslope side, into the grass. There they could hide without being seen, while hopefully being able to attract the attention of someone flying over the area. They could now see the magnificent and dangerous dark panorama of deep valleys, the rolling, forested hills and verdant meadows of tall waving elephant grass. There were purple ranges in the distance. Not a sound pervaded in the aching silence. They remained hidden, their keen roving eyes shifting everywhere to catch movement. They felt the wildness and loneliness of their position. A few minutes later, they heard the faint, familiar drone of an aircraft engine at low altitude, as yet unseen. Hope surged. It was the sound of the Forward Air Controller's engine in the distance, flying to their north.

The Forward Air Controller

Air Force Capt. Kenneth L. Kerr was extremely worried about the men of Team Roadrunner. He was patiently flying in an elongated orbit above the valley. He knew that Team Eskimo had been chased out of its operational area on the 28th. Now, only an hour-and-a-half ago, at 1500 hours, the two surviving members of Team Capital were extracted. It had been a busy day. As he flew, he drank his coffee to stay alert. He stared studiously at the terrain below, watching for a panel, flare, the flash of a mirror, smoke, or the waving arms of the men themselves--anything. On the ground, Huston and McKeithe watched the aircraft make about five passes around in the general area. They fired their pen flare straight up. The L-19 turned and started directly for them. Relief flooded into the two men. The aircraft was still heading their direction. They quickly pulled out their international orange/red panels. In the clearing, they flashed their orange panel at the FAC. The aircraft now began to fly in a large circle centered on them. They were spotted. Both men now knew that at least someone knew where they were. They also knew that their location was being communicated to the FOB.

SFC Hodgson's Split-team

Unknown to Huston and McKeithe, the other half of their team was not far below them. Terry, Gray, and Hodgson were moving at first light, slowly as shadows, in an absolute noiseless and stealthy course through the forest until 0800 hours. They stayed inside the timber, avoiding the top of the ridge. Then they entered into an open area, gradually traveling uphill in a large rocky area covered with very tall elephant grass, taller than their heads. They came upon a well-used trail in the tall grass and crossed it. It appeared to be well traveled, faint and flattened. Shallow prints of sandals could be seen there. They established a defensive position off the trail to rest and to observe any activity upon it. They sat closely by, facing to the north, within arm's reach of each other. Thoroughly confused and in a panic situation, they took their time to plot their present position on the map. They remained still in this position until about 1600 hours. Avoiding any noise in the dry grass, they kept a close watch on the time, and on the trail to their front. At one point, they thought they heard troops behind their position, but there was only the sound of the wind in the grass to Gray's rear. His sixth sense alerted him to danger behind them. Almost afraid to move, he heard a slight brushing sound to his rear, and the hair on his neck stood up. There it was again. It was the faint, but briefly distinct sound that men in uniforms would make, moving through the tall grass. He looked to his right rear and saw seven PAVN infantrymen looking at them. They had been trailed and possibly surrounded. Three PAVN, dressed in black, were lying down in the grass, in the prone position. Four others were standing behind them, two in black and two in their faded green uniforms. Using his left hand, Gray reached out and touched Terry on his left leg and whispered their predicament.

SSG Ronald T. Terry turned and immediately fired. Gray's rifle was lying between him and Terry. Gray now picked up his weapon, whirled to a kneeling position and fired. He saw three of the standing men hit, stagger and fall. Reloading, he heard the soapy smack of a bullet hitting flesh. Terry cried out. Gray saw Terry holding his now bloodied right side and his fluttering hands trying to plug the wounds. Blood was flowing freely between his fingers. There was another burst of AK-47 fire. Terry's body jerked and jumped again with the impact of the firing. He was again hit in the chest, which collapsed the other lung. Terry now experienced a shortness of breath and felt a sharp pain. His attempts to breathe harder only made his condition worse. Unknowingly, Terry was creating a larger vacuum and drawing more air into his chest cavity. Mercifully, shock was already setting in. The wound was fatal without immediate medical assistance. There would be no help. He rolled onto his side into a ball, his face pale, and slid into the darkness. His bladder relaxed in death.

After returning fire, Gray looked back. He saw that SFC Cecil J. Hodgson, 29, was already gone. Gray jumped up and ran to the west. The sound of firing, lent wings to his feet. Bullets whistled and smacked through the grass, kicking up the dirt around him. Gray ran a short distance, dove to the ground in the tall grass and turned, facing back to the east. He concealed himself now and watched his back trail, his weapon at the ready. About a minute later, the stillness was shattered. Gray heard one crisp staccato shot from the 9mm pistol carried by Hodgson and heard the hollow thump of a soldier hit. Then silence. The air was suddenly shattered with one short automatic burst. Gray heard Hodgson moan and fall. Then there was a pause, and then another burst. A burst of fire came from the direction where Terry had been positioned. MSG Gray twitched at the sound, all too evident of what had been done. With both men dead, he was very aware that he was alone. He waited and listened, sweating from the tension. He heard the sound of helicopters up on the mountain.

On Top of the Mountain

At 1610 hours, Huston and McKeithe stiffened. After a few harrowing moments, with the wind blowing in their faces, the distant sound returned. The sound of rifles, a heavy volume of small arms fire, broke out a hundred meters to the east and slightly down the hill from them. Both men could hear the faint sound of shouting Vietnamese. Rounds were popping over their heads. For a moment they thought they were under fire, but it was too high. They realized they could start running again, but this was the best place they would find to be picked up. They realized a firefight had developed, and during a lull in the firing, they heard voices shouting. Then they heard a chopper coming. Huston told McKeithe to get on first as he prepared a red smoke grenade. It was only minutes before the nearest available Huey was in the area, escorted and trailed by gunships. The chopper saw their panels and roared in fast, the rotor wash flattening the tall grass to the ground. Huston and McKeithe ran for the chopper. The two men were helped into the helicopter as gunships provided suppressive fire around their extraction point. The pilot pulled pitch. The chopper lifted, turned and made its run, lifting higher and climbing away. Aboard, Huston informed the pilot and gunners of the direction from which the PAVN were firing. As the chopper flew down the hill to the east, Huston threw the red smoke grenade. Both he and McKeithe had successfully evaded the

PAVN. They relaxed and let the cool wind flowing through the compartment help revive them.

One Man Left on the Ground

The circling gunships were firing on the red smoke and the area nearby. Hiding nearby, MSG Gray listened to the helicopter work the area over for five minutes, then leave. The pounding of blood in his ears almost deafened him, and he knew that he had to calm down or suffer the unthinkable: capture or death. He heard the sound of the PAVN chopping poles to use for litters to carry their dead and wounded. Gray chose to use the chopping sound to cover his movement and ran, spurred on by panic. Frightened of running into the PAVN, he finally stopped. His breath sucked in open-mouthed gasps. It was now growing dark, and Gray realized that he would be spending another night hiding out. Alone.

It was damp. Easing himself slowly through the grass, he crawled a few feet and then stopped and listened. He cautiously looked around, and then crawled some more. He moved through the tall elephant grass and found a hide among the boulders higher up on the slope, as the mist rose in the low ground. He eased himself around from one boulder to another to get a good look all around him. Satisfied that he was safe for the moment, he settled in and watched the last traces of the mysterious half-light of day's end sinking behind the western mountains. Never had he felt so alone and small, so very, very small, watching the light disappear. Waiting, listening, horribly frightened, Gray strained his senses in the smothering gloom. The silence was crushing. Without eating, he felt light-headed, and his stomach rumbled.

The night passed uneventfully. In the predawn chill, the trees were still dripping. Gray, lonely and frightened, fought against a dreadful lethargy trying to steal over his body. His muscles wanted to yield to their fatigue. He slipped into a fitful doze near dawn without turning off his senses. The first early morning chirp came from the canopy overhead. It startled him and brought Gray's drooping head up to listen. Now there was an occasional chirp that told him all was still normal. Because of the night's rain, the birds were mostly silent. The area was covered in a mist as he watched and listened, wet and cold, his eyes red-rimmed with fatigue. He shook as though with a chill, waiting for the shapes of searching soldiers to materialize out of the mist.

The PAVN "Trinh Sat"

Not far away from Gray, in the predawn gloom, a company of "bo doi" rose from the ground and stood silently, awaiting their orders. Nearby, three men stood apart, talking among themselves. The two with the "Sam Brown" belts were the company commander and the unit's political officer. The third was the commander of the small group of "Trinh sat" personnel.[2] They had been charged with running down the American recon team. The three men discussed the day's method of search while the radio operator was busy. Several radiomen squatted nearby, talking among themselves about their 15-watt, Chinese-issued, field radios. One sat and cranked a generator between his legs, producing the power for the operator to talk to a distant headquarters in the valley.

It was now the morning of 30 January 1966. Gray could feel the enemy's presence. They were close by. He worried about the damp ground muffling the approach of those searching for him, and remained still in his hide until 1200 hours, not deceived by the calm. As if in a bad dream, Gray again sensed movement to his rear. He turned and saw five PAVN almost within arms reach of him, attempting to capture him alive. Shocked and frightened, he fired one whole magazine into the soldiers, then turned and ran deeper into the 8-foot tall grass.

Death in the Tall Grass

Gray ran in long strides down the side of the hill and dove into the tall grass and rolled, uncertain of where he was going. He was knocking the dew off the long grass, revealing his direction. There was no way to restore it to its natural state. Near panic, Gray knew that he was now leaving a dark trail through the sea of silvered dew. Gasping for breath, he stopped and again turned, concealing himself, and studied his back trail. Listening to his ragged gasping, he realized that he had been running too fast and had to slow down. His heart was hammering. Fear regurgitated hotly in his throat. The last thing he needed was to be out of breath or fatigued, or to injure his legs. He had to calm down, sweating, his lungs afire with the need for oxygen, he tried to quiet his breathing as much as possible. MSG Gray waited until his heartbeat returned to normal. He now knew the full meaning of terror.

The NVA tracker would notify the commander that the American had entered and left a visible trail through the grass. The commander would then order a team of soldiers to follow it. Their eyes would easily see the contrast in color of the trail as the light reflecting off the tall trampled grass, pointed the way.

For a while, Gray heard only the mournful wind and its passage through the grass. Finally, he heard a faint, unnatural sound. His nerves on edge, he couldn't tell if it was something moving in the grass or just the wind. Then came the sound he had been dreading. Now his breath became faster. He heard the soft swishing sound of passage made by uniforms, and the faint, muffled sound of Vietnamese as they easily followed his trail. The sound stopped. His eyes narrowed. This was worse than any awful nightmare from which he could easily awake. Again, he heard the soft swish of movement coming closer, along the fresh trail he had made. He saw something stir back along his trail. A coldness in his blood stopped the beating of his heart as he quit breathing. He saw them. Just a dim outline slowly moving through the grass. He knew it was time.

Cold shivers up and down his spine, so scared he felt sick to his stomach, he drew down on the approaching figures and waited. The first of the shadowy figures appeared in the tall grass, two armed NVA regulars, along his back trail. Gray could see the sweat streaks on their chest. They were looking for their enemy, dead serious, focused, intent. Gray felt that he was going to die. He had no concealment, and they were looking right at him through the thick screening grass. They crept slowly along Gray's path. Now his fear and panic left him, as he let them get within six feet and fired. He dropped both men. Gray immediately came upright. His knees weak and trembling as doubt reared its vile head, he turned and fled down the side of the hill, adrenaline pumping, lending speed to his flight. He listened to the unseen NVA, firing for approximately three minutes into the grass in three directions. Gray's lips grew dry. They hadn't seen him move.

Hidden in a prone position and covered with grass, Gray listened and watched. His mouth was all dry inside, his palms sweating from the tension. He was afraid that they would hear his breathing. The agony of running on his tightening leg muscles and lungs was severe. His head throbbed. Gray took several deep breaths in order to regulate his breathing. His eyes were watching through the heavy long stems.

The PAVN began randomly firing into the tall grass. Many rounds thumped into the ground nearby. One individual shouted loud commands at the PAVN troops in the vicinity of Gray's last position. The waiting was torture. Gray heard the sound of movement in the grass again coming his way. Then he detected movement along his back trail. From deep within him came a hard, burning defiance. Again there were two men, one behind the other, slowly materializing in a cautious, upright advance, following the trace of flattened grass. One was wearing the "Sam Brown" leather waist belt with shoulder strap. Gray, creating as little motion as possible, looked down the axis of his rifle barrel. He waited until he was sure he would not miss. His weapon locked into his shoulder. He fired a sustained burst of fire, hitting both men.

Again, he leaped up and ran, and then threw himself into a roll down the hill. As his momentum stopped, he carefully moved a few feet and again hid himself completely in the grass to watch his back trail. He waited nervously for fifteen minutes. There was only the sound of the wind. Suddenly, he heard loud and sharp orders being shouted. Although startled, he did not move. He heard movement in the grass once more. It was slowly coming toward him. There were now more shouted orders. Gray could hear the voices plainly. Unknown to Gray, he had just killed the unit's commander, or its political officer. The PAVN troops were now passing on both sides of him unseen. He tried his best to stop his trembling. He hoped the "bo doi" would continue along the same line. Higher up the slope, he heard them talking. The only words he understood were the words "American," and "Officer." For two hours the troops remained in the area looking.

Gray could hear someone talking on a radio close by. As he listened, it seemed that most of the PAVN had moved on, still searching. Then the area became quiet. The fear was harder to manage all alone. He was overwhelmed by a sense of helplessness. Gray listened for two more hours, straining all his senses. He felt an overpowering dread of this place, as the thrill of fear pricked his spine. He knew he had to force his brooding mental state aside to deal with his problem. Anxiety already graying his tight-drawn face, he began to think again. He got his second wind. His breathing became normal. The piercing pain in his lungs had dissipated. He could again smell the clean, sweet air. A small surge of joy at still being alive overwhelmed him. He realized that if he were to attract the attention of a passing aircraft, he would have to be on the high ground. There was no other way without a radio.

Gray pulled out his map from his side pocket and studied it. He picked a high area and decided to go for it. Taped securely to the harness of his web gear were all the items that he would need to attract a passing aircraft or helicopter: smoke grenades, a pen flare gun with plenty of cartridges, a signal mirror, and an international orange and red panel. He had to find out if they had moved on or were merely waiting and watching for him to make the next move. His inability to predict what he would run into preyed upon his mind. He no longer heard any movement around him, only the sound of his rapidly beating heart. He stood and looked through the tops of the seedpods of the grass. The slopes were steep. He looked all around the grass-covered, rocky terrain and saw his selected high point. He prayed it was not occupied by the PAVN. Taking no chances and becoming more cautious, he moved slowly, conserving sweat and calories.

The soldier now shifted direction. Using the protective cover of the 8-feet-tall open grassland to mask his movement, he headed up the large, steep rolling finger ridge, to the top of the hill. His muscles began loosening up now as he moved toward higher ground. He worried constantly about scaring up ground birds and cause the PAVN to see or hear him. Using all the cover he could, he kept on at a slow, steady, cautious pace, stopping frequently to listen and watch. He could now view the waving grasslands and the rush of a constant wind, blowing through the forest below. He listened to the hissing in the breeze. As he moved higher, he exulted in his immediate escape, but then stared around his location anxiously. He was always watching his back trail. There was nothing he could do about his back trail. He just had to stay ahead of his trackers. He was bone-tired and weary, and in perpetual anticipation, watching and listening for any movement. He moved very slowly.

Gray finally arrived at the top, panting, exhausted, and dripping with sweat. The grass in this area collected the heat of the sun, making his physical condition almost unbearable. It was better than being dead. He was alone in an incredible silence. He checked his watch and hoped he would be more easily seen here from the air, while remaining unobserved from the surrounding terrain. It was now 1700 hours. As he sat down, he heard the distant whine. It was getting louder. His eyes tearing, he now hurried to assemble and cock his pen flare. The FAC was going to fly right over him. He fired his small, white flare straight up and to the front of the oncoming aircraft. The pilot would have to see it.

Flying along the top of the ridge, Captain Kerr's eyes were constantly moving in all directions so as not to miss any signal from the lost men still remaining on the ground. Starting his sweep from one side of the aircraft to the other, he saw a flare shoot up to his front. He waved his wings, marked the position visually and on his map and flew straight on, as he reached for the VHF to make his call. The FAC flew in a wide orbit around the area so as not to mark Gray's position to the watching NVA troops.

Extraction

An eternity passed. Then Gray heard the whopp . . . whopp . . . whopp of helicopter turbines in the distance. The deep, throbbing sound of four helicopters reverberated off the distant hillsides and then was gone, masked by the terrain. He heard it again, the rhythmic thumping getting closer. He knew it was now or never. When detected by the PAVN, the pyrotechnics would have them moving quickly to the area, where he would be easily captured or shot. Gray waited nervously. Soon, he heard the approaching helicopters again. Finally, Gray saw them. He fumbled for his pen-flare gun and waited until the chopper in the distance was pointed toward him, growing larger in the sky. He fired a white flare straight up, so that it would not be seen as a threat.

One of the four armed helicopters seemed to slow its speed, banking slightly into a gentle turn to the left and coming directly for Gray. The others now began a wide orbit of the area. He fired another white flare straight up. He fired two red flares straight up. He knew he had attracted their attention, and he tossed a yellow smoke grenade into the field to mark his position and to show the wind direction. Even Gray's assurances that he was "pretty safe" did little to ease the anxiety he felt. They were still circling warily at a distance for a better look. He took off his hat and held his weapon out so that its outline could be seen. The pickup chopper came closer and closer until they recognized him for what he was--an American soldier.

Gray watched the incoming chopper's nose go up to slow down its rate of descent. It flew low overhead and dropped a rope ladder. Due to the down force of the wind, the heat and rising humidity, each step Gray took lowered the helicopter. After several attempts, he realized he was too weak to climb. Aware of the problem, the pilot had the crew chief pull the ladder in. He brought the chopper into an outcropping on the steep slope and rested one skid against the hillside. Despite the terror still in his eyes, Gray was able to climb into the chopper. The pilot slowly lifted the chopper and turned in a sharp banking turn with its nose down. He made a low run to gain airspeed and power and lifted up and away with one more survivor. MSG Wiley Gray had made it.

Delta Tactical Operations Center

Immediately upon landing, Huston and McKeithe informed the Delta personnel about the firefight they had heard before being extracted. The sound of gunfire might have come from the rest of the team. Aircraft returned to the area but could not find any sign of them. SFC Huston knew that Badolati had saved lives by his determination to keep going. MSG Gray later confirmed that the firing below the hill had been their firefight with the NVA.

The 1st Cav's Captain Joseph L. Spencer, the man responsible for supplying the operation, stated that his unit had been reduced to semi-paralysis by the bad weather and attempts to logistically support the helicopters daily with a minimum of 1,000 air-to-ground rockets, 3,300 rounds of artillery and 40,000 gallons of fuel reduced his Cav to semi-paralysis. Spencer added that they could not help the Special Forces teams in trouble on the ground because they already had more than they could handle: they were trying to maintain their own shot-up helicopters and support their own troops engaged on Highway 1.

Binh Dinh Province was never pacified. In Phase I, 121 men were killed and 220 wounded. In World War II, this division had suffered 4,055 casualties. In the Korean War, the same suffered 16,498 casualties. By the end of the Vietnam War this division would suffer more than 30,000 wounded and dead.

Heavy casualties incurred in the DELTA Project depressed everyone. Gen. William C. Westmoreland, the commander of U.S. forces in Vietnam, personally debriefed the bitter Special Forces survivors. He heard the blunt truth about the broken promise of support and the lack of support. He was also informed of the failure to exploit the situation immediately with a quick follow-through, by the 1st Cavalry.

The bodies were never recovered, due to the heavy fighting taking place in the area. Later, PAVN POWs would confirm finding one large, decayed American skeleton still retaining remnants of its "Tiger striped" uniform and one smaller Vietnamese skeleton along with remnants of his khaki uniform still lying above ground at grid coordinates BS 806213. A PAVN infantryman, taken prisoner, reportedly took part in burying Badolati in a shallow grave next to the stream, which was later found in an excavation by an unknown source. Again, in December 1974, two remains were discovered at grid coordinates BS 806213 by South Vietnamese forces. However, plans to recover them could not be carried out, because massive numbers of PAVN occupied the entire area in March 1975.

The 1st Cavalry had its problems with other American units during the war. After returning from my leave in the United States, I learned about the Bong Son Operation and the problems with the 1st Cavalry. I would eventually learn that other units had problems with them also. In September 1965, during Operation Gibraltar, the commander of the 2/320 Artillery, of 101st Airborne Division, could not get help from the 1st Cavalry to move their guns with their helicopters.

During September 1965, another 101st unit, the 2/502 Airborne, needed support during a battle at An Ninh, having been pinned down by interlocking fields of fire from enemy machine-guns. The 1st Cavalry refused to help. During the same operation, a 1st Cavalry artillery unit fired on the 2/320 Artillery position.

On that day in January, Major Charlie A. Beckwith again passed out somewhere in flight to the hospital. He regained consciousness in Triage. Triage-the word loomed heavy in his mind. Where they screen and classify the incoming wounded and determine their priority of treatment. If they get treated. There were many wounded men awaiting treatment, more than they could handle. In this emergency situation, they had to determine who they could save and who was put aside to wait. To die. He had regained consciousness just in time to overhear two doctors discussing his condition. Evidently while he was unconscious, the triage nurse had already checked his vital signs and listened to the weakening lubb-dup--lubb-dup sound of his heart and felt the slowing in his pulse. Seeing that he was still bleeding, they had decided he had lost too much blood and was too far-gone to help. He was still unconscious. There were others the doctors felt they could save. That's when the great bear of a man fought through his shock and startled the doctors. In his typical fashion, he became violently profane and told them to do their job. The doctors, now aware of his great fighting spirit, immediately prepared him for operation.

The human body contains five quarts of blood, with two pints to a quart. During Major Beckwith's operation, due to an unclosed bleeder, he went through twenty-three pints of blood. They removed a damaged twenty-one inch section of his 22-feet-long small intestine and his gallbladder. Although Colonel Harold G. Moore, the commander of the Cav's 3rd Brigade, visited his men at the hospital, he was too ashamed and lacked the military courtesy to visit with Charlie, who was in the same hospital. Once Major Beckwith's wounds were stabilized, he was flown to the Philippines, then to Chicago, to the Great Lakes Naval Hospital.

The Bad News

I returned from my one-week leave to Project DELTA's compound in Vietnam. The first question I asked the first member of the team that I saw at the team house was, "Where is everyone?" He related the story of Operation Masher to me. I was stunned. It had been my unit that the TV news in Sacramento had reported. I had sat at home in the living room, watching and listening to the news. At that time, I thought that it was just another war statistic being reported. I had been at home, safe. Now I was frightened, woken to the reoccurring nightmare. I felt my superstitious fears raise their heads. Getting married had sapped my enthusiasm for voluntarily risking my life.

The unit now received a new commander as we continued our training. It now consisted of patrolling missions in the surrounding dry mountains overlooking Nha Trang to our southwest and west.

The enemy was well dug in there. The entrances to their tunnel complexes were skillfully concealed, and rarely found. They remained hidden underground by day. One underground system was discovered above Nha Trang. We kept it under observation for a length of time to make sure it was being used. When we determined that it was, a generator was airlifted in. Smoke was pumped into it to locate other entrances and air holes. Then except for one, all the small, hidden entrances and air holes were permanently sealed and gassed. Then the team sealed the last one for good.

In the mountains, the nightmares left me alone. On our recon patrols there were too many things to worry about. Exhaustion claimed body and mind during the brief respites. But safe back in the compound at Nha Trang, the dream would again cling to me.

The new commander called in the men of Delta to meet and interview them over a period of time. After asking us about ourselves, he explained how he wanted the unit to operate. The team would run trails to see where they would go. This was contrary to staying alive. In my heart, I knew that I was uniquely qualified to do this job, but when he asked me if I was willing to do that, I said, "No." I added that to do this was not using good sense. I also told him that I was not willing to run trails, and that he would get more men killed.

During the day I could feel the reality of the dreams that I had been experiencing. I continued to try to put it out of my mind. But what I tried to force away during the day was being revealed to me in my dreams at night. I knew dreams come for a reason, and I had to accept them for what they were. The vivid and gripping message was clear to me. I felt that my dreams were showing me my fate. At some future time, I would face capture or death. I was now afraid and definitely did not want to die. I felt quitting would be the only way I would be free of it and the possible reality of crossing an invisible line. Dreams don't have to come true. I greatly feared being ostracized by the new and old men on the team as much or more than the reality of the dream's message. For the first time in my life, I was learning what it was like to really appreciate and value life. My idealistic zeal had diminished with the casualties of my friends. I was afraid, but I was more afraid of not doing what I knew I should. So I asked to be relieved from duty with the DELTA Project. I wasn't going to let some officer who didn't know the realities of this war determine my fate. No one said anything about my decision, because I wasn't the only one to do so. Those of us who had made this decision did so on our own.

I reported to the 5th Special Forces Group Sergeant Major. He asked me where I wanted to go and what I wanted to do. Since I had learned that my old unit had arrived in country, I replied that my choice would be the 1st Brigade, 101st Airborne. This Brigade was deployed to Vietnam in July 1965. It fought as a separate brigade, the only brigade of the 101st Airborne Infantry Division in Vietnam, until 1967. I felt they could use my experience. Personally, I felt that I had demeaned and humiliated myself for leaving. I didn't know it at the time, but I was jumping out of the frying pan and into the fire.

The 1st Brigade

The infantry primarily used trails. On 21 March 1966, I was welcomed into the 1st Brigade. It was made up of three units--the 1/327, 2/327 and 2/502 infantry battalions--and had been in Vietnam for eight months. When I had looked at the Brigade personnel manning board, I saw that they had almost a complete change over in personnel. Nearly 1500 men had been KIA, WIA and MIA. Sickness of one kind or another had taken its toll. The brigade was already well blooded in Vietnam. It had paid an extremely high price for getting itself acclimated. In World War II, this division suffered 9,328 men killed or wounded. By the end of the Vietnam War, this division would suffer almost 20,000 wounded or killed. It would be the last Army division to leave Vietnam.

The 1st Brigade had just completed Operation HARRISON. The Personnel Section decided I would skip the eighty-hour bloc of instruction normally given to the new trooper to help him survive a little while. I already had more operational time in country than anyone serving in the Brigade. My experience took me straight to a line unit. In the following two months, my new unit, Company "C" 1/327 Infantry, moved from place to place by C-123 aircraft and helicopter. One of the most notable facts pressed upon me in these early days in the infantry was the fact that our issued .45 cal. pistols, 5.56 cal M-16 rifles, 7.62 cal M-60 machine guns and our 30-06 cal sniper rifles were not standardized. They all fired different caliber ammunition. To top it off, the M-16 rifle was an unreliable weapon. On the other hand, the PAVN weapons system fired a standardized 7.62mm round in their SKS rifle, AK-47 assault rifle and their RPD light machine gun, and all were very reliable weapons. The M-16 could not always be counted upon to fire, and therefore was not a dependable system. It cost too many soldiers their lives.

In April, Operation FILLMORE started in the Lang Biang Mountains outside the fishing port of the seacoast city of Phan Thiet. The city, capital of Binh Thuan Province, with its colonial villas, is located on Highway 1. The surrounding roundish mountains were rocky and heavily forested. It was the most arid region in Vietnam and the heat was intense. We endured long, hot and dry days, conducting an exhaustive search for a large PAVN stronghold. Known to operate in the area were the 482nd and the 840th Main Force Battalions. They were elusive or underground. Our companies operated in the field separately, reacting to the reports of reconnaissance patrols. The days and nights seemed to run together as we searched the rugged terrain.

Like the rest of the mountain areas in Vietnam, the terrain evoked a feeling of immense distance, monotonous and infinite remoteness at all times. The mountains were dry. The intermittent streams we came across had only trickles of water in them, if anything. The standing water was bad. We conserved our water, by taking only a trickle into our mouths from our canteens and holding it there to thoroughly wet and soak our mouth. Then we'd swallow and wish for more. Those who drank the most were soon without water and became our first casualties, prostrated from the heat. Because water was scarce, we ate little. It takes water to digest food, which is needed more to keep the core organs and brain hydrated. Our nights were full of weary and watchful waiting and listening. Many imagined the shadows moving. They had to be told to keep their eyes moving back and forth and not to concentrate too long on any one object or their minds would play tricks on them. Though low on water, we did manage to find a cache of 300 quart bottles of warm Tiger beer. It was wet. There was no threat of real contact with the enemy. As we secured our landing zone site, I found an American jungle boot right in the trail, with the foot still inside. I broke my men down into lifts and sat back to wait my turn. I was on the last lift. Just before the helicopters returned, I heard a bugle blow not far away. We lifted out seemingly without incident. As we got together later, one of my men told me that a bullet struck the lower compartment where he was sitting--between his legs.

Next, in Quang Duc Province came Operation AUSTIN. We searched for the PAVN forces near Nhon Co and along the Cambodian border. This was located in the southern part of the II Corps area. One afternoon I saw a very large bear there. The only incident I remember was when an Indian friend of mine, Sgt. Amont, asked me how to set up an ambush, since he had this assignment. I told him to look at his ambush site as he moved through it, but not to stop; go a little way and set up until dark while keeping his ambush site under observation; as soon as it gets dark, go back and set up. This was just in case he was being trailed. He would be able to see the location where he would set up for the night, and thereby avoid a nasty surprise. I explained to him that his M-18A1 Claymore antipersonnel mines should be in the linear portion of his ambush; to stick them in the ground and tilt them slightly. The 60 degree fan-shaped spray pattern of 600 pellets per mine covered an area 50 yards wide. They had to be aimed about three feet off the ground in the killing zone. I told him to put a large tree between him and the mine, and to be sure that he had 360 degrees of security. When my friend returned, he told me he had set up a linear ambush. He had gone straight to his picked ambush site and set up in the daylight, instead of following the procedure I had outlined. During the course of the night a rain and lightening storm had developed. Once, while the sky was lit up, he saw two men standing behind his position listening and watching. The rest of the night he felt very insecure. He had learned his lesson.

It was during my time at the airfield at Nhon Co that I was informed of my time for R & R, or as the young soldiers called it: "Rest and Recreation." The older soldiers called it "I & I," after our two principal pastimes: intercourse and intoxication. I was worn out. Since I am light skinned, I also had the worst case of jungle rot seen by our medic. I had it on my face, neck, arms and legs. They were runny sores. Wherever the fluid from the sore ran, a new and larger sore developed. The sleeves of my shirt were stained with the discharge from the sores.

We could go anywhere we wanted. My wife told me that she would meet me in Japan. She would be at Camp Zama, in Kanagawa Prefecture, where I was scheduled to check in. She would be waiting with clean underwear, shoes and a suit. I was extremely worried about how I was going to look to my wife, but during the flight to Japan, the jungle rot just seemed to start disappearing.

R & R

My wife had reservations at the Palace Hotel in Tokyo. It was in front of the Imperial Palace. We stayed there two days. I had the luxury of crawling into bed, enjoying the darkness and my wife. After all the years of sleeping on the ground in all weather conditions, I was now warm and cozy. I quickly passed from full consciousness and drifted off to sleep. I slept for ten hours straight each night. The most memorable thing was drinking the coffee. It was real coffee, not like what passes in the United States as coffee. There was real cream and the golden, natural cane sugar from Hawaii. It was very expensive and served in small cups, but soooo good.

We then departed by the bullet train for Kyoto and then on to our family hotel in the city of Nara, the Seikanso Inn. Nara was Japan's old capital, and the present home of the largest statue of Buddha in the world, the Daibutsu of Todaiji Temple. All too quickly my time flew by and it was time to return.

Back in Vietnam

The 1/327 started searching in Phuoc Long Province in the Central Highlands near Bu GhIa Map to the south and east, ten miles from the Laotian border in the II Corps area. We found only a deserted headquarters and hospital complex. I found myself walking over more of South Vietnam's terrain than I had ever imagined possible. Our operation terminated on 18 May, and we were airlifted to a staging area southeast of Pleiku. Our new location was in Phu Bon Province near Cheo Reo in the central part of the II Corps area.

Footnotes:

1. The term CS is a code name for ortho-chlorobenzylidene malonitrile.

2. The "Trinh sat" were men specially schooled in tracking and scouting. They were trained in the Military Intelligence School in North Vietnam's Hoa Binh Province southwest of Hanoi.

**Passing through
Silent and empty forest
Then shadows moved
Time stopped
Azrael looks on, satisfied.**

Author

CHAPTER 11

TOU MORONG

There is an old Asian saying, "If you plan to ride the tiger, then you must go where the tiger goes." Known for good reason as the "Assassins," we were heading for another rendezvous with destiny. In early June 1966, we were loading into the rear of a long-range C-130 Hercules assault transport aircraft. This medium Air Force transport could fly into strips that would make you shudder. I quickly tore open a letter from my beautiful and kind Japanese wife in Sacramento, California, one which I had not had time yet to read. Her letters always had a red rose in the upper left corner. As always it began "Dearest Charles." She had just returned from class at the college she attended, and expressed her joy at receiving a letter of mine after not hearing from me for so long. There was the welcomed petty gossip of her family in Japan and mine in Sacramento. Most important, there was much needed spiritual support, always to be found in her many letters. She promised to continue to write me often. I was overcome with emotion.

Her letters kindled a soft feeling in my heart that lasted throughout the war, because of this eventual promise of a renewed life. She went on to tell me not to worry about the timing, that whenever it was time for my R & R she would be there waiting at the door for me in Japan.

The pilot made a typical gut-wrenching assault landing with the aid of reverse-pitching the props. The aircraft taxied and parked, then an explosive silence rushed in as the aircraft shut down. The plane's ramp went up, like the steady, foreboding sound of our inevitable doom, threatening our existence. We were part of a multi-battalion force of U.S. and Vietnamese troops, being flown into the rugged western highlands to the Special Forces camp at Dac To, some 35 miles north of Kontum, the provincial capital. This airstrip is overlooked by a 4,593-foot mountain, located near the junction of the northern and southern Cambodian borders. We were about to initiate "Operation Hawthorne." The Vietnamese would call it Dan Tang 61. It was here that the sore and weary paratroopers of Company C, 1st Brigade, 327th Airborne Infantry Battalion, 101st Airborne Division, were going to search for the elusive phantom, the 24th North Vietnamese Army Regiment. They were thought to be hiding in the remote areas of these nearby mountains waiting for us to get tired and walk into the wrong place. The 1st Brigade also had the mission of withdrawing the Special Forces camp of Tou Morong back to Dac To.

Since the 1st Brigade arrived in Vietnam on 8 July 1965, it had conducted operations on 294 of its 321 days in Vietnam, killing 1,898 by body count of the enemy in action. The PAVN tactical doctrine was to fight positional warfare whenever its regular or main force units had adequate strength, weapons and sufficiently trained personnel to do so. Regular or main force units would conduct a maneuver attack whenever they were capable of achieving surprise on a vulnerable position. Elements of the North Vietnamese Army had reportedly moved into position for their monsoon offensive in Kontum Province. The well-camouflaged PAVN regiments had reportedly moved into their newly assigned area of operation in November 1965 and had spent seven months digging in preparation for a knockdown, drag-out fight. Unreported was the fact that after early 1966 the communists were sending 100,000 men south each year. Our present mission was to seek out and destroy this unit before the monsoon season started and before the NVA had time to mass their indirect fire weapons on the ridge known as "Rocket Ridge" above Dac To. Whoever controlled the Highlands controlled Vietnam.

SGT Christian G. Girard (Right)

Dac To was situated below an impressive sweeping mountain ridge, above an equally long, wide green valley surrounded by a vast forbidding wilderness of black-green mountains almost 6,000 feet tall. The low clouds of the coming bad weather would limit the time that fixed-wing aircraft and helicopters could operate, or ground them altogether. The few existing roads would wash out in some places and become mud pits in others and limit the use of supporting light and heavy vehicles. It was a beautiful area with numerous large pine trees on the ridges. The terrain raised concerns about the M-16 rifle and its lack of penetration in moderate to heavy cover. The weather was good. The rainy season had not started yet. The strong summer southwest monsoon, from the Indian Ocean that dominates the climate, blows from mid-May to mid-October and drenches the region west of the Annamite Mountains with heavy rain. A month or so of unsettled weather would exist in the western highlands at each end of this time period, but the rainstorms had not set in early.

Digging In

When we first arrived at the airstrip at the Special Forces camp at Dac To II, we dug our defensive positions in deep on the north side of the airstrip from the camp. The Special Forces camp was on a bluff overlooking the Dak Poko River to it's immediate south. On the north side of the airstrip, Communal Route 512, which starts at the town of Kon Hojao about 5,000 meters to our east, ran westward past the airstrip to Dak Mot Kram. Dac To, was dominated by a high 3,085-foot ridge immediately to the north. Our early patrols left from the airstrip on foot and worked up the immediate higher ground to Suim Ngok Tu, overlooking Dac To. A lonely and hard country, its beauty was terrifying, for it was here that the ugliest of realities and our fate would be determined, whether we were to live or die. It was over a 4,000-meter straight-line distance from Dac To to the top of the ridge. With all the ups, the downs and the arounds, it was a long move. At least the intermittent streams had good water in them. We searched day and night and found nothing on the mountain, then returned to the airfield.

Our battalion commander, Colonel David H. Hackworth, inspired great confidence in all the infantrymen who served under him. This charismatic commander was one of the few officers I saw in the war who r[1]eally led the way. Under his leadership, the mountains were no longer a place that offered sustenance and a peaceful place to rest to the North Vietnamese. Colonel Hackworth, being patient and persistent, used a strategy of small-unit patrolling to saturate the mountains in a pattern looking for the NVA, who were spread out and concentrated in small isolated pockets.

The night before our operation was to begin, I noticed far across the darkened sky in the distance the brief brightening under cumulus clouds, underlit with bright-tinted flashes, and thought a storm had come early. Then I felt the slight tremble of the earth, indicating a B-52 strike. *Carpet-bombing.*[1] I was watching the flickering, eerie half-light reflection in the clouds of the bomb strike. The NVA would not see or hear the aircraft from the ground. Over three hundred bombs were falling, silently; five seconds before the bombs were to impact, the scream of the falling bombs would be heard, but it would be too late. It would be the last thing the PAVN would hear. The three bombers would disgorge their bombs in 30 seconds. In a B-52 bomb strike, the landscape erupted in an area one-mile long and a half-mile wide, leaving permanent craters thirty feet deep. Bunkers located one-half kilometer away would collapse on the NVA.

It was a thick-misted morning. We flew northwest of the mountain top Special Forces outpost of Tou Morong (Tu Mo Rong), some twenty-five kilometers, for our initial insertion by helicopter. The name of the map we were operating on was KON HO'NONG, map Sheet 6538 I, named for a non-existent village in the Ta Kan Valley. The map covered a virtual wilderness area of no roads, except one far to the south. I watched the map closely as we flew over high, steep, rugged, infinite mountains. There were eight of us. I realized that I was living with darkening prospects. The immense valley of fallow ground lay unfurled in startling clearness below, all the way toward the horizon. Soon the silent loneliness of this great wilderness would be broken. I had a feeling of doom, a fear that I would never get back home. We flew along cool, serene mountain ridges of shady mountain pines. It seemed wild and grand from up there. I saw part of a silvery ribbon of a stream below, a magnificent panorama of endless forests of mountain range upon mountain range, appearing purple in the distance. The nearest ridge was covered with pine trees. I looked at the great space before me and shivered--not from cold, but from fear.

In one valley we found signs of the ancient presence of man, forgotten by time--long-unused bronze pots or drums that were very large, laying right out in the open. Somehow, they seemed more significant than our impending battle. Along the side of a ridge we found signs of a more recent presence. Bamboo animal traps were placed periodically in an opening along a staked fence, and in the streams there were 4-feet-long conical fish traps made from rattan palm strips. The fish traps placed along the edges of streams had very limber twigs that allowed a fish to enter but prevented its leaving. All had been woven with great skill.

    In a thick brushy area among the trees, I managed to brush a vine or limb on the ground that triggered a huge red ant ball in a tree to fall directly on me. I had to hurry a few feet ahead and tear off my equipment to get my jacket off and shook out. I had help in brushing them off myself, but they bit, emitting a strong formic acid that everyone could smell. They stung like hell. Agricultural evidence of the presence of man was found in the form of a very large pineapple grove that covered one side of a semi-open ridge. The pineapple was not yet quite ripe enough to harvest, but it was still sweet and we were starved for it. We were always starved for fruit. In the bottomland in the wet areas of a creek were the large-leafed taro plant, the tall cassava plants, and sweet potato plants. This hidden agricultural area had been under cultivation for some time. After my earlier years in this country, I had learned to recognize the plants that were cultivated for food. The elephant ear shape always gave away the taro plant. Its underground tuber was rich in starch and gave those who ate it a lot of carbohydrates. The leaf helped account for the white teeth of those who ate it. The tall, 5-feet high, slender-stalked cassava plant was grown for its large, fleshy, tapering roots filled with milky juice. All these cultivated plants meant that troops were close by.

    Generally, with experience and teamwork, we could usually speculate where the NVA could be found, based on surrounding cover and geographical terrain. However, we were spent and discouraged, suffering from too little to eat while constantly staying on the move with great caution and finding nothing. We slept when we could on the cold, dry ground. We were wet constantly from the dripping dew or perspiration. All we had found was some of the most spectacular scenery in these Central Highlands. I had also seen one of the great spectacles of nature, which we carefully avoided: a colony of large red ants on the march. Always curious, I would have liked to see how far their column stretched and how far they went in a day. We later moved our search further northeast into the wilderness of mountains around the Special Forces camp. While insects generally agitated and attacked us mercilessly in the lowlands, the mosquitoes were almost absent from the dry forest of the highlands this time of year. However, I was periodically sick, experiencing real discomfort. I needed rest and was greatly fatigued.

Forest Creature

One night, the silence of the forest broken by the rustle of the wind, sighing through the trees, I gradually became nervous, then suddenly fully alert. I knew I had felt a sound rather than hearing it. Perhaps it was only the breeze rustling the branches. My pulse quickened, as I tried to put an image and a name on whatever was there. I could see nothing, but my sensitive early warning system was working. *I must be hallucinating*, I thought. I could smell something. Then I heard it clearly, a sound just ahead. The soft pad of broad feet! The sound was followed by softer exhalations. Something walked within the night--something huge. Slowly a liquid shadow congealed at the limit of my vision in the black of night. The stillness was broken by a slight snuffling sound, closer and closer. The wind had picked up. My heart skipped two beats. There was a slight movement at the edge of my field of sight. I tried to focus. The shadow's form sharpened, an enormous black silhouette against a lighter background in the dim light. I saw and smelled a huge, round, lumbering animal, dark in color--the shadow of the great Asian bear. The beast was only scant yards away. It looked immense. I heard the effortless suck of its breathing, the snorting, snuffing, grunting grumble at the back of the large creature's throat. I could make out the sound of heavy, furry, soft-padded paws making contact with the dry hard ground, the low snorting sound, sniffs and a cross growl as he rooted around. I wondered if the smell of our bodies had attracted the bear. Its large snout was close to the ground, picking up our scent, possibly thinking we were just more dead bodies lying around. The creature drew closer, snuffing and pawing. It stopped. Its huge head started swiveling eerily back and forth. I could now smell it and just make out the white V on its neck and chest. Then someone made a very slight sound. It suddenly stopped grunting in ravenous anticipation, grumbled at the back of its throat and quickly lumbered from the area. As quickly as it had risen, silently like a spirit, it had disappeared. The next morning I asked those closest to my position if they had heard or seen any movement during the night. It turned out that I was the only one. I kept my silence about the bear.

Meanwhile, on 3 June, "B" battery, 2nd Battalion, 320th Field Artillery had been inserted into an abandoned, burned out Montagnard village designated LZ Lima Zulu on the map, to support the infantry.[2] The 320th artillery position was out of range of any other American and Vietnamese artillery positions, therefore no preplotted concentrations were registered. The location and lack of a planned fire support system literally invited an attack. The men quickly erected their fighting walls where the gun crews could defend their position, should the PAVN penetrate their position. After seeing them into position, their commander, LTC Braun, kissed them good-bye, boarded a helicopter and flew to Brigade headquarters near Dac To. He was letting them act as a target of opportunity for the PAVN, leaving them in extreme danger. Unknown to the 320th FA, a special reconnaissance unit was observing them. During the daylight, the PAVN were making detailed sketches of the position, at night they made verification of sentry positions and recorded close-in measurements for their future approach during their planned night attack.

Sick

During our fruitless search through the mountains, my flu-like symptoms returned. I was experiencing severe headaches, fever, intense chills, sweating and then my body would ache. I vomited and defecated. I alternately perspired and shivered. I periodically had a high fever, the shaking chills, severe headache, and could barely keep anything in my stomach. I fought to keep my muscles relaxed. I passed mucus and blood. It didn't seem to matter which end it came out. I had to split the seat of my jungle pants because the attacks came fast. Sometimes it came out of both ends at the same time. I couldn't get enough water to drink. Each cycle of these symptoms would come and go, and now they were attacking me every other day. I was just praying that we would not be in heavy enemy contact when I came down again because it was affecting my ability to think. My mental state was now very weak. Each day now required a supreme effort; there was little time for the blessed unconsciousness of sleep. The fundamental act of walking became a mesmerizing narcotic that numbed my mind.

Our strong bonds for each other were often demonstrated in sharing what little food we had with each other. Yet I knew if I couldn't eat and keep something down, I was on my way to the grave. I had heaved up again and again what little my stomach held, until there was nothing left but the spastic, wrenching seizures of dry heaving. My platoon would donate their own needed solid items of tinned food, such as cheese, peanut butter and crackers, to me. It kept me going, though we were all now exhausted. I was almost accidentally shot twice by my own men, because of the noise I made in my small watery elimination's during the dark.

I remember once during a stream crossing, I waved them on and stopped in agony to clean myself. I squatted in the lukewarm water of the stream to wash the bloody stool dripping from my bottom and fell asleep in that position. Luckily I awoke and found myself all alone in that position in the middle of the stream. My heart began to race. It was like a terrible dream to wake up and see myself all alone and understand what I had been doing. I looked at the position of the sun. It looked the same. I checked my watch and with some relief realized that only about 10 minutes had passed. The platoon worked slowly, and I knew they wouldn't get too far. I worried about getting shot by the rear security. Their legs had cut deep depressions through the grass, which made my way easier. I stopped twice and turned around and squatted, waiting. I listened and watched for the sounds and a glimpse of anyone dogging our back trail. Only once was I startled. I though someone was approaching me from my flank. I prepared myself. Then came the mating call of the peacock, *"may-awe, may-awe,"* with its rapidly fluctuating amplitude. I followed their trail slowly and caught back up. No one knew what had happened, and I was too sick to tell. The rear security had not been alert to anyone behind him. I would speak to him later about what could happen if he wasn't closely watching the rear of the formation.

On 6 June, dawn broke red over the North Central Highlands. The 2nd platoon of Company "C" 1-327 Infantry led the way, heading southeast, until we came out of the mountain onto a dirt road in the low ground. We then turned southwest and moved up the road of a long finger ridge, higher and higher, getting a good view of the area we had been searching so hard, without success. Finally, at the top, we reached a bend in the road and stopped. A road spur to our left led south immediately into the entrance of the small, isolated Special Forces camp of Tou Morong. Although the camp was named Tou Morong, it was just one more unmarked place on the map. The Special Forces personnel and their CIDG were unable to pull out of this campsite due to the presence of the NVA. The CIDG also had their women in this camp.

The North Vietnamese had been attacking Tou Morong since May, but with little effect, because there was only one way into the camp, which was by the road entrance. The other three sides of the camp were steep drop-offs. The day before, elements of a South Vietnamese unit, elements of the 42nd ARVN Infantry Regiment, had attempted to come up this road and had been ambushed and had taken some 23 casualties before withdrawing.

This day I felt tired but a lot stronger. It was here at Camp Tou Morong that our battalion commander, Col. Hackworth, received the information as to where the enemy was located. The information came from an old mountaineer tribesman. Col. Hackworth, on point with my platoon, was now pointing us to move over the top and use the road for speed. We had to move fast, some 14,500 meters through the mountains toward the Dak Ta Kan River Valley and Landing

Zone Lima Zulu. Moving in the open, on a road through the mountains filled with "Little Brown Motherfuckers" waiting to kill you is not easy to think about or do when you are actually doing it. Evidently the PAVN were all bunkered up on the mountain ridges, because we were not ambushed once.

We passed by the overlooking dangerous high ridge of the 4,852-foot high Ngok Hroe Mountain on our left flank to our immediate south without any incident. On the afternoon of 7 June, we arrived on foot in the Ta Kan Valley 320th FA position at grid coordinates ZB 089347, overlooked by the finger ridges of Hill 872.

One of my men, P.F.C. Wordlow, had been severely stung about the head by the large black bees that inhabited this country and could not see out of one eye. I told him to wait until we linked up with the artillery unit and he could receive medical attention and evacuation if needed. When we arrived, we held up short of their position while our unit commanders conferred. I told my severely stung Wordlow to go to the artillery aid station. In a very short time he returned to me, looked at me for a minute, and then said, "Sgt. McDonald, I'm staying with you. There isn't anything over there except dead people, body fragments and shell casings." These bodies were seen all over the perimeter. Unknown to us, earlier that morning of 7 June around 0230 hours, a North Vietnamese battalion-sized unit of the 24th NVA Regiment had conducted a surprise night attack just after midnight and overran our only supporting artillery unit. The artillery unit was "B" battery, 2nd Battalion, 320th Field Artillery (FA) commanded by Captain Don Whalen.

We asked the Redlegs what had happened and were informed that a few days earlier, on 5 June, their unit had been lifted into the valley at a site called LZ Lima Zulu. The CH-47 Chinook helicopters landing zone (LZ) positioned them on the north side of the road just above where Dak Djram stream ran into the Dak Ta Kan stream.[3] Everything had been fine until early this morning, when one of the artillerymen had heard a muffled noise at his gun position and looked over the waist-high sandbag parapet into the faces of several NVA sappers preparing their charges for his position. The sappers had passed through the infantrymen guarding the artillery position without being detected. The battle then started from the inside and developed all around the artillery position at the same time with NVA mortar fire. As the firing started inside the perimeter, the NVA infantrymen fronting 502nd infantrymen could be heard blowing bugles and whistles to coordinate their assault. The PAVN attacked through their own mortar fire and quickly passed through the thinly defended outer 502nd defensive perimeter.

Meanwhile, during the early morning at 0200 hours at Dac To, "B" battery, 1st Battalion, 30th Field Artillery (FA), hearing on the radio the 320th FA call for help, immediately loaded their trucks in anticipation of orders to relocate their six gun positions forward. The strong, young men labored mightily, loading ammunition. Each 155mm round weighs 96 pounds. The towed 155mm battery, commanded by Captain Joseph Toth, was prepared when the orders to move their guns came.

The 320th had lost two of their gun positions to the PAVN. Both had been retaken after a prolonged small arms fight. Some 100 NVA were killed in this fight. The American Infantry unit and artillerymen suffered greatly in the two hour battle. The Devil had already knocked at our door.

Carefully camouflaged, these commandos had moved down from the north to link up with their reconnaissance personnel. They had watched it all. During the daylight hours, they followed parallel to the Dak Sia stream, up the hill and over the top overlooking the American position, the artillery site. As the sky darkened in imperceptible stages, the PAVN carefully observed their objective, the 320th FA. For days, the PAVN had been taking note of where and how the sentry system was placed. Dark and silent the men stripped themselves of unnecessary equipment, the order came, and the assault unit moved forward.

Alert and ever cautious, they felt a sense of relief, as they started their methodical advance. It was right after dark, at 7:15 p.m. It would be a long, slow journey, to maintain absolute silence. At the perimeter, they waited for the moon to come up to have enough light to infiltrate through the defensive perimeter. After careful examination of the ground immediately within reach, the NVA would creep a foot forward before freezing to listen again and repeat the slow process over and over again, until they were at the perimeter. They initiated their attack from inside the American perimeter and the higher finger ridges of Hill 872 immediately to the 320th FA front. The PAVN knew that their artillery could not be effectively used. The NVA had every intention of annihilating the men manning the artillery position and securing the five 105mm howitzers' gun-positions.

Baptism in Blood

The PAVN had completely surrounded the artillery position. Their main approach had been from behind the hill. The early warning tripflares and listening posts were easily avoided, making the use of command-detonated claymore mines useless. They had laid above and just outside the artillery position quietly watching and listening. The PAVN knew that the Americans would feel better and see better once the moon came up around ten. By 2 o'clock in the morning, the poor noise discipline and finally the lack of movement from dozing guards told the sappers everything they needed to know. Six hours had passed. The Americans were unaware that death was coming quickly and without warning. With enough knowledge of the gun position, the PAVN now set about achieving surprise by moving into the defended position with great stealth. The main suicidal attack was initiated on the 320th FA in the area of their number six gun position located at the base of the hill. The night suddenly erupted with enemy fire, explosions and the scrambling of feet. The sappers, once detected, utilized small charges as a prearranged signal to receive supporting mortar fire. The PAVN now delivered highly effective fire on the men in the Howitzer positions. This forced the shocked young infantrymen to take cover. The well-coordinated night attack achieved tactical surprise, and the NVA moved rapidly in among the battery, destroying artillery and infantrymen with grenades and automatic weapons fire at close range. When their fire support element fired into the American positions, the sappers continued their attack through their own mortar fire. The battle intensified and the disciplined NVA quickly gained fire superiority, their momentum and weight in numbers carrying a second wave into the defensive line and reaching the gun positions. The night came alive with the rattle of machine guns, rifles, mortars and exploding grenades, as well as shrill voices on both sides of the wounded and dying. The staccato roar of battle was terrifying. The air was thick with smoke, flames, dust, screams and flying lead. Men briefly silhouetted in the dark from the explosions were quickly fired upon. The Americans were dying hard.

The cannon-cockers were momentarily stunned. The bright-white light of exploding grenades and rattle of blazing automatic weapons at close quarters in the dark was blinding. Smoke from the ChiCom grenades was drifting about everywhere. The firing, heard everywhere, continued at a terrifyingly hectic pace. However, the fear quickly passed. The brave men and their commander did not collapse under the stress. The PAVN troops were now inside the perimeter, everywhere in the dark. The ultimate terror filled everyone. The Americans had to be careful about individual movements and stay low to the ground. The faintest movement brought fire directed at you. Any upright and skylined movement brought fire. Sweeping, suspicious eyes questioned every motionless man in the shadows: PAVN or friend? On both sides, many were afraid to make a movement that would betray them. A flareship arrived overhead and started orbiting the area, dropping flares. Faced with a superior enemy force, the artillerymen counter-attacked in short rushes.

Initially, the Americans realized that reinforcements or supporting fire from another battery were out of the question. Captain Don Whalen, pleading for support over the radio, was told he would have to fight on alone for the time being. His anger, born of frustration, was quickly overcome as he now applied himself to the defense of his artillery position. He sent a radio message to Brigade Headquarters monitored by the 30th FA. The 30th, anticipating their next order, starting preparing to move. This meant loading a great amount of ammunition and equipment. No other American or Allied unit was within range. They had to make a dangerous night move without security to Brigade Headquarters, to provide fire support for the 320th FA at LZ Lima Zulu. With several miles to go in the dark, Captain Toth ordered the vehicle lights turned on, and the unit hauled butt up the road as fast as they could.

The NVA pressed the attack on the 320th FA and after a hotly contested fight, captured the number six gun.[4] The artillerymen, fighting and dying, quickly recovering from their shock, retook the gun. They fought back valiantly to keep the NVA from capturing the number three gun. All sense of time was lost in the struggle. A series of hand grenade duels and counterattacks for the number three gun, surged back and forth. The tide of the battle began to turn when the area around LZ Lima Zulu erupted from the fiercely crashing 155 mm shells, even wounding some of the defenders led by Billy Colwell. The incoming artillery was directed at the facing rugged slope and finger ridges overlooking LZ Lima Zulu. The NVA, after lobbing their stickhandled, potato-masher grenades, would rush while firing their assault rifles and take the number 3 and number 6 guns.

Then the Americans buried their fear. In many, the anger turned to rage. Small groups of artillerymen lobbed their M-26 grenades and, firing their M-16s, rushed the Howitzer positions. They would take them back. Both sides, amid the screams of pain, locked into a fight to the death, executed stunning displays of personal courage. The 105mm howitzers exchanged hands twice.

Redlegs

Meanwhile, both 155mm guns of B/1/30 FA arrived safely in the dark at their new position, Brigade headquarters. The gun trails (legs) were quickly unhooked from the trucks and unlocked. Then they were manhandled into position after the trails were spread. These heavy guns had a range of 14,600 meters. The guns were positioned 25 yards apart in "open positions," and laid parallel. The crew then quickly dug in the spades on the trails to stabilize the weapons for firing. Now all the guns ammunition had to be unloaded and fused, ready for action. The Fire Direction personnel from the 30th joined the Brigade FDC personnel in their tent. The Fire Direction

Officer, 1Lt. Bill McMakin, and SP-4 Fox utilizing the slipstick would be plotting all the rounds to be fired while the rest of the battery was still somewhere back on the road. The gun crews quickly started setting up and laying the hefty cannons on their proper azimuth with their optical instruments. They knew that they could decide the battle. The gun crews quickly emplaced a line of aiming posts in the ground: their artificial aiming points. Ammunition was stood at hand and made ready to fire. Illumination and Point Detonating (PD) rounds were prepared. All fires were to be directed from the 320th as soon as the 30th FA battery was ready. Knowing that the many lives of B/2/320 FA were at stake, the well-trained crews worked quickly in the dark. The 30th FA was ready for action in minutes. The Fire Direction Officer communicated by field telephone to the gun crews. A sudden stab of flames momentarily lit the sky. The trundling passage of the large rounds, streaking high overhead, reverberated throughout the valley. The deafening sound of the guns would remain constant now, an assault on the senses.

    The 320th FA directed the 30th FA fires at the two ridges immediately fronting the battery position, on top of the finger ridges and on their reverse slopes. As the 155mm rounds slammed and flowered into the ground, the enemy fire gradually slackened. Surrounded by ear-splitting explosions and smoke, the ground shaking beneath them, some North Vietnamese soldiers could be seen fearfully crouching and attempting to escape into the exploding darkness, carrying off their dead and wounded. The artillerymen and supporting infantry scrambled to retake both guns. The 320th now lowered their guns to fire the antipersonnel (APERS) XM546 BEEHIVE rounds point blank into the still attacking PAVN. Each Beehive round coughed death into a fan-like shower of 8,000 one-inch long steel darts called flechettes, shredding flesh at close range and leaving hundreds of tiny holes in the bodies of any enemy at any distance directly in front of the perimeter. After a bitter battle, there were thirteen dead NVA remaining inside the number six-gun position. Capt. Don Whalen, effectively controlling the supporting fire, allowed the "Redlegs" to consolidate their position.

The 30th FA fired four rounds a minute, placing a ring of steel around the isolated artillery position at LZ Lima Zulu, rendering screaming men to torn flesh and splintered bone. Each 155mm round had a bursting radius of 50 meters. The order was given to expend all the ammunition. All officers, radio operators, mechanics and cooks began carrying all the ammunition available into the firing positions to be fired. The gunners slaved at the guns. Muzzle flames lit the night. The thunder of the guns echoed hollow and malignantly over the valley. The smoke hung like a sea fog above them as it slowly settled. On this dark night, there was a constant glow surrounding the battery. Between each of the rounds, the breech blocks were yanked open, the old primers removed and the bores swabbed with water so the next powder bag will not cook off. More smoke continued to be pumped relentlessly from the huge guns. Then the guns were loaded with another projectile. The battery of six guns fired a maximum rate of fire, firing four rounds a minute for three minutes, flames and smoke contracted writhing shapes all around. The noise seemed to go on forever. A thick cloud of cordite hung low to the ground in the night air, and the men choked on the smoke, gas and dust as they labored.

The powder-stained gun crews of B/1/30 FA strained and sweated in the cool of the night. They continued their overwhelming, accurately aimed and controlled fire for four hours, straining with dedication at their hard labor. The stabbing flames lasted until the dawn's early light, at which time the 30th FA received word over the radio in the Fire Direction Control (FDC) center that the PAVN had broken contact with the American artillery unit. They had saved some of the men of the 320th. At first light, 5:30 a.m., amid sporadic firing, the PAVN, now fearing the worst and knowing that they would be hunted, started disappearing back into the mountains. The dust drifted slowly away. Men checked their dead and wounded friends and their ammunition. The wounded, now horribly thirsty, were tended to by their grieving comrades.

After the 30th FA fire mission ended in the half-light of dawn at 6:30 a.m., the exhausted and dirty artillerymen slept at their guns amidst the heavy cloud and smell of cordite. The litter of fuse cans and powder canisters were strewn about everywhere, a mute testimony to their intense and gallant effort. They had accomplished their fire mission without burning up their tubes or developing hydraulic problems. The big guns had won the night. Hours later, B/1/30 was ordered to join their fellow artillerymen at LZ Lima Zulu. They remained at LZ Lima Zulu for the rest of the campaign.

Between midnight and dawn, the battered, reinforced PAVN battalion and their well-trained sapper units had lost some 86 men whom they had not been able to drag away.[5] Now, some of the fresh NVA troops would set up ambush positions and those battered in the attack would go to ground, sit back in their underground bunker positions and wait, true to their doctrine. After hearing the artilleryman's story, I kept my thoughts to myself, believing that the Red Legs had been hit and overrun by a sapper battalion.

Our commanders in Vietnam had a habit of placing lone, small units out where they became targets of opportunity to draw the PAVN forces out, specifically artillery units. To draw out the tiger, they needed a Judas goat. B/2/320th FA was the Judas goat. While the communists were doing their best to annihilate the cannoneers and the small attached infantry unit and seize their 105mm guns, the waiting American commanders would then converge on the sound of the guns, often too late. Our brave artillerymen in Vietnam very often fought just as much as infantrymen, and all too often, very intensely.

"Charlie Company" was given the word to move north. At this point, my body was again acting like it was healthy. We now knew that there were tigers in this valley. At the artillery position, the battalion separated, each company going its own way. The battalion commander preferred to operate in small units to locate the enemy and then, when found, consolidate on them. We followed the blood trails and drag marks on the high-speed trail up the Dak Ta Kan Valley, leading away from the artillery battery. This was the direction in which the NVA had gone. Giving some quick orders as to the order of march, I noted the stoic look on the haggard faces of the platoon. We knew we faced a violent death at any time and had to concentrate on preventing it. There were many blood trails along the way. Their blood trails were in a relative straight line, and their splatter marks pointed out their direction of travel. We followed in the same general direction. My 2nd platoon was to lead the way. As we passed the artillery position, the smell of the dead hung so heavily, I could taste it. I realized that we now had to kill without hesitation, without conscious thought in order to survive.

The trail up the flat valley was mostly covered with brush and at times spotted with large timber. At some points there were large unobstructed open spaces and closed-in areas of brush, all of which had us paying close attention to our surroundings. The sun was out in full force in a beautiful blue sky, and it was hot and dry. In the distance outside our immediate area, in every direction we could see the light green color of large groves of bamboo standing out against the darker green of mature hardwoods. My few men had gone quiet. Each man, myself included, was dealing with this new situation inside. I had to pay close attention to all my senses. To ignore them now would be to die. I felt attuned to my environment, frightened, but trusted my judgment and instinct about the reality all about me. If there was a need to talk during movement, it was done in a whisper. Cautiously, but aggressively, we began to dog the North Vietnamese force. I noticed the wide, shallow and smooth print of the NVA sandals in the trail. The prints maintained their heel width through the instep, spreading at the ball of the foot until rounding toward the toe. The heel and toe areas were hardly noticeable in the dry dirt of the trail, because of the way they were cut.

We had only progressed a little over a mile, when I got a powerfully felt uneasy feeling, then a sense of alarm. After spending so much time patrolling incountry, I had a lot of confidence, and often felt a sense of threat before seeing anything. There was a distinct absence of normal sounds. I stopped, motioned the man behind me forward, and told him, "Something's here, keep a sharp watch." Our first encounter with the NVA came. I had barely noticed a flash of white, deep in the brush about 50 yards away. Suddenly my muscles contracted nervously. My eyes grew big as saucers. Warning enough, I put my arm up to motion for a halt. Everyone went down, facing both directions. *Possibly a bird flittering from place to place!* Something in the back of my mind said "look closer." I turned with my weapon at the ready on a patch of scrub brush. A twig broke softly. I froze, muscles tensing, and then I moved slowly forward. My first squad was up and beginning to slowly spread out, moving in the direction my rifle was pointed. I locked my eyes into the concealed direction where I had heard the sound. Three of us saw the NVA soldier at the same time and fired.

We searched the area. He had been alone. The body was stripped of its weapon, ammo, and grenades. I had seen a white field dressing on his head as he watched from deep in the brush. On his person, aside from his weapon, he had all his possibles in his pack--cooked rice with meat and peppers--indicating a unit on the move. We dragged him out to the trail and left him there for his comrades to pick up and carry away in the night. The NVA scouts were to constantly lurk on our edges throughout this campaign.

Much later, our commander, Captain Dill, stopped the company in the low ground for the night in an open basin, a valley-like depression covered with high grass near the edge of the surrounding forest where there was a little grassy area near a stream at the bottom of a higher ridge. This low ground had high ridges three-quarters of the way around us and was sure to be bug-ridden and under NVA observation. The tallest peaks in the mountain ridges on our move up the valley would reach from 5,430 feet to 7,802 feet. I remember just shaking my head and wondering how anyone in combat could choose the low ground to set up a night defensive position. Watching the leaves rustle in the twilight, I sniffed the air. I could not smell the acrid tint of wood smoke in the light breeze that touched my face. The NVA uniforms could often be smelled because the smoke from fires and incense was so strongly embedded in their clothes. Wind could often be the nemesis of the hunted. In spite of the lack of evidence lingering in the air, I knew that they were there. We all knew that they were there.

The commander wanted several ambush positions put out for security. The platoon leader selected me to take an ambush team out from our platoon. Thank God, I wouldn't have to spend the night in this area. I told him that I would go back and ambush the dead body on the trail. Just in case I was being followed, after arriving back in the area opposite the dead body, I kept slowly moving while selecting my ambush site. I moved further away to a point that I could keep the body and surrounding area under observation and waited for darkness. After it was good and dark, I quietly moved my men back into the previously selected ambush site and set up. A bright moon had risen and light shined through the rustling and creaking branches moving gently in the wind. An opalescence flooded the open area to our front. Inside our cover and concealment, invisible in the mottled moon shadows, we watched in the barred and broken moonlight. At times, we could see the moon-silvered reflection in each others eyes. We listened to the stillness of the night, through the vibrating chorus of night creatures. We waited all night without hearing any unusual sounds, except for the wavering of the treetops in the wind and the peeping of the tree frogs from the wet area along the river to our back.

Our only incident came late in the night. I had been forced to take an inexperienced staff sergeant with me on the night ambush, which I strongly protested. Captain Dill just as strongly stated that I had to do it. During the night the staff sergeant fell into sleep and started moaning, "Mama, Mama," loud enough to be heard by anyone within hearing. I had to have him quickly awakened. He was told to remain awake, that our lives depended upon it. He argued, and I sensed immediately that to push the issue would only force a confrontation, and that might get us all killed. Mistakenly, I trusted him to stay awake. As soon as three-quarters of an hour went by, there again came this loud moaning sound of "Mama, Mama." This time I had one of my most trusted men remain with him, with orders to keep him awake. When the eastern sky had begun to gray, I made sure each man was ready and waiting. This part of the day always smelled the very best, the fresh, fertile smell of the earth.

Early in the morning, the air was heavy and wet with a chill. I returned the squad to the company area. It was now the

8th of June. The 2nd platoon was ordered by Captain Dill to patrol a high ridge. I took the time to clean my rifle thoroughly before leaving, otherwise I could count on the M-16A1 jamming. I checked the pins of my grenades carried in my canteen pouch. The content of these M-26 grenades were filled with Composition B, a high explosive whose detonation velocity was terrible at close quarters. An accident with one of these would shred you to pieces. Most of us were mentally prepared to expect the worst. If we were going to be ambushed, it would be at a long range. I prayed it wouldn't be while we were still in the low ground. I knew that the North Vietnamese were more likely to have us under observation because of our being near this stream. And occupying the low ground made it easy for them.

    We moved off from the rest of the company toward the stream and a fording place, without our staff sergeant in tow. Through the foliage, I could see the glint and sparkle of the stream. We chose a snaking bend of the stream to cross. It offered the most concealment. I squinted from the cover at the promontory overlooking the stream with my heart beating loudly, praying that no one was there. The uphill side across the stream was covered in dark shadows. This section of stream for several miles had a slow taper.

    I studied the lay of the surface water upstream, straight across and below from my covered position. The current flow changed in a subtle manner due to bottom conditions. Our inside bend would offer us the most cover from observation. The bend had a sand bar extending out into the stream. There were riffles, current breaks and boils in the water, indicating a rocky bottom. The further out from the shore, the larger the rocks became, with eddies of dead water below them. It was better to cross straight across than above or below from where I watched. The slick flow of water in the middle of the stream indicated it was deeper there. I pinpointed the deeper channel on the far bank where the water ran faster. Below, the current grew swifter and formed a backwater area with a soft bottom that we didn't want to get into. Straight across from me was a wide area of ripples where the stream was rocky and shallow, and the best solid footing. I sent a security team across first.

They got into the shallows of the stream and plunged into the current and were able to cross quickly without any trouble. They left the water and worked their way up. Two security teams would cover the crossing, one on the near side and one on the far side. Kneeling in a concealed position, I turned toward the few faces I could see behind me and extended my arm, palm outward, signaling "Ready?" then motioned with my hand to my head to "Follow me."

Gray mist steamed upward as the air began to warm. We crossed the stream. The shaded water was cool with a dark, full current flowing. I was amazed at the size of the foot-long, dark but colorful poisonous centipedes found clinging to the side of the large rocks in the shade. Their many orange-red legs along their body gave them a sinister appearance. Their bite was reportedly painful. I scanned the entire top of the ridge that was within my view. I felt the thermals on my face flowing downward, dissipating the wispy fog. The sun cleared the tops of the hills, bathing the dark ridge to our front in a glorious, vivid early morning light.

The only sound was the constant murmur of the stream. Water is an important component in hunting the NVA. Every base area requires basic needs, and water is important as a food source, and for bathing, cooking, and drinking. It also serves as a hidden trail for an approach into an area or retreat from an area. If there were a camp or defensive area above, it would be upstream of this crossing site, so that its use would not make for bad water at the campsite. The sun would soon reverse this flow of air. As we were midstream, I suddenly heard a familiar whirring song. The very loud shrilling sound of the tropical sap-sucking cicadas started as the sun was starting to filter through the leaves of the tallest trees. What concerned me was the fact that the noise started over a hundred yards away from us. I stopped and turned my head and eyes in every direction. The cicada is the noisiest insect in the world. It makes a frightening noise, sorting out the sounds into the threatening or non-threatening variety. I was hoping it wasn't a disturbance squawk to alert the North Vietnamese. Generally, when one of these insects was disturbed and started up his shrilling, the others responded. And they did. The sound came as a low drone, accelerating to a roar that was nearly deafening, staying steady for a prolonged period and then falling to a whisper and then into silence. This is one of the few insects capable of hearing, and it produces the loudest sound of any insect. I was wondering who had disturbed them. Maybe it was only the wind and temperature change that set them off. I knew that most of our serving soldiers did not know what to listen for, or how to interpret the sounds of the forest. It was important to identify the source of a sound or movement in order to be able to respond to danger. Most were hearing these sounds for the first time, if they were even registering in their minds.

We left the stream, again merging with the shaded darkness, and started climbing up the opposite bank, moving as cautiously and quietly as nature would allow and striking out into the forest. Our gradual, crouched ascent up the ridge through the brushy evergreen laurel undergrowth was slow. The creeper vines and scrub were changing to a thick and deepening full-foliated dark forest as we neared the top. I was hoping the NVA were not set up above us. I stopped everyone moving as soon as my eyes cleared the top and visually searched the surrounding area. Then, upon silent command, our shadowy profiles slowly disappeared into the heavy timber above the stream's banks. The wind was down and the sky had blown clear blue. Our pants and boots, sopping wet, were soon dry. Now, if we were ambushed, we were at least in the trees where it would be close up, and we would be able to fight back from cover. While we were stopped, paying attention in the directions of the variations of terrain around us, I cupped both hands behind my ears to listen--swiveling my head slowly, letting my eyes rove for any movement. I detected only the natural sights and sounds. We called the crossing security teams back in. Although it was not treated as such by most American commanders in Southeast Asia, jungle warfare, more so than any other type of warfare, was a war of wits.

The Cook Shack

At the top of the ridge, the first thing we found was an elaborate trench system with individual fighting positions and a path. Luckily for us, it had not been occupied. The NVA on the move always had prepared positions to move to. A solid leaf shelter served as a cook shack. The thick walls of packed leaves would hold the smoke of the small fireplace inside. The leaf walls allowed the smoke to dissipate slowly without revealing any outward physical sign of its presence. No telltale rising smoke. Any small amount of escaping smoke would hang low to the ground and, in the strong morning updrafts and evening downdrafts, leave a narrow scent trail to be found. Mountain wind eddies and the great number of large trees would further alter the scent trail and dissipate the small amount of smoke, rendering it less easily observed. Any amount of rising smoke would further diffuse through the ample foliage of the forest canopy overhead. *There would be no smoky haze*. The NVA had only to add more leaves as they became matted down with time. Leaves insulate effectively when dry. The walls smelled of smoke. This type of quickly built shelter could be used for weeks, until the rainy season. The hut had the closest access to the source of water below. I pulled some of the leaves from the frame and tested their decomposition by rolling them in my hand. Lifting them to my nose, the acrid scent of smoke grew stronger. They were old, crispy-dry, and came apart easily. The hut passed its first test.

Entering the hut, I noticed the soot-blackened leaves of the interior walls, and wood saplings used as support framework overhead, dark where black curls of smoke had often risen upward. It passed its second test. At the fireplace, where the acrid scent of dead ashes hung faintly, I put my splayed hand palm-down low over the gray-white ashes. Feeling no heat, I put my palm in the ashes of the old fire in the baked mud hearth. They were cold. I scraped away the dead coals and ashes and placed my palm to the ground under the fire. It was cold. It was at least 24 hours or more. From the looks of the old fireplace, I guessed that it was at least three days old. If it had been only one day, the ground would still retain some warmth where the fire had burnt. There were no broken pieces of mud shells that the food items had been baked in, which might have left evidence of decomposition. The cook shack was swept clean. Now I was suspicious. Although this defensive position had existed here for some time, it was a relatively, newly constructed position. It was a converging site sitting on a high-speed trail. However, there was no container to check for water. My suspicion grew. It had to be a company-sized, remain-overnight position, or else it concealed the entrance to an underground tunnel. I went back to the fireplace. The fireplace in many villages covered the entrances to underground tunnels. Tunnel entrances needed an elevated and dry area. The cook shack was in an elevated area and the inside was dry. More suspicious than ever, I spent a little time with my knife, first probing and then digging down and around to check the ground under the fireplace. No tunnel entrance.

I moved a little way ahead of the main body of the platoon along the dim trail as our patrol took a silent break. I studied the trail before we would enter the dark tunnel-like course through the forest. The ground ahead elevated gradually. I stood listening, unmoving. Looking back at the abandoned camp, my mouth went dry. I could not hear one soldier in our platoon fidgeting around; they knew better. The younger soldiers were growing spookier and spookier. Only their red eyes, filled with growing despair, were talking, flashing those wordless messages. Eyes watched other eyes. I could smell their fear and see their faces strained with fatigue. They were scared: they were in a world where the weak, slow and unwary would die. I could see them gripping their weapons so tightly their knuckles were white. I think we were all paranoid by this time anyway. But it was plain on every soldier's face beneath their helmets: dull, red eyes set in grime-smeared faces haggard from fatigue, betraying the dark, unspoken truth of their private premonitions that contact was imminent. I swept away the leaves from the ground and put the palm of one hand flat against the bare earth to feel and listen for movement above and below ground. I could detect nothing. The morning had broken clear and cool.

Sandal Tracks

We traveled further north along the gradual ascending crest of the ridge above the stream, marked with undulating folds of thicketed ravines here and there. Trying to move carefully and silently, I tried to see through and beyond the screening foliage. Some brush patches were to be seen in the patches of light that managed to shine through the stately trees. There were many smaller, slender young trees with smooth bark of good size that were interspersed between the larger trees. They were reaching up for the light. A high mountain current of air offered us a cool relief. Late in the morning, we moved up on a semi-open flat and stopped. I moved as point with two other men ahead of the main body of the platoon. Briefly looking down, my eyes suddenly caught something. My eyes noticed the shiny, unmistakable, fresh and faint sandal prints with plain soles. Where they had first entered the trail, I didn't know. Human traffic. I held my hand up, signaling to stop the patrol. My number two man, Cook, watched while I went down on one knee, thoroughly examined the view through the vegetation, then, checked the tracks in the trail. This particular portion of the trail was harder and drier than the rest. I fixedly stared at where it disappeared into the deep shadow of trees. My eyes made a quick cast ahead, watching for a breakaway point. The outline was that of a flat, plain sole, characteristic of that worn by the NVA and very difficult to see unless it was fresh. *No antitracking effort has been made to conceal their passing!*

The impressions of the tracks were sharp, with well-defined, sharp edges, except for the toe and heel. A small twig had been dislodged from its bed in the trail where one of the NVA had stepped on it. A twig's bed imprint was clearly visible and the scuffed twig itself had been kicked out, pointing in the direction they were going. I squatted where I was for a little time, touched the edge of the faint track, studying the trail immediately ahead of me intently, and then noticed the shine caused by the flattening of the dirt. There were better-defined sandal prints in the trail, the sharp edges still unmarred by the wind, sun, presence of leaves or crossing of insect tracks.

These plain, unpatterned prints were straight or slightly toe-in prints, about a foot and a half apart. The wind had not had time to mar the rim of the tracks, meaning that they were only minutes ahead of us. The tracks headed straight up the trail, headed in our same direction at a steady pace. Judging from the size of the prints, the men were small. Their short strides and the depth of the tracks showed they were traveling slowly and lightly.

They feel safe and confident!

The absence of their toe marks digging into the ground also verified their slow pace. The lack of scuffmarks indicated they were in good physical condition, unhurried and confident of their surroundings. My eye boxed off a distance of two paces and then counted the number of prints. Sixteen prints. There were four men walking the trail ahead of us. They would be trying to link up with the element engaged with the tiger force, or they would wait for us somewhere ahead if they were already aware of us. Worried that we were already the hunted, I remained sharply focused on the tracks as far ahead as I could see them to make sure they were maintaining their direction of movement. I had to slow down. I had to think. Once the tracks disappeared, we would possibly be ambushed. I signaled to move forward again, now very much afraid.

Our lives were now determined by the smallest decisions. I stopped every three or four steps so we would not be caught in an awkward shooting position. I tensed at a second open meadow and stopped the patrol. The other men remained quiet and unmoving behind me, watching. There had been no sound. I did not know what I had seen, but a premonition, a mystical intuition manifested and settled into me. Something was there. Almost daring not to turn, I stretched my eyes as far to the right as they could go in their sockets without moving my head. My educated thumb of my right hand constantly caressed the fire selector switch and my index finger rested gently on the trigger guard. I would frequently and subconsciously move the selector switch from its forward position of safe to its straight-up position of semi-automatic to its rear-pointed position of automatic to insure that I could select its firing position without thinking about it when the emergency came. My senses were turned on and tuned in to the quietness of the mountain forest. I did not trust the silence. All my senses were suddenly alert as I listened to the cool wind with a sense of foreboding. I raised my rifle to the ready position, moving my head slowly all about, scanning the area. I stood quietly to listen for a long time. I tried to focus my eyes beyond my immediate front and see through the forest into the shadows. I listened and tried to smell whatever it was. But there was only the clean, pleasant, thick air and the fragrance of the forest. But the forest had grown quiet. My mouth went dry. A sickening premonition grew in my gut. I got that eerie feeling that something was watching me. There was something there. It was now late morning and the thermals were moving up the ridge. I stood suddenly transfixed. I felt something had moved in the tall grass. A second warning, as I opened my mouth and cocked my head in that direction to hear better. I took a step toward the area that was troubling me. I stopped in midstep. At first, there was only a mini-flicker in the thick vegetation. At the limits of my peripheral vision, I caught the physical movement of the stirring of tall grass, and my heart quickened. I held my breath, listening. I felt my stomach constrict. There was the faintest whisper of something treading lightly through the grass just off the trail to my right. I finally saw him but it was too late. A khaki-clad North Vietnamese soldier jumped up running like a deer, arms pumping, and feet pattering. The tall grass flowed out and back around him as he ran into the better cover of the forest around him, gone before I could shoot.

Tiger Force.

As my eyes continued to search, I was told to forget this NVA soldier-the Platoon Leader had received word that the reconnaissance platoon (Tiger Force) had been ambushed by two NVA companies and had sustained large casualties and was slowly running out of ammunition.[6] This last radio transmission probably saved us from being drawn after a decoy and getting ourselves trapped. We were ordered to move further north to their position to relieve them since we were the nearest element.

The 2nd platoon was moving toward superior enemy forces, to contact. Alone! No one else was remotely close. I realized *all the other units were now engaged by North Vietnamese forces!* My eyes quickly boxed off two stride lengths again and counted. *Sixteen prints!* The same number of fresh sandal tracks, were still in the trail. The size and shape of the sandal prints were etched in my mind. The NVA spotted back in the grass had not been part of this group. I looked everywhere for motion. Nothing else stirred. I suffered from an intense pain in the pit of my stomach, like a rock sitting there, pain in the base of my neck at shoulder level and a terrific headache from anxiety. This pain had, over time, become chronic on all of our operations, and this time it was no different. I knew death was inevitable and unavoidable.

As silently and as slowly as a shadow, I moved on up the trail. My nerves were worn thin, my eyes examined every yard of ground immediately below the trail, as it came into view. I studied the folds in the ground on the upper side of the trail and ahead as far as I could see and came back to study them again. These depressions had a way of suddenly disclosing what had not been there a moment before. I felt breathless. A small muscle beneath my left eye twitched uncontrollably. The mountains rose steeply on both sides of us. There were few spots of flat terrain anywhere. Where it was flat, there was ample evidence of the NVA in the form of rubber sandal tracks.

The nausea came and went and came again. I would spike hot and then cold. We wound our serpentine way up a series of steep ravines and slopes along the ridge, our eyes constantly on the move, sweeping over and into the concealing shadows of the terrain. I could smell the lingering dampness of the semi-dark forest. In rare places the light penetrated the dark foliage of the overhead canopy, shining in arrowed shafts like strips of thin, translucent silk, hiding whatever was beyond the light. No birds flittered away, no creature moved. The silence was now absolute. I had to be prepared to expect the unexpected.

The valley was narrowing down and the mountain forest was now darkening with even larger trees. My slow-paced steps were second nature, like those of the great cat. We watched where we placed our feet, moving between the trees by instinct, making no sound, eyes looking into the depths of the shadowed forest. Extremely wary, conditioned by months of combat, we moved in a slightly balanced crouch, taking short fluid steps at a dead slow pace. On razor-edge nerves, I eased forward a few feet at a time, then stopped, trying to identify any hidden person or position, then got my breath and nerve back and moved on again. We moved without sound. I was extremely frightened, and had little enthusiasm for what I was doing, having to coax myself onward. I had stopped moving to listen, waiting, with a presaging sense of events, for what was coming. I had not really heard anything. But there was no doubt something was there, ahead. I was aware of the danger now. There had been no definite sound; it was a far away warning. I had the feeling that somewhere a motion had occurred. I stood quietly, remaining motionless for a long time, moving my head slowly in different directions to catch the next warning; there wasn't one. Far in the distance ahead, we could hear the mad rattle of automatic weapons fire. I listened to the sound signature of the different weapons. The thump of grenades, the high velocity chatter of M-16 rifles answering the coarser, staccato ripping of the communist AK-47 assault rifles told us that Americans were still alive and fighting. It was hard to tell how far away the gunfire was. *Sound travels at a speed of about eleven hundred feet per second. The forest will slow it down a little. The Tiger Force was over three hundred yards away!*

I could hear the rapid beat of my bloodstream echoing in my ears. Then after a time, it was again quiet. With my throat constricting, I motioned again for movement forward. I watched our flanks. Again, I briefly heard the slow, faint rattling staccato beat and sharp cracks of AK-47 fire, and then silence.

NVA Taking a Break

My insides clenched and my heart beat faster, sensing something. I could not see. My thumb flicked at the safety, as my heart beat faster and my breath became shallow. I sensed the presence of the NVA before I saw them. The sandal tracks were still there. My men, following, had silently stopped, watching me. Our second encounter with the NVA came. My eyes were searching frantically; again I was sensing something unseen in the shadows. Slowly my hearing was being stimulated by a barely audible, distance-thinned sound and I didn't know what it was. It seemed to be coming from the direction ahead. The muscle under my left eye was out of control. I was now moving in a deliberate, upright crouch, in the ready position. My feet felt their way along. The intensity of the sound changed in pitch. The grip of my right hand tightened on the rifle's pistol grip, and my index finger now tickled the trigger. I froze, heart pounding in my ears. Standing still, head cocked slightly to the right, I had that prickly sensation up and down my spine. I could feel the hair on my neck rise. I willed myself to complete and absolute immobility and silence. My brain was firing a wave of warnings in a steady rhythm now. The indistinct muffled murmuring that a moment later I knew was the sound of men talking. I heard the familiar, tonal rhythm of low-spoken Vietnamese, only 15 feet further along the trail, around a finger of the hill, my head turned off to my side, I caught them in my peripheral vision. I turned my head slowly. I stopped dead in my tracks, and remained perfectly still. The trail became clearly distinct in my eyes. The muzzle of my rifle shifted. The man behind me saw them at the same time. He stepped to my right and my third man on the point came up and stepped to my left. We stood there silently watching them, our black rifles leveled at them. Time seemed to stand still.

They were unaware of our presence, taking a break and quietly talking among themselves. I had heard their voices. I scanned their faces as the first one looked up in surprise, then the startled response--almond eyes widened and mouth opened as the jaw moved downward. Then the other two NVA soldiers repeated the performance. Our eyes met and locked. My teeth were set hard. Then all three were staring at us, unbelieving, for a brief second. No one moved. They raised their arms up slowly in surrender as our rifle muzzles indicated. And then he moved. The first NVA soldier who had seen us was now slowly starting to drop one hand toward a stick grenade. I commanded "Dung lai" (stop) in Vietnamese. He did not stop. The forest silence was shattered by the blast of our three rifles. We watched as pieces of their uniforms blew outward, the neck and chest areas of their bodies were perforated with holes, blowing misting streams of blood out the other sides of their bodies. I saw his head snap back as pieces of the jaw shot away. The other two collapsed and fell straight backward limply and my man half-turned sideways as his body tried to slump forward. I slowly advanced on all three bodies and saw the looks on their dark, contorted faces.

The one with the jaw shot away was still alive, in a welter of blood and pain. A barely audible moan rose from him. He raised one arm and his fingers told him that there was nothing below his now exposed upper teeth. His breathing, already raspy from his shattered lungs, was magnified now as he began to gag, gurgle and choke with his tongue gone. Already in an impersonal state of self-hypnosis, I ordered him shot again. The NVA were very young looking. PFC Cook took his backup firearm, a .45 caliber pistol, put it to his head and ended his terrible misery. My third man on point turned and stared into my eyes and stated that we had been on point long enough. With his body shaking, he stated he wanted another squad to resume this job. I looked back into him and saw that primal look that strained his face. I knew! *A reflection of myself.* He was frightened. We were all frightened. He had done a good job, and I told him to fall in behind the squad. We left the dead for the platoon leader to quickly search. All I wanted was to be away from this place, to escape somehow, wake up and find it was a bad dream. The bad dream was reality. I could feel Death and Destruction holding out their hands for more, and all I could do was move forward to meet them. I took the point and continued on. I felt sick. The platoon had no trouble maintaining their distance from each other, because it was only a matter of time before we were ambushed again. The NVA knew we were there. Despite the presence of my men, I felt alone as I moved along, on up the ridge slowly. Again my premonition of impending danger was at a high pitch. My sense of vision, hearing, and smell were now more intensified. I felt a sharp pain building up behind my eyes. I wanted to live. Like a harbinger of doom, the ominous sound of weapons fire ahead in the distance was growing louder. Nerves now raw and exposed, I moved, wondering when and where the next encounter would take place.

NVA Trail Watcher

I was now measuring our progress and time by the westering sun. Again I had a prickling in my senses. I signaled with my hand for the platoon to stop and stood still, my eyes and ears searching everywhere. The only sound and movement was the rustling of foliage in the tops of the trees from a light breeze. I felt the presence of the enemy near. I detected no sign of movement anywhere in my range of vision. With a frightened feeling and a declining day warning me, I noticed two important things. One was that the stream was no longer directly below us. The other, more troubling was the footpath, beaten hard by many feet. A clear, small outline of a smooth-bottomed sandal prints made in a patch of clear ground, the kind worn by the NVA. I motioned my second man to me. I was distracted from my immediate surroundings and bending in anxious scrutiny.

Our third encounter came quite suddenly from ambush only a few feet away from our immediate flank. I just had a chance to silently ask my second man if he had noticed when and where the stream had veered away from the ridge, when it happened. A carefully concealed North Vietnamese soldier armed with an SKS 7.62 mm semi-automatic rifle had been watching us from a natural ground blind that blended with the terrain right on the trail against the hillside. It had several shooting holes to see from to reduce his tendency to fidget. His blind was wide, high and solid enough to allow himself movement and was cleaned of all the leaf litter, so as not to create any noise accidentally. The entire platoon could have all walked by him and not detected him had he remained still. We were both standing still. The NVA soldier had been in the kneeling position, low to the ground, waiting patiently until we were both looking in a different direction down the ridge and at the track. Then he fired a volley on us. Luckily we were not standing too close to each other. The SKS sent smoke blowing past us. He had narrowly missed us both at extremely close range.

With blistering speed, I seized the opportunity and pulled my rifle into a quick-reaction shooting position; with my left forearm extended and the butt-stock locked into my right side by my elbow, I found my target and pointed, firing my M-16 almost simultaneously. My aim was better than his had been. With a terrible thrill, I knew I had killed him. After firing on him, I went into the prone position and before the echoes of the shots had died away, I pulled a grenade from inside my canteen cover. This was one pound of death. Its serrated sheet metal body blows into small pieces from its filler of composition B. I armed the grenade before throwing by pulling the pin, allowing the lever to fly and the striker to hit the primer. With the delay element now burning through its length, I counted one, two, and three. I lobbed an M-26 fragmentation grenade at him. By this time the delay element had now burned into the detonator. It landed right next to him, exploded and sent debris everywhere. My number two man had run back to his position from where I had motioned him forward, to take cover. Thin clouds of blue smoke were floating on the somewhat still air, gradually thinning. I was shaken up and still reacting to the shock. I slowly walked over to him at the ready with my rifle. Anytime you think you have a dead man, you're the one that's apt to be dead soon. I placed the flashhider on the muzzle of my rifle into his back, caught the material of his blouse and, applying downward pressure, twisted it. His chest didn't move. I reached down with my left hand and placed it on his neck. I had to check him to be sure he was dead. He was already dead; his last spasms were finished. Moving to one side, I carefully rolled him over, watching for a grenade. Seeing nothing, I retrieved his weapon. The unblinking almond-colored eyes stared at the sky overhead. They were slowly losing their luster and glazing over. I closed his eyes for him and searched his body, noticing that all my rounds went into his chest. One moment you were among the living and the next you were somewhere else.

    I looked at his wallet and color pictures of his family. I choked up. I felt sad for him and them. For the first time in the war, I had come to realize that these enemy soldiers were not just like me. They were just young boys doing a man's job. These young soldiers were more violent and loyal. They were easily controlled by their leaders and obeyed orders. His only mistake was being too young, miscalculating when to shoot us.

He probably became unnerved by the ordeal and had tried to get us both at the same time instead of concentrating on one target at a time. His worn khaki uniform was neatly patched and repaired, and blended perfectly with the surrounding brush and bare dirt of the embankment where he was hidden. The bluing on his weapon was worn in places from the metal from long usage, but was clean and well maintained. I handed the dead soldier's Simonov 7.62 mm semi-automatic, gas-operated carbine to one of the other men. It had a long, flat-bladed, folding bayonet and a ten-round nondetachable box magazine. He could have shot us coming up the trail, at broadside or as the rear security man quartered away from him. I sat down and saw that my hands were shaking. The shaking spread as I started to experience an adrenaline rush.

When I looked up and around at the platoon still crouched in cover and waiting, I saw in their faces the same thing I had just felt, and still felt. I saw doubt and gut-crimping fear. Nothing is easier to detect in a man than fear. It is also contagious. I tried my best to stop my trembling for their sake, to force my present mental state aside. My heart was still palpitating. Their faces registered the shock of what had happened for a second time. The pain between my shoulder blades and in the pit of my stomach was now worse. My head felt like a tight band was wrapped around it. I felt weak. I sat down on a little berm and took a few minutes to calm down. No one else moved. Slowly, I again became aware of the forest. There was no sound.

Miraculously, by some peculiar chance, I was safe from destruction and eternity. This phenomenon of emerging unscathed from such a close encounter was incomprehensible to me. My fear was working for me; it had sharpened my reactions. No one should have had a chance of living. I began to wonder how long it would be before it all ended, fatally. The sun had long passed its zenith and could no longer be observed. I had lost its directional guidance with which I'd maintained my heading through this wild terrain. Moving slowly as a shadow and absolutely silent, we resumed our ascending course. Gradually, the landform began to descend. Sporadic volleys from small-arms fire gave away the specific area and direction of the Tiger Force. I prayed for strength and courage. My Grandmother's favorite Bible verse popped into my head, "Lift thine eyes to the hills from whence cometh thy help!"

Linkup

The retreating glow of impending night now backlighted the ridge above us. The place was wild, dismal, a shallow vale between dark, heavily timbered slopes. The gunpowder smell was sharp and pungent. With nerves worn thin, we now moved into the maw of death, a low place with many bodies covered in blood, lying sprawled where they had fallen, in grotesque angles that only dead men killed violently could achieve. Their blood soaked black in the dark soil. Most had not suffered too greatly, dying quickly. Those who had suffered long and greatly before they died lay curled up. We had reached the isolated Tiger Force, a site of violent death. My mind was momentarily diverted by the stench of blood. The source was everywhere. This was a scene of gruesome mass slaughter. Too late, if at all, had they noticed the fighting positions of this NVA base camp, dug into the sides of the draw.

The Tiger Force, reconnoitering for enemy forces, their movement, base areas and trail networks, had been caught in a deadly ambush by two NVA companies at very short range. The site was located beneath great, high-branching trees, cleaned of underbrush. The NVA occupied well-camouflaged prepared ambush positions in the slope above the trail that the reconnaissance unit was on and initiated heavy crossfire on the unsuspecting men. As all too often in this war, the PAVN forces had again chosen the time and place to fight on their terms, nearly always keeping us on the defensive and exacting maximum casualties. Many of the troops were hit at near point-blank range. The Tiger Force was unable to retreat from the narrow base of a hill, caught in the low ground, between two steep surrounding hills of the ridge, suffering terribly in the confused fighting and paying a terrible price for entering this low area. They were unable to secure their seriously wounded. Any attempt to retrieve their wounded was met with heavy fire. The wounded had to suffer alone and in silence. The fighting had been close and savage. From the start, the frantic battle could not have lasted very long. The silent NVA had placed devastating fire upon them. They had no way out. No escape. There were 12 men killed and 19 others very badly wounded, hit multiple times in the upper body areas. I could see from the scattered equipment all over the area that they had become addle-brained with panic. Starlight scopes, packs and weapons were lying where they fell. There were no AN/PRC-25 radio sets lying around, though. Since joining the 1st Brigade, I had noticed that whenever we policed an area where Americans had been ambushed, that the PAVN had not left without the radios and spare batteries. The young and mostly inexperienced Tiger Force, in their baptism of fire and blood and their abandonment of so much necessary equipment, demonstrated the deteriorated mental condition of the troops at the time of the ambush. I looked around us, our position in this location was desperate. Once more we were in the low ground with a slaughterhouse of death surrounding us. We spread ourselves out defensively, and our men made themselves obscenely comfortable among the dead and awaited the next move. There was an ominous quiet.

It was cool and damp in the forest with moss growing on the trees, for the roof of leaves and creepers shut out the sun. The low spot widened in a fan shape as it descended into a sloped bench divided by ridges. Further down, the ravines were covered with brush. There was only one man unwounded among the few hideously mutilated survivors that I saw. Nothing affects morale more than seeing the misery of many other wounded men. This was a bloody, carcass-littered draw, where bloody limbs stuck out at strange angles. I could smell the oppressive and overwhelming foul, sweet copper-scent of blood thick in the air from the many shredded bodies. There was the stench of soiled clothing and protruding bones. I caught my first whiff of sweet-sickening decay and could feel it on the back of my tongue. Flesh was moldering and beginning to rot. War's carnage was mixing with the aroma of damp compost, mold and the rotting vegetation. We had to consolidate the wounded and dead.

A medic had, not as yet attended to the first casualties I saw. With a quick look at the first live trooper I saw, I knew that treatment no longer mattered. He had been shot through the side of the mouth, the bullet scoring its way through his teeth. Evidently his tongue wasn't hit, because he wasn't choking. He was sitting with his upper body leaning slightly to the side, his head slumping back grotesquely. His forehead and face were very white and streaming with sweat. A trickle of scarlet blood was flowing down. He was also hit twice in the chest region and once in the leg. He was still barely alive, moaning very low, and touching his face with one hand. I could hear his near silent mewling and labored breathing. I could see the white of ragged and splintered bones. He slowly raked the leaves and dirt with the fingers of his other hand. The light flitted from his eyes, dull with pain. His gaze was vacant. A final ray of sunlight lit his face. He looked like he would faint and go into shock. Another, staring the stare of death, wallowed in his own blood while gazing upward as life slipped unerringly from his child-like eyes. The first spasms of death jerked at his body. Most of the men had taken multiple hits. Now they were just grimy, blood-spattered soldiers sprawled along the ground everywhere. There was the stench from their bowels having voided, from dying violently. All of the men showed great inner strength, evident as they tried to ignore the spasms of terrible pain racking their badly wounded bodies. Some twisted in a dark abyss of pain. Too many had a death pallor staining their faces. It hurt my eyes and heart to look at them. Our medic would have his hands full.

The huge trees in this location stretched a canopy of foliage, which denied the sunlight from reaching the forest floor. The dark shade was almost like twilight. Consequently there was little ground cover. This allowed for long-distance viewing through the woods. Already the forest shadows were lengthening to purple shadows. Time raced. The forest darkened as our nearby wounded were hurriedly consolidated, but more were spread over a wider area. The wounded were quiet, except for a low groaning which could not be helped. The most seriously wounded were put together. We could see throughout the canopy that there wasn't much daylight left. The sun would soon be gone. The Regular North Vietnamese Army infantrymen, the Bo Doi Chu Luc, were already throwing hand grenades at our position and we were not going to be able to pull them all into our perimeter. I was called to report to my platoon leader's position at the base of a tree. I was ordered to the thankless task of leading and rooting out the North Vietnamese soldiers, from their defensive positions on the side of the hill by Lieutenant Kirby Young. The Lieutenant offered me his flask. I took it. *A little of this is strength, too much would be weakness.* I took one swallow and felt its sting as it fired the belly and the numbing of the taste buds on my tongue. The effect was almost immediate on my starved body and trembling hands. The liquid burned wonderfully, dulling the pain and providing my soul with a manufactured false courage. My shaking hands stilled. This is it, I thought, this is the end, as my heart loudly thumped in my chest.

Attack the Hill

The NVA were firmly entrenched in the ill-lit forest with a commanding view from well-concealed foxholes. I knew now that I didn't have to worry about the Devil knocking at our door; we were now about to go knocking at his. We all had to reach down into our souls for courage. The veins on the bottom side of my wrists now tingled. After I got the platoon assembled, I turned to give the skirmish order and, looking into their stoic faces, told them we were going to look them in the eye. I told them to spread out well and to stay on line with the man on either side of them. I would be on the exposed left flank leading the way up. I instructed each man to low-crawl going up the hill and keep his head down next to the ground, and when encountering a spider hole, one man was to cover it with his rifle or pistol. The other man would pull the pin on a hand grenade and release the grip on the safety lever. The striker would rotate, flipping the safety lever off. We would count to three and flip it in the hole, praying that the NVA soldier wasn't quick-witted enough or that there wasn't enough time for him to get his hands on it and toss it back. The fuse of the M-26 grenade burns for five to seven seconds before activating and exploding. Our way was clear. The tension was now electrifying. I sensed their fear. Some were visibly shaking, but tight-lipped and silent. My eyes touched the eyes of each man in that small gathering of warriors, seeing the clean narrow streaks under their eyes on their dirty faces. I saw in their eyes a spiritual energy kindled by the grim task before them. Forming to attack the hill quickly had strung our mental strength to its highest pitch. Without a word, but with a dark, sinister resolve, the men fanned out into position among the close trees, grim and silent, and like a great serpent we started our crawl up the hill.

A stick grenade, its wooden handle turning end over end, hit the ground to my front and bounced toward me and ended its journey to my right front less than five feet away. I stared at it, as I flattened my body as much as I could. It suddenly exploded in a brilliant light, showering the area with chunks of iron and dirt. Their cast-iron fragmentation grenades were of a low explosive power. The serrated grenade sat upon a hollow wooden cylinder with a waterproof-cap at the bottom of the handle. The cap removed, the NVA soldiers looped the string onto one finger and threw. The string remaining with their hand ignited the friction fuse. It was my past experience that many of their grenades were unreliable and failed to explode. However, none of these stick grenades presently were having that problem.

As the light faded from the forest, we received our first warning that the North Vietnamese were aware that we were coming up the hill. We were immediately welcomed by a short, wicked burst of automatic fire from the ridge on our left flank, profanely smacking the ground and tree trunks around us. They were likely using a 7.62 mm RPD light machine gun. The RPD gunner was well trained. The muzzle flashes blinked rapidly as he periodically fired short burst, to keep his barrel from overheating and jamming, scything the ground litter with a stream of lead. One thing I will say for the AK-47 assault rifle, if we were watching we could see from where the enemy was firing. The AK-47 had a shorter barrel, producing more muzzle flash. They also had no flash suppressor, and then the sonic crack definitely let you know you were under fire. Our M-16 had a long 20-inch barrel that allowed the hot gases released by firing longer to dissipate and cool producing a smaller muzzle flash. The flash suppressor also helped with the muzzle blast. However, none of this technology would be worth much in the dark under these great trees, as the glittering of light would be easily seen. The flesh-hunting rounds whickering and careening through the foliage hardly deflected, they just chewed right into whatever they hit. Bark and splinters exploded in all directions. They would pick you right up off the ground if they hit you. Trying to see as much as possible and as quickly as I could, I shifted my eyes from left to right and tried to focus on objects at the edge of my peripheral vision. Bullets chewed into the foliage just above our heads. The volume of fire whipped at the low branches and shredded bark from the tree trunks. It was coming from the same ridge we were on and it made a bend and came back around, overlooking our position at a distance. Then small arms fire and the "Made-in China" stick grenades welcomed us with their coughing roar. The dank air was full of concussions; rank with the bitter stench of powder smoke from the gunfire and Chinese stick grenades. The heavy timber and foliage gave us some cover and concealment as we continued our way through the machine-gun fire toward their dug-in positions. Bullets exploded into the tree trunks around us, others ricocheting from rocks. Bark, twigs and leaves rained down upon us. There was the high-pitched whine going past our ears and the sonic crack popping over our heads as we crawled forward. One round ripped into the ground near my head and exploded dirt into my face and eyes and filled my mouth with debris.

  More machine-gun bursts came stitching the ground from our left front and across our line, barely missing the man on my immediate left and over my legs. There were dull thuds of rounds impacting into soft parts of the ground everywhere. The distinctive rush, like a ripping sound of the RPD light machine gun, and peculiar whining of ricocheting rounds sang through the trees. Forest litter and humus raised impacted against us and misted over us. I gave little attention to the firing on my flank, only on the dug-in fighting positions to my immediate front. As I looked up the hill, I saw the quick motion of just a hand, then the Chinese stick grenades turning end-over-end. A desperate resistance on the part of the besieged was now taking place. The grenades caught the fading sunlight; thrown from directly ahead uphill and coming directly for me, they completed their arc and fell around me. I yelled "grenade" and flattened, turning my face away from the area they landed. The flash of the Chinese hand grenade explosions rocked the ground but only a blast of wind and forest litter hit me. Luckily, the cast iron body of the stick grenade exploded into large chunks. A bitter grenade exchange took place. Smoke from the many stick grenades drifted among us. As if a demon spirit were present, the cacophony of war sounds engulfed us. My men had become something different now in the face of the enemy. As the attack intensified, an endless storm of small-arms fire rose to a steady crescendo followed by shrieks, groans, screaming of the wounded. Filtering through the darkened forest up on the hill, we could hear the NVA shouting their rage at us. They were determined to keep us from coming up the hill. Some of the NVA spoke in English. With an icy determination, angry obscenities, we shouted taunts at the enemy. The challenge was flung back at the enemy. I yelled "du-me" (mother fucker) and "an-ket" (eat shit) at them. Now, we constantly taunted each other, to distract each other, while one or the other silently moved to gain a killing advantage from another angle. Yelling helped us to rid ourselves of the paralyzing fear. It also encouraged us. We had all gone mad.

  Covered with sweaty dirt, I started crawling upward again from tree to tree. I looked up and saw two stick grenades flipping through the air as we pressed closer and closer. I knew they were going to land behind me. They exploded, sending more smoke and geysers of dirt and debris leaping up and then wafting through the air. The closer we got, the hotter their small-arms fire became. We had reached the edge of their fighting positions. These individual NVA fighting positions were what the enemy called "Frog holes" (Ham ech); they were just big enough for one man, what we would call a spider hole. I heard the flat metallic snap of a round being chambered from the hole just ahead. The best weapon for clearing the dug-in fighting positions, was the hand grenade and the standard-issue

Colt Model 1911A1 .45 ACP caliber semi-automatic pistol. The man nearest me covered the fighting position to my front with the pistol as I pulled the pin on an M-26 fragmentation grenade, allowing the handle to pop off and the striker to arm the grenade. The acid fuse now burning inside, I counted to four and flipped it into the hole. I prayed that it wouldn't be thrown back out. The short wait was painful. The pound of high explosive, Composition B, exploded into over seven hundred pieces. The NVA soldier was blown into a red shower of shredded flesh above me. The North Vietnamese machine gunner continued to stitch the ground around us again. The man on my left started yelling, "I'm gonna die, I'm gonna die." I told him to shut up and change his position by crawling further up and the machine gunner would probably not be able to see him. That worked, because the NVA machine gunner continued to fire but now it was stitching the ground behind us. I saw the first NVA hole blown by one of my men about three men down on the right. I saw the blast and saw shredded NVA flesh hanging from some limbs overhanging the position. Fighting just feet apart, the North Vietnamese and my platoon hurled curses at each other. We were fearful, but we suffered more anger than fear. In defiance, we taunted the Vietnamese by shouting at them in their own language that they ate shit. I encouraged the men close by to do the same. Up and down the line of low-crawling men slowly moving forward, their voices called out, working themselves up for this task. The shooting had become controlled. I suffered from thirst. Others were suffering from wounds.

    We had crawled through the first tier of defensive positions, having cleared every position with grenades and fire. The firing was so fast and furious that it blended as a continuous roar. I looked up in time again to see three stick grenades in the air tumbling end over end toward us. We immediately stopped crawling and turned our heads from the direction of the explosions. Suddenly, the firing abruptly ceased. Only an occasional taunt was hurled by the other side. It would soon be too dark to see well. A smoke mantle drifted above us. A silence fraught with suspense ensued. I felt that the NVA had silently pulled back under the cover of darkness, just before we were ordered to pull back. Strange. At this point we were ordered to return to our perimeter. At the bottom of the hill, my platoon leader, Lt. Kirby Young, was already seriously wounded in the head and had lost an eye. Eventually he would be replaced by a less experienced officer, further reducing the "cream of the crop," the seasoned soldiers' life expectancy.

One small force of men joined us just before it got too dark to see under the trees. They had managed to find their way on the trail in the dark by the sounds of the fighting without getting ambushed. They conducted an attack on the hill above us, the muzzle flashes ripping the night open and strobing the trunks of the trees, but they did not receive any return fire. Evidently the NVA had delayed us long enough from their spider holes to withdraw from the immediate area of their circular-constructed hilltop fortifications with the essential supplies they needed.

The remaining few frightened men of the Tiger Force and the 2nd Platoon of C Company 1/327th, now completely surrounded, went into a night defensive position again in the low ground. The NVA still held the high ground all around us. We were told that the closest element was an under-strengthed platoon from Alpha Company 1/327, and that they would be here to join us if and when they could. Nighttime is the right time for most activity and with night's arrival the silence deepened. Surrounded at night, we were colder than usual with the presence of the thermals moving down from the top of the ridges. Once the sun had disappeared, the air had cooled at an amazing pace. The damp night cold was penetrating. Insects didn't bother us. For a while it was peaceful, as a cool wind blew down from the mountain with the coming of night. We began to hear the periodic rustle of foliage and familiar sounds of movement in the leaves around our front in the shifting shadows. The NVA were still close. I felt an eerie pall settle around me. We listened with practiced ears and were hearing the NVA quietly, wraith-like, searching around the dead, for equipment and survivors. Hopefully they wouldn't find those still alive or the starlight scopes. It was worse for our wounded still out there, the torture of lying powerless and untended outside our line. Where earlier they felt little, only a numbness, from their fresh wounds, which is common, they now felt great pain. They had to endure their pain; to move or make a sound, even under the cover of darkness, would mean death. Hopefully their wounds would put them into a cataleptic state, until they could be recovered.

    The rhythmic, cosmic clock continued to tick. As the dark womb of night surrounded us, we could feel and smell the transition from day to night. We set up a night defense for an attack that we were sure would come. I moved over to the one level area where we expected the NVA to come from, since this was where we were hearing the most movement. I was in an NVA foxhole with my good friend, "Frenchy," Sgt. Christian G. Girard.[7] We were both cold and shivering from exposure to the elements. He watched while I quickly cleaned my rifle. The NVA's Russian-designed Kalashnikov AK-47 assault rifle weighed about nine and a half pounds and was less complicated and tended to break down less often than our M-16 rifle. The chrome barrel of the Kalashnikov made it impervious to neglect. Our rifle was lighter, eight and a half pounds, and fired more accurately but that didn't matter because we were constantly engaged at very close quarters. The M-16, unless kept clean, just did not function well. This included the cleaning of our 30-round magazine and the individual rounds. The only magazine we cleaned was the one carried in the rifle, the other being secure in our pouches. Our weapons cleaned, we both wished we had a cup of hot coffee.

    The dew would usually soak things through completely and by morning we would be thoroughly chilled. I remembered earlier seeing a discarded pack from one of the dead soldiers. The only sound I could hear was the mumbled delirium from the wounded behind me. Like a huge snake, I slowly and quietly wormed my way along out into the dark and got it and returned to the position with it. It was a blood-soaked camouflaged poncho liner rolled in a poncho, which we would both use to stay warm through the night.

    We readied our grenades around the top of the hole along with all the Chinese stick grenades. With growing despair and hopelessness, we settled in to wait for the coming attack in the darkness--for the shadowy profiles to emerge. We were painfully aware of every slight new sound in the misty night in this pitiless and foreboding range of mountains. There was little to do but wait and let the scenario that fate had in store for us play itself out. At least we had a good foxhole. I felt as if it were our grave. At least it had been dug for us. I experienced a sensory elixir. I could taste the air, the pungent, wet, earthy smells flared from the fresh dirt of our foxhole. The breeze coming down the mountain now seemed to invigorate me. I wanted to live. We waited and waited, thinking that the NVA moment by moment were inching closer, drawing tighter and tighter around us.

Evacuation

We had received an adrenaline punch when the Army med-evac flights, attempting to come in and fly out the wounded. Flying into the teeth of enemy ground fire, they were quickly shot up from the surrounding high terrain by the North Vietnamese heavy .51-caliber machine guns. We watched as the green tracers went overhead and heard the slapping sound as they stitched the choppers. The NVA machine guns followed their path as they very bravely tried to come flying into our narrow and enclosed area between the ridges. Finally the word was received that the Army pilots refused to fly the mission. We felt alone and desperate, knowing that night the Army would not attempt any further missions to fly out the many seriously wounded. We were also aware that there were more enemy troops around us than we thought, supported by anti-aircraft units.

Later we received word that the crew of a Kaman's HH-43 B Huskie helicopter had volunteered to brave the fire.[8] The HH-43B lacked armor and armament because the Air Force had envisioned it only for the airborne fire fighting and air base crash rescue role. This fire-fighting Air Sea Rescue helicopter was equipped with twin intermeshing rotors, eliminating the need for a tail rotor and facilitated hover control. It was the last helicopter to have wooden blades. It was referred to as "Pedro" because that was their call sign. Only one squadron of HH-43s was stationed in the country. They were broken down and assigned in detachments of two's throughout the country. This aircraft saved more personnel than all the other Air Force choppers together, and after being alerted they could be on their way in 30 seconds. The huskie had a jungle penetrator, with which it lowered a wire basket, known as a Stokes litter. The HH-43B carried 11 passengers. This particular helicopter crew was from a detachment of the 37th Air Rescue and Recovery Squadron. These unlikely heroe's in the Air Force flying this type of helicopter flew more air rescues than any other aircraft in the war. One of the great hazards of this mission was the fact that the Huskie had very limited fuel.

  The night wore on as we listened to the night sounds. Our eyes accustomed to the starlit darkness, I realized moonrise would be coming soon. Death could now come quickly and without warning. We lay there fearfully in our dark perimeter defense, staring and listening into the pitch-blackness in a daze, trying to pay attention to detail. Alertness now depended upon ear. I got a jolt and my heart jumped. A slight sound caught my attention, startled me, and then was gone. My heart began to thump with a hard rhythm. I worried about the shape of a particular dark shadow. Was someone standing there, motionless? I gripped a grenade. A sound froze me. Crouching, I started to prepare to arm the grenade. I tried to breathe normally. I looked away for a few minutes and then, when I looked back its appearance was unchanged. I relaxed and decided it was just the trunk of a tree, not a man standing there. The worry and strain were affecting my nerves. Again a sound came, this time in the distance. This was the sound that had first taken my attention, only louder now, as it gradually became more audible, this very faint sound told us we were not forgotten. Soon it was the heavy "thwap-thwap-thwap" arising as the whirling rotor blades of a large helicopter bit into the mountain air turbulence--swirling air that tumbles off the blade in front of it. We prayed for the crew. Then the sudden flurry of automatic fire from the NVA's Chinese-made .51-caliber heavy machine guns, lit by green tracers, formally announced his arrival as they began to follow the low-flying black blob in. We could tell from the sound that he had to be flying close to the canopy of the trees. The sound of his engine remained steady on course, never wavering. Then he was upon us. We heard his air speed drop. He came in lower and settled into our narrow area between the ridges in our hollow. The roar of engines was loud. The fearless pilot was completely resolved; he had not wavered once from his dark path. In chilling awe and terror we watched and listened to the helicopter as the pilot eased down on the collective, whipping the uppermost branches violently and blowing leaves and small limbs up into the rotor-wash. Finally into position above the wounded, he now sat there accepting the small-arms fire and giving the men on the ground instructions that when the wire basket was lowered and secured, he would then turn off his ground light. I marveled at his self-control. This was a brave Air Force pilot. He could not afford to waste any time. The ground crew loading the wounded would have to work fast. In the light of the helicopter, I found that the shadow to my front that had spooked me was in fact a tree.

The basket was lowered through the dense trees and caught by the men on the ground. There were many brief cries of pain as the wounded were prepared for loading and strapping into the basket. The lights on the helicopter were turned off while the large ground light on the chopper was turned on. The great light lent an ethereal glow to the surrounding area, and portrayed the bravery of the helicopter crew. We hugged the ground, knowing we were now silhouetted in the ghostly hue. The NVA, however, seemed more interested in the helicopter.

The trees waved their branches frantically as we glanced up periodically amid the great downdraft from the thwap-thwap-thwap of the constant beat of the rotor blades. We had to look up periodically; we were afraid he was going to be shot down and crash on us. The resounding sound of the beat of the whining engine and blades echoed off the high surrounding terrain rising on every side. The heavy machine guns, located on top of the ridge, had quit firing. Evidently they were not in a position to continue to fire into the low ground. However, there was still periodic small-arms fire. We didn't receive any fire support this night because the other small friendly infantry platoons were out there somewhere, still trying their best to get to us in the dark without being ambushed, forced to use maps of this area which were so bad.

The men had to work fast as the silhouetted chopper hovered there waiting patiently, taking fire. The Para rescue crewman maneuvered the hoisting cable with attached basket through the waving branches. As each load of wounded was secured, the chopper would bring the engines to full power, then ease up on the collective, rising amid the cloud of branches and leaves being sucked up, and slip sidewise, turning away from this treetop effect. As his airspeed climbed, the pilot skimmed along the treetops in the dark of the night, then up into the illuminated clear night air. The helicopter departed the area, leaving us alone again. We listened as he flew away, sounding as if he was even lower than when he came in. The helicopter was not fired on while immediately leaving, because he was so much lower than the heavy machine gun positions taken by the NVA, who surely had a forest of trees in front of their guns. The NVA could not depress their muzzles too much. After the helicopter was gone, the smell of cordite would then flood the forest once more, drifting down to us in dead silence on the night thermals, and hang in the air from the NVA positions. When the helicopter returned for another load, the cordite would dissipate with the wash of the rotors. Sometime during the night, late, the under-strengthed platoon from Alpha Company reached us. Misery loves company, but thank God for them.

A Last Cup of Coffee

I had not been conscious of when the moon had poked its head over the ridges and illuminated the treetops, providing some light at ground level. Exhaustion ran very deep, with little sleep and little to eat. We were catching ourselves nodding and blinking to stay awake. We peered into the night. The chill inside me wouldn't go away. *This is it*, I thought. *We're going to die.* My mouth was painfully dry. Not knowing if we would survive the night, we decided on a last cup of coffee together. Its stimulating effect had to last us several more hours.

I always carried two baby bottles of Folgers coffee, one of sugar and one of powdered cream. They were my most precious possessions.

Christian got out of the foxhole and made sure the hole was sealed for light, while I quickly brewed us a hot canteen cup full of coffee with some of my plastic explosive (C-4). The soft C-4 looks like white modeling clay and will not detonate without a blasting cap. I broke off a small piece and lit it with my lighter. It took only a minute. Just the rich aroma of the coffee boosted our spirits. Few things in this world are so comforting and so warming to the heart as a cup of coffee. The coffee was a natural mood booster, quickly alleviating our headaches and pain from too much being demanded of us, and best of all, kept us alert. *Thank you Folgers Coffee Company!* Christian and I shared a warm companionship found only in the Army among men at war. We watched for shapes as we listened to several muffled approaches growing louder at various times, but they always retreated. We were silent and ready.

We had already spent days without sleep. Going without it for another night, while watching for the NVA to attack us was not a hard thing to do. Our eyes searched the darkness for a flicker of movement--just a hint of something. Our ears sensitive to every faint rustle. The cooling night air was still except for the hum of insect. Later, we watched in silence and awe as the other strange platoon conducted a night attack on the NVA positions. We did not see any return fire. The NVA had withdrawn, but we did not yet know this. We assumed they withheld their fire for another reason. Our body temperatures had already taken a dip and it took some extra effort for me to stay awake. The cold air was penetrating. It had brought a light fog into the bottom. By this time, I knew that those wounded who survived the night on the forest floor would mercifully be the least sensitive to the pain of their wounds. They would be our first priority. We knew other units were fighting their way to us.

There was a fresh breath of wind, which announced the coming of dawn. At the first graying of day's light, shortly after moon set, I gently squeezed Girard's shoulder until he was alert. We stared ahead into the ghostly light of predawn, waiting for flitting shadow-like forms to emerge. Nothing stirred. I felt the hairs on my neck rise stiff and tingly at the threatening atmosphere. Our imaginations worked overtime, making our fears real. Everything was made to look unearthly in the light, gray fog. I could just make out the defining edges of the solid dark trunks of trees to my front in the shades of gray, giving depth to the darkness under the dark solid canopy. The dark gray sky was getting brighter. We had spent a miserable and virtually sleepless night. The sun had finally broken the horizon. Shadows were created in the forest and closely watched. The normal nearby and distant carrying sounds of birds indicated that all was well. The PAVN had pulled away during the night. We could now see the reddish-orange through the few holes in the canopy and then suddenly it was light. We were all chilled. The sun had come up! Warm sunlight streamed through the branches. I was euphoric. We had survived another night to see another day. Truly the light was a sweet and pleasant thing for my sore and tired eyes, hardly able to focus, to see again. Later it would become hot. We were given the word to saddle up. I forced myself up. The cold, fatigue and hard ground were taking their toll. I was getting old. I saw the obvious reality of war as we collected to move. The horror, exhaustion, tension and tragedy, was imprinted on the gray, grim and haggard faces of my platoon, no longer young and clean-cut or fresh. Their blind faith and idealistic zeal was gone; only survival mattered now. They were exhausted, drowsy and red-eyed from being too long without sleep. Dark circles surrounded their sunken eyes as the word was given to prepare to leave. We had been surrounded by absolute chaos and the platoon had suffered no social breakdown. Their faces were weirdly drawn and pale under their helmets. Only the streaked lines beneath our eyes marked our dirty faces, where tears had welled beneath our lids and run down our cheeks in salty rivulets, telling of our individual stress. We had remained tightly together. Comrades.

Footnotes:

1. Carpet bombing was used for close air support in ground operations against troop concentrations and enemy base camps. The standard formation of three bombers would fly at 30,000 feet, each carrying a load of 108 conventional 500-pound bombs.

2. The 320th was reinforced by a platoon from Company A 2/502nd Infantry. It was under the command of Lt. Karl Beach. The 1st Platoon of Company A 326th Engineer Battalion was reorganized as infantry, led by Billy Colwell.

3. In Vietnamese, "Dak" means stream.

4. Gun number six was fought over and lost twice. It was recaptured each time. The near 600 hits by rifle rounds on the 105-MM gun attest to the viciously fought battle.

5. Sappers were made up of carefully selected and trained personnel, specializing in explosives, detecting and disarming early warning systems, and attacking fortified defensive positions. Sappers, used primarily to conserve forces, were organized into battalions and Regiments.

6. The Tiger Force was the division short-range reconnaissance element. This unit consisted of 42 men, and was commanded by Capt. Lewis Higinbotham. Of the original 42 men, only 7 men in the Tiger Force were not killed or wounded.

7. SFC Christian G. Girard was killed in action on 8 April 1968. He was serving with the Studies and Observation Group (MACSOG), conducting a cross-border mission.

8. The HH-43B was stabilized by four vertical tail surfaces. The prop wash from the two rotors helped beat down flames and foliage in its mission role. This helicopter was fitted with skids to each wheel allowing it to land on swampy or marshy ground. It had a crew of 2-3. Its cruising speed was 105 miles-per-hour. It had a maximum range of 276 miles.

I still feel the bite of battlegrounds,
momentary awe of hills, hollows,
mountaintop's, and men who hallowed
the ground without regret.
Their souls now free
We few remaining must climb on

Author

CHAPTER 12

HOSPITAL

Usually the NVA, after being engaged in battle, broke up into smaller-sized units and retreated into hidden and isolated base camps to avoid any sizable strike to follow. As we were leaving, I had the feeling we had worn out our warm welcome. I had lived, but for how long I didn't know. We would fight these NVA soldiers another day. I didn't know it, but our bad days were about to get worse. The fighting was just beginning. Again, my temperature was spiking and the shakes returned.

It seemed a long time before the gray dawn lightened the sky. The surrounding landscape was full of potential menace. When it was finally light enough, our company commander of Charlie Company 1st Battalion, 327th Airborne Battalion, 101st Airborne Division, had us following a narrow, well-used trail, zigzagging in a serpentine single file over the ridges in the growing, dispiriting dawn light. It was early June 1966 at Dac To in the impenetrable mountain forest of Kontum

Province. There, we had already found the 24th North Vietnamese Army Regiment numerous times, and were attempting to maintain contact. We had boldly pushed ahead at the start of this operation, but now we were very cautious, fearful. The NVA had again eluded us, for a time.

The Ants

At sunrise, the forest was still and lonely. We glided in file through the silent shadows under the great storied layering of dense hardwood trees. Exhausted from the perpetual anticipation and tension, I still had enough presence of mind to notice that there were no morning sounds. It was a time when there should have been the sounds of many birds. I was struck by the silence, and wondered if anyone else noticed.

The worst thing we had encountered in the forest was similar to P.F.C. Wordlow's earlier encounter with the nests of hanging colonies of red ants. Their nests were in the soil and leaf mold or in their massive balls high in the trees. This formidable predator, when triggered in passing by a vine or limb on the ground below, dropped in mass on whatever was below. This generally occurred if the weather was too hot, say near 100 degrees Fahrenheit, when the ants could be found in their massive balls. I often wondered if it wasn't just one female being "gang-banged" by the males like I had been taught in school. The thousands of hardy and prolific swarming red ants injured soldiers with their many bites from their curved, razor-sharp pincers. The large ants inspired much fear in the other soldiers. Those of us unlucky enough to be their target had to run ahead and quickly remove our web-gear and take off our jackets to shake them out. Their many bites and the strong smell of their formic acid was not soon forgotten. Those lucky enough not to be their targets watched incredulously as the ants virtually covered several men at the same time. The sight was awesome.

At night, if the temperature was above 55 degrees, they were out and about. When they were out in search of food, insects, small snakes, lizards and nesting birds, if you were lying close enough to a thickly lined ant trail, you could fall prey. The first warning was the smell of formic acid, then their chirping sound. Then if you disturbed them and listened closely, there was a noticeable whirring sound as their soldiers snapped their mandibles in the air. They could eat almost anything, including wood and leaves. On the few occasions I got caught, they bit the living hell out of me.

But now, the forest was quiet. Every aspect of the wilderness seemed intensified. Strangely, not one bird fluttered about. The usual social bird life and their melodious sounds were not there. Nothing flew above our heads. The air was heavy and expectant. The broken ground of the rugged ridges grew steeper and dense with trees, causing the wind to swirl in the morning updraft. At least the wind favored us. We seemed to blend with the dark colors and become a part of the wild, richly timbered woodland. Our many encounters with the NVA had induced a state of mind approaching paranoia, but with one difference: we knew it would happen again, soon. We stopped only to listen and watch the green-walled foliage and the deep grotesque shadows to ferret out the slightest movement and sound where the light and dark merged. The only movement was that of the wind and leaves.

We penetrated deeper into the forest. Its general appearance remained uniform as we ascended into rockier and rougher country. Visibility was down to fifteen yards. The ridges ran like washboards, walled with brush and rock and choked with dense bottom thickets, above which the leathery leaves of the lofty hardwood trees towered, blotting out the sun. It was hauntingly dark, still and lonely. Ridge after ridge we alternately climbed and descended along a crooked trail. Once more I sensed a menacing presence, just waiting for someone to make a mistake. Bending under the weight of ammunition, grenades, and our packs on our backs, we worked our toilsome way through thickets and thick-stemmed liana vines that twisted their tendrils from tree to tree and spread a network in our path. The physical discomfort of our mistreated, sleep-deprived bodies was overridden with more immediate thoughts. We had all accumulated a large sleep debt and suffered attention lapses.

Exhaustion

A frightening cacophony erupted as the cicadas continued to sing loudly. We stopped in the low ground. The forest had warned us. With that odd feeling of brooding danger, I lay back on my pack. I was panting on the verge of collapse, my ill body drained by stress, fever, hunger, sheer physical exhaustion and sleep deprivation. My back and legs screamed for relief. I was in a stupor, but knew I had to stay awake. My body fought for rest. I had trouble concentrating. My thinking had slowed and my attention span was gone. My vision was becoming blurred. I felt like being trapped in the nether world between sleep and reality.

The cumulative loss of sleep over a long period of time had now become a palpable danger to us. It had finally caught up with me, and had broken me down. I slipped into a paralytic slumber of total exhaustion. The cicadas' warning went ignored and I fell into a merciful unconsciousness in the middle of the trail.

The prickling of my senses gradually awakened me. I became aware that my chin was resting on my chest. In my foggy sleep, from beneath eyelids heavy with need of sleep, I saw vivid images of an ambush: as the mist cleared within my mind, I slowly awoke; men were firing at each other across the trail. It looked so real. It was real. Luckily, I must have looked dead to anyone who looked my way. There was the frenzied wail of men being torn apart. Blood was flowing freely. Men were instantly transformed, suffering intense physical pain. They were bloody and lifeless, their unseeing eyes staring up at the sky. Then it was over and we were moving back up to the high ground again. My mind was still numbed and groggy, after I was hurled from a deep sleep into panic. My responses were now impaired. Then someone was shaking me. I awoke. The ambush had not been reality. I really had been dreaming.

Utterly miserable and stiff in the joints, our bodies wanting, we headed slowly up the point of a steep shoulder to the top of the ridge. We followed a narrow trail, twisting and ducking. We worked around obstacles and through the latticework of hanging vines covered by giant trees whose interlacing branches formed a solid canopy overhead. The canopy crowned the brow of a precipice on both the left and right. The wild, lonely ridge was covered with growths of open understory that overlooked a deep mountain glen and many miles of richly forested mountains. All the other creatures of the jungle were silent, except for the cicadas. Suddenly, I wondered if the dream had been a warning. The path in the rain forest made it easier to walk without noise. It was narrow, but opened up the higher we went. Another platoon was leading. As we moved in file, we were painfully aware that we were in the least defensible formation. I had butterflies in my stomach.

The Mountain Top

I was at the head of my platoon just behind the lead platoon's last man. I couldn't believe my eyes and ears as we rounded a curve in the trail and ascended onto the top of the ridge. Here was the point man, faint of heart and coming unglued, losing his emotional self-control. His mind was unable to handle the stress, and now, broken with fear, he came running back through the formation from the platoon ahead of us and back through mine, yelling "VC, VC," and kept right on as if the devil were on his tail. Unknown to the rest of us, our company commander had placed a green private and a new replacement NCO on point. He had made a serious mistake.

Experience comes by making mistakes and usually good judgment grows from experience, but this takes years of development. Company commanders in Vietnam spent only a few months on the line before being rotated to another job. Therefore, there was a great lack of the good judgment that usually gives birth to wisdom. This was supposed to give a lot of officers combat time. Consequently, the professional infantrymen eternally suffered from these inexperienced officers and their leadership in the realities of the battlefield. I imagine the terrified private was stopped in the middle of the company by the company commander. I never had a chance to find out.

During our relief of the surrounded Tiger Force, I knew we would meet the NVA another day, soon. That day had not been long in coming. It was here, and now. The air seemed to be oppressed with a terrible charge. The roaring sound of automatic fire ahead engulfed us, breaking the silence. There was a rush of wind as the air came alive with the sound of flying lead. Bark and leaves fluttered down upon us as the dirt kicked up around us, all settling on us. I dropped to one knee and crouched at the ready. Now there was a breathless silence. My vision narrowed as I searched into the surrounding forest, tense and still. Another surprise encounter had just taken place. It came off badly due to inexperience, and we lost the initiative we needed. The point man had walked right up on a khaki-clad North Vietnamese infantryman looking out at a ninety-degree angle from the direction in which we were approaching on the trail. The NVA unit was dug in and holding in defense. Waiting.

The NVA were evidently expecting us to come cross-compartment through the forest terrain. The young point man merely turned and ran instead of firing at point-blank range. Gripped by panic and shock, he'd made a bad situation worse, increasing the danger to the other bewildered soldiers, who weren't aware of the immediate threat. The second man in the lead platoon was a new arrival, a buck sergeant I had taken the opportunity to meet because, like myself, he had a Japanese wife. Encountering the frightened point man, the NVA soldiers merely turned and killed the next man. The sergeant. His body was picked up by the force of the AK-47 rounds and thrown backward.

Several NVA soldiers were already positioned in the thick trees ahead and above us. My platoon went down to the ground, taking what available cover there was--mostly the base of the trees and the lip of the well-worn trail that covered the lower half of our prone bodies. Most of the lead platoon had already run back through us. My breathing became rapid and my pulse quickened. I experienced a heightened awareness, like a rush. I could hear my heart hammering in my ears. I was as low to the ground as I could make myself. The lower I was, the better I could see through the leafy trees. I turned my head and checked to my rear to make sure we had no skylight behind us. Luckily we were in the long shadows of the trees. My head and eyes could sweep the ground to my front without being seen too easily.

I concentrated on the area immediately ahead and to the sides, listening, eyes straining into the dark understory and foliage. Deafening automatic fire and clouds of acrid cordite filled the air. We fired into the area to allow the rest of the lead platoon to come back. With the smell of gunpowder and dust clogging my nostrils, I grew absorbed in my own part of the battle: the chattering sound of 7.62 mm Kalashnikov AK-47 assault rifles and SKS Siminov semi-automatic rifles to our sides and front. The sound of the battle was unbelievable.

The NVA snipers and lookouts were the ones to take us under fire. There was a period of silence. The mountain forest around us was still. Our eyes moved back and forth, searching for a target. One ashen-faced wounded soldier, his rib cage open and splattered with blood, was being quickly carried through to the rear. The unmistakable smell of fresh blood filled my nostrils. *More blood and death!* I remained frozen and very slowly eased my head up to look around. From the feel of the close smack of rounds, hitting near me before I heard them, and from the way the debris was being thrown up, I could tell that someone was above us. My eyes were right at ground level and I could see plenty of light through the trees above, but could not detect any movement above or on the ground. With the hair on my neck bristling, and feeling a cold dread, I searched hard into the foliage of the trees but could see nothing. I searched the ground shadows well ahead of me in the distance, but I could not see into the dense shadows. I slowly and cautiously maneuvered my position and searched the lighter patches. Now I saw shadowy forms and slight movement. I caught only glimpses of bobbing sleek black heads, flashes of tan uniforms, and glints of light reflected from rifle stocks and barrels, amid the crack and ricocheting of bullets. When possible, I directed my own fire at individual targets.

The Lead Element

My second platoon was now the lead element. We were all pinned down in the semi-open forest. Instead of boldly and speedily following his own senses, aggressively seizing the initiative and keeping our momentum by an envelopment with the platoons in the rear to keep the NVA off balance, the company commander was now calling for us to withdraw. At this point, a show of determination and purpose was needed, along with a frontal attack, since the enemy had little time to prepare. At this point we would have gained all control of the high ground since we were already on top, and we could have made a stand there. So much for independent initiative. This commander lacked the ruthlessness and determination essential to command. I guessed that the company commander was already worried about over-committing himself, and about what headquarters would think. He was already in contact with them, calling for air support and advice. Headquarters, fearing casualties, would be worried about the numbers, and would want to hold down our losses. Tactical flexibility in battle is lost when commanders are worried about taking the risks.

I wasn't too worried about the NVA on the ground--they could not see any better than we could. The snipers could probably see everything, but could not afford to expose themselves too long. I had gained a general idea where the sniper's bullets were coming from by watching the striking angle in the humus. A sniper fired one too many times when no one else was firing. My eyes traced his shots back. I concentrated my observation back along their path in the trees above, searching the areas of the trunks large enough to hide a man. I finally spotted a movement, catching a glimpse of the muzzle flash against the trunk of a tree as the weapon was fired through the branches. Well ahead to my front and above was an NVA khaki uniform, well within range. He was located about 50 yards ahead, up where the tree forked. He aimed and fired quickly. He was careless, because his silhouette was against the sky. The contrasting background of light behind him gave his body outline away when he moved to fire. Rounds from everywhere were cracking overhead and into the leafy humus around me. Luckily, the PAVN, like so many other soldiers when firing downhill, were firing too high.

I had seen him shift to the location where he kept his cover and concealment, where he could barely look at us. He was behind the left fork in the tree. My eyes were glued to that area as I alerted those around me, but they could not see anyone or anything. The NVA soldier in the tree stayed well under cover. Surprisingly, I was able to quickly find the correct tree trunk in the large aperture of my rear sight. The dark mountaintop now took on a grotesque appearance. I saw movement again, as he looked in our direction for a target in preparation to fire. I did not have much of a target, but took careful aim and fired at the position in the tree without seeing any results, except for a short scream of pain. At any rate, he knew someone had seen him. The air came alive with a roar of sound, as bullets slapped the trunks and branches around and over us. My heart was hammering in my chest and it seemed that all I could hear was my pulse. The rounds from the AK-47s, with their muzzle velocity of 2,330 feet per second, blew the bark off the trees and plowed straight into their trunks. We were in serious trouble. I searched the surrounding area as I moved to the edge of the hill.

Something moved in the darkness ahead, just over the lip of the hill. My heart quickened. I raised my head slightly. Suddenly, the soft sound of many scurrying feet and the rustle of branches. A crunching noise caught my ear, then the flash of motion of running NVA arrested my eye. Again, I heard the sound of quick feet scattering leaves. Through the drifting debris and smoke, I barely noticed the dim bare tops of the heads of two NVA caught in the sunlight just over the lip of the hill, swiftly slinking past back down behind us, like phantoms, on our left flank. The sound of the many feet told me there were a lot more of them than I had heard and seen. Taking advantage of all the suitable cover and concealment available, they were now flanking us and would soon move in behind us. We had to attack and seize the high ground or withdraw and reorganize on the hilltop to our rear. Either way we were going to be isolated and surrounded.

In the shadows of the great trees, these well-disciplined NVA seemed ghostlike and ethereal to me: unreal, seemingly everywhere at once, as rounds from their weapons flew by us. How many more there were, I didn't know. In almost total silence, they were quick and light-footed. I instantly realized they were going to envelop us. Without further hesitation, I told the men nearest to me to crawl back down the trail until they were under the crest from those above us. Bullets slapped off the tree next to me, ricocheting with a whine, while others thudded into the ground with a muffled thump, spraying me with leaf litter and dirt. Slowly, while firing and reloading, we inched backward at any let-up in the NVA fire. The NVA were too strong at this point. I knew that our situation was totally desperate. Intense fire caused our withdrawal. We backed off into the shadows, over the lip of the hill and out of their sights, momentarily. Now we had to hurry downward and up the next hill before they encircled us and attempted to split our force.

Wounded

A defensible position was chosen on top of the next hill and we now quickly organized our defense. The enemy, meanwhile, had the luxury of both time and the terrain to work slowly but persistently around our position. We knew there would be a counterattack. For just a bit of time, there existed in the forest an unexpected, eerie and menacing silence. Inevitable as destiny they loomed, now taking advantage of our commanders' timidity. The occasional quick glimpse of the khaki-uniformed NVA bobbing in and out of sight revealed how, in very little time, they had come down the steep rolling landscape, using the best-covered route, and then forward, following us toward the line of trees that hemmed the base of the hill. Now more NVA, with the scent of blood and battle fresh in their nostrils, were attracted by the firing and were seen creeping, bent over double, or on hands and knees, running where brush and foliage would not betray them. Then they disappeared, as if they had never been there. Nothing moved. They were closing in on us. Once again we were surrounded and facing down the barrels of the NVA. Charlie Company was about to fight for its life.

It had a chilling effect on our attached troops. I still remember seeing two of our attached engineers with their faces fixed in a rictus of terror; the unnatural pallor of their faces, white-lipped and shaking, surveying us with frightened, unnaturally round and wide eyes, racked with doubt and uncertainty. There was nothing ambiguous about what their faces communicated: pure fear. On the brink of panic, they seemed to be ineffective and useless, talking with a half-choked sobbing and crying with strangled gasps, while sucking hungry draughts of air. Still, they did not panic. Those engineers were desperately needed. In order to stem their panic, they were given something useful to do, like cutting timber down and widening an open area for a landing zone for helicopters to take out our wounded. They managed to stay in control. The faces of the men around me were also tight with tension. Our fear made us defiant. I was alerted that an air strike was going to take place any minute on the next forested hill.

Sporadic small-arms fire had broken out around the perimeter, amplified by the mountain ravines. The automatic-weapons and small arms fire reached a crescendo on the left flank. No sooner had it died than it rose and ceased and rose again. The first jet, glinting in the sun, streaked in, dropping two of its sinister-looking, six-foot-long napalm canisters too close to our position, and the gooey fuel hit several of our troopers in the splashdown. Napalm tanks don't always go where you want them to and sometimes a tank would literally fly. There was as much as a 70-yard distance between where two tanks released at the same time would hit. Piercing screams, were heard by most everyone. This close air strike with its napalm and 250-pound bombs would undoubtedly serve us well, even if it did cause friendly casualties. I could now hear and see the green tracers of the NVA's 12.7mm anti-aircraft machine guns streaking over our position, as bullets whistled and popped over us. The tracers were aiding the gunner in putting his rounds on an approaching target. One of the troopers yelled that he could just make out NVA moving below us. When I slowly turned and focused directly, straight out under the hill, I got a quick look at two khaki-clad soldiers trying their best to avoid being seen. Briefly exposed, they had melted back into the cover of the thick foliage. I could smell a smoke grenade. Then came the sound, a distinctive sound of popping blades, of a helicopter fast approaching for a landing back on the top of the hill. He was the target of the antiaircraft gunner. The smoke thickened and spread around the area.

I made a mistake and stood erect, directing the placement of one of my machine guns on the military crest, just far enough forward that I could see the bottom of the hill. I was pointing with my left arm when a bullet passed through it. I did not realize that I had been hit. It was merely an annoyance that I unconsciously scratched and rubbed and the palm of my hand came away bloody. When I looked down in surprise at my hand, I was in a state of amazement, for I had not felt anything. Blood was trickling down my arm, my sleeve was now wet. *I was wounded!* I had been hit in my left arm. At least it wasn't spurting blood!

It would take a short while for the pain to begin. The bullet had merely passed through the fleshy part of the back of my arm without hitting any bone. It had torn up the flesh a little. I wiggled my left hand experimentally. They responded a little slowly. The shot had been fired from somewhere to my front and to the right. I had said nothing about my wound, since there was very little pain or numbness. Evidently someone around me had said something, for I was soon ordered to report to the company commander back on the top of the hill. The captain appeared nervous and pale. He asked about the situation, and in a tone veined with disgust, I related it to him. He ordered me out on the next medical evacuation helicopter (medevac) to come in. I told the captain that I would stay, that he needed every man he had. I was told to go out. A low-flying helicopter was making a stealthy approach in the distance, racing in just above the trees. I felt that a bold initial envelopment on top of the ridge would have cost us fewer men and gained us the PAVN's high ground position. After seeing and talking to the captain, I now felt he lacked the cool objectivity and reflexes needed to handle the situation. You either knew what you were doing or you didn't. I was stripped of any confidence I had earlier had in him. It was FUBAR, "fucked up beyond all reality."

The medevac helicopter, known as "dustoff" to all the troops, was now on site and already full of wounded. The noise was tremendous as the downdraft from the blades whipped small branches and dirt in all directions. Weary with the toil and hunger, and grimy with sweat and blood, I sat down in the evacuation area with my back to a tree, and stared at the absolute waste of bloody, torn bodies. On the faces nearest me I saw nausea and pain. I noticed the medic trying to stanch the flow of blood: blood spurted, entrails oozed and steamed. His bloody hands worked rapidly, trying to stem the tide of death. His clothes were bloodstained, his face flecked with blood. Looking at the other wounded, some grotesque from bullet wounds, he quickly and expertly tore the brown paper package covers off the thick sterile battle-dressings. He had an intense responsibility. I watched the medic--uniform bloody, dirt and blood streaking his face--talking to each man, showing confidence and imparting faith. Many wrappings were already sodden, saturated with blood. The 3/4-inch-thick dressing would absorb the wounds' lost fluids, protect against infection, and cushion the wounds. He swabbed at a purple, oozing stomach wound. I stared at the soaked brownish film of the rectangular dressing pads on the exposed parts of the writhing, wounded bodies. Without these dressings covering their massive gunshot wounds, they could die.

A gray-faced trooper sitting up with a wound between his chest and shoulder had blood bubbling up at the corner of his wheezing mouth. I saw one soldier as his breathing became strained, intermittent; near death, he convulsed once, his feet kicked and he was dead. The trauma was magnified as three men quickly lumbered in with a wounded man, all flinching as bullets ricocheted with a whine, one man on each arm and one carrying the legs. The wounded man's head was slung back, wagging loosely in semi consciousness, mumbling in delirium. They set him down and were gone; as yet another urgent cry for a medic could be heard. These self-sacrificing medics, pushing the bounds of bravery, were primary targets, mainly because they were usually the only ones crouched upright, moving targets while going to the aid of someone else.

The next chopper landed quickly. One of the napalm-burned victims convulsed in agony. His breathing was very slow, rhythmic, to control his pain-racked body. I could hear his small weak voice. "Help me. Please." He was quickly carried to the waiting chopper. I watched the "dustoff" climb and the green tracers of the NVA anti-aircraft machine guns follow him. I prayed they would make it out safely. It was very plain that the communist soldiers did not respect the Red Cross. It was merely an aiming point. North Vietnam was not a signatory to the Geneva Convention in this respect. Thanks to the helicopter, most all of our wounded would survive, saved by quick delivery to the hospitals and the miracles of modern medicine.

I watched the nearest pale, white face going into arrest-- his breath, coming in short, shallow, irregular spurts, suddenly had stopped. I saw the first frightened reaction of the medic's face. I felt an impulse come over me to help. I managed to get a hold on myself and started to get up. Seconds for that soldier were now vital. The medic, however, responded quickly and efficiently by pinching his nose, then blowing into his mouth, filling his lungs, letting out the pressure and inflating them again. I settled back. I watched as the medic worked and the wounded soldier responded. The air was filled with the smell of blood and bowels released in death. My wound and my head had begun to throb, but it did not seem to matter.

A nearby trooper lay on his back, his shirt open, no bandage: he was dead. A small black-bloody hole in the upper right part of the abdominal cavity indicated a hit in the liver.

My left arm and hand still responded. I could move them properly. I was a little frustrated because I was now so weak. The fever, and now the loss of blood, left my whole body exhausted. I had hardly slept for days, and my body was crying out for rest. I looked up and saw that the clouds were breaking away, showing blue sky. I heard the distant sound of rotor blades coming toward us. A smoke grenade was popped. Another brave helicopter crew was flying in fast and straight, unwavering, in our direction. From the sound of the approach, I could tell he was probably flying at 120 miles per hour. The pungent odor of the drifting smoke, the clattering sound of disorganized automatic fire from the NVA's 7.62 cal. AK-47s Kalashnikov assault rifles and grenade explosions were now building up stronger. The green NVA .51 caliber tracers were again working the sky. Suddenly, from the volume of sound, I knew he had dropped down to treetop level for his final approach. The "dustoff" came in fast, the pilot lifting the

Huey's nose and dropping its tail; flaring to lose speed, quickly turning, the rotor wash of disturbed air was causing the trees and bushes to whip violently back and forth, as he settled to the ground. Whoever he was, he was an excellent pilot. His rotors continued to turn; he was now facing the proper direction for a fast departure. The sound of sporadic firing was slowly turning into a raging battle. The fear, dust, and smoke had suddenly made me very thirsty.

Evacuation

The helicopter's rotary wings turned faster and faster, the turbine roared, the power grew, causing the Huey to tremble and shudder as the engine labored. I felt a wet spray and checked myself and noticed spots of blood. The wind draft blew streaks of blood around the inside of the helicopter from the dead on the floor from the downdraft of the blades. The vibration of the tortured machinery reverberated through me. Finally, the pilot had pulled pitch, nose lifted a few feet off the ground, and then we rose straight up, the rotors clawing for altitude. I stiffened up in the seat, waiting for the impact of rounds to come. It would only take seconds to gain altitude, leaving us difficult to track with automatic weapons. I heard the loud pop, pop, popping of the .51 caliber rounds, and saw the bright flash of their passing. The North Vietnamese anti-aircraft heavy machine guns were now shooting at my ship.

Terrified, I watched as another sudden stream of green tracers went by. In an aircraft, you never see most of the rounds fired at you unless it is hit or they are close enough to hear. I had no trouble hearing and seeing the streams of tracers. There were any number of metallic ticks of small arms rounds going through the skin of the helicopter. I tightly adjusted the seat belt again, in case we went down. A cold shiver of apprehension slipped down my spine, my gut tightened. I felt so vulnerable. I felt and heard my heart pounding in my chest and throat. Then the Huey pulled pitch, dipped its nose and accelerated, making a long, low run forward to avoid the fire directed at us.

As we gradually lost altitude, we built up enough air speed and then climbed up very quickly. It seemed to take forever to get clear of the range of small arms and the anti-aircraft guns, but it was only seconds. Then we were gone, away from the killing ground. I knew I had been lucky, again. He was a good pilot.

Constant battles would rage over this terrain with other infantrymen. It would be another two years and eleven months before the experiences of another unit, the 173rd Airborne, here at Dac To, would enter people's consciousness.

At altitude, it was cool and quiet. The sky was a cloudless blue. Now I could see how the landing zone was hemmed in by the immense, lofty mountain masses, stretching out below the helicopter as far as I could see. A primal forest covered the mountainsides and valleys. I watched range upon range of a vast sea of silent green loneliness of wilderness as we sped away. I had gotten out of the shadows of the unbroken forest alive. Its images were locked in my mind. It was over, for now. My thoughts were filled with fear and dreaded doubt for those left behind. I pondered the grim reality of what lay ahead for them, wondered how many old faces I would see, if and when I eventually returned. Many were to die; the outlying mountains surrounding Dac To had become a dark and bloody ground.

Battalion Aid Station

We quickly approached the 1-327 Battalion aid station tucked between green, rolling hills. I watched through the open door as we came closer to the landing zone area. We dropped and flared, and the helicopter changed its pitch as we began to descend. Then it lowered itself gently to the ground. Army medical line units, being able to move at any time, were deployed into our operational area. I had first been evacuated to our battalion aid station. It was here that vital surgery was performed to stabilize and save critical cases.

The ordeal of the wounded was by no means over when they had reached the battalion aid station--it was just beginning. The wounded inside the hospital tents had their hemorrhaging brought under control by tying off the bleeder vessels and being hooked up to intravenous fluids or plasma, or both. I could hear someone unconscious, raving and calling out in delirium. As soon as each patient was stabilized, he would wait his turn to be evacuated by helicopter to Pleiku and the network of the many hospitals throughout Vietnam. The aid station was overflowing with badly wounded troops, waiting for treatment. Those whose ghastly wounds were too complicated for the overworked surgeons were sent out as quickly as it took to get a chopper in. They would linger in the dark tent, their faces whitening with the pallor of coming death. I detected the pathogenic odor of decomposition, a mixture of septic wounds, an acidic, sickly, and fetid smell arousing nausea in me. How many would die before reaching the hospital would never be known. I could wait, and that is what I did.

My wound had initially been attended to. It was washed, disinfected and wrapped, and then my arm was put into a sling to immobilize it. An unknown sergeant walked up to me and handed me an ice-cold soft drink. A can of Coca Cola. I sat down and appreciated this simple elemental pleasure. I fastened my mouth on the top of the can and took two eager swallows. My stomach told me that it was not going to handle it too well. I felt bloated. My stomach had shrunk considerably. I sat there for some time, just feeling that wonderful cold feeling on my hands and face, and sipping on it until it was gone. My mind slowly settled. I felt much better. Now I would wait until transportation was provided to evacuate me beyond the combat zone. I sat staring at the dead, a leaden sensation at the back of my throat. I felt a quiet communion with them.

I rested and remained waiting in the pickup area. I observed the new replacements and their attitude of watchful waiting with a sense of foreboding until I decided they really needed someone to talk to. I could see the graying fear written clearly on their youthful faces. I spent the rest of my time talking to the new replacements, who were waiting to go out to the line units, trying to ease their fears. They were visibly frightened. They were getting their first truly religious experience. For some, sadly, it would be their last. I heard the whopping sound of a number of slicks approaching at a more normal speed, and watched the faces of the replacements as the Hueys were landing individually in the small landing zone.

The dead were unceremoniously thrown off on to the ground from each helicopter as if they were so many bags of feed, some already cold and stiff, their skin already turned a unique shade of green-gray. I felt the muscle at my temple pulsing. This aroused great resentment in me that turned to a silent anger, but I knew the helicopter crews were hard pressed for time to support all the units in trouble. They had a difficult job to do. In between helicopter landings, the bluebottle flies collected and fed on the dead and laid their eggs. Each bloodied body lay mute against the darkening ground. I could smell the light, floral sulfur release of gases. The replacements were shocked at the many dead American bodies and their rough treatment, their first full scent of death and decay. The terror-filled facial expressions of some wounded, accompanied by the pained, anxious expressions of others, had their terrifying effect on the staring replacements. Their faces blanched in a fixed consternation as they received their first true visceral flash of warning of what lay ahead of them. The sweet smell of blood spread over the area.

Then the signal was given for the new replacements to load. Their eyes had a wild, distraught look, and they hesitated before loading; the helicopter floor was covered in blood, and it ran in fresh red rivulets off the frame of the doorway. With visibly trembling hands and legs, the replacements began to load. I saw the graying fear written clearly on their youthful faces. In the helicopter, filled to capacity, some of the replacements had to sit on the floor in the blood.

Loaded first were the critical cases requiring more extensive care. Finally it to came our turn, the walking wounded. In the chain of evacuation, we were flown to Pleiku, where we remained overnight.[1] Our wounds were cleaned and debrided. Then we were loaded on a C-123 and flown to the complex at Cam Ranh Bay, which was one of the best-defended areas in South Vietnam. This was the home of the 12th Tactical Air Wing. Cam Ranh Bay in Khanh Hoa Province, south of Nha Trang, is located 180 miles northeast of Saigon. It was home to the U.S. Army's First Logistical

Command, which supplied some 72,000 American troops in the southern half of II Corps. I would learn much later that the harbor anchorage's there were even protected by the U. S. Navy's specially trained and equipped killer dolphins. We were loaded on buses for the trip to the 6th Convalescent Center.[2] This unit, under the 43rd Medical Group, had just arrived and become operational. The 6th provided the facilities for convalescent care and physical reconditioning of the wounded and sick, with well over one thousand beds. By this time I no longer had an appetite because food made me sick, and my head ached the whole way. We traveled almost blindly, moody, suffering from delayed shock.

On 13 June 1966, with the infantry withdrawn to Dac To, the commander of the 1st Brigade, 101st Airborne Division, assessed the approximate center of the PAVN operational area and gassed it, just minutes before the earth-shattering explosions of a massive B-52 raid took place. The infantry again launched into the area and tried to police up what was left. The PAVN had temporarily withdrawn for the time being. Operation HAWTHORNE was terminated on 20 June 1966, after the 24th NVA Regiment withdrew across the border into Laos. It was officially reported that only 239 members of the 1st Brigade, 101st Airborne Division, had been wounded and 48 killed in action.

The Hospital

I turned in my seat and faced the center aisle in preparation for getting off. With a tremendous effort, I attempted to stand. For a moment there was a sudden blackness that descended upon me. My ears rang. My dizziness became so intense that I could not remain standing without holding on to the backs of the seats on both sides of the aisle. I sat awhile, exploring the edge of my physical capability. Again, I slowly tried to get up and managed. I tottered on my unsteady legs. My head swam to stand there a few minutes until the vertigo went away. Looking at the long-unshaven men waiting to get off, I noticed their haunted, ashen faces with a dark, somber cast, scared young innocents showing signs of being anxious, overexcited, worried and depressed. Their inwardly suffering wounded and aching, tired bodies were now in need of medical care and rest.

No longer was there a fiery arrogance to be seen in them as their ragged, thin and pale, slouching ranks began to move off the bus. Many faces were pointed, liver-colored and contorted with caved cheeks from weeks of unending fatigue. Their hollowed, sunken eyes, tired and pinched at the corners, had whites that were too sallow for health. Their teeth were loose like mine. Some had spongy gums that were touchy; evident by the way they kept a hand to their mouth, fearing they would lose their teeth. Emotional damage from the horrors and sudden shocks and prolonged strain of combat had occurred in everyone. It had been weeks since we had bathed or shaved. Our clothes were sweat-stained, ragged and torn. Fever's moisture beaded on foreheads and necks.

For a minute, I caught the look in the eyes of the staff as they took their first darting, examining look at us. The moldy stench exuded by our uniforms aroused a brief noticeable revulsion. I'm sure they saw us exactly as we were, as underfed, filthy bundle of rags who desperately needed their attention. Then the look was gone as they quickly went about the job of attending to us very professionally. In addition to being wounded, most of us were desperately sick from exposure, and from all manner of illnesses, fevers of unknown origin (FOUO), dysentery, malaria, and typhus. We looked older than we were, and smelled badly.

The Ward

We were deathly tired, too utterly bone-weary with fatigue to do anymore than collapse into the beds and fall asleep. After we were buck-naked in the clean beds, we were all washed laboriously by hand. I watched the nurses' faces and could see them physically assessing each patient. It took a long time to clean us; our bodies were caked with black grime. It was startling to see yourself become white under the cloth of the medical personnel. They checked our skin for any breakdown; there were a lot of problems, mainly jungle rot that formed new sores and scabs wherever it drained onto uninfected skin. The doctors slowly poured a clear solution onto the bloody crust of the stiffened bandages and then slowly pulled back. The fresh-formed scabs were stuck to the old dressings. The scabbed wounds came away with the dressings inch by inch. Together, the staff labored with a devotion borne from compassion as the patient stiffened and hissed with agony. The ward exuded a strong, fetid odor of dried blood and disinfectants. I detected the sweet smell of the nurses as they watched each man's face for the faintest sign of pain, their faces contorting in sympathy with the patient. Each man would moan and cry from the excruciating pain of the ripped, drying raw nerve endings that made up the newborn flesh of their wounds where blood had coagulated. Other dressings were pulled back from the stench of wet sticky wounds. The face of each man, in turn, especially of the more seriously wounded, twisted with their desperate assertions in their beds. I noticed that the soldier next to me had fouled himself. The nurses and doctors, instead of trying not to breathe, were using their noses to smell. I was to learn that the medical personnel smelled the stool, for a byproduct of bleeding into the gastrointestinal tract, a sign of an undiagnosed wound. Blood has a distinct odor. Even if they couldn't see it, the doctors could smell it.

As I watched the medical team move from patient to patient, giving physical examinations--checking pain, temperature, pulse, blood pressure and respiration--I observed the ashen faces of the patients, contorted with agony. Bandages were dried and stuck to the wounds. Men with the large wounds trembled. They gritted their teeth, keeping their eyes tightly closed while tearing, some crying from rising spasms of pain brought on by the lifting of bandages stuck to the wounds. At that moment, nothing existed except for absolute and intense pain.

They were always fighting for their breath. I could hear one man crying out as he sobbed and his chest fluttered "Please, oh God---no, no, wait, stop!" Some oozing wounds were taking longer to heal because infection had taken its toll on them. But bandages were being changed. The raw, angry flesh that was slower to heal was rewrapped in clean surgical dressings. Many in this ward could not move their limbs more than a few trembling inches; the healing skin was so tight. This process of changing dressings would be repeated many times in the hospital. Finally, the last soggy dressing came away and the nurses left us. My brain relaxed and my spirit became tranquil: now, for a short time, life was not a battlefield.

I don't even remember my first night in the hospital; we slept like the dead. I had drifted into sleep so deep even dreams were shut out. We had accumulated a large sleep debt and must have slept more than twelve hours, for it was near the end of the next day when my eyes opened. I had to urinate badly. A beautiful young nurse helped me. I awoke with I.V. tubes in each of my arms. My blood was drawn to be tested. Finally, I had a blood smear taken.

I well remember my second night. For once, I was sleeping very soundly. A harsh, dry crying woke me in the night. My hands had been slowly searching for my weapon. They found nothing. Breathless and hardly daring to breathe, I lay there in the dark, listening, confused and unsure of where I was or what was happening. My heart hammered in my ears. The despair came rushing back to me. I lay there shaking and listening. I dreaded to look around. I was in that place where nightmares and reality become indistinguishable. I don't know how long I'd laid there, before the sleep went out of me and I could figure out what the noise was. Then, I realized the air was pleasantly warm and had the tangy smell of salt. I had been startled awake with a sudden jump by the wounded patient in the bed next to me. He was crying out hoarsely in his sleep, his voice quaking and curdled with horror. Slowly I realized where I was. I was safe. I was in the hospital. I was in a bed. I choked and my eyes began to pool, and then the tears of misery rolled down my face at the relief. Safe.

I lay there for a while, with my eyes shut, awash in memory. Then I relaxed. I was so comfortable. I listened in the dark and realized that any number of the men in this ward, in their painful delirium, were also dreaming and reliving the vivid horror--the terror of their hideous nightmare experiences, photographed in their memories for all time. Someone was always tormented by nightmares, sitting upright and rigid, eyes wide but unseeing and calling for something or someone. Their slumbered cries always reminded us of men back in the blood and smoke of the mountains, reliving their experiences. Men frightened and alone. Men hit and bleeding. They were calling out for someone to help them in the dark. Another man was sobbing in the far end of the ward, dreaming of ceaseless flight from some unidentifiable pursuer. Nightmares made some men afraid to go to sleep. For the first time, I realized that we were not only suffering physically, but also emotionally from the weight of trauma and loss of friends. This was damage that no amount of medical attention could ever again heal us from. My soul hurt.

Then came the hours I dreaded, when the silence and solitude would fall oppressively on me. The hospital was a fearful place at night. It was always so dark that one was afraid to go to sleep, afraid to dream the dreams. Those who were awake listened to the wild talk of those that did sleep. We could not escape the haunting shadows of our minds. The only light, in the opposite ward, a small light, shone from where the night nurse was on duty. For those who could turn their bodies and head, the pallid light could barely be seen. We were only aware that it was there because we were told it was there. It must have been some comfort for those on the other side of the ward. Now and then, someone would be heard making the rounds quietly in the dark, moving from ward to ward, and then would briefly be seen with a small light. Finally, I became warm and drowsy and fell into a deep sleep.

Doctors' Rounds

Everyday was followed by doctors' and nurses' rounds. They checked the four vital signs: temperature, pulse, respiration and blood pressure. They were always talking to us and asking how we felt and if we were experiencing any pain or other symptoms. It would be well after daylight when I awoke. None of the on-duty staff had arrived yet, but we all knew it was time to change bloody bandages again. The first man next to me was slowly rolling his wild, wide eyes, registering his immense fear. He had already started crying again, afraid and suffering the anxiety of the pain to come. The pain would be caused by slowly ripping the last bandage, saturated with dried scabs, away from the extensive debridement of his wounds. He had two large gaping wounds. Each day, as the layers were removed, the wounds beneath were growing smaller, and pink, healthy flesh was revealed.

Each of us suffered each man's pain. Others began to whimper. A few minutes before changing bandages, several nurses who had assessed the level and characteristic of pain in every patient would come in a little early to hold the hand of the first few men, to comfort them as they began to whimper and cry. It was said that this positive nurturing stimulated the release of the body's natural pain suppressors, known as endorphins. Then the doctors arrived. I would watch as they slowly poured a solution onto the smelly dressings to ease the tearing of the scab before they lifted them off. I watched their hands flutter over the crusted bandages with gentleness, trying not to tear the new skin. Sweating faces were twisted with pain. The patients pleaded, tears streaming from their eyes. Then I would see their faces suddenly show restraint, as they sucked in air in shallow breaths, gasping in pain, summoning their strength to keep from crying out. I wrinkled my nose as an odor swept over me.

From the puffed area and the throbbing, many of the men knew that when the bandages were removed, it might reveal more inflammation and swelling that had redeveloped. Fever always threatened. It meant that another instrument would be used upon them to cut open and drain the infected area. I recovered slowly from my wound. My left arm and hand still responded. I could move the fingers properly. I could not effectively use the arm, though it was possible to move it a little. I still had the fever. Each visit left me with a headache. We were in agony most of the time, except for when we fell asleep with exhaustion.

The Forgotten Blood Smear

I woke with a chill and an uncontrollable shaking. I could not catch a good breath. I could not call out. My muscles shook like jelly and I could not control my body. I found it very difficult to breathe. I tried to force myself to breathe. I knew that unless someone helped me, I would die. I needed air. I tried to swing my legs from the bed, but only succeeded in slumping back against my pillow, as sweat popped out on my face. When you need your body to work, you make it work. With great effort I rolled myself to the edge of the bed and let my body drop onto the floor. I managed to pull myself to my feet with my weakened arms. I realized that my body wasn't going to give out. I managed to hold on to the bed and get my feet under me. Panting for breath and feeling faint, I managed to move on wobbly knees that threatened to fold unexpectedly at any moment, staggering from bed to bed to the doorway frame. From my hut, I tottered and stumbled across the boardwalk and into the next tent, where the night nurse was stationed.

    It took all my effort to keep from falling. If I fell, I didn't know if I would get back up. It was very dark and there was only one small weak light on in the ward. It was now only a matter of feet to the desk. The small light was ghostly on the night nurse's desk. She was talking to one of the male medics when she heard me and looked up. The look that twisted her face startled the medic. As I slowly emerged and approached into the light, bent and shaking, the night nurse stood and stifled a scream. The medic jumped up and supported me so that I wouldn't fall. He told the nurse it was O.K. that he would take care of me. He picked me up in his arms and carried me back to my bed. I told him I could hardly breathe. He told me to just try to relax and he would help. A thermometer found its way into my mouth, which was followed by instructions not to let my mouth close. My teeth rattled on it, but I managed not to break it. He stayed and rubbed my neck, shoulders and back to relieve the tenseness, until I relaxed and was able to breathe normally. The massage helped reduce my heart rate and lower my blood pressure. At last, I fell into the deep, dreamless sleep of total exhaustion. I never saw that medic again to thank him. The two on-duty nurses, however, had failed to take my blood for a blood smear at the critical time of the raging fever. Identification of what was really wrong had escaped them. My blood was drawn again in the morning when the doctors came on duty for testing. It was then studied with the use of a centrifuge, microscopes and a blood-count machine in the laboratory. Nothing that they knew of was identified.

The days and nights passed. Permitted only to sleep, we slept most of the days and nights, interrupted only by the body's need to urinate or defecate, by pain, by the other discomforts of illness, or by our terrible dreams. We received no mail during this time, except a letter from General Pearson, the Division Commander, acknowledging the fact that we were wounded and hoping we would be returned to duty soon. Each night, upon awakening I was always afraid to close my eyes again, afraid of the horrific dreams. Much of the night was spent thinking and listening until becoming exhausted, and again dropping off to sleep. Periodically I would awake from a dream. In these fevered dreams, the images of the NVA--the individual faces and the equipment--had been so real, and the feelings I had experienced were so clear that I found myself sweating and my heart pounding.

Many times the NVA were just moving bushes; they were well camouflaged, as they were in reality throughout the war. It always seemed that there were more NVA in my dreams than we could handle, and just before the end of me, as they approached with light reflecting off their bayonets, I would come awake suddenly. Upon awakening, I was frozen, listening, until I became aware of where I was. This dream would remain with me for many years. Always a nurse was close by, watching us. I was alive and safe. Tears would roll down my face as she smiled at me. In the ward you could always hear those others at night who were swallowed up by the nightmares behind their flittering eyelids.

The Air-Conditioned Ward

Late one night, I awoke shaking. I had no control of my muscles. A watching nurse took my temperature. It was 106 degrees and spiking. A body temperature of 107 is nearly always fatal. They quickly rubbed me down with rubbing alcohol mixed with water. I was carried to a tub, my robe quickly removed, and gently lowered into it. I was frightened. Then three different people were dumping ice cubes into the tub until I was completely covered with ice except for my head. I knew that if my brain cooked off, I would be left a vegetable. After a while, I began to cry because I was so cold. It was more than I could bear. The doctor told me to bear it. I told him I was. I felt I was being tortured. The hospital had only two air-conditioned wards. They transported me there and put me into a bed under the air-conditioner. They turned it on full blast and also turned the vents so all the air hit me. My I.V.s were re-inserted, and there I was left, with a nurse on watch.

Eventually my arms began to ache. The I.V.s in each vein of my arms had begun to ache from the point of insertion to under my armpit. They felt hard, as if they had turned to wood. I begged for them to be taken out. Eventually one was. At least in this ward I didn't have to listen to the suffering from intense pain, because the men's moans were quieted by the pain-obliterating drip of morphine. A powerful painkiller, morphine was usually avoided for fear it would cause respiratory failure and death.

Each day was the same. Not daring to stretch the tender arm too much, I lay in my bed, listening and watching. The dreaded time would eventually come. The other men, in turn, tried to be brave only to be betrayed by the slight, silent tremble as they shuddered with sobs at the lifting of the dried scabby bandages covering their wounds. Some would watch, but most tried not to. Everyone could hear. Their pillows were wet from their translucent fear running from the corners of their eyes. Their turn was coming.

I was growing stronger. As I recovered, I grew restless. My need for rest was still present, but the periods of sleep were shorter and less frequent. I always seemed at my best in the morning, after a night's sleep. I became more impatient with the frustration that I now faced, thinking of returning to my unit in the field. I had had enough and did not want to return to the war. As the days passed, I had eventually been given permission to get up and walk around for exercise and keep my hospital wristband on. My muscles were atrophying and needed exercise. Some men just disappeared from the wards forever.

It was pleasant for me to go out into the sunlight. I stood there, watching the clouds, feeling the wind and sun on my face, and slowly moving toward the latrine with my left hand gripping the silver pole of the IV stand. The wheels squeaked of my approach. The container of glucose was still attached to my forearm. Generally, when I came back from the latrine, I looked in the tent at the corner of the boardwalk, where those who had just died in the hospital were taken. I usually only saw a tagged toe. Now and then, I would see a complete body. No one was ever around or in the tent. They were always alone and unattended. One day I was shocked to see a black soldier in this tent. I had just talked to him while using the latrine. He smiled when he left. He had collapsed and died while walking back to his ward. It was depressing. I swallowed hard. I felt as if no one cared. I would stare at the sky and watch the clouds to close my mind to the image of tagged toes.

Eventually the raw, red flesh around our wounds became new, pink skin that could gently stretch more each day. Finally, I was told that I could go to the Air Force mess hall, eat and come back. Patients, not experiencing pain rehabilitate faster if they are able to get up and walk, causing them to breathe deeper. I went out and discovered an incredibly beautiful day. The air was crystal clear and hot. I went to the latrine to shave and wash before taking the walk. I put my few toilet articles down on the shelf above the basin and looked into the mirror. I saw a much older man. Wrinkles creased the skin on my cheeks, and there were crow's feet around my eyelids, and new lines etched deeply into my forehead and the corners of my mouth. My face had subtly changed with lines of pain and worry. I was twenty-eight years old when I had first left for the war. Now, at the age of 31, my hair was already white. There was no way to go back, to heal the early aging process. Worse, I knew that eventually I would be going back to the line unit again.

As I walked, I noticed the heat for the first time. Cam Ranh Bay was all sand--mountains of it. I was extremely weak from lying in bed for so long without exercise, and the heat didn't help. I had to stop frequently on my short journey to the mess. I really enjoyed the freedom of the walk. As I entered the mess hall, the pleasant but acrid scent of the coffee came to my nostrils. I wanted to enjoy a good meal. I would be served anything I wanted. I remembered my daydreams of food in the mountains. The pleasing sight of so much food was too much. Tears came down my face as the cooks stared at me.

As I sat slowly eating, I watched the fresh young faces around me and listened to their conversation. I realized that their concerns consisted of the normal everyday interactions of their jobs, their trips off base to town and places and activities back in the United States. How different! Only a short distance away, men lay in bed, living their nightmares, brought back to reality only by the daily routine of the nurses and doctors and the changing of bandages, men wanting only to escape the agony and suffering of the metal tweezers pulling away the dead skin from their wounds.

I finished eating and just sat there being entertained by the activities of the mess hall. I didn't want to go back to the hospital, but had nowhere else to go. I realized from watching these young men that I had lost a lot of my physical sensation, that something dark had entered my soul forever. I began to feel lightheaded and knew that I had to go back. After returning to the hospital, the nurse asked me how I felt. I told her the truth and was told to get in bed and stay there. No more walks. For once, I slept the sleep of an exhausted and well-fed man.

The Good News and the Bad News

I spent 33 days in the hospital. Upon being released, I weighed 140 pounds and was told by the doctor that they could not identify the fever that I had. So it went into my medical records as FOUO (Fever of Unknown Origin). The doctor told me never to volunteer my blood for anything. The good news was that I was cured for the immediate future of the rot and corruption of the mountain jungle. I wanted to resume a normal life. I wasn't entirely happy about leaving, however, besides not wanting to go back to the mountains, I felt they were discharging me too soon. I was not combat effective. But then, I was just a lowly enlisted man. After 33 days in the hospital without any mail, I felt abandoned and was very much feeling sorry for myself. I had received one letter, dated 11 June 1966, from Brigadier General Willard Pearson, the commanding general of the 1st Brigade, wishing me a speedy recovery. I knew in Special Forces that if I had been a suspected malaria case, I would have been hospitalized for a full six weeks. The bad news was that I was going back to the mountains again, and that of the four types of malaria, the nonfatal types can hide in the body outside the liver for up to 30 or 40 years, waiting for some unknown signal to trigger its emergence and cause a recurrence of symptoms. My fever had proven vexing and mysterious, and the doctors never diagnosed it. However, I did learn from the hospital staff of a little known viral disease called chikungunya that infected many of the troops.

It was mid-July, and with several inches of clean, pink puckered scar tissue, I was going back to my line unit. Again, I felt the old fear grab at me. I felt trapped. I had fought my mental and physical pain, and now it was time to face cunning and cruel reality. The superbly trained medical personnel and staff of the 6th Convalescent Center had done a terrific job in caring for all of us. They had eased the pain and saved my life, and had treated me well. Still sick, with a mysterious fever that defied explanation and took its toll on my mind and body, I was transported back to my unit and immediately inserted back into my company in the mountains north of Tuy Hoa. I was finding that trying to overcome the physical and mental challenges was becoming insurmountable.

Attack on the Hospital

Sometime later, after I left, I had heard that the hospital complex at Cam Ranh Bay had been attacked and that there had been a large loss of life among the staff and wounded personnel. Communist forces had attacked, killed two patients, and wounded 99 others, running through the wards and placing satchel charges.

I was back to living on the edge, where the world consisted of nothing but suffering and trying to survive. The company was then engaged in "Operation John Paul Jones" to secure Vung Ro Bay, the highway north out of Tuy Hoa, and the rice harvest in Phu Yen Province. This operation ended in early September.

Footnotes:

1. The 71st Evacuation Hospital, stationed at Pleiku near the Cambodian border, provided hospitalization for all classes of patients and prepared patients for evacuation to other medical facilities. The hospital inspired the television show "China Beach."

2. The 6th Convalescent Center at Cam Ranh Bay was a complex of Quonset huts. It provided convalescent care and physical reconditioning for wounded personnel.

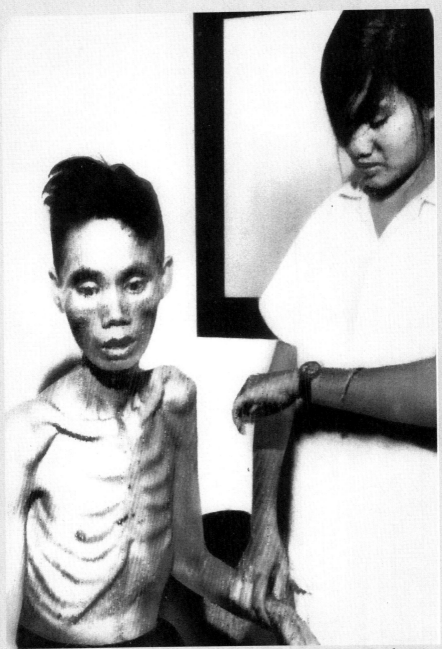

Prisoners Liberated During the Phu Yen Prison Raid

**Hope-drained men become meat
with bowed heads, greeting death
as father and friend. Discarded
souls in overgrown mountain graves
beg to be remembered.**

Author

CHAPTER 13

THE PHU YEN PRISON RAID

The prison camp was shrouded in mist and clouds on a small, level place atop the ridge. The tall trees with thick dark trunks and large spreading branches formed an almost impenetrable darkness, beneath the canopy that blocked out any light of the tropical monsoon. The well-camouflaged camp was made only of materials found locally, and could not be seen from above.

There were three open-air cages that could easily accommodate thirty prisoners per cage. They were built up off the ground, similar to a small house, but they were not designed for comfort. The camp was constructed in order to force the occupants to live in the open. Each large cage had a solid teak frame, with corner posts made from stripped and squared tree trunks, solidly planted in the ground. The floors and walls were made of two-inch saplings with about three-inch separations, and the roof was made of palm leaf thatch.

All the construction of the wood had hand-cut locking joints. The wooden bars of the floors and walls had natural bindings made from thin, soft pliant fiber green strips. The strips had been cut from the bark of green saplings, softened by pounding then cut and peeled off. These were strapped around the poles that formed the bars, where they crossed over the larger stronger supports. As the binding strips dried, they became tight and strong.

The guards could see everything that went on inside the camp. Only the close sides of the mountain ridge that went down in every direction from the camp, except the south side, where the spine of the ridge continued on, limited their vision. The prison contained some fifty prisoners. Its purpose was to indoctrinate the people with the communist's unworkable ideology at the point of a bayonet. They isolated severely weakened prisoners, already in a state of depression, to obtain information and confessions, to indoctrinate and compel them to inform on other prisoners and, in all too many cases, to kill them or let them die as an example to others.

On 22 September 1966, under the cover of darkness, former Popular Force (PF) PFC Hoang Kim Chinh, 31, and a friend escaped. They'd been prisoners for just over a year and a half. The Popular Forces were a South Vietnamese Army Territorial Force, a countrywide outpost system, manning critical points. They were known to the Americans as "Ruff-Puffs." The area the two men moved through was covered with long golden-brown grass that extended well out into the valley. Under normal circumstances, the sight of the valley, surrounded by mountains, filled with the waving, two-foot tall green stalks, and their heavy golden heads bowed with kernels, would have been beautiful to behold. While they made their way down the densely wooded mountain ridge to the valley's unworked area, Chinh's friend quickly fell behind and became lost.

Chinh was heading straight across the valley, past scattered, distant villages, to the worked area of ripe rice paddies, when he was spotted from the air by an American helicopter. The officers in the helicopter directed the pilot in for a closer look and found a man with his hands held in surrender, a surrender leaflet fluttering in one hand. He was immediately flown to our area for interrogation. Popular Force's soldiers serving with our unit recognized him and verified that he had worked as a clerk in Hieu Xuong District Headquarters. During the interrogation, he related how he had gone to visit his family, and had been taken prisoner by the Viet Cong, who had been watching his house. He had been given a trial and sentenced to four years imprisonment for serving the government of South Vietnam.

The following day found us 200 miles northeast of Saigon in the upper end of the Hieu Xuong Valley, the southernmost district of Phu Yen province, participating in Operation Seward. The mission was to protect the rice harvest and conduct search and destroy operations.

The valley runs inland from the coast at Tuy Hoa. The small town of Tuy Hoa is located between Nha Trang and Qui Nhon cities, and is the capital of Phu Yen province. We had relieved the 28th Infantry Regiment, the Republic of Korea's famed 9th Infantry Division (White Horse).

Our Worst Enemies

When it rained, the mosquitoes were active night and day descending on us in a sopranic cloud of misery. The lowland Aedes Aegypt mosquito transmitted Dengue fever, a common viral disease, for which there is no cure or vaccine. We had lost a lot of men due to one kind of debilitating sickness or another, but dengue fever was the most common.

Its nickname is "breakbone fever." In its mild form, it was accompanied by excruciating and agonizing bone pain, high fever, rashes, severe headache, eye pain, nausea, vomiting and painfully disabling muscle and joint spasms that would last several weeks. After the onset of the fever, if you weren't sure what you had, all you had to do was check for the telltale small red spots four days after you felt bad. The organism required the living cells of a host organism in order to multiply. It usually lasted around two weeks, sometimes longer. A subsequent infection could lead to dengue hemorrhagic fever or

Dengue shock syndrome, which caused soldiers to bleed from the mouth, nose and gums. This could lead to a circulatory collapse, characterized by increased permeability of blood vessels, which in turn led to plasma leakage, shock, and death. The good news was that anyone infected developed an immunity to the virus. The bad news was there were four strains of it. We all suffered from it, but the only way we got to see a doctor about it was if we were lucky enough to get wounded.

We also lost men to Malaria. The parasitic disease transmitted from person to person was caused by Mrs. Anopheles P. Falciparum. She was our greatest threat, because she was a source for the most severe symptoms of malaria parasites prevalent in the world's four endemic areas. There was just no way for the infantrymen to avoid her bite. She waited until it became dark to attack, although if you spent any amount of time hiding in the heavy shadows during the daytime, she was there too. She followed your breath and she loved dark colors. Her malaria seeds lived in her salivary glands. They dodged a soldier's immune system to seek out his liver and burrow inside the cells there. In four weeks, these developing merozoites ruptured the cells in the liver and started flowing into the blood stream. Within 48 hours the red blood cells burst. The victim then suffered severe fevers with hot and cold chills.

You came down with headaches, diarrhea, muscle and joint pain, stomach pain, sweat-drenching fevers, teeth-rattling chills and suffered just plain ill health. All this while trying to keep from being shot. You could fall into a coma, have seizures, suffer from anemia or kidney failure, or your spleen could rupture. One responsibility of a good leader was to pay attention when your men casually took a leak, without seeming to do so; blood in the urine portends kidney failure and death. Those who fell victim would suffer chronic, relapsing waves of infection. It took our immune systems about a year to get it under control. Because it primarily affected the brain, if someone was unlucky enough to get cerebral malaria (*Plasmodium falciparum*), he stood the chance of becoming retarded.

Most of the time, we had no medical care unless wounded, so the army used Chloroquine-Primaquine, which was developed after quinine. One tablet was taken weekly. Many of us drank quinine water in the clubs if we were lucky enough to get some time off. The problem was we were never in the clubs, and never had any time off in the infantry. The army issued anti-malarial drugs that helped fight the parasite, but no malaria vaccine or drug offered substantive relief, and for some, the tablets induced nightmares. You could always detect the long-term soldiers: the whites of their eyes were no longer white from taking the tablets. The bad news was that most of us were very far from medical care, and as usual, if suspicious symptoms developed, the unit could not afford to lose one man, even if the unit commander cared. Even if you were lucky enough to get to a hospital, the medical personnel might not be able to diagnose you successfully. The good news was if Mrs. P. Falciparum didn't kill you the infection would burn itself out in a year or two.

The mountain range on the south side of the valley was occupied by the 95th North Vietnamese Army Regiment. Also in the area was the 18B Regiment, as well as main force VC battalions. The NVA's 5th Division headquarters, which had operational control over the 95th and 18B regiments, was also thought to be in the province. Most of the time, they remained underground in caves dug deep into the rocky and thickly forested coastal mountains, which dominated the lowland plains bordering the valley. The NVA occupied the high ground and we, the low ground. Much of the central coastal strip's winter monsoon came from the northeast between October and March, bringing approximately 79 inches of rain. The further west you went toward the Central Highlands, the more rain there was. However, between July and November unpredictable and violent typhoons often developed. During the transitional period of September there was always great enemy activity everywhere, until the next month brought the wet chilly winter. We always worried about the weather, about bad flying conditions for air support or medical evacuation, but at present the sky was beautifully clear.

We had been briefed that two concentration camp prisoners had walked into our perimeter just hours before. During interrogation, they had given their personal information and had finally been asked where they had come from. The next question to follow naturally was: "Are there more prisoners there?" The answer had been: "Approximately 50 prisoners." He had reported that earlier there had been as many as 200 prisoners. Now, there were fewer, but there were two Americans and one Korean marine. The rest were Vietnamese. The unit commander, Colonel Meinzen, had been alerted to the information coming out of the interrogation. He was wary; the escapee may be a North Vietnamese soldier leading us into a trap. Nevertheless, he had decided to react quickly to the intelligence, knowing that time was now a critical factor for success. The walk-in prisoner, PFC Hoang Kim Chinh, had volunteered to lead the way back to the prison.

Early in the year, during February, two members of the Tiger Force, one white and one black soldier, from HHC 1/327th Infantry, on a route reconnaissance, were engaged in a firefight. The firing could be heard at the patrol base some 250 yards away. The two never returned. Sources revealed that the black sergeant had been killed, stripped of his clothes and gear and thrown into the nearby Da Rang River. At the rivers mouth is the provincial capital, Tuy Hoa, and the South China Sea. The other soldier wounded and captured, was last seen being led across the river about 10 km NW of the prison camp.

My platoon, the 2nd Platoon of Charlie Company, 1st Battalion, 327th Airborne Infantry, 101st Airborne Division, was located on the north side of the Tuy Hoa Valley. I was quickly briefed on the known background information and ordered to cross the valley, to link up with the Tiger Force to the east of Hill 51 in front of the mouth of the large canyon located there and wait. When informed that one of the former communist soldiers was going to lead us back, I got goose bumps. I had served in Vietnam long enough to know that trick. *"Here we go again, another ambush."* I felt that the NVA were just targeting the commander.

There was an additional cause for caution. Our briefing revealed that an old, unmarked anti-personnel French barrier minefield, well covered, by years of vegetation, would delay our movement enroute. No record or graphic pattern of this minefield existed. As always, for infantrymen, the first indication of mines came when someone stepped on one.

* * *

With the sun resting low on the western horizon, I assembled my 15-man platoon. They were weary from constantly running daytime patrols and conducting night ambushes. I informed them of what we were going to do. I looked at the melancholy faces of my hollow-cheeked young men--their pallid, stoic, gaunt faces, with vacant stares from red-rimmed hollow eyes. They stood loosely formed, with the butts of their rifles resting on their boots, so as not to pick up any more dirt than they had to. They patiently waited, watching me. They were tired and dirty, but their rifles and magazines were clean. They realized that today was just another bad news day. They remained calm and still. This under-strengthed, hardened platoon had stood up exceptionally well under months of intensive combat actions, and had accepted and endured their fatigue and psychological shocks. They had fought to keep alive. They were the survivors.

Long shadows were sneaking over the mountains as we got started. We crossed the wide valley, crossed the paddies toward the fallow fields that were no longer worked. I cast a glance at the sun. It was too low in the sky. The distant mountains to the west were a glowing haze. There was a dazzling sunset of vivid colors. I could see the canyon, but the sun's last crescent had already gone down behind the mountains.

We moved like the wind that rippled the brown water in the rice fields. The area closest to the mountains was now nothing more than tall, golden-brown grass. As we moved quickly across the open fields, I watched the mountains turn from gold to blue, then indigo. Wisps of orange could be seen across the sky. The shadows had grown long across the valley, and the mountains were now hidden in darkness. The golden air of the evening was gone. I wanted to live. In the fading light

I headed straight for the front of the mouth of the canyon, stopping minutes before it was too dark to see. The sun had dipped beyond the horizon, leaving only a mystic gloaming in the valley. We tried and were unable to establish contact with the other unit. They had not yet arrived.

Darkness had engulfed the valley while I had carefully watched our back trail. The light had drained from the sky, taking the day's heat with it. I waited until it was completely dark, sitting in the tall grass. Then I silently picked up the platoon and moved our position. Out of caution, I would always pretend to settle for the night in one place while it was still light enough to see, and then after full darkness move back to an area visually selected earlier. This type of move depended upon each man understanding what we were doing and why. I made a 90-degree turn and with only a whisper of sound, moved about 200 yards to the east. This was just in case we were followed. The NVA would only know where we had been, not where we were.

The vast sea of grass could easily swallow up a platoon, especially at night. Gradually, the hour came and the moon rose. I studied the landscape in the white air of the bright moon. Much of the illness that we suffered came from this tall grass, filled with mites that caused Rickettsia. Moving through it and lying in it, we would pick them up on our uniforms. Mites were also a potential source of fever of unknown origin, FOUO. These parasitic microorganisms live in the bodies of mites, lice and ticks, and easily infect animals and man. They lived on chickens and rats, and in the nasal passages of dogs, on birds, in the lungs of monkeys. They could also cause scrub typhus, which, could lead to death. As usual, there was nothing we could do about it but keep our pants tucked securely in our boots. Someone was always getting sick.

My own particular horrors were the hopeless misery of mud, water, the wet cold, and our black rat-hole bunkers. Now, we were wet from the waist down and hungry, but it wasn't so bad; at least the ground was firm. At times like these, I would take off one boot at a time, and dry and powder my feet. I could easily see them in the dark; they were their usual off-colored white, and very wrinkled. We suffered constantly from immersion foot, but drying them always removed a lot of dead skin, which we could not afford to lose. It was a constant battle at times just to stay on your feet.

I had to focus my concentration, listen to the night sounds, to the swooping of the winged night hunters, the song of chirping insects, very faint and low, and the barking of deer, to determine if we had been followed. The best way to observe sounds at night around you is first to clear the cobwebs out of your head, to put you in the proper mental attitude. If your mind was wide-awake, your eyes and ears were as well.

The Starlight Scope

The night was a mix of pyrotechnics and potential menace. While scanning for an unusual sound, I would freeze periodically, my hands cupped behind my ears, and rotate my upper body to focus reception on the particular sound. Gnats whined, and mosquitoes droned. It was not difficult to classify the sounds, because there was little wind. I made a habit of enjoying the trilling, croaking song of frogs and toads. Once, I was briefly worried by the brief silence of the frogs. It was probably the other element arriving late and setting up for the night, not far from us. The frogs began to sing again. I smelled only the acid odor from our own bodies, and the sweet earthy scent of the wet grassland. I was responsible for this small, young platoon. I had to be prepared emotionally for anything to happen, ready to act and react.

The AN/PVS-1 starlight scope normally operated well off the light given from the stars, pale and small. At times, depending upon the phase of the moon, the scope worked much better than normal. Its main drawback was its batteries, which didn't last very long. If illumination rounds were being fired anywhere in the distance, it worked beautifully.

To the west, about a mile away from my position, the night sky suddenly blossomed into an incandescent brightness. Flares drifted slowly down, lighting the valley in peaceful silver. I made good use of my starlight scope, scanning the area. The visual acuity of the scope was very clear. The problem was that if I used the starlight scope very long, I lost my night vision for some time. For a while, I was on edge, having heard a deer bark in the distance. The NVA often communicated in the darkness in this way. I listened carefully for answering barks, which would mean they knew we were here. Nothing. The same deer barked again. It was a real deer after all. While my men rested, I spent nearly three hours evaluating the night sounds for danger, until fatigue crept in. With eyelids drooping, I changed the watch. The night passed uneventfully.

Sometime later, my internal clock awoke me as usual. The moon had gone down and the night was growing pale. I silently moved around, making sure all my people were awake. It was still more night than day, but the stars were fading as the eastern sky grayed. Finally there was just the pale predawn. To the west, the sky and the mountains were still dark, mysterious. Before long, the first streaks of crimson shone, and the gray mountains loomed up out of the dark. I studied the landscape. We remained alert and hidden in the tall grass until the sun came up. The chilly morning air was thick with the damp, lingering scent of night. We were silent, watching, listening.

I looked over at the quiet mountains, growing more dramatic now as the light grew stronger. The low clouds misted the mountain like a blanket, an obscuring shroud making visibility poor for anyone up there. They would feel safe.

The coolest part of the day is in the early morning hours just before daylight. Many species of animals are most active at this time. The early morning sounds were good, reassuring and normal. A few songbirds were starting to trill nearby and many more were flying high, indicating that there was little wind. The weather would be good.

We stood up from the damp ground, stretching our stiff muscles preparing to move. Suddenly, I saw and heard the startled and noisy alarm of some small birds, taking flight in the distance. I quickly motioned with one arm while verbally giving a warning to get down. I felt the initial burn of gall at the back of my throat. Then there was the Tiger Force, not too far from us, standing up, looking at us and ready to go. My instincts were good, but I felt worn out. Link-up was completed. Looking up at our destination, the ridge, I could see the morning sun had finally warmed the air above the mist-shrouded timbered ridge. The slow shudder and dance of the mist was thinning and disappearing.

Saturday, 24 September 1966

As we quickly moved toward the recon element, leaving the shadow of a dark green trail through the dew-covered grass, I looked all around to see if there were other, similar trails of dragged or bent vegetation leading away from us. Although dew will re-inflate dry stems to their original position, the taller the grass, the harder it is to stand back up, and this grass was tall.

Such trails would give a clear sign that we had been followed and watched. There were none. Our fatigue pants were sopping wet. There was one good sign so far--the heavy early morning dew indicated that we would have good weather and no rain. Our uniforms would soon dry. The dew would be burned off by the sun.

The first thing we had to do that day was to get through the minefield safely. We knew that there was still no means for a swift search and elimination of mines, but luckily, ahead of us was an attached three-man mine sweeping team, from Company "A," 326th Engineers. They would clear only a narrow path.

The Minefield

As we slowly made our way through the minefield, looking for any discoloration of the natural earth or vegetation, variations in the vegetation, small depressions in the ground, or any old disturbance of the earth, we had to remember all that we had learned during our training. We made a good visual inspection that could provide clues to where something was buried, but we were on our own as usual. Needless to say, whatever appeared to be the most natural trail would be the most dangerous to us.

I listened carefully for the sharp metallic "thip" sound of a mine being activated by someone ahead or behind. To stay alive in this war, you had to depend more on your brains than brawn, and had to smell, see, listen and step light-footedly, or the Devil would come knocking. As every infantryman knows, it only takes a few pounds of pressure to set a mine off. Depending upon the type, it could take off the foot or leg. They are designed to maim rather than kill.

In the case of the M16 "bounding mine," or Bouncing Betty you hear the click when you step on it. When you remove your foot, the projectile bounces up into the air, where it leaps out of the ground and explodes between waist and chest height, spraying shrapnel in every direction. It can shred the legs of an entire squad. I had the old eerie feeling, knowing that death lurked in this tranquil setting. The casualty-producing radius would be about 35 meters, but the mine could still hit you at 200 meters. Mines never sleep, they just wait with limitless patience. Despite all the advances in minefield technology, we employed the time-honored method of probing in the soft ground with a bayonet and hands at a 45-degree angle, covering a one-meter front to clear a footpath through the field. The search was conducted by several men, with sweat dripping off their faces. Appearing calm and confident, but inwardly frightened, we walked through that invisible doorway, leaving the relative safety of the open fields. We entered into the mountain range, the home of the 95th NVA Infantry Regiment, and knew that once again we were in great danger.

The Outpost
At its start, the trail was vine-entangled and rock-studded, but it soon developed into a high-speed trail up the mountain that appeared to be well traveled. We could see the skyline above, and thought ourselves to be near the top. I was surprised that it favored us with so much cover and concealment. On the way up, I had expected a warning shot to be fired at us at any time, alerting the NVA to our presence. However, there was only silence. It led me once again to think it was a trap, that the NVA had indeed targeted the commander with this story and had deployed a guide to show the way to an ambush. Another large battle would result. We had just barely recovered from the last one, at Dac To in Kontum Province in June.

We stopped near the first outpost on the trail, our uniforms sweat-soaked, our thighs burning, to relieve our altitude-aggravated shortness of breath. Several men from the Tiger Force checked a cave out and found it empty. We then continued to move until we neared the second outpost, and stopped again. We could now see that the skyline had proved to be a false crest. Although we were close to the top, we still had a way to go. The smells of woodsmoke and cooking hung in the air. A narrow scent trail of smoke coming down the trail had given its warning. The enemy was close.

Sgt. Christian G. Girard, my friend from Tiger Force, with whom I had shared a foxhole and coffee that one terrible night, came back to tell me exactly what was going on with the delays. He had once been a member of the 2nd Platoon at Dac To. We had just finished talking when our ears rang with the vibrant shock of a rifle report. It echoed across the quiet hills. Our heads all jerked up. Members of the recon element had found an NVA outpost occupied by several guards. One of the younger members of the Tiger Force had shot one of the guards. With the lives of prisoners at stake, the inexcusable bravado of an inexperienced young soldier was going to cost. That shot, served as a warning, alerting the NVA. The decision was made to race toward the camp, still a good distance away. There was no deployment of our force. None was now possible. Still, we had to cover the distance as quickly as possible. We moved as fast as we dared, straight up the trail.

The Reign of Terror

As the shadows lengthened and crept up the slopes, we reached the final crest, arriving at the prison camp late in the afternoon. We gained the top of the trail, disappeared into the trees, went a short way and stopped. The forest closed over us. The prison camp now lay before us.

Streams of light painted a confusing mosaic through the leaves, making it difficult to take in the whole prison camp in one view. We fell motionless and silent. We were left expressionless and speechless. Then my eyes widened, bulging in surprise at what they saw, at the full sad, subhuman, grotesque picture of human misery in the murky gloom.

Everyone was silent. Most of the prisoners were already gone. Among those that remained, their faces were unmoving, with eyes distant and dead, sitting on deflated torsos. The prisoners had already slipped into passivity and resignation from their confinement-induced torpor. Our eyes narrowed to angry slits. A smell came to my nostrils. I detected a familiar stench.

The reek of death profaned the air. Nothing smells quite as bad as the sickening stench of rotting flesh in the early stages of decay. Our eyes became accustomed to the darkness and the obvious structures of the camp, and we saw the many elongated mounds around the camp's perimeter. They were for those who had already died here. The recent dead were wrapped and waiting to be carried to a shallow grave. Here in this isolation was an example of how and where the self-righteous communists enforced their vindictive rule over the people, suppressing opposition of those who held contrary beliefs, and demonstrating their strength and lack of government control. Here was where communism, based on Maoism and Stalinism, was carried out to the extreme, without remorse, pity or fear, destroying all social fabric. This was the place where dissident re-education took place. After they had segregated the prisoners, debased them, humiliated them and slowly starved them with meager diets, inflicted pain, restricted their movement, and left them only monotony and a minimum of sleep, the NVA gained either compliance and collaboration, or fatally exhaustive labor. Starvation was slow. It takes a long time and is very painful. You could plainly see how it had deteriorated their bodies and souls. Skeletal and semiconscious, many were in a state not far from death, where their spirits were already leaving their bodies, where they would find it hard to come back.

One horrible example of this was Le Van Than, 23. He had been a former member of the Viet Cong forces that had defected because he did not believe in their cause. He deserted and returned to his family, but was made to work for the communists. After repeatedly refusing to become a Viet Cong soldier, the communists again came to his house in the night and put him into their prison system. Of all the prisoners in this camp, he had been here the shortest time; however, he had been treated the worst. The starvation, overwork and constant beatings had taken a great toll on his body.

This brutish daily regimen of sleep deprivation, constant fear of their captors inflicting painful punishment, and total dependency on their captors, was the key to confusing, bewildering and tormenting the prisoners, to the point of long lasting personality changes and ultimate cooperation and confession of any subject desired by a professional interrogator. Psychopathic communist cadres terrorized them. The NVA used systematic and savage brutality to stifle opposition; extermination, long hours of forced labor from dawn until late night, torture by sexual psychotics and sadists, long stretches without water, strangulation, beatings, letting them die, hemorrhaging from too many blows. All this was perpetrated on defenseless people, who were treated like animals. No hope, no dreams, no promise of a future. I couldn't imagine what it would be like to look each day into the eyes of someone who hated you and denied you your humanity. This was where prisoners were forced to choose between cooperation and slow death.

One such woman, now before our eyes, was Mrs. Vo Thi Han, 37, an ordinary housewife. She had given up in the prison and was dying when we arrived. But the little nourishment we managed to provide her saved her life, and she experienced rebirth. This is what she had later told everyone from her bed in the hospital. Mrs. Han's prison duty was maintaining the prisoners' quarters. Her only crime had been that her brother worked for the Government Information Office in Tuy Hoa. Her brother had convinced her to move to the city for her own safety, and she had been captured enroute, without trial or any explanation, other than that she was considered an enemy follower. Her husband disappeared, never to be found. She had been a prisoner for eight months when liberated.

I saw Sgt. Girard again, and he explained to me what the rifle shot had been about. As we talked, we looked around. From the appearances and stench of the prisoners before us, you could tell that from this camp there was no return. They were very pale and drawn, a prison pallor. Their bodies shriveled, reduced to skin and bone from inadequate diet, and from the efforts of nature to rid itself of its sickness through their bowels.

There was Nguyen Bo, 48, a rich property owner, who served on the provincial intelligence staff, making himself a major communist target. Mr. Bo had been captured by the communists while making a map of his hamlet. He spent almost his entire imprisonment shackled. During the 13 months he was a prisoner, his family disappeared, never to be seen again. The very air we breathed shocked our senses with its stench. I was stifled by the horrible animal odor these people exhaled.

A farmer, Nguyen Hang, 18, had been cutting grass when captured. Mr. Hang had been accused of passing information about the communists to the agents of the South Vietnamese government. He said he was closely watched and would be repeatedly beaten and kicked by the guards while making charcoal, if he was not working hard enough. Asking questions of the guards also brought the same treatment.

Another Popular Force prisoner, PFC Pham Thang, 39, was captured in his family home while on leave. Tried and sentenced by the communists, he had served for 18 months of his four-year sentence as a prisoner when liberated. His only crime was being in the South Vietnamese military. At his debriefing in the hospital, he stated that his goal was to return to his unit.

Yet another Popular Forces soldier, PFC Truong Tung, 38, had been captured while on pass to see his family and had been a prisoner for nine months when we arrived in the prison camp. He was not permitted to work, and spent his entire time shackled. His hands were only freed to eat. The former prisoners later explained that in the prison system they had been provided two meals a day, rice with salt. However, a food shortage developed and their rice ration was thinned and made into soup. They had been allowed to bathe only once a month.

Another surviving prisoner, the Ho Thin hamlet chief, Nguyen Phu Xuan, 34, had spent eleven months in this prison and later stated that he personally saw 75 prisoners die there, mostly from malnutrition. He knew of 10 others who had been shot trying to escape. During Mr. Xuan's time in the prison there had been 200 prisoners, whose only crime had been loyalty to the South Vietnamese Government. He had been captured in his home during the night and sent to this camp. Often beaten and kicked for not working hard enough, he had endured the forced labor and charcoal-making until liberated. He eventually returned to his wife and four children, who were moved to a more secure house.

A Regular Army soldier and former paratrooper, PFC Tran Van Dinh, 38, was on his way for Special Forces training in 1965, enroute to Nha Trang from Nam Dinh when he was captured. A former refugee from North Vietnam, he was a prisoner for 14 months. Afterwards, in the hospital, his goal was to go to Nha Trang and complete training.

The remaining haggard prisoners in the camp were so skinny, wasted and weakened that their skeletal frames were ridging the skin. They could scarcely walk, their limbs swollen, their bones and joints racked with excruciating scurvy pains and weakness. I felt the now familiar pulse of a muscle at the temple. There was an aura of animal fetidity about them. But it was their sunken eyes that struck me most. The exhaustion of body and spirit showed across the eyes. Normally Vietnamese have dark almond eyes, but the eyes of these gaunt-faced prisoners were idiotic, glassy and preternaturally bright, remained fixed on the ground. There was only a terrible black emptiness to be seen in them.

The prisoners were not even aware that they had been liberated, and continued to work, producing charcoal with a detached and visible indifference. They didn't cry, laugh or indicate that they even saw us. You could tell from the prisoners' actions that they had a long traumatic experience with fear and physical hardship. Their humanity and dignity gone, their actions showed a loss of motor function and psychological changes. Like zombies, they made no attempt at communication of any kind. No emotion was shown on their faces, save for depression and apathy. Some of the prisoners with their starved faces—all the bones sticking out—just watched us with huge, hollow dark eyes. They were just too tired. Their narrow faces, framed with dirty black hair, were pinched and emaciated, and etched with lines of starvation.

Their cheekbones protruded sharply beneath the skin, and their ribs stood out like stripes on their chest.

Apart from indoctrination and interrogation, the only function that this camp had, was to serve as a factory, to use these enslaved prisoners to produce charcoal until they died. At least a hundred men and women had died here. We found a sewing machine and lots of blue and gray cotton cloth, the kind supplied by the Chinese, for the prisoners to make their own prison uniforms. Much else of what had been used in the camp had been supplied by China: the ammunition, weapons, medicine and Chinese troops. The Chinese soldiers wore PAVN and Viet Cong uniforms. The Chinese communists supplied three-quarters of the total military aid given to the People's Army of Vietnam (PAVN) during the war.

The prisoners had been deprived of all human dignity, insulted, starved into their weak condition, and eventually left to grow sick and die of disease. The grim efficiency of their communist guards was apparent. Subsisting on a diet that would not sustain life, broken down physically, these prisoners were no longer capable of escape on their own. I wondered if these prisoners were people who the communists considered to be collaborators or informers. The longer I looked at the graves, the uglier their deaths became in my mind.

Everyone stopped and listened. We could hear Vietnamese shouting. We didn't need a picture drawn for us. We realized that it was the guards shouting at the prisoners down the trail. When they evacuated the camp, the guards had taken those strong enough to walk and were now driving them like animals further into the mountain forest. We all knew that someone had to go after them, and fast, but we were also aware that we had been ambushed too many times before while moving recklessly along the trail. The NVA guards were now moving some forty prisoners away from us as fast as they could.

When silence returned, I was told to go down the trail with my men and see if I could catch up to them before it got dark. My insides clinched, as a chill went through me, as my heart beat faster and my breath became shallow. Thin-lipped and with white knuckles gripping the pistol grips on our rifles, we started moving down the trail. We all knew the open trail was now very dangerous, so we kept our silent, easy movement at a slow, fluid pace. I knew that if I hugged the inside of the curves as I moved, using the brush and tree-lined bends for concealment, the NVA would not hear me as quickly, and given only a short field of straight-away vision, they might miss seeing my movement altogether in the low light. My eyes constantly moved from place to place, every sense tingling. Here in the mountains every boulder, every fold of ground was a possible prepared enemy fighting position to be minutely inspected before allowing my feet to go forward. I moved a hundred yards, two or three steps at a time, gearing my advance to the difficult terrain. The trail was siding downhill in a southeasterly direction. I stopped to listen in the dull and diffused light, letting my senses drink in the surroundings. I dreaded the thought that the first warning I would receive would be the wicked crackle of an RPD light machine gun, firing at a rate of six hundred rounds per minute.

An instinctive uneasiness came over me, as I waited and listened in the fading light to the voices still far ahead. While pivoting my head to search the surrounding terrain, I eased silently forward, a few feet at a time, looking, listening and watching as I went. I could smell their passing. Just ahead and to the right, I heard a faint rustle of leaves. I sidestepped to the left slowly, a step at a time. My educated thumb had instinctively put my rifle on full automatic without a thought. It was in the ready position, three-quarters of the way to my shoulder. I neither heard nor saw anything, but the hair on the back of my neck and forearms rose on end, as I felt a presence. My flesh began to crawl as a shiver rolled up the length of my body. I had grown used to the feeling of being watched over the years as my eyes quickly scanned the immediate area. I now felt other eyes upon me with great intensity. I was looking down the top of the barrel for a target, knowing I was already one myself, as I was standing in the open trail, compelling my senses to reach out beyond their capabilities to tell me something. I was again being too rash. A movement and a low black object appeared at the side of the trail. I froze in a low crouch, holding my breath. I was being watched. My index finger tightened on the trigger, as my eyes surveyed to the sides of the trail ahead. Then it was clear--the shoulders and head of a black clad figure. I stared for a long moment.

It was a dropout: a prisoner who was too weak to keep up and had been left. I had almost shot him. I knew that if it had been an enemy soldier, I would now be dead. I moved up and stopped by the black-clad prisoner, who turned out to be a Vietnamese woman. The woman was Lam Thi Ao, 65, a housewife who maintained the cages and grounds. She would be reunited with a son in nearby Tuy Hoa, and eventually with the rest of her family. I ordered one of the men to carry her back to the camp on his back. I could see he was happy to go. I had to be more cautious. I glanced up at the top of the opposite side of the narrow canyon. The shadows cast by the sun indicated that no matter how tense I felt, no matter how the minutes seemed like hours, time was flying by.

I moved a little further down the trail, and again felt the eyes. I felt as if any moment I would be dead. Then, there was another prisoner dropout right in the middle of the trail. Again, I had almost fired on a helpless person. A farmer, Nguyen Huong, 23, who had decided to move with his two brothers to the nearby town of Tuy Hoa because of the repeated communist pressure to join their army. Enroute to the city, they were stopped by the communists. Knowing that the best time to escape is when first taken, his two brothers jumped into the nearby river. He told a story of being repeatedly beaten and kicked, while performing hard labor for five months.

As I continued to move, I was wondering if those two prisoners had snuck off from the main body as it passed, waited until it was gone, and then came back to the trail, or if it was a kind of trap, that the next figure would be a North Vietnamese Army soldier waiting for me. The NVA would not allow themselves to be run down without an effort to strike back. They would lay an ambush soon, or one was already in place close by. I ordered another soldier to carry the second dropout back to camp. Realizing my force was now quite small, I moved extremely slowly, even though I knew that the main body of prisoners was getting even further away. Again, I looked around the tightening canyon and to the tops of the ridges without seeing any rays of sunlight. I knew that the sun was already going down behind the mountains to the west. The terrain about me harbored deep shadows, black and ominous. Time was running out. I cocked my head, listening. Not a sound from the prisoners ahead. In the distance to the west, higher up the ridge, I heard a swarm of bats, all lifting up before sunset. Far above, I saw dark silhouettes of trees shutting out the night sky. As the insects whispered their night song in the fading light, I made the decision to return to the camp. My 2nd Platoon was moving too slowly to catch up with the main body of POWs and it was finally getting too dark to see. "To this day, I still think about that decision."

Our own bellies cramped with hunger, we collected what little canned food and water we had on us, and distributed it through the medic out to the prisoners before we left the camp for the return trip. Other soldiers set about opening the containers for them. The prisoners, stomachs aching for nourishment, seeing our intent to give them food, began to fight and quibble with each other for the food in slow motion, and then to manhandle the medic in the same way. Although their voices were weak and inaudible, the intent was clear. Staggering on wasted muscles and almost falling from dizziness, they had to be separated so that the food could be given out individually. The prisoner's hungry eyes followed every movement of the soldier handing out the food. Clawed hands received their ration. These poor people were subsisting on two hands full of rice daily. Their monotonous diet was 600 calories a day. Bare subsistence is 1,200 calories a day. The prisoners were meant to die. It was a good thing that we didn't have much food, because they were not used to eating, and eating too much would have ruptured their stomachs and killed them.

We liberated twenty-three helpless prisoners who had only a faint will to live. The NVA had left behind only those too weak to walk. All the prostrated prisoners suffered from exposure, pneumonia, malnutrition, and dysentery. More than likely, they also suffered from respiratory infection, infectious hepatitis, beriberi, and perhaps typhus from the lice they carried. They could only remain on their feet briefly without help. We got them on our backs and started carrying them out of the mountains. This part of their life, with its prolonged suffering, was over. We left the prison camp intact. The pervading aura of human suffering and misery still persisted, emanating from the structures. It made my skin crawl. The cicadas and other insects were already singing their congregational night song. It pervaded the air.

Like a black mantle, nightfall swallowed us up. Things grew quiet as we moved back down the trail. Soon we turned off the trail and entered the semi-dry creekbed of a gully. The creekbed, a confusion of large boulders, was difficult to negotiate in the dark. We scrambled awkwardly around and over the slippery boulders and rocks. We spent part of the night moving until the moon came up, when we finally had to stop and rest. When we were far enough away from the trail to put us out of hearing range, we stopped along a solid wall of limestone. We were no longer so afraid that the NVA would find us. They would expect us to take the easy way out, on the trail. The moon-blanched treetops were serene and full of silvered light, which filtered down to the forest floor in places. There had been a time when the moonlight soothed me--no more.

Hidden in the rocky cleft, we managed to find a little seepage of water dribbling in the overhang with which to satisfy our thirst. We avoided stagnant pooled water, full of flat, parasitic flukes, which would eventually bore into your bloodstream, causing much misery before making you a statistic. After drinking, we silently sat in the dark on the rocks of the dry creekbed and listened to the night sounds, waiting for daylight. A silent chill came from the dark and impenetrable gloom of the forest. The cicadas had ceased to whisper their melancholy night song. The only sound to be heard was the familiar, feeble, high-pitched clicking "Awk Oooo" of the small green gecko lizards, darting on their urgent errands, catching mosquitoes. I had watched them many times in the past, as they licked their eyes, moistening and cleaning them with their tongue. They couldn't close their eyes.

Every set of eyes strained into the dark. The long hours dragged by. Sometime during the night, the grunting of wild pigs, foraging far below us, could be heard. We waited. During the early morning hours, looking up through breaks in the trees, I watched the stars glow like diamonds in the black sky overhead. Then, ever so faintly, to the east came a finger of light--the first sheen of dawn. Finally our long vigil was almost over. The moon had long since set. The stars slowly faded. Dawn wasn't too far distant. We continued to watch and listen. There was a welcome light growing in the east. As we picked up and moved downward, we felt a breeze fanning our faces.

The dawn light crept across the eastern sky and lit up the top of the opposite ridge with shafts of gold. Deep in the shadowy dark canyon, we picked up our few liberated emaciated prisoners and moved slowly, quietly, downward. We knew that any sound would carry a long way. We listened intently to the jungle chorus of silvery birdcalls, while other birds chirped and squawked, to the accompaniment of dripping dew from the canopy above. Thousands of insects chattered and clicked. Others were buzzing. All was well nearby. To the east, the canyon rim was orange with light. I could now see plants sprouting from every visible rock cranny--a wild tangle of plants growing upon plants. Black, foot-long centipedes, an inch wide, with bright orange legs, clung to the sides of the huge moss-covered boulders and rock walls of the creek. Finally, we reached the bottom of the narrow canyon. Staying among the taller straight trees, we came to the winding stream. It gleamed bright where touched by the sun. The morning was cool, sweet and fresh. The red sun, presaging a hot day, gilded the rising morning mist that sifted above the stream in the warming air, giving the area a surreal appearance.

We wove our way among the large trunks, northward along the creek. Light penetrated the thick, dark foliage of the old forest, shining in vertical shafts like strips of translucent gauze. Our eyes concentrated on nothing but took in everything, as we made our way to the mouth of the canyon. Finally, the liberated prisoners, bruised and covered with running sores, were assembled and evacuated to our 1/327th headquarters by helicopter. Flown to freedom, they were administered and checked by one of our units' doctors, Captain Stephen M. Wilson, the medical platoon leader, and were fed a nourishing soup. Before being moved on to a hospital in Tuy Hoa, Gen. Westmoreland and Gen. Willard Pearson, the commanding general of the 1st Brigade, were able to see and talk to them.

I know that one of the malnourished men, Le Van Than, 23, died in the hospital. Mr. Than had not been able to furnish much information, because he had not always been coherent. I often wondered if the spirit of the other prisoners had been able to stand the test of strength and willpower required to live. I have already seen and experienced how easy it is for many to give up and die. The hard part is fighting to live, especially under the strain of post-traumatic stress disorder, which would follow them the rest of their lives.

I led my dirty, ragged, and weary mud-stained infantrymen, back across the open fields to our camp. They were suffering from too much stored-up fatigue and tension. I could see it in the way they moved. There were no thanks when we returned to the company. No, "Well done." There was a near physical indifference by our command structure for what we had done. But the platoon didn't really need it: we were back with the unit and alive. However, I couldn't help but ponder what must have been a nightmare existence for those many who filled those graves around that prison camp, now sadly forgotten. I knew that most of Asia is eclectic in its faith, and the majority of Vietnamese have traditional shamanistic beliefs. In Vietnamese culture, the people seriously attend to the dead, believing that their ancestors will otherwise unhappily roam the land as lost souls.

Eight of the prisoners, in critical condition, were further evacuated to a hospital in Saigon, where doctor's records from Tuy Hoa and Saigon estimated that they had lost 30-40 percent of their original weight. In Saigon, the prisoners came in contact with the media. It was reported from an interview in the New York Times on 5 October 1966, on page eight, that one of the two suspected NVA soldiers that reportedly walked in and furnished the information for this raid was actually one Private Hoang Kim Chinh, a 31-year-old member of the national militia. He had been sentenced by the communists, to nine years in the prison system for working for the South

Vietnamese Government. He further related during interrogation that prison guards were all local men; some of them known to him, and a few had been his friends. The liberated prisoners did not have any knowledge about American prisoners.

Years after I retired from the service, the American media was full of distraught relatives wanting their prisoners, their fallen sons and husbands who were dead and missing returned, or at least accurately accounted for. I decided to call an acquaintance of mine at the Pentagon and inform him of this camp's location. I also wanted to suggest that the great number of graves surrounding this camp should be checked out, and that they should be opened and identification should be attempted. We agreed to meet one day, and he signed me into the Pentagon. He led me into his office. The correct map was found. "Show me," he said. I got a sharp pencil and pinpointed the exact spot. He then went to the correct file and pulled an after action report on this raid. The only Americans listed as having participated in this raid were the names of the Tiger Force personnel. About two months later, he called to tell me that it was verified that a camp was reported to be in that area. That's where I thought it ended.

I also communicated this story to another friend of mine, Garnett Bell, at his office in Thailand. He was then serving on the "Joint Casualty Resolution Team," responsible for locating and recovering the missing prisoners. I learned that the Joint Casualty Resolution Center/Joint Task Force-Full Accounting had assigned to me source number 2920 for the information I provided at the Pentagon. Since the Communist, were known to keep accurate records of American burial sites, we might some day get this soldiers remains back.

We Could Not Win Their Hearts and Minds

**Soldiering is an ugly business.
But the soldiers' grim choice,
between killing and being killed,
is one more burden they carry.**

D.J. Tice

CHAPTER 14

EAGLE FLIGHT

For the combat soldier, there is no insulation from the reality of war: those entrapped in a war often pay a great physical cost. Those who survive pay a greater psychological cost for killing. For me, this violent period is one that will be with me vividly the rest of my life.

I had spent the day resting. The sky was mostly blue over the Tuy Hoa Valley. Piles of silver clouds rested upon the distant green mountains. I thought of many things far away, and wished myself far away from this place. As I sat there eating a can of lima beans and ham garnished with hot sauce, I watched two young peasant boys in the distance, herding their large flocks of ducks in the valley's rice paddies. In Vietnam, they have a perfect ecological system at work. The ducks, are an adjunct to rice farming, they eat the insects and crabs without eating the rice.

Alerted

By evening, our camp had turned quiet. There was only the croaking of the frogs in the nearby paddies and ponds. A runner had found me and summoned me to the command post (CP) to see my company commander. I didn't know why they'd sent for me, but knew I was headed into harm's way again. I also knew I couldn't run away from the war--I just had to bear it. As I made my way to the CP, the sun hung low over the valley, casting a red glow on the surrounding peaks. I estimated that a half-hour's daylight was left. I was informed that my platoon had been designated to make a night combat assault.

The Loading Zone

I had received a short briefing on the ground tactical plan concerning our objective area and the landing plan. Naturally, my men and I were in the first serial of the combat assault. I was again leading my men toward the loading zone. I had been told that a helicopter had received heavy ground fire from a distant village. They didn't mention the type of fire, probably because they were in a hurry for us to get there. As it was, we couldn't get there before dark.

I checked and made sure that everyone had sufficient ammunition, and that each man had at least four of the standard issue M26 grenades. The grenade was deadly when used in crowded places because of a coiled inner liner that was notched to fragment. Coiled under tension, this weapon is ideal for causing great numbers of casualties.

I cocked my head in a listening attitude, hearing the distinct, unmistakable sound of a rotor starting to revolve slowly. The helicopter quickly built up to speed, its shrill high whine of the mighty turbo engine was soon followed by another and then another. Our transportation was starting their engines, warming them up, as the men were broken up into their chalks for loading. The turbines of the waiting helicopters wound up and were soon in a penetrating howling whine. Soon there was only the sound of the rotor blades beating the evening air. Within minutes, we scrambled forward into the open hatchways and were loaded, as a garish blood-red sunset fired the sky. The pilot, watching his gauges, rotated the throttle. The blades spun faster, and rose in pitch. We lifted a few feet. The chopper lowered its nose, making its forward run, picked up airspeed, and then surged upward. We were airborne.

We climbed fast as the pilot pulled back on the stick. The cool wind of the open compartment felt good. Once in the air, we lifted in a lazy spiral. Then the choppers tilted forward in their tail-up position and poured on the horsepower. Darkness quickly engulfed us, as we sat quietly wondering about what was to happen.

The Flight

We had flown east and then turned north, coming in toward the village from the south. We cruised at around 60 miles per hour. I hated these "vertical envelopment approaches," as our staff officers called them. The surrealistic glare of the burning village stained the dark sky. There was an eerie calm with a shroud of mist below as our troop carriers descended. During the landing zone prep, the sky was suddenly lit by the brilliance and glittering flood of the enemy's streams of green tracers. Enemy 12.7 mm anti-aircraft machine-gun tracer fire rained on our formation and the gunships from around the village. I wondered if they purposely forgot to tell us the type of fire that initially brought us here. I watched the muzzle flashes, tracers and vapor trails from rockets of the aerial rocket artillery being fired in a methodical pattern. The glare and cacophony of battle was loud and horribly beautiful.

The UH-1 Huey Iroquois that we flew in on served as an aerial weapons' platform and could place a great volume of effective fire on the target in just a short period of time. Armed with 40-mm grenade launchers, 7.62-mm machine guns, 2.75" rockets, the pair of UH-1 Huey gunships below and forward of us hovered like predatory sharks, flaring the black night into a panorama of hell. I felt sorry for those NVA gunners. I could imagine the terror and controlled panic of those NVA gunners as they continued to fire back. Smoke boiled up, yellowed by the jumping light of flames. There was a quality of unreality about the scene below. An instant later I could see the orange and yellow glow across the rice paddies, and against the dark woods beyond the village. Like most of the villages in Vietnam, these structures were all roofed with thatch and ignited easily, providing a ghostly yellow-orange light to our assault landing. Flames, whipped by the wind, turned into a roar. I worried about the illumination from the fires exposing us. Again, I felt the effects of stress and tension. Fear, my familiar companion, was back. My stomach was tight with tension. My heart was thumping and a muscle twitched in my left cheek. With my eyes missing nothing, I prayed.

Dear Lord, you know what I must do this day. If I forget thee, do not forget me.

The Initial Insertion

Thick smoke thrust itself above the village. We started our run for the ground tactical phase, losing altitude rapidly as we approached the landing zone. The noise of the rotor pitch was now deafening as the chopper lost altitude in our final approach. I knew that at the first sign of trouble, the peasants would take shelter in their bunkers. They had probably been there a good while, since the original aircraft had been fired upon. Our landing zone was to be right in the NVA's field of fire, in front of the village. The tension magnified as the ground came up fast on our lead ship. We flew fast over the low-lying, fallowed rice fields, The sound of the rotors whined in a finer pitch, as the pilot slowed the machine, then the helicopter shuddered as it decelerated, flaring out, 'raising its nose' and dropping its tail to slow its forward motion. It settled into a fast hover before landing on its skids.

Even before it could land, we had already exited the chopper. We felt the down-thrust from the rotors as we bailed out both sides. The helicopters were now vulnerable, the obvious target of any NVA gunner. We sprinted away from them, for the protection of the paddy dike, our first and only available cover. The fiery blur of muzzle flashes blinked rapidly, reaching out of the darkness ahead. I heard the sonic cracks and felt the disrupted air of passing rounds. Moving quickly forward in the dark, our legs pumping in unison, in short precision bursts, we were answered by the clatter of Kalashnikov on full automatic and the distinctive wicked crackling rush of a RPD light machine gun. A stream of bullets scythed the ground, showering me with geysers of dirt. We safely made the cover of the forward paddy dike, our breath coming in harsh rasps. The sound of the gunships' return fire was audible. The wind brought the scent of wood smoke. As we again moved forward during a lull in the firing, the AK's again returned our fire, slapping into the forward side of the paddy dike above our heads as we took cover on the opposite side of the next dike. I could smell the smoke lingering in the air and see the sparks crackle and dance. Fire was now raging on all sides of the village, sweeping over it without regard for its inhabitants. A veil of smoke hung over this remote part of the valley. We flattened out as harsh, flat cracks ripped over our heads like an ocean wave. For the next two hundred yards, we would keep our eyes directly ahead, toward the firing and the burning village. The fires outlined the tops of the forest just behind the village. The silence was broken every few seconds by sporadic bursts from the enemy. Then the enemy fire picked up. Muzzle flashes blinked rapidly ahead followed by the rattling din of AK blazing widely, as the second wave of helicopters approached. I felt the flow of adrenaline thick in my blood at the sound of disrupted air from rounds cracking overhead.

The Second Wave

The second wave had landed behind us. As the rotor noise of the departing helicopters faded, I heard the distinctive hammering rattle of an M-60 machine gun being fired on full automatic behind us. Dirt was kicking and exploding up in my face. A second burst of automatic fire hissed by. I slid all the way down into the paddy. Another rattling burst kicked up the dirt all around me on my side of the dike. I was momentarily overcome by the cruel perversity of the breath-stopping moment. After the initial shock of realizing that someone could see me, I knew. I saw in the burning glare from the village one of our young replacements shooting in our direction. The machine gun fire was being directed by our equally young, and new Lieutenant. Together, they were now unleashing fully automatic fire on me, and my men.

Rounds licked toward us across the paddy and then along the dike. For a moment my throat closed up and made it hard for me to breathe, as my new sergeants eyelids flew wide open as his eyes bulged from their sockets. The impact of a 7.62 round found the head of my sergeant and punched him forward. I heard his head pop. His head whiplashed, swelled, and altered shape. The bullet lifted him from the ground, and flung his arms and body forward, halfway across the dike. He rolled limply to one side. I saw his dead body convulse once and his feet kick. His eyes had rolled up into his skull. I could smell the rank smell of his body losing control, voiding its bladder and bowels. The hot, sweet stench of urine and stink of excrement was overpowering.

I warned them on the radio of what they were doing. I yelled at them in my bitter anger and despair of what was already done. I wanted to kill the lieutenant and that inexperienced machine gunner, as his body shuddered and legs kicked in a macabre dance of death. An almost triumphal relief took hold when I realized that I had solved that immediate problem on the radio and by yelling at them. Then my relief turned to immediate grief for my young sergeant. I was sick at heart. My head and neck began to ache. It was too much to be shot at by both sides, but it was all too common in an army that relied on an individual replacement system throughout the war.

The Burning Village

The burning huts threw foreboding reflections of wavering light over the nocturnal landscape of the darkened village like an army of shadows. The staccato hammering of machine guns and the roaring of the resinous orange flames was deafening. Pillars of flames and black smoke shot some forty feet up into the darkness from the older, wood-framed houses and huts. I could hear the rush and crackle of the tinder-dry houses. Huge curls of light, white ash and flying hot sparks drifted and floated down through the fire's light, igniting everything. Fires raged and smoke drifted everywhere. Red-hot embers of the beams from many other houses were beginning to crumble. I watched for movement in the narrow spaces between the huts, any movement that might be revealed by the flickering flames sweeping from one hut to the next. I saw bewildered animals, and a few quick glimpses of the moving shadows of people. Ammunition exploded in the huts as their burning roofs caved in and collapsed, sending up a high swirl of sparks. We ran into the bunkers, located between the village and the rice paddies. They were built into undisturbed ground, just on the outside of the village, in the open.

Checking the Bunkers

I yelled at my men not to bypass the bunkers without checking them. They checked them with grenades, and went on. The serrated, pressed steel-coil of the M-26 grenade would shred bodies of anyone who was in those bunkers. Ignoring the sounds of small arms echoing ahead, I checked the bunker nearest to me. In the distance from the line of bunkers came the screams and cries of anguish. From the sounds, the bunkers were filled with old and young people, who would be staring toward the entrance with eyes of trapped animals. *Too late!* I knew what had already been done. The screams and wails of despair filled my head. I made a mental note of it to go back and check these sites when I returned for the body of my new sergeant. I looked ahead knowing that the shadows moving to our front were the retreating NVA.

Into the Village

Well spread out, my squad led the way into the village. As we drew closer to the source of the fire, I found it difficult to breathe. The roofs of the unburned houses were now steaming. Smoke began to pour from them. My senses tingled in warning and I felt the short hairs on the back of my neck rise. I was being watched. Despite the dirty gray-black, acrid smoke that hung like a fog in the windless air, I tried to see through the light and movement of flames, to spot those shooting at us. Each sudden sharp sound made from the fire of the burning village made me jump. Tongues of bright yellow-orange flames were now leaping from the smoking roofs as the remaining unburned houses burst into fire. Sparks flew everywhere. The flames glimmered luridly on the surrounding forest, creating moving shadows, lending an eerie atmosphere to our surroundings. I moved forward. The sound of a bullet cracking close forced me back between the cover of two flaming huts. As my men advanced, firing, reloading against the unseen resistance, I listened to the screaming of people and livestock. There was a smell of roasted meat. The noise of the battle grew. Rounds popped overhead and ricocheted all around.

The Young Boy

My eyes and nose were now watering, my breath was rasping and my lungs felt seared from the acrid clouds of smoke. The flames became too hot, and almost blinding. The strong smell of burning flesh filled the air. I ran forward, taking the cover of an animal cart. My hearing warned me of the light footfalls ahead. I moved forward to an unburned hut. With my ear close to the side, I listened. No whispers or movement came from inside. I prayed it was empty. I waited in the shadows of the thatched hut and saw a movement ahead. Near blinded by tears from the smoke flooding my eyes, robbing everything of its familiar form, I fired as a dark shadow separated itself from the rest of the darkness on the far side of the corner of the house. I heard the sound of a bullet thunking into flesh.

I moved forward to check the body. I was shocked at what I saw. I prayed it hadn't been me that did this, but I knew the real answer. I could detect the metallic smell of his fresh blood; the odor left a sour tang tickling the back of my throat as my eyes searched for a weapon. There was no weapon. I tried swallowing it down. A young boy, clothes saturated with blood, was quickly bleeding to death. I tore my triangular bandage off my head that I used as a scarf/bandanna and applied a quick tourniquet. His arm hung by a shred of flesh. I carried him to a medic, back the way I had come. As I stood there with him in my arms, the medic looked and said, "He's dead, just leave him." He had quickly died of shock and loss of blood. Tears running down my face, I wanted to go home. I shook my head, then, turned again to watch the roofs caving in as the fire and smoke climbed higher than the surrounding trees. Exploding fireflies of sparks spiraled skyward.

The flames had built to a roar. Waves of light flickered and grotesquely danced through the surrounding forest. The flames greedily burned hot and glowed radiantly. The sick-sweet smell reeking of burned and charred human flesh was in the air. I felt as if the world were destroying itself. I needed a breath of clean air. The super-heated air was now almost too much; we would have to withdraw. Just then the word to withdraw came. We could not advance beyond the village for fear of being backlighted and cut down by the sure-to-be-waiting NVA. I reasoned that they had already disappeared into their underground tunnels anyway.

The Burning Man

The inferno sounded as if it were howling. It had happened so quickly. My eyelids were red and dry from the smoke. I heard a peculiar, hair-raising animal sound, as a horrific screaming erupted. It was the despairing scream of a human in mortal agony. I turned my eyes to the nearest billowing flames. I saw the dark figure of a man outlined in the heart of the flames. He was trapped inside the burning house.

I saw him just as the brilliant flare of his long hair fluttered up and caught on fire. His head was momentarily surrounded by a halo of gold, as the fire began to consume him. The screaming and roar of the fire became louder in my ears. His clothes had already burned away. The upper body blistered and burst and curled up and turned into charred crisps. He was already blinded and could not make it out. The flames quickly leaped closely around the hideously screeching man, now writhing in agony, dying in the fire. His body caught on fire and he sank to a kneeling position. The screaming stopped abruptly as he sucked the fire into his lungs. His blackened arms flailed out. Evidently he had been in a shallow underground hide-away inside when the smoke became too much for him. There had been other high-pitched and forlorn terrible screams, screams of women, but I don't know where they came from.

There must have been an underground bunker in the house. I moved closer to see. The sharp odor of smoke was overwhelming. The man had not quite made it out of his bunker under the house. I was horrified when I saw the silent, open-mouthed head frozen in place. Without any real conscious thought, I had my rifle at my shoulder. His body writhed as I realized I had fired. Too late! I had tried to end his suffering. To my unbearable dismay, I watched the hideous sight of the steaming torso twitching, shoulders bubbling, blistering and growing black, reveling unnaturally the exposed pink flesh of the discolored peeling skin. The body was jerking and sagging slowly as greasy black smoke billowed from the flames. Then it became still. In the intense heat, I knew his eyeballs would explode, and then his head. Little would remain. The arms and legs characteristically drew in close to the body as it continued to burn, and then the blackened flesh split, burned beyond recognition. I had to back up as ashes and smoke blew into my face. As the walls burned through and fell off to reveal the rib mahogany timbers, showers and swirls of sparks rose into the smoke and brightened it to yellow. Then the charred blackened human mass was gone; it became only a part of so much burning debris and ashes.

My eyes were stinging, my throat hurt, and my nostrils were full of wood smoke, singed hair and roasted flesh in the embers of the fire-lit darkness. The sickening, thick, sweet odor of human flesh would last for days once it was in the nostrils. I had seen a man burn to death and wondered how many others there were who met this same fate. We began to consolidate and leave the village area, our uniforms glittering in the garish firelight. The village was now an immense pyre; bright, twisting light reflected over our faces. The air was alive with feathers of soot and ash, floating down everywhere. The fire changed our faces: brows, noses and cheeks threw shadows that distorted eyes and mouths; the eyes grotesquely reflected the fires. Our passage through the fire-lit darkness and inhuman roar of the fire, with its strange groaning, was a birthing into some nether world.

I checked two bunkers on the way back for the body of my sergeant. The familiar smell at the entrance told me everything. I prayed it wouldn't be, but it was. Inside were mostly the very old and the very young that had taken refuge in the bunkers. The only sounds were the groans and wheezing of the seriously wounded, fighting for their lives from their wounds suffered in the bunkers. I saw the shredded dead bodies of those closest to the exploded grenades, and those scarred by the erratic pattern of grenade fragments at some distance from their explosions. They would die in pain and terror. Now, in the dark, I saw the hand of death, and saw the loss in everything. I was shaking and fighting off nausea. I developed a real headache and now felt a severe pain behind one eye. The muscle in my left cheek quivered.

The Extraction

The night sky was full of red smoke, when I found my dead sergeant. I cursed the green lieutenant and the machine gunner. I put my arms around him for a moment . . . wishing I could bring him back . . . I had had enough of this war. I felt sick. I lifted his great dead weight onto my shoulder. I could smell the sweet, malodorous smell of death and his excrement in his pants. He had followed me loyally, and had died without a sound. I started moving toward the pickup point, his head hanging and bobbing with every step. One of my men asked me if I had shit my pants. I turned and very rudely told him, "No." I told him about head wounds and just keeping a tight asshole if you're frightened. And that if you're not careful, this may happen to you. I was shaking, I was so mad and grief stricken. Immediately, the quiet of the mountains rushed in. There was a dark side to the inescapable solitude of the silence. Guilt. In the silence, the insanity of what we had done was foremost in my mind.

As we stood together, looking back, our eyes and faces glinted with the fire glow of the burning village, vivid against the night. We heard the unmistakable distant droning throb of rotor blades of the helicopters, quickly approaching up the narrow valley. Everyone was still, listening. The light from the fires guided their way in. The village and its still standing torches were just beginning to fall, whooshing and exploding, sending more eddies of sparks high into the air. Black smoke hung in the valley, as charred flakes fell everywhere. An oily stench filled our nostrils. I turned away to face the fast incoming sound of the helicopters, mesmerized by my dark thoughts. All the village huts and houses were now caving in. I saw the blinking lights in the night sky coming fast. We split up, half the men on one side of the paddies and the other half on the other, formed in our original lift loads. We smelled of the sour odor of urine, excrement, sweat, smoke and a trace of burned flesh. In the matter of just an hour, all signs of human and animal life were reduced to charred wood and skeletons of smoldering smoke and ash.

As soon as we were aboard, the stench of evacuated bowels arose. The pilot pulled back on the collective, lifting the ship into a hover. He quickly checked his gauges, then his eyes shifted out the windshield, checking his drift. He lowered the helicopter's nose to the red and yellow flames, and moved slowly forward, then rapidly accelerated, banking to the right, and then up in a quick climb. With the flow of cool air through the open compartment, the smell was gone. The best part of riding in the helicopters in Vietnam was getting the temperature change. It was like someone had turned on the air conditioning.

During the extraction, I knew this destruction was not necessary. Whoever had ordered this mission had made a major mistake, and something hideous and evil had happened. I knew that our commanders had been suckered again, had again lost control of the situation the minute the helicopters fired on the village and inserted us. The PAVN soldiers, who had occupied the village until we had attacked, had then withdrawn, their mission successfully accomplished. The surviving village people were now alienated from the government and would support the communists. Most of the dead were innocent villagers. When we were gone, the NVA would come out of their tunnels and blame the survivors' suffering on us, with good effect, convincing the people that they needed to protect themselves from the government and the American forces. The 1/327 commander had played into the enemy's hands.

The area surrounding the village could have been reconned for tunnel entrances; trails could have been marked and put under surveillance. The small village could have been cordoned off in a daylight operation, the villagers moved away from the immediate area and a thorough tunnel search of the village conducted, particularly the fireplace and stock pens, those places most often used for this purpose. Then at a future time, they could have isolated the village from a distance, and curtained it with ambushes. If that failed, we could again secure the village and use a small generator to pump smoke into a tunnel and locate the other tunnel exits by the outpouring smoke. Then, the entrance could be sealed off, gas pumped in and sealed up. Then the villagers could be relocated to another geographic area.

I never saw a thorough search of a village conducted by the 101st Airborne while I was with them. In Special Forces, we had ample diagrams of how tunnel systems were constructed and where you could start looking for them. The enemy was winning the battle of the "hearts and minds," with our help. Evidently, whoever the officers were that ran the S-3 operations at our division and brigade headquarters, were not mental giants.

I sat staring, sick at heart, looking back down at the fluorescent halo glow of the sky over the remains of the incandescent village below us. The village had been burned from end to end, and now mostly guttered smoke. The charred ends of timbers lay in a smoldering, glowing heap. The breeze kept the last of the embers glowing in the grisly scene. The underside of the low clouds on the western horizon reflected the dull fire glow as we flew away in the streaked and silted smoke of the sky. Whatever the provocation, the village was completely destroyed. We had left nothing but the ruin of charred poles and heaps of ashes behind us.

High up in the cool air, the smell still lingered in my nostrils--I could still smell it all. The sour odor of old sweat, smoke, blood, urine and excrement had permeated my dirty uniform and clung to me. I felt dirty. I was dirty. My young dead sergeant lay on the floor at my feet. His blood saturated the back of my battle blouse, sticking to my skin. I felt as if I were alone, in a world gone mad. I wondered when the young boy had been hit, if his weapon had been spirited away. The NVA would claim him as an innocent victim like all the others. It had been just another living nightmare. I realized how fleeting life could be and how precious my life was to me now. All illusions of my self-importance were gone. After landing back at our base, I had one last look as they unloaded my dead sergeant. I saw his face, distorted by the impact of the round.

His nose and eyes were swollen and his eyeballs were blood red. The skin had already gone grayish-green.

Upon returning to our unit area, the smoke was still rank in my nose, and its sour taste lingered in the back of my mouth. I felt bad, because I felt it had all been unnecessary. My singed, smoke-permeated uniform was still saturated, wet with blood, as I stood reporting to my Company commander about the events of that night's action. Ashen faced, and trying to blink the burned man from my mind, still hearing the crackle of the flames, still seeing the burning man, I made my report. In my commander's face, I did not see or feel that he felt any compassion or conscience about what I had told him.

Later, head bowed, suffering from emotional pain, I sat slumped and alone in my dark bunker, silent for a long while, absorbed in thought. I thought about hearing and smelling the life go out of the young sergeant, about his limp body lying in the rice paddy, about the young and old people sheltered in the bunkers, the reek of charred flesh, the burning man and the young boy. For the very first time in the war, my mind and my heart experienced a new kind of hate. Not for our enemy, but for the undisciplined action of my new platoon leader. A young lieutenant and a new private acting as a machine gunner were responsible for his death, and almost for mine. I blamed everyone but myself. Exhausted by fear and remorse, I fell into a deep sleep. In the morning the blood, dark against the uniform green, was stiff. It still had the smell of blood. I heard that the machine-gunner was sent somewhere else, but the lieutenant who gave him the order to fire was still with us. This particular officer had been a problem ever since I'd returned from the hospital after being wounded at Dac To, and would continue to present many more problems in the days ahead.

* * *

Someone touched me, and I opened my eyes. The stewardess was smiling at me, and asking me to fasten my seat belt. I looked out the window, and there was the coast of California. *I was safe! I was home!*

In This Valley There Are Tigers

*   *   *

I started writing this story long ago and then set it aside to gather dust, because it was too emotional for me to do. My wife followed me after the war to Schofield Barracks, Hawaii, and then to Fort Hood, Texas. In 1975, two years before I retired, Keiko traveled to Pittsburgh to seek a teaching position and eventually became tenured there. She taught at the University of Pittsburgh for 27 years. Keiko would never remain in Pittsburgh during the summer. She chose to teach for the University of Maryland in Japan. She felt that it was important to give something back by teaching American service men and women stationed abroad, to help them attain their college degrees. Keiko, held a "Secret" security clearance and a GS-13 rating, and taught at the Naval, Air Force, and Surveillance Base's. My wife loved fishing and spent most of her spare time fly-fishing. During the latter part of our years together, I began to notice a slight loss of her equilibrium. She had an abnormal rhythm that caused her heart to insufficiently send blood to her brain. It was while fishing, one beautiful day that a viral infection caused her to faint and have a significant heart attack. She fell into the water. Alone, when I found her, I fought to revive her with CPR and then went for a phone and an ambulance. In the ambulance, the life support system revealed she was still alive. I had brought her body back to life. Except for when the doctor and nurses were working on her, I remained by her side. I held her hand and talked to her continually and rubbed her feet and limbs. The doctor told me she was gone. Remembering the smile of the woman of my dreams, my loving wife of 42 year's, Dr. Keiko Iwai McDonald, I kissed her one last time. Keiko left this world at 8:56 a.m. on 14 September 2008, from a heart attack causing her to fall into the water, while fishing at Yellow Creek in Indiana County, Pennsylvania. To honor my wife, she was cremated the next day. With the fire that consumed her, the rising billowing smoke and her soul made its ascent into the blue-gray sky of dawn honoring the natural cycle, reducing the body to ash and the elements of which she was composed to become one with the sky and earth. I gathered my wife's medical files and sent them to one of her friends, a neurologist, Dr. Harriet Fellows in Connecticut, who had requested to see them. Dr. Fellows knew my wife's history of suffering as a child in Japan during World War II from starvation. Dr. Fellows consulted with some of her doctor friends and the conclusion was, that the virus from a shot given to Keiko by her doctor in Pittsburgh was the problem. The virus that had lodged in her enlarged heart and the loss of her equilibrium was actually a small heart attack taking place. The day she fell into the water, she suffered a large heart attack.

* * *

Now, alone, I picked up this manuscript that my wife had encouraged me long ago to write and decided to finish it to rid myself of the ghosts and disappointments in the Veterans Administration.

Agent Orange.
After my wife's death, I decided to move to Buffalo, Wyoming. I met a beautiful American Indian woman, Louise Bertha, and married her there in the famous Occidental Hotel. After my Indian wife was refused service for her life threatening disease in the local clinic, we sold our home, packed our bags and moved to Cheyenne. It was one of the best moves I've ever made. I processed into the Cheyenne Veterans Administration facility, and after receiving a thorough physical examination, I learned that I am twenty percent disabled. I was also shocked to learn I was suffering from the effects of Agent Orange. My mind swiftly went back to all those years spent in the mountains of looking up hearing and seeing low-flying C-123 aircraft or a formation of three flying overhead spraying dioxin and other toxic substances to defoliate the trees providing cover for the enemy. In the year 2010, I learned that the U.S. military in Operation Ranch Hand sprayed some 20 million gallons of Agent Orange, Agent White, Agent Blue, and other herbicides across Indochina.

Forty years later, I find that I no longer have to wonder why I suffer from fatigue, rashes and blistering sores that some doctors passed off as shingles. As the list of my diagnoses grew longer to find out prostate cancer and worst of all chronic ischemic heart disease, all linked to Vietnam. Thousands of us are suffering and dying from various ailments.

To name just a few, the VA would list AL amyloidosis, Chloracne, Type 2 diabetes, Ischemic heart disease, Parkinson's disease, Peripheral neuropathy, Porphyria cutanea tarda, kidney problems, Hodgkin's lymphoma, Non-Hodgkins lymphoma, Prostate cancer, Chronic Lymphocytic Leukemia, Lung, larynx, trachea, and bronchus cancer, and some soft-tissue sarcomas.

So, the horrors of war and this noxious miasma will permeate my everyday thoughts for the rest of my life, and those of you who think the Vietnam War is over, it still goes on, the dying and suffering continues at an incredible rate. Only those who have experienced the maelstrom and horror of battle can truly understand what we have gone through and experienced in battle.

I learned to live with the psychological effects of the war that overwhelmed my mind. These vivid, traumatic dreams lasted many years, always making my heart race and my body sweat leaving me tired and tense during the day. The horrifying nightmares that made me afraid to go to sleep at night and filled my mind by day, have mostly ended. *"Thank God."* But still my daytime functions are impaired with depression. The psychological, physical and emotional trauma suffered in combat, has left me wounded for life.

After years of sleeping on the cold ground in the rain and snow, putting arthritis in my joints and looking at my swelled knuckles and bent finger and toe joints, going near deaf, the VA still won't pay me for it. The VA says there is no record of me ever going on sick call to complain about all this. In the military we were taught to put our mission and unit first, our needs came second. So after all these years when it comes my turn, they turn a deaf ear to me, and others.

Talking of deaf ears, I now have hearing aids issued by the Veterans Administration long after the war. But the VA says that my deafness is not service connected. Yet our ears are the sensitive indicator of exposure to blast and concussion. All the loss of equilibrium, hearing loss and tinnitus, caused by the direct exposure to blasts and concussion effects of incoming bombs, artillery, rockets, mortars, hand grenades, and heavy and light infantry weapons in three years of combat have nothing to do with the loss of my hearing. Vertigo, anxiety, fatigue, headaches, pain, and dizziness, were the side effects that went along with these circumstances. The celebrating sounds on the 4th of July and the normal yelling and screaming sounds of children at play are disturbing to me. Severe stress led to sleep disruption for many years, and now and then, still does.

(L to R) LTC Phuong-Chief North Vietnamese Delegate, Sr Lt. Ngoc-Interpreter, Col James R. Dennet-Chief U.S. Delegate, Sp6 Garnett Bell-Interpreter.

They say that the only glory in war is surviving, and that old age has its dignity, maybe so, but it's dammed inconvenient. But my experience has taught me to value life.

This makes me think of an old friend, another survivor, Larry Dring, like many others, his life, was shortened by his war wounds, but, that's a whole nother story.

Ironically, a good friend of mine, Garnett (Bill) Bell, sat at the negotiating table representing the United States at Gia Lam Airport on the outskirts of Hanoi in 1973, ending the Vietnam War. Later, Bell went on to negotiate with the Communists officials concerning the American POW/MIA issues. In March 1982, in China, Bell interrogated North Vietnamese Army prisoners of war captured by the Chinese, prior to their release.

Garnett Bell on Right Negotiating End of Vietnam War

Charles A. McDonald

(March 1982)

Garnett Bell in China on Mission of Interrogating Prisoners of War Belonging to the North Vietnamese Army Prior to their Release.

Glossary of Terms and Abbreviations

AK-47: Designer was Mikhail Timofeevich Kalashnikov. He was born in the village of Kurya in the Altai Territory, located 1,860 miles east of Moscow, on the border of southern Siberia and Mongolia. The 7.62x39mm M43 Russian Avtomat Kalashnikov AK-47 assault rifle with a 30-round magazine is superior to the clones produced by other countries. It is rugged, reliable and simple to maintain, and requires less training to master than American weapons. In 1949, mass production of this selective fire rifle began in Russia, at Izhmash and Izhevsk. It has a chrome-plated bore and firing chamber to counter the corrosive primers of communist ammunition. The long-stroke gas piston above the barrel and attached to the bolt carrier, reduced muzzle rise when fired on fully automatic fire. This simple effective weapon is characterized by an explosive popping sound.

Ao dai: Vietnamese national dress for men and women. The women's high necked, tight-fitted smock, split at the waist, reaches down to their high heel shoes. The pants were full, loose cotton trousers. The men loose-fitted smock only comes down to the knees.

Ap Bac: A village located in the Mekong Delta. It became the scene for the most publicized battle of the war in January 1963, when the American 3rd Radio Research Unit (ASA) located a North Vietnamese radio transmitter sending messages.

APC (Armored Personnel Carrier): A light armored infantry vehicle designed to ferry infantry on the battlefield.

ARVN: Army of the Republic of Vietnam. Founded on 2 July 1949 by the French. On 11 February 1955, the French officially turned over financial and training control of this army to the Americans.

BAR: World War II .30-caliber infantry weapon. The Browning Automatic Rifle, loaded with a 20-round magazine, weighs 19.4 pounds.

Binh Xuyen: A military sect, and mafia-like crime syndicate with forty thousand followers. They maintained financial control over Saigon when President Diem came to power. They refined crude opium supplied by French Intelligence and sold it through the Chinese and Corsican Mafia on the world market. They wore black uniforms and had a snarling tiger badge on their berets.

B-52: First flown in 1952. This high-altitude bomber with a crew of six and a range of 7,500 miles unrefueled is used in support of ground operations. It has a 185-foot wingspan, weighs 184,000 pounds when empty and can carry eighty-four 500-pound bombs, or forty-two 750-pound bombs. The bombs from one B-52 would devastate an area a mile long and a half-mile wide.

B-57: Royal Australian Air Force Canberra Medium bomber. A British Martin-designed, straight-winged, two-engined jet tactical bomber with a range of 805 miles and known for its bombing accuracy. With a crew of two it carries six 750-pound bombs, used to attack strategic targets throughout Vietnam and Laos. American General Dynamics also built B-57s. These bombers also employed laser-guided ordinance and airborne radar.

Bo doi: Northern soldiers or North Vietnamese soldiers.

Browning M1919A4 Machine Gun: Standard 30 caliber U.S. light-weight, air-cooled machine gun that served throughout World War II, Korea, and Vietnam.

Bru: A friendly, but secretive tribe of the northwestern mountains in Vietnam. In 1968, the Bru fought with great bravery in a major battle against North Vietnamese tanks.

Buddhism: The religion founded by Gautama Buddha (563-483 B.C.) in North India. Later it was divided into two schools: the Hinayana and the Mahayana. While the Hinayana spread into Southeast Asia, the Mahayana spread into China, Tibet, Korea and Japan.

Cao Dai: Indigenous Vietnamese politico-religious sect founded by So Ngo Minh Chieu in 1926. It was a combination of Buddhism and Christianity and communicated with spirits through séances.

COSVN: An American acronym for the Central Office of South Vietnam, the highly mobile North Vietnamese headquarters that controlled all communist forces in Tay Ninh Province. It was an extension of the ruling Central Committee in Hanoi. The headquarters maintained several operational radio units, which moved after transmission.

Can Lao Party: A covert political party created in 1954, and commanded by Col. Le Quang Tung, the Special Forces commander. Controlled by President Diem's brother, Ngo Dinh Nhu, it was made up of thousands of Catholic refugees from North Vietnam.

C-123 (Provider): A twin-engine, medium assault cargo/troop aircraft that operated out of small unimproved, short-field airstrips. This workhorse, well suited for special warfare operations, was tested in South Vietnam as a counterinsurgency aircraft.

Cell: The basic underground unit of the National Liberation Front (NLF), its size dependent upon function.

C-4: M5A1 Composite Explosive Four "plastique" issued in 2.5-pound blocks. White in color, it is a safe explosive with the consistency of molding clay. Commonly used to heat C rations and coffee water.

Chinese medicine: Made extensive use of arsenic, lead and mercury.

Cholon: Saigon's Chinese twin city forming the western district 5 of Saigon. Cholon means "Big Market." The Chinese name is "Di An" (Embankment).

Cochinchina: The Southern French colonial administrative region.

Covert Action: CIA jargon for attempting to influence the affairs of another country.

CV-2: The Caribou, a STOL aircraft (short takeoff and landing) developed by de Haviland Aircraft Corporation in Canada. It could take off in 250 feet. Used as a light, cargo aircraft, it was capable of flying a 5,000-pound payload. Later designated the C-7.

First Indochina War: French phase of the 30-year-long War.

FAC: Forward air controller, a pilot who flies over the battlefield, relaying calls, acting as a "spotter" and marking targets with smoke rockets for attack aircraft.

Guerrilla: Member of a small organization who lives and operates outside the control and surveillance of the government and performs paramilitary operations such as assassination, sabotage, ambushes and raids.

Gulf of Tonkin Resolution: The resolution became the sole legal basis for the prosecution of the war. On 7 August 1964, after nine hours of deliberation, the House approved of the resolution by a vote of 416-0. In the Senate, only two senators, Wyane Lyman Morse (D) of Oregon and Ernest Henry Gruening (D) of Alaska, voted against it.

Hanoi Hannah: A group of communist radio personalities that broadcasted an English-language propaganda program to South Vietnam from the Democratic Republic of Vietnam. The most famous personality was Ngo Thi Trinh.

Helicopters: A total of 4,869 helicopters were lost during the war.

Hoa Hao: An armed militant sect of Buddhism founded in 1939 by Huynh Phu So. It had about 1 million followers.

Ho Chi Minh Trail: Chinese and North Vietnamese engineered infiltration and supply route in Laos and South Vietnam. It was developed by a 30,000-man work force from trails into a complex network of highways with all types of underground facilities to support troops and vehicles.

Indochina: North Vietnam, Laos, South Vietnam and Cambodia. The name acknowledged the early influence of Indian and Chinese cultures.

Jungle Antenna: The jungle antenna was made of coaxial cable or WD-1, with ceramic insulators and three sticks. When erected, it consisted of one vertical radiator and 3 ground plane elements connected at the bottom with the sticks and the five insulators. The formula for the construction of the jungle antenna was the constant (234) frequency in megacycles equaling the length of our radiator (center conductor).

Karst: Rocky, limestone terrain characterized by water-filled sinkholes, underground rivers and cave systems.

Khe Sanh: Small town in the remote northwestern corner of South Vietnam, known as the site of a Special Forces camp from July 1962 to late 1966.

Laterite: A porous, clay-like rock, black-brown to reddish in color, which hardens on exposure.

Lemon grass: An important herb, flavoring Vietnamese stir-fry cooking. It adds a lemon/lime like tang to food. Looks like a green onion with long, thin, green-gray leaves and a lighter bulb at the tip. The woody, outer layer of leaves, are removed before use as you would a green onion.

Local force: Insurgent force composed of villagers performing guerrilla tactics at the local level.

MAAG-V: Military Assistance and Advisory Group-Vietnam, originally established as MAAG-Indo-China in 1950 to assist and supply the French in their fight against the communists in Indo-China.

Main Force: Insurgent military force organized along conventional military lines, such as squads, platoons and companies, and using conventional tactics.

Meo Tribe: Tibeto-Burman tribesmen that call themselves "Hmong." "Meo" is the derogatory term used by ignorant foreigners.

Montagnards: The Nguoi Thuong, or People of the Plateau, who lived in the Central Highlands. A French term for 33 ethnically, distinct mountain tribes of Thailand, Laos, and Vietnam.

M-1 Carbine: Reliable World War II semi-automatic, caliber .30 infantry weapon.

M-2 Carbine: Reliable World War II semi-automatic and automatic infantry weapon identified by its selector switch on the left side of the operating slide handle.

M-1 Rifle. U.S. Rifle, Caliber .30 M1, was the first semi-automatic rifle issued to U.S. troops. It was the standard issue rifle during World War II and Korean War. During the Vietnam War, it was also issued to Montagnard and Vietnamese troops.

M-16: Standard American small-caliber 5.56mm (.223 caliber) infantry rifle. The smaller size of the ammunition allows for greater magazine capacity. This high-velocity weapon could be fired on semi-automatic and automatic, but easily broke and malfunctioned. It is 39-inches long. Over the objection of the Army Ordnance Corps, Robert S. McNamara, ordered the rifle for use by the U.S. Armed Forces. The weapon has been under constant modification for years.

M-26: Standard American infantry fragmentation hand grenade. Identified by its olive drab color and yellow markings. Weighs one pound.

M-60: Standard American 7.62mm light machinegun. It is gas operated and belt-fed by a 50-round link belt.

M-79: Standard American infantry shotgun-style, single shot, breech-loaded, 40mm grenade launcher. It was an effective weapon.

M1911A1: Caliber .45 automatic pistol. Loaded, it weighs 2.9 pounds. This pistol remained in service until 1985.

National Liberation Front: Formed in South Vietnam by the Communist Party of North Vietnam at a secret meeting in December 1960. It was used to disguise its communist leadership in recruiting support to help overthrow the South Vietnamese government. In reality it did not exist.

NVA: Soldiers of the North Vietnamese Army.

Operation Ranch Hand: U.S. Air Force aerial defoliation program in which 20 million gallons of the herbicides Agent Orange, Agent Blue, and Agent White containing dioxin were sprayed. The Vietnamese and the Americans were exposed to it from breathing, cooking, drinking and bathing in it. Congress passed the Agent Orange Act of 1991, stipulating that any veterans who served in Vietnam from 9 January 1962 to 7 May 1975, is presumed to have been exposed to Agent Orange and automatically qualifies for a disability rating for a list of specified diseases.

O-1: Aircraft used by the U.S. Army for air support of ground troops and for aerial reconnaissance. A single-engined, aircraft known as *Birddog*.

PAVN: Military establishment of the Democratic Republic of Vietnam (DRV), and known as the People's Army of Vietnam (North Vietnam). It evolved originally from a guerrilla army in 1945 into one of the world's largest armed forces, and trained at six training centers in southern China.

People's Self-Defense Force (PSDF): In April 1968, President Nguyen Van Thieu activated the South Vietnamese PSDF, a civilian militia. Some 3.5 million people: those too old or too young to serve in the regular military were enrolled. The PSDF enhanced security within South Vietnam's villages and employed guerrilla tactics against the communist and their guerrillas, saboteurs, and terrorists infrastructure. This program established and proved the South Vietnamese government had the support of the people.

PRC-25: FM field radio, AN/PRC-25, portable radio. Line-of-sight transmission, its range was 25-30 miles. Used by American troops in South East Asia.

RECONDO School: Ranger and Commando training school initiated in the 101st Airborne Division at Ft. Campbell, Kentucky, to prepare selected personnel for the Vietnam War. On 15 September 1966, Detachment B-52 (Project DELTA) established it in Vietnam to prepare selected allied personnel from major combat units for long-range reconnaissance patrolling (LRRP) techniques. It also conducted a combat orientation course for all Special Forces replacement personnel.

Revolutionary Military Council: The November 1963 junta that overthrew President Ngo Dinh Diem, attempting to establish peaceful coexistence between North and South Vietnam.

RPK: The 7.62mm Russian light machinegun, 40-round or 75-round box magazine, drum fed.

Regional Force: Insurgent military force that uses guerrilla tactics. Supported by the local population, it has the responsibility of an area comparable to a province.

Rice: The Vietnamese short-grain rice calls for less water in cooking than long grained Chinese rice.

RVN: The republic that was formed on 26 October 1955, as a result of the 1949 Elysee Agreement which gave Vietnam "independence" within the French Union.

Rung Sat Special Zone: A maze of rivers and thick mangrove, shallow water swamps in the northeastern Delta. Located south of Saigon, it was a PAVN stronghold for units directly threatening and operating in the capital city and its port. Known as the "forest of the Assassins."

Saigon: The largest city in Vietnam, the capital of French Cochinchina, with 17 urban districts. Renamed Ho Chi Minh City after the war in 1975.

SCUBA: Self-contained underwater breathing apparatus.

Second Indochina War: The American phase of the over 20-year-long War.

Skyraider: A counterinsurgency aircraft known as the A-1E. It carries four 20-mm cannons in its wings and four tons of varied ordinance.

SKS: The two variants of the SKS were used in the war: the 7.62mm SKS-45 Russian Simonov semi-automatic carbine and the Chinese SKS was the Type 56 carbine. The rugged and reliable SKS shortcoming was its fixed 10-round magazine and its lack of a select-fire capability. It was 40-inches long, and remained in production until 1954.

Special Forces Qualification Course: Three-phase training course that must be passed to become a member of Special Forces. Records of qualified personnel are kept separately in the Special Categories section of the Pentagon.

STARLIGHT: The August 1965 code-name for the first large-scale U.S. Marine engagement against North Vietnamese regulars in South Vietnam.

Terrorism: A political instrument that commits coercive acts of violence. It is directed toward disrupting government control over the citizenry and creating a state of mind--terror--which makes the citizenry acquiesce to subversive demands.

Tonkin: Northern administrative region of Vietnam in the French colonial era.

Truong Son Range: The Vietnamese name for the mountain highlands that stretched the western length of Vietnam. The Troung Son Mountain range was known to the Pathet Lao, as the Saiphou Louang. To the western world, they were known as the Annamites.

Underground: A covert, insurgent organization living within the control and surveillance of the government, while supporting the guerrillas with intelligence and logistical support.

United Front: A common communist tactic, which creates an alliance against the government or all organizations or forces of discontent.

USARYIS: United States Army Ryukyu Islands.

VC: Viet Nam Cong San (Vietnamese communists), a derogatory name for the National Liberation Front. The National Liberation Front (VC) was a strategic deception designed to deceive world opinion, specifically the anti-war faction in the United States.

Vietnamese Names: The family or clan name comes first, followed by the given name.

Vietnamese Zodiac: Vietnamese astrology that follows the lunar calendar. The 12 zodiacal signs are: rat, ox, tiger, rabbit, dragon, snake, horse, goat, monkey, rooster, dog and pig.

Appendix: Cast of Characters in the 1 November 1963 Coup

The reader, no doubt, may be bedazzled by a dizzying array of exotic names of places and persons. To prevent the reader from drowning in this sea of proper names, I have added a cast of characters involved in the 1 November coup. I have also added a brief summary of the salient events.

Averell Harriman (1891-1986): President Kennedy and President Johnson's ambassador-at-large, who opposed the war in Vietnam. As undersecretary of state for political affairs, he helped draft the August 1963 cable to U.S. Ambassador Henry Cabot Lodge that authorized the Generals of South Vietnam's Revolutionary Command Council that it was okay to go ahead with the planned November 1963 coup that assassinated President Diem. While at the State Department, Harriman maneuvered to deny Military Assistance Command Vietnam (MACV) authority to operate against the Ho Chi Minh Trail. President Johnson, dissatisfied with Harriman, made him a roving ambassador for everything but Asia.

Emperor Bao Dai (22 October 1913-31 July 1997): Prince Nguyen Vinh Thuy was born in Hue. He was the son of Emperor Khai Din. He was the 13th Emperor and the last of the Nguyen Dynasty. In July 1954, Emperor Bao Dai, was deposed by Diem after he won 99 percent of a referendum. He died in Paris, France. Served as Emperor of Annam (1926-45), and as Chief of State of Vietnam (1949-55).

Col. Bui Dinh Dam: Col Dam served in the 7th Division commanded by Gen. Huynh Van Cao, during the Battle of Ap Bac on 2 January 1963. The battle was an early major victory for the Communist. The disgruntled advisor Col. John Paul Vann was Col Dam's American counterpart.

Lucien Emile Conein (1919-1998): A French-born American commissioned in 1943 into the U.S. Army. Served in the OSS in World War II in Vietnam. Served in Special Forces.

In This Valley There Are Tigers

In 1954, he returned as a CIA agent to work in Vietnam, and was closely connected to the Corsican syndicate in Saigon. He served as an adviser to Nguyen Khanh and acted as go-between for Washington and the Revolutionary Military Council in the 1963 coup in Saigon. In early October he informed the council that the funds were cut off to Col. Tung's Special Forces, signaling Washington's approval for the coup, and in late October, passed on the funds for the coup.

Maj. Gen. Do Cao Tri: From May 1954 to March 1955, Maj. Do Cao Tri commanded the *Groupement Airport 3* (G.A.P.3) the Vietnamese Airborne unit equivalent of an airborne Regimental combat team and was promoted to Lt. Col. In early 1963, Gen. Do Cao Tri was the commander of the 1st Division. In August 1963 he was the commander of I Corps. In December 1963, he was the commander of II Corps. In August 1968, he was commander of the III Corps area. On 23 February 1971, he was killed in a helicopter crash.

Maj. Duong Hieu Nghia: He was one of two executioners, in the M-113 Armored Personnel Carrier (APC), who brutally tortured and executed President Diem and his brother, in the 1 November 1963 coup. The other executioner was Capt. Nguyen Van Nhung, who drove the APC away from the Cha Tam Church in the Cholon section of Saigon. Duong Hieu Nghia later became a Colonel in ARVN Armor and served as the Chief of the RVN Delegation to the Four Party Joint Military Team from 1973 to 1975. Nghia was stranded in Saigon in April 1975. After some 14 years of "re-education" in prison camps, in 1992, he was allowed to resettle in the area of Seattle, Washington.

Col. Duong Van Minh (1916-1997): Known to Americans as "Big Minh." In 1956, he executed the guerrilla leader, Ba Cut, of the Hoa Hao sect. He was the ARVN commander for Saigon-Cholon in 1955, during the battle with the Binh Xuyen. In 1963, Minh was removed from troop command by President Diem. In October of that year, he started conspiring a coup with the American CIA against Diem.

He became chairman of the Revolutionary Military Council the same year, and convinced Washington to cut off funding to the loyalist Vietnamese Special Forces unless they removed themselves from Saigon in order to overthrow the government of President Diem. The order for the removal of the Special Forces from Saigon on 29 October was key to the overthrow of Diem. He gave the approval for the coup and Diem's assassination. In October 1971, due to U.S. pressure, he withdrew his candidacy in the presidential elections. On 28 April 1975, he was appointed President of South Vietnam, and on 30 April he announced the unconditional surrender of South Vietnam. Arrested by the communists on 2 May, he was sent to a reeducation camp. He later emigrated to France.

Gen. Paul Donal Harkins (1904-1984): Appointed by President Kennedy as the first Commander of Military Assistance Command, Vietnam (MACV), in Saigon. He served from 1962-1964. Gen. Harkins was a positive commander who stood completely behind President Diem, and wound up being circumvented by members of the Kennedy Administration. Two such people were Ambassador Lodge and Averell Harriman, who insisted on replacing President Diem without a qualified successor. On 20 June 1964, Gen. Harkins, was replaced by Gen. Westmoreland.

David Halberstam: Harvard-educated know-it-all who arrived in Vietnam in 1962, working for the New York Times and marked as a left-wing journalist by the U.S. government. Spent only one year in Vietnam and helped provide the American people with much of the bad press generated there. Most closely associated with journalist likely to criticize the United States and the Vietnamese. Wrote the story concerning the immolation of Thich Quang Duc.

Malcolm Browne: The 30-year-old Associated Press photographer who was called in advance by the Buddhists of Thich Quang Duc's scheduled self-immolation. Browne took the pictures as two assisting monks poured gasoline over Duc and lit the match. Browne took the pictures from twenty feet away.

Ho Chi Minh (1890-1969): President of the Democratic Republic of Vietnam (DRV). He adopted and was known by dozens of pseudonyms throughout his life. Starting in 1911, he traveled to France, United States, London, and after World War I, back to France. He was one of the founding members of the French Communist Party. In 1923, he traveled to Russia, China, and by 1927 was in Thailand living as a Buddhist monk. In 1930, in Hong Kong, he founded the Vietnamese Communist Party before returning to China. In 1941, he was in the mountains of northern Vietnam resisting the Japanese occupation. In August 1945, the Japanese defeated, Ho consolidated control of the northern and central part of Vietnam, and on 2 September declared the Democratic Republic of Vietnam in Hanoi. From 1954 to 1969, he led the DRV on its path of war for Vietnam's reunification. He died on 2 September 1969.

Huynh Van Trong: Minister under Bao Dai. Trong, was recruited by the Communist A22, secret agent group in South Vietnam. Trong helped Nguyen Van Thieu to become the President of the Republic of Vietnam, which gave him access to Top Secret documents. These documents were turned over to North Vietnamese secret agent Vu Ngoc Nha.
Note--See Vu Ngoc Nha below.

Capt. Ho Tan Quyen: President Diem's loyalist Navy commander, and Chief of Naval Operations. Assassinated at the naval station on 1 November 1963 at the fuel farm on the Saigon River.

Gen. Huynh Van Cao: In March 1959, Col. Huynh Van Cao was the commanding officer of the 7th Division at Can Tho in IV Corps. On 1 January 1963, he was the commander of the South Vietnamese 7th Division at the battle of Ap Bac. In late January 1963 he was the commander of IV Corps that was responsible for the entire Mekong Delta. He was relieved of duty in the aftermath of the 1 November 1963 coup against President Diem. In May 1966, Maj. General Huynh Van Cao was again the IV Corps commander.

Lyndon Baines Johnson (1908-1973): A Democrat who assumed the presidency after the assassination of President Kennedy. His wife owned the large construction firm, RMK-BMJ, which had all the construction contracts in Southeast Asia. In his re-election campaign he promised that, unlike his opponent Senator Barry Goldwater, he would not carry the war to the north. He successfully requested Congress pass the Tonkin Gulf Resolution, then ordered sixty-four air sorties against North Vietnam to destroy the patrol boat bases and sent conventional ground combat forces to South Vietnam. He gradually escalated the war until 1968, without the full support of the American people. His greatest failure, was not understanding his enemy.

John F. Kennedy (1917-63): On 20 January 1961, JFK replaced Eisenhower as president. He was assassinated on 22 November 1963.

Gen. Le Van "Bay" Vien (-1972): French-backed leader of the Binh Xuyen river pirates who controlled the highway from Saigon to Vung Tau. He shared his profits from opium, gold smuggling, gambling, currency manipulation, real estate, and prostitution with Emperor Bao Dai. Became the national police chief. He was considered as the most direct threat to President Ngo Dinh Diem. In April 1955, when ordered out of Saigon by President Diem, he refused, and in the fighting between the Binh Xuyen and the South Vietnamese Army, hundreds of people were killed and entire neighborhoods destroyed leaving thousands homeless. By the end of May, the Binh Xuyen had retreated southwest into the swamps. In 1955, his money secured safely abroad, he fled to France.

Lai Van Sang: A military commander of the Binh Xuyen until April 1954. In that same year he became director-general of the Saigon police (1954-55).

Col. Le Quang Tung (1918-1963): Commander of the loyalist Vietnamese Special Forces (Luc Luong Dac Biet, or LLDB) used to suppress Buddhists. Led the raid on the Xa Loi pagoda in Saigon. Assassinated on 1 November 1963, along with his brother Maj. Le Quang Trieu.

Gen. Mai Huu Xuan: Member of the Military Revolutionary Council that overthrew President Diem. General Mai was the ranking officer of the small convoy of troops that picked up, arrested and assassinated Diem and his brother Nhu. General Mai reported directly to Gen. Minh after the two brothers were killed.

Robert McNamara: Served as Secretary of Defense from 1961 to 1968. An unconscionable managerial statistician, who wanted to run the Vietnam War like a business corporation.

Ngo Dinh Diem (1901-63): A Catholic, who was vehemently anti-communist. Diem served six months in a communist prison. In 1945, Diem refused Ho Chi Minh's offer of a cabinet post in the new Democratic Republic of Vietnam, because the communists had assassinated his brother Khoi. On 7 July 1954, Diem, was appointed prime minister by the former Emperor, Bao Dai. His Anti-Communist Denunciation Campaign drove the communists underground. On 23 October 1955, the nationalistic Diem became President and announced the creation of the Republic of Vietnam. His special adviser was Vu Ngoc Nha, a communist agent. Diem was executed on 2 November 1963.

Ngo Dinh Kha: The father of President Ngo Dinh Diem. In 1896, Kha founded the most famous secondary school in Hue, Vietnam, The National School (Quoc Hoc High School). This school located on the southside bank, faces the

Perfume River, on the western end of town. The school was attended by Ho Chi Minh (1895-1901), Gen. Vo Nguyen Giap and commander-in-chief Pham Van Dong, Party Secretary Le Duan, Ngo Dinh Diem and former Prime Minister Do Muoi. It is still open.

Ngo Dinh Nhu (1910-63): Organized the Can Lao Party that enabled the family to remain in power and acted as political adviser to his brother, President Diem. Brutal head of the secret police, who maintained control over the Vietnamese Special Forces. Because he would not voluntarily step down from power, he caused himself and his brother to die during the coup.

Ngo Dinh Nhu, Madame (1924-2011): Born Tran Le Xuan, she became the wife of Ngo Dinh Nhu, the president's brother. Madame Nhu, as she wished to be called, served as President Diem's official host. She fancied herself a modern-day trung, defending her country against the communist. In 40 A.D., the fabled Trung sisters rode elephants into battle to free Vietnam from the Chinese invaders. The sharp-tongued lady was the sister-in-law of South Vietnam's bachelor president, Ngo Dinh Diem. Madame Nhu was the de facto first lady of the Diem regime. Her husband was head of the secret police. She was living in Los Angeles, California, during the execution of her husband.

Ngo Dinh Canh (1911-9 May 1964): Younger brother of Ngo Dinh Diem. He controlled his own personal army and secret police. Cahn was a virtual warlord in central Vietnam. He dealt in black market rice and opium. Ambassador Lodge ordered him turned over to the military junta, the Revolutionary Command Council. The junta ordered Canh executed in public on 9 May 1964.

Ngo Dinh Luyen (1914-1990): President Diem's youngest brother. Served as Ambassador to Britain.

Ngo Dinh Thuc: Thuc was the second oldest of the Ngo brothers. He wanted an independent Vietnamese state centered on Catholics. Appointed as Roman Catholic archbishop of Hue in 1963, and forbid Buddhist flags being displayed on Buddha's birthday. This action culminated in the Buddhist led coup on 1 November 1963. He helped found Dalat University with the help of Cardinal Spelman of New York. The university was seized from the church in 1975 and closed. In 1977, the university reopened after becoming a state-run institution. Thuc was supported by the U.S. Department of State as a go-between the United States and his brother Nhu. He was eventually excommunicated in Rome.

Ngo Dinh Khoi: The eldest of the six Ngo brothers, Khoi served as the governor in charge of the provinces south of central Vietnam, from 1933 to 1943. Khoi was assassinated by the Communists in August 1945, to remove all potential rivals for power in the new Democratic Republic of Vietnam.

Nguyen Cao Ky (1923-23 July 2011): The flamboyant former air force general who ruled South Vietnam with an iron fist. In 1959, he commanded the 43rd Air Transport Group. In January 1964, Ky joined Gen. Nguyen Khanh in a coup against Duong Van Minh's government. In June 1965, elected by the Armed Forces Council, he became prime minister after helping Gen. Nguyen Van Thieu and Gen. Nguyen Chanh Thi to oust Premier Phan Huy Quat. On 3 April 1966, Ky announced that the Buddhist movement had fallen into communist hands. In May, Ky violently crushed Buddhists in Danang. In June, the Buddhist opposition in Hue and Saigon was put down. In September 1967, Ky became vice president. On 29 April 1975, Ky flew to the U.S. evacuation fleet and landed his helicopter aboard the USS Midway, and settled in the United States. Ky split his time between his home in California and Vietnam. He was 80 years old and died in the hospital in Kuala Lumpur, Malaysia, of respiratory complications.

Gen. Nguyen Chanh Thi (1923-): A Buddhist. In early 1964, he was the commanding officer of the 1st Division. Took command in November 1964-65 of the five northern provinces that made up the "I Corps" area that included Hue and Danang. He was a close friend of Buddhist leader Thich Tri Quang. Fled to Cambodia after being relieved of command of I Corp for participating in the November 1960 coup, which failed. Returned to Vietnam after the 1963 assassination of President Diem. Thi was one of the members of the powerful ten-member National Leadership Committee. On 4 March 1966, Thi was discharged from command by Prime Minister Nguyen Cao Ky for launching the "Struggle Movement" against the government in Saigon and fled to the United States. The Buddhists and communists subsequently took control of the radio station in Hue and Danang. Ky announced the area controlled by the communists. The government suppressed the revolt and made Gen. Ton That Dinh the commander of I Corps.

Col. Nguyen Khanh (1927-): Former member of the communist Viet Minh. Dismissed for poor discipline. Joined the French forces. In December 1962, Lt. Gen. Khanh served as the commanding officer of the II Corps area. In December 1963, Lt. Gen. Khanh served as the commanding officer of I Corps area. From 1964-65, he served as Prime Minister of South Vietnam and during the 7 August 1964, Gulf of Tonkin Crisis, proclaimed himself president. Riots in Saigon over Khanh's self-appointment forced him to resign. Serving as deputy chief of staff, he participated in the coup against President Diem. On 30 January 1964, Khanh had Minh's bodyguard, Captain Xuan (Van) Nhung, executed. In the summer of 1964 he promoted himself to the presidency. In December 1964 and in January and February 1965, Khanh had secretly contacted the communists to negotiate and end to the war. He was forced to emigrate to the United States.

Nguyen Van Thieu (1924-2001): Fought for the communists against the French. In December 1962, Col. Thieu commanded the 5th Division. Troops of the 5th Division commanded by Col. Thieu promoted him to general in 1962, and he participated in the 1 November 1963 coup that overthrew President Diem. In September 1964, Maj. General Thieu was the IV Corps commander. In September 1967 Thieu became President and ruled the Republic until resigning on 25 April 1975. President Thieu's special adviser and top aide was Vu Ngoc Nha, a communist agent. Thieu died in the United States on 29 September.

Gen. Nguyen Duc Thang: In October 1961, as a colonel, he commanded the 5th Division, headquarters in Bien Hoa. In 1968, as a Lt. General, he was the IV Corps commander. Served as the minister for pacification. The Ministry of Revolutionary Development (RD) was created in 1966 under Maj. Gen. Nguyen Duc Thang. RD was responsible for showing the governments' presence and contesting communist control. The cadre lived where they worked for a period of six months. There were teachers, medics, construction, and sanitation workers. There were those responsible for organizing the village Popular Forces and Regional Forces for defense and ferreting out the communist infrastructure. Populated areas undergoing pacification efforts had 59-man RD Groups and later to cover more areas, it was organized into 30-man teams deployed at the hamlet and village levels. Later, in February 1968, Lt. Gen. Nguyen Duc Thang was the IV Corps commander.

Captain Nguyen Van Nhung (-1964): Gen. Minh's bodyguard. During the 1 November 1963 coup, he executed Col. Le Quang Tung, Maj. Le Quang Trieu, President Ngo Dinh Diem and his brother Ngo Dinh Nhu. During the military coup on 30 January 1964, General Khanh ordered Captain Nguyen Van Nhung to be executed.

Capt. Nguyen Xuan (Van) Nhung: Duong Van Minh's bodyguard. At Gen. Duong Van Minh's orders, he executed the Special Forces commander, Col. Le Quang Tung. He executed Maj. Le Quang Trieu, Maj. Duong Hieu Nghia and the President of South Vietnam, Ngo Dinh Diem, and his brother Ngo Dinh Nhu.

Nguyen Ngoc Tho: A Buddhist, who in 1963 was serving as the vice-president to Ngo Dinh Diem. He was also a member of the Revolutionary Military Council that overthrew President Diem. Vice-President Tho was a wealthy landlord, who oversaw the land reform policies that favored other wealthy landlords.

Gen. Nguyen Van Hinh (1915-): He was a French citizen and served as a French Air Force officer. In 1949, he volunteered for Vietnam's Air Force. In 1952, he was promoted to Maj. General and served as the Chief of Staff until 1954. Threatened an abortive coup against President Diem in October 1954. Soon after, he departed to France and rejoined the French Air Force and retired in 1969.

Col. (Albert) Pham Ngoc Thao (-1965): Former communist officer in the First Indochina War. Remained a communist, serving as a colonel in the South Vietnamese Army. Responsible for destroying the credibility of the South Vietnamese governments due to the misinformation he passed onto the Western Press Corps reporters, like **Browne** and **David Halberstam**. Thao was assassinated while serving as Ben Tre Province chief by men loyal to Nguyen Van Thieu.

Captain Antoine Savani aka "Corsican bandit.": Corsican commander that ran the French Army 2eme Deuxieme Bureau in Vietnam. It was a branch of military intelligence within the French Army that organized and controlled the underground opium monopoly. This clandestine narcotics trade and its flow of money to the communists, known as Operation X, coordinated the intelligence and operation of the French cooperation with the Binh Xuyen. The Deuxieme Bureau carried out a terror campaign in Saigon against the CIA. French intelligence officers of this organization are key figures today in the International Narcotics trafficking.

Thich Tri Quang (1922-): Communist sympathizer. Instigated the 8 May 1963 Buddhist demonstration in Hue, in which he told his followers to be prepared to die. Headstrong Buddhist agitator in Hue, who in 1963 helped bring down the Diem government. Tri Quang, a close associate of Ambassador Lodge, was protected in the U.S embassy during the period of time leading up to the 1963 coup. Conspired against all South Vietnamese governments. In 1966, Gen. Nguyen Cao Ky defeated the major Buddhist and student revolt and placed Tri Quang under house arrest, ending Buddhist activity. Actively tried to force the withdrawal of American troops.

Gen. Ton That Dinh (1926-): In August 1958, Maj. Gen. Ton was the commanding officer of II Corps. In December 1962, Maj. Gen. Ton was the III Corps commander. In 1963, he commanded the Capital Military District, controlling the forces surrounding Saigon. He was responsible for commanding the removal of Loyalist Col. Le Quang Tung's and his Special Forces out of Saigon to pave the way for the overthrow of President Diem. In April 1966, Lt. Gen. Ton was the I Corps commander.

Gen. Tran Van Don (1917-): In October 1957, Lt. Gen. Tran was the I Corps commander. On 20 August 1963, he became the Chief of the Joint General Staff of the South Vietnamese Army, he was the key participant in the 1963 Diem coup. Responsible for recruiting Gen. Duong Van Minh into the 1963 coup. Gen. Tran became the RVN Deputy Prime Minister and Minister of Defense under President Thieu. He departed from the roof of the U.S. Embassy in Saigon with his family by helicopter on 29 April 1975.

Gen. Tranh Thien Khiem: In February 1960, he commanded the 21st Division. The 21st Division under Col. Tranh helped put down the 11 November 1960 coup attempt against President Diem. He became the prime minister under President Nguyen Van Thieu. Khiem was popular with the Catholics. He was evacuated from Saigon during April 1975.

Thich Quang Duc: Monk from Hue's Thien Mu Pagoda, whose photograph of self-immolation shocked the world on 11 June 1963. Thich Quang Duc assumed the Lotus position at the busy intersection of Phan Dinh Phung and Le Van Duyet streets, as two monks poured gasoline over him and lit a match. His sacrifice inspired a number of other monks to burn themselves to death in the Lotus position in the Buddhist war against President Ngo Dinh Diem. The army eventually toppled and killed President Diem. The photos were taken by Malcolm Browne and the story was written by David Halberstam.

Gen. Vang Pao: Hmong leader of the Royal Lao Army, and Commander of the CIA's 39,000 Meo mercenaries in Northeastern Laos, helping fight the Communist in Laos. In January 1961, U.S. Special Forces personnel were working with the Meo tribesmen. In 1962, Vang Pao's headquarters were located at Long Tieng. By 1971, due to increasing casualties, Vang Pao had to recruit Lao Theung tribesmen into his army. He settled in the United States after the war. The United States Government arrested him in a sting operation on terrorism charges 5 June 2007 for planning to oust the Laotian Communist Government. He was free on bail 14 July 2007.

Vu Ngoc Nha: (1928-7 August 2002): Born in Thai Binh province, North Vietnam. A communist agent assigned in 1955 to infiltrate the South and set up an intelligence network. He served as special adviser to two presidents of the American-backed government of South Vietnam. He served as a top aide to Presidents Ngo Dinh Diem and Nguyen Van Thieu. He was the COSVN intelligence agent of a Saigon spy ring, directed against the Office of the President of South Vietnam. This spy regularly passed information to the North Vietnamese Communists. One of his best sources of information was **Huynh Van Trong**, the special assistant of political affairs to President Thieu. He was discovered by the American Central Intelligence Agency and arrested on 16 July 1969.

John Paul Vann: (2 July 1924-9 June 1972) A disgruntled senior American advisor in Vietnam to Col. Bui Dinh Dam of the 7th Division, during the Battle of Ap Bac. Lt.

In This Valley There Are Tigers

Col. Vann started the credibility gap in Vietnam between the military, American government and American people by talking to the press, calling the Vietnamese incompetent. The media began to portray the Vietnamese in the worst light and played upon this theme for the rest of the war. This attitude led to the end of his military career.

About the Author.

Charles A. McDonald grew up on a ranch in California. He enlisted in the army in July 1954. McDonald attended Arizona State University, and graduated from Chaminade College in Honolulu, Hawaii. He was awarded two Presidential Unit Citations. Today, he enjoys his retirement on an Iowa farm, where he lives with his wife, Louise, and continues to work on writing projects.

Printed in Great Britain
by Amazon